The Perfect Online Course

Best Practices for Designing and Teaching

a volume in
Perspectives in Instructional Technology and Distance Education

Series Editors:
Charles Schlosser and Michael Simonson
Nova Southeastern University

Perspectives in Instructional Technology and Distance Education

Charles Schlosser and Michael Simonson, Series Editors

The Perfect Online Course: Best Practices for Designing and Teaching (2009)
edited by Anymir Orellana, Terry L. Hudgins, and Michael Simonson

Connected Minds, Emerging Cultures (2009)
edited by Steve Wheeler

Online Learning Communities (2007)
edited by Rocci Luppicini

Research on Enhancing the Interactivity of Online Learning (2006)
edited by Vivian H. Wright, Cynthia Szymanski Sunal,
and Elizabeth K. Wilson

*Trends and Issues in Distance Education:
An International Perspective* (2005)
edited by Yusra Laila Visser, Lya Visser,
Michael Simonson, and Ray Amirault

*Toward the Virtual University:
International On-Line Learning Perspectives* (2003)
edited by Nicolae Nistor, Susan English,
Steve Wheeler, and Mihai Jalobeanu

Learning From Media: Arguments, Analysis, and Evidence (2001)
edited by Richard E. Clark

The Perfect Online Course

Best Practices for Designing and Teaching

edited by

Anymir Orellana
Nova Southeastern University

Terry L. Hudgins
Nova Southeastern University

and

Michael Simonson
Nova Southeastern University

Information Age Publishing, Inc.
Charlotte, North Carolina • www.infoagepub.com

KH

Library of Congress Cataloging-in-Publication Data

The perfect online course : best practices for designing and teaching / edited by Anymir Orellana, Terry L. Hudgins, and Michael Simonson.

    p. cm.

    Includes bibliographical references.

    ISBN 978-1-60752-120-4 (paperback) — ISBN 978-1-60752-121-1 (hardcover)

1. Instructional systems—Design. 2. Distance education. 3. Computer-assisted instruction. 4. Teaching—Computer network resources.

I. Orellana, Anymir. II. Hudgins, Terry L. III. Simonson, Michael R.

    LB1028.38.P47 2009

    371.35'8—dc22

                                2009014750

Printed in the United States of America

1/27/11

CONTENTS

Preface: In Search of Perfection
Anymir Orellana and Terry L. Hudgins   *ix*

PART I:
INTRODUCTION

1. We Need a Plan: An Instructional Design Approach
   for Distance Education Course
   Michael Simonson and Charles Schlosser   *3*

2. Does it Matter? Analyzing the Results of
   Three Different Learning Delivery Methods
   William N. Chernish, Agnes L. DeFranco, James R. Lindner,
   and Kim E. Dooley   *23*

PART II:
BEST GUIDELINES AND STANDARDS

3. In Search of Quality: An Analysis of
   e-Learning Guidelines and Specifications
   Atsusi Hirumi   *39*

4. Learning Online: Adapting the Seven Principles of
   Good Practice to a Web-Based Instructional Environment
   Christine K. Sorensen and Danilo M. Baylen   *69*

5. Instructors' Self-Perceived Pedagogical
   Principle Implementation in the Online Environment
   Jinsong Zhang and Richard T. Walls   *87*

6. Key Instructional Design Elements for Distance Education
    Lihua Zheng and Sharon Smaldino   *107*

7. Class Size and Interaction in Online Courses
    Anymir Orellana   *127*

8. What Works: Student Perceptions of Effective Elements
    in Online Learning
    Marcy Reisetter and Greg Boris   *157*

9. Design and Implementation of a Web-Based
    Learning Environment: Lessons Learned
    Alaa Sadik and Sorel Reisman   *179*

10. A Framework for Analyzing, Designing,
    and Sequencing Planned e-Learning Interactions
    Atsusi Hirumi   *201*

11. Designing Effective e-Learning:
    Guidelines for Practitioners
    Angelene C. McLaren   *229*

PART III:
BEST INSTRUCTIONAL METHODS AND MODELS

12. An Analysis of Team vs. Faculty-Based Online
    Course Development: Implications for Instructional Design
    Mark Hawkes and Dan O. Coldeway   *249*

13. Getting it Right Gradually: An Iterative Method for
    Online Instruction Development
    Douglas A. Kranch   *265*

14. Towards a Person-Centered Model of Instruction:
    Can an Emphasis on the Personal Enhance Instruction in
    Cyberspace?
    Christopher Miller and Joan M. Mazur   *275*

15. Enhancing Web-Based Instruction Using
    a Person-Centered Model of Instruction
    Christopher T. Miller   *297*

16. Evaluating College Students' Efforts in
    Asynchronous Discussion: A Systematic Process
    Dave S. Knowlton   *311*

17. Pragmatic Methods to Reduce Dishonesty
in Web-Based Course
Newell Chiesl   327

18. Organizing Instructional Content for Web-based Courses:
Does a Single Model Exist?
Joi L. Moore, Richard E. Downing, and David L. York   341

19. An Instructional Design Approach for Effective Shovelware:
Modifying Material for Distance Education
Gary R. Morrison and Gary J. Anglin   359

20. Investigating the Use of Advance Organizers as an
Instructional Strategy for Web-Based Distance Education
Baiyun Chen, Atsusi Hirumi, and Ning Jackie Zhang   377

21. Streamlining the Online Course Development Process
by Using Project Management Tools
M'hammed Abdous and Wu He   389

22. The Learning Contract Process: Scaffolds for Building
Social, Self-Directed Learning
Naomi R. Boyer   401

PART IV:
BEST ENGAGMENT STRATEGIES

23. Interaction in Online Learning Environments:
A Review of the Literature
Constance E. Wanstreet   425

24. Interaction Online: A Reevaluation
John Battalio   443

25. Online Learner's Preferences for Interaction
Pamela T. Northrup   463

26. Learner Support Needs in Online Problem-Based Learning
Steve Wheeler   475

27. Deep Learning: The Knowledge, Methods,
and Cognition Process in Instructor-Led Online Discussion
Byron Havard, Jianxia Du, and Anthony Olinzock   487

28. It's The Same Only Different: The Effect the
Discussion Moderator has on Student Participation
in Online Class Discussions
Vance A. Durrington and Chien Yu   503

29. Does Sense of Community Matter? An Examination
of Participants' Perception of Building Learning
Communities in Online Courses
Xiaonjing Liu, Richard J. Magjuka,
Curtis J. Bonk, and Seung-hee Lee   521

CONCLUSION

30. And Finally ... Designing the "Perfect" Online Course
Michael Simonson   547

Author Affiliations   551

Original Publications   555

PREFACE

In Search of Perfection

Anymir Orellana and Terry L. Hudgins

"To improve is to change; to be perfect is to change often."

—Winston Churchill

Often times, one thinks of something *perfect* as something flawless, something unattainable. But perfect is also defined as accurate, as "satisfying all requirements" (*Merriam-Webster Online Dictionary*, 2008). On the other hand, the term *best practices* is commonly used to connote a set of documented strategies, procedures, or methods employed by highly successful organizations to effectively achieve results in particular circumstances. In this book, a perfect online course is one that is designed and taught to accurately satisfy a course's learning requirements. Best practices in online education are methods and strategies used to produce predetermined learning outcomes.

The Perfect Online Course: Best Practices for Designing and Teaching was edited under the assumption that a perfect online course can be delivered

The Perfect Online Course: Best Practices for Designing and Teaching
pp. ix–xvi

following different instructional methods and models for design and for instruction, and by implementing different teaching or instructional strategies. Such methods, models, and strategies are framed within quality educational guidelines and must be aimed toward attaining the online course's learning goals.

For the purpose of clarification, it is necessary to explain key terminology used throughout the book. Although arguably different in meaning, the terms *online education* and *e-learning* have been used interchangeably by the authors of the works here presented. It was considered that authors have used both terms to refer to Internet-based distance education, particularly Web-based, and basically describe the same processes with only subtle differences. Distance education is defined as "institution-based, formal education where the learning group is separated, and where interactive telecommunications systems are used to connect learner, resources, and instructors" (Simonson, Smaldino, Albright, & Zvacek, 2009, p. 7). Analogously, the term *teaching* is used similarly to the term *instruction*, which is defined as "a set of events or activities presented in a structured or planned way, through one or more media, with the goal of having learners achieve prespecified behaviors" (Dick, Carey, & Carey, 2005, p. 365).

The Perfect Online Course: Best Practices for Designing and Teaching is a volume in the series Perspectives in Instructional Technology and Distance Education, from Information Age Publishing. The book seeks to make a contribution to the existing body of literature related to best practices and guidelines for designing and teaching distance courses, specifically online education. The process of selecting works suitable for this compilation included an extensive review of the journals *Quarterly Review of Distance Education* and *Distance Learning*. These two sources provided both evidence-based research and expert commentary concerning designing and teaching online courses.

To provide a coherent organization of the works into chapters, the book was structured following a top-down approach. The book begins by covering literature related to general approaches and guidelines, continues with proposed methods and models for designing and instruction, and ends with instructional strategies to achieve engagement through interaction. The book is divided into four independent, yet interrelated, parts and a concluding section: Part I: Introduction; Part II: Best Guidelines and Standards; Part III: Best Instructional Methods and Models; Part IV: Best Engagement Strategies; and the concluding section, And Finally ..., with words from Simonson who delineates the structure of a perfect online course. Following is a brief description of each part that can guide the reader to obtain the most from this book.

PART I: INTRODUCTION

Part I contains two chapters that present the need for effective approaches to instructional design in distance education. Both chapters emphasize the importance of good instructional design for effective learning. In chapter 1, Simonson and Schlosser present an introductory overview about best practices in distance education. They stress the importance of the "correct instructional design" for effective distance education, and propose an "easy-to-apply" approach for designing an online course called the U-M-T (Unit-Module-Topic) Approach. In chapter 2, Chernish, DeFranco, Lindner, and Dooley address the issues that arise when the same course is delivered using three different methods (traditional face-to-face classroom activities, instructional television, and Internet) and conclude that online education can be more effective than face-to face, but special attention must be paid to instructional design and ensuring a sense of community. Although the authors use the term *delivery method* to mean *delivery media*, the findings were consistent with the literature that shows that the instructional medium does not contribute directly to learning achievement.

PART II: BEST GUIDELINES AND STANDARDS

A "perfect" instructional design should be guided by quality standards. Nonetheless, a common concern that arises is determining which quality guidelines or specifications allow for best practices and, more important, how these guidelines can be implemented. Part II contains literature with recommendations related to guidelines, standards, and specifications for designing and teaching online courses. Additionally, the concept of interaction is introduced in Part II as a key element of best practices, and is expanded upon in Part IV as a necessary and purposeful element to achieve an effective online learning environment.

In chapter 3, Hirumi presents a thorough literature analysis of current educational guidelines and industry specifications for quality e-learning published by professional organizations. Hirumi concludes that the "search for quality" is an ongoing task and that the setting of guidelines and practices is a solid step towards attaining quality. Hirumi's work on quality guidelines and specifications serves as a preamble to the rest of the chapters in this second section.

Teaching is the key element in successful distance education, and instructors' perspectives, philosophical orientation, and practices can have an effect on the learning environment. In chapter 4, Sorensen and Baylen describe the application of Chickering and Ehrmann's "Seven

Principles of Good Practice" for effective learning to a Web-based environment. They conclude that these principles can be effectively adapted to the online environment, but this plan requires "teachers to overcome obstacles, to develop new strategies, and to look at their craft from new perspectives." In the following chapter, Zhang and Walls explore instructors' perceptions of their implementation of the seven principles and find that the perceptions vary from one principle to another. In chapter 6, Zheng and Smaldino present a literature review related to key design elements for effective online teaching. Continuing with the theme of the significance of the instructor's role in successful education, in chapter 7 Orellana presents findings of instructors' perceptions of optimal class sizes for online courses according to levels of interaction. Orellana's work is connected with best practices and accreditation standards for course design that promote interaction and is framed within a multidimensional model to examine the construct of interaction.

In chapter 8, Reisetter and Boris study effective design elements in online learning from the perspective of students. The findings show that the major factors that contribute to successful online course design are student-course and student-teacher interactions in accordance with Moore's types of interactions. Chapter 9, by Sadik and Reisman, focuses on design elements that should be evaluated in a Web-based learning environment. The authors describe issues with respect to the lessons learned during design and implementation, and connect their experiences to the literature. Among the key elements was the "understanding [of] the spectrum of interactions."

The last two chapters of Part II present theoretical frameworks for designing effective instruction. Based on the significance of interaction in online education, Hirumi proposes a three-level framework that can be used to effectively design, analyze, and insert interactions in an online course. Finally, McLaren presents practical guidelines for designing effective instruction based on several instructional methods and design models. McLaren's work serves as theoretical preamble to Part III, where instructional methods and models are presented.

PART III: BEST INSTRUCTIONAL METHODS AND MODELS

The chapters in Part III address methods and models that focus on the instructor (chapters 12 and 13), the student (chapters 14 to 17), course content and materials, and on design process management (chapters 18 to 20). It is worth noting that *instructional design methods* are tied to specific *instructional design models* and frequently both terms have been used interchangeably in the literature, including in the chapters of this book. However, the difference between these terms lies within the definitions of *model* and *method*. A model is "a simplified representation of a system ... showing selected features of the system" (Dick et al., 2005, p. 365). A method consists of "a procedure or process for attaining an object: as ... a systematic plan followed in presenting material for instruction" (*Merriam-Webster Online Dictionary*, 2008). Thus, an instructional design model represents a simplification of the instructional system and an instructional design method is a plan that defines how to organize the whole design process.

In chapter 12, by Hawkes and Coldeway, two approaches for online course development (team versus faculty-based development) are compared. The authors discuss design implications for online education and for the role of faculty as designers. In chapter 13, Kranch proposes an Individual Iterative Instructional Design (I3D) that sees the instructional design process as one that "does not wait ... to finish before using the product." Kranch bases this proposal on the need to aid the individual instructor, "who is both the developer and presenter of distance education," when designing instruction in formal education environments.

Chapters 14 to 17 present methods and models that focus on the online student. Miller and Mazur describe in chapter 14 a person-centered model for online instruction that emphasizes the "learners' interests, personal ability, and prior knowledge on a given topic." The authors theorized that three outcomes result when designing under this model: creative, useful, and original products; significant learning; and increase of self-actualization. Then, in chapter 15, Miller evaluates the person-centered model and compares its implementation to non-person-centered instruction. Differences in experiences were found between the groups under each approach. Continuing, and completing with the emphasis on the students, chapters 16 and 17 make a contribution to best practices by describing methods for specific instructional activities: evaluation of asynchronous discussions and reduction of online academic dishonesty.

Chapters 18 to 20 focus on course materials, course content, and design management. In chapter 18, how instructors organize the material in an online course was compared to where students expect to find these materials. Discrepancies were found and the authors present recommendations "for alleviating student confusion" when finding materials in a Web-based course. In chapter 19, Morrison and Anglin identify shovelware as "content taken from any source and placed on the Web as fast as possible with little regard for appearance and usability." Morrison and Anglin then provide tools such as reverse engineering and instructional disassembly to help designers evaluate the instructional soundness of traditional courses presented in an online format. Chapter 20 introduces the use of graphic and text advance organizers to assist learners in linking what they already know to new information and then applying this information in new contexts.

In Chapter 21, Abdous and He introduce Enterprise Project Management as a tool to assist in blending a systematic approach to planning, designing, and producing online courses. Abdous and He also provide suggestions for staff training and server configuration. To round out Part III, Boyer provides evidence for scaffolding techniques such as learning contracts, diagnostic instruments, and reflective components.

PART IV: BEST ENGAGEMENT STRATEGIES

An instructional strategy is "an overall plan of activities to achieve an instructional goal" (Dick et al., 2005, p. 365). Instructional strategies should be tied to the interest and needs of the student. As noted in previous sections, purposeful interaction is a key instructional strategy for the perfect online course. Student engagement can be obtained when well-planned instructional strategies for interaction are inserted in the design. In chapters 23 to 25, the need for different types of interaction is discussed. Wanstreet provides an extensive review of the literature as it pertains to the conceptual and operational definition of interaction. This includes areas of interaction as an instructional exchange, interaction as computer-mediated communication, and interaction as a social/psychological connection. In contrast, Battalio in chapter 24 suggests that some types of interaction may not be necessary for all students; both articles emphasize student-instructor interaction. In chapter 25, Northrup addresses learners' preference for interaction. Northrup found that students most valued timely feedback from the instructor and intrapersonal/metacognitive interaction.

Problem-based learning (PBL) is another strategy to achieve interaction that may be used in the perfect online course. In chapter 26, Wheeler describes how PBL can be used to provide learners with real-world simulations. Student-student interaction within these simulations mirror situations the learners may encounter in their work environments. Havard, Du, and Olinzock bring deep learning into the dialog of interaction as they provide evidence for instructor-led discussions. In Chapter 27, Havard et al. identify three roles of the instructor and how the instructor can use these roles within the course to model desired discussion behavior, create a supportive learning environment, and enhance students' adaptive learning. Chapter 28 further emphasizes strategies for moderating a discussion forum in online courses. Durrington and Yu compare discussions moderated by the instructor versus peers. Study results indicated that students participated significantly more when the discussions were student-moderated, as opposed to instructor-moderated.

Students in online courses have reported a sense of isolation; therefore, the final chapter of this section—chapter 29 by Liu et al.—is presented as a resource for strategies to enhance community building within groups, the class, and beyond the class. The spirit of community lies in the commitment and mutual engagement of community members, instructors, and program administrators.

CONCLUSION

Simonson closes our exploration of the perfect online course by admitting that the perfect online course is a "pipe dream." As editors exploring the current research involving the guidelines, standards, methods, models, and strategies for online course designing and teaching, we have found that by following the recommendations provided, an online course can "satisfy all requirements." Those requirements start with establishing learning outcomes, followed by the use of a solid instructional design that is guided by quality standards and best practices. Effective methods and models presented here provide developers and instructors with a starting point. Finally, by using the strategies for interaction to achieve engagement, the perfect online course can be satisfying to both the instructor and the learner. The perfect online course may not be flawless, but it is attainable. However, as Winston Churchill noted, "to be perfect is to change often." As new technologies, new perspectives, and more research become available, we must be willing to reevaluate "The Perfect Online Course."

REFERENCES

Dick, W., Carey, L., & Carey, J. (2005). *The systematic design of instruction* (6th ed.). New York: Allyn & Bacon.

Merriam-Webster Online Dictionary. (2008). Retrieved December 10, 2008, from http://www.merriam-webster.com/dictionary/method and December 8, 2008, from http://www.merriam-webster.com/dictionary/perfect

Simonson, M., Smaldino, S., Albright, M., & Zvacek. S. (2009). *Teaching and learning at a distance: Foundations of distance education* (4th ed.) Upper Saddle River, NJ: Prentice-Hall.

PART I

INTRODUCTION

CHAPTER 1

WE NEED A PLAN

An Instructional Design Approach for Distance Education Courses

Michael Simonson and Charles Schlosser

On October 25, 1965, downtown St. Louis stopped in its tracks and thousands watched as the last piece of the mammoth Gateway Arch was put into place. The weight of the two sides required braces to prevent them from falling against each other. Fire hoses poured on water to keep the stainless steel cool, which kept the metal from expanding as the sun rose higher. Some horizontal adjustments were required, but when the last piece was put into place and the braces released, it fit perfectly, according to plan, and no one was surprised (Liggett, 1998).

Just like the Arch, distance education programs require a careful planning process that includes systematic design and implementation. There will be success if all the pieces of the plan receive the same attention as the most obvious. The base sections of the Gateway Arch required more engineering savvy and study than any other component. The last and most visible span that connected the two halves received the most attention from the thousands of onlookers, but success was directly related to how the original supports were positioned.

The Perfect Online Course: Best Practices for Designing and Teaching
pp. 3–21

One key to effective distance education is correct instructional design, a systematic process that applies research-based principles to educational practice. If the design is effective, instruction will also be effective. This chapter presents a review of what we know about "best practices in distance education," and proposes an easy-to-apply approach to guide those who are designing classes.

DISTANCE TEACHING AND DISTANCE LEARNING

Distance education has two major components: distance teaching and distance learning. Distance teaching is the efforts of the educational institution to design, develop, and deliver instructional experiences to the distant student so that learning may occur. Designers of instruction concentrate on distance teaching, while students are responsible for learning.

EFFECTIVE DISTANCE EDUCATION: A SYNOPSIS OF WHAT WE KNOW

Distance education has been practiced for more than 150 years, passing through three phases: first, correspondence study, with its use of print-based instructional and communication media; second, the rise of the distance teaching universities and the use of analog mass media; and third, the widespread integration of distance education elements into most forms of education, and characterized by the use of digital instructional and communication technologies. Peters (2002) has suggested that "the swift, unforeseen, unexpected and unbelievable achievements of information and communication technologies" will require "the design of new formats of learning and teaching and [will cause] powerful and far-reaching structural changes of the learning-teaching process" (p. 20). Peters' views are well-accepted, but there is also consensus that the most fruitful way of identifying elements of quality instruction may be to reexamine "first principles" of distance education and mediated instruction.

Perhaps the first of the "first principles" is the recognition that distance education is a system, and that the creation of successful courses—and the program of which they are a part—requires a "systems" approach. Hirumi (2000) identified a number of systems approaches, but noted a concept common to all: that "a system is a set of interrelated components that work together to achieve a common purpose" (p. 90). He described a system that involved the efforts of faculty, staff, administrators, and students, and consisted of eight key components: curriculum, instruction, manage-

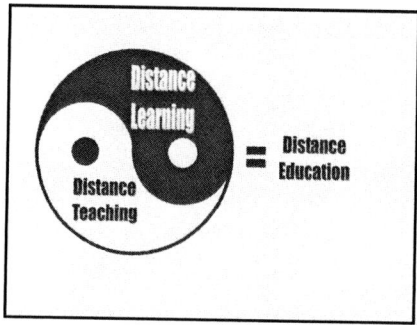

ment and logistics, academic services, strategic alignment, professional development, research and development, and program evaluation.

Bates (in Foley, 2003) proposed 12 "golden rules" for the use of technology in education. These offer guidance in the broader areas of designing and developing distance education:

1. Good teaching matters. Quality design of learning activities is important for all delivery methods.
2. Each medium has its own aesthetic. Therefore professional design is important.
3. Education technologies are flexible. They have their own unique characteristics but successful teaching can be achieved with any technology.
4. There is no "super-technology." Each has its strengths and weaknesses; therefore they need to be combined (an integrated mix).
5. Make all four media available to teachers and learners. Print, audio, television, and computers.
6. Balance variety with economy. Using many technologies makes design more complex and expensive; therefore limit the range of technologies in a given circumstance.
7. Interaction is essential.
8. Student numbers are critical. The choice of a medium will depend greatly on the number of learners reached over the life of a course.
9. New technologies are not necessarily better than old ones.
10. Teachers need training to use technology effectively.
11. Teamwork is essential. No one person has all the skills to develop and deliver a distance-learning course; therefore, subject matter

experts, instructional designers, and media specialists are essential on every team.

12. Technology is not the issue. How and what we want the learners to learn is the issue and technology is a tool (p. 833).

A number of these "rules" are overlapping. Three of them (1, 2, and 11) address course and program design. Any examination of "first principles" should first examine instructional design. While it has been noted that instructors, even those new to distance education, can learn to adapt courses and create materials for online delivery (Ko & Rossen, 2003), and the author-editor model has long been an element of correspondence study programs, "what is strikingly missing in these arrangements, usually, is an instructional designer and many good features of the instructional design approach" (Moore & Kearsley, 1996, p. 104). The team-based approach to distance education course development is generally regarded as more likely to result in high-quality materials, experiences and, hence, more satisfactory teaching and learning experiences (Hirumi, 2000).

Bates' triumvirate of subject matter expert, instructional designer, and media specialist is the standard core of the course design team, which may be expanded—one source (Hanna, Glowacki-Dudka, & Conceicao-Runlee, 2000) has suggested as many as eight members— based on the particular needs of the program and the media employed. No one approach to course design is ideal; as Moore and Kearsley (1996) noted, the course team approach results in "materials [that] are usually much more complete and effective. Furthermore, [it] tends to emphasize the use of multiple media in a course" but is "very labor-intensive and therefore expensive, and it involves a lengthy development period" (p. 106). Of the two approaches, "the author-editor approach is the only one that makes economic sense if courses have very small enrollments or short lifetimes, while the course team approach is justified for courses with large enrollments and long-term use" (p. 107).

Foley (2003) has noted "there are general principles of good design that can be applied to all distance learning activities" (p. 831) but noted the following influences:

- the target audience of the activity;
- the content of subject matter to be delivered; and
- the outcomes or objectives desired (p. 831).

Other considerations having "profound effects on the design of the learning activities" (p. 831) include:

- the cost effectiveness of the system;
- the opportunity costs of alternative systems and methods;
- the availability of technology to the provider and to the learners;
- the geographical location of the learners; and
- the comfort level of the learners with any technology that is used (p. 831).

Foley notes that these factors apply equally well when designing instruction for any given audience, from children to adults. When designing the World Bank's Global Development Learning Network, "results of more than 30 years of research on adult learning were applied to the distance learning programs" (p. 832). The criteria included:

1. They are based on clearly established learning needs and built around succinct statements of outcome.
2. They are based on a variety of teaching and learning strategies and methods that are activity based.
3. Effective distance learning materials are experiential ... they address the learner's life experience.
4. Quality distance learning programs are participatory in that they emphasize the involvement of the learner in all facets of program development and delivery.
5. Successful distance learning programs are interactive and allow frequent opportunities for participants to engage in a dialogue with subject matter experts and other learners.
6. Learner support systems are an integral part of any successful distance learning program (p. 832).

The Indiana Partnership for Statewide Education (IPSE, 2000) proposed "Guiding Principles for Faculty in Distance Learning":

- Distance learning courses will be carefully planned to meet the needs of students within unique learning contexts and environments.
- Distance learning programs are most effective when they include careful planning and consistency among courses.
- It is important for faculty who are engaged in the delivery of distance learning courses to take advantage of appropriate professional developmental experiences.

- Distance learning courses will be periodically reviewed and evaluated to ensure quality, consistency with the curriculum, currency, and advancement of the student learning outcomes.
- Faculty will work to ensure that incentives and rewards for distance learning course development and delivery are clearly defined and understood.
- An assessment plan is adapted or developed in order to achieve effectiveness, continuity, and sustainability of the assessment process. Course outcome assessment activities are integrated components of the assessment plan.
- Learning activities are organized around demonstrable learning outcomes embedded in course components including: course delivery mode, pedagogy, content, organization, and evaluation.
- Content developed for distance learning courses will comply with copyright law.
- Faculty members involved in content development will be aware of their institution's policies with regard to content ownership.
- The medium/media chosen to deliver courses and/or programs will be pedagogically effectual, accessible to students, receptive to different learning styles, and sensitive to the time and place limitations of the students.
- The institution provides appropriate support services to distance students that are equivalent to services provided for its on-campus students.
- The institution provides its students at a distance with accessible library and other learning resources appropriate to the courses or programs delivered via technology. It develops systems to support them in accessing and using these library and other learning resources effectively.
- It is important to provide the appropriate developmental experiences for faculty who are engaged in the delivery of distance learning experiences.
- The institution implements policies and processes by which the instructional effectiveness of each distance learning course is evaluated periodically.
- Timely and reliable technical support is vital to the success of any distance learning program.
- It is recommended that a system of faculty incentives and rewards be developed cooperatively by the faculty and the administration, which encourages effort and recognizes achievement associated with the development and delivery of distance learning courses.

- The institution will communicate copyright and intellectual property policies to all faculty and staff working on distance learning course development and delivery.
- The institution complies with state policies and maintains regional accreditation standards in regard to distance learning programs. (www.old.ihets.org/learntech/facprinc.html)

Commonalities between these principles and those suggested by other authors and organizations may be readily perceived. For instance, careful planning and the need for teacher training are cited by Bates (in Foley, 2003), and the emphasis on the unique needs of students in a variety of contexts is mentioned by Foley (2003). The IPSE principles make an important contribution by highlighting need for consideration of copyright law and policies, intellectual property ownership, faculty incentives, and state policies and accreditation standards.

Because education (including distance education) is a system, each of its elements interacts with other elements, making the isolation of elements difficult. Interaction (its type, quantity, quality, timing, etc.), for instance, cannot be separated from instructional philosophy, choice of media, and other factors.

Whatever media are selected to facilitate instructor-student and student-student interaction, it should be recognized that these forms of mediated discussion should not completely replace the face-to-face element in courses. As Peters (1998) noted, those who believe that new, digital media will "supply the interactivity and communication lacking in distance education … cherish a hope here that will prove to be serious self-delusion" (p. 155). Peters' comments on the topic (in the context of videoconferencing, a relatively rich "high bandwidth" form of communication), trenchant and incisive, are worth quoting at length:

> Communication mediated through technical media remains mediated communication and cannot replace an actual discussion, an actual argument, the discourse of a group gathered at a particular location. Mediated communication and actual communication stand in relationship to one another like a pencilled [sic] sketch and an oil painting of the same subject. What takes place in a discussion between two or more people can only be transmitted in part electronically. What is missing is the consciously perceived presence of the other persons, their aura, the feeling of being together that differs each time the participants meet. All this supplies genuineness and liveliness to the communication. A virtual university that does without face-to-face events by referring to the possibility of videoconferencing can only ever remain a surrogate university.
>
> A distance teaching university in a multimedia system, with its face-to-face study counselling [sic] and its tutors in the study centres, is much more

fortunate in this regard. Even the most extensively developed virtual university cannot do without these meetings. This is not an argument against video-conferencing as such. It is a new medium for learning and teaching in distance education, with particular advantages and disadvantages, whose effect has still to be developed. There is no doubt that to a certain extent [videoconferencing] will improve the structure of communication in distance education—but it cannot ever take the place of personal communication in distance education. (p. 155)

Peters' views on virtual communication have not been significantly modified with time. More recently (2002), he has noted that the losses inherent in mediated communications are serious:

They reduce, surround, parcel out, spoil or destroy experiences gained at school or university. For this reason, it may be concluded, learning in virtual space will never be able to replace completely teaching in real spaces. (p. 104)

The effective use of a variety of media to facilitate communication, combined with critical quantities of well-structured face-to-face instruction and learning, have characterized many distance-delivered programs. They are two key elements of the Nova ITDE model of distance education, what has been called "the best of both worlds" (Schlosser & Burmeister, 1999).

As important as is the appropriate selection and use of technologies of instruction and communication, Moore (1998) has noted that these technologies are not critical elements in shaping students' satisfaction with their distance courses. Rather, satisfaction is determined by "the attention they receive from the teachers and from the system they work in to meet their needs" (p. 4). Those needs, "what all distant learners want, and deserve" include:

- content that they feel is relevant to their needs;
- clear directions for what they should do at every stage of the course;
- as much control of the pace of learning as possible;
- a means of drawing attention to individual concerns;
- a way of testing their progress and getting feedback from their instructors; and
- materials that are useful, active, and interesting (p. 4).

At the same time, it should be noted that frustration with the use of complex, inadequate, malfunctioning equipment, as well as perceptions of emotional distance engendered by the use of distance education technologies, have negatively affected students' attitudes toward—and, in some cases, achievement in—distance education.

Bates' seventh "golden rule," that "interaction is essential," is well-accepted by the field, and is a central element in most definitions of distance education (see, for instance, Keegan, 1996; Schlosser & Simonson, 2003). Keegan (1996) noted that distance education must offer "the provision of two-way communication so that the student may benefit from or even initiate dialogue" (p. 44). Initial provisions for interaction were primarily for student-instructor interactions but, with the availability of expanded communication technologies in the 1990s, came an increasing emphasis on additional forms of interaction. Three forms of interaction are widely recognized by the field: student-content, student-instructor, and student-student. It is this third form of communication, reflecting, in part, andragogical and constructivist perspectives, that has increased dramatically with the rise of online education.

Concurrent with the expansion of online education and the diffusion of new communication technologies, there arose the mistaken belief that, if interaction is important, "the more interaction there is in a distance education class, the better" (Simonson, 2000, p. 278). As Simonson (2000) has noted, early research in the field had "demonstrated clearly that the provision for interaction was critical" (p. 278), but later research indicated as clearly that "interaction is not a magic potion that miraculously improves distance learning" (p. 278). Indeed, "the forcing of interaction can be as strong a detriment to effective learning [as is] its absence" (p. 278).

When quantifying and qualifying student-teacher and student-student interaction, perceptions may be less than reliable. In a study comparing distance students' perceptions of interaction (as compared with observations of their interaction), Sorensen and Baylen (2000) noted that students accurately noted that: across-site interaction was very low, that within-site interaction was very high, that interaction changes with instructor location, that remote site students participate less, and that group activities increase interactions. However, students perceived that less interaction occurred over time (when, in fact, interaction increased), and that technology inhibits interaction (when, more accurately, it seems to create different patterns of interaction.

Although Sorensen and Baylen examined interaction in the context of an interactive television course, their findings have implications for other distance education modalities. The researchers concluded that a sense of community formed among students at the distant sites, but interaction increased when the instructor was present at a given distant site. Having instructors rotate among sites encouraged interaction. Interaction was hampered when students were unable to see or hear their distant class-mates. Allowing constant displays of distant students would likely increase interaction. Maintaining students' attention in a distance-delivered course "appears to be a more difficult task than perhaps in the traditional class" (p. 56). Sorensen and Baylen noted that "varying activities and including hands-on exercises and small and large group discussions were instructional methods appreciated by the students" (p. 56). Students in the Sorensen and Baylen study expressed satisfaction with the "distance learning experience," but suggested that the course include "at least one opportunity for students to meet face-to-face" (p. 57).

Distance-teaching institutions (and their students) have a wide variety of instructional and communication media from which to choose. These two categories (instructional and communication) may be, to some extent, addressed separately, but they are often one and the same. Bates' fourth "golden rule," that there is no "super-technology," is well-accepted and understood by experienced instructional technologists and distance edu-cators, but often less so by those new to the field (and many of today's practitioners fall into this latter category). For this reason, it is important to invoke the findings of Clark (1983), who noted, two decades ago, that "media do not influence learning under any conditions" (p. 446). Indeed, "The best current evidence is that media are mere vehicles that deliver instruction but do not influence student achievement any more than the truck that delivers our groceries causes changes in our nutrition" (p. 446). Clark's conclusions have been bolstered by Russell (1999), whose well-known "No Significant Difference Phenomenon" articles have summa-rized the conclusions of decades of media-comparison studies.

If, as Clark (citing hundreds of studies and decades of research) main-tains, the application of any particular medium will neither improve stu-dent achievement nor increase the speed of learning, what criteria might a distance-teaching institution apply in the selection of media for the delivery of instruction and the facilitation of communication? Cost (to both the institution as well as to the student) is an obvious criterion. Less obvious, perhaps, are the culture of the institution and expectations of students (or potential students).

At a very practical level, Ko and Rossen (2003) suggested that, prior to selecting media and instruction for online education, the institution's resources be assessed and the following questions asked:

- What's already in place (what, if any courses are being offered online; who is teaching them, etc.)?
- What kind of hardware and operating system does your institution support?
- What kind of network has your institution set up?

- What kind of computer support does your institution provide? (p. 19).

As Ko and Rossen noted, "the tools an institution uses and the support it offers very much influence the choices [the instructor will] need to make" (p. 18).

Other guidelines for selection of media for synchronous communication, in the context of one "best practice" in distance education—collaborative, problem-based student work groups—have been offered by Foreman (2003). Foreman noted the usefulness of a wide variety of synchronous technologies: chat, telephone conference, Web conferencing and application sharing, voice-over-IP, virtual classrooms, and videoconferencing. Of the technologies at either end of the spectrum—chat and videoconferencing—"neither works especially well as a tool for collaborative teamwork" (para. 5) because chat is slow and awkward, and because videoconferencing is expensive, is frequently of low technical quality, and often fails to capture many of the visual cues so helpful for communication.

Telephone conferencing, however, "is highly effective for organizing small-team distance learning experiences," as it "provides immediacy, a high rate of information exchange, and complex multiperson interaction facilitated by a familiar audio cueing system" (para. 6). Foreman recognizes that telephone conferencing can be expensive, but counters that significant savings may be realized through inexpensive three-way calling options—which, "despite its name, four or more people can use ... at once" (para. 7)—available through most telecom providers.

Commercially provided Web conferencing, combining telephone and Web technologies, overcomes the limitations of voice-only technologies through the provision of "application sharing," but its telephone component is costly. Voice-over-IP is a promising technology but, at its current level, is "intrusive and clumsy" because of sometimes-lengthy lag time and overall low fidelity (para. 15).

Virtual classrooms focus on synchronous teacher-student and student-student interaction through application-sharing and voice-over-IP. Virtual classrooms have been available for several years, but only recently has usability advanced to a level considered acceptable by many. Foreman suggests that this final category is most promising, as it can

create inexpensive cyberspaces where geo-distributed students can perform their learning work through the preferred medium for intense communication—talk. Their talk will focus on shared screen objects ... that facilitate the dialogue.... Under the best circumstances, the students will divide the work, perform it separately, and then gather online to share their findings and integrate them into a deliverable product that can be assessed by the instructor. This is the decentered classroom taken to a logical extreme by an emerging technology. (para. 21)

Adams and Freeman (2003) have noted the benefits of the virtual classroom, noting that the interactions within them "in addition to allowing for the exchange of information, provide participants with a shared feeling of presence or immediacy that reinforces their membership in the community" (para. 12).

In the end, all of the above criteria are considered and, frequently, a pragmatic approach is adopted. As Bates recommends in his fourth "golden rule," "each [medium] has its strengths and weaknesses, therefore they need to be combined (an integrated mix)" (Foley, 2003, p. 843).

The literature abounds with guidelines for distance education and identified "best practices" of distance education. Sometimes these are based on careful research but are, in most cases, the products of practitioners relating practices that have proven successful for that author. Still, some common threads have emerged.

Graham, Cagiltay, Lim, Craner, and Duffy (2001) have offered seven lessons for online instruction:

1. Instructors should provide clear guidelines for interaction with students.
2. Well-designed discussion assignments facilitate meaningful cooperation among students.
3. Students should present course projects.
4. Instructors need to provide two types of feedback: information feedback and acknowledgment feedback.
5. Online courses need deadlines.
6. Challenging tasks, sample cases, and praise for quality work communicate high expectations.
7. Allowing students to choose project topics incorporates diverse views into online courses.

In his eighth "golden rule," Bates notes that "student numbers are critical." While this observation is made in the context of cost and media selection, student numbers are, indeed, critical in at least two other respects: class and working- (or discussion-) group size. Distance education has been embraced, in some quarters, as an opportunity to reduce costs by increasing class sizes. The literature clearly indicates that there are practical limits beyond which the quality of instruction and learning are compromised. As Hanna et al. (2000) noted, "demand for interaction defines the size of face-to-face classrooms and the nature of the interactions within those classrooms; the demand for interaction has a similar effect upon online classrooms" (p. 26). Palloff and Pratt (2003) have suggested that experienced online educators can "handle" 20 to 25 students in an online course, while "instructors who are new to the medium, or instructors teaching a course for the first time, should really teach no more than fifteen students" (p. 118). Chat sessions should be smaller, with perhaps 10 to 12 students (Palloff & Pratt, 2003), and work/discussion groups might have four or five members (Foreman, 2003; Hanna et al., 2000).

On a larger scale, institutions of higher education should understand that distance education is not the "cash cow" that some have mistakenly suggested (Berg, 2001). Indeed, the development and support of distance-delivered courses and programs is normally more expensive than for similar traditional courses and programs. When exceptions are occasionally noted, it is usually found that a difference in scale could explain the savings, as in the University of California-Davis study that found that preparing and offering a large (430 students) general education course at a distance was less than the cost of the same course delivered traditionally (Sloan Consortium, 2002). A second exception is the instance of the very large distance-teaching universities, such as the Open University of the United Kingdom, where large enrollments and a long "product cycle" reduce the unit cost per student to about half that common among traditional graduate programs (Moore & Kearsley, 1996).

Care should be taken when schools search the field for suitable models. As Garon (2002) has noted, "academic attempts at providing universities online have been marketing failures and academic distractions. New York University, Temple University, and other famous universities have closed their virtual doors" and "highly touted start-ups such as Columbia University's Fathom.com and Western Governors University ... [have] dramatically downsized the attempts to provide online degrees" (para. 2). Garon cites two successful for-profit institutions—the University of Phoenix and DeVry University—while noting that their success may be because, given their model for instruction, they "are much closer to large, national community colleges than traditional four-year colleges, but the model serves their community of adult learners well" (para. 6). Schools, then, should clearly identify the type of students they wish to attract, the needs of those students, and the type of university they aspire to be.

Distance education is a broad field with a long history. It is important to remember that, the views of some authors notwithstanding, there is no one "right" way to conduct distance education. At the same time, it would be foolish to ignore the insights and recommendations of longtime practitioners of distance education, as well as those whose field is the study of distance education. Distance education has experienced a marked expansion—and, to a certain extent, reinvention—in the past few years (coinciding with the rise of the Web and entrepreneurial forces in education). However, it should be borne in mind that online education is not the sum of distance education, that the field existed long before the Web, and that enduring principles of education did not become obsolete with the development of new, electronic technologies.

DISTANCE-DELIVERED INSTRUCTION: THE U-M-T APPROACH

This section includes recommendations that are intended to provide a way to organize a course. These recommendations are guiding principles to help make courses with equal numbers of semester credits equivalent in terms of comprehensiveness of content coverage, even if these courses are offered in different programs, cover different topics, and are delivered using different media.

Organizational Guidelines

In traditional university courses, the 50-minute class session is the building block for courses. Usually, 15 classes are offered for each semester credit. This is the Carnegie unit, which usually means that for each semester credit, a traditional course must have 15 50-minute class sessions, for a total of 750 minutes of face-to-face instruction.

Distance-delivered courses do not normally have class sessions, as such. It is proposed that the designer of distance instruction use the topic as the fundamental building block for a course. Topics are then organized into modules that are further organized into units that are roughly equivalent to a semester credit.

The designer can organize a course like this:

- each semester credit = 1 unit,
- each unit = 3-5 modules,
- each module = 3-5 topics, and
- each topic = 1 learning outcome.

When applied, a typical 3-credit course might have 3 units, 12-15 modules, 48-60 topics, and 48-60 learning outcomes.

Working definitions of unit, module, and topic are:

Unit. A unit is a significant body of knowledge that represents a major subdivision of a course's content. Often, one unit of a course would represent 4 or 5 weeks of instruction, and would be equivalent to a semester credit. For example, in a 3-credit educational statistics course a unit might be the study of descriptive statistics.

Module. A module is a major, distinct, and discreet component of a unit. Generally, a unit such as descriptive statistics might be divided into 3-5 major components, such as statistical assumptions, measures of central tendency, measures of variation, and the normal curve. Modules generally are the basis for several class sessions and are covered in about a week of instruction and study.

Topic. A topic is an important supporting idea that explains, clarifies, or supports a module. A topic would be a lesson or a presentation. Three topics in a module on central tendency might be median, mode, and mean.

These three terms can be used in a variety of ways. Of importance is the idea that topics form modules and modules form units, and units are the main subdivisions of courses.

Assessment Guidelines

Assessment is defined as the determination and measurement of learning. Ultimately, assessment is used for grading. Assessment is directly related to learning outcomes. Normally, there is at least one learning outcome for each course topic.

A typical 3-credit course might have the following assessment strategy:

- 1 examination,
- 1 10-page paper,
- 1 project,
- 3 quizzes,
- 3 small assignments (short paper, article review, activity report), and
- graded threaded discussions, e-mails, and chats.

Learning Outcome

A learning outcome is observable and measurable. Learning outcomes are a consequence of teaching and learning—of instruction and study. Often, learning outcomes are written with three components: conditions under which learning is facilitated (instruction), observable and measurable actions or products, and a minimum standard of expectations. Usually, there is at least one learning outcome for each course topic. For example, a learning outcome for a topic in a statistics course dealing with median might be:

> After studying the text, pages 51–53, reviewing the PowerPoint with audio presentation on measures of central tendency, and participating in synchronous chats, the student will analyze two sets of test data to identify the median for each.

Content Guidelines

Traditionally, instructors have offered content by making presentations during face-to-face instruction. Additionally, readings in textbooks and handouts are commonly required of students in courses.

In distance teaching situations, readings in texts, handouts, and information on the Internet are often used to deliver content. For high-quality courses, there often is an emphasis on the use of various forms of visual media to offer instructional content. Videos, visual presentations with accompanying audio, and other graphical representations of important topics are important in a well-designed course. A variety of delivery systems for content can be considered, including the use of compact disks, electronic files posted to Web sites, and streaming.

As described above, content is organized into topics. Topics are combined into modules of similar topics and modules are used to form units.

Modules might have 3-5 topics presented in the following ways:

- readings in the text or other written materials;
- videos supplied on CD, DVD, or streamed;
- audio recordings of speeches or presentations supplied on a CD, as an e-mail attachment, or streamed;
- recorded presentations using PowerPoint with prerecorded audio; and
- synchronous chats with content experts.

Instruction/Teaching Guidelines

The pace of instruction for learners is a critical concern for the distance educator. Because many distance education students are employed full-time, it is important to offer instruction in a way that complements their other responsibilities. These guidelines relate to the pace of instruction and the need for continuing interaction between instructors and students:

- 1 module per week;
- Instructor e-mail to students each week;
- 1 synchronous chat per week;
- 2-3 threaded discussion questions per topic, or 6-10 questions per week;
- Instructor comments on discussions as part of threaded discussion; and
- Progress reports (grades) submitted to students for each module.

These course design guidelines are based on the literature of distance education and are derived from the analysis, review, and discussion of quality courses delivered at a distance.

A FINAL WORD

The simplicity of the Carnegie Unit has made it the standard for course design, primarily because it is easy to apply. It is easy to count class sessions in order to determine if a course "measures up." Distance education, with few if any face-to-face sessions, does not have such a widely accepted standard. The unit/module/topic approach is being used in courses, and seems to be quickly and accurately applied, while establishing a standard of quality.

The successful placement of the final section of the St. Louis Gateway Arch depended on planning and design that was completed years earlier. Distance learning is facilitated by distance teaching, if distance teaching is well planned and designed, often months before the course is taught.

REFERENCES

Adams, E., & Freeman, C. (2003). Selecting tools for online communities: Suggestions for learning technologists. *The Technology Source*. Available online at http://ts.mivu.org/ default.asp?show+article&id=994

Berg, G. A. (2001, April-June). Distance learning best practices debate. *Web-Net Journal.*

Clark, R. E. (1983). Reconsidering research on learning from media. *Review of Educational Research, 53*(4), 445-459.

Foley, M. (2003). The Global Development Learning Network: A World Bank initiative in distance learning for development. In M. G. Moore & W. G. Anderson (Eds.), *Handbook of distance education*. Mahwah, NJ: Erlbaum.

Foreman, J. (2003, July/August). Distance learning and synchronous interaction. *The Technology Source*. Available online at http://ts.mivu.org/ default.asp?show+ article&id=1042

Garon, J. (2002, August). A new future for distance education. *Interface Tech News*. Available online at http:// www.interfacenow.com/syndicatepro/ displayarticle.asp?ArticleID=180

Graham, C., Cagiltay, K., Lim, B. -R., Craner, J., & Duffy, T. M. (2001, March/ April). Seven principles of effective teaching: A practical lens for evaluating online courses. *The Technology Source*. Available online at: http://ts.mivu.org/ default.asp?show+article&id=839

Hanna, D. E., Glowacki-Dudka, M., & Conceicao-Runlee, S. (2000). *147 practical tips for teaching online groups: Essentials for Web-based education*. Madison, WI: Atwood.

Hirumi, A. (2000). Chronicling the challenges of web-basing a degree program: A systems perspective. *Quarterly Review of Distance Education, 1*(2), 89-108.

Indiana Partnership for Statewide Education. (2000). *Guiding Principles for Faculty in Distance Learning*. Available online at: www.old.ihets.org/learn-tech/facprinc .html

Keegan, D. (1996). *Foundations of distance education* (3rd ed.). London: Routledge.

Ko, S., & Rossen, S. (2003). Teaching online: A practical guide (2nd ed.). Boston: Houghton Mifflin.

Liggett, R. (1998, October 2). A prescription for telemedicine. *Telemedicine Today*.

Moore, M. G. (1998). Introduction. In C. C. Gibson (Ed.), *Distance learners in higher education: Institutional responses for quality outcomes*. Madison, WI: Atwood.

Moore, M. G., & Kearsley, G. (1996). *Distance education: A systems view*. Belmont, CA: Wadsworth.

Palloff, R. M., & Pratt, K. (2003). *The virtual student: A profile and guide to working with online learners*. San Francisco: Jossey-Bass.

Peters, O. (1998). *Learning and teaching in distance education: Pedagogical analyses and interpretations in an international perspective*. London: Kogan Page.

Peters, O. (2002). *Distance education in transition: New trends and challenges*. Bibliotheks- und Informationssytem der Universitat Oldenburg.

Russell, T. L. (1999). *The no significant difference phenomenon*. Montgomery, AL: International Distance Education Certification Center.

Schlosser, C., & Burmeister, M. (1999). Best of both worlds: The Nova ITDE model of distance education. *Tech Trends, 43*(5), 45-48.

Schlosser, L. A., & Simonson, M. (2003). *Distance education: Definition and glossary of terms*. Bloomington, IN: Association for Educational Communications and Technology.

Simonson, M. (2000). Myths and distance education: What the research says (and does not). *Quarterly Review of Distance Education, 4*(1), 277-279.

Sloan Consortium. (2002). *Practice: Comparing the cost-effectiveness of online versus traditional classroom cost per student pass rates.* Available online at http://www.aln.org/effective/details5.asp?CE_ID=21

Sorensen, C., & Baylen, D. (2000). Perception versus reality: Views of interaction in distance education. *Quarterly Review of Distance Education, 1*(1), 45-58.

CHAPTER 2

DOES IT MATTER?

Analyzing the Results of
Three Different Learning Delivery Methods

**William N. Chernish, Agnes L. DeFranco,
James R. Lindner, and Kim E. Dooley**

The increasing diversity of learners and their preferences, coupled with increasing usage of the computer and Internet, prompted the need for testing and verifying the ways that knowledge can be delivered and learned effectively. This research addresses these concerns by comparing the results of a college course, hospitality human resource management, which was offered by the same instructor, to the same student pool, in one semester, with the same text and common examinations, but using three different delivery methods: traditional classroom, instructional television, and Internet. Implications for the instructors, instructional designers, and the use of technology are also discussed.

INTRODUCTION

Profiles of college students can be very diverse. Some students are the traditional 18-year-old first-time incoming freshmen. Families support some

The Perfect Online Course: Best Practices for Designing and Teaching
pp. 23–35

students entirely, while others are on their own and have to work various part-time jobs or hold a full-time position to pay bills. There are also others who are married. Some may have young dependents. There are still others who come back to college after having been in the work force. With all the different types of learners, contemporary college instructors are faced with using various methods, both inside and outside the classroom, to impart knowledge and help students learn and master subject matter.

At the same time, the impact of a new emphasis on instructional design and technology has generated great interest in applying new or different ways of delivering information and instruction. Education in the traditional classroom has been enhanced and supplanted by the use of instructional television (ITV) and various other forms of distance learning delivered by computer and the Internet (online instruction).

"Instructional designs serve as mediators between the realms of learning theory and instructional practice, providing a means of developing interventions through which changes in learned capabilities can occur" (Wagner, 1994, p. 20). Instructional designers must consider learner-centered and self-directed approaches. Learner-centered instruction considers a myriad of characteristics, processes, interactions, and delivery methods that result in effective teaching and learning. For example, asynchronous delivery strategies allow learners to complete work in their own time and location rather than being in the classroom at a specified time.

Related to learner-centered instructional design is the notion of self-directed learning. "As a person matures, his or her self-concept moves from that of a dependent personality toward one of a self-directing human being" (Merriam & Caffarella, 1999, p. 272). Adults prefer self-directed or self-designed activities, more than one medium for learning, and to control the learning pace (Zemke & Zemke, 1984). Self-directed learning does not mean isolation but, in fact, involves several resources, professionals, lectures, seminars, and face-to-face interactions. According to Gerald Grow (1991), adult learners progress from dependency to self-direction. "Some features of self-direction are distinctly situational: Few learners are equally motivated toward all subjects. Some features appear to be deep, familial, perhaps even genetic traits of individual personalities—such as persistence" (p. 128).

Instructional designers have introduced new ways in which instructors can work with students. There has been a paradigm shift from the mode where a teacher delivers information to a mode where responsibility for learning and learning activities is shifted to the learners. While these are all happening, the ubiquitous appearance of generally affordable personal computers that are interconnected by the Internet has made possible the dispersion of learning and a paradigm shift to distributed learning and distance learning.

While there is no single best technology for distance delivery of instruction, instructional designers are interested in making the technology as seamless and transparent as possible. Distance education technologies expand options for interaction among faculty and students. Kochery (1997) noted that by creating an environment that advocates peer interactions, social support, and interpersonal communications, cooperative learning models can help attain the sense of a learning community which is frequently lacking in distance education experiences.

Born and Miller (1999) noted that faculty were concerned about the lack of student-teacher interactions in Web-delivered courses. Lindner, Kelsey, and Dooley (2002) found that students were happy with their relationships with their professors, stating that interactions were generally adequate with a few exceptions. Other studies, however, have shown that distance education students were dissatisfied with isolation, inaccessible resources and educational materials, registration and technology problems, and amount of time required to complete course requirements (Kelsey, Lindner, & Dooley, 2002).

Skeptics and scholars alike would like to know whether the shifting paradigms and the new delivery tools have had an impact on the outcomes of the educational process, especially in the higher education arena. Learners have their own perceptions. While some find these new delivery tools beneficial, enhancing the learning experience, others do not rank effectiveness as high. Since evaluation in distance education efforts can identify program effects, helping staff and others to find out whether their programs have an impact on learners' knowledge, skills or attitude (Nickols, 1999), it is prudent to collect data on how these new tools might affect the level of learning.

The increasing diversity, needs, and preferences of learners, coupled with increased access to knowledge via the Internet, prompted the need for comparing various ways that knowledge can be delivered and learned effectively.

PURPOSE OF THE STUDY

This study compared multiple sections of a college course at the junior level, Hospitality Human Resource Management, which was offered by the same instructor, to the same student pool, in one semester, with the same text and common examinations, but using three different delivery methods: traditional classroom, instructional television, and Internet. Specifically, the researchers were interested in the following:

1. Are the three different delivery methods equally effective?
2. Will the different methods affect the learners feelings regarding being "part of the class," communicating and interacting with each other?
3. Will the different methods affect the learners' access to learning resources?

LIMITATIONS

This is an exploratory study, which was conducted with one class that had three different sections with the same instructor during a semester. This study would be greatly enhanced if a longitudinal study could be performed and/or more data collected either with different instructors from different types of classes, and with a larger number of learners. Students chose the course section (delivery method) themselves rather than by random assignment to a particular delivery method. Future studies would be enhanced by using random assignment.

REVIEW OF LITERATURE

In the last 10 years or so, distance education has been accepted into mainstream education. More than a third of colleges in the United States are offering degrees and/or courses on the Internet, including universities such as Columbia, Stanford, the London School of Economics, and the 181 year old University of Virginia (Eggen, 2000). Current literature suggests that some 54,000 courses enrolled 1.6 million students in distance education programs in 1998 (National Center for Educational Statistics, NCES, 1999; Merisotis, 1999), and was expected to exceed 2 million by the year 2002 (Stewart, 2001). Between 1994 and 1998, the proportion of colleges and universities offering online distance education rose from about 11 to 44% (NCES Fast Facts, 2001).

The reason for this trend is simply the demand from a particular segment of the student population: nontraditional students. Is distance education the cure-all for education? No, but it does offer alternatives. Kathleen Burke stated that undoubtedly, distance education, in its various forms, opens opportunities to many, especially to women with children and military personnel who are moved often (Brown, 1999). Distance education offers learners the convenience and flexibility to learn at anytime, anywhere. Knowledge is available 24-7 for those who want it. For those who cannot travel long distances, it also opens the door for knowledge (Owston, 1997).

Some reports have been published with encouraging results that student dropout rates can been decreased using online education (Carnevale, 2000, January), while others (Johnstone & Krauth, 1996) mention no significant learning outcome differences in distance education compared to traditional classroom methods (Russell, 2001; Young, 2000).

Distance education has experienced some growing pains and is not for everyone. The success stories may come from those who are more disciplined and able to follow a schedule on their own. Because learners are not required to be in a class at a certain time to *listen* to the lecture, the less-disciplined groups may soon fall behind the class progress. Simply learning to use the VCR to tape classes when they are being broadcast or using programs on the Internet to communicate with the professors and fellow classmates can be challenges for the distance learners (Carr, 2000).

Educators are coping with the new delivery techniques to ensure that the quality of education is not being compromised. Numerous articles and textbooks explore such concerns in detail. Solloway and Harris (1999) discuss the importance of creating a learning community online using Lotus Notes threaded discussion group, and document their success in working with students through this *discussion community*. Carnevale (2000, October) supports the same idea, stating that a social bond is pertinent in the success of distance education. Others view this community concept as important but they extend the idea of a physical community in a traditional classroom to a cyber-community, where people do things together without regard to location (Wellman, 1999).

Besides the sense of community, educators need to modify their traditional classroom teaching techniques to the new distance education environment. Abbey (2000) compiled 16 insightful discussions on topics ranging from designing technology enhanced learning environments to cognitive effects of Web page design. Lau (2000) explored methods of evaluation, digital video usage, and some essential conditions to success in distance education. White and Weight (2000) put together an online teaching guide to discuss how to communicate online, facilitate individual and group learning, and even adapt the regular syllabus to the distance learning mode. Educators need to ensure that there is a sense of community within the class and provide a means of communication among participants.

METHODOLOGY

A pretest, posttest quasi-experimental design, and a survey instrument were used to compare how traditional classroom, instructional television, and the Internet affect the academic achievement of college students in a hospitality human resource management class, and to assess the learners' perceptions of these delivery methods.

The model considered the independent variables as: the traditional classroom instruction, instructional television, and the Internet. At the beginning of the semester, each student was administered a common pre-test to assess the baseline knowledge in hospitality human resource management. At the end of the semester, the same set of questions was administered and evaluated as part of a common final examination for all sections.

The traditional face-to-face class consisted of students meeting in a classroom. Traditional interactions took place between the learners and the instructor and between the learners themselves. In addition, the face-to-face course included a threaded discussion and PowerPoint slides, which were available online.

The instructional television group met in the television studio. The studio sessions were broadcasted at three other remote sites in the city. Further distribution was made through delayed broadcast on the citywide cable system on an educational channel, where many students viewed the televised class from home or videotaped the classes for later viewing. Students enrolled in the ITV course were required to participate in a threaded discussion that was available online.

Students in the online course were asked to connect to a course-related Web site that provided access to the course content. The online course was developed using the software IntraKal, an online course management and delivery package, adopted by the university at that time. Students enrolled in the online section only met face-to-face for an orientation meeting prior to the beginning of the course, and for a final examination. Like the other two sections, students in the online delivered course also participated in a threaded discussion.

The dependent variable in this research design was the achievement of the learners. Analysis of covariance was used to analyze the results. The pretest was covaried with the outcome variable, or posttest, in order to remove variability or noise.

An assessment of the perceptions of the learners with respect to the quality of interaction was examined through three surveys, one for each respective delivery method. Each survey contained common questions but also included questions that were related to the specific delivery mode. All learners were asked to provide demographic information such as age, gender, classification, and the like. Each was asked to determine the effectiveness of the course and the amount of interaction with the instructor and other learners in the course. They were asked to rate the effectiveness of course-related resources and indicate if they felt they were part of the class. The data were entered into SPSS to run descriptive statistics such as frequency and percentages.

RESULTS AND ANALYSIS

"Classes" were for one full semester with the same content delivered and common assessment measurements administered to the groups in the three different sections based on delivery method. A total of 83 students participated in this study.

Demographics of the Three Groups

Of the 83 participants, 34 were in the traditional class, 31 were in the ITV class, while 18 were in the Internet class. In the traditional classroom where lecture-discussion was the norm, 72% of the group was 23 years of age or younger, while 28% were in the age group of 24-29. The female to male ratio was 59% to 41%. In the ITV class, the 23 and younger age group was only 56%, with 33% in the 24-29 age group, 6% in the 30-35 group, and another 6% in the 42-47 group. Once again, the female group had the higher percentage in the ITV mode, with 61%. These students could participate in the studio, at remote sites, or in the comfort of their own home. Finally, the online group had half of its learners below age 23, 33% between age 24-29, and 17% in the group of 30-35. The female-male ratio was 58%-42%, again with the female group being the dominant (see Table 2.1).

Table 2.1.   Demographics of Participants

	Traditional Classroom	Instructional Television	Online Via Internet
Number of learners	34	31	18
Age Distribution			
18-23	72%	56%	50%
24-29	28%	33%	33%
30-35	0%	6%	17%
36-41	0%	0%	0%
42-47	0%	6%	0%
Gender distribution			
Female	59%	61%	58%
Male	41%	39%	42%

Table 2.2.   Academic Achievement of College Students

	Adjusted Least Squares Means	SE	N
Traditional classroom	37.892	0.765	34
ITV	37.345	0.811	31
Online	34.833	1.091	18

Note: F ratio $= 2.667$, p value $= 0.075$.

Effects on Achievement

The analysis of covariance on the pre- and posttest showed an F ratio of 2.677 and a p value of 0.075, signifying that though there might be differences among the three groups, such difference was not statistically significant (see Table 2.2). Thus, the delivery method did not contribute to any difference in the learners' achievement level.

Perception of Comfort Level and Learners' Preferences

While it is interesting to note that the three methods did not contribute to any difference in learning achievement, the researchers were also interested in measuring the perception of the learners about the efficacy of each of the methods. When the learners of the ITV group were asked about their "comfort" with the instructional television method, 39% of them stated that they were not very comfortable at the beginning, although this number dropped to only 6% at the end. In the online group, 25% of the learners rated themselves "not comfortable" at the beginning, and this remained unchanged.

To record their preferences and see if there was any difference in the preference between the groups on the traditional method and distance education methods such as ITV and online, the learners were asked how they would rate the method they chose against the others. Seventy-nine percent of the traditional classroom group reported that they felt their own chosen method was superior to the distance education method. In contrast, only 66% of the ITV group thought that their delivery methods was superior to the traditional classroom method, and only 50% of the online group shared this same view. Thus, it appeared that this group of learners still slightly favored the traditional classroom delivery method (see Table 2.3).

Table 2.3.   Interaction Response Distribution (by Percentage)

	Traditional Classroom		Instructional Television		Online Via Internet	
	Strongly Agree	Agree	Strongly Agree	Agree	Strongly Agree	Agree
Felt comfortable in class	31%	45%	11%	33%	17%	17%
Communicate easily with others	24%	42%	11%	39%	0%	49%
Interface easily with others	24%	56%	11%	33%	0%	33%
Post my thoughts and opinions	17%	29%	17%	28%	18%	33%

The "Group" Sense

Questions were asked of the learners regarding their feeling of being part of a "group" in their respective delivery environments. When asked if they "felt as part of a class," 76% of the traditional classroom group agreed or strongly agreed with such statements, while only 44% of the ITV class and 34% of the online class shared the same perspective.

When asked about the ability to communicate easily with other learners, 66% of the traditional classroom group agreed or strongly agreed that this was true. The other two groups both reported at a level of about 50%. Thus, while half of the participants in both distance education methods felt that they could communicate easily with others, the other half did not.

Besides communicating, the learners were also asked about general interaction with classmates. Not surprisingly, the traditional classroom group posed the highest satisfaction level with 80% reporting a good level of interaction, and only 44% and 33% reporting positive perceptions for the ITV and online group, respectively.

The researchers then asked about the learners' experience in sharing thoughts and opinions through classroom discussion or postings on the Internet. Since all three groups had the chance to use the Internet to post discussions, the response to this question was quite even, with all three groups reporting "agree or strongly agree" in the range of 45% to 51%. Since the online group used the Internet as their primary communication method, it was expected that this group would view this question more positively than the other two groups.

It was interesting that, although the preferences of the learners differed, the learning achievement level did not. Thus, the outcome suggested that the use of various methods in delivery would provide choices needed for the varied learners and yet would not compromise the learning results. However, it was quite unsettling to see that the comfort level and communication among the learners were not high in the distance education delivery methods.

CONCLUSIONS AND IMPLICATIONS

So where do we go from here? This question can be divided into three areas: implications for instructors, implications for instructional designers, and applications of technology in general.

If instructors view learners as customers, the results of this study were not positive. For example, some learners did not feel comfortable in communicating with the class. Therefore, instructors may wish to pay more attention to learners' needs in all delivery methods, especially with distance learning methods, and try to establish closer contacts and interactions with the learners. Instructors may also want to encourage and monitor interactions among the learners so that the learners feel more comfortable using the new technology.

Referring back to Table 2.3, the comfort level was 76% for the traditional classroom, 44% using ITV, and 34% online. The interface is even more dramatic, 80%, 44%, and 33% respectively. With better interface design and an increased vigilance of instructors who teach online, we can further explore how to increase the comfort level and interface to improve instruction and learning.

Instructional designers may need to work with instructors more closely to develop learner-centered and learner-driven activities. In most cases, the instructional designer and the instructor are the same person. Thus, instructors need to develop skills or have them provided by other means. Many major publishers have their own instructional design personnel to create compact disks and other tools to enhance a traditional text. Perhaps these services can complement online instruction.

It is true that some view online education as a "glorified correspondence course," with interactions being few and far between. However, a well-designed distance education course does not fit such descriptions. The instructional designer can put in real-time chats with instructors, threaded discussions among the learners and the instructors, and even public or private e-mails to the other learners in the class and to the professors. One can tape a segment of a guest speaker to be streamed online or, better yet, have a real-time guest speaker sign on to the class to chat with the students. The advantage of this strategy in a distance environment is that this guest may be in a totally different state or country. As long as the time is coordinated, all students, instructors, and guests can log on and learning can begin.

The idea of synchronous and asynchronous learning plays a big part in distance education. Learners and instructors do not have to engage in a conversation at the same time. Instructional designers will need to keep this mind so that the instructors can provide various learning experiences to many different learning styles. Thus, there are many strategies that instructional designers can use to assist first-time or novice instructors to "reach out and touch" the learners.

Of course, one can never forget technology, as it is the facilitating force behind distance education, whether it is ITV or online. First and foremost, the comfort level of the learners must be raised. Most learners reported the comfort level low as they experienced difficulties with the technology. They were intimidated to ask questions or simply assumed that it was the "computer" that caused the delays or problems.

The software used in this study was IntraKal. Since the conclusion of this study, IntraKal has been improved, and the university and the individual colleges have begun using different software, such as WebCT and Blackboard. Each of these software programs has its advantages and disadvantages, from the ease of use, to the ease to learn, and the cost involved. In general, classroom support software has become much more user friendly and should elicit higher future responses to the comfort question. Educational institutions should spend ample time to assess their own needs before investing in particular software. Many of the programs available contain or facilitate a posting or bulletin board for threaded discussions, e-mails, and chat rooms. Some even have built-in functions such as an academic calendar and icons for assignments, texts, syllabi, and other course elements.

Further, studies suggest that distance-delivered education *can* be more effective than traditional face-to-face classroom activities (Russell, 2001). The data in this study and knowledge of the degree of sophistication and development of the distance learning activities gives credence to that notion. Improvements in software, telecommunications tools, knowledge of instructional design and learning principles, and greater interaction suggest that the future of distance learning may result in better learning for students and a more comfortable learning environment.

REFERENCES

Abbey, B. (2000). (Ed.). *Instruction and cognitive impacts of Web-based education*. Hershey, PA: Idea Group.

Born, K. A., & Miller, G. (1999). Faculty perceptions of Web-based distance education in agriculture. *Journal of Agricultural Education, 40*(3), 40-49.

Brown, J. (October, 1999). Distance learning for full-time lives. *Converge, 26*, 28.

Carnevale, D. (2000, January 28). Online instructor takes steps to reduce dropout rate. *Chronicle of Higher Education*. Retrieved May 9, 2005, from http://www.chronicle.com

Carnevale, D. (2000, October 13). Social bonds found to be crucial in online education. *Chronicle of Higher Education*. Retrieved May 9, 2005, from http://www.chronicle.com

Carr, S. (January 13, 2000). Learning to communicate online is a challenge for new distance-ed students. *Chronicle of Higher Education*. Retrieved May 9, 2005, from http://www.chronicle.com/free/2000/01/2000011301u.htm.

Eggen, D. (April 7, 2000). Logging on to college. *Washington Post*, p. B1.

Grow, G. O. (1991). Teaching learners to be self-directed. *Adult Education Quarterly, 41*(3), 125-149.

Johnstone, S. M., & Krauth, B. (1996). Balancing quality and access: Some principles of good practice for the virtual university. *Change, 28*(2), 38-41.

Kelsey, K. D., Lindner, J. R., & Dooley, K. E. (2002). Agricultural education at a distance: Let's hear from the students. *Journal of Agricultural Education, 43*(4), 24-32.

Kochery, T. S. (1997, February). Distance education: A delivery system in need of cooperative Learning. *Proceedings of Selected Research and Development Presentations at the National Convention of the Association for Educational Communications and Technology*. (ERIC Document Reproduction Service No. ED 409847)

Lindner, J. R., Kelsey, K. D., & Dooley, K. E. (2002). All for one and one for all: Relationships in a distance education program. *Online Journal of Distance Learning Administration, 5*(1). Retrieved May 7, 2002, from http://www.westga.edu/%7Edistance/ojdla/spring51/linder51.html

Lau, L. (2000). (Ed.). *Distance learning technologies: issues, trends, and opportunities*. Hershey, PA: Idea Group.

Merisotis, J. M. (1999). The "what's the difference" debate. *Academe, 85*(5), 130-145.

Merriam, S. B., & Caffarella, R. S. (1999). *Learning in adulthood: A comprehensive guide*. San Francisco: Jossey-Bass.

National Center for Educational Statistics, U.S. Department of Education. (1999). *Distance Education at Post Secondary Education Institutions, 1997-98*. Washington, DC: U.S. Department of Education. Retrieved November 10, 2001 from http://nces.ed.gov/pubs2000/2000013.pdf

National Center for Educational Statistics Fast Facts. (2001) U.S. Department of Education. Retrieved November 10, 2001, from http://nces.ed.gov/fastfacts/display.asp?id=80

Nickols, F. (1999). *Evalating training: There is no "cookbook" approach*. Retrieved May 9, 2005, from http://home.att.net/~nickols/evaluate.htm.

Owston, R. D. (1997). The World Wide Web: A technology to enhance teaching and learning? *Educational Researcher, 26*(2) 27-33.

Russell, T. L. (2001). *The significant difference phenomenon*. Retrieved November 11, 2001 from http://teleeducation.nb.ca/significantdifference/

Solloway. S. G., & Harris, E. L. (1999, March/April). Negotiating students' desires and needs in cyberspace. *Educom Review, 34*(5), 8-9, 12-13.

Stewart, E. M. (2001). *Higher education online*. Retrieved October 20, 2001 from http://wind.winona.msus.edu/%7Ebjg/papers/EileenStewartcsfinpaper.htm.

Wagner, E. D. (1994). In support of a functional definition of interaction. *The American Journal of Distance Education, 8*(2), 6-29.

Wellman, B. (Ed.). (1999). The network community: An introduction to networks in the global village. In *Networks in the global village* (pp. 1-48). Boulder, CO: Westview.

White, K. W., & Weight, B. H. (2000). *The online teaching guide: A handbook of attitudes, strategies, and techniques for the virtual classroom*. Needham Heights, MA: Allyn & Bacon.

Young, J. R. (2000, February 10). Scholar concludes that distance ed is as effective as traditional instruction. *Chronicle of Higher Education*. Retrieved October 14, 2001 from http://chronicle.com/free/2000/02/2000021001u.htm

Zemke, R., & Zemke, S. (1984, March). Thirty things we know for sure about adult learning. [Electronic version]. *Innovation Abstracts, 6*(8). Retrieved July 20, 2001 from http://www.hcc.hawaii.edu/intranet/committees/FacDevCom/guidebk/teachtip/adults-3.htm

PART II

BEST GUIDES AND STANDARDS

CHAPTER 3

IN SEARCH OF QUALITY

An Analysis of e-Learning Guidelines and Specifications

Atsusi Hirumi

Educational institutions across the country are adopting guidelines to help assure the quality of e-learning programs and courses. Corporations are also adopting guidelines, but their focus is on the interoperability and reusability of learning objects. While there are commonalities, there are also significant differences between how education and industry view quality and approach e-learning. This article analyzes education guidelines and industry specifications for e-learning published by professional organizations. Key factors within, as well as across both approaches are identified and discussed to inform those considering the adoption of standards and the establishment of a quality assurance system for e-learning.

In traditional classroom settings, good instructors can make up for flaws in the design of instructional materials by using their expertise to shed light on complex or confusing content matter, and their charisma to gain and sustain learners' attention. If students note a problem, the instructor can provide immediate feedback and clarify misconceptions in real time.

The Perfect Online Course: Best Practices for Designing and Teaching
pp. 39–67
Copyright © 2009 by Information Age Publishing

In contrast, during e-learning, most key interactions, such as elaborations, clarifications, discussions, and feedback occur asynchronously through reading and writing, rather than speaking and listening. Online distance educators can also make up for faults in design, but at what cost?

If the quality of e-learning materials is poor, educators may have to spend exorbitant amounts of time explaining requirements, clarifying expectations, correcting errors, troubleshooting, and otherwise filling in gaps in design. Consider the additional logistical and technical challenges that accompany e-learning, and it is understandable why so many educators feel overwhelmed with the prospects of teaching online, and claim they can only meet the needs of 15-20 online students in one class. Otherwise motivated learners may become frustrated and disenchanted, having to deal with logistical issues rather than course contents, leave dissatisfied with their experiences, and tell others to avoid certain courses or programs. Without quality materials, learners may also not achieve specified objectives, fail licensing examinations, and perform poorly on critical job functions. In short, distance learners and educators are more dependent on the quality of the learning materials and services than are students and teachers in traditional classroom settings.

High-quality programs (a cohesive set of quality courses coupled with responsive student and academic services) are also necessary to demonstrate that e-learning is a legitimate form of education and professional development. Even with the growing body of literature that indicates that there is no significant difference in learner achievement in distance and traditional classroom settings (e.g., Johnson, Aragron, Shaik, & Palma-Rivas, 2000; Machtmes & Asher, 2000; Saba, 2000; Wetsel, Radtke, & Stern, 1994), distance education degrees are still perceived by many as being inferior in quality: "a good number of educators remain skeptical [of distance learning]. Believing that teaching and learning are inherently social processes, these educators consider 'same-time same-place' interaction central to a successful educational experience" (American Federation of Teachers, 2000, p. 5). Distance learning programs must demonstrate quality and graduate skilled and satisfied students to convince people that e-learning is valid.

This article is written for K-12, college, and university administrators who are interested in establishing or improving an existing system to assure the quality of e-learning programs and courses. Instructional designers, developers, and managers in government agencies, companies, and corporations may also gain useful insights by looking at quality from an educational perspective. The article begins by comparing industry and conventional interpretations of "quality." It then details the derivation of, and analyzes the commonalities and disparities between, educational guidelines and industry specifications. Readers will see the interrelationships among the guidelines and specifications. They will be able to identify key factors to consider when adopting guidelines and make informed decisions when creating policies and procedures to ensure that e-learning courses and programs achieve their objectives dependably and efficiently with minimal cost and maximum effectiveness.

WHAT IS QUALITY?

So, what is quality and how can you assure the quality of your instruction? There are two contrasting views: conventional and industrial. Most educators in K-12 and higher education take a conventional perspective, discussing quality in terms of effectiveness, efficiency, and appeal. Tactics focus on enhancing learner achievement, retaining a greater number of learners, and promoting learner satisfaction. In distinct contrast, industry increases quality by reducing variance around set standards. Figure 3.1 begins to compare the two views, illustrating how increases in quality differ over time.

Two distinct movements characterize the quest for quality in distance education that parallel the conventional and industrial view; the adoption of education guidelines and development of industry specifications. Both movements include input from, and serve the interests of, education, government, and industry. The goals of both movements are to assure that e-learning achieves its objectives dependably (for students and users) and efficiently (with minimal cost and maximum effectiveness). Again, the primary difference is that education guidelines focus on the quality of e-learning courses and programs, whereas industry standards concentrate on the technical quality, reusability, and interoperability of learning

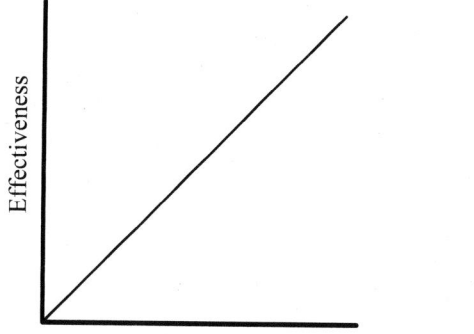
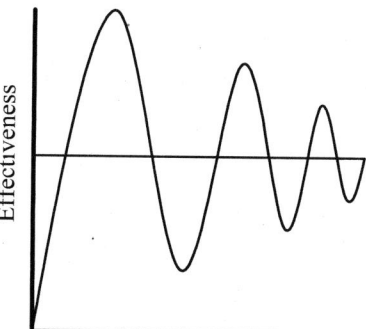

Figure 3.1.   A comparison of conventional and industry perspectives on quality improvement.

objects. The difference in focus, in turn, has significant ramifications for those considering the adoption of standards and the development of a quality assurance system.

EDUCATION GUIDELINES

Traditional indicators, such as teacher credentials and time spent in class with a teacher, may be inappropriate for assuring the quality of distance learning programs. "New delivery systems test conventional assumptions, raising fresh question as to the essential nature and content of an educational experience and the resources required to support it" (Council of Regional Accrediting Commissions, C-RAC, 2000, p. iii). To address the proliferation of distance learning programs, professional organizations are publishing new guidelines that are being adopted by states, regional accrediting associations, K-12 schools, and institutions of higher education. This study analyzes six sets of guidelines, including:

1. The Council of Regional Accrediting Commissions (2000). *Statement of the regional accrediting commissions on the evaluation of electronically offered degree and certificate programs* (http://www.wiche.edu/telecom/Guidelines.htm)

2. The Institute for Higher Education Policy (2000). *Quality on the line: Benchmarks for success in Internet-based distance education* (www.ihep.com/quality.pdf)

3. The American Council on Education (ACE, 1997). *Guiding Principles for Distance Learning in Learning Society* (www. acenet.edu/calec/dist_learning/dl_principlesIntro.cfm)

4. The American Distance Education Consortium (n.d.a., n.d.b). *Guiding Principles for Distance Learning* and *Guiding Principles for Distance Teaching and Learning* (www.adec.edu/admin/papers/distance-teaching_principles.html).

5. The American Federation of Teachers (2000). *Distance Education: Guidelines for Good Practice* (www.aft.org/higher_ed/downloadable/distance.pdf)

6. Open and Distance Learning Quality Council (ODLQC, 2001). *Standards in open and distance education* (http://www.odlqc.org.uk/st-int.htm).

The *Best Practices* generated by C-RAC (2000) seek to address concern that regional accreditation standards are not relevant to new distributed learning environments. Based on the *Principles of Good Practice*, initially drafted by the Western Cooperative for Educational Telecommunications (WCET, 1997), the *Best Practices* are meant to assist institutions in planning electronic distance education activities and provide a framework for self-assessment; they are not new evaluative criteria.

The National Education Association (NEA) and Blackboard Inc. jointly commissioned The Institute for Higher Education Policy (IHEP) to examine existing guidelines for distributed learning. An initial list of 45 benchmarks was then analyzed by faculty, administrators, and students from six colleges and universities. The final outcome of 24 *benchmarks for success in Internet-based distance education* was published by IHEP in 2000. Subsequently, 16 higher education leaders reviewed the IHEP benchmarks for a symposia sponsored by The Pew Learning and Technology Program, providing further insights into distance learning and quality assurance from a provider and consumer perspective (Twigg, 2001).

A national task force created by the American Council on Education and The Alliance: An Association for Alternative Programs for Adults generated *The Guiding Principles for Distance Learning in a Learning Society* (ACE, 1997) that focused on the changing nature of education and training, not on specific delivery systems or methods. These guidelines are neither a treatise nor a "how to" for distance learning; rather, they address the qualities of tomorrow's future learning society. The purpose of the guidelines is to "help learners, educators, trainers, technologists, and accreditors/state regulators to develop, deliver, and assess formal learning opportunities" (Sullivan & Rocco, 1997).

The American Distance Education Consortium (ADEC) published the *Principles for Distance Teaching and Learning* (n.d.a) and the *Principles for Distance Learning* (n.d.b) to evaluate Web-based learning environments and nonformal educational programs. Like ACE, ADEC recognizes that Web-based instruction may be designed for distance and face-to-face learners. As such, the principles are foundational to high-quality learning environments in general, no matter where the learner resides. The *Principles for Distance Teaching and Learning* concentrates on course design and delivery. The *Principles for Distance Learning* addresses service and administrative policies.

The *Guidelines for Good Practice*, published by the American Federation of Teachers (2000), is based on a 1999 survey of 200 members. Although the focus is on 2-year, 4-year, and graduate credit-bearing degree programs, the guidelines are said to be applicable to all types of distance education, including job and skill training "because they are simply about good teaching" (AFT, 2000, p. 6). The guidelines are designed to help faculty negotiate distance education issues with management, as well as to help administrators and public officers who want to put quality at the center of their initiatives.

Recognizing that technology has changed the face of distance and open education, European accrediting agencies are also reviewing and adopted revised quality standards. Set up by the British government in 1968, the Open and Distance Learning Quality Council (ODL QC) operates as a voluntary distance learning registration system. Course providers must meet the *Standards in Open and Distance Education* published by ODL QC (2001) to register courses.

This study analyzes the six guidelines and extends findings from the Pew symposia (Twigg, 2001) by elaborating on instructional design issues and illustrating how industry specifications for the development, reusability, and interoperability of learning objects may be applied to complement education guidelines.

FINDINGS: EDUCATION GUIDELINES

Analysis of the education guidelines reveals a number of important issues to consider if you are establishing a system to assure the quality of e-learning programs or courses.

Guidelines are Written for Similar Organizational Structures

In a review of standard-setting initiatives, members of the Pew Learning and Technology Program (Twigg, 2001) noted a high level of agreement among published guidelines. Table 3.1 illustrates that education guidelines posited by professional organizations center around five basic structures (i.e., institution, program, course, student support, and faculty support).

The convergence across guidelines suggests that those adopting quality standards should consider specifying guidelines for their institution, programs, courses, students, and faculty. However, there are a few points of divergence worth noting. Specifically, the guidelines proposed by C-RAC focus on program outcomes listed under *Curriculum and Instruction* and *Evaluation and Assessment*. They do not specify process-oriented standards associated with pedagogy and course design. In contrast, ODL QC specifies standards for course objectives, outcomes, and content, but do not offer guidelines for the design of programs or curriculum. Three sets of standards (i.e., ACE, 1997; ADEC, n.d.b; ODL QC, 2001) do not address faculty support, but all six sets recognize the importance of setting institutional and student support guidelines.

A closer look reveals greater congruence between guidelines than Table 3.1 suggests. Differences in guidelines may be more semantic than

Table 3.1. Comparison of Education Guidelines Posited by Professional Organizations

IHEP	C-RAC	ACE	AFT	ADEC	ODLQC
Institutional Guidelines					
• Institutional support benchmarks	• Institutional context and commitment	• Organizational commitment	• Encourage experimentation	• Administrative & organizational commitment.	• The Provider • Joint Provision • Accreditation • Learning Centres
Program Design and Curriculum Guidelines					
• Course development benchmarks • Evaluation and Assessment Benchmarks	• Curriculum and instruction • Evaluation and assessment	• Learning outcomes • Technology	• Class size • Student assessment • Full programs • Evaluation of coursework	• Technological and human infrastructure.	
Course Design and Pedagogical Guidelines					
• Interactions • Feedback • Research methods • Advisement • Technical requirements • Objectives. • Library resources • Expectations		• Outcomes • Content • Expectations • Interactions • Assessment • Complement Elements • Technology • Activities and assessments	• Potentials of medium • Personal interaction • Courses materials	• Outcomes and objectives • Learner engagement • Media use • Learning environments • Learning experiences • Social mission	• Course objectives & outcomes • Course contents
Student and Academic Support Guidelines					
• Student support benchmarks	• Student services	• Learner support	• Student requirements • Advisement • Research opportunities	• Learner support	• Publicity and recruitment • Admissions procedures • Learning support • Learner welfare
Faculty Support Guidelines					
• Faculty support benchmarks	• Principles of faculty support		• Academic control • Faculty preparation • Materials control		

actual variations in implementation. For instance, ODL QC does consider program and curriculum issues, but from an institutional and a course perspective, addressing staffing and resource availability under guidelines for *The Provider* and degree and certification requirements under guidelines for *Course Objectives and Outcomes*. Similarly, C-RAC addresses course design issues, such as learning outcomes, instructor-learner interactions, and learner assessment, but at a programmatic level under the headings *Curriculum and Instruction* and *Evaluation and Assessment*, rather than specifying guidelines under *Course Design or Pedagogical Guidelines*.

The congruence across published guidelines suggests that there are several basic categories related to organizational structure. However, Table 3.1 demonstrates that comparable guidelines may be categorized in different ways. Current guidelines tend to mix the primary target of analysis. Some statements address the institution, while others focus on programs, and still others address courses and learning experiences. If you are adopting quality guidelines, consider establishing guidelines for your institution, programs, courses, students, and faculty, noting that it is not necessary to specify five categories, rather to address key issues related to each category. Also, keep in mind that "consistency and clarity concerning the organizational level being addressed would improve any statement about quality indicators in distance learning" (Twigg, 2001, p. 7).

Guidelines are Written for Differing Levels of Organizational Effort

Traditional criteria used to accredit degree and certificate programs have assumed that learning would take place if institutions provided certain *inputs* or resources (e.g., limited class size, full-time tenure-track faculty, student seat time, documented policies, equipped classrooms and libraries). Accrediting bodies, such as NCATE and SACS, are now placing emphasis on learning outcomes, giving institutions flexibility over how they achieve the outcomes. Advances in technology also challenge traditional views on what constitutes quality. Distance learning guidelines no longer focus on inputs. But, rather than concentrating on results, the guidelines center on process-oriented variables. For instance, the guidelines posited by IHEP (2000), AFT (2000), ACE (1997) and ADEC (n.d.a.) all specify requirements for learner engagement, media use, interactions, assessment, and feedback. Outcomes are specified by ACE, ADEC, and ODL QC (2001), but there is a definite attempt to guide the teaching and learning process.

For now, process guidelines may be warranted. Educators may not have the knowledge necessary to define their own methods for creating e-

Table 3.2.   Five Elements of the Organizational Elements Model

Elements	Inputs	Processes	Products	Outputs	Outcomes
Variables	Resources, human, fiscal, material, time, existing needs, goals, objectives, policies, laws, values	Methods and means, procedures, tasks, functions, activities, techniques, support services	Discrete skills and knowledge, interim products and services, completed reports, trained staff	Products and services delivered to customers, educated students	Profit, off welfare, no addictive relationships, credit, contributing to self, and community, customer satisfaction
E-learning examples	Class size, instructor credentials, documented policies, equipment, library resources	Online teaching, e-learning, learner assessment, program evaluation, academic and student services	Skills and knowledge, completed courses and instructional unit	Educated and trained learners	Satisfied, self-sufficient, self-reliant graduates who enjoy self-selected, legal quality of life
Scope	Internal to Organization				External
Focus	Organizational Efforts			Organizational Results	

learning materials or facilitating the e-learning process. A balance between input-, process-, and outcome-oriented guidelines may be useful for assuring the quality of e-learning experience, at least for the immediate and near future.

To set quality guidelines, it is important to consider the level of organizational effort you want to measure. The Organizational Elements Model (OEM) (Kaufman & Hirumi, 1992; Kaufman & Watkins, 2000; Kaufman, Watkins, & Leigh, 2001) provides a useful framework for distinguishing different levels of organizational effort (Table 3.2).

Application of the OEM to e-learning illustrates how standards can be written for varying levels of organizational effort. Table 3.2 notes examples of inputs, processes, and three levels of results (i.e., products, outputs, and outcomes) relative to e-learning. If you are adopting standards, it is important to decide if you are going to specify guidelines for inputs, processes, products, outputs, and/or outcomes. Again, the key is the consistency and clarity with which guidelines are communicated and addressed.

Guidelines are Written as Minimum Requirements

Higher education leaders have expressed concern that published guidelines appear more like statements of adequate rather than best practice (Twigg, 2001). "Statements [of quality] do not say, 'you should have these outcomes.' They say only, 'you should have outcomes'" (Twigg, 2001, p. 17). In other words, published guidelines do not always specify the level at which distance educators, learners, or organizations are expected to perform. For example, IHEP (2000) benchmarks state that students should (a) receive information about programs (e.g., admissions, tuition, fees, books, supplies, technical and proctoring, services), (b) receive hands-on training and information for securing instructional materials, and (c) have access to technical assistance throughout course/ program. They do not specify the level at which educators should perform each of these functions. Compare such statements to a sample of student support standards published by Athabasca University (Abrioux, 2002) (Table 3.3). The differences between minimum requirements and high-quality standards are apparent. Athabasca not only specifies the services to be offered, but also defines performance standards and lists contact information for each service.

World-class benchmarks not only define what should be done but also delineate how well it should be done. When specifying quality standards, you should consider whether you want to define minimum requirements or identify world-class benchmarks that people within your organization should strive to achieve.

Course Guidelines Do Not Address Important Pedagogical Principles

The published guidelines do address important instructional variables, such as objectives, content, assessment, feedback, and media use. However, they ignore a number of evolving pedagogical and instructional design principles. For example, members of the IHEP (2000) study excluded 19 of the original 45 benchmarks because they felt they were not necessary for assuring quality. Pew symposium members acknowledged that the excluded benchmarks may not be essential, but also noted that several were "ones that lead to higher quality practices because they were more learner-centered and incorporated pedagogical approaches of proven effectiveness" (Twigg, 2001, p. 8). The following design principles are not addressed by published guidelines. To establish world-class benchmarks, consider specifying guidelines for:

Table 3.3.   Sample of Student Support Service Standards Published by Athabasca University

Service	Standard	Contact
Sample General Information Standards		
Telephone response time	1 minute during work hours	Canada/US: 1.800.788.9041
Calendar processing	2 business days	Other: 011.780.675.6100
Resolution or referral of problem/query	2 business days	Information Center: 780.675.6106
Sample Academic Support Standards		
Assignments marked	5 business days from receipt by marker	Coordinator Learning Services
Exams marked	5 business days from receipt by marker	780.675.6344 tutserv@athabascau.ca
Unofficial final grades	10 business days from receipt of final exam	
Sample Counseling and Advising Standards		
Acknowledge voice and e-mail	1 business day	advising@athabascau.ca
Urgent counseling appointments	Immediately on a business day	counseling@athabascau.ca
General counseling appointments	Within 1 business week	counseling@athabascau.ca
Sample Library and Course Material Standards		
Information desk response	1 business day	Library Information Desk 780.675.6254
Borrowing period	4 weeks	Circulation Supervisor 780.675.6232
Interlibrary loan	3 business days	Interlibrary Loans Officer 780.675.6251

1. *The alignment of objectives and assessments.* Have you ever taken a test and wondered, where the #&%@ did that question come from? Alignment between explicit objectives and criteria is fundamental to high-quality instruction (Berge, 2002; Dick, Carey, & Carey, 2005). If an objective states that students will be able to *list* key concepts, assessments should ask students to *list* key concepts. If an objective states that learners will be able to *analyze* a case, the assessment should ask learners to *analyze* a case. High-quality learning environments present learners with explicit and congru-

ent learning objectives and assessment criteria. To establish world-class guidelines, consider specifying the alignment of learner assessments with objectives.

2. *The alignment of objectives and instructional events.* Research suggests that how we teach should be based on what we teach. The methods used to teach verbal information should differ from the methods used to teach a procedure that, in turn, should differ from the methods to teach complex problem solving, and so forth. Smith and Ragan (1999) classify alternative instructional events that have been found to facilitate achievement of various learning outcomes (Table 3.4).

   High-quality learning environments present learners with instructional events based on targeted learning outcomes. To establish world-class guidelines, consider specifying the need to incorporate instructional events that are designed to facilitate the achievement of learning outcomes based on research and theory.

3. *The nature of feedback.* Feedback is vital to e-learning. At minimum, feedback is essential for closing message loops (Northrup & Rasmussen, 2000; Yacci, 2000), informing learners that communications are complete (Berge, 1999; Liaw & Huang, 2000; and Weller, 1988, as cited by Northrup, 2001). Feedback may also (a) increase response rates or accuracy, (b) reinforce correct responses to prior stimuli, and (c) change erroneous responses (Kulhavy & Wager, 1993). Feedback comes in two basic forms; confirmatory and corrective. Confirmatory feedback lets students know what they did correctly. Corrective feedback identifies areas and provides recommendations for improvement. Current guidelines recognize the importance of providing timely and appropriate feedback, but they do not detail the nature of the feedback. To develop world-class guidelines, consider delineating what is meant by timely and appropriate feedback based on research, theory, and documented best practices.

4. *The design and sequencing of e-learning interactions.* In traditional classroom settings, key interactions that affect learner attitudes and performance often occur spontaneously, in real-time. Good instructors interpret verbal and nonverbal cues, clarify expectations, facilitate activities, promote discussions, elaborate concepts, render guidance, and provide timely and appropriate feedback as they present content in a clear and engaging manner. Good instructors can also make up for flaws in design by utilizing their charisma to gain and sustain learners' attention and their experience to shed light on complex or confusing content matter. During

Table 3.4.   Grounded Events Related to Learning Outcomes

Learning Outcome	Grounded Event
Verbal information	• Mnemonics and metaphoric devices • Instructor or learner generated images • Rehearsal • Clustering and chunking into categories • Expository and narrative structures • Graphic and advanced organizers • Write meaningful sentences • Devise rule
Concepts	• Inquiry and expository approaches • Attribute isolation • Concept trees • Analogies, mnemonics and imagery
Rules	• Determine if the procedure is required. • List the steps in a procedure. • Complete the steps in a procedure. • Elaborate sequence • Check appropriateness of completed procedure.
Problem solving	• Presentation of the problem • Analyze problem space • Apply appropriate principles • Practice
Cognitive strategies	• Discovery and guided discovery • Observation • Guided participation • Direct instruction
Attitudes	• Demonstrate desired behaviors • Practice desired behaviors • Provide reinforcement for the desired behavior • Communicate persuasive messages from highly credible sources • Create dissonance
Psychomotor skills	• Massed versus spaced practice • Whole versus parts practice • Progressive parts practice • Backwards chaining

e-learning, opportunities to interact in "real-time" are relatively confined. Key interactions that occur spontaneously in traditional classroom environments must be planned and managed as an integral part of e-learning. Hirumi (2002a, 2002b) posits several grounded instructional strategies to guide the design and sequencing of e-learning (Table 3.5).

Table 3.5.   Sample of Grounded Instructional Strategies

Nine Events of Instruction	Student-Center Learning	Jurisprudential Inquiry
1. Gain Attention 2. Inform Learner of Objective(s) 3. Stimulate Recall of Prior Knowledge 4. Present Stimulus Materials 5. Provide Learning Guidance 6. Elicit Performance 7. Provide Feedback 8. Assess Performance 9. Enhance Retention and Transfer	1. Set Learning Challenge 2. Negotiate Learning Goals and Objectives 3. Negotiate Learning Strategy 4. Construct Knowledge 5. Negotiate Performance Criteria 6. Assess Learning 7. Provide Feedback (Steps 1-6) 8. Communicate Results	1. Orientation to the Case 2. Identifying the Issues 3. Taking Positions 4. Exploring the Stance(s), Patters of Argumentation 5. Refining and Qualifying the Positions 6. Testing Factual Assumptions Behind Qualified Positions

Simulation Model	Direct Instruction	Experiential Learning

1. Orientation
  • Present topic of simulation
  • Explain simulation
  • Give overview
2. Participant Training
  • Set-up scenario
  • Assign roles
  • Hold abbreviated practice
3. Simulation Operations
  • Conduct activity
  • Feedback and evaluation
  • Clarify misconceptions
  • Continue simulation
4. Participant Debriefing
  • Summarize events
  • Summarize difficulties
  • Analyze process
  • Compare to the real world
5. Appraise and redesign the simulation
	1. Orientation
	  • Establish lesson content
	  • Review previous learning
	  • Establish lesson objectives
	  • Establish lesson procedures
	2. Presentation
	  • Explain new concept or skill
	  • Provide visual representation
	  • Check for understanding
	3. Structured Practice
	  • Lead group through practice
	  • Students respond
	  • Provide corrective feedback
	4. Guided Practice
	  • Practice semi-independently
	  • Circulate, monitor practice
	  • Provide feedback
	5. Independent Practice
	  • Practice independently
	  • Provide delayed feedback
		1. Experience—Immerse learner in "authentic" experience.
		2. Publish—Talking or writing about experience. Sharing thoughts and feelings.
		3. Process—Debrief: Interpret published information, defining patterns, discrepancies and overall dynamics.
		4. Internalize—Private process, learner reflects on lessons learned and requirements for future learning.
		5. Generalize—Develop hypotheses, form generalizations and reach conclusions.
		6. Apply—Use information and knowledge gained from lesson to make decisions and solve problems.

(Table continues on next page)

Table 3.5. (Continued)

Inquiry Learning	Inductive Thinking	Problem-Based Learning
1. Confrontation with the Problem • Explain inquiry procedures • Present discrepant event 2. Data Gathering—Verification • Verify nature of objects and conditions • Verify the occurrence of the problem situation 3. Data Gathering—Experimentation • Isolate relevant variables • Hypothesize and test casual relationships 4. Organizing, Formulating and Explanation—Formulate rules or explanations 5. Analysis of inquiry process—Analyze inquiry strategy and develop more effective ones.	1. Concept Formation • Enumeration and listing • Grouping • Labeling, Categorizing 2. Interpretation of Data • Identify critical relationships • Explore relationships • Make inferences 3. Application of Principles • Predicting consequences • Explaining predictions • Verifying predictions	1. Starting a New Problem • Set problem • Describe requirements • Assign tasks • Reason through the problem • Commitment to outcome • Shape issues and assignment • Identify resource • Schedule follow-up 2. Problem Follow-Up • Resources used • Reassess the problem 3. Performance Presentation(s) 4. After Conclusion of Problem • Knowledge abstraction and summary • Self-evaluation

To establish world-class standards, consider specifying the need to design and sequence e-learning interactions based on grounded instructional strategies.

5. *Motivational design.* Educators recognize that motivation is essential to student learning. Students must be presented with the appropriate skills and knowledge *and* they must be motivated to learn and use them. Even though there are numerous theories of human motivation, published guidelines do not address motivational factors, at least not with the precision they attend to concept acquisition. Keller (1987a, 1987b) presents a systematic process for designing motivationally effective instruction that subsumes related theories. In short, Keller's ARCS model suggests that, to motivate students to learn, instruction must (a) gain and sustain learners' *A*ttention, (b) be *R*elevant to learners' needs and interest, (c) promote learners' *C*onfidence in their ability to succeed, and (d)

Table 3.6.   Tactics for Motivating Students to Learn

Motivational Constructs	Motivational Design Tactics
Attention	• *Perceptual Arousal*—Stimulate senses • *Inquiry Arousal*—Stimulate curiosity • *Variability*—Vary stimulus
Relevance	• *Goal Orientation*—Help students create and achieve goals • *Motive Matching*—Address specific needs • *Familiarity*—Relate to learners' past experiences
Confidence	• *Requirements*—Awareness of expectations and evaluation criteria • *Success Opportunities*—Opportunities to experience success • *Personal Control*—Link success or failure to student effort and abilities
Satisfaction	• *Natural Consequences*—Meaningful opportunities to apply skills • *Positive Consequences*—Positive reinforcement • *Equity*—Consequences perceived to be fair by all students

ensure that learners are *Satisfied* that their efforts were worthwhile. Table 3.6 depicts some of the tactics educators can apply to meet motivational quality guidelines.

To define world-class guidelines, consider learner motivation, using insights derived from research on instructional design (such as the ARCS model) to guide the development of related standards.

Education Guidelines Do Not Address Important Technical Issues

The development of high-quality learning materials requires considerable resources. To optimize return on investment, the materials must be reusable. In other words, educators must be able to use the materials multiple times in alternative contexts. The concept of reusing educational resources is not new. There are extensive databases housing lesson plans and distance learning initiatives that share both human and material resources. To facilitate the reusability of e-learning materials, the documents or files must be interoperable. In other words, educators must be able to readily transfer e-learning materials (or objects) across settings.

Education guidelines focus on pedagogical aspects of e-learning. Guidelines are written primarily to ensure the quality of educational programs and courses by concentrating on the teaching and learning process and the provision of academic services. Few guidelines are written to facilitate the sharing and reuse of materials. To garner a significant return on the investment in the development of high quality e-learning materials, consider adopting industry specifications to promote technical quality. (In other words, to ensure that learning objects meet technical specification to enable the interoperability and reusability of the objects.)

INDUSTRY SPECIFICATIONS

When considering industry approaches to quality, keep in mind that, in the strictest sense, standards can only come from accredited bodies, such as the Institute of Electrical and Electronics Engineers (IEEE) and the International Standards Organization (ISO). Many so-called "standards" are actually guidelines, specifications, or statements of good practice. In short, a standard is a sanctioned specification. A standards body must determine that a given specification meets broad, industry-wide needs before it can become a standard. None of the criteria analyzed in this article are true standards, although the Sharable Content Object Reference Model (SCORM) is on a fast track toward becoming an industry standard.

Industry specifications for e-learning are related to, yet distinct from, education guidelines. In industry, specifications for learning objects are set to assure quality, but from a technical rather than a pedagogical perspective. This is not to say that industry is not concerned with pedagogy. In fact, there is a great deal of work going on throughout industry to establish the "next generation" of e-learning, in which the educational quality of content is being addressed along multiple fronts (e.g., individualized learning, problem-based learning, learning-by-doing, etc.). However, such efforts are seen as instructional design issues and are not treated by the formation of technical specifications for guiding the development of e-learning resources.

High-quality instruction achieves its objectives dependably (for all students and users) and efficiently (with minimal cost and maximum effectiveness) (Advanced Distributed Learning, 2002). Industry specifications focus on facilitating development (efficiency) and minimizing cost. To better understand industry specifications, it may be useful to first review several fundamental assumptions and the basic premise for the development of reusable learning objects.

It is assumed that there are thousands of colleges, universities, and public schools that teach the same subjects, such as introductory biology. It is also assumed that many of these introductory courses cover similar topics, such as cell division, and that the properties of cell division remain fairly constant across institutions. As a result, we have thousands of similar lessons about cell division. Now, assume that each institution puts its introductory course online. Do we need thousands of similar online lessons on cell division? The basic premise behind the development of learning objects is that the world needs a few representations of basic instructional units.

Let's assume that it takes $1,000 to produce an interactive, multimedia instructional unit on cell division. If 1,000 institutions pay $1,000 to generate their own unit, it would result in a total expenditure of $1,000,000. In comparison, if the institutions shared development costs, the cell division unit would cost $1 per institution. The economic reasons for developing learning objects and establishing standards to ensure technical quality and interoperability are convincing. History also suggests that significant benefits are not realized without the widespread adoption of common standards (e.g., standard voltage and plugs for electricity; standard gauges for railroad track; common TCP/IP, http, and HTML standards for the Internet). The challenge lies in establishing useful standards and relatively seamless processes that can be readily adopted and maintained by a critical mass of people.

Industry specifications published by professional organization and analyzed in this study include:

1. The Instructional Management Systems Project (IMS, 2000). *Open specifications for facilitating online distributed learning activities* (www.imsproject.org/).

2. The Advanced Distributed Learning Initiative (ADL, 2002). *Sharable Content Object Reference Model (SCORM)* (www.adlnet.org).

3. The Institute of Electrical and Electronics Engineers (IEEE, 2002). *Learning Technology Standards Committee (LTSC) P1484* (itsc.ieee.org/).

4. The Aviation Industry Computer-Based Training Committee (AICC, 1999). *AICC Guidelines and Recommendation for Web-based Computer Managed Instruction (AGR-010* (www.aicc.org/).

5. ARIADNE (2002). *ARIADNE Educational Metadata Recommendation—V3.2* (www.ariadne-eu.org).

6. Dublin Core Metadata Initiative (DCMI, 2002). *Dublin Core Metadata Element Set Version 1.1* (www.dublincore.org).

Like education guidelines, industry specifications are not born at once; they emerge through consensus from related initiatives. For instance, the Instructional Management Systems (IMS) Global Learning Consortium is a coalition of academic, commercial, and government organizations promoting the development of open specifications for online learning activities. The goals of the IMS are similar to other industry initiatives: to define technical specifications for the interoperability of applications and services in distributed learning and to support the incorporation of specifications into products and services worldwide.

The Advanced Distributed Learning (ADL) Initiative, supported by the U.S. Government, released the Sharable Content Object Reference Model (SCORM) that is viewed as one of the best and most recent applications of e-learning specifications (Hodgins & Conner, 2000). According to Walker (president of the IMS consortium), ADL is not trying to dictate the definition of specification. Rather, it takes the specifications identified by other standards bodies into a test-bed and evaluates whether they have the desired effects (Barron, 2000).

According to Hodgins and Conner (2000), most groups creating learning specifications use the Institute of Electrical and Electronics Engineers (IEEE) Learning Technology Standards Committee (LTSC) P1484 to cover topics including object metadata, student profiles, course sequencing, computer managed instruction, competency definitions, localization, and content packaging. As one of the most recognized standards bodies, IEEE LTSC has initiated work toward establishing full International Standards Organization (ISO) standards for learning technology.

The Aviation Industry Computer-Based Training Committee (AICC) is an international association of technology-based training professionals. The AICC develops guidelines to (a) promote the implementation of CBT among airplane operators, (b) develop guidelines for interoperability, and (c) provide an open forum for discussing CBT and other training technologies. Although AICC focuses on the aviation industry, technology-based training and computer software and hardware vendors are adapting AICC guidelines for their own industries.

Comprised of partners from Belgium, Finland, France, Italy, Spain, Switzerland, the Netherlands, and the United Kingdom, and supported by the European Union Commission and the Swiss Federal Office for Education and Science, ARIADNE seeks to apply IEEE LTSC specifications for metadata in a European context. ARIADNE's goal is to develop an international system of interconnected knowledge pools (KPS) and to develop tools and basic methods for maintaining and exploiting the KPS.

The Dublin Core Metadata Initiative (DCMI) is also an open forum engaged in the development of interoperable metadata standards that have been adopted in Australia, Canada, Denmark, Finland, Ireland, and the United Kingdom. Originally conceived to describe Web resources, the DCMI has attracted the attention of museums, libraries, government agencies, and commercial organizations that often search for and access electronic resources. In December 2000, the IEEE LTSC on Learning Objects Metadata and the DCMI signed a Memorandum of Understanding announcing a joint commitment to the development of interoperable metadata for learning, education, and training.

FINDINGS: INDUSTRY SPECIFICATIONS

Analysis of the industry specifications reveals important variables to consider if you are establishing a system to assure the quality of e-learning programs, courses, or objects.

Industry Specifications Focus on Objects, Reusability, and Interoperability

Advances in technology and increased interest in just-in-time training has resulted in the disaggregation of content into smaller instructional units. Working professionals are now less likely to go to universities to complete courses and degree programs. The emphasis is on providing smaller chunks of instruction (referred to as learning objects) at the moment and location of need through the use of modern telecommunication technologies.

Brennan, Funke, and Andersen (2001) define a learning object as the smallest stand-alone piece of instruction that contains an objective, an activity, and an assessment, wrapped by descriptive metadata. Metadata describes the nature and purpose of each object and is used to index the objects so that others can search for, retrieve, and reuse the object. The nature of the objectives, activities, and assessments that comprise a learning object is still under debate. Adherence to specifications, however, should allow objects to be shared across platforms, increasing the efficiency of the production process.

Table 3.7 lists six sets of specifications published by professional organizations for assuring the technical quality and interoperability of learning objects. Clearly, industry specifications differ from education guidelines. The specifications are technical in nature, addressing variables such as the XML binding, metadata coding, and the packaging of learning objects, rather than the design and delivery of courses and programs.

A fundamental question must be answered: "Are you going to set quality guidelines for programs, courses, faculty, and students, and/or meet specifications for the storage and interoperability of learning objects?" The ramifications are considerable. Not only does the approach used to create and store courses differ significantly from those used to generate and manage objects, the purpose and nature of the quality assurance system also differ, as illustrated by a comparison of Tables 3.1 and 3.7.

Table 3.7. Comparison of Industry Standards Posited by Professional Organizations

ADL (SCORM)	IMS	IEEE (LTSC)	AICC (AGR-010)	ARIADNE	Dublin Core
Content Aggregation Model • Content Model • Meta Data • Content Packaging Run Time Environment • Launch • Application Program Interface • Data Model In Progress (IP) • Simple Sequencing • Learner Information Profiles • Assessments	• Content Packaging • Digital Repositories • Enterprise • Learner Information Package • Meta-data • Questions and Test • Competency Definitions (Draft) In Progress (IP) • Learning Design • Simple Sequencing • Accessibility • Competency Definitions	• Architecture and Reference Model • Glossary • Computer managed instruction • Learning objects metadata • Semantics and Exchange Binding • Data Interchange Protocols • Platform and Media Profiles • Competency Definitions In Progress (IP) • Digital Rights Expression Language	Internet CBT Courseware • CMI-to-lesson communications for CBT and CMI • Export and import course structure files • Lesson evaluation files • Authoring tools • CMI Guidelines for Interoperability • Difference between HTTP and file-based methods • CBT Assignable Unit • URL Command • HTTP Communications • HTTP	• Educational Meta Data • General information on the resource • Semantics of the resource • Pedagogical attributes • Technical characteristics • Conditions for use • Meta-meta data • Annotation	• Meta Data Elements • Name • Identifier • Version • Registration Authority • Language • Definition • Obligation • Data type • Maximum Occurrence • Comment

Industry Specifications Address Varying Aspects of an E-learning System

Similar to education guidelines that deal with different organizational structures, industry specifications address different aspects of an e-learning system. Figure 3.2 illustrates how SCORM v1.2 incorporates existing IMS, AICC, and IEEE specifications. The interconnectedness of the published specifications is further demonstrated by the SCORM metadata specifications that are based on IEEE Learning Object Metadata specifications that were developed as a joint effort between the IMS and ARIADNE.

SCORM differs from other published specifications in that SCORM addresses a complete learning system. IMS and ADL share the architecture embodied in SCORM, but focus only on components of an entire system. According to Walker (Barron, 2000), SCORM is applicable to large corporations, government agencies, or universities striving to establish a comprehensive approach to training and education. The focus of IMS and other standards organizations, such as the IEEE, is on specifications that may be used by everyone.

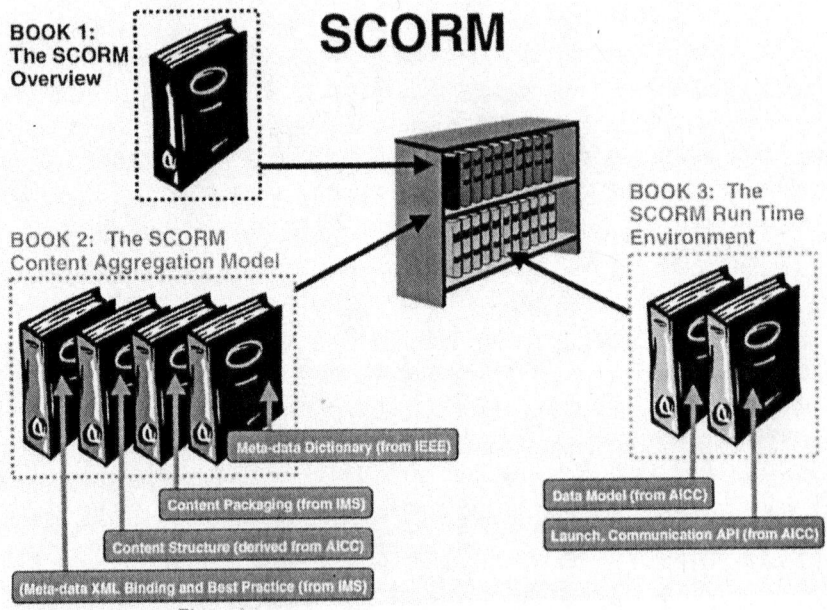

Figure 3.2.   Basic SCORM components illustrating relationship between published industry specifications.

If you decide to adopt specifications for e-learning objects, you must decide if you want to define specifications for the entire e-learning system (like those specified by SCORM) or for components of your e-learning system. You can concentrate on storing and accessing objects, meeting specifications for metadata (like ARIADNE and the DCMI), or you can adopt specifications for various aspects of an e-learning system (like IEEE and IMS), or you can meet specifications for aggregating content and creating a run-time environment (like the ADL initiative). If you go beyond the specification of metadata, additional human resources (or at least a redefinition or reclassification of job descriptions) may be required. Someone well versed in programming is necessary to apply and stay abreast of industry specifications.

Industry Specifications Fail to Delimit Learning Objects

Metadata recognizes that learning objects consist of pedagogical attributes. However, there is considerable debate as to what constitutes an object. Popular definitions posit that learning objects contain a measurable objective, an activity, and an assessment that are classified by metadata (e.g., Brennan et al., 2001). Other definitions quantify the size of the object using metrics such as duration (e.g., no more than 30 seconds to review) or the amount of information (e.g., no more than three individual screens of information). Recognizing that optimal object size depends on many factors, standards organizations neither specify the size nor composition of learning objects. Rather, they opt for broad definitions that approach size and composition based on need. For example, the IEEE (2002) defines a learning object as "any entity, digital or non-digital, that may be used for learning, education or training" (p. 5).

Such definitions are problematic. As Merrill (cited in Welsch, 2002) has noted, "If everything is an object, then nothing is a learning object" (p. 17). On an interpersonal level, the lack of a commonly-accepted definition can lead to confusion and miscommunications among experts and development team members. From an operational perspective, the lack of consensus makes it difficult to classify and assemble objects in a pedagogically sound fashion.

From a designer's perspective, failure to define the specific elements of learning objects makes it difficult to code objects. When a designer classifies an object, does he or she consider an entire instructional unit as an object or specific elements of a unit as objects? Is a graphic an object? How about an activity? Is a set of objectives an object or must an object contain an objective, an activity, and an assessment? Some specifications even refer to learning assets (e.g., ADL, 2002) that may or may not be considered elements of a learning object.

Effectiveness

Educators who seek to combine objects to create instructional modules or courses may neither have the time nor the expertise necessary to combine the objects in a cohesive manner. Let's say a biology teacher finds an excellent object that depicts cell division, but finds the object does not contain appropriate objectives or assessments. Will he or she have the time and knowledge necessary to add the key instructional elements? If not, learners who access objects may find them lacking and fail to achieve specified outcomes. Unless the size—or, more specifically, the composition of a learning object—is further delineated, it may be difficult, if not impossible, to realize the long-term vision of the ADL initiative: to create a system that will store sharable content objects from across the Web and assemble them in real-time to provide learning and assistance anywhere, at anytime (Figure 3.3).

If you consider adopting industry specifications for learning objects, you must keep in mind objects may vary in size and composition. Additional guidelines and/or specifications may be necessary to assure the pedagogical effectiveness of e-learning courses and programs that are based on learning objects.

Industry Specifications Do Not
Address Learning and Instructional Principles

Like education guidelines, industry specifications do not to address key principles derived from research and theory. Although considerable progress has been made to formalize the technical aspects of industry specifications (e.g., to assure interoperability), that does not mean that the objects are pedagogically sound. "The interoperability that they (ADL) are promoting is just plumbing, and they don't care what goes into the pipes. It could be spring water, or it could be sewage" (Anderson, cited in Welsch, 2002, p. 17).

Recognizing that existing specifications do not necessarily assure the pedagogical quality of instruction, the IMS (2000) is in the process of defining standards for Learning Design and Simple Sequencing. The ADL (2002) is also developing specifications for Learning Information Profiles to account for differences in learner characteristics, and generating additional specifications for delineating learner assessments. It will be

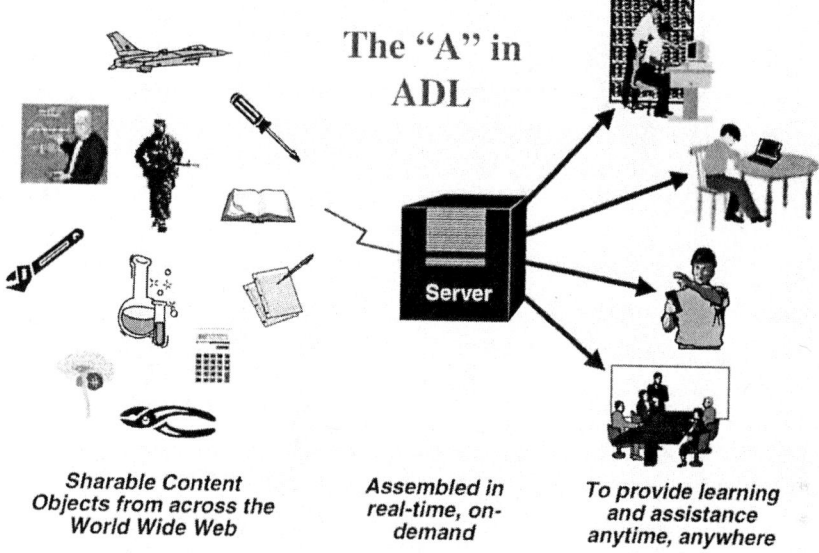

The "A" in ADL

Server

| Sharable Content Objects from across the World Wide Web | Assembled in real-time, on-demand | To provide learning and assistance anytime, anywhere |

Source: Advanced Distributed Learning, Sharable Content Object Reference Model (SCORM^TM) Version 1.2, Copyright 2001.

Figure 3.3.   ADL's long-term vision for use of sharable objects.

interesting to see if the new specifications address the pedagogical concerns expressed in this article.

Earlier, it was noted that education guidelines do not address important pedagogical principles related to alignment, feedback, sequencing, and motivation. Analysis of industry specifications yield similar concerns, but applied to learning objects and assets rather than academic courses and programs. Research and theory provide an empirical foundation for defining such specifications. The challenge lies in distilling and applying the plethora of findings in a manner that is specific enough to assure the pedagogical effectiveness of the instruction, yet simple enough to follow and flexible enough to promote creativity while accounting for differences in learning outcomes, learner characteristics, and educational philosophies.

CONCLUDING THOUGHTS

Renewed interest in distance education has given us an unprecedented opportunity to reflect on current and past practices and establish a dialog among practitioners and researchers to guide future activities. It has stimulated discussions on pedagogy, instructional design, and the use of technology across disciplines rarely seen in industry or academia. New initiatives have resulted in products that not only facilitate distance learning, but learning in traditional and hybrid settings. Return on investment is not limited to distance learners; significant benefits are also accrued by on-campus students as educators transfer skills and educational materials to enhance learning in alternative settings. However, benefits to both distant and on-campus students cannot be realized without the development and delivery of quality programs, courses, and/or objects.

To help ensure quality, one of the first issues that must be addressed is whether your organization wants to take an educational or industrial approach. In other words, will your organization define guidelines for programs and courses, or for learning objects and assets? Or, is a combination of approaches more appropriate? After establishing the basic approach, you must also determine which set of guidelines or specifications to adopt and/or adapt. This article identifies some of the key factors to consider as you answer these basic questions. However you proceed, there is still one fundamental question that must be answered that transcends both education guidelines and industry specifications; that is, will you define separate standards for distance learning and traditional classroom courses?

In the belief that new delivery systems require new standards, institutions and accrediting bodies have generated different requirements for assessing the quality of distance education and traditional classroom instruction. Certainly, from a logistical perspective, applying two sets of standards to assure the quality of instruction takes more time and money than one set and complicates the certification process. From an operational perspective, the increasing number of hybrid courses that combine distance and face-to-face components bring to question the validity of either set of requirements. Should a third set of standards be developed, is either set more appropriate or should we consider defining one set of standards for teaching and learning that transcends the method used to deliver the instruction?

The guiding principles posited by the American Council on Education and The Alliance (ACE, 1997) represent a movement toward outcomes or results-orientated guidelines that do not distinguish between delivery system. Rather than specifying how distance learning should take place, the guiding principles seek to address, "the qualities of tomorrow's future learning society" (Sullivan & Rocco, 1997). In the immediate future, the complete dissolution of traditional standards and the adoption of new standards may be too overwhelming for many. Maybe it is more practical to define separate standards first, then look to synthesize them over time. What we do know is that advances in technology will continue to outpace research and challenge conventional views of teaching and learning. The publication of guidelines and specifications is seen as a solid step toward assuring the quality of e-learning, but as the analysis reveals, our work is far from finished. The search for quality continues, and those who seek it may find the conversations resulting from the quest as—or even more— valuable than the actual adoption of quality standards.

REFERENCES

Abrioux, D. (2002). *The challenges of quality assurance in a distance learning environment.* Retrieved November 18, 2002, from http://www.athabasca.ca/presoff/ presentations/ SREB.ppt

Advanced Distributed Learning. (2002). *Sharable content object reference model (SCORM) version 1.2: Conformance requirements.* Retrieved April 18, 2002, from http://www.adlnet.gov/

American Council on Education. (1997). *Guiding principles for distance learning in the learning society.* Retrieved October 3, 2002, from http://www.acenet.edu

American Distance Education Council. (n.d.a). *Guiding principles for distance teaching and learning.* Retrieved October 3, 2002, from http://www.adec.edu/admin/ papers/distance-teaching_principles.html

American Distance Education Council. (n.d.b). *Guiding principles for distance learning.* Retrieved October 3, 2002, from http://www.adec.edu/admin/papers/ distance-learning_principles.html

American Federation of Teachers. (2000). *Distance education: Guidelines for good practice.* Retrieved October 3, 2002, from http://www.aft.org/pubs-reports/ higher_ed/distance.pdf

ARIADNE. (2002). *ARIADNE Educational Metadata Recommendation-V3.2.* Retrieved November 1, 2002, from http://www.ariadne-eu.org/en/ publications/metadata/ams_v32.html

Aviation Industry CBT Committee. (1999). *AICC Guidelines and Recommendation for Web-based Computer Managed Instruction (AGR-010).* Retrieved October 31, 2002, from http://www.aicc.org/pages/down-docs-index.htm

Barron, T. (2000, November). Ed Walker talks standards. *Learning Circuits.* Retrieved October 1, 2002, from http://www.learningcircuits/nov200/walker .html

Berge, Z. (2002). Active, interactive, and reflective elearning. *Quarterly Review of Distance Education, 3*(2), 181-190.

Berge, Z. (1999). Interaction in post-secondary Web-based learning. *Educational Technology, 39*(1), 5-11.

Brennan, M., Funke, S., & Andersen, C. (2001). *The learning content management system: A new e-learning market segment emerges.* Retrieved November 9, 2001, from http://www.avaltus.com/idc/index.html

Council of Regional Accrediting Commissions. (2000). *Statement of the regional accrediting commissions on the evaluation of electronically offered degree and certificate programs*. Retrieved October 3, 2002, from http://www.wiche.edu/telecom/guidelines.htm

Dick, W., Carey, L., & Carey, J. O. (2005). *The systematic design of instruction* (6th ed.). Boston: Allyn & Bacon

Dublin Core Metadata Initiative. (2002) *Dublin Core Metadata Element Set Version 1.1*. Retrieved November 1, 2002, from http://www.dublincore.org/documents/2002/07/31/dcmes-xml/

Hirumi, A. (2002a). A framework for analyzing, designing and sequencing planned e-learning interactions. *Quarterly Review of Distance Education, 3*(2), 141-160.

Hirumi, A. (2002b). The design and sequencing of e-learning interactions: A grounded approach. *International Journal on E-Learning, 1*(1), 19-27.

Hodgins, W., & Conner, M. (2000). Everything you ever wanted to know about learning standards but were afraid to ask. *LiNE Zine*. Retrieved October 1, 2002, from http://www.linezine.com/2.1/features/wheyewtkls.htm

Institute of Electrical and Electronics Engineers. (2002). *Learning Technology Standards Committee (LTSC) P1484*. Retrieved October 31, 2002, from http://ltsc.ieee.org/ index.html

Institute for Higher Education Policy. (2000, April). *Quality on the line: Benchmarks for success in Internet-based distance education*. Retrieved January 7, 2000, from http://www.ihep.com/quality.pdf

Instructional Management System Global Learning Consortium. (2000). *E-Learning Specifications*. Retrieved October 25, 2002, from http://www.imsproject.org/specifications.cfm

Johnson, S. D., Aragon, S. R., Shaik, N., & Palma-Rivas, N. (2000). Comparative analysis of learner satisfaction and learning outcomes in online and face-to-face learning environments. *Journal of Interactive Learning Research, 11*(1), 29-49.

Kaufman, R., & Hirumi, A. (1992). Ten steps to implementing total quality management "plus." *Educational Leadership, 50*(3), 33-34.

Kaufman, R., & Watkins, R. (2000). Assuring the future of distance learning. *Quarterly Review of Distance Education, 1*(1), 59-67.

Kaufman, R., Watkins, R., & Leigh, D. (2001). *Useful educational results: Defining, prioritizing, and accomplishing*. Lancaster, PA: Pro>Active.

Keller, J. M. (1987a). Strategies for stimulating the motivation to learn. *Performance & Instruction, 26*(8), 1-7.

Keller, J. M. (1987b). The systematic process of motivational design. *Performance & Instruction, 29*(9), 1-8.

Kulhavy, R. W., & Wager, W. (1993). Feedback in programmed instruction: Historical context and implications for practice. In J. V. Dempsey & G. C. Sales (Eds.), *Interactive instruction and feedback* (pp. 2-20). Englewood Cliffs, NJ: Educational Technology.

Liaw, S., & Huang, H. (2000). Enhancing interactivity in web-based Instruction: A review of the literature. *Educational Technology, 40*(3), 41-45.

Machtmes, K., & Asher, J.W. (2000). A meta-analysis of the effectiveness of telecourses in distance education. *The American Journal of Distance Education, 14*(1), 27-46.

Northrup, P. (2001). A framework for designing interactivity in Web-based instruction. *Educational Technology, 41*(2), 31-39.

Northrup, P. T., & Rasmussen, K. L. (2000, February). *Designing a Web-based program: Theory to design.* Paper presented at the annual conference of the Association for Educational Communications and Technology, Long Beach, CA.

Open and Distance Learning Quality Council. (2001). *Standards in open and distance education.* Retrieved October 3, 2002, from http://www.odlqc.org.uk/stint.htm

Saba, F. (2000). Research in distance education: A status report. *International Review of Research in Open and Distance Education, 1*(1), 2-9.

Smith, P. L., & Ragan, T. J. (1999). *Instructional design* (2nd ed.). Upper Saddle River, NJ: Prentice-Hall.

Sullivan, E., & Rocco, T. (1997). *A credo for going the distance.* Retrieved October 3, 2002, from http://www.pbs.org/als/agenda/articles/credo.html

Twigg, C. A. (2001). *Quality assurance for whom? Providers and consumers in today's distributed learning environment.* The Pew Learning and Technology Program. Center for Academic Transformation at Rensselaer Polytechnic Institute. Retrieved October 2, 2002, from http://center.rpi.edu/pewsym/mono3.html

Weller, H. G. (1988). Interactivity in microcomputer-based instruction: Its essential components and how it can be enhanced. *Journal of Educational Technology Systems, 28*(2), 23-27.

Welsch, E. (2002). SCORM: Clarity or calamity? *Online Learning, 6*(6), 14-21.

Western Cooperative for Educational Telecommunications. (1997). *Good practices in distance education.* Retrieved September 27, 1998, from http://www.wiche.edu/telecom

Wetzel. D. D., Radtke, P. H., & Stern, H. W. (1994). *Instructional effectiveness of video media.* Hillsdale, NJ: Erlbaum.

Yacci, M. (2000). Interactivity demystified: A structural definition for distance Education and intelligent computer-based instruction. *Educational Technology, 40*(4), 5-16.

CHAPTER 4

LEARNING ONLINE

Adapting the Seven Principles of Good Practice to a Web-based Instructional Environment

Christine K. Sorensen and Danilo M. Baylen

Increasingly, colleges and universities are offering courses on the Internet, and enrollments in online learning opportunities are soaring. Research on distance education in general, including online learning, indicates that students can learn effectively in technology-mediated environments. Growth in online, or virtual, education is expected to continue. However, we are just beginning to examine the impact of these technologies on pedagogy. Some argue that these technologies will transform the way learning occurs in college classrooms, both traditional and online (Newman & Scurry, 2001). While some point to earlier technologies (overhead projectors, films, television) and claim that such transformations are overstated, those earlier technologies did not actively engage students in the learning process, something that Internet and Web-based technologies can do (Newman & Scurry, 2001).

The Perfect Online Course: Best Practices for Designing and Teaching
pp. 69–86

TECHNOLOGY AND TEACHING

While technologies, such as the Internet, can be used to perform routine and traditional tasks (providing syllabi, linking to readings, providing communication channels), they can also be used to implement teaching methods that are as effective or more effective than traditional lecturing. Newman & Scurry (2001) discuss how online technologies can engage students in active learning through software that allows hands-on experiences, such as "virtual labs." Computer-based simulations can help connect learning to real life. Students can gain access to massive amounts of information, including graphics, pictures, and videos, in addition to text-based materials. Teaching styles can be tailored to individual student needs as the technology provides mechanisms for faculty to access student profiles and compare student performance. The role of the faculty member changes from that of the source of all information to a learning coach, providing greater individualized attention and allowing students to choose from a variety of online possibilities. Students can easily retrieve and review material. And, technologies such as virtual reality allow students to gain early experiences in a safe setting (Newman & Scurry, 2001).

As online technologies become more prevalent in society, traditional classrooms and online courses may begin to look more and more alike as both incorporate active learning strategies and online resources. As technologies continue to improve and to become more available to the masses, students will begin to expect their use in learning environments. Higher education must face this challenge, and faculty must become proficient in the use of technologies. However, just using the technology is not enough; faculty must use it in ways that truly enhance learning. Faculty must engage in sound pedagogical practices in a new, technology-based environment.

These pedagogical practices may be better aligned with what is known about adult learning, or andragogy (Robles, 1998). Andragogy implies a more equal and reciprocal relationship between the student and teacher and uses more variety in methods. Andragogy allows for the interests and needs of the learner and deliberately introduces experiential, collaborative, and interactive learning strategies. The principles of andragogy seem consistent with what has been identified as principles of good practice in collegiate education.

PRINCIPLES FOR GOOD PRACTICE

The "Seven Principles for Good Practice in Undergraduate Education" were first published in 1987 by the American Association for Higher Education. The "Seven Principles" evolved as a result of a sponsored Wingspread meeting attended by Alexander W. Astin, Howard Bowen, Carol M. Boyer, K. Patricia Cross, Kenneth Eble, Russell Edgerton, Jerry Gaff, Joseph Katz, C. Robert Pace, Marvin W. Peterson, and Richard C. Richardson, Jr. and emerged from a study supported by the American Association of Higher Education, the Education Commission of the States, and the Johnson Foundation (Chickering & Ehrmann, 2003; Chickering & Gamson, 2003; Winona State University, 2003). The "Seven Principles" form a sound model for quality collegiate instruction. While these principles have formed a foundation for traditional classroom instruction, it is important to consider them when developing and designing instruction in technology-based environments.

The "Seven Principles" are general enough in their perspective that they can be adapted to many learning environments. They support the notion that good teaching is good teaching. They describe some essential components that are important in effective learning environments. The "Seven Principles of Good Practice":

1. encourage student-faculty contact
2. encourage cooperation among students,
3. encourage active learning,
4. give prompt feedback,
5. emphasize time on task,
6. communicate high expectations, and
7. respect diverse talents and ways of learning.

The authors of the "Seven Principles" document assert that student motivation, involvement, and intellectual commitment result from student-faculty contact both in and out of class. They maintain that creating collaborative, cooperative learning environments increases student involvement in learning, enhances the sharing of ideas, and improves understanding (Winona State University, 2003; Chickering & Gamson, 2003). "Good learning, like good work, is collaborative and social, not competitive and isolated" (Chickering & Gamson, 2003).

Active learning is a key in the "Seven Principles." "Learning is not a spectator sport" (Chickering & Gamson, 2003). Students need to do more than take lecture notes and memorize facts. Active learning incorporates past experiences, requires application, and allows students to talk about and write about what they are learning (Winona State University, 2003; Chickering & Gamson, 2003).

Timely feedback and time on task are other essential components of a good learning environment. Students need frequent feedback and suggestions for improvement and assistance in learning to assess their own performance, including opportunities to reflect. Students must also learn to use time effectively. According to Chickering and Gamson (2003), "there is no substitute for time on task" and "time plus energy equals learning."

High expectations for students can become a self-fulfilling prophecy, thus setting appropriate learning goals contributes to a successful learning environment (Chickering & Gamson, 2003; Winona State University, 2003). Appreciating and recognizing individuality, allowing students to learn from their strengths while still pushing them to learn in new ways can enrich learning opportunities (Winona State University, 2003). "There are many roads to learning" (Chickering & Gamson, 2003) and a positive learning environment acknowledges these various paths.

APPLYING THE "PRINCIPLES" TO A WEB-BASED ENVIRONMENT

We talk in higher education about the profession of teaching, and about our obligation to making knowledge available to others. As Lee Shulman (2000) states, "teaching, fully understood, is an extraordinary process" (p. 6). We in the profession also have an obligation to study teaching and share our knowledge with others as we seek to enhance student learning (Hutchings, 2000). This article provides suggestions and strategies for incorporating the "Seven Principles of Good Practice" into online learning environments based both on the literature and on the authors' six years of online teaching experience, both developing and delivering online instruction. Using methods recommended by Angelo and Cross (1993) for examining teaching practice, the authors learned from experiences teaching in Web-enhanced traditional classes as well as delivering full online courses.

Principle 1: Student-Instructor Contact

Student-instructor contact can be encouraged through a variety of strategies, including setting up specific communication structures that allow for both social and academic contacts as well as mechanisms for information distribution. Chickering and Ehrmann (2003) note that using communication technologies can increase student access to faculty, promote resource sharing, and encourage shared learning. They note that interactions are particularly strengthened for shy students who may be reluctant to speak openly in class and for commuting part-time students whose opportunities for face-to-face interactions are constrained by work and family obligations. Both synchronous and asynchronous communication can be used successfully.

> Electronic mail, computer conferencing, and the World Wide Web increase opportunities for students and faculty to converse and exchange work much more speedily than before, and more thoughtfully and "safely" than when confronting each other in a classroom or faculty office. (Chickering & Ehrmann, 2003)

Chickering and Ehrmann also maintain that these media allow more equitable and widespread participation from diverse students.

The authors of this article have identified several successful strategies in teaching in a Web-based environment for encouraging student-faculty contact and increasing interaction. One of the most important lessons was in how to set up asynchronous communication spaces to accommodate different learner needs. After several years of experimentation and student feedback, a structure was designed to allow for five discrete areas of communication within an asynchronous Web environment such as WebBoard, Embanet, Blackboard, or WebCT. These five areas included:

1. announcement space,
2. question and answer space,
3. content discussion space,
4. social space, and
5. team space. These areas are set up to address specific needs.

Announcement space is used for instructor messages to the students. This might include reminders, instructions, additional connections to online resources, and class announcements (for example, class cancellations due to weather). Students are instructed to check this area routinely.

Question and answer space is designed to address questions students may have about course content or about assignments. If one student has a question or is unclear about something, odds are that others in the class are experiencing similar questions or concerns. Thus, rather than individually e-mailing the instructor questions, students are instructed to post their questions in this space. The instructor checks the space daily and provides answers to the students' questions or expands on explanations that it appears may be unclear to students.

Content discussion space is an area set aside for graded discussions. In this area, the instructor posts topics for group discussion or poses questions to initiate group interaction. Students are required to respond during a set time period and a grading rubric is provided that sets

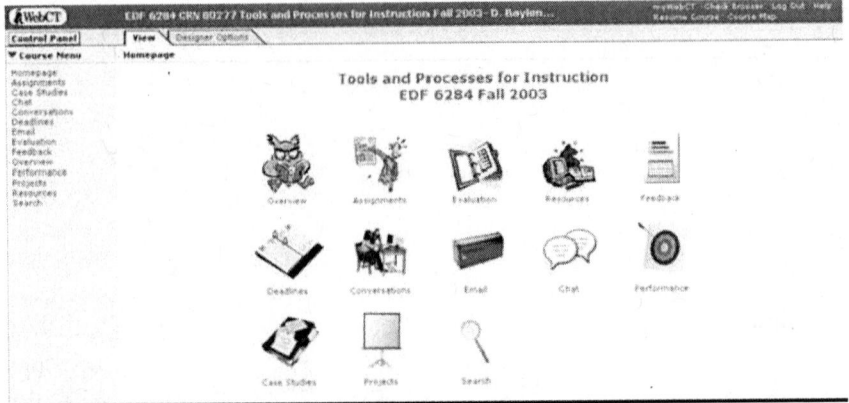

Figure 4.1.   Opening page of a course where students can access information about course content, instructions about different activities, and various ways of communicating with the course facilitator and students.

expectations for interactions in this space. Levels of communication and levels of interaction (see Baylen & Sorensen, 2002) are established.

Social Space (often named, e.g., the Coffee Shop, the Courtyard, etc.) was added to encourage nonformal interactions between the instructor and the students and among the students. The instructor observed that content-related course space was often sprinkled with personal information and messages between students or non-course-related questions to the instructor. To keep the other areas focused and yet not discourage this informal "chatter," the instructor instead set up a space especially for this purpose and, indeed, encouraged students to participate. It was found that such spaces enhanced the sense of community established in an online class.

Team space was the final area established. Students were assigned or selected teams during courses taught by the instructor. Each team named itself, and a separate (and private) discussion area was established for each team. Communication about team assignments could occur in the team space. The instructor could interact with the team on issues connected to the team's work. Team space often included a chat area as well that allowed for real-time student interactions on tasks and projects.

In addition to setting up specified spaces in the online environment, the instructor also used other methods to encourage student-instructor contact. Students were given information to allow individual contacts with the instructor via e-mail or telephone. The instructor also set up regular chat office hours. These hours varied by day of the week and by hour, allowing for differences in students' schedules. Day and evening hours, weekday and weekend hours were used. Finally, e-journaling was used in several classes. Students were required to submit weekly reflective journals using e-mail or assignment submission tools (e.g., in WebCT) that maintained privacy and were not available for classmates to review. These journals were read by the instructor and comments were returned to the students.

One strategy that proved particularly effective in a completely online course was a midterm telephone contact made by the instructor. Each student was called by the instructor for a midpoint "check." Students were asked how their assignments were coming along, whether they had any questions, and whether they had any concerns about the class. End-of-course evaluations indicated that students truly appreciated this contact and that it enhanced their perception of the level of interaction between the student and the instructor.

Principle 2: Cooperation Among Students

Technology-based communication tools can facilitate cooperation among students, opening up communication channels among classmates who are not physically together (Chickering & Ehrmann, 2003). Cooperative strategies used in traditional classrooms, such as study groups, group problem solving, and assignment discussion, can also occur in an online environment. The authors of this article have found several teaming strategies that promote cooperation among students in an online learning environment.

Reciprocity and cooperating in an online course can be enhanced through the development of teams and team identities. Depending on the nature of the course, teams can be assigned or students can self-identify teams. To create a team identity, teams were asked to name themselves. Over several courses, teams came up with such titles as "Sneakers," "Four Gals and a Guy," "Negative Space," and "Superstars" to name a few. Teams were also encouraged to develop a visual representation, icon, or graphic to place on the Web site as a team identifier. This, too, enhanced team identification among the team members.

It is important for instructors to realize that students may not understand how to operate in an online team, nor understand the dynamics of group processing. Setting up team expectations, roles for individuals in the team, and team evaluation and monitoring processes are key elements in developing effective teams. Initial orientation to team work is generally necessary. We have found it useful to outline expectations for team behavior. These expectations can be developed by the whole class or by the instructors and provided to the class. Expectations that we have found useful include such things as "all team members participate in online discussions and no one person dominates." Depending upon the tasks or group assignments for which the team is responsible, defining and assigning such roles as facilitator, recorder, summarizer, process manager, timekeeper, reporter, and instructor liaison may be useful.

Two mechanisms have been found useful for monitoring the group process. A student assigned as process manager has the responsibility to report group difficulties to the instructor and seek guidance in strategies to move the group forward. In one case, this person reported an interpersonal interaction that required instructor intervention. A second mechanism is to ask for periodic feedback from group members related to the functioning of the team and for evaluation of their individual and peer contributions to the team. We have developed an online tool that students complete at midpoint in the class to assess the functioning of the team. In addition to evaluating the functioning of the team, we have found it important to assess individual accountability in the team's performance. Thus, we request each team submit with assignments a summary paragraph briefly outlining each team member's contribution to the final product. The instructor retains the ability to adjust an individual's grade (e.g., an individual may receive a grade higher or lower than the overall group grade) on the basis of the individual contribution to the group project.

As mentioned earlier in this article, providing teams with private space, both asynchronous and synchronous, can facilitate group interactions. Which spaces are used by the team typically depends upon the nature of the group assignment. Types of assignments we have used include: development of a case study, analysis of a case study, problem-solving assignments, development of a group presentation (generally using PowerPoint with audio/video components) that can be shared online, peer review of individual assignments, and sharing of resources (for example, sharing URLs for useful Web sites, or sharing citations and abstracts for articles).

Building a sense of community in the online class contributes to cooperation among students. The authors have used several strategies to try to enhance community. Students can be asked to provide introductory e-mails to the class or to develop their own Web pages with photographs to share with the class. Icebreaker games can also be used to introduce students to one another. One game we have used asks students to e-mail to the instructor one thing no one else in the class knows about them. The instructor then makes a list of these items. A class assignment is to try and figure out which item goes with which classmate. Students can make use of the social space described earlier to ask questions that may help them identify their classmates.

Principle 3: Active Learning

Active learning uses procedures that increase student participation in the learning process (Kochery, 1997). A tremendous range of strategies can be used in traditional classrooms to involve students in active learning. Some of these strategies can be adapted to online environments, and online environments can also take advantage of technologies to engage students in the learning process. Evidence indicates that students actively involved in learning remember more and remember it longer than when they are engaged in passive listening activities (Newman & Scurry, 2003). Some claim that, unlike earlier technologies such as overhead projectors, films, and television, technologies available in an online world have the capacity to engage students in active learning (Newman & Scurry, 2003).

Active learning techniques can be experiential, hands-on, participative, or inquiry-based. Active learning strategies can include such things as animations, virtual labs, graphing technologies, role playing, problem- or project-based learning, case studies, portfolios, analysis activities, debates, virtual field trips, games, online expert interviews, reactor panels, structured online discussions or reflections, and more. The authors of this article have incorporated these active learning strategies into their courses. For the purposes of this article, only two of these strategies will be described, one targeted to individual students and one to teams of students.

The first example is a way to engage individual students in structured online discussions. Each student may be assigned a topic (or students may be allowed to choose a topic) related to the course. The student then poses a question on the discussion board. Other students in the class (either the entire class or a portion of the class depending upon the enrollment) must respond to the question and engage in a discussion. The student who posed the question is responsible for moderating the discussion and for contributing additional Web links to information on the topic. After a pre-assigned time period, typically one week, the student who posed the question is responsible for synthesizing and summarizing the key points of the discussion and posting the summary for the entire class. This summary may be graded. In addition, students may be asked to write a personal reflection on the experience and e-mail it to the instructor. We have found this strategy to be most effective in an asynchronous environment, although we have used it in a modified form in a synchronous chat environment as well.

The second example has been used to engage small groups of students in analysis of case studies. Each small group is assigned a case study for development and analysis. After the small group has analyzed the case, they are asked to present the case to the larger group using a Web page or downloadable format. Using a rubric and criteria provided to the class, a second group is asked to critique the original group's response to the case study. The original team is then asked to provide a response. Again, we have found the case study format to be most effective in the asynchronous environment; however, an alternative may be a live chat discussion of the case following the analysis and critique.

The opportunities for developing active learning strategies in an online environment are as plentiful as in a traditional teaching environment. While we have provided two fairly simple strategies, the variations and variety of techniques possible are constrained only by the instructor's imagination.

Principle 4: Prompt Feedback

"Knowing what you know and don't know focuses learning" (Chickering & Gamson, 2003). According to Chickering & Gamson (2003), and Chickering & Ehrmann (2003), students need appropriate feedback, frequent opportunities to perform and receive suggestions to improve, chances to reflect on their learning, and assistance in assessing themselves. Establishing mechanisms for acknowledgement of assignments or assignment receipt protocols is important in enabling prompt feedback in online environments. We have found students demand immediate feedback in an online course, often e-mailing repeated messages asking whether an assignment was received or whether the instructor feedback is completed.

The authors have used several strategies to ensure prompt feedback in an online course. Students in the online course are required to submit assignments electronically, either via e-mail attachment or via an assignment support tool available in the course environment (e.g. WebCT or Blackboard have secure areas where students can submit work). Guidelines are provided to students indicating that the instructor will acknowledge receipt of the assignment within 48 hours of submission. This is typically done via e-mail. Students are asked not to contact the instructor with a question about whether the assignment has been received unless 48 hours have passed and no acknowledgement has been received. Not only does this reduce the number of panicked e-mails sent by students who want assurance the assignment has been received, but it also provides documentation of assignment receipt. Students are provided guidelines on

You need to do the following as part of your discussion participation:

1. Read or view (<u>powerpoint</u>) first the information provided on discussion roles (initiating, supporting, challenging, monitoring, and summarizing).

2. For discussion participation, **you need to make a minimum of at least 10 postings beyond the "Initial Post" with this configuration --**

- 1 Initiating
- 5 Supporting
- 2 Challenging
- 1 Monitoring
- 1 Summarizing (pertains to a specific thread in the conversation)

NOTE: If you are not sure what role supports your posting, you can use the designation OTHER or you CHOOSE THE ROLE you want it to represent that is not in the list (initiating, supporting, challenging, monitoring or summarizing). If you do this, the posting with this role will count as one posting with a supporting role.

3. For each of your posting in this discussion, you need to add your role. After the heading, type a dash and your role. Make sure you remove the previous role unless you are using the same role. **Please stick to one role per posting -- again, avoid typing more than one role in the heading of your posting.**

For example, the posting has heading that states "Baylen-Initial Post". When you make reply that is supportive or challenging to that posting, your new heading for that reply should be "Baylen-Supporting" or Baylen-Challenging".

4. If you are doing an Initiating role, please click on compose message to allow you to start a new thread.

NOTE: Posting headings without accompanying roles will not count as discussion participation.

Figure 4.2.   This is a set of instructions for students to follow as they participate in a specific online discussion in a given course.

when to expect instructor feedback on the assignment, typically a one-week time period. Students are asked not to contact the instructor about feedback unless the week is past and no feedback has been received. Giving students guidance on the turnaround time to expect for assignments helps reduce their anxiety level and decreases the number of individual e-mails directed to the instructor. Such guidelines for timeliness of responses also are useful related to online discussions and responses to general e-mails in addition to assignments.

Technology can assist the instructor in providing prompt feedback. We have found it useful to set up protocols for assignment submission, such as appropriate software package and version to use (e.g., Word 97 or higher) and how to name the file (e.g., E Smith assignment 1). This enables the instructor to more easily manage the files and better track submissions. Editing tools, for example, those available in Word, can be

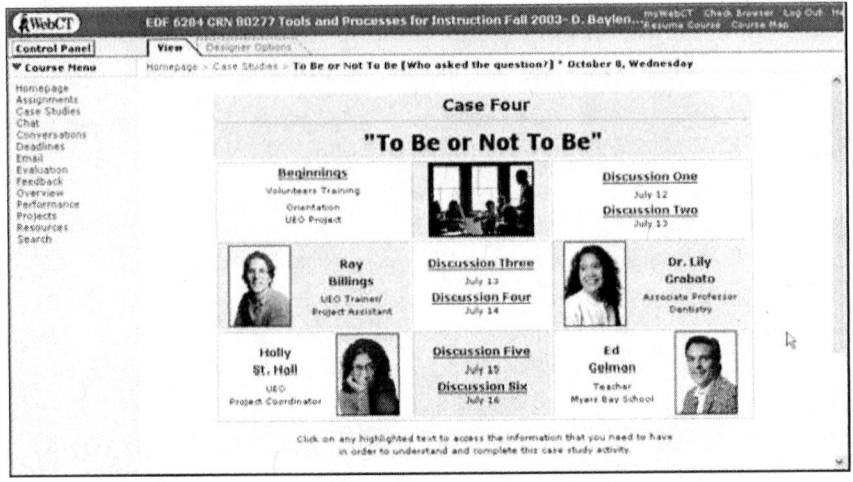

Figure 4.3.   Case studies are set up (like the one above) to facilitate active learning, problem thinking, and teamwork among students enrolled in a course. In this example, the case study is a nonlinear fashion where students can choose to access information that they believe can support the direction they are heading in finding solution to a problem.

used to embed feedback to the student. "Hidden" comments can be embedded using options in the word processing program. We have found that, with brief instructions, these editing tools and "hidden" comment functions can be used for peer reviews as well. While it took some time for the instructors to become used to reading and commenting on assignments that were not printed, we have found that managing assignments electronically and responding electronically now saves us time and that we are able to more quickly provide feedback to students.

With the move to electronic management of assignments, we have also found it easier to provide students with early feedback and revision options. For some assignments, students are allowed to respond to the initial feedback with a second draft (E Smith assignment 1 revision) in order to improve their performance.

In the online environment, we have found that students often seek more and prompter feedback than in a traditional classroom. We have posited that perhaps this is due to the lack of visual cues for the students to rely on in the classroom, or the loss of a particular classroom time (e.g., Mondays from 9-10 a.m.) when students in traditional classrooms can request or expect feedback from the instructor. Students in an online class seem to have a tremendous need for feedback, constant feedback.

Principle 5: Time on Task

Learning to use time well is critical for students, and they often need assistance with effective time management and allocating realistic amounts of time for specific activities (Chickering & Gamson, 2003). Technologies can help students manage time and can document student time on task. Time on task can be focused through the use of tools that can track student participation. Most course delivery tools such as WebCT or Blackboard have tools that allow instructors to monitor when students are accessing materials and for how long. Students can be shown how to use these tools to monitor their own behaviors. In addition, instructors can look at threaded discussions to determine participation levels of individual students. A number of other strategies have been found useful to keep students focused and on task.

Setting up frameworks for discussions and protocols for interactive time can keep students focused. For example, for asynchronous discussions, setting up specific dates for the beginning and end of the discussion (when postings are allowed) ensure that students participate in a timely manner. For synchronous discussions, or even telnet time that might be used in the course, we have found it useful to set time expectations and a framework for discussion initially. For example, a framework might be established that the first five minutes of time would be spent with the instructor presenting information, followed by 15 to 20 minutes of discussion, and concluding with 15 minutes of application or connection to real-world contexts. Setting time limits keeps the activities moving and keeps students focused. Limiting the numbers of students in chat rooms also can keep discussions better targeted. The experience of the authors would indicate that chat rooms with 5 to 10 participants are manageable.

Using organizational strategies and teaching them to students can assist students in maintaining focus in the class. Strategies such as the use of online calendars, organization of online files, posting reminders for events or assignment due dates, sending e-mail reminders, and the use of checkpoints to determine whether students are adequately moving through the materials can be important in maintaining attention. Online calendars can be effective in reminding students of assignment dates, dates of synchronous chats, dates when asynchronous discussion topics are open, dates by which materials are to have been reviewed, and more. Posting reminders in the "instructor" space described earlier in this article can be effective if students adhere to instructions to check that space regularly. An e-mail reminder may be used to remind students of an assignment or to notify a student that an assignment has not been

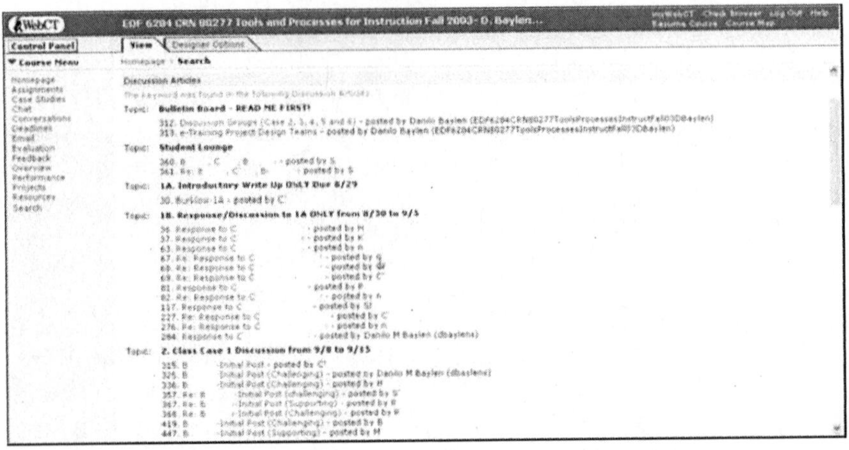

Figure 4.4.   The search function of the course management system (WebCT) used in this particular allows students to monitor their participation in the different online discussions. Students reported that they find this WebCT feature helpful in getting them organized with the task at hand.

received. Checkpoints can be used in two ways. One way is to provide the students a summary of what assignments have been received and where they are in terms of progressing through the course at specified points in time. We have done this through an e-mail with a table attachment. A second way is to require students to self-evaluate at specific points in the course and summarize their progress.

How the materials are structured in the course can also affect time on task. Using course mapping or indexing helps students to see the course as a whole and identify where they are in terms of the course. Arranging the course in discrete units focused on particular topics and establishing guidelines for completion of the units keeps students focused. In general, online courses that provide access to instructor notes, PowerPoints, additional exercises and activities, and links to resource materials encourages students to spend additional time with the content. Students have ready access to materials and can review materials on their own time if they are having difficulty with a particular concept or unit.

Principle 6: High Expectations

"Expect more and you will get it" (Chickering & Gamson, 2003). It is important to set explicit expectations for students in an online instructional environment. Setting appropriate goals for both online behaviors

5B. Discussion Synthesis and Reflection - Case 4
Last day to post in Conversation: October 18, Saturday

Part 1. Synthesis Paper -- As a group and with the leadership of your discussion facilitator, you need to prepare a synthesis paper (minimum 2 page, maximum 5 pages) of what your group discussed given the 3 guide questions --

- What did this case study miss to address given the instructional design concepts and principles presented in the Piskurich book?

- How will you go about teaching the major concepts and principles addressed in this case study to a group of 20 Thai, Saudi Arabian, Swiss, and South African adults?

- Based on your reflections of this learning experience, how come many of our experiences in university and college settings end up as lectures by faculty members?

Part 2. Reflection Paper -- Each group member will take the synthesis paper that the group put together and add his/her own reflection (at least a page, maximum 3 pages) using the following questions as guide --

- How similar or different is this learning experience from the first 3 case discussions?

- In what ways did this experience enhance or hinder the acquisition of new knowledge and skills pertaining to instructional design?

- How did the shared websites and online articles contribute to expanding your knowledge base as an educational technologist, instructional developer, and/or facilitator of learning?

3. Finally, **add as a separate page a list of selected references** (at least 3 websites and 3 online articles) that were shared by your group members during the case discussion that strictly follows an APA format.

Figure 4.5.   The example above demonstrates how students can be engaged in reflective practice (reflection paper), higher-order thinking (synthesis paper), teamwork, and evaluation of online resources.

and academic performance can contribute to a successful learning experience for all students. The authors have found a number of strategies to be effective in communicating high expectations in an online class.

First, students seem to need more detailed information in an online class than in a face-to-face class. We recommend use of online study guides that include detailed information about the course, including course objectives; course, department, college and university policies (sometimes accessed through links to the relevant documents); assignment information; performance expectations; the basis for grading in the course; and sample grading rubrics. Students have a high need for structure in an online course. This need can be partially met though detailed information provided as part of the course.

We have used very detailed assignment instructions, often with links to resources (such as the APA rules) embedded in the instructions. Each assignment will have defined levels of performance expectations with rubrics for assessing individual or group performance. We have even developed rubrics for assessing the quality of online discussions. These rubrics demonstrate acceptable levels of performance. Providing links from the rubrics to sample documents or sample discussions that demonstrate various levels of performance (high performance versus adequate performance versus low performance) clarifies expectations. In setting expectations for online discussion, it is useful to define the types of responses you wish students to make, such as analysis, synthesis, application, and evaluation, and to post sample comments that reflect these levels of communication.

Using criterion-referenced grading communicates high expectations for students, as does allowing for revision of assignments in order to reach higher levels of performance. As mentioned earlier, technology can enable faster turnaround time for assignments and opportunities to revise papers and projects. Setting up clear communication expectations, also described earlier, and posting expectations for online etiquette in both synchronous and asynchronous environments, can assist students in meeting high expectations for behavior in the online class.

Principle 7: Diverse Ways of Learning

The final principle of good practice respects diverse talents and ways of learning. Students need the opportunity to learn in ways that work for them (Chickering & Gamson, 2003). Chickering and Ehrmann (2003) point out that technological resources can provide

> for different methods of learning through powerful visuals and well-organized print; through direct, vicarious, and virtual experiences; and through tasks requiring analysis, synthesis, and evaluation, with applications to real-life situations. They can encourage self-reflection and self-evaluation. They can drive collaboration and group problem solving.

As an online instructor, a variety of strategies can be used to address the diverse ways in which students learn. Providing tasks that require students to analyze and evaluate information can be accomplished online just as well as in face-to-face settings. Assignments that require application of concepts can be developed. The use of self-evaluation activities and activities that require collaborative group problem-solving address different needs for students. Online environments can provide activities that appeal to visual as well as aural learners. A key to addressing diverse

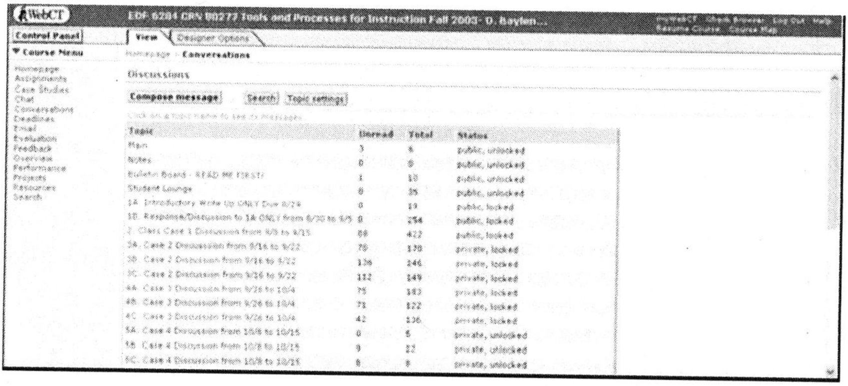

Figure 4.6.   The sample above illustrates different ways students build a sense of community in this course—from public spaces such as bulletin board and student lounge to private spaces for small group case discussions.

learner needs is to provide a learning environment that includes options within structure. Individual assignments and the ability to move through topics at one's own pace appeal to some learners. Group activities and projects and the ability to get peer feedback appeals to other learners. All can be accommodated in an online learning environment.

In our experience, accommodating diverse ways of learning can also mean accommodating cultural differences. In teaching an online class with international students, instructors must be aware of differences that may affect learning. Use of certain language or terminology can create miscommunication in terms of meaning. Phrasing can create misinterpretation of tone. In some cultures, deadlines can be misunderstood as time is interpreted differently. And the nature of the relationship between students and between student and instructor may vary and be more or less formal.

CONCLUSION

Implementing the Seven Principles in online courses can require teachers to overcome obstacles, to develop new strategies, and to look at their craft from new perspectives. Doing so can lead to an improved student experience and to enhanced learning. These principles were not developed for online environments, but they can be adapted and applied to multiple learning environments. We hope that the ideas we have presented here may benefit others as they seek to provide a learning-rich environment online.

REFERENCES

Angelo, T. A., & Cross, K. P. (1993). *Classroom assessment techniques. A handbook for college teachers* (2nd ed.). San Francisco: Jossey-Bass.

Baylen, D. M., & Sorensen, C. K. (2002). Examining online interactions in two graduate courses. In M. Simonson & M. Crawford (Eds.), *Research Proceedings of the 2002 Association for Educational Communications and Technology Conference, 1,* 29-36.

Chickering, A. W. (2000). Creating community within individual courses. *New Directions for Higher Education, 109,* 23-32.

Chickering, A. W. (1991). Institutionalizing the seven principles and the faculty and institutional inventories. *New Directions for Teaching and Learning, 47,* 51-61.

Chickering, A. W., & Ehrmann, S. C. (2003). Implementing the seven principles: Technology as lever. *American Association for Higher Education.* Retrieved November 1, 2003, from http://www.tltgroup.org/programs/seven.html

Chickering, A. W., & Gamson, Z. F. (2003). Seven principles for good practice in undergraduate education. *Wingspread Journal* (special edition). Retrieved November 1, 2003, from http://www.uncg.edu/tlc/seven.html.

Chickering, A. W., & Gamson, Z. F. (1999). Development and adaptations of the seven principles for good practice in undergraduate education. *New Directions for Teaching and Learning, 80,* 75-81.

Chickering, A. W., & Gamson, Z. F. (1987). *Seven principles for good practice in undergraduate education.* (ERIC Document Reproduction Service No. ED 282491).

Hutchings, P. (2000). *Opening lines: Approaches to the scholarship of teaching and learning.* Menlo Park, CA: The Carnegie Foundations for the Advancement of Teaching.

Kochery, T. S. (1997). Distance education: A delivery system in need of cooperative learning. In *Proceedings of Selected Research and Development Presentations at the 1997 National Convention of the Association for Educational Communications and Technology.* (Albuquerque, New Mexico, February 14-18, 1997).

Newman, F., & Scurry, J. (2001, July 13). Online technology pushes pedagogy to the forefront. *Chronicle of Higher Education.* Retrieved November 1, 2003, from http://chronicle.com/weekly/v47/i44/44b00701.htm

Robles, H. J. (1998). *Andragogy, the adult learner and faculty as learners.* (ERIC Document Reproduction Service No. ED 426740.)

Shulman, L. S. (2000). *Fostering a scholarship of teaching and learning.* Athens, GA: University of Georgia Institute of Higher Education.

Winona State University. (2003). The seven principles for good practice. Retrieved November 1, 2003, from http://www.winona.msus.edu/president/seven.htm

INSTRUCTORS' SELF-PERCEIVED PEDAGOGICAL PRINCIPLE IMPLEMENTATION IN THE ONLINE ENVIRONMENT

Jinsong Zhang and Richard T. Walls

This study explored online instructors' perceptions of their implementation of Chickering and Gamson's Seven Principles and the factors that influenced instructors' implementations. Results reveal that endorsement of the Seven Principles by online instructors varied significantly from one principle to another. The least-endorsed of the principles was encourage cooperation among students, and the most endorsed was communicate high expectations. Instructional strategies and technology features positively influenced implementations of the Seven Principles, while time and distance negatively influenced the implementations. Significantly more implementation of the encourage active learning principle occurred for participants teaching courses in humanities than for those teaching science and technology.

The Perfect Online Course: Best Practices for Designing and Teaching
pp. 87–106

In 1987, Chickering and Gamson proposed "Seven Principles for Good Practice in Undergraduate Education" (hereafter referred to as Seven Principles). These Seven Principles that have been found to dictate good practice in undergraduate education are: (1) encourage student-faculty contact, (2) encourage cooperation among students, (3) encourage active learning, (4) give prompt feedback, (5) emphasize time on task, (6) communicate high expectations, and (7) respect diverse talents and ways of learning.

These Seven Principles are based on 50 years of higher education research on "the way teachers teach and students learn, how students work and play with one another, and how students and faculty talk to each other" (Chickering & Gamson, 1987, p. 3). One of the primary purposes of the creators of the Seven Principles was to identify instructional practices. The principles provide substantive research-based advice that can enrich our understanding and practice of higher education (Sorcinelli, 1991).

Gamson and Chickering secured Johnson Foundation sponsorship and invited a small task force to meet in July 1986 "to identify key principles which characterize the practices of educationally successful undergraduate institutions ... [and to] identify research which supports those characteristics and create a draft statement of principles" (Gamson, 1991, p. 7). The task force members included scholars responsible for some of the most important research on the impact of the college experience (Gamson, 1991, 1995). In 1987, the final version of the Seven Principles appeared as the lead article in the March issue of the AAHE Bulletin (Chickering & Gamson, 1987; Gamson, 1991, 1995).

The response to the principles was immediate, enthusiastic (Gamson, 1991, 1995), and overwhelming (Chickering & Gamson, 1999). These principles were widely used as the criteria for assessing classroom instruction. The passionate reaction to the principles encouraged the authors of the Seven Principles to develop a self-assessment instrument for faculty members and a second instrument for campus practices and policies assessment (Chickering & Gamson, 1999). These inventories have helped faculty members as well as their colleges and universities to examine and improve their pedagogical practices (Graham, Cagiltay, Lim, Craner, & Duffy, 2001).

The purpose of this study was to explore and describe the experience of university faculty members who participated in the practice of online distance instruction for undergraduate students. The study (1) explored the instructor's perception of the seven pedagogical principles in the online environment, (2) determined factors that influenced implementation of the principles, and (3) discovered the relationship between the influencing factors and the online implementation of the Seven Principles. This study examined faculty implementation of Chickering and Gamson's (1987) Seven Principles when a course was conducted over the Internet.

Distance education refers to education when an instructor and students are separated by geographic distance (Lewis, Snow, Farris, Levin, & Greene, 1999; Moore & Kearsley, 2005; Willis, 1993) or by time (Lewis et al., 1999; Moore & Kearsley, 2005) and communications technologies are used to bridge the instructional gap. Although distance education may seem like a contemporary development, it can be traced back to its origin more than a hundred years ago. Educators at different times have put to use the latest communications technologies to deliver instruction to learners at a distance. Moore and Kearsley (2005) believed that distance education evolved through five generations, namely, correspondence, broadcast radio and television, open universities, teleconferencing, and Internet.

Internet-mediated distance education witnessed a great expansion with the arrival of the Internet and the World Wide Web. According to the results of *2003 Sloan Survey of Online Learning*, during the fall of 2002, more than 1.6 million students took at least one online course, and more than one third of these students (about 578,000) took all of their courses online. This enrollment of at least one online course was projected to reach 1.9 million for the fall of 2003, a yearly growth rate of 19.8%. This survey also indicated that more than 81% of all institutions of higher education were offering at least one fully online or blended course (Allen & Seaman, 2003). In addition to online courses, there are also online programs that range from associate to doctorate. Nevertheless, online instruction is still in its formative years of development, "characterized by trial and error" (Williams, 2002, p. 263). University faculties sometimes are reluctant in the acceptance of the online teaching phenomenon. Their attitude toward the quality of online education and its ability to equal the traditional face-to-face instruction is still conservative (Allen & Seaman, 2003).

Distance education differs from face-to-face instruction in several ways. First, classroom teaching relies on the visual and unobtrusive cues and clues from the student. The communication between an instructor and students occurs spontaneously. An instructor and students have many opportunities for interaction, both inside and outside of class. But in distance education, an instructor has very few or even no visual cues of the students. In some situations, the cues are filtered out because of the technology used. Second, distance education settings impact the relationship between an instructor and the students (Willis, 1993) in that the community normally formed between an instructor and students on campus does not exist in distance education. Third, in a distance education system, the interaction sometimes may be conducted by a specialist instructor who does not design or teach the course (Moore & Kearsley, 2005).

The major advantages of distance education include (1) its ability of reaching out to a greater and wider student audience, (2) its flexibility and customized learning and teaching, and (3) greater interaction between instructor and students (Higher Education Research Center, 2001). But there are also concerns and negative feelings among instructors about the technology. These negative feelings generally include (1) lack of human contact, (2) more work for the instructor, (3) unreliability of the technology (Higher Education Research Center, 2001), and (4) technological skills requirement for the students (Beard & Harper, 2002).

Some research indicated the learning outcomes of online distance students are similar to, or better than, those of traditional on-campus students (Bates, 1997; Fallah & Ubell, 2000; Keeton, 2004; Lanza & Roselli, 1991; Lynch, 2002; Neuhauser, 2002). Other studies revealed different results. Brown and Liedholm (2002) argued that online courses represented an inferior technology compared to traditional face-to-face instruction, and online students performed significantly worse than the live students. Terry, Owens, and Macy (2001) joined them in providing results which suggested that students perform better in traditional courses than in virtual ones. They argued that "Internet-based instruction is not as effective" (p. 4). However, meta-studies of distance education tended to favor the distance. Shachar (2002) conducted a meta-analysis of 86 experimental and quasi-experiment studies. He discovered that in two thirds of the cases, distance students outperformed their traditional counterparts. Allen, Mabry, Mattrey, Bourhuis, Titsworth, and Burrell (2004), in another meta-analysis comparing the performance of students in distance education and students in traditional classes, found that distance education students slightly outperformed traditional students on exams and course grades. Nevertheless, other researchers believe that comparative studies of learning outcome between on-campus and off-campus students overlooked the essentials of the issue. Clark (1983, 1994) believed that technology did not influence learning, and he argued that "media are mere vehicles that deliver instruction but do not influence student achievement any more than the truck that delivers our groceries causes changes in our nutrition" (1983, p. 445).

Williams (2002) believed that using new technologies does not automatically guarantee learning or improve learning. She argued that "the first and most important issue … when transferring courses to a Web-based form of delivery, is that of pedagogy" (p. 264). In search of pedagogically sound strategies for online education, the Seven Principles are referred to from time to time. Graham et al. (2001) used the Seven Principles to evaluate four online courses in a large Midwestern university. They believed that using the Seven Principles as a general framework for the evaluation would provide insights into important aspects of online teaching and learning. Wood (2002) found through her study that instructor beliefs are strongly related to their selections of strategies for Web-based instruction. Her findings indicated that teaching conceptions, teaching experience, type of technology, and instructor behaviors influenced instructors' selections of instructional strategies. The seven pedagogical principles for good practice in undergraduate education summarize the research on teaching and learning of half a century. These Seven Principles have been used as a framework for evaluating conventional classroom instruction ever since their creation in 1987.

The present investigation sought to evaluate the implementation of the Seven Principles in the online environment. It investigated instructors' perceptions of their implementation of the Seven Principles and the major factors that enhanced or barricaded their implementation when instruction was delivered primarily through the Internet: (1) What are online instructors' perceptions of their implementation of the Seven Principles? (2) What factors are influencing an online instructor's level of implementation of the Seven Principles? (3) What is the relationship between demographic factors and instructors' perceptions of implementation of the Seven Principles?

METHOD

Participants

The population of the study was defined as the faculty members who taught undergraduate online courses at a major university. These were distance courses for undergraduate students with more than 50% of the instruction being delivered through the Internet. The participants of this study were instructors who taught undergraduate online courses during spring, summer, and/or fall semesters of 2005 at the university. There were a total of 107 instructors who were identified as teaching 282 sections of 132 undergraduate online classes in 2005.

The participants were divided into two groups: (a) humanities (e.g., economics, psychology, English) and (b) science and technology (e.g., mathematics, chemistry, nursing) based on the discipline of the course they were teaching. The researcher relied on standard library classification methods (Taylor, 2000) for the grouping scheme.

Procedure

An online survey was sent to the 107 potential participants in September 2005. In order to obtain a higher response rate, both ordinary mail and e-mail were sent to invite the instructors to participate. The invitation package contained a cover letter and a copy of the IRB approval. This invitation assured participants confidentiality, and it provided the participant with the URL of the Web-based survey. About a week after the package was sent out, a follow-up strategy (Berdie, Anderson, & Niebuhr, 1986) was employed by sending e-mail reminders to all the 100 nonrespondents. Ten days later, another e-mail message was sent out to the 47 identified nonrespondents. In all, invitations were sent to 107 participants, and responses were received from 49 of the 107 instructors. The response rate was 45.79%.

The items in the survey questionnaire asked instructors to report their implementation of pedagogical principles in their online instruction. Demographics included course subject and course number, instructor classroom teaching experience, online teaching experience, student on-campus participation, instructor age, gender, highest degree obtained, instructor job classification, class size, and instruction delivery technology.

The pedagogical principles section was made up of seven parts, each of which dealt with one of the Seven Principles. In every part of the pedagogical principles section, there were five questionnaire statements (all 35 of which are shown in Table 5.1) and two open-ended questions. Each questionnaire statement was rated on a 5-point Likert scale in which the choices were 1 = never, 2 = rarely, 3 = occasionally, 4 = often, 5 = very often. At the end of each of the seven parts were two open-ended questions. The first open-ended question asked the participant to indicate the factors that promoted the implementation of that particular one of the Seven Principles. The second open-ended question asked the participant to indicate the factors that hindered the implementation of the same pedagogical principle. These open-ended questions were asked seven times, once for each of the Seven Principles.

The questionnaire statements were based on the Faculty Inventory (Chickering, Gamson, & Barsi, 1989). Since the original inventory was intended to assess traditional face-to-face instruction, modification to the inventory was made so that the items were meaningful for online instruction. Several major procedures were involved in the development of the present inventory. These procedures included: (a) selecting some items verbatim as written in the Chickering et al. (1989) instrument, (b) rewriting items from Chickering et al. (1989) to make them more applicable to undergraduate online education, (c) eliciting expert suggestions and comments to the first draft of the inventory, (d) rewriting or adding items based on expert suggestions, and (e) assessing content validity of each of the items in the resulting draft instrument. After incorporation of expert suggestions, there were 64 items in the draft. Only 35 items were finally selected for the online faculty inventory, five items for each of the Seven Principles. These items represent content validity in which there is: (a) fair sampling of items from the domains of instruction, and (b) expert judgment regarding the items that can be used to assess each principle. Content validity was assessed by: (1) selecting an expert panel (4 content experts and 3 lay experts), (2) submitting the draft instrument to the expert panel, (3) having the expert panel rate each item on a 1 to 4 scale for content validity related to the Seven Principles for online education, and (4) selecting the five highest-rated items for each the Seven Principles. The four-point scale in the expert response form was dichotomized (Davis, 1992; Lynn, 1986; Rubio, Berg-Weger, Tebb, Lee, & Rauch, 2003) to determine interrater agreement for an item, combining values one and two and values three and four. For online faculty inventory, the scale interrater agreement reached 0.94; that is, 94% of the 35 items in the inventory had an item interrater agreement score of 0.80 or higher.

Content validity index of an item indicated the proportion of experts who rated the item as content valid (Lynn, 1986; Rubio et al., 2003). Content validity index for each item was determined by the proportion of experts who gave the item a rating of 3 or 4. The content validity index for online faculty inventory was 0.92 or 92%. To sum-up, the online faculty inventory had a mean of 3.73, a scale interrater agreement of 0.94, and a scale content validity index of 0.92.

1. What are online instructors' perceptions of their implementation of the Seven Principles? The data source for Research Question 1 was the Likert scale ratings. The Likert scale for each of the rated items ranged from 1 (Never) to 5 (Very Often). Each rated item generated a mean across all the participants. This mean indicated the implementation of the strategy stated by the item. A total score was generated for each of the seven pedagogical principles. This score indicated the implementation of one of the Seven Principles in the online environment.

2. What factors are influencing an online instructor's level of implementation of the Seven Principles? The data source for research question 2 was the two open-ended questions, which elicited the participants to report the major factors that promoted or obstructed their implementation of the principle concerned. The positive and negative statements were categorized for each of the seven pedagogical principles separately. Because of the scoring judgments involved in categorizing responses to open-ended questions, a second scorer

was invited to categorize the responses (blind to the researcher's scoring). Interscorer reliability was tested to measure the agreement between the ratings. The coding process included four major steps: (1) reviewing all responses from the 47 participants, (2) highlighting words or phrases with high frequencies, (3) setting up draft categories, and (4) revising the category list.

3. What is the relationship between the influencing factors and instructors' perception of the implementation of the Seven Principles? The data sources for research question 3 were the Likert scale ratings of the questions (rated 1 to 5) and the demographics. Analyses of variance (ANOVAs) were used to explore the relationship between the major influencing factors and the implementation of the Seven Principles. The independent variables included course subject, classroom teaching experience, online teaching experience, student on-campus participation, instructor age, gender, highest degree obtained, instructor job classification, and class size. Instructor self-reported pedagogical practices (ratings) were the dependent variables. An initial multivariate analysis of variance (MANOVA) was calculated for each independent variable with the ratings of the implementation of the Seven Principles as the dependent variables. MANOVA was used to protect against experiment-wise error rate and thus allow multiple statistical tests at a $p < .05$ alpha level.

RESULTS AND DISCUSSION

The average age of the respondents was 45.35 years, ranging from 26 to 70. By gender, 14 were male (29.79%), and 33 were female (70.21%). Instructor teaching experience varied from 0 to 40 years, and online teaching experience ranged from 0 to 10 years. Class size of the online courses varied from 1 to 250. All courses used a course Web site for instruction delivery, through either WebCT Vista™ or SOLE (Secure Online Environment). Streaming video ($n = 6$), streaming audio ($n = 2$), and CD-ROM ($n = 2$) also were used. More than half of the participants ($n = 24$) had no face-to-face interaction.

Research Question 1: What Are Online Instructors' Perceptions of Their Implementation of the Seven Principles?

Faculty self-reported implementation of the Seven Principles in the online environment was determined through the computation of means and standard deviations of questionnaire items in the pedagogical princi-

Table 5.1.   Online Implementation of Seven Principles

Principle and Strategy	M	SD
Principle 1: Encourage Student-Faculty Contact		
1. I advise my students about career opportunities in their major field.	2.74	1.21
2. I share my past experiences, attitudes, and values with students.	3.55	1.28
3. I know my students by name by the end of the first 2 weeks of the term.	3.68	1.22
4. I serve as an informal advisor to students via e-mail.	3.51	1.25
5. I invite or take my students to attend professional meetings or other events in my field.	2.04	1.25
Principle 2: Encourage Cooperation Among Students		
1. I encourage my students to prepare together for classes or exams.	3.02	1.42
2. I encourage students to do projects together.	2.98	1.57
3. I ask my students to evaluate each other's work.	2.57	1.54
4. I ask my students to discuss key concepts with other students whose backgrounds and viewpoints are different from their own.	3.53	1.50
5. I create "learning communities," study groups, or project teams within my courses.	2.81	1.58
Principle 3: Encourage Active Learning		
1. I ask my students to relate outside events or activities to the subjects covered in my courses.	4.15	1.25
2. I encourage students to challenge my ideas, the ideas of other students, or those presented in readings or other course materials.	3.87	1.21
3. I give my students concrete, real-life situations to analyze.	4.38	0.85
4. I encourage my students to suggest new readings, research projects, field trips, or other course activities.	3.32	1.38
5. I carry out research projects with my students.	2.30	1.37
Principle 4: Give Prompt Feedback		
1. I prepare online activities which give students immediate feedback on how well they do.	4.17	1.07
2. I return examinations and papers within a week.	4.66	0.81
3. I give students detailed evaluations of their work early in the term.	4.13	1.08
4. I ask my students to schedule conferences (phone calls, chat room, or on-campus) with me to discuss their progress.	3.32	1.46
5. I give my students written comments on their strengths and weaknesses on exams and papers.	3.85	1.38
Principle 5: Emphasize Time on Task		
1. I expect my students to complete their assignments promptly.	4.66	0.73
2. I clearly communicate to my students the minimum amount of time they should spend preparing for classes.	3.83	1.20
3. I underscore the importance of regular work, steady application, sound self-pacing, and scheduling.	4.40	0.83
4. I contact students who fall behind to discuss their study habits, schedules, and other commitments.	3.89	1.15
5. If students miss my classes, I require them to make up lost work.	3.53	1.52

(Table continues on next page)

Table 5.1.   (Continued)

Principle and Strategy	M	SD
Principle 6: Communicate High Expectations		
1. I tell students that I expect them to work hard in my classes.	4.30	0.91
2. I emphasize the importance of holding high standards for academic achievement.	4.28	1.06
3. I make clear my expectations in writing at the beginning of the course.	4.74	0.71
4. I help students set challenging goals for their own learning.	3.68	1.14
5. I explain to students what will happen if they do not complete their work on time.	4.62	0.85
Principle 7: Respect Diverse Talents and Ways of Learning		
1. I encourage students to speak up when they don't understand.	4.60	0.71
2. I use diverse teaching activities to address a broad spectrum of students.	3.87	1.10
3. I select readings and design activities related to the background of my students.	3.49	1.18
4. I integrate new knowledge about women and other underrepresented populations into my courses.	3.32	1.51
5. I try to find out about my students' learning styles, interests, or backgrounds at the beginning of each course.	3.47	1.50

Notes. $N = 47$. Multiple comparisons by the Tukey test indicated significant ($p < .01$) differences between strategies. For Principle 1: $1 > 5$, $2 > 1$, $2 > 5$, $3 > 1$, $3 > 5$, $4 > 1$, and $4 > 5$; for Principle 2: $4 > 3$ and $4 > 5$; for Principle 3: $1 > 4$, $1 > 5$, $2 > 5$, $3 > 4$, $3 > 5$, and $4 > 5$; for Principle 4: $1 > 4$, $2 > 4$, $2 > 5$, and $3 > 4$; for Principle 5: $1 > 2$, $1 > 4$, $1 > 5$, and $3 > 5$; for Principle 6: $1 > 4$, $2 > 4$, $3 > 2$, $3 > 4$, and $5 > 4$; and for Principle 7: $1 > 2$, $1 > 3$, $1 > 4$, and $1 > 5$.

ples section of the Online Faculty Inventory. Table 5.1 includes seven sections indicating the mean and standard deviation for each item. For each of the Seven Principles, separately, to determine if there was a significant difference among the practice of the five strategies for that principle, a one-way within-subjects analysis of variance (ANOVA) was computed in which strategy was the independent variable (the five strategies), and rating (possible range 1 through 5) was the dependent variable. The F value for each of these principles was significant ($p < .01$). Tukey test multiple comparisons (alpha of $p < .01$) are reported at the bottom of Table 5.1.

The most commonly implemented pedagogy for each of the Seven Principles included: (1) to know the students by name by the end of the first 2 weeks of the term, (2) to ask students to discuss key concepts with students with different backgrounds and viewpoints, (3) to give concrete, real-life situations to analyze, (4) to return examinations and papers within a week, (5) to expect the students to complete their assignments on time, (6) to make clear the expectations in writing at the beginning of the course, and (7) to encourage students to speak up when they don't understand.

The least commonly implemented pedagogy for each principle included: (1) to invite or take the students to attend professional meetings or other events in the field, (2) to ask students to evaluate each other's work, (3) to carry out research projects with students, (4) to ask students to schedule conferences (phone calls, chat room, or on-campus) with the instructor to discuss their progress, (5) to require students to make up lost work if they miss a class, (6) to help students set challenging goals for their own learning, and (7) to integrate new knowledge about women and other underrepresented populations into the courses.

Thus, in answer to research question 1, *What are online instructors' perceptions of their implementation of the Seven Principles,* significant ($p < .01$) differences were found for the strategies that the participants used to accomplish each of the Seven Principles. These differences are summarized in the previous paragraphs and reported in detail in Table 5.1.

Results indicate a significant difference in the implementation of the "Seven Principles for Good Practice in Undergraduate Education" (Chickering & Gamson, 1987) among the undergraduate online instructors. Some principles received more emphasis than others. As is shown in Table 5.2, of all the Seven Principles, communicate high expectations was implemented with significantly higher frequency than other principles, and encourage cooperation among students and encourage student-faculty contact were least frequently practiced. Significant differences ($p < .01$) also were found for the degree of implementation of the Seven Principles (Table 5.2). The order of implementation with reference to the means, from most to least, was (6) communicate high expectations, (5) emphasize time on task, (4) give prompt feedback, (7) respect diverse talents and ways of learning, (3) encourage active learning, (1) encourage student-faculty contact, and (2) encourage cooperation among students.

High expectations for academic excellence are of crucial importance for creating a learning environment that values and rewards academic achievement. When an instructor "expects students to perform at high levels and supports their efforts to meet their high standards, students generally strive to rise to the occasion" (Kuh, Kinzie, Schuh, Whitt, & Associates, 2005). This emphasis of principle 6 reflects the general consensus over the importance of communicate high expectations. The five strategies that constitute this principle include (1) I tell students that I expect them to work hard in my classes; (2) I emphasize the importance of holding high standards for academic achievement; (3) I make clear my expectations in writing at the beginning of the course; (4) I help students set challenging goals for their own learning; and (5) I explain to students what will happen if they do not complete their work on time. These strat-

Table 5.2.   Overall Implementation of the Seven Principles

	Principles	M	SD
1.	Encourage student-faculty contact	3.11	0.90
2.	Encourage cooperation among students	2.98	1.24
3.	Encourage active learning	3.60	0.95
4.	Give prompt feedback	4.03	0.72
5.	Emphasize time on task	4.06	0.67
6.	Communicate high expectations	4.32	0.72
7.	Respect diverse talents and ways of learning	3.75	0.92

Notes: $N = 47$. Multiple comparisons by the Tukey test indicated significant ($p < .01$) differences between Principles (3 > 1, 3 > 2, 4 > 1, 4 > 2, 5 > 1, 5 > 2, 5 > 3, 6 > 1, 6 > 2, 6 > 3, 6 > 7, 7 > 1, and 7 > 2).

egies may be easier to implement than some of the others. Scott and Tobe (1995) argued that although all students may not do equally well, all can do better. The role of an instructor is "to encourage improvement, not expect equal results of all" (p. 81).

Overall, as noted, principle 6 was rated highest, but of the five component strategies for principle 6, "help students set challenging goals for their own learning" received relatively low ratings in comparison with the other four. Students enrolled to take distance courses are usually "independent, older, married, or having dependents" (National Center for Education Statistics, 2002). They are "autonomous," "self-directing" (Knowles, Holton, & Swanson, 2005, p. 149), and have their objectives and goals when they decide to return to school. Consequently, instructors may not feel the necessity to help them in regard to setting learning objectives and goals for themselves, as they do for the traditional onsite students.

Principle 2, encourage cooperation among students, received the lowest rating from the online participants. The rating was significantly lower than the implementation of Principles 3, 4, 5, 6, and 7 (see Table 5.2 for Tukey test details). Cooperative learning experience is "an important part of a student's intellectual and personal growth" (Hatfield & Hatfield, 1995, p. 28). It can promote student learning, retention, satisfaction, social skills, and self-esteem. Palloff and Pratt (2001) argued that "students should be expected to work together to generate deeper levels of understanding and critical evaluation of the material under study" (p. 115). Research has indicated motivational and learning outcomes of collaborative learning in higher education (Alavi, 2005). There are studies of the possible ways in which computers can be used in promoting student collaborative learning (McAlister, Ravenscroft, & Scanlon, 2004). Such being the case, then what has caused the online instructors to treat this principle differently?

In answer to the open-ended question for this principle, some participants indicated that they did "not promote" the practice of this principle, or they believed that this principle "does not apply to an online course." One participant made it clear that he did "not encourage cooperation among students," and considered any form of "collaboration ... as cheating." Another commented that "This [cooperation] was impossible because the course was online." Concerns about cheating or other forms of academic dishonesty are legitimate for online instructors at a distance, since there is very little means to rely on for an instructor to check on the students. Nevertheless, concerns over academic dishonesty cannot explain everything. Instructional activities can be designed in such a way that cheating is not an issue. Case studies and group discussion, for example, can be implemented online. Palloff and Pratt (2001) believed that the failing of many online programs "stems from the instructor's inability or unwillingness to facilitate a collaborative learning process" (p. 115).

Principle 1, encourage student-faculty contact, also received low ratings from the participants. The average score was significantly lower than the implementation of principles 3, 4, 5, 6, and 7 (see Table 5.2 for Tukey test details). Frequent student-faculty interaction in and out of class is considered the most important factor in student motivation and involvement. In the face-to-face environment, an instructor can invite a student to drop by his or her office, give advice about career opportunities, share past experiences with students, attend events sponsored by student groups, or have informal talk outside the class. When an instructor is teaching online, some of these possibilities are eliminated. Of the five strategies, two that received lower ratings are "advise my students about career opportunities" ($M = 2.74$) and "invite my students to attend professional meetings or other events" ($M = 2.04$).

Studies indicate that instructor *immediacy* behaviors are strongly correlated with student learning outcomes (Arbaugh & Benbunan-Fich, 2005). Immediacy refers to behaviors that reduce social and psychological distance between people (Arbaugh, 2001). It includes verbal and nonverbal behaviors. While online courses severely limit the instructor's demonstration of nonverbal immediacy, verbal immediacy is still possible. An instructor teaching over the Internet can still "use humor, encourage discussion and feedback, or address students by name" (Arbaugh, 2001, p. 44). Social presence is interpreted as the degree to which a person is perceived as "real" in mediated communication (Swan, 2003). Bischoff (2000) suggested that an online instructor communicate social presence by providing regular feedback, maintaining public course visibility, and selecting and directing students to high-quality learning materials.

Research Question 2: What Factors Are Influencing an Online Instructor's Level of Implementation of the Seven Principles?

The data sources for research question 2 were items 6 and 7, the two open-ended questions at the end of each principle. Responses to these open-ended questions were qualitative data. Since subjective judgment was involved, a second rater participated in the categorization process.

In answer to this research question, "instructional strategies" and "instructional activities" were reported as positive factors for five of the Seven Principles. "Technology features" and instructor "accessibility and availability" also were portrayed prominently as factors that helped online implementation of the Seven Principles. "Time and distance" was reported as a negative factor for all seven of the principles. "Lack of student involvement," "Motivation and negligence," and "technology competence" were described as factors that barricaded the implementation of the Seven Principles in the online environment. Of all the factors that were reported as helping the implementation of the Seven Principles, "instructional strategies" was mentioned 59 times, which accounted for 23.60% of all the positive factors reported. "Technology features" was mentioned 38 times, accounting for 15.20% of the total. Of all the factors that were reported as barricading the implementation of the Seven Principles, "time and distance" was mentioned 85 times, which accounted for 41.87% of all the negative factors reported. "Lack of student involvement" was mentioned 33 times, accounting for 16.26% of the total.

The top four *positive* categories identified from research question 2 (factors influencing implementation) were (1) instructional strategies, (2) technology features, (3) accessibility and availability, and (4) rules and encouragement. These four categories were determined based on the overall responses from across the Seven Principles.

With regard to positive category 1, instructional strategies, participants reported such approaches as (a) interactive discussion, (b) exposure to diversity in race, political thought, and media, (c) photo assignments in shared Web galleries, and (d) fast turnaround for grades and comments on weekly assignments. With regard to positive category 2, technology features, participants reported features such as (a) e-mails, (b) synchronous chat discussions, (c) discussion boards, (d) interactive lessons, and (e) automatic grading for exams, were useful for the implementation of the Seven Principles. With regard to positive category 3 accessibility and availability, participants emphasized the importance of (a) frequent communication with the student, (b) online office hours, (c) phone advising appointments, (d) synchronous chat discussions, and (e) "speedy reply" to student e-mails. One participant commented that he found "students tend to care more about an online class and do better in such a class when they know a 'real' person is behind the class and ready to help them if they need it." With regard to positive category 4, rules and encouragement, participants reported that they believed the use of (a) reminders, (b) deadlines, and (c) rule enforcement as well as (d) congratulations, was facilitative.

The top four *negative* categories identified for research question 2 include (1) time and distance, (2) lack of student involvement, (3) motivation and negligence, and (4) technology competence and technical difficulties. These four categories were determined from the overall responses from across the Seven Principles.

With regard to negative category 1, time and distance, some participants noted that online instruction was so time consuming for preparing materials, replying to e-mail, and grading assignments that it became "a 24/7 job." Also, they strongly felt the inconvenience of the geographic distance in the implementation of the Seven Principles. Partee (2002) said that technology cannot duplicate the richness of direct human interactions. With regard to negative category 2, lack of student involvement, participants noted that "reticence of students" in such activities as discussions or chats can make it difficult for an instructor to conduct a class. With regard to negative category 3, motivation and negligence, some participants commented that some students are "willing to get by with just doing the minimum." But for some, it may not be a problem of motivation or negligence, but just a matter of how much time they have for the online courses they are taking. With regard to negative category 4, technology competence and technical difficulties, examples included student or faculty lack of understanding of how to use the tool, hardware/software problems, Web site problems, (e.g., delay on quizzes), system reliability, lack of connectivity, and inadequate technical support.

Research Question 3: What is the Relationship Between the Demographic Factors and Instructors' Perception of the Implementation of the Seven Principles?

To answer research question 3, several independent variables were analyzed in connection with the dependent variables. A MANOVA was computed to determine whether difference existed for course subject area of humanities versus science and technology (independent variable) on the mean ratings by each participant on the Seven Principles (seven dependent variables). This one-way MANOVA revealed a significant multivariate main effect for course subject area [Wilks' $= .68$, $F (7, 38) = 2.60$, $p <$ .05]. The follow-up ANOVAs indicated a significant course subject area difference in the implantation of principle 3, encourage active learning [F $(1, 44) = 4.20$, $p < .05$]. Participants in the humanities group reported significantly higher than their science and technology counterparts in implementing the principle of encourage active learning.

Class size (< 15 vs. 15 to 30 vs. > 30) was not found to be related to implementation of the Seven Principles. Instructor age (< 40 vs. > 39) was not found to be related to implementation of the Seven Principles. Instructor gender (M vs. F) was not found to be related to implementation of the Seven Principles. Teaching experience in years (< 5 vs. 5 to 10 vs. > 10) was not found to be related to implementation of the Seven Principles. Online teaching experience in years (< 3 vs. > 2) was not found to be related to implementation of the Seven Principles. Instructor education Level (with doctorate vs. without doctorate) was not found to be related to implementation of the Seven Principles. Job classification (tenure track vs. other instructors) was not found to be related to implementation of the Seven Principles.

Participants' self-reported ratings were consistent across class size, instructor age, gender, teaching experience, online teaching experience, highest degree obtained, and instructor job classification. Participants teaching humanities were more likely than those teaching science and technology to implement encourage active learning.

A potential limitation is that the study relied on participants' truthful and accurate report about their professional practice, and any deceit or bias in responding to the items of the online faculty inventory may skew the result. Also, all the participants taught undergraduate online classes at a single university, which may limit generalizability. Future research may consider the use of multiple institutions, both onsite and online instruction, and use of a student survey of their instructor's competence and practice of the Seven Principles. Such an evaluation of "how good" the instructor is could be compared to his or her ratings in the online faculty inventory.

In conclusion, undergraduate online instructors indicated that they implemented five of the Seven Principles in the "often" range (principle 3, encourage active learning, principle 4, give prompt feedback, principle 5, emphasize time on task, principle 6, communicate high expectations [the most implemented], and principle 7, respect diverse talents and ways of learning). These five principles may be recommended, based on both the literature and the current findings. The other two principles were implemented in the "occasionally" range (principle 1, encourage student-faculty contact, and principle 2, encourage cooperation among students [the least implemented]). As noted, however, even these two principles can be used to the advantage of instruction and learning. Thus, overall recommendation may be advanced for incorporation of Chickering and Gamson's *Seven Principles for Good Practice in Undergraduate Education* as adapted to the online environment (online faculty inventory).

ACKNOWLEDGMENT

This study is based on the doctoral dissertation of the first author.

REFERENCES

Alavi, M. (2005). Technology-mediated collaborative learning: A research perspective. In S. R. Hiltz & R. Goldman (Eds.), *Learning together online: Research on asynchronous learning networks* (pp. 191-213). Mahwah, NJ: Erlbaum.

Allen, I. E., & Seaman, J. (2003, September). *Sizing the opportunity: The quality and extent of online education in the United States, 2002 and 2003.* Needham, MA: Author. Retrieved April 24, 2004, from the Sloan Consortium Web site: http://www.sloan-c.org/resources/sizing_opportunity.pdf

Allen, M., Mabry, E., Mattrey, M., Bourhuis, J., Titsworth, S., & Burrell, N. (2004). Evaluating the effectiveness of distance learning: A comparison using meta-analysis. *Journal of Communication, 54*(3), 402-420.

Arbaugh, J. B. (2001). How instructor immediacy behaviors affect student satisfaction and learning in Web-based courses. *Business Communication Quarterly, 64*(4), 42-54.

Arbaugh, J. B., & Benbunan-Fich, R. (2005). Contextual factors that influence ALN effectiveness. In S. R. Hiltz & R. Goldman (Eds.), *Learning together online: Research on asynchronous learning networks* (pp. 123-144). Mahwah, NJ: Erlbaum.

Bates, A. W. (1997, June). *Restructuring the university for technological change.* Paper presented at the conference of the Carnegie Foundation for the Advancement of Teaching: What Kind of University? London, UK. Retrieved March 7, 2005, from http://bates.cstudies.ubc.ca/carnegie/carnegie.html

Beard, L. A., & Harper, C. (2002). Student perceptions of online versus on campus instruction. *Education, 122*(4), 658-663.

Berdie, D. R., Anderson, J. F., & Niebuhr, M. A. (1986). *Questionnaires: Design and use* (2nd ed.). Metuchen, NJ: Scarecrow Press.

Bischoff, A. (2000). The elements of effective online teaching: Overcoming the barriers to success. In K. W. White & B. H. Weight (Eds.), *The online teaching guide: A handbook of attitudes, strategies, and techniques for the virtual classroom* (pp. 57-72). Boston: Allyn & Bacon.

Brown, B. W., & Liedholm, C. E. (2002). Can web courses replace the classroom in principles of microeconomics? *The American Economic Review, 92*(2), 444-448.

Chickering, A. W., & Gamson, Z. F. (1987, March). Seven principles for good practice in undergraduate education. *AAHE Bulletin, 39*(7), 3-7. Retrieved April 25, 2004, from http://aahebulletin.com/public/archive/sevenprinciples1987.asp

Chickering, A. W., & Gamson, Z. F. (1999). Development and adaptations of the *Seven Principles for Good Practice in Undergraduate Education. New Directions for Teaching & Learning, 80,* 75-81.

Chickering, A. W., Gamson, Z. F., & Barsi, L. M. (1989). *Faculty inventory: Seven principles for good practice in undergraduate education.* Racine, WI: The Johnson Foundation.

Clark, R. E. (1983). Reconsidering research on learning from media. *Review of Educational Research, 53*(4), 445-459.

Clark, R. E. (1994). Media will never influence learning. *Educational Technology Research and Development, 42*(2), 21-29.

Davis, L. (1992). Instrument review: Getting the most from a panel of experts. *Applied Nursing Research, 5,* 194-197.

Fallah, M. H., & Ubell, R. (2000). Blind scores in a graduate test: Conventional compared with Web-based outcomes. *ALN Magazine, 4*(2). Retrieved March 7, 2005, from http://www.aln.org/publications/magazine/v4n2/fallah.asp

Gamson, Z. F. (1991). A brief history of the seven principles for good practice in undergraduate education. In A. W. Chickering & Z. F. Gamson (Eds.), *Applying the seven principles for good practice in undergraduate education* (pp. 5-12). San Francisco: Jossey-Bass.

Gamson, Z. F. (1995). The seven principles for good practice in undergraduate education: A historical perspective. In S. R. Hatfield (Ed.), *The seven principles in action: Improving undergraduate education* (pp. 1-8). Bolton, MA: Anker.

Graham, C., Cagiltay, K., Lim, B., Craner, J., & Duffy, T. M. (2001, March/April). Seven principles of effective teaching: A practical lens for evaluating online courses. *The Technology Source.* Retrieved March 2, 2005 from http://ts.mivu.org/default.asp?show=article&id=839

Hatfield, T., & Hatfield, S. R. (1995). Cooperative learning communities. In S. R. Hatfield, D. G. Brown, D. W. Krueger, S. J. Poulsen, R. A. Scott, & M. Nemko (Eds.), *The seven principles in action: Improving undergraduate education* (pp. 23-38). Bolton, MA: Anker.

Higher Education Research Center. (2001, March). Focus on distance education. *Update 7*(2). Retrieved March 19, 2004, from http://www2.nea.org/he/heupdate/images/vol7no2.pdf

Keeton, M. T. (2004). Best online instructional practice: Report of phase I on an ongoing study. *Journal of Asynchronous Learning Networks, 8*(2), 75-100. Retrieved July 4, 2005, from http://www.aln.org/publications/jaln/v8n2/v8n2_keeton.asp

Knowles, M. S., Holton, E. F. III, & Swanson, R. A. (2005). *The adult learner: The definitive classic in adult education and human resource development.* Boston: Elsevier.

Kuh, G. D., Kinzie, J., Schuh, J. H., Whitt, E. J., & Associates. (2005). *Student success in college: Creating conditions that matter.* San Francisco: Jossey-Bass.

Lanza, A., & Roselli, T. (1991). Effects of the hypertextual approach versus the structured approach on students' achievement. *Journal of Computer-Based Instruction, 18*(2), 48-50.

Lewis, L., Snow, K., Farris, E., Levin, D., & Greene, B. (1999). *Distance education at postsecondary education institutions: 1997-98* (Publication No. NCES 2000-013). Washington, DC: U.S. Department of Education. Retrieved March 19, 2004, from http://nces.ed.gov/pubs2000/2000013.pdf

Lynch, T. (2002). LSU expands distance learning program through online learning solution. *T.H.E. Journal, 29*(6), 47-48.

Lynn, M. (1986). Determination and quantification of content validity. *Nursing Research, 35*, 382-385.

McAlister, S., Ravenscroft, A., & Scanlon, E. (2004). Combining interaction and context design to support collaborative argumentation using a tool for synchronous CMC. *Journal of Computer Assisted Leaning, 20*, 194-204.

Moore, M. G., & Kearsley, G. (2005). *Distance education: A systems view* (2nd ed.). Belmont, CA: Wadsworth.

National Center for Education Statistics. (2002, November). *A profile of participation in distance education, 1999-2000: Postsecondary education descriptive analysis reports* (Publication No. NCES 2003-154). Retrieved September 11, 2004 from http://nces.ed.gov/pubs2003/2003154.pdf

Neuhauser, C. (2002). Learning style and effectiveness of online and face-to-face instruction. *American Journal of Distance Education 16*(2), 99-113.

Palloff, R. M., & Pratt, K. (2001). *Lessons from the cyberspace classroom: The realities of online teaching.* San Francisco: Jossey-Bass.

Partee, M. H. (2002). *Cyberteaching: Instructional technology on the modern campus.* Lanham, MD: University Press of America.

Rubio, D. M., Berg-Weger, M., Tebb, S. S., Lee, E. S., & Rauch, S. (2003). Objectifying content validity: Conducting a content validity study in social work research. *Social Work Research, 27*(2), 94-105.

Scott, R. A., & Tobe, D. E. (1995). Effective undergraduate education communicates high expectations. In S. R. Hatfield, D. G. Brown, D. W. Krueger, S. J. Poulsen, R. A. Scott, & M. Nemko (Eds.), *The seven principles in action: Improving undergraduate education* (pp. 79-94). Bolton, MA: Anker.

Shachar, M. (2002). Differences between traditional and distance learning outcomes: A meta-analytic approach. *Dissertation Abstracts International, 63*(10) 3465A.

Sorcinelli, M. D. (1991). Research findings on the seven principles. In A. W. Chickering & Z. F. Gamson (Eds.), *Applying the seven principles for good practice in undergraduate education* (pp. 5-12). San Francisco: Jossey-Bass.

Swan, K. (2003). Developing social presence in online discussions. In S. Naidu (Ed.), *Learning and teaching with technology: Principles and practices* (pp. 147-164). London: Kogan Page.

Taylor, A. G. (2000). *Wynar's introduction to cataloging and classification* (9th ed.). Englewood, CO: Libraries Unlimited.

Terry, N., Owens, J., & Macy, A. (2001). Student performance in the virtual versus traditional classroom. *Journal of the Academy of Business Education, 2*, 1-4.

Williams, C. (2002). Learning on-line: A review of recent literature in a rapidly expanding field. *Journal of Further and Higher Education, 26*(3), 263-272.

Willis, B. (1993). *Distance education: A practical guide*. Englewood Cliffs, NJ: Educational Technology.

Wood, V. L. (2002). What influences selections of instructional strategies for Web-based instruction? Relationships between approaches to teaching, concerns with technology, and selections of strategies (Doctoral dissertation, University of Colorado at Denver, 2002). *Dissertation Abstracts International, 63*(05), 1802A.

CHAPTER 6

KEY INSTRUCTIONAL DESIGN ELEMENTS FOR DISTANCE EDUCATION

Lihua Zheng and Sharon Smaldino

Distance education professionals need to play multiple roles, one of which is instructional designer (Thach, Murphy, & Korhonen, 1994). However, there is little literature that reflects the instructor's views on the application of the different types of design elements in distance education courses (Koszalka & Bianco, 2001). The authors argue that distance education instructors need to understand and apply some important instructional design elements in order to exert a successful role of an instructional designer. This article reviews the most recent literature pertaining to designing instruction in distance education, identifies some key instructional design elements for teaching at a distance, and provides some suggestions on their application in the distance teaching process.

INTRODUCTION

Distance education has been growing rapidly in the past decade. Olgren (2000) points out that one of the major changes occurring on the front-line of distance education is the increasing number of distance education programs. He reports that over the past decade, there has been "a dramatic increase in the adoption of distance education methods" (p. 20). In the academic year 1994-1995, nearly 26,000 distance education courses were delivered via audio, video, or computer technology, enrolling more than 750,000 students. A total of 690 degree programs and 170 certificate programs were offered exclusively at a distance (Olgren, 2000). Also according to some estimates given by Griffiths and Gatien, "the distance learning market is now growing at a 25 percent annual rate in the U.S. and represents $ 3.5 billion in annual revenues for postsecondary education" (cited in Olgren, 2000, p. 20). Therefore, great progress has been made in distance education offerings in the past decade. Because learning at a distance can bring many advantages, there has been a growing demand for distance education.

The instructor's role is very important in terms of teaching at a distance. Willis (1994) states that to a great degree, "the success of any distance education effort rests squarely on the shoulders of the faculty" (p. vi). When teaching at a distance, according to Willis (1994), the instructor is confronted with special challenges that include: develop an understanding of the characteristics and needs of distant students with little first-hand experience and limited, if any, face-to-face contact; adjust teaching styles and course content and consider the needs and expectations of multiple, often diverse audiences; develop a better understanding of delivery technology and staying focused on teaching role; and work effectively as a skillful facilitator as well as content provider. Willis implies that instructors play a key role in the distance education process. Thach, Murphy and Korhonen (1994) identify 11 roles for distance education professionals. These roles might be assumed by one individual or by several individuals. One of these roles is instructional designer. However, there is little literature that describes how distance instructors engage in this role in their distance teaching process. Thus, additional attention needs to be paid to how they look at their role as instructional designers and how they apply instructional design elements in distance teaching courses. We argue that distance education instructors need to understand and apply some important instructional design elements when they teach at a distance. The goal of this article is to provide some guidance on what design elements distance education instructors need to understand and how they should apply them in distance education courses. This article will offer some suggestions that may help to direct instructors' efforts in meeting such challenges when teaching at a distance by identifying some important design elements through analyzing some of the most widely used instructional design models and key design issues related to teaching at a distance and examining how those elements can be applied in the distance teaching process in an attempt to clarify issues related to such an application.

TOWARD THE SOLUTION: DESIGN OF DISTANCE EDUCATION BY APPLICATION OF KEY INSTRUCTIONAL DESIGN ELEMENTS

Instructional design is highly valued by faculty when designing learning experiences. Piskurich (2000) explains the importance of instructional design as follows:

> The instructional design will help you create good, clear objectives for your program that can be understood and mastered by your trainees. It will help you develop evaluations that truly test for the knowledge and skills that our objectives are based on. It will help you or whoever instructs that course to facilitate the participants' learning effectively and efficiently and, most important, it will help your make sure that what is in your program is what your trainees need to learn. This reduces wasted time, wasted money, and wasted opportunities for helping to develop more effective employees who, through their knowledge and skills, increase corporate profitability. (p. 3)

Piskurich' views identify the worth of instructional design as a process to ensure quality instruction.

Dijkstra (1997) gives an explanation of the relationship between process and product in terms of instructional design by asserting that instructional design refers to "a certain mode of producing or developing instruction as well as to a product that defines an educational setting" (p. 27). This means that instructional design is a process in which a product is generated in an educational setting. Thus, instructional designers have to be concerned both with the aspects of process and product when designing instruction.

Instructional design or development models are useful in the instructional design process. Several models can be used to design instruction of units and lessons. In 1990, Dick and Carey developed one of the most widely used models (Gustafson & Branch, 1997). This model involves nine stages: identifying an instructional goal, conducting a goal analysis or instructional analysis, identifying entry behaviors and characteristics of learners, writing performance objectives, developing criterion-referenced (objective-referenced) test items, developing an instructional strategy, developing and selecting instructional package materials, designing and conducting formative evaluations, and designing and conducting summative evaluation. This model is valuable because it introduces the concepts and applications of the systematic design of instruction to people who are new to the field (Gustafson & Branch, 1997).

Kemp, Morrison and Ross (1994) identified nine elements that should receive attention in a comprehensive instructional development plan: identifying instructional problems, and specifying goals for designing an instructional program, examining learner characteristics that should receive attention during planning, identifying subject content, and analyzing task components related to stated goals and purposes, stating instructional objectives for the learner, sequencing content within each instructional unit for logical learning, designing instructional strategies so that each learner can master the objectives, planning instructional delivery within three patterns for teaching and learning, developing evaluation instruments to assess objectives, and selecting resources to support instruction and learning activities. This model emphasizes subject matter content, goals and purposes, and selection of resources (Gustafson & Branch, 1997).

Smith and Ragan (1993) created an instructional design process model that is "becoming increasingly popular for students and professionals in the fields of instructional technology who are interested in the cognitive psychology base of the ID process" (Gustafson & Branch, 1997, p. 68). Their approach includes eight steps: analyzing the learning context, analyzing the learners, analyzing the learning task, assessing learner performance, developing instructional strategies, producing instruction, conducting evaluation, and revising instruction. This model is useful when introducing the philosophy and theory of the systematic design of instruction to practitioners in educational field (Gustafson & Branch, 1997).

Though the models emphasize different aspects of the instructional design process, they all include the following elements: learner considerations, content organization, instructional strategies, and evaluation (see Table 6.1). Thus, these four elements are four key elements in the instructional design process.

Instructional design is important to distance education. The most critical aspect of successful distance education is good planning, because planning for effective teaching is necessary for learning to occur (Smaldino, 1999). Instructors who teach at a distance are confronted with many new challenges. Limited instructional design knowledge and skills are a factor in faculty development of quality instruction (Moore, 1997). However, instructors will obtain a lot of benefit if they understand and apply instructional design elements in their design for distance teaching. Therefore, it is essential to take key instructional design elements into account when designing instruction at a distance. To secure the success of the planning, distance learning faculty should pay attention to some key

Table 6.1.   Key Elements of the Instructional Design Process

Instructional Design Elements	Dick & Carey	Kemp, Morrison, & Ross	Smith & Ragan
Instructional goals	X	X	
Learner characteristics	X	X	X
Learning context			X
Learning task/content	X	X	X
Instructional objectives	X	X	
Selecting			
Instructional strategies	X	X	X
Media and materials	X	X	
Assessing learner performance	X	X	X
Resources		X	
Producing instruction			X
Revising instruction			X

issues regarding designing instruction at a distance. According to Simonson, Smaldino, Albright, and Zvacek (2000), the following issues need to be considered:

1. Who are the learners? The instructors need to have knowledge of learner characteristics. This knowledge about the learners can help the instructor handle the separation of instructor and students successfully.

2. What is the essential content? The content of a course should reflect where this content relates to the rest of the curriculum. Thus, instructors need to consider the nature of the content, and the sequence of information. Generally, the scope of the content for a course needs to be sufficient to ensure that the entire learning experience will result in the desired outcomes. Thus, the identification of goals and objectives for instruction is necessary.

3. What teaching strategies and media should be used? It is essential to make the learner participate when distance educators decide which strategy or strategies to use. The instructor needs to think about selecting those instructional strategies that enable all the learners to participate in active learning. Doing so can ensure that students will be harmonious with the class.

4. What is the learning environment? To completely understand distance education, one must examine not only the technology, but

also the learning environments that are created (Herring & Smaldino, 1998) because learning environments, as a class of systems, integrate, to different degrees, tools, resources, and pedagogical features that enhance student comprehension (Hannafin, 1992).

5. How do you determine the quality of the instruction? Here, the issues the instructor needs to address, when teaching at a distance, include general learner characteristics, the nature of content, teaching strategies and media selected, the learning environment, and evaluation.

Moore and Kearsley (1996) stated that many questions need to be addressed in the design of a distance education course or program, including:

- What content should be included or left out?
- What is the best way to sequence and organize the material?
- What are the best media to use to present the material?
- What kind of teaching strategies should be employed?
- How can learning be measured most appropriately?
- What feedback should students receive about their progress?
- What methods should be used to create the materials?

Moore and Kearsley stressed such issues as content organization, media selection, teaching strategies, evaluation, and materials creation that are all connected with how to meet needs of learners.

Sherry and Morse (1995) also argue that teachers take interest in specific areas of the instructional system design process, such as determining how much content to put into a single lesson, diversifying types of presentation and course activities, designing ancillary materials, developing courseware, assessing teacher effectiveness and student learning, and revising learning modules to fit student needs. Sherry emphasizes the issues including content, instructional strategies, the development of materials, the use of media, and assessment. These issues need to be considered surrounding how to address learner needs as well.

When discussing the issues related to the design of instruction in distance education, the cited authors all address the issues associated with learner considerations, content organization, instructional strategies, distance education technology characteristics, and evaluation (see Table 6.2). These issues match those identified earlier as essential to instructional design with one added element, the distance education technology environment. Therefore, these issues can be considered as key elements for designing instruction at a distance. We suggest that distance education

Table 6.2.   Key Elements for Designing Instruction at a Distance

Instructional Design Elements	Simonson, Smaldino, Albright, & Zvacek	Moore & Kearsley	Sherry & Morse
Learner considerations	X	X	X
Learning task/content	X	X	X
Selecting Instructional strategies	X	X	X
Media	X	X	X
Learning environment	X		
Assessing quality of instruction	X	X	X
Materials		X	X

instructors understand and apply these identified key elements in their distance teaching process in order to ensure the optimal learning outcomes take place.

APPLICATION OF THE IDENTIFIED INSTRUCTIONAL DESIGN ELEMENTS FOR TEACHING AT A DISTANCE

Since teaching at a distance is not an easy task, our purpose is to find a solution to help distance education instructors design distance education courses. To achieve this aim, it is necessary to elaborate on those common identified instructional design elements in order to provide a better framework for faculty to comprehend and apply those elements when designing instruction in a distance education setting.

Learner Considerations

It is important to consider learner characteristics and needs in the design of instruction in distance education because "it is not just the learners' presence but also the characteristics and needs they bring with them that influence the design, structure, and operation of a distance learning system" (Chute, Thompson, & Hancock, 1999, p. 66). These characteristics and needs affect the system as a whole because "any action in one part of the system cannot help influencing (in at least a small way) the other parts" (Chute, Thompson, & Hancock, 1999, p. 66). In the following, some of the most important aspects associated with the distance learners in terms of addressing their needs are examined.

General Learner Characteristics

Simonson, Smaldino, Albright, and Zvacek (2000) claim that each individual learner is unique and those unique characteristics need to be identified. Those characteristics can have a great impact on the distance learning outcomes. Those characteristics include attitude or interest, prior skills, knowledge, experience, and learning styles.

Interactivity

Interactivity is one of the crucial elements regarding learner considerations in terms of distance education. As Belanger and Jordan (2000) state, instructors and participants should facilitate all types of interactions in distance learning courses because interaction can reduce the sense of isolation of individual participant attending distance courses, make participants adjust themselves to new environment more flexibly and add the variety of experiences individual learners have, which may include multicultural environments, broader age range of learners, or greater expertise of all learners combined. Moore and Kearsley (1996) propose three types of interaction in distance education. They are learner-content interaction, learner-instructor interaction and learner-learner interaction. Learner-content interaction refers to the interaction that the student has to deal with about the subject matter presented in the course. Education is a process of learning provided by a teacher or institution. Each learner has to obtain knowledge by personally modifying information to fit former cognitive structures. It is just a process of interacting with content that causes the changes in the learner's understanding in perspective, and their constructs in knowledge. Learner-instructor interaction is a communication between the instructor and student and can be reinforced by face-to-face talk, phone conversation, e-mail, etc. The third kind of interaction is learner-learner interaction that is interaction between one learner and other learners, alone or in group settings, with or without the concurrent presence of an instructor (Moore & Kearsley, 1996). Learners need this kind of interaction because of the complicated circumstances for the learners related to their age, experience, and level of learner autonomy. Learner–learner interaction among members of a class or group can be an extremely valuable and essential resource for learning; individual interaction can be enhanced through peer group interaction by asynchronous e-mail and by synchronous computer conversations (Moore, 2000/2001).

When distance instructors address the issue of learner considerations, they need to take these three kinds of interaction into account. Specifically, they need to design and organize courses to ensure that there is each type of interaction and provide the types of interaction that is most appropriate for the various learning tasks for different content areas for learners at different stages of growth. The major weakness of many distance education programs is that they commit to a particular communications medium; when there is only one medium used, probably only one kind of interaction is facilitated well. This indicates that distance instructors need to think about using all three kinds of interaction by using a variety of media (Moore & Kearsley, 1996).

How Faculty Support Distance Learners and Meet Their Needs

Instructors teaching at a distance need to be aware of providing frequent and adequate feedback to support these learners (Gibson, 1998, p. 49). Student needs and limitations need to be understood in every aspect of the distance education program. Successful student support is an indicator of the result of every aspect of the program, "from a prospective student's first awareness of the program to graduation day, working in an integrated fashion to maintain the student's engagement and progress" (Granger & Benke, 1998, p. 128). Distance students find programs supportive because faculty and staff design the program with the consideration of their needs and expectations of a responsive program (Granger & Benke, 1998).

Faculty need to be involved in program design and delivery. The faculty who teach the courses often connect the academic program and the student with academic and support services. Because distance learners need knowledge of assignments in advance, structure, and prompt feedback, faculty should be prepared to prepare those elements effectively in distance instruction. The instructors also need to incorporate experiences, goals and expectations of the learners into the learning activity. Faculty who assess expectations and skills of distance learners through administrative and support services can also assist students in the learning processes. (Granger & Benke, 1998)

Rowntree (1992) states that distance learners probably need more individual personal support than general support (as cited in Reid, 1995). Dekkers and Cuskelly (1990) stress that distance learners are not generally isolated by choice, and that open learning centers play an important role in facilitating interaction with staff and student instead of taking mere minor responsibility sometimes ascribed by institutions. They identify four important areas associated with a student perspective (as cited in Reid, 1995): access to academic support and other students—preferably by direct contact; student learning characteristics—adaptation of a variety of learning styles instead of mere stress on study packages; access to library and other resources to learning—particularly for independent study materials; understanding of the student learning environment and background—realizing the family and work commitments of students. These statements indicate that there is a need for student support in the aspects such as direct interaction with teachers and other learners, instructor studying and adapting different kinds of learning styles, having access to library and other resources, and getting familiar with learner background. However, how to help distance learners accomplish the above mentioned learning support will bring many challenges.

How Faculty Help Students
Get Comfortable With Distance Learning

When implementing distance learning, it is important to get people to use and support the system (Chute, Thompson, & Hancock, 1999). Thus, it is important to make distance students feel comfortable with distance learning. The distant instructors can help distance learners to get used to using the distance learning system and become comfortable with learning in distance learning environment. They can help students bridge the gap by providing channels for interaction, access to resources, and help with technology.

Students as Factors of Design

Distant learner satisfaction is an important aspect in understanding the success of distance education. Thus, distance instructors need to consider student satisfaction factors when designing instruction at distance.

One of the basic instructional design principles is to plan the content around the needs of the audience and engaging the learners (Fisher, 2000/2001). Distant instructors need to choose effective teaching strategies to deliver instructional content to achieve the ideal learning outcomes. The major barriers Kelsey (2000) shows for the successful organization of content in interactive compressed video classes are associated with students publicly asking questions before the larger learning community and time constraints for processing content. These barriers are possibly caused by the particular features of distance learning such as the separation of the learners from instructors, and the use of electronic communication technologies. Instructors need to work out some related instructional strategies intended to fit their teaching format in the unique distance-teaching environment for the purpose of ensuring learner participation.

The students' perception of interaction is essential. Courses designed for distance learning should produce successful interaction since interaction provides assistance for students to get over the sense of isolation and loneliness distance learners might have in the distance learning setting. Fulford and Zhang (1993) also emphasize that a crucial indicator of distance students' satisfaction was their perception of overall interaction. The survey conducted by Sorensen and Baylen (2000) shows two problems concerning interaction: teacher-student and student-student interaction. These findings imply that instructors need to be more involved in the across-site activities so as to increase the interaction with the students and that the instructors also need to create more opportunities for students at the host site to interact with the students at other sites. Kelsey (2000), in a study investigating participant interaction in a course delivered by interactive compressed video (ICV) technology, identified some of the student perceived barriers to interaction in such a course. One of those barriers related to the use of the technology is camera shyness. Sixty-two percent of the students reported that they had anxiety about being seen on camera. When the site facilitator did not display the picture-in-picture (PIP) feature on the ICV monitor, the students felt more comfortable asking questions, for they could not see themselves. Students at the original site indicated that camera shyness was a more serious issue for them than for remote site students, as their larger-than-life-size image was displayed on a screen in the front of the room.

One characteristic of distance learning is its association with high dropout rates at least in comparison with conventional institutions. Clearly there will always be some dropout. As distance learning opportunities grow, so competition mounts. Where students have a choice they will judge institutions by the quality of the design product they produce. Therefore, in order to maintain retention, it is essential to acquire student perceptions of the designed product.

Lockwood (1995) conducted a qualitative study by collecting data through interview, questionnaire, and self-recorded audiotape with the purpose of exploring students' perceptions and response to assessment material. He observed, through the analysis of the interview transcripts, questionnaire responses, and self-recorded audiotapes, three common features students regarded as benefits to their study. They are course-focused, self-focused, and assignment-focused benefits. Course-focused benefits are those regarding students' learning from the course—the concepts, ideas, and arguments under discussion. These activities help students to understand the course material. Self-focused benefits are those related to a student's learning and development as a person; "the opportunities they provided for ideas and arguments to be explored or reconsidered, previous assumptions challenged and personal interest awakened, developed or extended" (Lockwood, 1995, p. 202). The essential feature is that one thinks critically, or question the materials. Assignment-focused benefits indicate those associated with directly answering an assignment that offers an opportunity to think about the issues to be discussed in an assignment or which supplies materials to be used in it. These perceived benefits indicate that if the learning activities help students to understand the course material, think critically, or answer the questions regarding assignments, students would consider the course as a good one. Otherwise, they would feel unsatisfied with the quality of the course or the product of the instructor's design. Lockwood's findings are significant because they provide important implications on those aspects in which distance instructors need to examine and evaluate their course product.

There are factors perceived by students which instructors need to take into account while addressing student needs when they design instruction at a distance. These issues need to be addressed in order to ensure the quality of learning in the distant environment.

The Design for Content Organization in Distance Education Courses

Content organization is very important in achieving learning objectives: the way in which to organize the content may affect the learning outcomes directly. In a distance education setting, how to organize content seems even more important. As Willis (2000/2001) explains, classroom instructors depend on a number of "subtle visual cues from their students to enhance their delivery of instructional content" (p. 197). This is true because it is easy for them to distinguish students who are carefully taking notes, thinking about a difficult concept, or prepared to comment from students who are frustrated, confused, and tired. The thoughtful teacher consciously and subconsciously observes and analyzes these visual cues and adjusts the delivery of content to meet the needs of the students. The distant teacher, however, may have access to few visual cues. Thus, it is difficult to implement an exciting teacher-class discussion, especially when technical requirements and distance change the spontaneous state of the class (Willis, 2000/2001). Distance instructors need to realistically assess the quantity of content that should be effectively delivered in the course, since delivering information in a distance course often takes more time than presenting the same amount of information in a traditional classroom setting (Willis, 2000/2001).

Gibson (1998) believes that all distant learners need: content that meets their needs; obvious directions for their actions at each phase of the course; as much control of the pace of learning as possible; a means of drawing attention to individual concerns; a method of investigating their progress and acquiring feedback from their instructors; materials that are useful, active, and interesting. Here, Gibson stresses the importance of taking learners' needs into account when discussing course content in distance education.

Instructional Strategies

Distance education is an opportunity for instructors to revisit techniques for teaching, for it incorporates both place and time shifting (Herring & Smaldino, 1998). A place shift indicates that all the participants in the class are not in a single location; a time shift suggests that the instruction is not live. Even the most experienced educators are faced with the instructional challenges of these two aspects of distance learning (Simonson et al., 2000). Instructors often feel that "the focused preparation required by distance teaching improves their overall teaching and empathy for their student" (Willis, 2000/2001, p. 197). This implies that though encountered with great challenges it is still possible that instructors who teach at a distance will overcome the related obstacles and achieve teaching effectiveness through constant effort.

Willis (2000/2001) claims that "for the most part, effective distance teaching requires the enhancement of existing skills, rather than developing new abilities" (p. 199). According to him, some of the issues distance instructors need to pay special attention to include the following:

- Diversify and pace course activities; do not use long lectures. Combine content presentations with discussions and student-centered activities.

- Use locally relevant examples as often as possible to help students to comprehend and apply course content. The earlier this is done in the course, the better.

- Be concise. Employ short, cohesive statements and direct questions because using technical equipment may take more time for students to respond.

- Cultivate strategies used for student reinforcement, review, repetition, and remediation. To reach that aim, one-on-one phone discussions and electronic mail communication are particularly favorable.

- And finally ... relax. Participants will quickly become comfortable with the process of distance education and effective teaching will be resumed.

These effective teaching strategies can be used to facilitate effective distance learning. However, what is important in determining which strategy or strategies to use is the issue of engaging the learner (Smaldino, 1999). Since distance education is a learner-centered approach, methods that focus on the learners and incorporate interactivity have been shown to be most successful. Instructors need to consider a variety of techniques in order to involve learners in active learning experiences (Simonson et al., 2000).

Issues Related to Using the Internet and ITV for Teaching and Learning

According to the U.S. Department of Education, National Center for Education Statistics (1999), the Internet and ITV are the two most popular delivery technologies used in distance education. They have greatest potential in the application of teaching at a distance. However, while using them in instruction, instructors frequently come across different kinds of problems that prohibit them from using the two technologies smoothly. Therefore, it is necessary to investigate issues and concerns regarding the distant instructor using the Internet and ITV for teaching content.

Wang-Chavez and Branon (2001), in their study, investigated the instructors' participation in Web/Internet-based instruction. They observed the visible interaction occurring on one course Web site. Through the analysis of the evaluation data, they identified three general major difficulties with the instructor use of the Web for instruction. First, very little interaction took place on the course message boards during the early part of the semester. One of the causes for this lack of interaction with students lay in the fact that most of the students had never had the experience of taking an online class before; they did not know how to communicate by using the related courseware. The instructor did realize this lack of student involvement in the class; however, he did not have more time to promote the students' online communication due to the heavy teaching work. The second major difficulty was connected with the quantity of feedback students were getting from the instructor. The same reason (time shortage) restricted the amount of individual student feedback students got from the instructor. The professor hoped students would interact more with each other and learn from each other instead of depending on him to get plenty of the feedback. The third major problem refers to standards for the class. Students stated that they were not clear about how the instructor was evaluating them. This was especially the case with the participation part of their grade. They suggested that clear and specific guidelines about how participation was being evaluated (for example, by number of message board postings, depth of the posts, etc.) would be helpful with the clarification of the students' confusion. Similarly, students also need clear guidelines for group projects to address their concerns about group work. This would result in more participation from group members.

Moore and Koble (1995) offer some implications for training of faculty who use interactive television. The need for training of faculty before teaching an interactive television course is obvious. First, instructors identified traditional instructional methods as ineffective in the televised courses. However, instructors kept using these methods. Furthermore, the instructors suggested that instructional methods that integrate more audio-visual materials are effective in the interactive television classroom, but they failed to use such materials. Future research should determine if instructional methods that students identify are as effective as those identified by the instructors. A much stronger case can be established to combine audio-visual materials, and to train the development and use of such materials, when instructors and students both consider them to be effective methods of instruction in an interactive television course. Another training issue concerns the instructors' perceived need for hands-on training. Instructors do not like to be told how to teach; instead, they intend to get a feel for the equipment and the effective specific techniques they need to use in interactive television classrooms. Finally, there was the need for good system support. This embraces properly trained technicians, remote-site coordinators or facilitators, technical trouble-shooting personnel, and orientations of students to the system prior to the class. The findings of Gehlauf, Shatz, and Frye's study conducted in 1995 which investigated faculty perceptions of interactive television instructional strategies support what Moore and Koble have found here.

The issues and concerns discussed by Wang-Chavez and Branon, and Moore and Koble should not be neglected by instructors who teach at a distance. These issues and concerns generally include student lack of interaction with each other because they were inexperienced in taking an online class or because they did not know how to use the related courseware, students getting insufficient feedback from the instructor who is too busy with the coursework, students are unaware of appropriate standards by which their coursework is evaluated; instructor need for training students in using equipment, developing effective audio-visual materials and handling system issues such as dealing with technicians and remote site coordinators, and the need for good system support.

Investigating student perceptions of the use of the Internet and ITV in learning is very important, for it can help to identify the related problems or issues which need to be solved or addressed. Wang-Chavez and Branon (2001) did formative research on improving an online undergraduate business course to facilitate Web-based instruction. One of the consistent results of their research is that students enjoyed the flexibility and convenience of attending an online course. Other findings suggest that students also valued the professor's patience and understanding in dealing with problems they faced. Some students enjoyed the group work and online discussions. However, students identified some prominent themes regarding problems and concerns that occurred from the qualitative data analysis which included concerns about taking an online exam for fear of technical problems, the fairness of the group work assessment, etc. Student perceptions of an online course presented here provides some valuable insights into how involved parties improve future online courses.

Thomerson and Smith (1996), who did a study to investigate student perceptions of the affective experiences encountered in distance learning courses in which ITV was used, found that there are some areas that need to be improved in the distance program at Valdosta State University. They indicated that many remote-site students found difficulty hearing at off-campus sites. Both the remote- and host-site groups suggested that the distance learning equipment led to distractions. Down time was the biggest problem. Many remote- and host-site students found variety of equipment problems that interrupted class. Other distance learning students complained about making adjustments in the equipment in order to get all sites together online appropriately led to the loss of some class time. Host-site students did not understand these problems better. Many host-site students did not want to tolerate these problems since they could not find any benefits for themselves. Findings from this study have shown that instructors need to develop appropriate strategies to improve the affective aspects of students' learning experiences, specifically those of both remote- and host-site students. Strategies for improving the host-site experience are essential. Host-site students were not willing to take a distance-learning course. One possible suggestion might be simply to not include the host-site group so that the instructor would be able to concentrate entirely on students at the remote sites. Host-site students could attend traditional-classroom courses in order not to be disturbed by any of the distractions caused by the distance learning experience (Thomerson & Smith, 1996).

The above issues and problems related to using the Internet and ITV for teaching or learning are critical for the success of distance education programs. To make distance education more effective, these concerns need to be addressed.

Evaluation of the Design Product

Evaluation is an important procedure in the instructional design process in distance education because, as Morgan and O'Reilly (1999) state, teachers need

- to know if students are attaining the intended learning outcomes;
- to know if course materials and teaching activities are effective;
- to be able to certify that students have achieved standards or met requirements.

There are many benefits to doing evaluation as a continuous process. Belanger and Jordan (2000) suggest three benefits:

> First, it is the only way to determine whether or not, and to what degree, instructional objectives have been met. Second, it is the only way to determine, post hoc, what the actual return on investment has been. Third, evaluation results provide valuable feedback so that the program can be continually improved. (p. 186)

These benefits of doing an evaluation indicate the chief purposes for doing evaluation in an educational program. They can be considered as the starting-point from which to think about evaluation of an educational program.

How to Monitor and Evaluate
the Quality of Instructional Design

Chute, Thompson, and Hancock (1999) confirm that evaluation is an important part of the design of distance learning systems and programs. They continue to state that the most direct measure of program effectiveness should center on the quality of the individual learning experience. They propose three factors requiring consideration for assessing such effectiveness: the amount learned, the integration of learned skills into practice, and self-reported satisfaction with the learning experience. First, distant instructors need to consider the amount learned by the learner. The evaluation or assessment activities should concentrate on measuring the extent to which students have accomplished the assignments or met the requirements described in the course objectives. The rationale for measuring the amount learned by a distance learner is the same as that for assessing the learning of a student in the traditional classroom. However, the strategies and procedures used in such measurement have to be revised to fit in the distance learning setting. Second, the distant instructors need to think about integration of learned skills into practice. Training and formal education provide opportunities to gain skills and knowledge that can be used in practical situations. Thus, the distance instructor should assess the extent to which distance learning can make such transference. Workplace setting can provide opportunities for a more direct assessment of learning outcomes. Third, the distant instructors need to examine learner satisfaction with distance learning. Satisfaction with the media and processes that form the learning environment is a major element to evaluate whether students are willing to continue to attend distance education courses.

Designing Assessment Tasks

Designing assessment tasks is a crucial activity in the earliest stages of subject design and development, and distant instructors can follow some ways to start to design assessment tasks (Morgan & O'Reilly, 1999). These approaches include aligning assessment with the objectives, and selecting appropriate assessment tools to ensure that the assessment process is possible in a distance-learning environment. Morgan and O'Reilly indicate that when instructors teaching at a distance are involved in designing assessment tasks, they need to consider if the assessment is clearly aligned with subject aims and objectives because content, teaching, and learning activities for a well-aligned subject are more likely to bring about a deep approach to learning. In addition, instructors also need to consider broadly knowledge, skills, and attitudes that can be developed in learners through assessment and seek diversity in methods that enhance the broadest range of vocational and disciplinary skills. They also need to choose methods that are appropriate to desired outcomes and think creatively about perceived difficulties—just about everything that can be assessed at a distance.

CONCLUSIONS

Distance education continues to exert its potential in the educational setting, "educators and designers need to increase their innovation in distance education by designing for instructional effectiveness" (Carr & Carr, 2000, p. 324). In order to be successful in meeting the new challenges that distance education instructors are faced with and make the learning outcomes more optimal, they need to understand and incorporate some important instructional design elements in their distance education courses. A better understanding and application of the identified instructional design elements discussed in this article will help the instructors who teach distance education courses accomplish successful design of instruction in their distance teaching process.

REFERENCES

Belanger, F., & Jordan, D. H. (2000). *Evaluation and implementation of distance learning: Technologies, tools and techniques.* Hershey, PA: Idea Group.

Carr, C. S., & Carr, A. M. (2000). Instructional design in distance education (IDDE): A web-based performance support system for educators and designers. *Quarterly Review of Distance Education, 1*(4), 317-325.

Chute, A. G., Thompson, M. M., & Hancock, B.W. (1999). *The McGraw-Hill handbook of distance learning.* New York: McGraw-Hill.

Dick, W., & Carey, L. (1990). *The systematic design of instruction* (3rd ed.). New York: Harper Collins College Publishers.

Dijkstra, S (1997). Theoretical foundations of instructional design: Introduction and overview. In R. D. Tennyson, F. Schott, N, Seel,. & S. Dijkstra (Eds.), *Instructional design: International perspectives* (V. 1: Theory, research and models) (pp. 19-24). Mahwah, NJ: Erlbaum.

Fisher, S. (2000/2001). Web-based training on a shoestring. In K. Mantyla, *The 2000/2001 ASTD distance learning yearbook* (pp. 76-82). New York: McGraw-Hill.

Fulford, C. P., & Zhang, S. (1993). Perceptions of interaction: The critical predictor in distance education. *The American Journal of Distance Education 7*(3), 8-21.

Gehlauf, D. N., Shatz, M. A., & Frye, T. W. (1995). Faculty perceptions of interactive television instructional strategies: Implications for training. In M.G. Moore & M. A. Koble (Eds.), *Video-based telecommunications in distance education* (pp. 85-93). University Park, PA: American Center for the Study of Distance Education.

Gibson, C. C. (1998). *Distance learners in higher education: Institutional responses for quality outcomes.* Madison, WI: Atwood.

Granger, D., & Benke, M. (1998). Supporting learners at a distance from inquiry through completion. In C. C. Gibson (Ed.), *Distance learners in higher education: Institutional responses for quality outcomes* (pp. 127-138). Madison, WI: Atwood.

Gustafson, K. L., & Branch, R. M. (1997). *Survey of instructional development models.* Syracuse, NY: Center for Science and Technology.

Hannafin, M. J. (1992). Emerging technologies, ISD, and learning environments: Critical perspectives. *Educational Technology Research and Development, 40*(1), 49-63.

Herring, M. C., & Smaldino, S. E. (1998). *Planning for interactive distance education: A handbook.* Washington, DC: Association for Educational Communications and Technology.

Kelsey, K. D. (2000). Participant interaction in a course delivered by interactive compressed video technology. *The American Journal of Distance Education, 14*(1), 63-76.

Kemp, J. E., Morrison, G. R. & Ross, S. M. (1994). *Designing effective instruction.* New York: Merrill.

Lockwood, F. (1995). Students' perception of, and response to, formative and summative assessment material. In F. Lockwood (Ed.), *Open and distance learning today* (pp. 197-207). London: Routledge.

Moore, M. G. (1997). Quality in distance education: Four cases. *The American Journal of Distance Education, 11*(3), 1-7.

Moore, M. G. (2000/2001). Tips for the manager setting up a distance learning program. In K. Mantyla, *The 2000/2001 ASTD distance learning yearbook* (pp. 133-136). New York: McGraw-Hill.

Moore, M. G., & Kearsley, G. (1996). Distance *education: A systems view*. Belmont, CA: Wadsworth.

Moore, M. G., & Koble, M. A. (1995). *Video-based telecommunications in distance education*. University Park, PA: The Pennsylvania State University

Morgan, C., & O'Reilly, M. (1999). *Assessing open and distance learners*. London: Kogan Page.

National Center for Education Statistics (1999). *Distance Education at Postsecondary Education Institutions: 1997-1998*. (NCES 2000-013). Washington, DC: U.S. Government Printing Office.

Olgren, C. H. (2000). Distance learning in higher education. In K. Mantyla, *The 2000/2001 ASTD distance learning yearbook* (pp. 19-25). New York: McGraw-Hill.

Piskurich, G. M. (2000). *Rapid instructional design*. San Francisco: Jossey-Bass Pfeiffer.

Reid, J. (1995). Managing learning support. In F. Lockwood, *Open and distance learning today* (pp. 265-278). London: Routledge.

Sherry, L., & Morse, R. (1995). An assessment of training needs in the use of distance education for instruction. *International Journal of Educational Telecommunications, 1*(1), 5-22.

Simonson, M., Smaldino, S., Albright, M., & Zvacek, S. (2000). *Teaching and learning at a distance: Foundations of distance education*. Upper Saddle River: NJ: Prentice-Hall.

Smaldino, S. (1999). Instructional design. *Tech Trends, 43*(5), 9-13.

Smith, P. L., & Ragan, T. J. (1993). *Instructional design*. New York: Macmillan.

Sorensen, C., & Baylen, D. (2000). Perception versus reality: Views of interaction in distance education. *Quarterly Review of Distance Education, 1*(1), 45-58.

Thach, L., Murphy, K. L., & Korhonen, L. (1994, April). *Identifying competencies for distance education professionals*. Paper presented at the Annual Conference of the American Educational Research Association, New Orleans, LA.

Thomerson, J. D., & Smith, C. L. (1996). Student perceptions of the affective experiences encountered in distance learning courses. *The American Journal of Distance Education, 10*(3), 37-48.

Wang-Chavez, J., & Branon, R. (2001). Facilitating web-based instruction: Formative research on improving an online undergraduate business course. *Quarterly Review of Distance Education, 2*(3), 209-220.

Willis, B. (1994). *Distance education: Strategies and tools*. Englewood Cliffs, NJ: Educational Technology Publications.

Willis, B. (2000/2001). Strategies for teaching at a distance. In K. Mantyla, *The 2000/2001 ASTD distance learning yearbook* (pp. 197-201). New York: McGraw-Hill.

CHAPTER 7

CLASS SIZE
AND INTERACTION
IN ONLINE COURSES

Anymir Orellana

This article presents findings of a study conducted to determine instructors' perceptions of optimal class sizes for online courses with different levels of interaction. Implications for research and practice are also presented. A Web-based survey method was employed. Online courses studied were those taught sometime in the last 5 years by a single instructor in undergraduate or graduate programs from U.S. higher education institutions. Instructors described the level of interactive qualities in their most recently taught online course using a Web version of Roblyer and Wiencke's (2004) Rubric for Assessing Interactive Qualities in Distance Courses, and they indicated optimal class sizes according to such qualities. Responses from 131 instructors were analyzed. On average (a) instructors described their online courses as highly interactive, (b) the actual class size of the online courses was 22.8, (c) a class size of 18.9 was perceived as optimal to better achieve the course's actual level of interaction, and (d) a class size of 15.9 was perceived as optimal to achieve the highest level of interaction. No relationship was found between online courses' actual class sizes and their actual level of interaction.

The Perfect Online Course: Best Practices for Designing and Teaching
pp. 127–156

Modern distance education is a means for higher education institutions to increase enrollments and students' access to learning (Lewis, Alexander, & Farris, 1997). Between 1997 and 2001, the percentage of American higher education institutions that offered distance education courses increased from 34 to 56, and course enrollments increased from 1.7 million to 3.1 million (Wirt, Choy, Rooney, Provasnik, Sen, & Tobin, 2004). Institutions also seek to implement quality distance education that often translates into high initial fixed costs and variable costs related to delivery of instruction (Bates, 2000; Bates & Poole, 2003; Morgan, 2000). These variable costs depend on course enrollments and, hence, class sizes.

Setting class-size limits is a budget-related matter for administrators (Parker, 2003; Thomas, 1984). Administrators are faced with the issue of determining an optimal class size to balance the cost-benefit relationship, while maintaining manageable faculty workloads and ensuring quality education. Administrators often believe that the number of students can be as large as hundreds because there is no physical space limitation in distance education (Simonson, 2004). Conversely, in a report of a year-long faculty seminar (University of Illinois, 1999), the following was concluded:

> Because high quality online teaching is time and labor intensive, it is not likely to be the income source envisioned by some administrators. Teaching the same number of students online at the same level of quality as in the classroom requires more time and money. (p. 2)

Class size research is important to educational policy development. Despite the growth of distance higher education, little research has been reported regarding class sizes for online courses (Boettcher & Conrad, 2004; Parker, 2003; Simonson, 2004). Simonson (2004) suggested that claims of "smaller is better [or that] it really makes no difference how many, if the course is organized correctly" (p. 56) are "myths" of distance education. Most of the class sizes recommended in the literature for distance education are based on anecdotal evidence (Simonson, 2004).

In this study, the online class-size problem was approached from the perspective of the instructor. It was assumed that different online courses may have different interactive qualities. Hence, the concern was not to determine a "one-size-fits-all" optimal class size for online courses, but to determine optimal class sizes according to the interactive qualities present in online courses. For the purpose of the study, interaction was defined as "a created environment in which both social and instructional messages are exchanged among the entities in the course and in which messages are both carried and influenced by the activities and technology resources being employed" (Roblyer & Wiencke, 2003, p. 81). Interaction is achieved "through a complex interplay of social, instructional, and technological variables" (p. 1).

The purpose of this study was to determine instructors' perceptions of optimal class sizes for online courses with different levels of interaction. The level of interaction was measured with Roblyer and Wiencke's (2004) Rubric for Assessing Interactive Qualities in Distance Courses (RAIQ). The RAIQ is a validated instrument that measures interactive qualities through five observable indicators (Roblyer & Wiencke, 2004): (a) social rapport-building designs for interaction, (b) instructional designs for interaction, (c) interactivity of technology resources, (d) evidence of learner engagement, and (e) evidence of instructor engagement. The RAIQ was not used in the study as a means to imply that the highest levels of interaction were optimal, needed, or desired in an online course. As Moore and Kearsley (2005) suggested, the RAIQ was used in the study as a "means of thinking about what kind of interaction you [the instructor] want to facilitate for different types of students and different subject areas" (p. 145).

Online courses studied were those that (a) counted for credit toward a degree in a bachelor's, master's, or doctoral program from an American higher education institution; (b) were taught at a distance at least 80% of the time using interactive telecommunications systems, perhaps with occasional traditional face-to-face activities; and (c) were taught by one instructor with no teaching assistant, or the like, sometime in the past 5 years. Class size was defined as the number of students maintained during instruction after the drop period. Class size did not necessarily reflect the number of initially enrolled students, or the limit set by the institution.

The study employed a Web-based survey research method. Instructors were asked to determine the level of interactive qualities in their most recently taught online course using a Web version of the RAIQ. Instructors were then asked to indicate what they perceived as optimal class sizes to better achieve the course's actual level of interaction and to better achieve the highest possible level of interaction, as measured by the RAIQ. Qualitative comments were also collected from instructors.

It was anticipated that findings would be useful as an initial approach to the class size problem in the field of distance education, specifically for online courses in higher education. It was also anticipated that results might be applicable to policy development regarding class-size limits for online courses. The importance given to interaction in the research, in best-practice guidelines, and in accreditation standards for online education served as the main framework for the study.

REVIEW OF LITERATURE

Research on class size in traditional education has been conducted for more than a century (Achilles, 1999). Research in elementary education has demonstrated that smaller classes allow for better student-teacher interaction (Achilles, 1999; Laine & Ward, 2000; Pritchard, 1999). More than 20 states in the United States have developed and implemented statewide policies that limit class sizes in public schools (Pritchard, 1999). On the other hand, class sizes in higher education usually can be as large as the institution deems necessary. According to Borden and Burton (1999), most studies focused on higher education have reported mixed results. Class size mostly affects what goes on in the classroom and not student achievement, per se (Gilbert, 1995; Hancock, 1996; Pascarella & Terenzini, 1991; Raimondo, Esposito, & Gershenberg, 1990; Toth & Montagna, 2002).

Gilbert (1995) advocated for large classes in higher education where group collaboration is best done. According to Gilbert, "Instruction which is intimate, interactive and investigative produces the most positive educational outcomes. The importance of interaction, participation and involvement of student learning are widely recognized ... and are, in fact, a part of effective large class instruction" (p. 5). On the other hand, Gilbert also suggested that quality instructor-student interaction is perhaps best achieved in smaller classes. Brown (as cited in Pascarella & Terenzini, 1991) and Smith and Malec (as cited in Pascarella & Terenzini, 1991) found that students' experiences in large classes negatively impacted student-faculty interaction. Also, Pascarella and Terenzini concluded that evidence suggested that smaller classes are better than larger ones if the goals of instruction are "motivational, attitudinal, or higher-level cognitive processes" (p. 87).

The question as to whether smaller classes are more conducive for learning than large ones is also important in distance education. Instructors also believe that quality of online instruction is questionable for large class sizes (Olson, as cited in Olson, 2002; Parker, 2003; University of Illinois, 1999). Sugrue, Rietz, and Hasen (1999) conducted a study across three learning sites to determine relationships among class size, instructor location, student perceptions, and performance. Two classes were taught at a distance via two-way video and differed in class size and the third class was taught face-to-face with 36 students. Results indicated that performance in the two smaller classes was better than in the large class. The authors concluded that, without considering individual differences among learners, class size influenced performance more than location did. Also, the authors indicated that small classes must be kept for successful multisite distance learning with two-way video. However, it was not clear to them what the optimum class size was.

Due to perceived higher demands of student-teacher interaction in online courses, many (e.g., Ko & Rossen, 2004; Sellani & Harrington, 2002; University of Illinois, 1999) have considered that instructors' workload increases with class size. In a descriptive study conducted by Berge and Muilenburg (2001), faculty time and workload were reported as main barriers for the adoption of online courses at any stage of the institution's maturity in implementing distance education. Instructors' perceptions of more work in online courses might be due to the instructor's unfamiliarity with the use of the media (Anderson, 2003; Hislop & Ellis, 2004). Accordingly, Simonson (2004) called the instructor-perceived-more-time issue the "'more work' myth" (p. 56) that is claimed among distance education practitioners. This group usually advocates for smaller classes. However, small classes might not be appropriate for course designs with emphasis on collaborative or group learning activities (Bates & Poole, 2003; Ko & Rossen, 2004; Vrasidas & McIsaac, 1999).

Survey research conducted by the National Education Association (NEA, 2000) showed that instructors perceived that time, or effort, is greater when teaching an online course, as opposed to a face-to-face course. However, the NEA report also showed that class size was not related to the amount of online teaching time estimated by surveyed faculty members. DiBiase (2000) concluded that the normalized teaching time per student in the online course was not greater than in the traditional version. Similarly, Hislop and Ellis (2003) found no significant difference in the total time spent by instructors teaching online versus face-to-face when time was normalized for class size. Visser (2000) conducted an experimental case-study to analyze the time to develop and teach the graduate-level distance course compared to a similar traditional course. Time was adjusted for class size. Visser concluded that online courses do seem to take more teaching and development time than the traditional course, but also noted that delivery time and effort may depend on the instructor experience and the level of institutional support.

Determining an optimal class size depends on multiple factors. According to Bates (2000), the driving factor that determines the ideal class size for an online course is the "amount and nature of the interaction between the tutor and students [and] student-teacher ratio is as much determined by educational philosophy, course design, and student numbers as by technology" (p. 129). In addition, a considerable body of literature presents sets of best practices and guidelines for course designs and for interactive strategies that promote quality distance education. Online strategies range from collaborative group activities, where interaction among students is essential, to activities in which more individualized instructor-student interaction is needed. Additionally, conventional wisdom suggests that large class sizes for online courses impact the amount of individual instructor-student interaction (Simonson, 2004). On the other hand, small class sizes negatively affect interaction in online community building (Vrasidas & McIsaac, 1999).

The importance of interaction in the design of distance courses is also highlighted in accreditation standards of the Southern Association of Colleges and Schools (2000) and the Western Cooperative for Educational Telecommunications (WCET, 2000). Accreditation is the means by which American higher education institutions are reviewed for quality (Council for Higher Education Accreditation, 2001) and recommended accreditation standards should be taken into account in the development of distance education policies (Simonson, Smaldino, Albright, & Zvacek, 2003). The Accrediting Commission of Career Schools and Colleges of Technology (2004) developed standards of accreditation that "sets forth the criteria under which the Commission will recognize programs or courses of study offered via distance education" (p. 29). Class size and interaction were addressed under the following faculty-related standards:

> The school ensures that faculty and students interact, and provides adequate means for such interaction
>   The school must have developed policies addressing teaching load, class size, time needed for course development, and the sharing of instructional responsibilities which allow for effective teaching using distance education methods. (p. 29)

The American Association of University Professors (AAUP, n.d.) has posted suggestions and guidelines for a sample language for distance education institutional policies and contract language. The AAUP recommended the following language for policies concerning faculty workload and teaching responsibilities: "Determination of class size for a distance education class should be based on pedagogical considerations. Large sections should be compensated by additional credit in load assignment in the same manner as traditional classes" (Workload/Teaching Responsibility section, ¶ 1). This recommendation is based on anecdotal evidence:

> In the absence of more definitive data, workload provisions should take into account the anecdotal evidence that distance education course development is taking two to three times as long as comparable courses taught in the traditional manner. The same evidence suggests that the investment of faculty time involved in teaching a distance education course is substantially greater than that required for a comparable traditional course. The time spent online answering student inquiries is reported as being more than

double the amount of time required in interacting with students in comparable traditional classes. (Workload/Teaching Responsibility section, ¶ 1)

In summary, research findings, practical guidelines and standards, and anecdotal evidence suggest that interaction is affected by class size. Determining an optimal class size for an online course is complex and depends on several factors. Instructors involved in the design, delivery, and administration of courses are key elements to successful distance education and their perceptions of optimal class sizes would be useful information to policy makers. A goal of this study was to determine such perceptions as they relate to interaction in online courses.

THEORETICAL FRAMEWORK

As in traditional classrooms, interaction is considered necessary and desirable for successful online learning (Bates, 2000; Fulford & Zhang, 1993; Lock, 2002; Moore, as cited in Gresh & Mrozowski, 2000; Offir, as cited in Gresh & Mrozowski; Roblyer & Wiencke, 2003; Sorensen & Baylen, 2000). Consequently, a model that captures the essence of theoretical and practical fundamentals of interaction is useful. In this respect, Roblyer and Wiencke (2004) developed and validated a RAIQ. The model is based on findings from theory and research related to interaction in distance education (e.g., Moore, 1989; Wagner, 1994; Yacci, 2000). Roblyer and Wiencke's (2004) RAIQ served as the main framework for this study. According to Roblyer and Wiencke, the rubric can be used by instructors as a "tool to allow more meaningful examination of the role of interaction in enhancing achievement and student satisfaction in distance learning courses" (p. 77). As Roblyer and Wiencke pointed out, the RAIQ might help the "design and research of optimal distance learning environments by helping to define and quantify observed interaction and allow empirical assessment of its contribution to course effectiveness" (p. 95).

METHOD

The study examined the following questions: What are instructors' perceptions of optimal class sizes for online courses with different levels of interactive qualities? What are typical class sizes of online courses? What are typical levels of interactive qualities in online courses? A Web-based survey research method was employed. The Class Size and Interaction

Questionnaire (CSIQ) was the Web-based instrument used for data collection.

Participants

According to Fowler (1993), "people who have particular interest in the subject matter or the research itself are more likely to return mail questionnaires than those who are less interested" (p. 4). Hence, in addition to faculty members who teach college-level online courses, groups of researchers in the field of distance education were also considered as potential participants. Participants were instructors who, sometime in the past 5 years, had taught an online course as defined in the study and were sampled from five groups of interest: (a) presenters of distance education-related topics at the 2004 National Convention of the Association for Educational Communications and Technology, (b) researchers who have published in the journal *Quarterly Review of Distance Education*, (c) researchers who have published in the journal *Distance Learning*, (d) researchers who have published in *The American Journal of Distance Education*, and (e) faculty members of U.S. higher education institutions that offer online courses.

Procedures

The Web-based software Surveyor was used to construct and administer the CSIQ via the Internet. Invitations and follow-ups to participants were also administered by Surveyor. Confidentiality, anonymity, and one-time responses were guaranteed by means of a secure Web-server, automated invitation and follow-up to participants, and randomly-generated-password access to the CSIQ. A multistage clustering was conducted to compile a list of 659 e-mail addresses from the five groups of interest based on the professional profile that was published on the selected journals or posted on the Web. The initial e-mailed invitation for participation in the research used Surveyor's features for survey invitation. Thirty-four messages were automatically returned to the researcher because of invalid e-mail addresses. These 34 addresses were deleted from the invitation list. Hence, a total of 625 composed the final list of invitation recipients.

After receiving the invitation, participants had 2 weeks to visit the URL that granted access to the CSIQ. Participants had to use the unique password randomly generated by Surveyor to access the CSIQ. To reduce the nonresponse rate, a follow-up e-mail was sent to nonrespondents as a reminder to complete the CSIQ. Surveyor automatically e-mailed the invitation letter to those who had not replied 1 week after the initial invitation. Eighty-six individuals submitted answers to the CSIQ before the follow-up reminder, and 68 more after the reminder. A total of 154 responses were collected. The response rate was 33.8%. The response rate was computed considering a total of 625 actual invitation-recipients and 211 replies to the invitation (i.e., 154 actual respondents to the CSIQ and 57 self-reported unqualified individuals).

According to Fowler (1993), "The effect of nonresponse survey estimates depends on the percentage not responding and the extent to which those that not responded are biased—that is, systematically different from the whole population" (p. 40). To maintain a nonbiased nonresponse rate, several aspects were considered: (a) sampled individuals were selected based on their professional profile (i.e., instructors or faculty members of college-level online courses), (b) individuals who did not meet the inclusion criteria were expected to reply to the e-mailed invitation and follow-up messages, (c) a conditional question in the CSIQ automatically directed respondents to the rest of the CSIQ questions only if they met the inclusion criteria, and (d) five nonrespondents were contacted by telephone to determine why they did not respond to the CSIQ.

From the five nonrespondents who were telephoned, two indicated that they usually do not take the time to answer online surveys. One did not read the e-mailed invitation or reminder, but indicated that he usually supported this kind of research and would have been pleased to participate. Another indicated that she did not teach online courses. The last nonrespondent telephoned indicated that she did not believe that the research problem was worthwhile or appropriate, and was not willing to participate.

Instruments

The CSIQ was designed following guidelines recommended by Gall, Gall, and Borg (2003) and by Schonlau, Fricker, and Elliot (2001) for Web-based questionnaires. The questionnaire consisted of an initial question to verify that the respondent met the inclusion criteria (i.e., sometime in the last 5 years, he or she had taught an online course as defined in the study) and four main parts: demographics, general questions related to the instructor's most recently taught online course, Web version of the RAIQ, and optimal class-size questions and comments

Demographics
Questions were formulated to collect respondents' age, gender, highest academic degree, number of years since degree was awarded, number of

years teaching in higher education, academic rank in faculty position, general area of teaching from the United Nations Educational Scientific and Cultural Organization's (UNESCO, 1997) Web site, level of expertise in online teaching on a scale from 1 (*novice*) to 5 (*very experienced*), number of years teaching online courses, and number of online courses taught. Respondents also indicated whether they had received formal training in online teaching methods.

General questions related to the instructor's most recently taught online course. Questions were formulated to collect the course's actual class size, academic level of the program (bachelor's, master's, or doctoral), duration in weeks, and semester credits. Questions were formulated to collect the number of credit-bearing courses that the instructor taught during the same academic term, the Carnegie classification from the Carnegie Foundation for the Advancement of Teaching (2005), and type of the institution that offered the course (public, private for-profit, private nonprofit).

Web Version of the RAIQ

Roblyer and Wiencke's (2004) RAIQ was used in its complete original form, but with a different layout format suited for the Web. Specifically, the five elements or indicators for interactive qualities in a distance course were separately displayed, as opposed to the original matrix-like display. Following is a brief description of each element:

1. Social rapport-building designs for interaction. This element is measured by the strategies designed for social interaction among participants. The instructor has control of the strategies during the design and implementation phases of instruction.

2. Instructional designs for interaction. This element is measured by the activities "designed to encourage, support, and even require interaction [among participants]" (p. 87). The instructor has control of the activities during the design and implementation phases of instruction.

3. Interactivity of technology resources. This element is measured by the various levels of interactivity that are offered by various technologies. The technologies "become meaningful components to promote interaction only in the context of course designs that make effective use of them" (p. 88).

4. Evidence of learner engagement. This element is measured by "the number of students who reply and who initiate messages on a frequent basis; send messages both when required and spontaneously; and send detailed, informative, well-developed communications that are responsive to discussion purposes" (p. 89).

Table 7.1.   Highest Levels of Interactive Qualities in a Distance Course in the Rubric for Assessing Interactive Qualities in Distance Courses (RAIQ)

Element in the RAIQ	Description
1. Social/rapport-building designs for interaction	In addition to providing for exchanges of personal information and encouraging student-student and instructor-student interaction, the instructor provides ongoing course structures designed to promote social rapport among students and instructor.
2. Instructional designs for interaction	In addition to the requiring students to communicate with the instructor, instructional activities require students to develop products by working together cooperatively (e.g., in pairs or small groups) and share results and feedback with other groups in the class.
3. Interactivity of technology resources	In addition to technologies to allow two-way exchanges of text information, visual technologies such as two-way video or videoconferencing technologies allow synchronous voice & visual communications between instructor and students and among students.
4. Evidence of learner engagement	By end of course, all or nearly all students (90-100%) are both *replying to and initiating messages*, both when required and voluntarily; messages are detailed, responsive to topics, and are well-developed communications.
5. Evidence of instructor engagement	Instructor responds to all student queries; responses are always prompt, that is, within 24 hours; feedback always offers detailed analysis of student work and suggestions for improvement, along with additional hints and information to supplement learning.

Source: Roblyer and Wiencke (2004). Copyright 2004 by M. D. Roblyer. Adapted with permission.

5.   Evidence of instructor engagement. Measured by the "consistent, timely, and useful feedback to students [from the instructor]" (p. 89).

Optimal Class-Size Questions and Comments

Two open-ended questions were formulated to collect instructors' perceptions of (a) an optimal class size that allows for the actual level of interaction in their most recently taught online course, and (b) an optimal class size that allows for the highest level of interaction in the RAIQ (i.e., a maximum score of 25). Table 7.1 presents the interactive qualities that characterize a course with the highest level of interaction in the RAIQ. An open-ended question was formulated to collect participants' comments that they believed would contribute to the study.

Data Analysis

Data collected from Surveyor were input to a spreadsheet. The spreadsheet data were then input to SPSS Student version 7 for Windows to obtain descriptive statistics. Following is a description of how the data were organized and analyzed:

1. Determining levels of interactive qualities in the RAIQ. The overall level of a course's interactive qualities can be low, moderate, or high (Roblyer & Wiencke, 2004). To obtain the course's interactive level, points were assigned to each level-option under each of the five elements. There were five options of levels under each element: low, minimum, moderate, above-average, and high. Low interactive qualities were worth 1 point; minimum interactive qualities were worth 2 points; moderate interactive qualities were worth 3 points; above-average interactive qualities were worth 4 points; and high interactive qualities were worth 5 points. Participants could only select one level per element. The five resulting scores (i.e., one per element) were totaled, and according to the interval where the total fell, the course had one of three interactive levels: low (1 to 9 points), moderate (10 to 17 points), or high (18 to 25 points). This calculation was done for each entry in the spreadsheet (i.e., for each online course described by respondent) and saved as the course's level of interactive qualities.

2. Determining class sizes. Descriptive statistics were obtained for class sizes of respondents' most recently taught online courses. Class-size statistics were grouped according to (a) the course's level of interactive qualities, (b) academic level of the online course's program, (c) type of institution that offered the course, and (d) Carnegie classification of the institution that offered the course.

3. Determining perceived optimal class sizes. Respondents' perceptions of optimal class sizes were grouped according to levels of interactive qualities previously calculated, and to the highest possible level in the RAIQ. Hence, four possible data groups of perceived optimal class sizes resulted according to the course's level of interactive qualities. Descriptive statistics were obtained for each group of data. Subgroups were analyzed and descriptive statistics were obtained according to (a) the course's level of interactive qualities, (b) academic level of the online course's program, (c) type of institution that offered the course, and (d) Carnegie classification of the institution that offered the course.

DISCUSSION OF RESULTS

From 154 CSIQ response-cases to the CSIQ, 23 were not analyzed. The reasons for removing the 23 cases were as follows: (a) 5 respondents provided a negative answer to the initial question of the CSIQ, indicating that they did not meet the inclusion criteria (e.g., they had teacher assistants, they had not taught in an American institution, or the face-to-face component of the online course was greater than 20%); (b) 17 respondents gave an affirmative answer to the initial question of the CSIQ, but did not answer the rest of the questions; (c) 1 respondent indicated a class size of 100, and the corresponding answers were removed because they were considered outliers. Therefore, the final sample was 131 ($N = 131$).

From 131 respondents, most (61.8%) were female, had doctoral degrees (82.4%), taught in the area of education (47.3%), on average perceived themselves as very experienced in online teaching (4.2 over 5), and had received formal training in online teaching (52.7%). Most of respondents' online courses were taught in public (71.8%), doctoral-research universities (68.7%), and in graduate programs (53.4% master's and 17.6% doctoral).

Following is a discussion of results related to the study's research questions. Results were interpreted bearing in mind demographics of respondents, the type of online courses studied, and the scope and purpose of the RAIQ and of the CSIQ.

What Are Typical Class Sizes of Online Courses?

Results from the CSIQ indicated that actual class sizes (CS) for the 131 respondents ranged from 4 to 81. The mode was 20 and the average was 22.8. Almost 62% of respondents' courses had 20 or fewer students, and only 2 courses had a CS greater than 65. From the results, it can be concluded that for online courses, as defined in the study, the average CS was approximately 23, the most frequent CS for an online course was 20, and most courses (61.8%) had a CS smaller than or equal to 20.

According to data posted in *U.S. News & World Report* ("E-learning," 2005), accredited higher education institutions that offer online graduate-programs in education have reported class size limits of 23, on average. Even though the CSIQ did not examine the accreditation status of the institution, the average CS identified by the CSIQ is consistent with the data posted in *U.S. News & World Report*. On the other hand, the NEA (2000) reported that one third of online courses had 20 or fewer students, and two thirds had 21 to 40. Similarly, according to the Higher Education and Policy Council of the American Federation of Teachers (2000), only

Table 7.2.   Characteristics of Online Courses According to Respondents to the Class Size and Interaction Questionnaire (N = 131)

Measure	Min	Max	Average	Standard Deviation
Actual class size	4	81	22.8	13.7
Number of weeks	4	20	14.2	2.8
Interactive level*	9	25	18.8	3.8
Semester credits	1	6	3.2	0.7

Note: Min = Smallest score reported, Max = Largest score reported.
*Interactive level = Sum of points of the five elements of interactive qualities described in the questionnaire; low interactive level = 1 to 9 points, moderate interactive level = 10 to 17 points, high interactive level = 18 to 25 points.

Table 7.3.   Descriptive Statistics for Class Sizes of Online Courses According to Respondents to the Class Size and Interaction Questionnaire (N = 131)

Classification	Min.	Max.	Average	Standard Deviation	n
Carnegie Classification of Institution					
Doctoral	4	81	24.7	15.4	90
Master's	4	37	19.5	7.4	29
Other	8	35	17.3	7.7	12
Type of Institution					
Public	4	81	24.4	15.1	94
Private for-profit	8	35	20.3	7.7	10
Private non-profit	7	45	18.4	8.8	24
Other	13	23	17.0	5.3	3
Academic Level of Online Courses					
Bachelor's	7	81	31.5	18.3	38
Master's	4	55	19.7	9.7	70
Doctoral	7	35	18.0	7.8	23
Interactive Level of Online Courses*					
Low	8	20	14.0	8.5	2
Moderate	7	81	25.8	15.9	43
High	4	65	21.6	12.4	86

Note: Min = Smallest score reported, Max = Largest score reported.
*Interactive level = Sum of points of the five elements of interactive qualities described in the questionnaire; low interactive level = 1 to 9 points, moderate interactive level = 10 to 17 points, high interactive level = 18 to 25 points.

one third of instructors taught online courses with 20 or fewer students. In contrast, results of this study indicated that most respondents (61.8%) reported a class size of 20 or less, and only a 27.8% reported a class size from 21 to 40. It seems that more recent courses, taught during the years 2000 and 2005, are smaller than those taught before the year of publication of the NEA report. However, the specific characteristics of the online courses studied (see Table 7.2) and the limitations of the sample of participants prevent making a generalization to other distance courses. Therefore, it is not appropriate to draw conclusions about typical class sizes of online courses from comparing these studies.

Table 7.3 presents descriptive statistics for class sizes. A more in-depth analysis indicated that, in public doctoral-research universities, the largest average class size resulted for courses in bachelor's programs (43.5), and the smallest average class size resulted for courses in doctoral programs (15). These results were to be expected. Public institutions usually have higher enrollments than private institutions, and bachelor's programs usually enroll more students than doctoral programs. Hence, class sizes were expected to be larger for online courses in bachelor's programs, and for courses in public institutions.

What Are Typical Levels of Interactive Qualities in Online Courses?

It was assumed that online courses may have different interactive qualities and, hence, different interactive levels (IL), as measured by the RAIQ. Results from the CSIQ showed that most respondents (65.6%) perceived that their online course had a high IL, 32.8% a moderate IL, and only a 1.5% a low IL. On average, respondents perceived that their online courses had a high-interactive level (18.8 over 25 possible points). Specifically, the online courses studied could be characterized as having above-average levels of social/rapport-building designs for interaction, of instructional designs for interaction, of evidence of learner engagement, and of evidence of instructor engagement. On the other hand, these online courses could be characterized as having a moderate level of interactivity and of technology resources. The standard deviation of interactive levels was 3.8. From these results, it can be concluded that almost all online courses (98.5%), that were taught during the years of 2000 and 2005, were moderately to highly interactive without much variability in their interactive qualities, as measured by the RAIQ.

Some respondents to the CSIQ commented that the RAIQ might not be an appropriate instrument to measure interaction in online courses. Moreover, respondents who commented about the interactive level in online courses indicated that the highest levels, as measured by the RAIQ, are not necessarily needed, feasible, or desirable. Some indicated that a high level of interaction did not necessarily require synchronous communication, video technologies, or such a demanding instructor engagement as described for the highest level of the RAIQ (e.g., 24 hours turnaround response time and instructor's detailed responses to every student query). As previously mentioned, it was not implied in this study that the highest interactive level was needed or desirable in an online course. The purpose of the study was to use the RAIQ to determine interactive levels of online courses and obtain information about class sizes according to these levels.

Most respondents described their online course as moderately and highly interactive. Also, results indicated no statistical relationship between CS and IL (see Table 7.4). The latter might indicate that CS does not seem to have an effect on the course's interactive qualities. Results also indicated that the average CS (21.6) of highly interactive online courses was smaller than the average CS (25.8) of moderately interactive ones. Generally speaking, because it has not been agreed upon in the literature what actually constitutes a *large* or a *small* online class, it cannot be concluded from these results that a small CS allows a higher IL than a large CS, or that highly interactive online courses have smaller CS than moderately interactive ones. From the results, it can be concluded that, even though highly interactive online courses that were studied had a smaller average CS than moderately interactive courses, CS does not seem to be related to the level of interaction. Respondents commented that other factors, which were also suggested in the literature, might affect interaction. Some of the mentioned factors were instructors' time commitment and workload in face-to-face traditional activities (e.g., administrative and teaching), course content, students' characteristics, and limitations of technology.

The CSIQ did not measure instructors' teaching-time commitment or workload in traditional face-to-face-activities. The CSIQ measured the number of online courses taught during the same term (NOCT) including the online course described. The NOCT did not measure instructor's workload completely, but it was considered to be an indicator of instructor's commitment in online teaching during an academic term. The average NOCT was 2.4 and ranged from 1 to 9. Most respondents' (66.9%) taught, at most, two online courses at the same time. No relationship was found between the interactive level and NOCT (see Table 7.4).

The CSIQ did not examine characteristics of students, per se. However, to some extent, the academic level of the course is related to the type of students (e.g., students are usually younger in bachelor's programs than in graduate programs). Common wisdom suggests that graduate

Table 7.4. Intercorrelations for Selected Measures Examined With the Class Size and Interaction Questionnaire (*N* = 131)

Measure	Age	CS	YTHE	NOCT	LE	OCS	OCSL5	IL	NCST	FT	YTO
Age	—										
CS	-.25**	—									
YTHE	.51**	-.12	—								
NOCT	-.05	.06	.12	—							
LE	.13	-.03	.17	.34**	—						
OCS	-.19*	.79**	-.07	.00	.04	—					
OCSL5	-.20*	.66**	-.14	-.02	.08	.81**	—				
IL	.04	-.12	-.13	.13	.25**	-.18*	.08	—			
NCST	-.03	.02	.07	.15	.08	.03	-.02	-.09	—		
FT	.05	-.16	.06	-.01	.01	-.15	-.10	.01	-.01	—	
YTO	.06	.03	.28**	.70**	.43**	.02	.02	.14	.13	.09	—

Note: CS = class size, YTHE = years teaching higher education, NOCT = number of online courses taught, LE = level of expertise, OCS = optimal class size, OCSL5 = optimal class size for highest interactive levels, IL = interactive level of the course, NCST = number of online courses taught during the same term, FT = formal training in online teaching, YTO = years teaching online courses.

*p < 0.05. **p < .01.

courses are more interactive, or should be more interactive, than under-graduate courses. However, results from the CSIQ indicated only two online courses with a low interactive level, and both were reported at the master's academic level. Fifty-nine percent of the total number of highly interactive courses was taught in master's programs, and 21% in doctoral programs. Bachelor's online courses were reported as moderately (55.3%) and highly (44.7%) interactive. Furthermore, no relationship was found when analyzing differences among average scores of interactive levels within groups of courses, per academic level.

These results indicate that there is not a strong relationship between the academic level of the course and the interactive levels of the studied online courses. Moderate and high interactive qualities reported for bachelor's online courses might be a reflection of younger students that have embraced technology-meditated courses in different ways than, perhaps older, graduate students. The assumption that traditional students at the bachelor's level are not as interactive as graduate students might not be applicable for online undergraduates. Nonetheless, highly interactive online courses were more frequent in graduate level programs than in undergraduate programs.

What Are Instructors' Perceptions of Optimal Class Sizes for Online Courses With Different Levels of Interactive Qualities?

In distance education, anecdotal class-size evidence is mostly related to two aspects that Simonson (2004) denominated "myths of distance education" (p. 56): (a) It takes more time to teach online, therefore smaller classes are needed—the "more-work myth" usually advocated by instructors; and (b) as long as the course is organized right, it does not matter how big the class is because there is no physical space limitation—a myth usually advocated by administrators. Results from this study seem to support the more-work myth of distance education.

Respondents indicated that, on average, an optimal class size (OCS = 18.9) should be smaller than the actual class size (CS = 22.8). Results indicated a strong positive correlation (r = .79) between CS and OCS to support this conclusion. On the other hand, a very low negative correlation (r = −.18) between the interactive level and OCS seems to indicate that the higher the interactive level the smaller the OCS. Hence, it can be concluded that, in general, respondents perceived that a smaller OCS than CS was needed to allow for moderate and high levels of interactive qualities in their online courses. Table 7.5 presents more detailed descriptive statistics for optimal class sizes for online courses.

Table 7.5.   Descriptive Statistics for Optimal Class Sizes for Online Courses According to Respondents to the Class Size and Interaction Questionnaire (N = 131)

Category	OCS				OCSL5				n
	Min.	Max.	M	SD	Min.	Max.	M	SD	
Interactive Level of Online Courses									
Low	15	25	20.0	7.1	6	15	10.5	6.4	2
Moderate	10	80	21.1	15.9	5	40	15.6	6.2	43
High	7	50	17.7	7.6	6	50	16.1	6.9	86
Carnegie Classification of Institution									
Doctoral	7	80	19.4	10.1	5	50	16.4	6.9	90
Master's	8	40	18.2	6.3	8	40	15.1	6.6	29
Other	8	35	16.2	6.8	8	35	13.5	3.9	12
Academic Level of Online Courses									
Bachelor's	10	80	25.3	12.6	5	40	19.3	8.4	38
Master's	7	50	17.0	5.7	7	50	14.8	5.8	70
Doctoral	7	20	14.0	3.4	8	20	13.5	2.8	23
Type of Institution									
Public	7	80	20.2	10.1	5	50	16.6	7.4	94
Private F-profit	10	25	15.9	4.5	10	20	13.9	3.0	10
Private N-profit	8	25	15.5	4.1	8	20	13.9	3.4	24
Other	10	20	15.0	5.0	8	20	14.3	6.0	3

Note: OCS = Perceived optimal class size of online course according to its interactive qualities, OCSL5 = Perceived optimal class size of online course if it had the highest level of interactive qualities in the questionnaire, *Min* = Smallest score reported, *Max* = Largest score reported, *M* = Average of scores, *SD* = Standard deviation of scores.

A more detailed analysis of the data revealed that 23% of respondents believed that the optimal class size should be greater than the actual class size. Out of this 23%, 73% taught courses with an actual class size less than or equal to 15. Most of these courses (74%) were perceived as highly interactive. This might indicate that, for class sizes of less than or equal to 15, most respondents felt that more students were necessary to better achieve the highly interactive qualities present in their online courses.

Hence, from the results of this study, it cannot be absolutely determined that higher interactive courses, as measured by the RAIQ, require small classes. These findings might be an indicative that instructors perceived that they needed smaller classes than what they actually had in order to better achieve moderate and high interactive level, but large enough (e.g., larger than 15) perhaps to increase the level of interaction in low-interactive courses.

In addition to identifying a smaller average of optimal class sizes than average actual class sizes, results indicated that online courses at the highest interactive levels should have an average class size of 15.9, which was smaller than the average optimal class size (18.9). Also, a strong positive correlation ($r = .81$) between optimal class size and optimal class size for highest interaction was found (see Table 7.4). A closer examination of the data revealed that every respondent perceived that a smaller class size than the optimal class size was needed to achieve the highest possible level of interactive qualities in the RAIQ. The latter might indicate that respondents perceived that achieving the highest levels of interaction in the RAIQ might demand from them more effort per student and, thus, teaching a course with the highest interactive qualities would require a much smaller class size.

Results from this study seem to support the literature that reports on instructors' beliefs that online teaching takes more time or effort than face-to-face courses. On the other hand, experimental studies have reported mixed results about online teaching time or effort. The literature has also suggested that perhaps this more-work perception is because of instructors' unfamiliarity with technology, or little experience in online teaching. Perhaps less-experienced instructors prefer smaller classes. However, results from this study indicated no relationship between instructors' level of expertise and both types of perceived optimal class sizes (i.e., OCS and OCSL5). The before-mentioned precludes concluding that teaching experience is related to instructors' perceptions of smaller classes to allow for higher levels of interactive qualities in online courses.

On the other hand, as seen in Table 7.4, a very low negative relationship resulted between respondents' age and CS ($r = -.25$), between age and OCS ($r = -.19$), and between age and OCSL5 ($r = -.20$). These correlations indicate that older instructors perhaps prefer smaller classes than do younger instructors. No statistical relationship was found between respondents' age and their perceived level of expertise in online teaching. Also, the number of years teaching in higher education, the number of online courses taught, the number of years teaching online courses, and the level of expertise were not related to any measure of class size. In traditional face-to-face settings, it is customary for department heads to assign larger classes to new instructors and smaller classes to instructors with more years teaching experience. Nonetheless, results of the study indicated that for online teaching, regardless of any of the studied indicator of teaching experience in higher education, instructor's age was the factor related to CS. These results might indicate that, regardless of instructors' level of expertise in online teaching, older instructors taught smaller classes, and preferred smaller OCS and OCSL5 than younger instructors.

IMPLICATIONS FOR RESEARCH AND PRACTICE

The theoretical framework for this study was Roblyer and Wiencke's (2004) RAIQ, which was based on several theories of interaction. Because of the applied nature of the study, results had implications for practice. Such implications are mainly related to the decision-making of class size-related policies that meet accreditation standards for online programs.

Accreditation is the means by which American higher education institutions are evaluated for quality. Institutions seek accreditation through their policies, among which are class size-related policies. As stated in the literature review, regional accrediting commissions have developed a set of guidelines, or quality assurance standards, to reflect current best practices in electronically offered programs that affect more than 3,000 colleges and universities in the United States (CHEA, 2001). The following standard exalts the importance of interaction in the design of distance courses and programs: "The importance of appropriate interaction (synchronous or asynchronous) between instructor and students and among students is reflected in the design of the program and its courses, and in the technical facilities and services provided" (WCET, 2000, p. 8).

From the mentioned standards, a main aspect that can be related to results of the study is how appropriate interaction and effective teaching can be achieved through the design of online courses. Interaction has been a concept defined and measured in multiple ways in different practical and theory-based publications. Hence, the appropriateness of interaction can be a vague term that may be measured in any way an institution decides. If the appropriateness of interaction is to be measured by the RAIQ, and moderate and high interaction were appropriate levels, then almost all online courses studied had an appropriate interaction. However, if the appropriate level is the highest possible level in the RAIQ, then very few courses met this standard for quality. Moreover, most respondents commented that the highest level in the RAIQ was not necessarily needed, feasible, or desirable.

Hence, two major implications for practice can be derived from this study: accrediting organizations might need to clearly indicate how they expect institutions to measure the appropriateness of interaction; and the highest interactive level of the RAIQ is not always an appropriate level of interaction for an online course. Inherent to these implications is that a design of the online course that reflects the appropriateness of interaction is subject to the characteristics the course. Once again, if the RAIQ is to be used to assess the design of the course through each of its five elements, then multiple combinations (i.e., scores for each element in the RAIQ) yield a certain level of interaction. That is, each element contributes to determine the level of interaction of the course. Thus, determining whether the design reflects an appropriate interaction is a complex task.

Results from this study, in addition to the literature about interaction and class size, could be used by accrediting organizations to indicate that different levels of interaction can be appropriate for an online course, and that different course designs can allow for appropriate levels of interaction. Furthermore, the literature and research does not support that more interaction in online courses is necessarily more conducive to learning, party because of the different ways to define and measure interaction.

Regarding class size and interaction, common wisdom has held that smaller class sizes for online courses allow for more interaction. In their recommended standard for distance education courses, the AFT (2000) stated that "class size should encourage a high degree of interactivity [and that] given the time commitment involved in teaching through distance education, smaller class sizes should be considered, particularly at the inception of a new course" (p. 11). However, experimental research has not supported that smaller classes allow for a high level of interactivity. Furthermore, it has not been agreed upon in the literature what actually constitutes a large or small online class. In essence, determining what actually constitutes a large or a small class is a complex task that does not depend on absolute criteria, but the perceptions of instructors might give some insight to approaching the problem. In this sense, results from this study could be used to set practical lower and upper bounds of class sizes for online courses with moderately interactive and highly interactive levels.

Other implications for practice are similarly related to institutional policy-making. Results indicated no statistical relationship between actual class size and the interactive level of the studied online courses, but results did indicate a low negative correlation between optimal class size and interactive level. Generally speaking, respondents seemed to have perceived that they would require more time and commitment if the number of students increased, when they indicated smaller optimal class sizes to achieve the highest levels of interaction in the RAIQ. However, it cannot be concluded from these results that class size alone determines the levels of interaction in an online course.

Respondents to the CSIQ commented that other factors might determine the level of interaction in online courses. Some of the mentioned factors were instructors' time commitment, instructors' workload in face-to-face traditional activities, and the role of the adjunct figure as part-time faculty. In this regard, Gellman-Danley and Fetzner (1998) considered that policies related to labor-management (e.g., class size, assignment of full-time or adjunct faculty, and workload) were among the most difficult to develop and included the toughest questions to ask. Johnstone (2004) raised the question on whether full-time faculty members are completely ready to adapt to online teaching, or whether they were really the best ones to assist students online. The figure of readily skillful professionals, as part-time adjunct faculty, is an alternative for institutions to fill this possible gap. As Johnstone pointed out,

> One institutional practice that is challenged by distance learning focuses on who should be doing the "teaching" [and that] if part-time faculty members, or adjunct faculty, are to be the core workforce for online instruction, then institutions that use a lot of online teaching may need to develop a new category of professional employees. (p. 396)

Nonetheless, adjuncts usually hold other full-time jobs that prevent them from trying to reach higher interactive levels in their online courses, regardless of class size. Respondents to the CSIQ commented the following: "If I'm teaching a class (as an adjunct) in addition to my 'regular' full-time job, I may not incorporate as many interactive activities, regardless of class size" (Respondent 32); and "most adjunct professors have other jobs and tend to do feedback two or three times a week ... not daily" (Respondent 7). Incorporating this kind of professional workforce, in addition to the new required roles of full faculty, suggest that institutions need to develop better ways to determine teaching workloads that adequately measures the effort, time-commitment, and dedication of the instructor in online teaching tasks, especially interacting with individual students.

RECOMMENDATIONS FOR FUTURE RESEARCH

More research in online education is needed to support or reject the assumption that smaller class sizes are needed for higher interactive levels, or even that higher interactive levels are more conducive to learning than lower interactive levels. Examining the following questions might support or reject the commonly held belief that more interaction is better for learning, and might also help examine whether what instructors perceived as optimal class size is better for interaction and learning outcomes: Is there a relationship between class size and learning outcomes? Is there a relationship between the level of interaction, as measured by the

RAIQ, and learning outcomes? Are there significant differences in levels of interaction and learning outcomes among different online courses with the same perceived optimal class size? Are there significant differences in levels of interaction and learning outcomes among similar online courses with different perceived optimal class size?

On the other hand, respondents' perception of smaller optimal class size than actual class size, on average, might be an indicator that instructors believed that a larger class size implies more time commitment and workload. Nonetheless, class size itself might not be an aspect that affects online-learning outcomes. The literature in traditional education has suggested that what happens in the class is what is actually affected by the class size. Respondents commented that the characteristics of the online course and of the students, as well as instructor's workload, are elements that affect interaction in an online course. As the IHEP (2000) suggested for online courses, "Maximum class size relates more to faculty course workload than student outcomes. It appears, therefore, that a specific benchmark for class size is ill advised, and much more experimentation needs to be conducted" (p. 18).

Hence, additional research questions can be examined to determine relationships between instructor's workload and online class size: Is there a significant difference between online-teaching time commitments among online courses with the same class size and taught by instructors with different workloads? Is there a significant difference between online-teaching time commitments among online courses with different class sizes and taught by instructors with similar workloads? How is online teaching time-commitment affected by class size? How is interactivity affected by the overall workload of instructors?

Results of this study did not support the commonly held assumption that graduate students interact more than undergraduate students. Considering students' characteristics is paramount when designing any instruction. Online instruction poses new challenges to designers because younger generations of students have practically embraced communications technology as living style. Online education requires a self-motivated student capable of using communications technology, regardless of the program's academic level. Both types of students (i.e., graduate and undergraduate) in online courses that were offered no more than 5 years ago were perhaps more technology savvy than students of online courses that were offered longer ago. Results indicated a larger average class size for undergraduate online courses, and that undergraduate online courses were also moderately and highly interactive, as measured by the RAIQ. Future research could be conducted to support or reject the assumption that larger class sizes are adequate for younger undergraduate students because, perhaps, they do not interact as much as older graduate students.

Some of the before recommended research issues involve exploring the interactive level of online courses, as measured by the RAIQ. Other instruments that have been reported in the literature can also be used to measure interaction. Moreover, respondents to the CSIQ commented about possible limitations of the RAIQ to measure interaction. Results of this study indicated no relationship between actual class size and interactive levels of the studied online courses, but perhaps different indicators of interactive levels would show a relationship. Thus, future research is recommended to examine the relationship between interaction and class size as measured by other instruments.

Qualitative research can also contribute to examine the optimal class-size problem. From the standpoint of quality in online courses, students and instructors might have different perspectives of what is an optimal class size. On the other hand, as respondents to the CSIQ commented, administrators usually establish class-size limits and then the instructor must accommodate the teaching methods accordingly. If results of optimal class size from this study are taken as benchmarks, a qualitative study might examine the question: How do instructors and students behave in similar online courses with the average optimal class size?

An assumption that was derived from the literature is that perhaps less experienced instructors prefer smaller classes. Results of this study indicated that regardless of instructors' level of expertise in online teaching, older instructors taught and preferred smaller classes than did younger instructors. Also, more experienced instructors seemed to have perceived their courses as having higher levels of interactive qualities. Some research questions that arise from these results are related to instructor's age: If older instructors perceive themselves as having similar levels of experience in online teaching than younger instructors, why do they prefer teaching smaller classes? If older instructors can achieve similar interactive levels in their online courses, why do they prefer teaching smaller classes? Should department heads assign larger classes to younger faculty members?

CONCLUSIONS

Results of this study were intended to be practical. Optimal class sizes from the perspective of the instructor were thought to be helpful to policymakers who are trying to establish class-size limits for online courses. Limitations of the study were inherent to the research method employed (i.e., recruitment of participants, availability and credibility of respondents, and limitations of the instruments), and results are likely to be applicable to online courses as defined in the study. Future research is recommended to examine class size and interaction from the perspectives of administrators and of students.

Findings indicate that, even though the actual class sizes of the studied online courses were not related to their actual interactive qualities and that most respondents perceived their online courses as moderately and highly interactive, respondents still believed that they needed smaller classes to achieve higher interactive levels (i.e., an average class size of 22.8 versus a perceived average optimal class size of 18.9). Furthermore, the data indicate that every respondent believed that even smaller class sizes were needed to achieve the highest interactive level possible in the RAIQ (i.e., an average of 15.6).

Because interaction is a concept that has been measured in different ways in research and practice, accrediting organizations might need to clearly indicate how an institution is to measure for appropriate interaction reflected in the design of the online course in order to meet quality standards. Also, institutions should take recommendations from consortia cautiously. Specifically, recommendations of having smaller classes to allow for high interactivity because it has not been supported by research and it has not been agreed upon what actually constitutes a large or a small online class. However, respondents perceived that smaller classes were needed to achieve the actual interactive level in their online courses. This might be because of a perceived increased effort if they had more students. Hence, for future research, it is highly recommended to examine the relationship between class size and instructors' workload and between class size and online teaching time commitment.

REFERENCES

Achilles, C. (1999). *Let's put kids first, finally: Getting class size right*. Thousand Oaks, CA: Corwin Press.

Accrediting Commission of Career Schools and Colleges of Technology. (2004). *ACCSCT standards of accreditation*. Retrieved January 14, 2005, from http://www.accsct.org/library/fullstandards.pdf

American Association of University Professors. (n.d.). *Sample distance education policy & contract language*. Retrieved September 9, 2004, from http://www.aaup.org/AAUP/issues/DE/sampleDE.htm

American Federation of Teachers. (2000). *Distance education: Guidelines for good practice*. Washington, DC: Author. Retrieved April 7, 2004, from http://www.aft.org/pubs-reports/higher_ed/distance.pdf

Anderson, T. (2003). Modes of interaction in distance education: Recent developments and research questions. In M. G. Moore & W. G. Anderson (Eds.), *Handbook of distance education* (pp. 129-144). Mahwah, NJ: Erlbaum.

Bates, A. (2000). *Managing technological change*. San Francisco: Jossey-Bass.

Bates, A., & Poole, G. (2003). *Effective teaching with technology in higher education: Foundations for success*. San Francisco: Jossey-Bass.

Boettcher, J., & Conrad, R. (2004). *Faculty guide for moving teaching and learning to the Web* (2nd ed.). Phoenix, AZ: League for Innovation.

Borden, V., & Burton, K. (1999, May/June). *The impact of class size on student performance in introductory courses*. Paper presented at the annual forum of the Association for Institutional Research, Seattle, WA. (ERIC Document Reproduction Service No. ED433782)

Berge, Z., & Muilenburg, L. (2001). Obstacles faced at various stages of capability regarding distance education in institutions of higher education. *TechTrends*, 45(4), 40-45. (ERIC Document Reproduction Service No. EJ631362)

Carnegie Foundation for the Advancement of Teaching. (2005). *Category definitions*. Retrieved February 2, 2005, from http://carnegiefoundation.org/Classification/CIHE2000/defNotes/Definitions.htm

Council for Higher Education Accreditation. (2001). *Fact sheet #2: The role of accreditation and assuring quality in electronically delivered distance learning*. Retrieved April 29, 2004, from http://www.chea.org/pdf/fact_sheet_2_dist_learn_02.pdf

DiBiase, D. (2000). Is distance teaching more work or less? *The American Journal of Distance Education*, 14(3), 6-20.

E-learning, online graduate degrees: Education regionally accredited. (2005). Retrieved May 29, 2005, from http://www.usnews.com/usnews/edu/elearning/tables/edu_reg.htm

Fowler, F. J., Jr. (1993). Survey research methods (2nd ed.). In L. Brickman & D. J. Rog (Series Eds.), *Applied social research methods series: Vol. 1*. Newbury Park, CA: Sage.

Fulford, C. P., & Zhang, S. (1993). Perceptions of interaction. *The American Journal of Distance Education*, 7(3), 8-21.

Gall, M., Gall, J., & Borg, W. (2003). *Educational research: An introduction* (7th ed.). Boston: Allyn & Bacon.

Gellman-Danley, B., & Fetzner, M. (1998). Asking the really tough questions: Policy issues for distance learning. *Online Journal of Distance Learning Administration*, 1(1). Retrieved April 29, 2004, from http://www.westga.edu/~distance/danley11.html

Gilbert, S. (1995). Quality education: Does class size matter? *Association of Universities and Colleges of Canada research file*, 1(1). Retrieved June 2, 2004, from http://www.aucc.ca/_pdf/english/publications/researchfile/1995-96/vol1n1_e.pdf

Gresh, K., & Mrozowski, S. (2000, October). *Faculty/student interaction at a distance: Seeking balance*. Paper presented at EDUCAUSE 2000: Thinking IT Through, Nashville, TN. (ERIC Document Reproduction Service No. ED452805)

Hancock, T. (1996). Effects of class size on college student achievement. *College Student Journal*, 30, 479-481.

Hislop, G., & Ellis, H. (2004). A study of faculty effort in online teaching [Electronic version]. *Internet and Higher Education, 7*(1), 15-31. Retrieved May 27, 2004, from http://www.sciencedirect.com

Johnstone, S. M. (2004). A policy perspective on learning theory and practice in distance education. In T. M. Duffy & J. R. Kirkley (Eds.), *Learner-centered theory and practice in distance education: Cases from higher education* (pp. 395-403). Mahwah, NJ: Erlbaum.

Ko, S., & Rossen, S. (2004). *Teaching online: A practical guide* (2nd ed.). Boston: Houghton Mifflin.

Laine, S., & Ward, J. (Eds.). (2000). *Using what we know, a review of the research on implementing class-size reduction: Initiatives for state and local policymakers.* Oak Brook, IL: North Central Regional Educational Laboratory.

Lewis, L., Alexander, D., & Farris, E. (1997). *Distance education in higher education institutions* (NCES 98-062).Washington, DC: U.S. Government Printing Office. Retrieved May 19, 2004, from http://nces.ed.gov/pubs98/98062.pdf

Moore, M. (1989). Three types of interaction. *The American Journal of Distance Education, 3*(2), 1-6.

Moore, M., & Kearsley, G. (2005). *Distance education: A systems view* (2nd ed.). Belmont, CA: Wadsworth.

Morgan, B. (2000). *Is distance learning worth it? Helping to determine the costs of online courses.* (ERIC Document Reproduction Service No. ED446611)

National Education Association. (2000). *A survey of traditional and distance learning higher education members.* Washington, DC: Author. Retrieved April 28, 2004, from http://www.nea.org/he/abouthe/dlstudy.pdf

Olson, C. (2002). Leadership in online education: Strategies for effective online administration and governance. In K. Rudestam & J. Schoenholtz-Read (Eds.), *Handbook of online learning: Innovations in higher education and corporate training* (pp. 237-256). Thousand Oaks, CA: Sage.

Parker, A. (2003). Motivation and incentives for distance faculty. *Online Journal of Distance Learning Administration, 6*(3). Retrieved April 27, 2004, from http://www.westga.edu/~distance/ojdla/fall63/parker63.htm

Pascarella, E., & Terenzini, P. (1991). *How college affects students.* San Francisco: Jossey-Bass.

Pritchard, I. (1999). *Reducing class size: What do we know?* (SAI 98-3097) [Electronic version]. Washington, DC: U.S. Department of Education. Retrieved May 7, 2004, from http://www.ed.gov/pubs/ReducingClass/title.html

Raimondo, H., Esposito, L., & Gershenberg, I. (1990). Introductory class size and student performance in intermediate theory courses. *Journal of Economic Education, 21*(4), 369-381.

Roblyer, M., & Wiencke, W. (2003). Design and use of a rubric to assess and encourage interactive qualities in distance courses. *The American Journal of Distance Education, 17*(2), 77-98.

Roblyer, M., & Wiencke, W. (2004). Exploring the interaction equation: Validating a rubric to assess and encourage interaction in distance courses. *Journal of Asynchronous Learning Networks, 8*(4). Retrieved December 21, 2004, from http://www.sloan-c.org/publications/jaln/v8n4/v8n4_roblyer.asp

Schonlau, M., Fricker, R., & Elliot, M. (2001). *Conducting research surveys via e-mail and the Web*. Retrieved December 8, 2004, from http://www.rand.org/publications/MR/MR1480

Simonson, M. (2004). Class size: Where is the research? *Distance Learning, 1*(4), 56.

Sellani, R., & Harrington, W. (2002). Addressing administrator/faculty conflict in an academic online environment [Electronic version]. *The Internet and Higher Education, 5*(2), 131-145. Retrieved December 8, 2004, from http://www.sciencedirect.com/science/journal/10967516

Simonson, M., Smaldino, S., Albright, M., & Zvacek. S. (2003). *Teaching and learning at a distance: Foundations of distance education* (2nd ed.). Upper Saddle River, NJ: Prentice-Hall.

Sorensen, C., & Baylen, D. (2000). Perception versus reality: Views of interaction in distance education. *Quarterly Review of Distance Education, 1*(1), 45-58.

Southern Association of Colleges and Schools. (2000). *Best practices for electronically offered degree and certificate programs*. Retrieved April 27, 2004, from http://www.sacscoc.org/pdf/commadap.pdf

Sugrue, B., Rietz, T., & Hasen, S. (1999). Distance learning: Relationships among class size, instructor location, student perceptions, and performance. *Performance Improvement Quarterly, 12*(3), 44-57.

Thomas, E. (1984). *Class size*. Eugene, OR: ERIC Clearinghouse on Educational Management. (ERIC Document Reproduction Service No. ED259454)

Toth, L., & Montagna, L. (2002). Class size and achievement in higher education: A summary of current research. *College Student Journal, 36*(2), 253-260.

United Nations Educational, Scientific and Cultural Organization. (1997). *International standard classification of education: ISCED 1997*. Retrieved February 2, 2005, from http://www.unesco.org/education/information/nfsunesco/doc/isced_1997.htm

University of Illinois. (1999). *Teaching at an internet distance: The pedagogy of online teaching and learning*. Retrieved June 3, 2004, from http://www.vpaa.uillinois.edu/reports_retreats/tid_final-12-5.pdf

Visser, J. (2000). Faculty work in developing and teaching Web-based distance courses: A case study of time and effort. *The American Journal of Distance Education, 14*(3), 21-32.

Vrasidas, C., & McIsaac, M. S. (1999). Factors influencing interaction in an online course. *The American Journal of Distance Education, 13*(3), 22-36.

Wagner, E. (1994). In support of a functional definition of interaction. *The American Journal of Distance Education, 8*(2), 6-29.

Western Cooperative for Educational Telecommunications. (2000). *Statement of the Regional Accrediting Commissions on the evaluation of electronically offered degree and certificate programs and guidelines for the evaluation of electronically degree and certificate programs*. Retrieved January 14, 2004, from http://www.wcet.info/resources/publications/Guidelines.PDF

Wirt, J., Choy, S., Rooney, P., Provasnik, S., Sen, A., & Tobin, R. (2004). *The condition of education 2004* (NCES 2004–077). Washington, DC: National Center for Education Statistics. Retrieved March 3, 2005, from http://nces.ed.gov/pubs2004/2004077.pdf

Yacci, M. (2000). Interactivity demystified: A structural definition for distance education and intelligent computer-based instruction. *Educational Technology, 40*(4), 5-16.

CHAPTER 8

WHAT WORKS

Student Perceptions
of Effective Elements in Online Learning

Marcy Reisetter and Greg Boris

Online education holds great potential for rural states like South Dakota, which has been recognized for advances in distance education. To maximize the potential of online learning, design elements that students believe are needed for successful online learning experiences must be identified. In this study, we present the qualitative and quantitative results of a survey administered to students in 7 School of Education graduate courses at the University of South Dakota. Course coherence, clear goals, teacher voice, and extensive teacher feedback were the most important elements for learner success. Student-to-student communications ranked lower than expected in students' analysis of their experiences.

The market for distance education is growing and profitable, fueled by the potential of these approaches to provide access to higher education for an underserved group of individuals (Leasure, Davis, & Thievon, 2000). As this group values the asynchronous variety of online learning because of the flexibility it affords (Billings, Connors, & Skiba, 2001),

The Perfect Online Course: Best Practices for Designing and Teaching
pp. 157–178

many colleges and universities are racing to develop online learning in this "rapidly emerging cybereducation market" (Navarro & Shoemaker, 2000, p. 16). However, it is important to note that distance education is more than an issue of geography; it is an entirely new education environment in which learners and teachers are distanced from their typical expectations for the education process (Lally & Barrett, 1999). With appropriate modifications, many educators believe this mode of course delivery can be as effective as traditional approaches (Burch, 2001). Exactly what are these modifications and how can the content and processes of traditional education be effectively translated into the ecology of the Internet setting?

Advocates emphasize the more efficient and individualized instruction that can be tailored to meet unique needs, with emphasis placed on individual responsibility and development of self-regulation (Navarro & Shoemaker, 2000). It offers valued opportunities for individual pacing and interaction with course materials when necessary and convenient for the learner (Perreault, Walman, & Zhao, 2002). The mode is flexible and dynamic, placing the student rather than the teacher in control of the timing and communication (Burch, 2001).

Ewing, Dowling, and Coutts (1998) in their analysis of the STARS Project, explained that online delivery provides opportunities to apply constructivist theory because it encourages individual meaning making. In their analysis, six constructivist premises—that learning is contextual, demands active engagement, is collaborative, incorporates autonomy and control, includes personally preferred modes of learning, and results in individually meaningful constructions—are potential processes in online learning systems (Ewing et al., 1998). Critics, however, point to the lack of genuine interactions, depersonalization, and mechanical pedagogy that can characterize online course delivery (Navarro & Shoemaker, 2000).

Because the movement toward online learning appears to be inevitable, it is essential that colleges and universities carefully consider how to meet the growing demand for this mode without compromising the quality of student learning, (Lindner, Dooley, & Murphy, 2001). Improvement of the quality of online learning experiences has been the focus of many studies, with emphasis on understanding the changing student population, student learning, student satisfaction, the role of learning preferences, and design issues including course organization, communication, and the role of the online learning community. Retention in online courses has also become a matter of concern. A brief summary of current research of each of the topics follows.

CHANGING STUDENT POPULATION

An increasing number of students in higher education have work and family responsibilities in addition to their academic work (Bunn, 2001) and are trying to balance these responsibilities with their education goals. Studies show that the participants in online classes are typically females with some computer experience who have limited access to traditional education because of these responsibilities (Lim, 2001). Online learning gives a more diverse group of students the opportunity to participate in higher education (Bickle & Carroll, 2003.)

Advantages listed by participants in Web courses are often personal. Numerous studies indicate that convenience, time flexibility, lack of a commute to campus and the need to "sit through" a class, and opportunities to be independent learners are frequently given as reasons for participation in online education. (e.g. Bickle & Carroll, 2003; Billings et al., 2001; Cooper, 2001; Navarro & Shoemaker, 2000; Perreault et al., 2002).

In addition, those who choose online education describe themselves as self-directed learners (Garrison, 2003; Leasure et al., 2000). These individuals prefer to choose when and how to work, to be personally responsible for their learning, and to determine for themselves how much time they needed to spend on each task to be successful (Cooper, 2001).

Lindner et al. (2001) described three kinds of online learners: self-directed learners see program offerings as congruent with their own goals, motivated learners want to earn degrees, and personal learners simply relish the experience of learning. Navarro and Shoemaker (2000) found that online learners believe in an internal locus of control, in the efficacy of effort, and view themselves as independent learners.

STUDENT LEARNING

Although indications about the efficacy of electronically-delivered courses are mixed, most studies have found that there are no significant differences when learning outcomes of online students are compared with those of traditional students (Allen, Bourhis, Burrell, & Mabry, 2002; Leasure et al., 2000; Navarro & Shoemaker, 2000; Neuhauser, 2002; Thirunarayanan & Peres-Prado, 2001-2002). Characteristics such as gender, ethnic background, academic preparation, aptitude, or computer skills do not appear to influence success in online learning (Navarro & Shoemaker, 2000). However, Cooper (2001) found that one third of the students who were successful in an online course thought they would have learned more in a traditional setting.

STUDENT SATISFACTION

Learners consistently report satisfaction with online courses (e.g., Moore, 2002), which has been linked to course success (Sherry, Fulford, & Zhang, 1998). Researchers have discovered that the key factors related to learner satisfaction with this delivery mode include performance-based orientation, group work, collaborative strategies, clear instructor presence, opportunities for reflection, clear directions, a concentration on ideas rather than facts, and equal opportunities to participate (Moore, 2002). Computer self-efficacy plays a role in satisfaction (Lim, 2001), as does opportunity to ask questions (Cooper, 2001). Billings and colleagues (2001) found that older students tended to be more satisfied with online learning than were younger ones.

Although some studies have indicated that, overall, students prefer traditional delivery to distance format, measured satisfaction levels do not show significant differences (Allen et al., 2002). However, at least one study has shown that as more channels of information (such as video) are added, the less satisfied learners report they are (Allen et. al, 2002).

STUDENT PERCEPTIONS OF BARRIERS TO LEARNING

Muilenburg and Berge (2001) summarized three types of barriers that block students' success and persistence in online learning. These are: situational, including the individual's environment, responsibilities, and obligations; institutional, which include the procedures for access and use as determined by the offering institution; dispositional, including personal background, perceptions, attitudes, and selfregulation skills; and epistemological, comprised of sets of beliefs about the efficacy of the learning process via online delivery.

A critical area of difficulty for some learners is in the lack of face-to-face communication with professors and peers (Perreault et al., 2002) that they have typically relied on as an important component of learning. These learners cite isolation and lack of connectedness as detrimental to their learning; the more isolated they felt, the less satisfied they were (Billings et al., 2001).

Other problems (Perreault et al., 2002) have been in technical areas, particularly in communication with instructors and peers through Web resources. Course delivery issues sometimes result from course designs not adequately converted to the demands of the delivery system, inadequate course development, and students' occasional overestimation of their own technical skills.

LEARNING PREFERENCES

Common sense may imply that online education is more effective for students with some learning preferences, less so for others. Studies have not supported this position. No learning styles/preferences dimensions have been shown to make a difference in learning outcomes (Neuhauser, 2002), although it is possible that we simply have not identified the critical learning differences that have an impact (Dillon & Greene, 2003).

Allen and colleagues (2002) pointed out that students are inclined to self-select their preferred mode of learning. Those who recognize their need for face-to-face interactions do not enroll in online courses or opt out of them when they perceive that their learning will suffer in this mode.

DESIGN ISSUES

Two major issues frame recommendations for course designs. The first is course organization, accessibility, structure, and pedagogy, and the second is integrating online communications and interactions within the class structure.

Organization

Without exception, the many sets of recommendations for course design emphasize that content must be organized around goals (e.g., Billings et al., 2001; Hall, 2002). Courses must also be student centered, creating a customized environment that allows learners to make their own choices in pacing, activities, and time expenditure (Perreault et al., 2002). Important elements include multimedia lectures, threaded bulletin board discussions, online discussion groups, and immediate feedback assessment (Navarro & Shoemaker, 2000).

Palloff and Pratt (2001) identified supportive factors as good organization, clear procedure and expectations, clear timelines, understandable texts, helpful supplementary materials, and quickly accessible technical support.

Goldman, Williams, Sherwood, Hasselbring, and the Cognition and Technology Group at Vanderbilt (1999) University listed four principles for course design. Instruction should be: (1) organized around the solution of meaningful problems; (2) provide scaffolds for achieving meaningful learning; (3) provide opportunities for practice with feedback, revision and reflection; and (4) promote collaboration, sharing of expertise, and independent learning.

Studies also support the importance of understanding the shift in teacher role in order to create a design that works. Instructors provide materials, procedures, and activities, and give thorough feedback (Perreault et al., 2002). Online instructors should view the Web as more than just a way to deliver information. According to Hall (2002), it is a medium to support essential dialog among all participants through emphasis on discussion, interaction, adaptation, and reflection.

INTERACTIONS

There have been ongoing efforts to create the benefits of an online learning community in a virtual classroom (e.g., Rovai, 2001). Moore and Thompson (1997) distinguished between three types of interactions that are critical to successful online learning: learner-instructor, learner-learner, and learner-content interactions. These must be carefully built into course designs to enhance meaning making, move learners to critical thinking skills, aid processing of content, and support motivation (Navarro & Shoemaker, 2000; Rovai, 2001). These are not easy tasks; they require a balance of academic and social discussion, effective use of time, academic focus, clear procedures that support and enable full student participation, and careful structuring of learning events (Lally & Barrettt, 1999). Students consistently emphasize the role of instructor feedback in guiding their online learning, but also value an accessible course design in which directions for participation are clear and allow them to proceed independently (Billings et al., 2001).

RETENTION

In spite of the extensive research on components of successful online courses, course design principles, and positive information about student learning and satisfaction, the dropout rate in online learning remains a significant problem (Chyung, 2001; Lim, 2001, Navarro & Shoemaker, 2000). National trends reveal that as many as 50% of enrolled online students fail to complete their courses (King, 2002), indicating that problems exist in electronic delivery that impair students' management of courses delivered in this mode (Carr, 2000). Reasons for this dropout rate are not clearly understood (Berge & Mrozowski, 2001). Some research indicates that students drop out because of interest discrepancies, lack of confidence in their learning without face-to-face interactions, difficulties with online technical tools, and feeling overwhelmed by too much information available simultaneously (Chyung, 2001). Others seem to find the mode unattractive, the courses irrelevant to their interests, or have low satisfaction with the nature of the online interactions (Chyung, 2001), particularly with lack of timely feedback (Hara & Kling, 2000).

THE PROBLEM

It is important to understand who participates in these courses, why they chose to participate in this mode of delivery, and what they need in order to be successful online learners. Online course designers must take into account these situational needs, as they influence the online environment and their perceptions of the most effective roles for all participants (Berge & Mrozowski, 2001). We also need a clear picture of the nature of students' experiences online in order to maximize learning potential and mitigate limitations inherent in the delivery medium (Lim, 2001). In other words, we need a better sense of what works and what does not to facilitate students' learning in online settings (Perreault et al., 2002).

METHODS

The Case

Because South Dakota is a rural state, there is a real need to offer a variety of distance courses (Christensen, 2001). In the last decade, the state has been recognized nationally for the extensive development of distance learning systems of all types and has been used as a model for development of a comprehensive distance education system (Simonson, 2001). State-led programs for wiring public schools and development of interactive video systems throughout the state began in 1994. These efforts continue to be supported by state programs and funding throughout all levels of education.

At the university level, these technological initiatives also include creation of Governor's Electronic Classrooms at each of the six state universities, which provide technologically sophisticated classrooms for distance delivery. A variety of programs are also intended to enhance faculty development (Simonson & Sparks, 2001). Since 1995, faculty members in the state systems have been eligible to apply for grants to develop technological applications in their courses, as appropriate. A funded proposal releases the faculty member from summer teaching responsibilities by supporting 3 months of technology research and development. Grant proposals have addressed many dimensions of teaching with technology, ranging from development of specific distance delivery skills to creation of entire classes that are Web based.

As a result of these opportunities to concentrate on creating and refining courses for distance delivery, the state universities have developed numerous courses that are delivered entirely online, using Web Course Tools (WebCT). Accordingly, the University of South Dakota has made a commitment to electronic course delivery and has dedicated extensive resources to meeting the needs of students who are unable to travel to campus for traditional classes. Systematic course design and standards for offering these courses are in place, increasing the likelihood that the Web courses delivered through the university meet rigorous standards.

The School of Education at USD has been a leader in development of these online courses. The school offers more than 30 courses that are entirely online, and three degrees can be earned completely through this medium. More than 300 different students have enrolled in the online courses since 2001, drawn from across the United States. Student evaluations, completed through the state's Electronic University Consortium (EUC), rate the electronic courses provided by the School of Education at USD very highly. According to Statewide Education Services at the university, discounting students who enroll and drop before courses begin, approximately 95% of our students complete their online courses.

Research Questions

Although we were confident that the online courses we offered met statewide needs, we were interested in gathering specific information about our individual courses and the online program as a whole in order to improve them and to continue with the effective elements. More accurate group descriptions and understanding of the experiences and perceptions of the viability of the courses were needed if we were to appropriately address these goals. We wanted to know:

1. Who takes these courses and why?
2. What course characteristics and factors support online learning?
3. What makes learning more difficult?
4. What course resources are most helpful/effective learning online? How frequently are they used?
5. How do students assess their learning, their teachers, the technical support, and their own skills in electronic learning?

The Instrument

We created an extensive survey, based on a review of the literature and our own experiences as online teachers. The instrument was available for online completion and consisted of 94 items, including demographic information. The survey was divided into sections with specific purposes, all scored by Likert scales with various descriptors appropriate to the nature of the questions, with space for comments included after each section. Open-ended questions were included at the end of the survey.

Seven online teachers in the program volunteered to have their students complete the online survey, with a total of 59 students. Six were educational administration courses, and one was a research methods course. All classes were required in the program for a master's degree in educational administration, although students were not drawn exclusively from that group.

FINDINGS

Demographic Information

This group of students was very similar to those described in other research. They were 73% female, 27% male. Twenty-nine percent ranged in age from 25-35, 27% were 36-44, and 27% were 45-55. Almost three quarters (73%) were currently enrolled in a graduate program. Although 7% were taking three online courses at the same time, 68% were taking only one, and 22% were handling two.

Students were asked to describe their situations in terms of work, family responsibilities, and study focus. Seventeen percent described themselves as full-time graduate students; 3% selected part-time graduate student, part-time work; 3% chose part-time graduate student with family responsibilities, another 3% were full-time graduate students with family responsibilities, and 7% marked part-time graduate student, part-time work, family responsibilities. The largest group (64%) described themselves as part-time graduate students with full-time work.

Seventy-five percent of the students lived more than 50 miles from campus, and almost all students worked on computers in the home or work setting. The students who took these classes were grateful for access. Comments included "Thank you for offering so many classes over the Internet. I would be unable to work toward my degree if you did not have classes online." "I really like the convenience of online courses. Because I ... have a family to care for, this allows the freedom to work on the course material when I can and not have to drive to campus several times a week." A traditional experience for these students was "not an option!"

Important Components for Online Learning

Our initial questions asked students to consider the importance of particular course features, specifically as they apply to online learning. Four survey items addressed students' perceptions of the importance of course organization: 95% believed that the structure and coherence of the course was very or somewhat important, and that expectations had to be explicit. Clear course procedures were equally important to 91% of the learners, and 89% indicated that the selected text needed to be understandable. The courses also include various online resources, some of which are linked to the course structure and some that have been uploaded into the course itself. Ninety-six percent of the students found these resources helpful. Interestingly, only 74% of the students indicated that technology assistance was important; their comments indicated that few technological problems were encountered during these courses.

Course Design

In addition to comments on the importance of coherence overall, we asked students to evaluate the framework of the specific courses they took. We were interested in understanding some basic elements of effective course design—expectations, coherence and organization, text choice, and effectiveness of included online materials. Once again, 98% strongly agreed or agreed that the expectations of the course they took were reasonable and 100% saw that course as coherent and well-organized. The text was rated as well chosen and accessible by 93%, whereas supplementary materials aided the learning of 88%. Students commented on the thoroughness of the courses they took. "I enjoy [this instructor's] willingness to master the electronic domain ... a wonderful learning opportunity."

The structure and coherence of the courses defused a good deal of student anxiety. "I was pretty worried at the beginning of the course since this is my first online class. But it was very organized and I turned out to really like it," said one. Students also made it very clear that they appreciated the coherent presentation of the courses. "The instructor was very organized, knowledgeable, and clear in expectations, and seemed to really want everyone to learn the material." Another first-time online student said "Thanks to [this instructor] I will definitely take more courses online ... well organized ... obvious that [this instructor] has carefully thought through the curriculum and presentation of the course."

Resources

Students were asked to evaluate the resources included in the courses from two perspectives. First, they were asked how important the resources were for them and, second, how frequently they used them. For all courses, the required text was viewed as the most important and frequently-used source of information, with 93% of students indicating it was a critical or important component, frequently or often used.

Because our courses make use of different resources within the WebCT format, it is somewhat misleading to assess overall importance by the percentages that follow. What is of interest, however, is the comparison between importance and frequency of use for each resource. Students consistently reported that they wanted these resources available, even though they did not make extensive use of them. However, illuminated by student comments, these data offer some important insights.

Online resources.   Online resources were considered important by 83%, and regularly used by 81%. Those who made use of the resources were positive in their comments: "All the support materials for the course were excellent ... the instructor created introductions were excellent supplements to the book ... the student work examples [were] very helpful." Students viewed the supplementary materials as another connection with the teacher: "Thank you for taking the time to provide the supplemental materials. They helped to make sense of the more technical terms and ideas." Although 42% thought that the technical assistance provided was very important or critical, only 8% used it frequently or often. The availability of university library reserves was considered important by 51% of the students, but regularly used by 34%.

Communications.   Virtual Office Hours (VOH), teacher availability in a chat room at a predetermined time to address student questions, were considered important by 69% of the students, and were often used by 36%. Peer chats were highly valued by 41% and frequently used by 25%, and e-mail was important to 85% and regularly used by 73%.

Some students responded very positively to these opportunities—"I loved the interaction components!" said one. Some recognized that the Virtual Office Hours held by instructors and the opportunities to interact in an online discussion format were critical to their learning and listed these resources as vital to course success. These students insisted that it was important to attend VOH, to ask questions, to contact the teacher immediately if they felt frustrated or confused, and to chat frequently with their partners. "Attend VOH," one student advised future course members, "even if you just 'listen in' because often things come up that you can use. Ask questions if you have any—the instructor is very willing to help steer you in the right direction." Others emphasized that the online chats with instructors and students made the course they took more interesting. One said "I found myself logging on several times a day to see how the threaded discussion was going and to check supplemental material." One said she found herself "wishing for more group discussion." Some who did not make use of the communication options later recognized that they might have made the task easier for themselves if they had done so. "I learned that too late," said one.

Teacher Competence

The personas of the course teachers were critical for the success of student learning. Level of knowledge and helpfulness was rated as very important or somewhat important by 98%, teacher accessibility at 95%, and clear teacher-established timelines at 97%. Peer interaction, which takes different forms in these courses, was perceived to be important by 90% of the participants. Responses to questions dealing with teacher competence were strongly positive. Teachers were judged to be knowledgeable (100%), helpful (98%), and accessible (98%). Students saw their online exchanges with the teacher as helpful (97%) and response time as reasonable (92%).

Student comments suggested that the teacher was a most important factor in the course. They valued the effort it took to create an online course and recognized the person behind the effort. "Thank you for all your efforts. I really appreciate all the work you put into making this an excellent course. Prior to taking this course I was terrified of online classes, but know I have new courage and would actually take another course … I leaned [sic] a great deal." They also appreciated the nature of the interactions they had with the teacher, which they perceived as "organized, supportive and helpful." For example, "You are very knowledgeable and easy to talk to, you didn't make me feel uneasy or uneducated at any time. I came into this class knowing very little and you made me feel adequate in the subject area by provoking good thoughtful questions that required me to think." Although students thought they had excellent feedback from their instructors—"I felt that my assignments were read carefully and your responses were detailed and specific," they wanted even more than they got. "[The instructor] was very helpful when connected but it would have been nice to hear more often," said another from the same class.

Assessment of Learning and Effort

Three items were aimed at understanding students' assessment of their own learning in the various courses. We wanted to know if they felt they had learned, if they felt the course content was important, and if they were confident that they understood the material.

All of the students—100%—agreed that they had "learned a good deal" in the class they took. Ninety-three percent believed that the content was important for them to know, and 95% were confident that they understood the course content.

We also asked questions specifically aimed at comparison of the course they took to traditional delivery of the same content. Asked if they had learned as much in this mode as they would have in a traditional class, 71% agreed. Approximately 10% disagreed. These students commented that the learning was "comparable" and "maybe even more." Other strongly believed that "[t]here is no way ... to replace that face-to-face interaction between students and instructor ... that is where the quality is for me." "Teacher's explanation [in a face-to-face setting] and examples are very valuable." This sentiment seemed to be especially strong when the course material was considered difficult. "I got a great deal out of [the course]. But a live course would have helped."

Students perceived that more effort was required in an online class than in a traditional course because they "couldn't rely on classmates or the teacher for immediate answers to questions" and because "working independently always takes more effort." The effort was also "more concentrated" and "dedicated." One student pointed out that there was "more effort expended in actual learning that was relevant, compared to busy work" (presumably in contrast to the busywork found in traditional learning settings). Another stated, "In the online course, I covered exactly what was expected, maybe not much more than that, but I learned it very well because I was worried that I wouldn't know what I was supposed to. I feel that I worked harder to understand the material, probably better than I would have in a live course because there I could have waited to see if things would come up during class or in discussion. That was less of an option here."

We also asked students if they would have preferred to take the course in a traditional setting. In this case, 41% indicated that they would have preferred a traditional setting. In one student's words, "I like the flexibility and using the technology. However, I do not feel the quality of my experience was what it could be because of the lack of face-to-face interaction with other students and the instructor." It was noted that the education field is person centered, and it was problematic to lose that dimension of learning.

This set of findings is particularly interesting. Although the survey indicated they were overwhelmingly positive about the quality of the course, the teaching they experienced, and the WebCT format, a large group indicated that they would have preferred a traditional setting, a quarter of the students were neutral to the mode of delivery, leaving roughly a quarter who would have chosen electronic delivery over a traditional class setting. The perspectives of the hefty proportion of students who would have preferred traditional delivery had it been available to them, but still valued the online experience, can be summarized in the following student's comments: "I don't think that anything can make up for the learning involved in the classroom. However, the materials presented were clear and if I had a question, it was answered as soon as was possible. I think that although a traditional classroom may be better, this one worked very well for me."

Self-Assessment

Items designed to allow the students to assess their own course processes, including time management and keeping up with the work, revealed that 88% of the students agreed that they learned well in an independent setting. Most (92%) believed that they had managed their time effectively and had kept up with the work. Those who did not think they were particularly effective were neutral rather than negative. Ninety-eight percent were satisfied with their skills in the WebCT electronic format; 86% believed that they had learned to handle the electronic medium by participating.

Most students credited some of their success in the course to their own willingness to put forth the necessary effort and to manage their time well, with being "self-motivated and independent learners." They saw the need to take a "proactive role" and be "committed to meeting the requirements" and relied on user-friendly course structure to ensure their learning. "I relied heavily on the calendar, syllabus and chapter intros to keep on top of the due dates and for explanations on the assignments," one student said, but added, "It also helped that I knew [and had face-to-face access to] someone that was taking the course and could talk to her when I had some questions."

Students recommended that future participants make use of all the resources. "Work on the course regularly, and utilize all the supplementary materials and communication tools. Don't be afraid to ask questions, both to the instructor and to other students." Many emphasized the amount of time online classes take and recommended that future students be aware of the pitfalls of poor time management. The major point was

"Don't fall behind.... Set up a schedule and stick to it!" Procrastination was seen as leading to certain failure. "This is not a weasy [sic] way out of a class!"

Enjoyment

Two students said they did not enjoy taking a course in this medium but, overall, students were positive; 88% of them found this an enjoyable way to learn. They liked the WebCT format. Some students apparently preferred online learning because of the independence and flexibility it afforded. Typical comments included "I enjoy learning independently, so I prefer this method." "I enjoyed this course because I could do it on my own time and was not confined to a classroom."

Frequently, comments about enjoyment were specifically addressed to the teacher—"Great job helping me get through this and actually enjoying it ... I never would have thought I would like this [course subject] but it definitely has my interest." "Great experience. Thank you." "[This] was my first experience with online courses of which I took two. It was so convenient, but also very thorough and I don't feel I missed anything in delivery." "I have the highest regard for the instructor and the course materials. I thought it was great." "Thanks for your help—I enjoyed this course much more than I expected!"

BARRIERS TO LEARNING

Various factors made progress through these online courses more difficult for some. Based on the literature and our experiences, we had identified technical difficulties, availability of materials, and personal time management as potential problems. However, only two students reported any important difficulty with their hardware and three identified their software or connections to the university server as problematic. Seventy-four percent indicted that technology assistance was important as they progressed through the course. According to this survey, no student had difficulties managing the technology within the WebCT system, 97% thought the technology was manageable, and 58% thought that the support they received for technology applications was good. However, 15 participants selected "did not use/did not apply" option for tech support. We can reasonably conclude that these students had no technology problems and no need to make use of support systems, which would further emphasize the accessibility of the WebCT format from a student perspective. Likewise, with a few exceptions due to late enrollment, books and materials were sent in a timely manner and students had necessary resources to work on the course.

Three barriers to learning were clear: time, personal need for the immediacy of face-to-face interactions, and the student-to-student interactions built into each course.

Time management. Twenty-seven percent of the participants reported that they were not prepared for the amount of time an online course took, and 25% had a difficult time completing the tasks on time. "This class took a lot of my time, far more than any other class that I took," one said. The comments directed to future students emphasized the need to manage time, meet deadlines, and avoid procrastination. Personal life factors also influenced available time to dedicate to learning. "My life was chaotic," said another, "but with the professor's flexibility and understanding it was not an issue. The professor wanted quality over just turning it in on time."

Need for face-to-face interactions. Although students indicated that their instructors were readily available, and they appreciated the feedback they received, some still voiced difficulty with the nature of the connection to the instructor." I think that I would have been able to ask more questions and get more direct answers in a traditional classroom setting—what I needed in order to understand this material better." The statements can be summarized by this student's comment: "Sometimes it would be nice to have the instructor right there to answer questions, but you can't complain when you're able to take a class online and live far away from campus." Students typically accepted the limitations of the interaction with the teacher in a distance mode, particularly when they connected through extensive feedback on course work.

Student-to-student interactions. We have all made serious efforts to involve our students in online communications, believing that the dialog that occurs between students and between students and teachers are essential for learning. So we were somewhat surprised to find the lower value that a large group of students apparently had for the interactive components built into the courses. Comments indicated that whether they used chat partners or bulletin board postings for threaded discussions, some found these course expectations less important for their learning. Technology glitches played a small role in their reactions—only two stated that they were not able to access the chat rooms. Others indicated that their chat partners were not very helpful for building understanding or that they did not contribute much in partner discussions themselves. Some participants recognized the potential of partner interaction, but felt limited by the delay in exchanges, especially when there were more than two in the chat room. "Chatting is easier for me with just one other person maybe because I haven't really participated in chats previously... lack of interest and time. Also it was difficult to make times set up for whatever reasons. Life in general."

Threaded discussions were perceived as initially valuable, but the learners who commented negatively thought the energy died quickly. "The original postings of the class members were helpful. I did not find the responses to members' responses helpful … just rehash of the original point." Another said "What peer interaction there was was mechanical in nature because most of the interaction was not in real-time."

Student Recommendation

In spite of the unexpected time demands and communication difficulties, 95% of the students said they would be interested in taking another online course from USD, and 93% would be interested in taking another course from the same teacher. The courses would be recommended to others by 93% of these participants. Students wrote that they had recommended *the medium*, the courses, and the USD online programs overall to friends. One student wrote "I am taking course from [two other universities]. I think USD is way ahead of the others." Another stated "This is my first course online and I will judge all other courses by the quality of this one. It was extremely well organized, online materials were very clear and helpful, the instructor is positive and supportive. I hope to take other classes from this instructor. A wonderful experience!" "Awesome!," said another, "This online course fit my current situation very well!"

DISCUSSION

Our study led to a number of conclusions that are supported by the literature. First, participants in these courses represented the same group that has been nationally noted as online course participants—young, professional, female, part-time students with family responsibilities (Bunn, 2001; Lim, 2001). This group was most strongly represented in spite of the proportion of educational administration courses, which generally include more males.

Also, our group members gave the same reasons for enrolling in online courses, as did those in other studies—accessibility, convenience, and flexibility. Participant comments indicated that, for some, distance education was the only possibility for pursuing a graduate degree (Bickle & Carroll, 2003; Billings et al., 2001; Cooper, 2001; Navarro & Shoemaker, 2000; Perreault et al., 2002).

Although we expected technological difficulties to be a source of frustration for at least some participants, few had difficulties in that area. The technical support offered was what they needed. The WebCT architecture was workable and intuitive for even first-time online students. We may also conclude that the technological sophistication of learners was sufficient for the task at hand, even when they expressed concern with this issue when they began the class (Lim, 2001).

Also in accordance with the literature, our students were satisfied with their experiences in online learning. They believed they learned the content well and were confident in most cases that they had learned as much taking a course through WebCT as they would have through traditional means, although many would have preferred a traditional class if it had been available to them. These responses also are congruent with other research (Allen, Bourhis, Burrell, & Mabry, 2002; Neuhauser, 2002)

Students also emphasized the importance of self-directed learning and personal responsibility for success in online learning. They recognized the different expectations and procedures necessary for online learning, which encouraged them to rely on themselves rather than on the teacher or fellow students. Time management and personal engagement were consistently mentioned as critical factors for successful learning, all of which were discovered in previous studies (Cooper, 2001; Leasure et al., 2000; Navarro & Shoemaker, 2000).

Two major factors that contributed to successful online course design and were vivid in this study have also been supported by other research. The first was coherent course design—organization, clear expectations, ease of navigation, and clear procedures for using the various courses (Hall, 2002; Moore, 2002). Our students were less impressed with bells and whistles than they were with clarity, usability, and coherence (Billings et al., 2001).

The second major insight, also supported by previous research, was the impact of the personal preference of the teacher in online learning (Moore, 2002; Tu & McIsaac, 2002). Although participants did not necessarily visit frequently with the teacher online or in chat rooms, or send an inordinate number of emails to the instructor, it was obvious that the teacher's voice in the course design was critical. The more often students had the opportunity to sense teachers' personalities in the course materials, the more connected they felt to the class. Posted information such as teacher-created unit introductions that made use of conversational style, personal examples, and responses to frequently asked questions, FAQs, in personal language were highly valued. Extensive and personalized feedback on assignments was critical and also contributed to connections with the instructors. Also important was a link to the instructor's homepage and vita. We have often been surprised at how well our online students feel they know us through interaction with these materials and how appreciative they are of the efforts of the person they perceive behind the technology.

In short, in accordance with Moore and Thompson's (1997) interactions, this group found the relationships of student-course and student-teacher to be critical. We were, however, surprised to find the relatively low value many students had for their interactions with their peers. This perspective is contrary to much of the current literature that deals with the significance of creating an online learning community (e.g. Carabajal, LaPointe, & Gunawardena, 2003; Goldman et al., 1999; Hall 2002; Rovai, 2001).

All of us have required some kind of peer interaction online, as we have a commitment to building a learning community as close as possible to that available in a traditional class. Perhaps we have not yet found a way to make these exchanges meaningful enough for the learner. Perhaps the perspectives of this small group were contrary to the majority of online learners in this respect and are therefore contrary to the bulk of current research.

Another possibility, however, is that the goals of online learners are different to begin with, and that their preferred mode of learning content online has less to do with the dynamic of a learning community than it does with learning course content well on their own. The idea that "nothing can replace" the dynamic of the traditional learning community seems to place the online experience in a different category—with a different set of expectations. Considering the groups who often enroll in graduate online classes—part-time students with both work and family responsibilities—the extra effort demanded to participate in an online community, whether through threaded discussions or online chats—may represent more time and group commitment than these learners value. The self-directed dimension of such classes is highly valued; perhaps the participation in a learning community, for some, is not an important dimension for learning.

This possibility poses a philosophical and pedagogical conflict for many of us who emphasize the learning potential of the dynamic and interactive environment of the traditional class. If we believe that the community itself enhances learning, can we accept a categorically different kind of learning online? It may be that the effects of technology in computer-mediated communication so drastically change the nature of the group interactions that other ways need to be found to define a learning community (Carabajal et al., 2003).

Further research is needed to better understand not only the mechanics for creating a meaningful online learning community, but also for addressing the needs and preferences of those who do not need this community to learn well. To what extent is the learning community fundamental to good online learning? Is it worthwhile to insist on development of this component of traditional learning settings within the online environment, in spite of differences in mode of delivery? Should we recognize that distance education might be fundamentally different education rather than impose expectations for a traditional learning community in an online environment? The issue is philosophical as well as pedagogical. Further research may be able to address some of these questions, but perhaps we also need to rethink some of our approaches to online learning and consider the environment, goals, and responsibilities of an online learner.

In this study, we sought to better understand our students and what they need for success in online learning. This group indicated that course coherence including clear expectations for learning and course navigation, and a vital voice of a teacher behind the technology were essential. The technology itself was effective and user-friendly, and our students were satisfied with their experience and their learning. Use of quantitative and qualitative data allowed us to develop a better understanding of not only what our students experienced, but also how they interpreted their experience and why. We are left with questions about the benefits of establishing an online learning community and to what extent student-to-student interactions contribute to student learning in this environment.

REFERENCES

Allen, M., Bourhis, J., Burrel, N., & Mabry, E. (2002). Comparing student satisfaction with distance education to traditional classrooms in higher education: A meta-analysis. *American Journal of Distance Education, 16*(2), 83-97.

Berge, Z. L., & Mrozowski, S. (2001). Review of research in distance education, 1990-1999. *American Journal of Distance Education, 15*(3), 5-19.

Bickle, M. C., & Carroll, J. C. (2003). Checklist for quality online instruction: Outcomes for learners, the professor, and the institution. *College Student Journal, 37*(2), 208-215.

Billings, D. M., Connors, U. R., & Skiba, D. J. (2001). Benchmarking best practices in web-based nursing courses. *Advances in Nursing Science, 23*(3), 41-53.

Bunn, M. D. (2001). Timeless and timely issues in distance education planning. *American Journal of Distance Education, 15*(1), 55-68.

Burch, R. O. (2001). Effective web design and core communication issues: The missing components in web-based distance education. *Journal of Educational Multimedia and Hypermedia, 10*(4), 357-367.

Carabajal, K., LaPointe, D., & Gunawardena, C. N. (2003). Group development in online learning communities. In M. G. Moore & W. G. Anderson (Eds.), *Handbook of distance education* (pp. 217-234). Mahwah, NJ: Erlbaum.

Carr, S. (2000, February 11). As distance education comes of age, the challenge is keeping the students. *The Chronicle of Higher Education*, p. A39.

Christensen, R. (2001). Wiring the schools: South Dakota does it right. *Tech Trends, 45*(3), 18-20.

Chyung, S. Y. (2001). Systematic and systemic approaches to reducing attrition rates in online higher education. *American Journal of Distance Education, 15*(3), 36-50.

Cooper, L. W. (2001). A comparison of online and traditional computer applications classes. *Technological Horizons in Education, 28*(8), 52-58.

Dillon, C., & Greene, B. (2003). Learner differences in distance learning: Finding differences that matter. In M. G. Moore & W. G. Anderson (Eds.), *Handbook of distance education* (pp. 235-244). Mahwah, NJ: Erlbaum.

Ewing, J. M., Ewing, J. D., & Coutts, N. (1998). Learning using the World Wide Web: A collaborative learning event. *Journal of Educational Multimedia and Hypermedia, 8*(1), 3-22.

Garrison, D. R. (2003). Self-directed learning and distance education. In M. G. Moore & W. G. Anderson (Eds.), *Handbook of distance education* (pp. 161-168). Mahwah, NJ: Erlbaum.

Goldman, S. R., Williams, S. M., Sherwood, R. D., Hasselbring, T. S., & Cognition and Technology Group at Vanderbilt. (1999). *Technology for teaching and learning with understanding: A primer.* Nashville, TN: Vanderbilt University.

Hall, R. (2002). Aligning learning, teaching and assessment using the Web: An evaluation of pedagogic approaches. *British Journal of Educational Technology, 33*(2), 149-158.

Hara, N., & Kling, R. (2000). *Students' distress with a web-based distance education course.* Bloomington: Indiana University—The Center for Social Informatics. Retrieved August 7, 2003, from http://www.slis.Indiana.edu/CSI/wp00-01.html

King, F. B. (2002). A virtual student: Not an ordinary Joe. *Internet and Higher Education, 5,* 157-166.

Lally, V., & Barrett, E. (1999). Building a learning community on-line: Towards socio-academic interaction. *Research Papers in Education, 14*(2), 147-163.

Leasure, A. R., Davis, L., & Thievon, S. L. (2000). Comparison of student outcomes and preferences in a traditional vs. World Wide Web-based baccalaureate nursing research course. *Journal of Nursing Education, 39*(4), 149-154.

Lim, C. K. (2001). Computer self-efficacy, academic self concept, and other predictors of satisfaction and future participation of adult distance learners. *American Journal of Distance Education, 15*(2), 41-40.

Lindner, J. R., Dooley, K. E., & Murphy, T. H. (2001). Differences in competencies between doctoral students on-campus and at a distance. *American Journal of Distance Education, 15*(2), 25-40.

Moore, M. G. (2002). Editorial: What does research say about the learners using computer-mediated communication in distance learning? *American Journal of Distance Education, 16*(2), 61-64.

Moore, M. G., & Thompson, M. M. (1997). *The effects of distance learning: A summary of the literature.* University Park: Pennsylvania State University.

Muilenburg, L., & Berge, Z. L. (2001). Barriers to distance education: A factor-analytic study. *American Journal of Distance Education, 15*(2), 7-22.

Navarro, P., & Shoemaker, J. (2000). Performance and perceptions of distance learners in cyberspace. *American Journal of Distance Education, 14*(2), 15-35.

Neuhauser, C. (2002). Learning style and effectiveness of online and face-to-face instruction. *American Journal of Distance Education, 16*(2), 99-113.

Palloff, R. M., & Pratt, K. (2001). *Lessons from the cyberspace classroom: The realities of online teaching.* San Francisco: Jossey-Bass.

Perreault, H., Waldman, L., & Zhao, M. A. J. (2002). Overcoming barriers to successful delivery of distance learning courses. *Journal of Education for Business, 77*(6), 313-318.

Rovai, A. P. (2001). Building classroom community at a distance: A case study. *Educational Technology Research and Development, 49*(4), 33-49.

Sherry, A. C., Fulford, C. P., & Zhang, S. (1998). Assessing distance learners' satisfaction with instruction: A quantitative and qualitative measure. *American Journal of Distance Education, 12*(3), 4-28.

Simonson, M. (2001). Guest editor's introduction. *Tech Trends, 45*(3), 3-4.

Simonson, M., & Sparks, K. (2001). Learning at a distance in South Dakota: Evaluation of the process. *Tech Trends, 45*(3), 38-43.

Thirunarayanan, M. O., & Peres-Prado, A. (2001-2002). Comparing Web-based and classroom based learning: A quantitative study. *Journal of Research on Technology in Education, 34*(2), 131-137.

Tu, C. H., & McIsaac, M. (2002). The relationship of social presence and interaction in online classes. *American Journal of Distance Education, 16*(3), 131-150.

CHAPTER 9

DESIGN AND IMPLEMENTATION OF A WEB-BASED LEARNING ENVIRONMENT

Lessons Learned

Alaa Sadik and Sorel Reisman

This article presents sets of observations and recommendations for Web-based distance learning, based on formative and summative performance and opinion data collected from participants involved in the design, development, and utilization of Wired Class, a Web-based learning environment that was developed to teach mathematics to Egyptian secondary school students. The discussion focuses on issues related to the nature of (1) Web-based learning materials, (2) the spectrum of learning/teaching interactions, (3) the Web as a learning environment, and (4) costs associated with delivering Web-based instruction. Examples are used to illustrate the basis for recommendations that evolved from the work on which this article is based.

The Perfect Online Course: Best Practices for Designing and Teaching
pp. 179–200
Copyright © 2009 by Information Age Publishing
All rights of reproduction in any form reserved.

Web-based instruction is a relatively new educational technology with many Web-based courses developed by people skilled in Web authoring but who "are not necessarily knowledgeable about educational concepts" (Janicki & Liegle, 2001). Powell claims that "despite the established base of online courses, online course design and facilitation is still uncharted territory for many college and university faculty" (2001, p. 44). Although much has been published about creating effective online learning, much of the literature does "not provide a comprehensive and practical guide to the challenges faculty encounter when designing complex Web modules" (Weston & Barker, 2001, p. 15). Online learning environments should meet many instructional, structural, and technical principles of design and development to be more than information dumping, and to avoid eyestrain from endless text screens, confusing navigation, and long download times (Spitzer, 2001). It is essential for responsible administrators to understand if their Web-based distance learning programs are meeting their design objectives or are merely alternative learning materials dumping grounds.

Many studies (e.g., Clark, 1994; Lockee, Burton, & Cross, 1999; Thorpe, 1998) have pointed out that that different levels of evaluation should be used to evaluate distance education programs. Clark (1994), for example, stated that two levels of evaluation that always provide useful feedback are measures of participant reactions, and the achievement of program objectives. Consequently, the "lessons learned" described in this paper are based on formative and summative student performance measures as well as student, instructor, designer, and "expert" opinion data collected during the 12 months of design, development, and utilization of *Wired Class*, a Web-based learning environment that was developed to teach mathematics to Egyptian secondary school students (Sadik, 2002). Constructivist epistemology provided the basis for the various instructional components and the related problem-centered and interactive activities used in *Wired Class*.

In this paper, "lessons learned" are discussed in terms of the following topics:

- providing a rich learning environment;
- understanding the spectrum of interactions;
- developing the presentation environment; and
- considering the cost benefits.

Each of these is discussed in terms of issues germane to specific characteristics of the topic.

PROVIDING A RICH LEARNING ENVIRONMENT

Web-based instruction is an instructional delivery mode that has evolved from traditional instructional delivery environments; hence, many online materials have been derived from traditional instructional material, typically textbooks. Unfortunately, converting textbooks to Web pages can result in digital versions of textbooks that provide no incremental benefit for learners. In this project, considerable time was spent converting and redesigning original textbook content to produce a rich online learning experience. Special efforts were made in terms of content design, the activities necessary to support and reinforce student learning, developing ancillary learning materials and resources, and utilizing Web resources. This section describes these efforts and some of the implications of each.

CONTENT DESIGN

In many (if not most) programs of instruction, course and lesson objectives are not always clearly presented to students, either initially or throughout the progress of a course. Course objectives are essential because they help instructors plan the structure of a course and develop learning activities and assessment methodologies (Berge, Collins, & Dougherty, 2000). The online learning materials developed in this project were derived from textbooks in which learning objectives were not stressed or made obvious to learners. This deficiency in the online materials was addressed by presenting learning objectives at the beginning of each lesson together with basic/new concepts and definitions to support those objectives. This was done continuously throughout the instruction to reinforce the learning of new concepts and to help students acquire and construct new mathematics meanings and principles.

Mathematical content is difficult for many students, particularly for those studying independently at a distance. Online content can provide learners with multiple forms of media (e.g., hypertext links, graphics, animation, real-time audio and video, and other hypermedia objects such as Java applets and Macromedia Flash presentations) to involve them in active learning activities (Weston & Barker, 2001). Other online tools/ effects that can be used are links to Web sites with authentic contexts or sites that afford access to primary source documents, and immediate automated assessment and feedback (Weston & Barker, 2001). Consistent with Harrison and Bergen (2000), *Wired Class* utilized such technologies to provide students with complete and up-to-date views of the subject matter, including main concepts, links to Web resources, examples, exercises, reminders, and so forth. The use of a variety of well-selected, real-life examples helped students focus on new concepts and understand difficult issues by applying them in new ways, especially when alone and with less access to instructor assistance than is common in face-to-face learning environments. Accordingly, more real-life examples were provided so that students could practice new concepts and skills in an independent and comprehensible manner.

Learning Support Activities

Web-based learning platforms provide an ideal environment in which to implement the principles of constructivist learning (Smith-Gratto, 2000); *Wired Class* was implemented on that basis. Constructivists assert that students construct their own learning in meaningful ways when they participate in individual and social activities, encounter and solve problems, interact with others, exchange information, and evaluate their understanding. Accordingly, different kinds of resource tools such as graphing calculators and situational problem solving exploration methodologies were provided to assist students achieve high-order learning objectives.

Although the mathematics content of *Wired Class* was accurate, addressed the learning objectives, and was thought to be interesting, rewriting the content for the Web with constructivist epistemology in mind required the development of strategies to encourage frequent and meaningful online student interactions in debates, problem solving, and general discussion. Students were involved individually in many real-life problem-solving activities through self-tests, exercises, and discussions. Through social interaction, facilitated by e-mail and discussion boards, students could learn others' points of view and assess their own understanding. However, it was felt that it was imperative for instructors to take an active role in helping students construct meaning and correct misunderstandings, and that discussions (via discussion boards) take place continuously throughout the lessons, and not be "add-ons" at the end of lessons.

Learning Materials and Resources

In *Wired Class*, course content was organized in a "conventional" yet flexible way. Each lesson was segmented into the lesson, further examples, self-tests, and exercises. Every module was segmented into smaller, labeled and interlinked submodules, each representing one concept, skill, or problem. This design was useful for students and instructors because the meaningful labels of the submodules provided easy to identify reference points that facilitated communication among instructors and students. The relatively fine submodule design also facilitated diagnostic action if students had problems and/or remediation was required.

One of the advantages of the World Wide Web is that ancillary technologies can provide media rich browser-based screens of information. *Wired Class* lesson material deliberately did not contain complex multimedia objects because most students accessed the Internet via slow phone line connections using hardware that was not state of the art. Additionally, and from an instructional development standpoint, it is expensive and time consuming to develop audio and video objects, most of which may not really be useful for subject matter that is heavily based on text, symbols, and graphs. Small and relatively low resolution still and animated GIF images were used to display figures, graphs, and mathematical formulae; interactive Java applets were used to illustrate abstract mathematical concepts and capture student interest. Although there are many other ways to generate and display mathematical formulae in HTML pages (e.g., HTML maths tags, Java applets and add-ins), GIFs were found to be more cost-effective and better able to represent attractive and accurate formulae. These other approaches can provide inaccurate results, require a long time for downloading, or require additional software (plug-ins) to be added to the Web browser. The only drawback to using images was the large amount of disk space they took up in the Web server.

Web Resources

Web-based education can provide learners with limitless information resources, but despite ease of access and probably because of the scope of the resources, expecting students to find and integrate them in a meaningful way may not be realistic. Instructional designers should pay attention to developing subject-specific directories or topic hot lists that are accessible and appropriate to students' academic levels. Lilla and Hipps (1999) highlighted the importance of a combination of subject-specific directories and search engines that they called "hybrids." The importance of hybrids is that they collect and categorize Web sites in a logical or subject-based structure so that the user avoids the false hits that can occur with search engines. The advantage of these hybrids is that they allow students to do all their information gathering from a single desktop connected to millions of computers all over the world (Green, 1997).

In a distance education context, Birmingham, Drabenstott, Frost, Warner, and Willis (2000) reported that the advantages of hybrids or "digital archives" are that:

- They reduce geographic, organizational, and time barriers of distance.
- They enhance collaborative and group-based activities.
- They provide access to collections of information in multimedia formats that are not available to off-campus students.
- They allow users to personalize or customize information access and representation.
- They provide information at any time and in any place.

In *Wired Class*, students were provided with an archive of preselected Web links and with access to powerful search engines (e.g., Google, Yahoo, AltaVista, etc.) to search for course-related information. Consistent with the literature cited above, students reported that they did not benefit very much from these tools or even from following preselected Web links. Feedback from instructors revealed that many of the resources were above the ability level of learners and did not seem to cover topics comprehensively. Instructors recommended that search engines and links be carefully selected with consideration of the subject matter (e.g., mathematics) as well as students' levels and needs. Although this is a time-consuming instructional design activity, it is now clear that it is important for curriculum designers to find and carefully select prescribed curriculum-specific Web resources. This was borne out by students' experiences where they reported that they found such links more appropriate and useful than general search engines. This result is also in line with results reported in the 10th GVU public survey (1999) approved by the World Wide Web Consortium which showed that the majority of users prefer and use links provided by other Web sites rather than using search engines to seek information themselves.

A no less important observation is that it is essential to verify the legitimacy and provide continued support of links in archives. In *Wired Class*, students reported that they found error messages instead of the resources to which they had been directed. According to GVU's 7th (1997) and 9th (1999) WWW User Surveys, in 1997 about 50% of Internet users reported broken links as their main problem in navigating the Web, and by 1999 this problem had become even worse. The only solution to this problem is for links to be regularly checked, and for there to be feedback mechanisms for students to report or comment on broken or difficult-to-follow links.

UNDERSTANDING THE SPECTRUM OF INTERACTIONS

A challenge of distance learning is overcoming the geographical separation of instructors from learners, and learners from other learners. Students in distance-delivered courses are expected to carry out a great deal of learning on their own (Baynton, 1992). It is essential for instructors to know whether remote students working alone and online are able to construct their knowledge successfully or not (R. Garrison, 1990). Because there is evidence that in classrooms with higher levels of interaction students have higher levels of achievement and more positive attitudes toward learning (Ritchie & Newby, 1989), it is also essential to optimize the learner/learner and learner/instructor quality of interaction. Too often, attention is given to the content and the delivery features of communications technologies rather than to the human dialogue that must take place in the online learning environment (D. Garrison, 1989). Nevertheless, participants must still be provided with a variety of explicit and implicit participatory methodologies in order to avoid feelings of isolation and to constructively participate in the online learning environment. The following section addresses the quality and effect of participants' interactions in *Wired Class*.

E-Mail

Students did not find e-mail to be a useful and easy method of interaction with classmates. A reason, as recounted by one student, was that classmates did not regularly access and check their e-mails nor quickly respond to others' messages. Feedback from a student who did not think that using e-mail was a good method of student-student interaction indicated that, "To contact my classmates I have to use the e-mail, but only a few students get into e-mail and use it. Contacting them is very difficult."

This experience suggested the need for a more reliable communication medium to encourage and facilitate interaction among online students. An asynchronous interaction tool, *Quick Messenger*, was developed to address this need, allowing students to send and receive messages using instant messaging (IM) tools. Students could check to see who was online and send quick messages to anyone currently connected to *Wired Class*. When the other party received the message, an alert to that affect displayed on the receiver's screen, allowing the message receiver to read it and instantly respond without having to close the main window or move to a new page.

Discussion Boards

In *Wired Class*, although discussion board participation was essential and tutors sent many reminder messages to students to participate, the average number of postings was very low (one message per student per two weeks), and many students "lurked" and posted fewer than three messages for 12 discussion topics. Students commented that they did not participate because (1) they could not post "correct answers" that would add meaningful value to discussions, (2) they had nothing to say, or (3) they did not consider discussions to be as important as conventional tasks. Other interesting characteristics of discussion communications were:

- The majority of students accessed discussion boards only in the last few minutes before a lesson deadline. This may have been because the discussion questions came at the end of each lesson.

- Because discussion questions varied in complexity, in discussions that addressed more debatable questions, students were motivated enough to engage actively in critical thinking processes and paid more attention to interaction with peers. Topics that required low cognitive effort did not help students use higher order thinking, interact with others, or learn from others' experience.

- Participation rates increased as the term went on. Flottemesch (2000) reported that students rarely interact via discussion boards because of a lack of opportunity to develop peer relations and/or because of intimidation about using new technology. After 4 or 5 weeks of studying in *Wired Class*, students who had not previously participated in discussions began to participate actively and become familiar with the new style of technology-based constructivist learning.

- The more the instructor participated, the more messages students posted. This is consistent with Harris (1999) who reported that the role of the instructor in discussion is as important as the role of the "chair of a conference." He argued that the instructor's role is essential to open and close discussions, to encourage students to participate and interact, to keep discussions on track, and to assess learning. Jonassen, Myers, and McKillop (1996) claimed that instructor-student interaction "exemplifies the constructivist design model" of online education, but the instructor's contributions should be only 9-15% of the message volume. Trentin called the instructor's modest participation the "initial approach" necessary to break "the ice between the students and those responsible for leading and assisting them throughout the course" (Trentin, 2000, p. 19). According to Trentin, the outcome of using this approach is that distance learners' sense of isolation is reduced and this helps to enrich and foster discussion. These findings suggest that online instructors should pay close attention to strategies that foster participation and build a sense of community. This can be achieved by directing questions to students, asking them to suggest new learning materials or Web links, or posting alternative points of view on discussion boards.

- The quality of social and cognitive-related interactions in the discussion groups appeared to be very low. This was apparent in students' superficial responses, which tended to (1) repeat information from others' messages without additional explanation, (2) support/reject others' opinions without adding personal comments or providing clear evidence, (3) offer solutions without providing clear interpretation, (4) provide solutions directly depicted from the text, and not from external Web resources or self-experience, and (5) ask questions that were not directly related to the discussion topic.

- Content analysis of students' discussion board messages showed that when students were challenged by discussion questions, they did not resort to Web links and this did not allow them to find information to clarify the discussion problem or respond to the discussion question.

- Although learner-tutor interaction is one of the key features of Web-based distance education and is interrelated to both learner/learner and learner/content interaction, it was found that it is not a significant factor in determining students' academic success unless there is a sufficient quantity of relevant, motivating, and content-related messages passing between and among correspondents.

In summary, because interactive and cooperative learning is a function of students' interactivity levels and social skills (Fisher, 2000), and since the learning process is influenced by proficiency in information manipulation (Henri, 1991), little educational effectiveness can be gained from involving students in group discussions if they are unable to carry out in-depth processing of discussion problems, are not interested in group-based learning, or do not have the necessary skills and experience to participate in such activities.

Interaction With Course Content

For learning to occur, students must interact and process the content of the course themselves (Bower & Hilgard, 1981). The design and development of the content is very important, not only to facilitate learner-content interaction but also to direct and foster other types of Web-based interactions which are vital for the success of learning (Kanuka, 2000; Moore, 1989). According to Moore, learner-content interaction is important in obtaining intellectual information and constructing knowledge from the course material. This type of interaction takes place in a variety of ways and many strategies can be developed to help students obtain information from the material.

In *Wired Class*, the most important issue considered in designing the content was learner-content interaction. Students were able not only to read the content in short and visually attractive chunks, but also to explore, browse, and choose before reading throughout the lesson. Students were able to choose and link among chunks and to previous lessons or support materials, use interactive visuals (elements, graphics, animations, and tools), search the library catalog, seek more information in links provided with each lesson, assess their learning and receive auto-feedback, submit their work, and receive immediate feedback from instructors.

As a result, it was not surprising to find that students' perception of student-content interaction was a significant factor in predicting and explaining their academic success. Student performance measures indicated that learners who were satisfied with interaction with the structure and format of course content earned higher grades than those who were not.

DEVELOPING THE PRESENTATION ENVIRONMENT

Too often, classroom-based research studies in education are unable to state that one treatment is conclusively superior to another. Researchers explain their results by asserting that there may have been uncontrolled and immeasurable effects introduced by the learning environment. Online learning environments may have an advantage over classrooms as research laboratories since there are more factors that can be controlled in online instruction. The controllable or manageable characteristics of online instruction should be used to try to optimize the learning experience for students, whether for research purposes or for real learning. This section of the paper describes some of these.

User Experience and Training

One issue that can affect student learning in Web-based environments is students' previous computer experience. Whether students possess substantial or minimal previous computer experience, the learning environment must be selected or designed to reduce the effect of that experience on the learning that is to take place.

Wired Class was designed for students with minimal Internet experience, so it was not surprising that student performance measures failed to indicate significant relationships between previous Internet experience and satisfaction and perception of ease of use of *Wired Class*. This means that if the design and structure of the learning environment are friendly and usable, students' previous Internet experience and skills may be discountable, and students can learn via the learning environment without their background influencing their expectations or their learning. However, this does not mean there is no need to prepare students or enhance their experience and skills to use computers and the Internet.

According to student and instructor feedback, a Web learning environment such as *Wired Class* should be acceptable if:

- It is appropriate to students' experience level and does not require prior experience in using the Internet or Web-based learning.
- No obvious technical problems are present.
- Students are able to learn to use the system in a very short time.
- It provides a variety of tools for students to access information and contact instructors and classmates.
- Communication tools are easy to use.
- It provides tools for instructors/designers to edit and publish Web pages without having to learn HTML or principles of Web design.

On the other hand, Web learning environments may have deficiencies. Some *Wired Class* users suggested that the following kinds of issues bear attention:

- Most learning management systems are text based and require learners to have good spelling, vocabulary, grammar, and typing skills. This can affect the kinds of constructivist learning activities an instructional designer might employ. For example, asynchronous rather than synchronous activities may be preferred by students who wish to perfect constructed communications before transmitting them electronically to other learners or instructors.

This is unlike chat rooms where spontaneity of responses is required for participation.

- Web-based learning environments require usually untrained learners (and instructors) to deal with hardware such as printers and modems. Users must also deal with the myriad software issues that inevitably arise from Web-based Internet connectivity issues such as plug-ins, viruses, spam, and so forth.

- There should be online help (preferably multimedia-enriched) to guide students through the learning environment, particularly at the beginning of instruction when the interface is likely to be unfamiliar, whether or not it is user-friendly. There should also be online content- and context-related help to direct learners to Web-based learning resources.

- Users should have access to online manuals that are searchable and linkable from online help. The online documentation should be printable for offline viewing when Internet connections are not available, or for use as adjunct material when online instruction is taking place.

Website Navigability

Today, most Web-based instruction in education is delivered via learning management systems such as WebCT or Blackboard. Such commercial systems are typically optimized for online learners and take into account the kinds of issues described above. However, often and for a variety of reasons institutions or instructors are unable or prefer not to utilize commercial systems, but instead create their own customized Web-based online learning environments. Whether a vendor or home-built strategy is adopted, there are many issues beyond content design that the instructional designer must consider: ease of site navigation must be a central aspect of instructional Web sites. In *Wired Class*, the aim was to help learners to understand the structure of the site so that they could logically locate content, learning resources, and tools. Following are some of the practices that were employed in *Wired Class*:

- In Web-based instructional delivery environments, the starting page must serve as a crossroad or origin point to guide learners toward exploring, understanding, and navigating through the site. In *Wired Class*, the starting page provided an overview of the whole site, categorizing the major areas, providing a brief description of each, together with its links. Well-designed homepages have been found to be essential for young and well-trained users who return to the homepage frequently to regain their orientation and to locate information (Meyer et al., 1997). Therefore, links in the homepage must be categorized and detailed, but with a moderate number of links to prevent learner confusion. These links should not take the learner too far from the starting page. At the same time, a homepage link should be available on each lesson page to take the learner back to a familiar place on the site.

- A number of navigation conventions were adopted in *Wired Class* to prevent learners from getting lost in the Web site. Rather than rely on either module presequencing or learner-controlled exploration, an index of links was provided. It was felt that the consistency of design as well as the ability for students to track their pathway in the site using pull-down menus, toolbars, and expanded/extracted menus would help them define their location and keep them visually oriented. Expanded/extracted Java Script menus were used to maintain the interest of the students (and even the instructors!). Labels were used to describe the function and destination of links, and back links to the starting page or high-level site categories were included on every page.

- Although frames seem to be a useful approach to reduce download time and to keep students visually focused, their use is not generally considered to be good design practice. In the design of *Wired Class*, there was concern about the ease with which frame-based resources or documents from other Web sites might distract learners and cause them to link out of the learning environment. Other problems with frames are that they cannot be bookmarked within the learning environment, their pages are difficult or impossible to reload/refresh, and in-site and Web search engines cannot easily search their contents.

Information Presentation

Whether an instructional Web-based learning environment is based on vendor learning management systems or home-grown implementations, the instructional designer has many options regarding the nature of the content presentation. The importance of a well-designed user interface is that it facilitates and improves the performance of learners in using the Web and helps them to focus their attention on studying and learning the information more closely (Najjar, 1998). Effective use of color, for example, can give the learner a good first impression of the site content and encourage his or her acceptance (Najjar, 1990). In addition, graphics and symbols are the most visible elements on the Web and if they are simple, well labeled, consistent, and displayed with an optimal resolution, they can increase learner motivation and concentration (Pellone, 1995). Similarly, the clear, uncluttered, and consistent layout of instructional screens makes the learners' task easier and helps them to focus on the content. Experience garnered from *Wired Class* revealed a number of other issues:

- Students do not like to scroll long pages; this implies that consideration should be given to optimizing the length of course pages when designing online material. Tradeoffs may need to be made regarding the relationship between optimal lengths of content display versus page download times. While it may sometimes be desirable from a learning standpoint to present larger amounts of content in one page, that benefit may be neutralized from lengthy page download times that negatively affect learners' perceptions of the overall learning experience.

- Another "lesson learned" with *Wired Class* concerns the design of image labels and captions. Students are familiar, from textbooks, with the use of captioning to provide brief descriptions of images, but this technique is inappropriate for visually impaired students who may require a screen reader to identify images. A guide for addressing this issue can be found at the U.S. Department of Justice's Section 508 Website (United States Department of Justice) which states:

    Section 508 ... requires that Federal agencies' electronic and information technology is accessible to people with disabilities, including employees and members of the public.

    Section 508 establishes requirements for any electronic and information technology developed, maintained, procured, or used by the Federal government. The term "electronic and information technology" has been defined by the Access Board in regulations published December 21, 2000.

In general, Web-based images such as those used in *Wired Class* require a precise and meaningful labeling strategy appropriate for students with special needs.

- Macromedia Flash is a popular a tool for Web page design, but as Nielsen (1995) claims, its use in Web-based learning content requires careful consideration. For example, some browser buttons/ functions (e.g., back, find in page, and font size) do not work within Flash. This can affect visually impaired students who may have to enlarge font sizes or search for specific words on the Web site. With Flash, hyperlink colors do not work consistently, thereby potentially affecting learners' perceptions of what they have seen or where they have been from links they have visited. Therefore, if Flash is used, for example to enhance interactivity, course designers (and students) must be made aware of such issues.

- The use of the Adobe PDF (Portable Document Format) has become widespread on the Web to distribute documents that must retain their original formatting. However, PDF documents are static and do not support interactivity and dynamic effects such as are possible from online Web pages. Instructional designers need to weigh the convenience of making materials available in PDF format against the more difficult to develop but pedagogically more valuable features of interactive Web pages. PDF should be used only if a large amount of information needs to be distributed and printed rather than read online.

Standardization of the Learning Environment

One of the issues that concerned *Wired Class* developers was how to ensure course material and client configuration (hardware and software) compatibility without precluding the use of Windows or Macintosh computers. An advantage to Web browsers is that, from a hardware platform standpoint, they are ubiquitous. Unfortunately, that is not true among different versions of browsers. A decision was made to try to use the most up-to-date browser functionality in the courseware while providing as broad base of access as possible to users of different browsers or versions of browsers.

Important tradeoffs had to be made to realize this goal, as creating text-only materials accessible from any browser would deprive students of many interactive capabilities of Web-based technology (e.g., style sheets, Java Applets, Java Scripts, ActiveX, and plug-ins). Developers compromised by using a minimal number of Java Scripts and Java Applets (for interactivity) accessible by Internet Explorer and Netscape Communicator browsers, both of which support Java Scripts and Java Applets. On the other hand, while ActiveX is a very useful, easy to use, and cost-effective tool for Web development, it was not used because it is supported by only by Internet Explorer.

Because no incompatibility issues were reported by *Wired Class* users, it can be concluded that:

- Standard HTML language, which is 100% compatible with all Web clients and standard Java and Java Scripts, is the best way to ensure that pages are compatible with browsers. Web browsers interpret the latest HTML tags, particularly Dynamic HTML (DHTML), differently, and do not support all types of scripts.

- Compatibility is essential, not only among different browsers, but also different versions of the same browser. New versions of browsers have features (e.g., cascading style sheets or DHTML) that are not available in older versions of the same browser. To reach the largest possible audience and to take advantage of DHTML, Web-based instruction should be designed in a way that takes advantage of the advanced features of DHTML while still maintaining compatibility with older browsers.

- Using standard client-side and server-side programming languages (e.g., Java Scripts, Java, and CGI Scripts) may be more useful than using cutting-edge technology (e.g., ActiveX, Flash, Shockwave, etc.) which requires additional software (plug-ins) to be downloaded and installed in users' machines. Browser incompatibility with different operating systems (e.g., Macintosh, OS2, and UNIX) reduces the value of many of the new functions that vendors release on a continuing basis.

- Although a screen resolution of 640×480 pixels displays less material than a resolution of 800×600, frames, pages and graphics should be optimized for Netscape Navigator 3.0+ or Internet Explorer 4.0+ at a resolution of 640×480 pixels.

- A workstation's operating system affects how colors are displayed; therefore Web pages should be designed to use only 216 colors, the common base for both Windows and Macintosh.

CONSIDERING THE COST BENEFITS

Decisions are often made to use new technologies such as the Internet in order to reach a wide population of learners for less cost than would be incurred using traditional instructional strategies (Inglis, Ling, & Joosten, 1999). However, from analyses of *Wired Class* cost elements, it was not possible to conclude that this is always the case. Internet-based instructional delivery costs are a function of many factors, some of which include the purpose of the distance education program, the nature of the learning objectives, the pedagogical approach, the quality of learning materials, the lifetime of the materials, and student enrollments.

Cost factors that need to be considered can be categorized as capital infrastructure costs, course materials design and development costs, and instructional delivery and support costs. Cost analyses are meaningless unless cost comparisons can be made between the technology-based delivery scenario and some other comparative base such as a traditional classroom environment. However, while it is reasonable to *construct* a framework to estimate costs of online learning based on each of the three cost categories, it might not be useful to *compare* these, one by one, with those of other instructional modes, such as classroom instruction. Consider, for example, that online learning requires a substantial investment in hardware, networking, software, and support training, while more conventional print and audiocassette programs are much less expensive to create. However, the higher investment required to create the online learning environment might be dramatically offset by the high cost of creating and supporting traditional classrooms in which the lower cost instructional materials would be used.

In *Wired Class*, a factor in the development and support costs was a desire to use high-quality online materials. Multimedia objects and interactive segments (e.g., input forms, interactive maps, etc.) were incorporated into the learning materials with the intention of improving student performance. More planning and programming time was needed to produce these materials than would have been required if only simple textual materials had been developed, and to develop the interactive materials required both the licensing of expensive and sophisticated production tools as well as employing skilled Web developers to use them.

However, the results of this study and previous research (e.g., Joy & Garcia, 2000; Spencer, 1999; Whittington, 1987) indicate that the use of interactive multimedia technology may not always enhance student learning. Spencer (1996) reviewed the effectiveness of media attributes in student performance and found that, overall, audio or visual media (e.g., radio, films, and television) that require expensive equipment, much time to develop and maintain, and skilled producers, may not improve student performance when compared with other static and low-cost media (e.g., textbooks and filmstrips). The information provided by these media "is often too much, in quantity or speed of delivery, and the student perceives only a fraction of it, and understands even less" (Spencer, 1999). Online developers should not assume that students will learn better from technology-based delivery systems. Rather, they should focus on instructional design strategies, regardless of the medium they choose (Joy & Garcia, 2000). Unless the use of multimedia (e.g., motion, sound, three dimensional images, simulation, etc.) to present specific concepts or skills (e.g., language) is considered to be essential for students to understand processes, achieve course objectives, or reduce study time, textual materials may be more cost effective than media-rich online materials, particularly for small population courses (Inglis, 1999).

It is not clear that even when high quality and/or sophisticated presentation is considered to be essential, that online learning is more reliable and efficient than if CD-ROM-based materials are deployed. The significant and recurring costs associated with Internet hardware, software, and network support as well as those concerned with administering and supporting online students may mitigate the cost savings that might be expected from using the Internet. In CD-ROM delivery, the ratio of fixed costs to variable costs is quite high, as the costs of delivery are much less than the development costs, thereby allowing for potential economies of scale to be realized (Inglis et al., 1999).

In *Wired Class*, the ratio of fixed to variable costs was relatively insignificant and offset by the high variable costs of support. This resulted from the design objective of maximizing the participatory role of instructors and facilitators to manage the learning environment, to solicit and monitor student participation, to process student inputs, and to respond to students' questions, and so forth. These activities can cause instructors to invest significant time in ongoing instruction, making the operating costs of even relatively simple online materials higher than those of print (Rumble, 2001).

Because offering distance students the opportunity for dialogue with the instructor is critical for social and academic support and reducing drop-out rates (Simpson, 2000), both synchronous and asynchronous communications should be implemented with care. Synchronous requires fast (expensive) connectivity and highly paid staff to arrange, moderate, and conduct live discussions. This raises the issue of the number of students that can be effectively supervised per course or per hour, and how these hours can be reduced without affecting the quality of learning (Rumble, 2001). However, asynchronous requires much time and also highly paid staff for planning students' activities and providing quality learning materials. Therefore, the best way to increase the ratio of fixed development costs to variable costs is to reduce instructors' levels of involvement and minimize student-instructor interaction. This can be done by using self-study and self-assessment materials, and by encouraging students to support each other via online discussions. To do this, students may need to spend more time learning from the online materials and from peers who substitute for instructors.

Other ways to reduce the per-learner effect of fixed costs are to spread the costs over more learners, maintain the instruction for more years, and/or offer more courses on the system in which the fixed costs have already been invested. Increasing course enrollment should be considered, if possible, particularly if the fixed costs of establishing the learning environment are higher than the variable costs. Extending a course's lifetime (for example, for 5 years), and deploying additional courses in the learning environment can spread the fixed costs of course development over a larger number of students, allowing the cost per student or study hour to decrease significantly. Moreover, by increasing the number of international enrollments per course, the potential for economies of scale can be exploited to offset online delivery costs when compared to the costs of copying and distributing CD-ROMs or print to world markets (Inglis et al., 1999).

Another set of cost factors that must be considered are the costs of *receiving* online instruction in the home or school. Access or reception costs include the costs of purchasing computers, support software, and cost of the Internet connectivity (e.g., modems, Internet service providers, phone lines). These costs should be considered as an integral part of all cost analyses, particularly in countries with poor and/or expensive network infrastructures.

Overall, the *Wired Class* experience revealed that it is unlikely that cost savings can be realized from converting traditional instruction to online Internet-based instruction. The design and development costs of highly interactive and high-quality online materials are less or similar to those for print/interactive CD-ROMs, but the variable and recurring costs of maintaining online materials, supporting, assessing, and administering online students, administering and connecting to Web servers, as well as the cost of student Internet access, can be significant. Instead of reducing costs, online learning systems can be more expensive than traditional instruction. However, if there is a need for Web interactivity and global access to the Internet, that need must be weighed against the inevitable costs described above.

REFERENCES

Baynton, M. (1992). Dimensions of "control" in distance education: A factor analysis. *The American Journal of Distance Education, 6*(2), 17-31

Berge, Z., Collins, M. P., & Dougherty, K. (2000). Design guidelines for Web-based courses, In B. Abbey (Ed.), *Instructional and cognitive impacts of Web-based education* (pp. 209-216). London: Idea Group.

Birmingham, W. P., Drabenstott, K. M., Frost, C. O., Warner, A. J., & Willis, K. (2000). *The University of Michigan Digital Library: This is not your father's library.* The University of Michigan Digital Library. Retrieved from http://www.csdl.tamu.edu/DL94/paper/umdl.html

Bower, H., & Hilgard, E. (1981). *Theories of learning.* Englewood Cliffs, NJ: Prentice-Hall.

Clark, R. (1994). Assessment of distance learning technology. In E. Barker & H. O'Neil (Eds.), *Technology assessment in education and training* (pp. 63-78). Hove, UK: Erlbaum.

Fisher, M. (2000). Implementation considerations for instructional design of Web-based learning environments. In B. Abbey (Ed.), *Instructional and cognitive impacts of Web-based education* (pp. 78-101). London: Idea Group.

Flottemesch, K. (2000). Building effective interaction in distance education: A review of the literature. *Educational Technology, 40*(3), 46-51.

Garrison, D. R. (1989). *Understanding distance education: A framework of the future.* London: Routledge.

Garrison, D. R. (1990). An analysis and evaluation of audio teleconferencing to facilitate education at a distance. *The American Journal of Distance Education, 4*(3), 16-23.

Green, D. (1997). The Web as a tool for research. *The Educational Technology Journal, 6*(4). Retrieved from http://www.fromnowon.org/

GVU. (1999). *10th GVU public survey, W3C.* Retrieved from http://www.w3c.org

Harris, R. (1999). Computer-conferencing issues in higher education. *Innovations in Education and Training International, 36*(1), pp. 80-91

Harrison, N., & Bergen, C. (2000). Some design strategies for developing an online course, *Educational Technology, 40*(1), 57-60.

Henri, F. (1991). Computer conferencing and content analysis. In A. Kaye (Ed.), *Collaborative learning through computer conferencing*, NATO ASI Series F, Vol. 90.

Inglis, A. (1999). Is online delivery less costly than print and is it meaningful to ask? *Distance Education, 20*(3), 220-239.

Inglis, A., Ling, P., & Joosten, V. (1999). *Delivering digitally: Managing the transition to the knowledge media.* London: Kogan Page.

Janicki, T., & Liegle, J. (2001). Development and evaluation of a framework for creating Web-based learning modules: A pedagogical and systems perspective. *Journal of Asynchronous Learning Networks, 5*(1). Retrieved from http://www.aln.org/alnweb/journal/Vol5_issue1/Janicki/Janicki.htm

Jonassen, H., Myers, J. M., & McKillop, A. M. (1996). From constructivism to constructionism: Learning with hypermedia/multimedia rather than from it. In B. Wilson (Ed.), *Constructivist learning environments: Case studies in instructional design* (pp. 93-106). Englewood Cliffs, NJ: Educational Technology Publications.

Joy, E., & Garcia, F. (2000). Measuring learning effectiveness: A new look at no-significant-difference findings. *Journal of Asynchronous Learning Networks, 4*(1). Retrieved from http://www.aln.org/alnweb/journal/Vol4_issue1/joygarcia.htm

Kanuka, H. (2000, May 3-6). *Learner-content interaction: The silent but active participant.* Proceedings of the 16th Annual Conference of Canadian Association for Distance Education. Retrieved from http://www.ulaval.ca/aced2000cade/english/proceedings.htm

Lilla, R., & Hipps, N. (1999) Searching for the Yahoos of academia: Academic subject directories on the Web. *Educational Technology, 39*(6), 33-39.

Lockee, B., Burton, J. K., Cross, & L. H. (1999). No comparison: Distance education finds a new use for "no significant difference." *Educational Technology Research and Development, 47*(3), 33-42.

Meyer, B., Sit, R. A., Spaulding, V. A., Mead, S. E., & Walker, N. (1997, March). *Age group differences in World Wide Web naviation.* CHI97, Conference on Human Factors in Computing Systems, Atlanta, Georgia.

Moore, G. (1989) Three types of interaction. *The American journal of Distance Education, 3*(2), 1-6.

Najjar, J. (1990) Using color effectively (or peacocks can't fly) IBM TR52.0018, Atlanta, GA, IBM Corporation.

Najjar, J. (1998) Principles of educational multimedia user interface design. *Human Factors, 40*(2), 311-323.

Nielsen, J. (1995, May 7-11). *Usability inspection methods.* Proceedings of ACM CHI'95 Conference on Human Factors in Computing Systems, Denver, CO.

Pellone, G. (1995). Educational software design: A literature review. *Australian Journal of Educational Technology, 11*(1), 68-84.

Powell, G. (2001). The ABCs of online course design. *Educational Technology, 41*(4), 43-47.

Ritchie, H., & Newby, T. (1989). Classroom lecture/discussion vs. live televised instruction: A comparison of effects on student performance, attitude, and interaction. *The American Journal of Distance Education, 3*(3), 36-45.

Rumble, G. (2001). The costs and costing of networked learning. *Journal of Asynchronous Learning Networks, 5*(2). http://www.aln.org/alnweb/journal/Vol5_issue2/Rumble/Rumble.htm

Sadik, A. (2002). *The design, implementation and evaluation of a Web-based learning environment for distance education.* Unpublished doctoral dissertation, Institute for Learning, University of Hull, UK.

Simpson, O. (2000). Supporting students in open and distance learning. *Open and Distance Learning Series*, London: Kogan Page.

Smith-Gratto, K. (2000). Strengthening learning on the Web: Programmed instruction and constructivism. In B. Abbey (Ed.), *Instructional and cognitive impacts of web-based education*. London: Idea Group.

Spencer, K. (1996). *Media and technology in education: Raising academic standards.* Liverpool, England: Manutius Press.

Spencer, K. (1999). Educational technology: An unstoppable force. A selective review of research into the effectiveness of educational media. *Educational Technology & Society 2*(4). Retrienved from http://ifets.ieee.org/periodical/vol_4_99/spencer.html

Spitzer, D. (2001). Don't forget the high-touch with the high-tech in distance learning. *Educational Technology, 41*(2), 51-55.

Thorpe, M. (1998). Assessment and "third generation" distance education. *Distance Education, 19*(2), 265-284.

Trentin, G. (2000). The quality-interactivity relationship in distance education. *Educational Technology, 40*(1), 17-27.

United States Department of Justice. Section 508 Home Page, http://www.usdoj.gov/crt/508/

Weston, T., & Barker, L. (2001) Designing, implementing, and evaluating Web-based learning modules for university students. *Educational Technology, 41*(4), 15-22.

Whittington, N. (1987). Is instructional television educationally effective? A research review. *The American Journal of Distance Education, 1*(1), 47-57.

CHAPTER 10

A FRAMEWORK FOR ANALYZING, DESIGNING, AND SEQUENCING PLANNED eLEARNING INTERACTIONS

Atsusi Hirumi

Published taxonomies for classifying distance learning interactions give educators valuable insights into the nature and range of potential interactions that may be used to facilitate eLearning. However, existing taxonomies neither depict the relationship between, nor provide practical guidelines for planning or managing a comprehensive set of interactions necessary to achieve a specified set of objectives. This article posits a three-level framework for classifying eLearning interactions. It illustrates how the framework may be used to design and sequence eLearning interactions, analyze planned interactions to reduce the need for costly revisions, and organize research on interactivity and eLearning to help interpret findings and guide future studies.

In traditional face-to-face classrooms, key interactions that affect learners' attitudes and performance often occur spontaneously in real-time. Good instructors interpret students' body language, answer questions, clarify

The Perfect Online Course: Best Practices for Designing and Teaching
pp. 201–227
Copyright © 2009 by Information Age Publishing
All rights of reproduction in any form reserved.

expectations, facilitate activities, promote discussions, elaborate concepts, render guidance, and provide timely and appropriate feedback as they present content in a clear and engaging manner. It is the ability to initiate and facilitate such interactions that often distinguishes a good instructor from a bad one. During eLearning, communications are predominately asynchronous and mediated by technology. Opportunities to individualize instruction and help learners' interpret content information based on spontaneous verbal and non-verbal cues are confined. Key interactions that occur in real-time face-to-face environments must be carefully planned and sequenced as an integral part of eLearning.

Various frameworks have been published for identifying and classifying distance learning interactions that may be grouped into four basic categories, including communication, purpose, activity, and tool-based taxonomies. Moore (1989) posited what may be the most widely known communications-based framework, defining the sender and receiver of three basic interactions: student–student, student–teacher and student–content. Student-student interactions occur "between one learner and another learner, alone or in group settings, with or without the real-time presence of an instructor" (Moore, 1989, p. 4). Student-teacher interactions attempt to motivate and stimulate the learner and allow for the clarification of misunderstanding by the learner in regard to the content. Student-content interactions are defined as a process of "intellectually interacting with content to bring about changes in the learner's understanding, perspective, or cognitive structures" (Moore, 1989, p. 2).

With the increasing use of computer-based delivery systems, Hillman, Willis, and Gunawardena (1994) argued convincingly for a fourth class of communication-based interaction (student-interface). The interface acts as the point or means of interaction between the learner and the content, instructor, fellow learners, or others. It includes learners' use of electronic tools and navigational aids as well as the layout of text and graphical elements.

Several authors posit additional classes of communication-based interactions. For example, Carlson and Repman (1999) defined learner-instructional interactions as those between the learner and the content that traditionally utilize strategies such as questioning, feedback and clarification, and control of lesson pace and sequence to facilitate learning. They further delineate social interactions as personal attempts to modify or enhance the quality of the instructional interaction by interpreting body language, promoting a sense of comfort, and developing class management routines. Northrup and Rasmussen (2000) stressed the importance of closing communication loops and distinguishing feedback from interactions with instructional materials, defining a total of four classes including student-to-student, student-to-instructor, student-to-instructional materials, and student-to-management (feedback) interactions. Mortera-Gutierrez and Murphy (2000) reminded us that we must also consider interactions from the instructor's perspective, extending the basic communication categories to include instructor-facilitator, instructor-peers, instructor-support staff and technical personnel, and instructor-organization interactions.

Alternative approaches codify interactions by purpose. For example, Hannafin (1989) posited five basic functions for computer-based interactions: confirmation, pacing, inquiry, navigation, and elaboration. With the emerging use of telecommunication technologies, Breakthebarriers.com (2001) identified nine basic purposes, including synchronous communication, asynchronous communication, browsing and clicking, branching, tracking, help, practice, feedback, and coaching. To guide the selection of online instructional strategies and tactics, Northrup (2001) proposes five interaction attributes (or purposes): to interact with content, to collaborate, to converse, to help monitor and regulate learning (intrapersonal interaction), and to support performance.

"Activity-based" interactions or *inter*activities are designed to stimulate active learning and the development of learning communities. For example, Bonk and Reynolds (1997) delimit three categories of interactivities based on a wide range of literature on learning and instruction, including critical thinking, creative thinking, and cooperative learning interactivities. Similarly, Harris (1994a, 1994b, 1994c) posits three classes, describing a variety of interactivities associated with information searching, information sharing, and collaborative problem solving.

Still others, such as Bonk and King (1998) take a "tools-based" approach, focusing on the capabilities afforded by various telecommunication technologies to facilitate eLearning interactions. They delimit five levels: electronic mail and delayed-messaging tools, remote access and delayed collaboration tools, real-time brainstorming and conversation tools, real-time text collaboration tools, and real-time multimedia and/or hypermedia collaboration tools.

The current frameworks provide valuable insights into the nature and range of interactions that may be used to facilitate eLearning. However, they neither illustrate the relationship between, nor provide practical guidelines for sequencing eLearning interactions to facilitate achievement of specified objectives. Within a lesson, when is it important for the instructor to contact the student? When should students interact with other students, with content information or with external resources? When should students be given the opportunity branch, or to receive help, practice, or feedback? How should each of these interactions be designed? What tools should be used to facilitate each interaction? This article seeks to help distance educators answer these questions by proposing a framework that delineates the relationship between fundamental communication-based interactions and by illustrating how the framework may be used to analyze, design, and sequence planned eLearning interactions.

PROPOSED FRAMEWORK

The framework posits three basic, interrelated levels of interactions that may be planned as an integral part of eLearning (Figure 10.1).

Level I interactions occur within each individual learner. Level II interactions occur between the learner and human and non-human resources. Level III interactions delineate an eLearning strategy; a set of Level II interactions that are designed and sequenced to stimulate Level I interactions.

The description of each level is given from the learner's viewpoint. This is not to say that the instructor's perspective (Montera-Gutierrez & Murphy, 2000) and other views are inconsequential. Rather, attention is placed here on the learners and their requirements in accordance with learner-centered approaches to instructional design, as discussed by Berge (in this issue) and others (e.g., APA, 1993; Dillion & Zhu, 1997).

Level I: Learner-Self Interactions

Learner-self interactions occur within each individual learner. They include both the cognitive operations that constitute learning as well as metacognitive processes that help individuals monitor and regulate their learning.

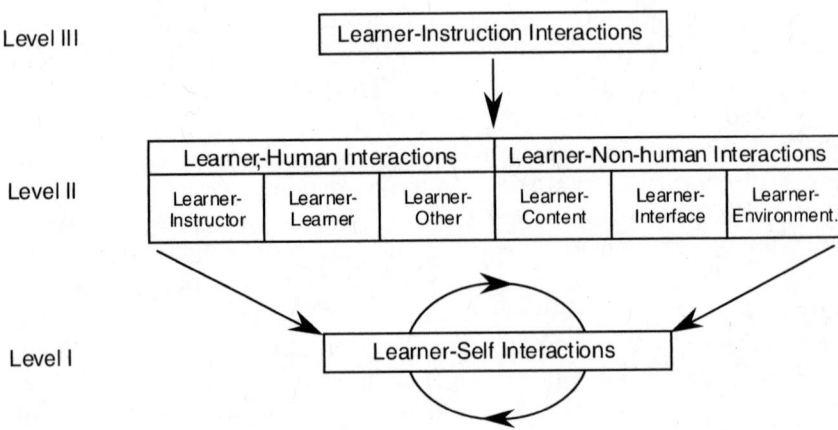

Figure 10.1.   Three levels of planned eLearning interactions.

The specific cognitive operations that occur within an individual depend on the instructional designer's epistemological beliefs. A behaviorist may recognize that some learner-self interactions occur, but chooses not to pay particular attention to them (e.g., Skinner, 1969). A behaviorist would concentrate solely on Level II and Level III interactions and how they reinforce or weaken particular behaviors. For someone who believes in information-processing theories of learning, key learner-self interaction may include sensory memory, selective attention, pattern recognition, short term memory, rehearsal and chunking, encoding, long-term memory, and retrieval (Atkinson and Shiffrin, 1968). Development constructivists (e.g., Piaget, 1971; Bruner, 1974) would key on learner-self interactions that result from adaptations to the environment which are characterized by increasingly sophisticated methods of representing and organizing information. In contrast, social constructivists would focus on learner-self interactions that occur when individuals interact with their social and cultural environment (Vygotsky, 1978). The proposed framework does not adhere to any particular learning theory or epistemology. However, the type of Level I (learner-self) interactions the designer ascribes to are important because they affect the selection of Level III interaction and the design and sequencing of Level II interactions as detailed latter in this article.

Studies identifying the characteristics of self-regulated learners underscore the importance of distinguishing learner-self as a primary level of eLearning interactions. Learners are self-regulated to the degree that they actively participate metacognitively, motivationally, and behaviorally in their learning (Zimmerman & Martinez-Pons, 1986). Self-regulated learners take responsibility for their own learning, initiate efforts to acquire desired skills and knowledge (Zimmerman & Martinez-Pons, 1988), access metacognitive strategies and take steps to correct learning deficiencies (Zimmerman & Martinez-Pons, 1995), activate, alter and sustain learning (Zimmerman & Martinez-Pons, 1986) and to plan, organize, monitor, and evaluate their learning processes (Corno, 1994; Hagen & Weinstein, 1995; Zimmerman & Paulsen, 1995).

Due to the relatively constrained nature of learner-instructor and learner-learner interactions in an online environment, self-regulation may be particularly important for distance learners. Self-regulated learners may have a substantially greater potential for success in distance education than those who have relatively poor self-regulatory skills because they may not need as much prompting from an instructor or help from other learners to monitor, regulate, and otherwise facilitate their learning. Fortunately, self-regulation may be learned and instruction may be designed to compensate for possible deficiencies (cf. Ley & Young, 2001;

Northrup, 2001; Corno & Randi, 1999; Butler & Winne, 1995; Iran-Nejad, 1990).

Level II: Learner-Human and Non-Human Interactions

Level II interactions occur between the learner and other human and non-human eLearning resources and are designed to stimulate Level I interactions. Six classes of Level II interactions are presented based on a framework for comparing instructional strategies posited by Reigeluth and Moore (1999). For this article, brief descriptions of Level II interactions are given to delimit each category. References to related literature are provided if further details are desired.

Learner-Instructor Interactions

Learner-instructor interactions are defined as student- or instructor-initiated communications that occur before, during, and immediately after instruction. Moore (1989) characterized learner-instructor interactions as attempts to motivate and stimulate the learner and allow for the clarification of misunderstanding by the learner in regard to the content. A recent study of distance educator competencies revealed seven key learner-instructor interactions: to establish learning outcomes/objectives; to provide timely and appropriate feedback; to facilitate information presentation; to monitor and evaluate student performance; to provide (facilitate) learning activities; to initiate, maintain and facilitate discussions; and to determine learning needs and preferences (Thach & Murphy, 1995). Literature on feedback is further examined because it is vital to learner-instructor interactions (Northrup, in this issue; Northrup & Rasmussen, 2000) and elemental to both behavioral and cognitive theories of learning.

Bangert-Drowns, Kulik, Kulik, and Morgan (1991) asserted that:

> any theory that depicts learning as a process of mutual influence between learners and their environments must involve feedback implicitly or explicitly because, without feedback, mutual influence is by definition impossible. (p. 214)

Feedback compares actual performance to set standards (Johnson & Johnson, 1994). It informs learners of the accuracy of their responses to instructional questions (Cohen, 1985; Kulhavy, 1977) and may be used to increase response rate or accuracy, reinforce correct responses to prior stimuli, or change erroneous responses (Kulhavy & Wager, 1993). In networked environments, telecommunication technologies are expanding feedback options. Immediate and delayed feedback may provide learning guidance, lesson sequence advisement, motivational messages, critical comparisons and information about answer correctness and timeliness (Hoska, 1993). At minimum, feedback is essential during eLearning for closing message loops (Yacci, 2000; Northrup & Rasmussen, 2000), informing learners that communications are complete (Berge, 1999; Liaw & Huang, 2000; and Weller, 1988, as cited by Northrup, 2001). An extensive review of feedback research (Mory, 1996) and a textbook on instructional feedback methods (Dempsey & Sales, 1993) yield further insights into the design of this essential learner-instructor interaction.

Learner-Learner Interactions

Learner-learner interactions occur "between one learner and another learner, alone or in group settings, with or without the real-time presence of an instructor" (Moore, 1989, p. 4). Typically, such interactions ask learners to work together to analyze and interpret data, solve problems and share information, opinions, and insights. They are designed to help groups and individuals construct and apply targeted skills and knowledge.

Assigning individuals to groups does not mean that they will work collaboratively (Johnson & Johnson, 1994). Considerations for effective learner-learner interactions are similar in traditional classroom environments and eLearning environments (e.g., group size, group goals, individual roles and responsibilities, group and individual accountability, contact information, communications, grading). The challenge lies in planning and coordinating such interactions during eLearning.

Much has been written about learner-learner interactions, including, but not limited to, literature on cooperative learning (Slavin, 1987) and social constructivism (e.g., Jonassen, 1995, 1994, 1991; Piaget, 1971; Vygotsky, 1978; Bruner, 1974; von Glasersfeld, 1989a, 1989b; Rorty, 1991). A meaningful analysis that includes implications of such work for the design of learner-learner interactions goes beyond the purposes of this paper. Those interested in additional information on the planning, management and facilitation of learner-learner interactions are referred to the works of Chih and Corry and Berge (in this issue) among others (e.g., Bonk and Reynolds, 1997; Harris, 1994a; 1994b; 1994c).

Learner-Other Human Interactions

Learner-other human interactions utilize the potential for telecommunication technologies to break down the barrier of classroom walls and enable learners to search for, access, acquire, and apply a wealth of information from a variety of external resources. Increasing numbers of online courses ask learners to review external websites, as well as to communicate with others outside of class to promote knowledge construction and social discourse (e.g., Bonk & King, 1998). Such interactions include exchanges with teaching assistants, mentors, and subject matter experts, as well as student and academic support staff.

Some argue that certain attitudes and behaviors must be modeled during face-to-face interactions with real people in real-time and thus, eLearning is not appropriate. In such cases, it is essential to keep in mind that just because a course or training program is put online, not all interactions must occur online. Distance learners may be asked to visit a designated facility and work with subjects and certified personnel. Thinking that face-to-face interactions must occur between students and the instructor of record can be somewhat egocentric. Suitable interactions may be arranged between learners and other experts as a required component of counseling, humanities, and education programs, for example. The key lies in distilling the nature of and designing such experiences.

Accrediting agencies, such as the Southern Association of Colleges and Schools (SACS), also remind us that distance learners must be afforded the same services provided to local students. During the design of eLearning programs, educators must consider how distance learners will be able to contact and garner support and services from staff, such as librarians, advisors, and counselors. The pervasive use of computer technology also makes ready, if not immediate, access to technical support staff essential during eLearning.

Learner-other human interactions may occur online or face-to-face depending on the location and configuration of the learners and the other human resources. They may be planned as an integral part of a lesson or learners may be given random access from within or outside of the eLearning program. The key is to provide ready access to the expertise, supports, and services necessary to enter, navigate, and complete the educational or training system in a user-friendly fashion.

Learner-Content Interactions

Learners-content interactions occur when learners access audio, video, text, and graphic representations of the subject matter under study. While it seems only logical to assume that media matters (e.g., what I hear, I forget; what I see, I remember; what I do, I understand), research suggests otherwise. Media selection guides, such as those proposed by Reiser and Gagné (1983) indicate that video and graphics (or more specifically, interactions with simulations or real objects) are critical when teaching psychomotor skills and may have a significant impact when trying to affect learner attitudes (e.g., modeling). Furthermore, if sensory discriminations (visual, tactile, auditory) are a required part of learning (e.g., music education), a specific medium or a combination of media is required during instruction. However, comprehensive reviews of media comparison research conclude that use of media, in general, has minimal effects on student learning (Clark, 1994a, 1094b). Research reviews, focusing on distance learners, yield similar results (Russell, 1993, 1999). It appears that instructional design has a greater impact on student achievement than the media used to deliver the content.

There are some practical criteria to consider when designing learner-content interactions. First, are the plug-ins and other software applications necessary to read various multimedia file formats readily available to learners? The use of Flash, Java, RealAudio, RealVideo and other specialized multimedia programs require updated Web browsers that may be difficult for novice computer users to configure. Second, is the expertise necessary to generate the desired multimedia resources available on staff or are funds available to outsource such development requirements? Third, how durable are the multimedia resources? If multimedia is used to communicate content information that is highly volatile, it may not be practical to continuously update and revise the files. Finally, what is the return on investment for creating such files? Creating and maintaining multimedia content costs a lot more than text. Is the resulting effect on student attitudes, learning or performance worth the price?

Learner-Interface Interactions

When a computer acts as the primary delivery mechanism, its interface serves as the principal point or means of interaction with the content, instructor, learners, and the larger community. Attention must be placed on how the interface enables learners to manipulate electronic tools, access information, interpret visual elements, and complete goal-oriented tasks. Hillman, Willis, and Gunawardena (1994) suggested that the extent to which a learner is proficient with a specific medium correlates positively with the success the learner has in extracting information from the medium. Metros and Hedberg (in this issue) also point out that poor interface design can place high cognitive demands upon the learner that may take his or her attention away from the subject matter at hand. Learners cannot deal with content information if they are unable to use the interface. Learners must possess the skills necessary to operate the delivery system before they can be expected to successfully interact with human and non-human resources.

Norman (1988) suggested that mental models form as users interpret the interface's perceived action and its visible structure. Then, as the model develops, it serves as the basis for understanding the interface, predicting its future behavior, and controlling its actions. The development of an effective mental model may be facilitated by instructional activities or tools that help the learner become familiar with the interface (e.g., in-class exercises, orientation sessions, technology credit courses, help screens or job aids).

The design of engaging learner-interface interactions is discussed in detail by Metros and Hedberg (in this issue). In short, key factors include learners' mental model that enable them to become proficient in interacting with the mediating technology, learners' understanding of specific communication protocol associated with the delivery system to transmit and receive information, and learners' potential fear of (or anxiety with) working with the technology. Gillani and Relan (1997), Jones and Farquhar (1997) among others (cf. Neilsen, 1993) have posited additional guidelines for Web interface design.

Learner-Environment Interactions

Learner-environment interactions occur when learners manipulate tools, equipment, or other objects outside of the computer interface during eLearning. As noted earlier, not all eLearning interactions have to occur online. Learners may be sent a package of manipulatives, field equipment, or laboratory instruments and asked to use them as an integral part of eLearning. Learners may also be required to seek or travel to specific locations to gather, observe, and otherwise inspect materials, complete activities, or participate in planned events to achieve specified learning objectives.

For example, gaining technical or problem-solving skills by interacting with highly specialized and sophisticated equipment may be necessary aspects of science, aerospace, and engineering courses or training programs. In such instances, distance learners may be asked to go to a remote facility and work with an experienced scientist or engineer. Such interactions may be difficult to manage at a distance but, when necessary, they can be arranged.

Like planning complex learner-other human interactions, the keys are to: clearly define the required learning outcomes and identify when such experiences are essential for the achievement of those outcomes; carefully plan and coordinate the interactions so that learners readily understand what is expected of them and why it is important for them to interact with their environment; and integrate the event with other interactions and embed them within a sound instructional strategy to optimize the experience and ensure that learners reach the specified objectives and achieve the greatest return from time and effort invested on arranging such learner-environment interactions.

Level III: Learner-Instruction Interactions

Learner-instruction interactions consist of a series of events (or eLearning strategy) that are necessary to achieve a defined set of objectives. Level III interactions are considered a meta-level that transcend and serve to organize Level II interactions. Like Driscoll's (1994) definition for instruction, Level III interactions involve a deliberate arrangement of events to promote learning and facilitate goal achievement. Learner-instruction interactions are differentiated from Level II and Level I interactions to illustrate how theoretically grounded instructional strategies may be used to help distance educators design and sequence planned eLearning interactions.

Educators often fail to ground their designs in research and theory (Bonk & King, 1998; Bonk & Cunningham, 1998; Bednar, Cunningham, Duffy, and Perry, 1995). While there is no substitute for practical experience, difficulties occur when eLearning strategies are based solely on past practices. Without sufficient time, training, or support, educators have little choice but to rely on what they know best (i.e., teacher-directed methods). The problem is that key interactions are not often planned as an integral part of traditional classroom teaching materials because instructors typically facilitate such interactions in real time based on their expertise and intuition. As a result, key interactions necessary to stimulate eLearning are frequently missing when traditional classroom materials are posted online to promote eLearning.

So, how do learner-instruction interactions help guide the design and sequencing of Level II interactions? A cursory review of literature on teaching methods reveals a number of research-based, theoretically grounded instructional strategies (Table 10.1).

Each of the events associated with an instructional strategy may be considered an interaction—a transaction that occurs between the learner and other human or non-human resources. Educators can select an instructional strategy, based on the learning objectives, learner characteristics, context and their epistemological beliefs and use the events to design key interactions and the strategy to sequence the interactions. The application of a grounded instructional strategy gives educators a foundation for planning and managing a comprehensive series of eLearning interactions necessary to achieve a set of objectives based on a combination of research, theory, and practical experience.

Table 10.1. Sample Outlines of Grounded Instructional Strategies

Nine Events of Instruction

1. Gain Attention
2. Inform Learner of Objective(s)
3. Stimulate Recall of Prior Knowledge
4. Present Stimulus Materials
5. Provide Learning Guidance
6. Elicit Performance
7. Provide Feedback
8. Assess Performance
9. Enhance Retention and Transfer

Student-Center Learning

1. Set Learning Challenge
2. Negotiate Learning Goals and Objectives
3. Negotiate Learning Strategy
4. Construct Knowledge
5. Negotiate Performance Criteria
6. Assess Learning
7. Provide Feedback (Steps 1-6)
8. Communicate Results

Jurisprudential Inquiry

1. Orientation to the Case
2. Identifying the Issues
3. Taking Positions
4. Exploring the Stance(s), Patters of Argumentation
5. Refining and Qualifying the Positions
6. Testing Factual Assumptions Behind Qualified Positions

Experiential Learning

1. Experience—Immerse learner in "authentic" experience.
2. Publish—Talking or writing about experience. Sharing thoughts and feelings.
3. Process—Debrief: Interpret published information, defining patterns, discrepancies and overall dynamics.
4. Internalize—Private process, learner reflects on lessons learned and requirements for future learning.
5. Generalize—Develop hypotheses, form generalizations and reach conclusions.
6. Apply—Use information and knowledge gained from lesson to make decisions and solve problems.

Simulation Model

1. Orientation
   1.1 Present topic of simulation
   1.2 Explain simulation
   1.3 Give overview
2. Participant Training
   2.1 Set-up scenario
   2.2 Assign roles
   2.3 Hold abbreviated practice
3. Simulation Operations
   3.1 Conduct activity
   3.2 Feedback and evaluation
   3.3 Clarify misconceptions
   3.4 Continue simulation
4. Participant Debriefing
   4.1 Summarize events
   4.2 Summarize difficulties
   4.3 Analyze process
   4.4 Compare to the real world
5. Appraise and redesign the simulation

Direct Instruction

1. Orientation
   1.1 Establish lesson content
   1.2 Review previous learning
   1.3 Establish lesson objectives
   1.4 Establish lesson procedures
2. Presentation
   2.1 Explain new concept or skill
   2.2 Provide visual representation
   2.3 Check for understanding
3. Structured Practice
   3.1 Lead group through practice
   3.2 Students respond
   3.3 Provide corrective feedback
4. Guided Practice
   4.1 Practice semi-independently
   4.2 Circulate, monitor practice
   4.3 Provide feedback
5. Independent Practice
   5.1 Practice independently
   5.2 Provide delayed feedback

Inquiry Learning	Inductive Thinking	Problem-Based Learning
1. Confrontation with the Problem	1. Concept Formation	1. Starting a New Problem
1.1 Explain inquiry procedures	1.1 Enumeration and listing	1.1 Set problem
1.2 Present discrepant event	1.2 Grouping	1.2 Describe requirements
2. Data Gathering - Verification	1.3 Labeling, Categorizing	1.4 Assign tasks
2.1 Verify nature of objects and conditions	2. Interpretation of Data	1.5 Reason through the problem
2.2 Verify the occurrence of the problem situation	2.1 Identify critical relationships	1.6 Commitment to outcome
	2.2 Explore relationships	1.7 Shape issues and assignment
3. Data Gathering - Experimentation	2.3 Make inferences	1.8 Identify resource
3.1 Isolate relevant variables	3. Application of Principles	1.9 Schedule follow-up
3.2 Hypothesize and test casual relationships	3.1 Predicting consequences	2. Problem Follow-Up
4. Organizing, Formulating and Explanation—Formulate rules or explanations	3.2 Explaining predictions	2.1 Resources used
5. Analysis of inquiry process—Analyze inquiry strategy and develop more effective ones.	3.3 Verifying predictions	2.2 Reassess the problem
		3. Performance Presentation(s)
		4. After Conclusion of Problem
		4.1 Knowledge abstraction and summary
		4.2 Self-evaluation

**Table 10.2. Six Step Process for Designing
and Sequencing eLearning Interactions**

Step 1—Identify essential experiences that are necessary for learners to achieve specified goals and objectives (optional);

Step 2—Select a grounded instructional strategy (Level III interaction) based on specified objectives, learner characteristics, context and epistemological beliefs;

Step 3—Operationalize each event, embedding experiences identified in Step 1 and describing how the selected strategy will be applied during instruction;

Step 4—Define the type of Level II interaction(s) that will be used to facilitateeach event and analyze the quantity and quality of planned interactions;

Step 5—Select the telecommunication tool(s) (e.g., chat, email, bulletin board system) that will be used to facilitate each event based on the nature of the interaction.and

Step 6—Analyze materials to determine frequency and quality of planned eLearning interactions and revise as necessary.

APPLYING THE FRAMEWORK

Three specific applications illustrate the utility of the proposed framework for designing and sequencing eLearning interactions, analyzing the frequency and quality of the planned interactions; and analyzing and organizing research on interactivity and eLearning.

Designing and Sequencing eLearning Interactions

Table 10.2 lists six steps for designing and sequencing eLearning interactions based on the proposed framework.

The steps result in an instructional treatment plan that is then used as a foundation for generating flowcharts, storyboards, and vertical and horizontal prototypes. Specific guidelines for applying the initial five steps within the context of an overall systematic design process are detailed in Hirumi (in press). An example is provided here to illustrate how the framework may be used to design and sequence eLearning interactions, as well as to analyze the planned interactions (Step 6).

Table 10.3 depicts an instructional treatment plan created by a professor during a two-day workshop on designing and sequencing eLearning interactions. The lesson is designed for undergraduate engineering students. The terminal objective is to write and present a feasibility report. The professor selected a WebQuest as the Level III interaction (or eLearning strategy) because one of the goals of the module is to engage students in searching the Web for scholarly articles in their field. Students are to synthesize the information from at least five sources into their feasibility report. A WebQuest seemed to be the most appropriate instructional strategy for integrating such an assignment.

Column 1 lists the key events associated with the WebQuest model (Dodge and Bober, in this issue). Column 2 provides a short description of how the professor plans to operationalize each of the events online. Italicized words represent the actual text that is to go online, plain text provides basic descriptions, and underlined words indicate links to additional information or resources. Column 3 identifies the type of interaction associated with each event, based on the classes of Level II interactions posited by the proposed framework. Column 4 denotes the specific telecommunication tools that were selected to facilitate each interaction. At this stage, an analysis of the planned interactions prior to flowcharting, storyboarding, or prototyping may reduce potential time wasted developing and programming instructional materials that may not be well designed.

Analyzing Planned eLearning Interactions

After generating a preliminary draft of an instructional treatment plan, an analysis can help determine the appropriateness of the planned interactions for learners and the instructor. A planned interaction analysis is particularly important during the design phase of the systematic process to reduce or eliminate the need for costly revisions after program development or implementation.

Web-based courses with greater interactions can be more complicated to use (Gilbert & Moore, 1998). For novice distance learners or anxious computer users, such complexity may lead to confusion, frustration, inadequate performance, and eventual drop out. Berge (1999) also noted that the overuse or misuse of interactions can lead to frustration, boredom, and overload. Students may become dissatisfied if they perceive online interactions as meaningless busy work. Too many interactions can also make it difficult for learners to discern the relative importance of content information and each interaction. Too many interactions may also overwhelm the instructor. A common concern expressed by educators is that it takes far more time and effort to manage the communications that occur during eLearning than during traditional classes. Two potential causes for such overload are: too many planned learner-instructor interactions, and poorly designed interactions that require considerable clarification, explanation and elaboration.

Table 10.4 represents a planned interaction analysis completed during the workshop of the sample treatment plan.

Table 10.3. Sample Instructional Treatment Plan Based on WebQuest Strategy

Event	Description	Interaction(s)	Tools
Introduction	Present students with series of questions to establish context, need for learning and guide completion of proceeding task.	• Learner-Content • Learner-Instructor • Learner-Learner	• WWW • BBS
	Ask learners to post message describing reports they have seen and/or written that work.		
Task	End products • feasibility report • oral debriefing report	• Learner-Content	• WWW
Process	1. Identify topic	• Learner-Content • Learner Instructor	• WWW • Email/BBS
	2. Perform *research*	• Learner-Content • Learner-Environment • Learner-Other (Librarian)	• WWW • Go to Library • Online Library
	3. Generate *problem statement*	• Learner-Content • Learner-Learner • Learner-Instructor	• WWW • BBS/Stu. Pres. • BBS/Mail/Stu. Pres.
	4. Identify *options*	• Learner-Content	• WWW
	5. Select *criteria*	• Learner-Content	• WWW
	6. Write *communication purpose*	• Learner-Content • Learner-Learner	• WWW • BBS/Stu. Pres
	7. Write *report body*	• Learner-Content	• WWW
	8. Conduct *peer reviews*	• Learner-Content • Learner-Learner	• BBS/Stu. Pres/Email
	9. Write final *report*	• Learner-Content • Learner-Instructor	• WWW Stu./email

		Interaction Types	Tools/Media
	10. Present *debriefing*	• Learner-Content • Learner-Learner (Synchronous) • Learner-Instructor	• WWW • Audiobridge, Chat, Desktop Video/ Audio Conferencing, Video (Asyn).
Resources	In addition to the information provided as links from each of the steps listed above, here are a series of resources that may help you complete your task. • *Engineering professors* • *Galileo (online library)* • *Engineering and scholarly journals* • *Product Websites* • *Textbook* • *Handouts* • *Sample reports*	• Learner-Content • Learner-Other (Professors) • Learner-Environment (Textbook)	• WWW • F2F, email, phonePurchase (F2f, or online)
Evaluation	*The following evaluation criteria will be used to evaluate your work and to determine completion of your task.* • *Grading Rubric for Report* • *Grading Rubric for Debriefing*	• Learner-Content • Learner-Instructor	• WWW • Email (feedback templates)
Conclusion	Learner to prepare and submit journal entry reflecting on experience.	• Learner-Content • Learner-Instructor	• WWW • Email

Table 10.4. Planned Interaction Analysis of Sample Treatment Plan

Interaction	Quan.	Quality	Design Decision
Learner-Content	21	• 1 lesson overview page that provides description of and links to information about intro., task, process, resources, evaluation, and conclusion. • Detailed descriptions of how to complete each of the 10 tasks associated with the process. • Links to 7 resources • 2 Detailed evaluation rubrics • Description of how to prepare and submit journal entry.	Interface very important to test prior to official course delivery.
Learner-Instructor	8	• Ask learner to post message • Review and provide feedback on topic • Review and provide feedback on problem statement • Provide guidance on writing final report • Provide guidance on preparing debriefing • Assess and provide feedback on final report • Assess and provide feedback on debriefing • Review and provide feedback on journal entries.	Far too many interactions to manage. Need to review and revise by grouping two or more interactions, grouping students, eliminating or further automating interactions).
Learner-Learner	5	• Share short description of previously seen or written reports • Share and discuss problem statements • Share and discuss purpose statements • Conduct peer reviews of reports • Participate and share comments on debriefings	Maybe too much, need review and pay particular attention during testing
Learner-Other	2	• Contact Librarian • Contact other Professors	Need to ensure Librarian prepared, need to ensure ready access to other professors.
Learner-Environment	3	• Go to Library • Acquire and read Textbook • Acquire and read journal articles	Need to ensure ready access to library resource and textbook

Column 1 lists each type of interactions specified in the treatment plan. Column 2 denotes the frequency of each type of interaction. Column 3 provides a brief description of the quality or nature of the interaction, and column 4 specifies any required revisions in design or factors to consider during development.

An analysis of each class of planned interactions contained in the sample treatment plan reveals several key factors that warrant further deliberation. To begin with, the frequency of learner-content interactions emphasizes the importance of the user interface, suggesting that resources spent conducting usability tests, such as heuristic and scenario-based evaluations (Nielson, 1993) during development may be worthwhile.

Moving to the second category of planned interactions listed in the analysis, eight learner-instructor interactions may be far too many for the instructor to manage. For each interaction, the instructor must acknowledge receipt of the initial communication, save and track relevant documents and messages, review each learner's work, and then generate and provide timely and meaningful feedback. If one takes into account the total amount of effort required to manage each interaction, multiply that by the total number of students registered for the course, and consider that the treatment plan represents just one unit in an entire course, it becomes readily apparent that eight learner-instructor interactions are far too many for the instructor to manage. In such cases, it may be helpful to group two or more interactions together to reduce the total number of interactions that must be handled by the instructor. Other options include grouping students to reduce the total number of assignments that must be reviewed by the instructor, eliminating some interactions or further automating the interaction so that preprogrammed responses are provided based on users' input.

The third category of planned interactions includes five learner-learner interactions that may be too much for learners, particularly in light of the number of planned learner-instructor interactions. During the workshop, the professor noted that students completed similar learner-learner interactions in her face-to-face course as defined in her treatment plan. However, bear in mind that in traditional classroom settings, such interactions occur through speaking and listening, two modes of synchronous communications that take far less time and effort than reading and writing, which are the predominate forms of communication during eLearning. Similar tactics for reducing the investment necessary to complete learner-instructor interactions are recommended here with one exception–grouping students. Because communications are predominately asynchronous, group work can take considerably more time and energy than individual assignments. Messages must be posted or sent directly to team members who must then access, organize, interpret and respond to the communications. If there are differences in opinion, an additional series of asynchronous communications may be required to reach group consensus prior to formulating a group response. Group processes may be facilitated through synchronous communications (e.g., chat), but such meetings may be difficult to schedule, particularly if team members live in different time zones. Therefore, to reduce learner-learner interaction requirements, it was suggested that the professor consider either grouping the interactions (e.g., requiring learners to share and discuss problem and purpose statements as two parts of one online activity) or eliminating one or more interaction.

An analysis of the third class of interactions specified in the treatment plan denotes two learner-other human interactions, potential interactions with a librarian and planned interactions with other professors. Such interactions are important to keep in mind during development and implementation. Librarians must be informed of such potential interactions with enough lead time to allocate sufficient resources so that they can respond in a timely fashion. The participation of other professors must also be solicited far enough in advance to ensure sufficient numbers and so they can properly plan for and address learner inquiries.

Analysis of the fourth class of interactions contained in the treatment plan identifies resources that must be made readily accessible to learners. In this case, the professor must make sure that all learners have ready access to a library and can obtain the course textbook and related journal articles in a suitable manner. Such considerations are also required in traditional on-campus classes. However, making sure that distance learners can readily access required resources may take additional time and noting such requirements during the design phase of the systematic process may help facilitate implementation.

Too few, too many, or poorly designed interactions can result in both learner and instructor dissatisfaction, inadequate learning, and insufficient performance, requiring additional time, effort, and expertise to revise instruction–resources that could have been spent on other projects. Improved interface design (Metros and Hedberg, in this issue) and the evolution of better Web course authoring and delivery tools may eventually make the technical aspects of online interactions transparent to learners. However, until such improvements are realized, educators must keep in mind that frequency does not equal quality (Northrup, 2001). Analysis of planned eLearning interactions specified in initial drafts of instructional treatment plans can help educators correct potential problems prior to programming as well as identify key factors to consider during development and implementation. Planned interaction analysis of prototypes and existing coursework may also be conducted to increase the overall effectiveness of eLearning materials.

Analyzing and Organizing Research

In addition to guiding the design and sequencing of eLearning interactions, the proposed framework may be used to analyze and organize research on interactivity and eLearning.

Several articles contained in this issue are examined to demonstrate how the framework may be used to analyze related research. For instance, Berge stresses the importance of aligning objectives, instruction, and assessment and the significance of evaluation and feedback (essential elements of Level III design). Berge also discusses how learner-learner, learner-instructor, and learner-content interactions (three Level II interactions) may be applied to facilitate active, interactive, and reflective eLearning and promote knowledge construction (Level I interactions). In comparison, Metros and Hedberg focus on interactions between the learner and the interface (Level II) and discuss how graphical interfaces may be designed to support constructivist views of learning (Level I). Chih and Corry discuss how social presence (Level II human interactions), technology (Level II non-human interactions), and instruction (Level III interactions) influence the development of eLearning communities. Their refined model also highlights the importance of community learning and suggests that it may be useful to add considerations for community-self interactions as a new form of Level I interaction.

Further analysis of the articles contained in this issue reveals several trends:

1. As noted by Bannon-Ritland (in this issue), studies typically do not focus on one type of interaction. Investigators usually concentrate on one category and discuss its effect on others.

2. Few studies address Level III interactions. Of the eight articles included in this issue, Berge and Chih and Corry allude to certain aspects of learner-instruction interactions, a comprehensive set of interactions (or eLearning strategy) that comprise an instructional unit designed to achieve a specified set of objectives.

3. None of the articles contained in this issue directly address learner-other or learner-environment interactions as defined by the framework.

Bannan-Ritland uses the proposed framework to analyze trends in research in her comprehensive review of literature, further illustrating the utility of the framework for analyzing, organizing, and guiding research on interactivity and eLearning.

SUMMARY

Key interactions that can affect student attitudes and performance must be carefully designed and delivered as an integral part of eLearning. While various taxonomies reveal a plethora of interactions that may be used to facilitate eLearning, relatively little has been done to synthesize related literature on, delimit the relationships between, and provide practical guidelines for planning and managing eLearning interactions.

This article presents a three-level framework for analyzing, designing, and sequencing eLearning interactions. Level I interactions consist of cognitive and metacognitive operations that occur within each learner's mind and is distinguished to further emphasize the importance of self-regulation. Level II includes six classes that are divided into human and non-human interactions (i.e., learner-instructor, learner-learner, learner-other human, learner-content, learner-interface and learner-environment). Level III (learner-instruction) interactions are viewed as a meta-level. Learner-instruction interactions provide educators with a set of events (an eLearning strategy) that may be based on research and theory to provide a grounded approach to designing and sequencing Level II and stimulating Level I interactions.

A higher education example illustrated how the framework may be used to analyze planned eLearning interactions. Additional guidelines for applying the framework to design and sequence eLearning interactions are described by Hirumi (in press). This article focused on how the framework may be used to analyze the frequency and quality of planned interactions during design and development to reduce the need for costly revisions after programming and to enhance the overall eLearning experience. Similar analysis may be conducted to optimize the design and sequencing of planned interactions in existing eLearning materials. Finally, several articles contained in this issue were analyzed to illustrate how the proposed framework may be used to analyze, organize, and guide research on planned eLearning interactions.

The creation of modern eLearning programs requires research and the development of new design methods that fully utilize the capabilities of telecommunication technologies and the potential they afford collaborative and independent learning (Bates, 1990; Mason & Kaye, 1990; Soby, 1990). While the effectiveness of the proposed framework has been demonstrated in several practical situations (e.g., workshops and in the design of secondary, undergraduate, and graduate eLearning coursework), much work is left. Further study is required to provide empirical evidence for its utility and to optimize the design and sequencing of planned eLearning interactions.

REFERENCES

American Psychological Association. (1993). *Learner-Centered Psychological Principles*. (ERIC Document Reproduction Service No. ED371994).

Atkinson, R. C., & Shiffrin, R. M. (1968). Human memory: A proposed system and its control processes. In K. Spence and J. Spence (Eds.), *The psychology of learning and motivation* (Vol. 2). New York: Academic Press.

Bates, A. W. (1990). *Third generation distance education: The challenge of new technology*. Paper presented at the XV World Conference on Distance Education, Caracas, Venezuela. (ERIC Document Reproduction Service No. ED332688).

Bangert-Drowns, R. L. Kulik, C. C., Kulik, J. A., & Morgan, M. T. (1991). The instructional effect of feedback in test-like events. *Review of Educational Research, 61*(2), 218-38.

Bednar, A., Cunningham, D. J., Duffy, T., & Perry, D. (1995). Theory in practice: How do we link? In G. Anglin (Ed.), *Instructional technology: Past, present, and future* (2nd ed., pp. 100-112). Englewood, CO: Libraries Unlimited.

Berge, Z. (1999). Interaction in post-secondary Web-based learning. *Educational Technology, 39*(1), 5-11.

Bonk, C. J., & King, K. (1998). Computer conferencing and collaborative writing tools: Starting a dialogue about student dialogue. In C. J. Bonk & K. King (Eds.), *Electronic collaborators: Learner-centered technologies for literacy, apprenticeship, and discourse* (pp. 3-23). Mahwah, NJ: Erlbaum.

Bonk, J. C., & Cunningham, D. J. (1998). Searching for learner-centered, constructivist, and sociocultural components of collaborative educational learning tools. In C. J. Bonk & K. S. King (Eds.), *Electronic collaborators: Learning-centered technologies for literacy, apprenticeship, and discourse* (pp. 25-50). Mahwah, NJ: Erlbaum.

Bonk, C. J. & Reynolds, T. H. (1997). Learner Centered Web Instruction for Higher-order thinking, teamwork, and apprenticeship. In B. Khan (Ed.), *Web-Based Instruction* (pp. 167-178), Englewood Cliffs, NJ: Educational Technology Publications.

Breakthebarriers.com (2000). *What is interactivity?* Retrieved March 02, 2001, from http://www.breakthebarriers.com/hottopic.html

Bruner, J. (1974). *Beyond the information given*. London: George Allen & Unwin.

Bulter, D. L., & Winnie, P. H. (1995). Feedback and self-regulated learning: A theoretical synthesis. *Review of Educational Research, 65*(3), 245-81.

Carlson, R. D., & Repman, J. (1999). Web-based interactivity. *WebNet Journal, 1*(2), 11-13.

Clark, R. E. (1994a). Media and method. *Educational Technology Research and Development, 42*, 7-10.

Clark, R. E. (1994b). Media will never influence learning. *Educational Technology Research and Development, 42*, 21-29.

Cohen, V. B. (1985). A reexamination of feedback in computer-based instruction: Implications for instructional design. *Educational Technology, 25*(1), 33-37.

Corno, L. (1994). Student volition and education: Outcomes, influences, and practices. In D. H. Schunk & B. J. Zimmerman (Eds.), *Self regulation of leaning and performance: Issues and educational applications* (pp. 229-254). Hillsdale, NJ: Erlbaum.

Corno, L., & Randi, J. (1999). A design theory for classroom instruction in self-regulated learning? In C. M. Reigeluth (Ed.). *Instructional design theories and models: A new paradigm of instructional theory* (Vol. II, pp. 293-318), Mahwah, NJ: Erlbaum.

Dempsey, J. V., & Sales, G. C. (1993). *Interactive Instruction and Feedback.* Englewood Cliffs, NJ: Educational Technology.

Dillion, A., & Zhu, E. (1997). Designing web-based instruction: A human-computer interaction perspective. In B. Khan (Ed.), *Web-based instruction* (pp. 221-224). Englewood Cliffs, NJ: Educational Technology.

Driscoll, M. P. (1994). *Psychology of learning for instruction.* Needham Heights, MA: Paramount.

Gillani, B. B. & Relan, A. (1997). Incorporating interactivity and multimedia into Web-based instruction. In B. Khan (Ed.), *Web-based instruction* (pp. 231-237). Englewood Cliffs, NJ: Educational Technology.

Gilbert, L., & Moore, D.R. (1998). Building interactivity into Web courses: Tools for social and instructional interactions. *Educational Techonology, 38*(3), 29-35.

Hagen, A. S., and Weinstein, C. E. (1995). Achievement goals, self-regulated learning and the role of classroom context. In P. R. Pintrich (Ed.), *Understanding self-regulated learning* (pp. 43-56). San Francisco: Jossey Bass.

Hannafin, M. J. (1989). Interaction strategies and emerging instructional technologies: Psychological perspectives. *Canadian Journal of Educational Communication, 18*(3), 167-179.

Harris, J. (1994a, February). People-to-people projects on the Internet. *The Computing Teacher.* 48-52.

Harris, J. (1994b, March). Information collection activities. *The Computing Teacher,* 32-36.

Harris, J. (1994c. April). Opportunities in work clothes: Online problem-solving project structures. *The Computing Teacher,* 52-55.

Hillman, D. C., Willis, D. J., & Gunawardena, C. N. (1994). Learner-interface interaction in distance education: An extension of contemporary models and strategies for practitioners. *The American Journal of Distance Education, 8*(2), 30-42.

Hirumi, A. (2002). Designing and sequencing elearning interactions: A grounded approach. *International Journal on E-Learning, 1*(1), 19-27.

Hoska, D. M. (1993). Motivating learners through CBI feedback: Developing a positive learner perspective. In J. V. Dempsey & G. C. Sales (Eds.), *Interactive instruction and feedback* (pp. 105-32). Englewood Cliffs, NJ: Educational Technology.

Iran-Nejad, A. (1990). Active and dynamic self-regulation of learning processes. *Review of Educational Research*, 60, 573-602.

Johnson, D. W., & Johnson, R. T. (1993). Simulation and gaming: Fidelity, feedback and motivation. In J. V. Dempsey & G. C. Sales (Eds.), *Interactive instruction and feedback* (pp. 133-57). Englewood Cliffs, NJ: Educational Technology.

Jonassen, D. H. (1995, June). *An instructional design model for designing constructivist learning environments*. World Conference on Educational Media, Graz, Austria.

Jonassen, D. H. (1994). Thinking technology: Toward a constructivist design model. *Educational Technology, 34*(4), 34-37

Jonassen, D. H. (1991). Objectivism vs. constructivism: Do we need a philosophical paradigm shift? *Educational Technology: Research and Development, 39*(3), 5-14.

Jones, M. G., & Farquhar, J. D. (1997). User interface design for Web-based instruction. In B. Khan (Ed.). *Web-based instruction* (pp. 239-244). Englewood Cliffs, NJ: Educational Technology.

Kulhavy, R. W. (1977). Feedback in written instruction. *Review of Educational Research, 47*(1), 211-32.

Kulhavy, R. W., & Wager, W. (1993). Feedback in programmed instruction: Historical context and implications for practice. In J. V. Dempsey & G. C. Sales (Eds.), *Interactive instruction and feedback* (pp. 2-20). Englewood Cliffs, NJ: Educational Technology.

Ley, K., & Young, D. B. (2001). Instructional principles for self regulation. *Educational Technology Research and Development, 49*(2), 93-105.

Liaw, S., & Huang, H. (2000). Enhancing interactivity in Web-based instruction: A review of the literature. *Educational Technology, 40*(3), 41-45.

Piaget, J. (1971). *Genetic epistemology*. New York: W. W. Norton.

Mason, R., & Kaye, T. (1990). Toward a new paradigm for distance education. In L. M. Harasim (Ed.), *On-line education: Perspectives on a new environment* (pp. 15-30). New York: Praeger.

Moore, M. G. (1989). Editorial: Three types of interaction. *The American Journal of Distance Education, 3*(2), 1-6.

Mortera-Gutierrez, F., & Murphy, K. (2000, January). *Instructor interactions in distance education environments: A case study*. Concurrent session presented at the annual distance education conference sponsored by the Texas A&M Center for Distance Education, Austin, TX.

Mory, E. H. (1996). Feedback Research. In D. Jonassen (Ed.). Handbook of research for educational communications and technology (pp. 919-956). New York: Simon & Schuster Macmillan.

Nielsen, J. (1993). *Usability engineering*. Boston: AP Professional.

Norman (1988). *The psychology of everyday things*. New York: Basic Books.

Northrup, P. (2001). A framework for designing interactivity in Web-based instruction. *Educational Technology, 41*(2), 31-39.

Northrup, P. T., & Rasmussen, K. L. (2000, February). *Designing a web-based program: Theory to Design*. Paper presented at the annual conference of the Association for Educational Communications and Technology, Long Beach, CA.

Piaget, J. (1971). *Genetic epistemology*. New York: W.W. Norton.

Reigeluth, C. M., & Moore, J. (1999). Cognitive education and the cognitive domain. In C. M. Reigeluth (Ed.). *Instructional-design theories and models: A new paradigm of instructional theory* (Vol. 2, pp. 51-68). Mahwah, NJ: Erlbaum.

Reiser, R. A., and Gagné, R. M. (1993). *Selecting media for instruction.* Englewood Cliffs, NJ: Educational Technology.

Rorty, R. (1991). *Objectivity, relativism, and truth.* Cambridge, England: Cambridge University Press.

Russell, T. L. (1999). *The "no significant difference" phenomenon: A comparative research annotated bibliography on technology for distance education.* Raleigh: North Carolina State University Office of Instructional Telecommunications.

Russell, T. L. (1993). *The "no significant difference" phenomenon as reported in research reports, summaries and papers.* Raleigh: North Carolina State University Office of Instructional Telecommunications.

Skinner, B. F. (1969). *Contingencies in reinforcement.* Englewood Cliffs, NJ: Prentice-Hall.

Slavin, R. E. (1987). Cooperative learning and the cooperative school. *Educational Leadership, 47,* 14-25.

Soby, M. (1990). Traversing distances in education: The PortaCOM Experiment. In A. W. Bates (Ed.), *Media and technology in European distance education. Proceedings of the EADTU workshop on media, methods and technology* (pp. 241-247). Milton Keynes, England: The Open University for EADTU.

Thach, E. C., & Murphy, K. L. (1995). Competencies for Distance Education Professionals. *Educational Technology Research and Development, 43*(1), 57-79.

von Glasersfeld, E. (1989a). Cognition, construction of knowledge, and teaching. *Syntheses, 80,* 121-140.

von Glasersfeld, E. (1989b). Constructivism in education. In A. Lewy (Ed.), *The international encyclopedia of curriculum* (pp. 31-32). Oxford, England: Pergamon Press.

Vygotsky, L. (1978). *Mind in society.* Cambridge, MA: Harvard University Press.

Weller, H. G. (1988). Interactivity in microcomputer-based instruction: Its essential components and how it can be enhanced. *Journal of Educational Technology Systems, 28*(2), 23-27.

Yacci, M. (2000). Interactivity demystified: A structural definition for distance education and intelligent computer-based instruction. *Educational Technology, 40*(4), 5-16.

Zimmerman, B. J., & Martinez-Pons, M. (1995). Self-monitoring during collegiate studying: An invaluable tool for academic self-regulation. In P. R. Pintrich (Ed.), *Understanding self-regulated learning* (pp. 13-28), San Francisco: Jossey Bass.

Zimmermen, B. J., & Paulsen, A. S. (1995). Self-monitoring during collegiate studying: An invaluable tool for academic self-regulation. In P. R. Pintrich (Ed.), *Understanding self-regulated learning* (pp. 13-28). San Francisco: Jossey Bass.

Zimmerman, B. J., & Martinez-Pons, M. (1988). Construct validation of a strategy model of student self-regulated learning. *Journal of Educational Psychology, 80,* 284-290.

Zimmerman, B. J., & Martinez-Pons, M. (1986). Development of a structured interview for assessing student use of self-regulated learning strategies. *American Educational Research Journal, 23*, 614-628.

CHAPTER 11

DESIGNING EFFECTIVE E-LEARNING

Guidelines for Practitioners

Angelene C. McLaren

INTRODUCTION

When discussing e-learning, there are a myriad of viewpoints about what it is or is not, depending on who you ask. According to Hall (2000), e-learning is the acquisition of knowledge and skills at a distance through a variety of technological mediums. Urdan and Weggen (2000), view e-learning as a subset of distance learning, and online learning a subset of e-learning. For the purposes of this article, however, the National Center for Supercomputing Applications' (NCSA) definition will be adopted: "e-learning is the acquisition and use of knowledge distributed and facilitated primarily by electronic means" (NCSA, 2000). As instructional design practitioners, there are usually six categories of consideration that must be addressed when designing, developing and implementing e-learning initiatives. These categories usually are: learner support and resources, online organization and design, instructional design and deliv-

The Perfect Online Course: Best Practices for Designing and Teaching
pp. 229–245
Copyright © 2009 by Information Age Publishing

ery, assessment and evaluation of student learning, innovative teaching with technology, and use of student feedback (Rubic for Online Instruction, 2003). This article will only address one of these categories—instructional design. It will address the designing of effective e-learning according the following topics: learning and performance outcomes, instructional methods, instructional media, e-learning and learning theories, e-learning and instructional system design, and e-learning and instructional theories. The article will also incorporate practical guidelines based on theory. This will enable e-learning instructional design practitioners to move toward a grounded "theory-to-practice" paradigm for design.

LEARNING AND PERFORMANCE OUTCOMES

When designing e-learning, or any type of learning for that matter, it is imperative that the learning and performance outcomes are understood and agreed on by the instructional design team and the client from the very beginning of the project cycle. By understanding the specific learning requirements, instructional designers can then map out successfully how to best meet these learning and/or performance goals according to the requirements of the learners. Each type of performance or learning outcome will require a different instructional strategy (Gagne, 1985).

Information Transfer

Information transfer is the most basic of learning tasks. During information transfer, learners are usually passive participants in the learning process. They are given information, either in verbal, written, graphic and/or pictorial forms. At the end of the transfer session, learners are then required to retrieving this stored information. Unfortunately, most of what passes as e-learning today is nothing more than the passive transfer of informational content from an electronic source to a learning population, regardless of the knowledge or performance outcomes expected. These learning modules usually have a fixed content and structure, offer no interaction or collaboration, and are usually not facilitated (eLearnity, 2001). There are instances, however, when this approach is logical and effective. These instances might include: teaching new policies, cultivating corporate culture, or giving directions.

Basic Skills Acquisition

Teaching basic skills can range from something as mundane as learning how to tie one's shoe, to something as complicated as learning how to use a new telephone transfer system. When creating e-learning geared to basic skill acquisition, the structure of the course should be fixed, the content can be fixed or flexible depending on the learners, and there should be supportive cooperation and directed facilitation (eLearnity, 2001).

Advanced Skill Development

Advanced skills development requires that learners be able to do more than read information from a screen or projector. It requires them to build on current levels of knowledge and expertise. As instructional designers, when creating e-learning for this learning and performance outcome, it is important to go beyond just providing static content and standard assessments. Learners here need dynamic course structure and content—one that can adjust or be modified according the level of expertise or need. Learners will need to be in collaborative learning environments where they can share and learn from their peers. Also, these e-learning initiatives need to be virtually facilitated. At this level, it would be easy for learners to get lost (eLearnity, 2001).

Adaptive Expertise Development

Adaptive expertise encompasses a range of cognitive, motivational, and personality-related components. The thing that separates adaptive expertise from mere competency is the ability to apply knowledge effectively to novel or atypical problems. When creating e-learning for this learning and performance category, designers must provide dynamic structure and content as well collaborative and facilitated learning experiences (eLearnity, 2001).

These four preceding performance and learning categories lead nicely into the next section of this article, which addresses the issue of instructional methods. As an instructional design practitioner, when addressing a particular learning or performance outcome (category of instruction), one must match it effectively to corresponding instructional methods for learning to occur (Gagne, 1985)

INSTRUCTIONAL METHODS

According to Clark (2002) there are three distinct elements to any e-learning lesson: instructional methods, instructional media, and media elements. Unfortunately, for a long time, a lot of emphasis has been placed on the latter two categories, with less emphasis on the former. Despite the fact that several studies have concluded that there are no significant differences in achievement between students who take courses face-to-face or via e-learning (Chute, Thompson, & Hancock, 1999; Clark, 2002), designers and clients often get caught up in the tools at the expense of how to best utilize those tools to achieve the learning and performance outcomes desired. E-learning lessons that are jam-packed with all the latest bells and whistles, but lack sound instructional design principles, will not maximize the effectives of information processing or learning (Shute, 2003). It is not the medium that causes learning to occur, but rather it is design and instructional methodology that make the difference (Clark, 2002).

Instructional methods are strategies, means, and ways to deliver new information in ways that foster learning. This could be through the use of examples, by providing opportunities for rehearsal and practice, and via simulations (Clark, 2002). When designing effective e-learning, the literature points most often to the following three instructional methods: learner-centered design, scenario-based learning, and problem-based learning. Learner-centered designs offer lots of practice with individualized feedback, while scenario-based and problem-based learning integrate self-study and collaboration, along with the use of simulation to accelerate learning (Clark & Mayer, 2003).

Learner-Centered Design

Learner-centered design is focused on the nature of the active learning process and the unique qualities of individual learners. A learner-centered approach builds the learning experience around the learners and not around the content. Don Norman states that, "The first step in learner-centric design is to understand how learning takes place.... It is very important that people learn not by reading a book and not by listening to a lecture, but by doing tasks that can engage the mind" (in Hsi & Gale, 2003, p. 7). Hsi and Gale also point out that learners need more "scaffolding" at the beginning of instruction. Scaffolding is an instructional technique in which the desired learning strategy or task is modeled by the instructor, then is gradually shifted to the students. This scaffolding serves as cognitive structural support, stepping stones and building blocks on which learners can comfortably constructs new knowledge and expertise. As learners grow in competency, this scaffolding should be faded out and then removed altogether (Hsi & Gale, 2003). Learner-centered design understands the need to offer learner support while at the same time encourages independent learning. Instructional methods should foster interest in the learning task and motivate further inquiry (Hsi & Gale, 2003).

Scenario-Based Learning

Traditional page-turner types of e-learning modules are increasingly being replaced by a more dynamic learning experience known as scenario-based e-learning. This approach does away with the telling and showing, and offers learners opportunities to learn by doing relevant tasks, making mistakes, and then redoing them until mastery is attained (Kindley, 2002). Scenario-based learning is learning that occurs in a contextual, situational, or social framework (Kindley, 2002). It springs from the concept of situated cognition, which proposes that knowledge cannot be fully understood outside of its context (Kindley, 2002). Knowledge then is constructed as a natural byproduct of doing natural tasks that are expected to be performed in the learners' natural learning, working or social environments. In this way, scenario-based learning is very similar to the experiential learning model. Accordingly, both adhere to the notion that learning occurs as a result of performance. The outcome, therefore, is focused on improved performance, not on the acquisition of knowledge and skills (Kindley, 2002). Scenarios may be built around a story, a role play, or a simulation. The focus of the activity must be to help learners contextualize the learning content. The more "authentic" these scenarios, the more likely it is that learners will transfer new knowledge and skills back to their real-world environments (Brodsky, 2003).

Problem-Based Learning

Problem-based learning is centered on solving "real-world" problems. Learners are given ill-structured, authentic problems to solve by finding the necessary knowledge and applying it appropriately. This approach encourages higher critical thinking, analytical, and reasoning skills. As in the learner-centered approach, problem-based learning utilizes scaffolding to reduce cognitive load and improve learning outcomes (Merrill, 2002a). This scaffolding comes in the form of instructor guidance that is faded out as learners attain competency. It is important to provide this guidance early on in the instructional cycle, because novices may spend a lot of time looking for solutions without actually learning (Sweller, 1988). The key to successfully utilizing this methodology is to move from the simple to complex and from guidance to independence. As learners gain expertise and ownership over the learning process, make the problems more realistic to reflect real world conditions (Merrill, 2002a).

At the root of every decision about the design of e-learning courseware should be the sound understanding of what is learning, how it takes place, and what research tells us about what factors lead to learning (Clark, 2002). Learning theories attempt to explain how learning takes place. The two learning theories that will be discussed here are behaviorism and cognitivism. How can behaviorism and cognitivism be best utilized for designing effective e-learning courseware?

APPLYING LEARNING THEORIES TO E-LEARNING

Behaviorism

According to behaviorist learning theory, learning is the ability to perform new behaviors (Skinner, 1954). These changes in behavior are a result of constantly manipulating environmental conditions. Pleasant experiences (such as rewards or praise) are positive reinforcements. The goal of the behaviorist is to cause learners to make desired connections between stimuli and responses. Unpleasant experiences (such as punishment) are negative reinforcements. The introduction of negative reinforcements causes learners to avoid undesirable responses to stimuli. Continuous reinforcement increases the rate of learning, while intermittent reinforcement contributes to longer retention of what is learned. Both positive and negative reinforcement can shape behavior, and result in learning.

Behaviorist learning theory has great influences on e-learning. Basic tenets, such as individualized instruction, operant conditions, feedback, a linear approach to instruction, and instructional prompts all work well in the context of e-learning. E-learning relies on observable changes in behavior as the basis for instruction. Performance and/or behavioral objectives are used to describe learning outcomes. Assessments, evaluations, feedback, and reinforcements are all geared toward facilitating new learner behaviors. Most online instruction is built around this behaviorist framework. Learners are given information, solicited for a response, they receive feedback, and then are either positively or negatively reinforced.

Cognitivism

Cognitive learning theories seek to explain how the brain processes and stores new information. Cognitive psychologists wanted to explain learning beyond the limitations of behaviorism and its focus only on observable behavior. Piaget (1985) suggested that the learning process is iterative. New information is shaped to fit with the learner's existing knowledge, and the existing knowledge is modified to accommodate new information. Interactive Web-based tools such as automatic feedback and interactive activities allow learners to modify their behavior by assimilating and accommodating new information from their peers and/or instructor.

This learning theory also has great impact on how e-learning is designed. One aspect in particular, cognitive load theory, is especially applicable in e-learning environments. Cognitive load theory revolves around manipulating intrinsic, extraneous and germane cognitive processes (Van Merrienboer & Ayres, 2005). The goal is to decrease extraneous cognitive load and to increase germane cognitive load. Strategies to accomplish this might include: taking learner expertise into consideration, moving from simple to more complex tasks, chunking information into easily assimilated chunks, presenting information bit by bit, and building on prior knowledge.

For e-learning to be effective, it must be grounded in sound learning, teaching, and design theory. According to Bednar, Cunningham, Duffy, and Perry (1991), "effective design is possible only if the developer has a reflexive awareness of the theoretical basis underlying the design" (p. 90).

APPLYING INSTRUCTIONAL DESIGN TO E-LEARNING

Designing effective e-learning requires that it be grounded in a sound design approach. The need for instructional design as a necessary component to effective e-learning design is now being realized (Siemens, 2002). The successful design of e-learning relies on the careful consideration of underlying pedagogy of how learning takes place online (Conrad, 2000). Instructional design, in this context, is "the act of combining the elements of content and display to effectively present the instructional content in a way that promotes learning through organized instructional resources and a user interface that is not confusing, dissatisfying, or cognitively taxing" (Mehlenbacher et al., 2005).

Instructional design models for e-learning closely follow those of traditional classroom learning. The steps of planning, implementation, and evaluation are present in most instances. From a design perspective, various models can be used, either alone or in tandem, during the design process (Siemens, 2002).

ADDIE

ADDIE is a generic model that is used by instructional designers as a guideline to building effective instructional materials. The acronym stands for analyze, design, develop, implement, and evaluate. The design phase deals with learning objectives, assessment instruments, exercises, content, subject matter analysis, lesson planning, and media selection. The design phase includes planning strategies for attaining the stated learning and performance outcomes. This process should be systematic and precise. It is this phase that instructional designers must apply instructional strategies that best fit the intended learning or performance outcome. The domain of learning must be considered, whether cognitive, affective, or psychomotor, for effective matches to be realized. The design phase then is focused on documenting specific learning objectives, assessment instruments, exercises, and content (Siemens, 2002). Many in recent years, however, have accused ADDIE of being too rigid, too systematic, and too linear, especially for use in online environments (Kruse, 2000). As an answer to this, many designers are modifying the traditional ADDIE model and utilizing rapid prototyping as a viable option.

Rapid Prototyping

Rapid prototyping
… involves learners and/or subject matter experts (SMEs) interacting with prototypes and instructional designers in a continuous review/revision cycle. Developing a prototype is practically the first step, while front-end analysis is generally reduced or converted into an ongoing, interactive process between subject-matter, objectives, and materials. (Thiagi, in Siemens, 2002, p. 2)

Rapid prototyping borrows from the best systematic processes of the ADDIE model, and is usually an extension of the design phase. In its simplest form, a rapid prototype is a quickly assembled instructional module that can be tested with the student audience early in the ISD process (Kruse, 2000). Designers are typically looking for how learners respond to instructional strategies, learning activities, and how well the technology chosen fits the learning requirements. Based on feedback, designers can then go back and make necessary changes as required. This process continues until there is agreement and confidence in the prototype. Designers do not move to the development phase until this process is completed (Kruse, 2000).

e-Learning Design Models

Just as there are many models for designing traditional classroom instruction, there are now many models for designing e-learning instruction. Many build on the traditional ADDIE model, with some modifications. Although they are varied in their approach, all emphasize the following issues (Engelbrecht, 2003).

Needs Analysis. A needs analysis is needed to answer questions related to the demand for instruction, the need for online delivery, and the cost of design, development and implementation.

Learner Analysis. A learner analysis seeks answers to questions about the learners. What are their ages, gender, culture, prior knowledge, learning patterns and styles, goal, and motivations?

Institutional Support. This investigates support structures related to the vision and the mission of the organization, implementation costs and sustainability, training for instructors, and technological infrastructure.

Pedagogical Choices. Pedagogy choices must meet the need of the learning outcome and the target audience. Key considerations include: learning models, delivery methods, interaction, and assessment (Engelbrecht, 2003).

Instructional design, when implemented correctly, serves the learning needs of students through effective presentation of content and the fostering of interaction (Siemens, 2002). Another component necessary in the designing of effective e-learning is the utilization of sound instructional theory.

APPLYING INSTRUCTIONAL THEORY TO E-LEARNING

What is instructional theory and why is it important to practitioners designing e-learning courseware? Well, as for the first, it depends on who you ask. According to Richey (1986), theory can either explain relationships among variables, or how to do a procedure. Seels (1997) describes theory as an explanation of phenomena that help us understand and deal with the world. Reigeluth (1997) says that design theory is goal-oriented and tries to offer means for accomplishing a given end. As for the second, Winn (1997) would argue that theory is important to practitioners because a lot of the things we design do not work. A discussion of the instructional theories of Gagne, Merrill, and Keller, and their application to designing effective e-learning courseware follows.

Robert Gagne

Robert Gagne's instructional theory was not rooted in any particular learning theory, although he was considered a behaviorist. Some of the major contributions of Gagne to the field of instructional technology are: cumulative learning theory and learning hierarchies, the domains of learning, the conditions of learning, the events of learning, and learning enterprises. Gagne is most famously known for his domain of learning, events of instruction, and conditions of learning.

The Domains of Learning. This theory illustrates Gagne's views about the different categories of learning outcomes and their influence on instruction (Richey, 2000). According to Gagne, learning can be categorized under the following outcome headings: verbal information, intellectual skills, cognitive strategies, attitude, and motor skills. Each learning outcome required a different instructional approach. Gagne felt this was a necessary component to the design of sound instruction because different parts of a content area are subject to different instructional treatments, similar parts can be found among different content areas, and different domains of learning require different techniques of assessment of learning outcomes. There can be no one way of measuring what has been learned (Richey, 2000). For example, in the cognitive domain, learners should be offered the opportunity to develop new solutions to problems; in the attitude domain, learners need be exposed to credible role models or persuasive arguments. Unfortunately, most e-learning concentrates on the basic level of learning, which is verbal information, and even skills that require changes in cognitive strategy or attitude are designed according to the verbal information domain. This explains a lot of why most e-learning is ineffective.

The Events of Instruction. Utilizing Gagne's nine steps of instruction in e-learning will aid learners' acquisition of the requisite knowledge presented (Gagne, Briggs, & Wager, 1992). These events of instruction are: gaining learner's attention, inform the learner of the objectives, stimulate recall of prior learning, present the learning stimulus, provide learning guidance, elicit appropriate performance, provide feedback, assess the learner's performance, and enhance retention and transfer (Gagne et al., 1992). These steps are necessary to designing effective e-learning, while providing e-learning that is chock-full of the latest technology that is not grounded in sound instructional design will not produce the desired learning and/or performance outcomes.

The Conditions of Learning. Gagne distinguishes between two types of conditions: external and internal (Gagne, 1985). The internal conditions observe attention, motivation, and recall, while external conditions focus on the arrangement and timing of stimulus events. His phases of learning included: receiving the stimulus situation, acquisition, storage, and retrieval. For practitioners designing e-learning, this is extremely important. Instructional design practitioners must pay close attention to how instructional events are designed. Aligning internal and external conditions in the learning environment is critical for designing effective e-learning.

M. David Merrill

David Merrill has evaluated hundreds of instructional products and have found that an alarming number of them are ineffective and do not teach at all. While reviewing a number of instructional design theories and models he tried to find fundamental principles to which all of these various approaches agree. As a result, he called these principles the "first principles of instruction." Merrill is also widely known for his component display theory and instruction transaction theory.

First Principle of Instruction. According to Merrill, in the instructional phase, the most effective learning environments are those that are based around a problem and offer learners four phases of learning: activation of prior knowledge, demonstration of skills, application of skills, and integration of these skills into the real world (Merrill, 2002b).

Component Display Theory. According to Merrill's component display theory (CDT), learning is sorted into two categories: content and performance. Content includes such this as facts, concepts, procedures, and principles; while performance focuses on remembering, using, and generalities (Merrill, 1983). The theory specifies four primary presentation forms: rules, examples, recall, and practice Secondary presentation forms include: prerequisites, objectives, helps, mnemonics, and feedback (Merrill, 1983). The theory asserts that instruction that contain all primary and secondary forms will yield more effective learning results. By first deciding on what learning and/or performance outcomes are to achieved, choosing the most appropriate strategies to reach those outcomes will then become much easier. For designers of e-learning, Merrill's CDT can be utilized effectively. One of the strengths of e-learning is the learner control. CDT stresses learner control. The theory propones that by giving learners control over the number of practices and examples they receive, this will result in more effective learning (Merrill, 1983).

Instruction Transaction Theory. According to Merrill, Li, and Jones, instructional transactions are patterns of learner interactions that are designed to facilitate the learning of a certain kind of knowledge or skill (Merrill, Li, & Jones, 1991). This theory asserts that different kinds of knowledge and skills require different kinds of transactions. A transaction shell is the structure of a transaction, which identifies the interactions parameters and knowledge representation needed for any given class of transactions (Merrill et al., 1991). The transaction configuration system provides instructional designers with a wide range of instructional parameters. These parameters control the nature of the interactions with the learner, and allow transaction shells to be tailored to a particular student population, learning environment, and learning task (Merrill et al., 1991). Transaction theory was created around the use of interactive technology, and thus is uniquely applicable to e-learning environments.

John Keller's ARCS Model

John Keller's ARCS model is a problem-solving approach to designing the motivational aspects of learning environments to stimulate and sustain students' motivation to learn (Keller, 1983, 1987). Motivation is a desire to reach a goal, and is divided into two parts: extrinsic and intrinsic motivation. Extrinsic motivation comes from outside the learner, while intrinsic motivation comes from within the learner. The four components of the ARCS model are attention, relevance, confidence, and satisfaction. Motivation is an essential variable in the successful completion of any educational task (Briggs, 1980). Keller asserts that his model offers instructional designers systematic guidelines for designing the motivational components of instruction (Visser, Plomp, Amirault, & Kuiper, 2000). Even though technology offers a variety of ways to deliver effective learning opportunities, learners face the same motivational issues in e-learning environments as they do in traditional classroom environments (Visser et al., 2000). Therefore when attempting to design effective e-learning, it is imperative that the designer keep learner motivation and the use of motivational strategies in mind. Motivational strategies should be incorporated in the design of instructional materials, as well as in the steps that guide learners through the learning process to deliver the best outcomes (Visser et al., 2000).

SUMMARY

E-learning involves the interplay of conceptual and procedural knowledge, in both the instructional content and the instructional environment. Care must be taken in the design phase to ensure that choices made are based on sound learning theory, instructional methods, instructional design practices, and instructional theory. E-learning is not about the technology, and should not be driven by the technology. Instead, effective e-learning is created only when the pedagogy of the course drives the design (Nichols, 2003). Therefore, instructional design practitioners should keep the following in mind as guidelines for effective e-learning design.

Know Your Learner

At the center of any e-learning environment is the learner. It is therefore imperative that e-learning courseware be learner-centered and not content-centered. By paying close attention during the learner analysis phase, will allow designers to create e-learning courses based on learner characteristics, and not based on the content and the technology.

Define Learning and/or Performance Goals

Unfortunately, many e-learning courses fail to identify learning and performance goals (Clark & Mayer, 2003). If design practitioners do not know where their learners are going, how can they affectively map out the best route to get them there? By neglecting this step, the result is courseware that does not build knowledge or skills. The result is e-learning that does not foster learning at all.

Select Appropriate Instructional Methods

A byproduct of knowing the learning and/or performance goal upfront is being able to select appropriate instructional methods. By selecting appropriate instructional methods, such as learner-centered design, scenario-based learning, and problem-based learning, learning is accommodated. E-learners will be more likely to reach the learning and performance goals more effectively and efficiently (Clark & Mayer, 2003).

Apply Appropriate Learning Theories

At the root of every decision about the design of e-learning courseware should be the sound understanding of what is learning, how it takes place, and what research tells us about what factors lead to learning (Clark,

2002). Learning theories attempt to explain how learning takes place. Utilizing concepts of behaviorism and congitivism appropriately will influence the success rate of e-learning courseware.

Apply Sound Instructional Design Methodology

Designing effective e-learning requires that it be grounded in a sound design approach. The need for instructional design as a necessary component to effective e-learning design is now being realized (Siemens, 2002). The successful design of e-learning relies on the careful consideration of underlying pedagogy of how learning takes place online (Conrad, 2000). In most instances, instructional design models for e-learning closely follow those of traditional classroom learning. The steps of planning, implementation, and evaluation must be present to increase effectiveness.

Apply Sound Instructional Theories

According to Richey (1986), theory can either explain relationships among variables, or how to do a procedure. Seels (1997) describes theory as an explanation of phenomena that help us understand and deal with the world. Reigeluth (1997) says that design theory is goal-oriented and tries to offer means for accomplishing a given end. It is important for practitioners to implement sound instructional theory into their everyday practice because a lot of the things we design just do not work (Winn, 1997).

By following these guidelines, e-learning designers will create learning courseware that delivers the learning and performance results wanted. They will also help to facilitate learning and build knowledge and skills that can be transferred back to the learner's real world environment (Clark & Mayer, 2003). Also, by following these guidelines, learning will be more effective and efficient for the learners. This will no doubt have a positive effect on learner motivation and decrease attrition rates (Clark & Mayer, 2003).

CONCLUSION

Emphasizing the systematic use and interaction between pedagogical models, instructional strategies, learning theories and instructional theories will produce a more grounded approach to design of effective e-learning. Practitioners must adopt a "theory-into-practice" design framework in order to craft effective e-learning courseware. E-learning, like all other forms of learning, must be grounded in sound epistemological frameworks in order to be effective (Bednar et al., 1991). As practitioners, e-learning designers must develop an awareness of what theories underpin learning and instructional design. By developing this awareness, a true marriage between theory and practice can take place. It is only through the systematic blending of sound learning theory, instructional design theory, and instructional design practices, that effective e-learning courseware can be obtained.

REFERENCES

Bednar, A. K., Cunningham, D., Duffy, T. M., & Perry, J. D. (1991, September). *Theory into practice: How do we link?* Paper presented at The World Conference on Educational Media and Hypermedia & World Conference on Educational Telecommunications, Frieburg, Germany.

Briggs, L. J. (1980). Thirty years of instructional design: One man's experience. *Educational Technology, 29*(2), 45-50.

Brodsky, M. (2003). E-learning trends, today and beyond. *Learning and Training Innovations.* Retrieved November 20, 2007, from http://www.elearningmag .com/ltimagazine/article/articleDetail.jsp?id=56219

Chute, A. G., Thompson, M. M., & Hancock, B. W. (1999). *The McGraw-Hill handbook on distance learning.* New York: McGraw-Hill.

Clark, R. C. (2002, September 10). Six principles of effective e-learning: What works and why. *Learning Solutions,* 1-8.

Clark, R. C., & Mayer, R. (2003). *E-learning and the science of instruction: Proven guidelines for consumers and designers of multimedia learning.* San Francisco: Jossey-Bass/Pfeiffer.

Conrad, K. (2000). *Instructional design for Web-based training.* Amherst, CA: HRD Press.

eLearnity (2001). *Design dynamics for e-learning: Making e-learning successful.* Retrieved November 19, 2007, from http://www.elearnity.com/index.html

Engelbrecht, E. (2003). A look at e-learning models: Investigating their value for developing an e-learning strategy. *Pregressio, 25*(2), 38-47.

Gagne, R. M. (1985.) *The conditions of learning and theory of instruction.* New York: CBS College.

Gagne. R. M., Briggs, L. J., & Wager, W. W. (1992). *Principles of instructional design* (4th ed.). Fort Worth, TX: Harcourt Brace.

Hall, B. (2000, January-March). How to embark on your e-learning adventure: Making sense of the environment. *E-learning, 1,* 10-16.

Hsi, S., & Gale, C. (2003, April). *Effective e-learning using learner-centered design (CHI 2003).* Tutorial notes of paper presented at the annual meeting Computer Human Interaction, Ft. Lauderdale, FL.

Keller, J. M. (1983). Motivational design of Instruction. In C. M. Reigeluth (Ed.), *Instructional design theories and models: An overview of their current status.* Hillsdale, NJ: Erlbaum.

Keller, J. M. (1987). Strategies for stimulating the motivation to learn. *Performance & Improvement Journal, 26*(8), 1-8.

Kindley, R. W. (2002). Scenario-based e-learning: A step beyond traditional e-learning. *Learning Circuits.* Retrieved November 20, 2007, from http://www.learnigcircuits.org/2002/may2002/kindley.html

Kruse, K. (2000) *Technology-based training: The art and science of design, development and delivery.* San Francisco: Jossey-Bass.

Mehlenbacher, B. Bennett, L., Bird, T., Ivey, M., Lucas, J., Morton, J., et al. (2005). Usable e-learning: A conceptual model for evaluation and design. In *Proceedings of HCI International 2005: 11th International Conference on Human Computer Interaction: Vol. 4. Theories, models, and processes in HCI* (pp. 1-10). Las Vegas, NV.

Merrill, M. D. (1983). Component display theory. In C. Reigeluth (Ed.), *Instructional design theories and models* (pp. 279-333). Hillsdale, NJ: Erlbaum.

Merrill, M. D., Li, Z., & Jones, M. K. (1991). Instructional transaction theory: An introduction. *Educational Technology, 31*(6), 7-12.

Merrill, M. D., (2002a). A pebble-in-the-pond model for instructional design. *Performance Improvement, 4*(7), 39-44.

Merrill, M. D. (2002b). First principle of instruction. *Educational Technology Research and Development, 50*(3), 43-59.

National Center for Supercomputing Application. (2000). *E-learning—A review of literature.* Retrieved from the Internet November 19, 2007 from http://learning.ncsa.uiuc.edu/papers/elearnlit.pdf

Nichols, M. (2003). A theory for e-learning. *Journal of Educational Technology & Society, 23*(3), 305-336.

Piaget, J. (1985). *The equilibration of cognitive structures.* Chicago: University of Chicago Press.

Reigeluth, C. M. (1997). Instructional theory, practitioner needs, and new directions: Some reflections. *Educational Technology, 37*(1), 42-47.

Richey, R. C. (1986). *The theoretical and conceptual bases of instructional design.* London/New York: Kogan Page/Nichols.

Richey, R. C. (Ed.). (2000). *The legacy of Robert M. Gagne.* Syracuse, NY: ERIC Clearinghouse on Information and Technology.

Rubic for Online Instruction. (2004). Retrieved November 20, 2007 from http://www.csuchico.edu/celt/roi/index.shtml

Seels, B. (1997). Theory development in educational/instructional technology. *Educational Technology, 37*(1), 3-5.

Siemens, G. (2002). *Instructional design in e-learning: elearningspace.* Retrieved November 19, 2007, from http://www.elearnspace.org/articles/instructionalDesign.htm

Shute, V. (2003). Adaptive e-learning. *Education Psychologist, 38*(2), 105-114.

Skinner, B. F. (1954). The science of learning and the art of teaching. *Harvard Educational Review, 24*(2), 86-97.

Sweller, J. (1988). Cognitive load during problem solving: Effects on learning. *Cognitive Science, 12*(2), 257-285.

Urdan, T. A., Weggen, C. C. (2000). *Corporate e-learning: Exploring a new frontier.* Berwyn, PA: W. R. Hambrecht.

Van Merrienboer, J. J. G., & Ayres, P. (2005). Research on cognitive load theory and its design implications for e-learning. *ETR&D, 53*(2), 5-13.

Visser, L., Plomp, T., Amirault, R., & Kuiper, W. (2000). Motivating students at a distance: The case of an international audience. *ETR&D, 50*(2), 94-110.

Winn, W. (1997). Advantages of a theory-based curriculum in instructional technology. *Educational Technology, 37*(1), 34-40.

PART III

BEST INSTRUCTIONAL METHODS AND MODELS

CHAPTER 12

AN ANALYSIS OF TEAM VS. FACULTY-BASED ONLINE COURSE DEVELOPMENT

Implications for Instructional Design

Mark Hawkes and Dan O. Coldeway

Instructional design literature for distance learning usually presents an approach deploying multi-disciplinary teams in course development. This model has been used extensively at distance learning universities for course and program development. Unfortunately, conventional instructional design views often ignore the role of the instructional designer when that designer is the sole course team member (i.e., the faculty member engaging in all functions of the process). Some conditions suggest that a single faculty-driven model may be a preferable to the team design approach. This article compares these two approaches to determine what those implementation conditions might be. The context for analysis is 3 online graduate degree programs in 2 disciplinary areas. The comparison of the team-based and faculty-driven approaches results in a discussion of design considerations for online education, graduate distance education, and the expanded faculty roles in design.

The Perfect Online Course: Best Practices for Designing and Teaching
pp. 249–264
Copyright © 2009 by Information Age Publishing

INTRODUCTION

The proliferation of online degree programs in the last several years accentuates the importance of distance education methods, systems, and design (Coldeway & Spencer, 1995; Erdelyi et al., 2001). The design lens is usually fixed on team-based approaches. However, an emerging faculty-driven design model hints of an equally dynamic approach to course and program development.

This article examines the team-based and faculty-driven approaches in the context of graduate education. A description of the variables that impact team-based instructional design are reviewed and discussed. Next, the faculty-driven approach to course and program design is analyzed as an alternative model to the team approach. The article concludes with a discussion of the expanded concept of instructional design for distance education informed by these models. The discussion is complemented with a description of the many roles and tasks required of instructional designers (or faculty serving as instructional designers).

Graduate Level Objectives

Most faculty teaching at the graduate level would agree that graduate programs and courses have at least two major goals. First, the programs must be capable of meeting course and program objectives as represented by the field of study. Second, a series of objectives that both interact and go beyond the content objectives must also be met. These objectives include the following:

(a) Interpersonal interaction
(b) Group work
(c) Written prose
(d) Analytical and interpretative skills
(e) Facility with distance delivery systems
(f) Use of outside resources for learning and instruction
(g) Presentation and discussion skills

Taken together, the above list suggests offering courses that cover only content is necessary but not sufficient at the graduate level. Moreover, in some cases, going beyond the fixed curriculum is sometimes more important than what is covered in course materials (i.e., thesis, project, and independent study activity).

Graduate course objectives and goals change the instructional design activities required for preparing both courses and programs. An instructor or instructional designer working at the graduate level must consider the following: sufficient analysis of learner needs, course materials meet minimum instructional design requirements, faculty readiness to teach at a distance, and a clear understanding of instructional technology for design and delivery of courses.

Coldeway and Hawkes (2001) discussed alternative ways by which distance-delivered graduate programs and their courses are designed and decisions regarding delivery of those courses are made. Using a somewhat simplified dichotomy, they suggest that instructional design decisions and resulting instructional development plans are accomplished in two distinct approaches. The details of this dichotomy and an evaluation of implementation results form the basis for a comparison, stipulating that the role of faculty, combined with distance delivery infrastructure and support for instructional delivery, come together to form a model for graduate education instructional design and delivery at a distance. Given that the instructional design role is often confounded with the faculty member's role in course design and delivery, a brief discussion of design basics precedes the comparison.

The Basics of Instructional Design in Distance Education

At the genesis of technology-supported distance education (DE), instructional designers were frustrated by their role in the course design and development process. This frustration was attributed to general confusion regarding their role in the wide scope of instructional design (ID). Most master's- and doctoral-level trained instructional designers learned the importance of systems thinking in the process of creating a learning environment. Their systems view, often referred to as instructional systems design (ISD), dealt with much more than the writing of objectives, organization of instructional materials, and helping with practice and test construction. In fact, the ISD process deals with every aspect of the teaching and learning process, beginning with content and learner analysis and continuing in a cybernetic fashion through instructional implementation (i.e., course delivery) and evaluation. Based on this ISD expertise, ID experts worked with content experts in subject matter they did not fully understand. This was important, because high-level ID expertise was not necessarily in the repertoire of a majority of content experts. Moreover, it was not, and currently is not clear that those responsible for distance delivery of courses have all the requisite skills required (hence the team approach used in many DE institutions that purport to span the spectrum of the ISD approach). Graduate programs at a distance emerged with differing views on the source, and sometimes importance, of instructional design and distance learning expertise in their efforts to design and deliver courses and programs. In an effort to characterize these differences, two approaches used in graduate course and program design are described in the following sections.

CHARACTERISTICS OF TWO
DISTANCE-DELIVERED GRADUATE PROGRAMS

The Team-Based Design

The team-based design approach is somewhat typified by the large course teams represented by broad-scale distance educational institutions (e.g., the UK Open University). In these large scale approaches, a team of experts is assembled to plan, design, develop, produce, and eventually deliver the course. A conventional list of team participants include the following:

(a) Subject matter expert (faculty expert)
(b) Instructional designer
(c) Editor
(d) Team manager (may be one of the above or someone else, usually someone responsible for the program)
(e) Graphics and media designer
(f) Webmaster
(g) Library consultant
(h) Outside reviewer (someone to provide quality control over content and design)

The merits and difficulty of the team-based approach to course and program design are illustrated in the development of graduate programs at two distinctly different universities. The Athabasca University Master of Distance Education Degree (MDE) Program (Alberta, Canada) began in the mid-1990s using a team approach that varied in composition, depending upon the experience and expertise of the faculty subject matter expert. Given that core faculty in the program are fairly experienced instructional designers, they often serve as both content and design experts in the development of new courses. Quality control involved a two-stage review process in which stage one calls for the review of the course blueprint by all university departments and individuals having a stake in the course. The purpose of this process is to appraise the course design draft before faculty is released to work on the full-scale version of the course. Stage two of the process invites experts to assist in various stages of the development, production, and delivery of the course as required. Computer programming experts, library technicians, media designers and artists, and support/management personnel are involved in a majority of courses that are eventually delivered to the MDE students at a distance.

This two-stage review process results in a physically and academically consistent product. Moreover, plans for delivery of that product are clearly understood before delivery begins. When outside faculty are used as instructors, they are typically given instructional packages and systems to use in the course. This level of quality control is atypical of conventional university courses at any level, but very consistent with large-scale distance educational delivery, especially at experienced distance education universities (e.g., in this case an educational institution with a 30-year history of distance education delivery without on-campus students).

A second approach to distance-delivered graduate education illustrating the team design model is the University of Wisconsin-Madison's Master of Engineering Professional Practice (MEPP) Program. MEPP began course delivery in the late 1990s. Although vastly different in content and structure from Athabasca University's MDE program, it shares some similar team design characteristics.

The MEPP program has a fixed curriculum that all students take in sequence over a 2-year period. Such progression makes it possible to identify all courses in the program, select faculty experts to design the course, and set up teams to help in the overall process. In this approach, the instructional design experts are not content experts (with limited exception). The design team consists of a compliment of the following:

(a) A faculty expert (in limited case more than one)
(b) An instructional design expert
(c) An editor
(d) A Webmaster or computer consultant (not a full-time team member, but used as needed)
(e) A team manager (the MEPP program director was an active team member in most courses)
(f) Support staff as needed
(g) Student counselor as a team member upon request (usually working on the entire program issues)

The MEPP program also uses a unique version of quality control. Each course is designed by the team and then tested with a comparable group of students before being offered in the regular curriculum to MEPP graduate students. This developmental test is useful for several reasons:

(a) Design teams achieve a sense of the quality of instruction
(b) Teams appreciate the volume and complexity of content
(c) Faculty members (not typically an expert in DE) gains skills in the delivery of distance instruction before the actual course is offered
(d) Dress rehearsal for technical and logistical problems can take place in preparation for problems students and faculty might encounter
(e) Homework, assignment, and exam structures can be piloted in a way that doesn't affect regularly enrolled program students

The team process, coupled with the developmental test approach, proved extremely valuable to the MEPP program success. The results of this approach suggest the following design considerations:

(a) The design team cannot anticipate all problems with the course before testing
(b) Teams are very good at finding problems and correcting them before testing and after testing for the regular course offering
(c) Team management is crucial, and having the program director as manager helped when persons in varying locations with varying needs were involved in a complex design process.

Both of the above programs utilizing a team design approach benefit from the expertise of team participation. However, in some cases the team complexity and interpersonal issues became difficult to deal with in day-to-day operations. It should be noted that in much of the above MDE and MEPP course design, team members are not working together in the same location. The value of working at a distance proved important, and communications systems such email, conferencing, and audio teleconferencing play a key role in all aspects of this work. When team members could meet in real time in the same location, issues such as team rapport, effective use of time, and future planning became important objectives.

Do too many cooks spoil the broth? Not always, especially when the above cases suggest the team approach can be effective when strong leadership, clear objectives, and substantial resources are available. But, when faculty lacking in DE experience take control of the design and delivery process, large-scale problems can arise. That does not suggest, however, that faculty alone cannot drive the design process.

Faculty-Driven Design

Faculty-driven design puts the instructor in the roles of the subject matter expert, the course designer, manager, and implementer. Very often in online programs, the faculty model requires the instructor to be the graphic artist, Web page designer and, occasionally, the programmer too. On the outset, the prospect of the "lone ranger" faculty as distance educator seems hazardous. But, this model may be necessary, or attractive—depending on the circumstances—when one of two conditions exists: when there is a lack of availability of experts with supplemental design skills, or when a faculty possesses the required development skills. For Dakota State University's (DSU) graduate program in educational technology, both conditions are present at some level.

Dakota State University built its masters degree program in educational technology on several foundational characteristics of the faculty design model. DSU is an institution specializing in programs in computer management, computer information systems, and other related undergraduate and graduate programs. The pervasive technological culture provides a solid foundation for a graduate degree in educational technology. And, since online courses have been provided by DSU since 1989, the delivery of a graduate program in the late 1990s was a natural evolution.

When the process of institutional application, self-study, and external review finally led to program approval, faculty scheduled to deliver program courses began the course development process with departmental review of their syllabi. Faculty course developers have extensive disciplinary knowledge and instructional design skill, and more than a general knowledge of Web site development, the use of synchronous and asynchronous communication tools, and online pedagogy. Given these tools, faculty work independently through the processes of course planning and course Web site development. Occasionally, technical expertise from campus computing support is provided. With a predetermined time set for course delivery, faculty aimed to reach those due dates. Courses were delivered, and processes and tools were often experimented with as the course progressed. Faculty pressed for real-time feedback from their students and often instituted revisions "on the fly."

The mostly K-12 educator and business trainer client base made for a tough audience on which to test the faculty-driven model. Yet, evaluation data collected over the first few years of program show some interesting results from both the student and faculty experience. These results are summarized in the points below:

(a) Short timelines to course development and implementation are usually observed

(b) Formative course evaluation information from students is rapidly transitioned into the course to improve the learner experience

(c) Course activities and communication modalities customized to students' unique skills and interests result in high student satisfaction

(d) Faculty as the primary source for addressing most content, pedagogical, and technical problems keeps student frustration low

(e) Flexibility to manage course pacing, scope, depth, interaction, and media partially offsets the pressure of an increased workload faculty feel in delivering an online course

(f) As attractive as faculty-driven distance delivery of courses is, distance-delivered courses continue to remain extremely time-consuming even when repeated delivery of the same course provides content and process familiarity.

Do too few cooks make the banquet a one-course meal? The evaluation data indicate probably not. Neither should the faculty-driven model of course development be regarded as the default model. Because the faculty-driven approach is the one-stop help center for content, assessment, technical, and procedural questions, it may in some cases be preferred if faculty have the necessary skills.

DESIGN CONSIDERATIONS FOR
ONLINE, GRADUATE DISTANCE EDUCATION

It's a broad generalization to describe the contrast between team-based and faculty-driven approaches to online program development as one typifying the team-based approach as mostly concerned with quality control and course standardization, while the faculty-driven model values short development timelines enhanced by the quick turnaround of formative feedback. Still, that simplification will have to suffice, because the key findings resulting from this analysis indicates that a fundamental understanding of the following instructional design principles for online programs at this level is useful, necessary, and relevant to both models. It is also important to note that these considerations are not often represented in conventional graduate course and programs, but take on added importance in programs at a distance with adult learners participating.

1. ***Needs and learner analysis.*** Numerous traits differentiate learners. An important design task is to identify significant characteristics that will lead to the acquisition of the learning objectives. Because online graduate-level learners are adults who are returning to higher education the working environment, there are several points to keep in mind. Adult learners have a high level of motivation to learn and appreciate a program that clearly articulates

requirements and objectives. Adult learners have a high need to know how the content will benefit them, and will test that content in their work environments. They bring extensive experience from personal and working lives and feel less restrained than young adults in sharing that information. Adults also seek flexibility in their learning experiences, which requires some level of shared decision making in the class environment.

2. ***Content and Task Analysis.*** The selection of appropriate and relevant content and eventual task performance at the graduate level is often difficult. Moreover, given the published nature of syllabi and requirements, faculty are compelled to spend more time on content analysis and determining relevant measurement of content and skill acquisition than on truly engaging the students in a professionally developmental experience. Quality design, often facilitated with outside instructional design assistance, can help avoid the fixation on objectives and assessment. However, as was described earlier, in some cases that outside assistance is simply not available.

3. ***Media selection and design.*** There is no shortage of Web site development standards. These standards are driven by good graphic design as well as the ergonomics of computing. Yet, just a few key design attributes of student/Web site interface pay large dividends. Students value minimum depth access to information. Server log files linked to courses show that resources requiring students to wade through several layers of Web pages see very little use. In all practicality, students prefer longer lists and menus to deeper layered sites. This principle holds true when designing for user diversity (desktops, TV, handhelds, etc.). Usability-focused Web-based course resources also suggest that commercial electronic course development products (WebCT, BlackBoard) have less appeal to DE students than self-developed and -maintained Web sites. While commercial products may be more advantageous for the less technologically literate faculty to use, commercial products also fail to accommodate and support complete user-controlled navigation.

The use of graphics should be as robust as can reasonably be made. Jonassen (2000) presents graphics as visualization tools that have immense power to convey meaning and communicate a set of beliefs. Yet, for low-bandwidth users, quality visuals can be a problem to access. A good guiding rule is to use visuals, media and other communication tools to improve the comprehensibility of ideas, and when they directly contribute to key ideas of the instruction. Designers should match graphics specifically to the context in which they are being used. Finally, message redundancy, using various forms of communication to reduce the event of overlooked content or key ideas, should be dutifully practiced.

4. ***Practice, feedback, and cybernetic systems within courses and programs.*** Often undergraduate-level courses use unit activity and exams to determine performance levels and recommend remediation. Given the less structured nature of many graduate-level courses, this form of design is often inappropriate. In contrast, methods that allow adult students to learn skills, demonstrate learning, and even add to the content knowledge base generate best results.

5. ***Smaller units of instruction with built-in evaluation.*** The distance learner is generally viewed as studying in isolation. Theories of distance learning have suggested that bridging this isolation through social interaction is essential to successfully engaging the remote learner. Because learners will use varying approaches to their study, depending on the their unique views and skills, Wheeler (2000) suggests interactions should be multi-modal. This analysis of team-based and faculty-driven development models supports this assertion and adds that increased interaction can be achieved by designing instruction into smaller segments that require asynchronous and synchronous reactions from the learner on a more frequent basis. The interaction itself can be formatively evaluative in determining the adequacy of the content, the practicality of the design, and the progress of the learner.

6. ***Discussion and interaction.*** Clark (1998) identified four different instructional styles (receptive, directive, guided discovery, and exploratory) that shed light on possible instructional architectures. The receptive style puts the learner in a passive role as end-user, for instance, of lecture material or Web site narrative. Directive instruction applies a very programmed mode of interaction like a computer-based tutorial, for instance, in which iterative cycles of information presentation are followed by installments of structured feedback experiences. Guided discovery is similar to the "hands-on" instructional strategy of primary-schoolers, in which the learner is encouraged to manipulate elements of his or her environment. Exploratory instruction poses issues and problems that require the learner to format and address using the array of networked and tangible resources at their disposal.

In explaining the interaction between instructional architectures and learner characteristics, Clark suggests that a directive style is more appropriate for novice learners, while guided discovery may be more appropriate for more experienced learners, and the exploratory style more suited to expert learners. Jonassen and Grabowski (1993) contend the same by citing studies that show that cognitive-flexible learners do better in a guided discovery or exploratory style. The characteristics of the adult learner, coupled with information about preferred learning styles, and our experience in developing and delivering online coursework at three institutions confirms a guided discovery or exploratory style appears best matched to adult-learner, graduate level needs. This approach suits the adult learners' experientially wide knowledge base and the flexibility, independence, and applicability of content they desire in a course of study. The approach requires an instructor who is fully knowledgeable about the subject and who has the skills to provide an adaptive learning environment.

7. *Going beyond stated objectives through interaction.* Objectives guide the learner, they provide a framework for evaluating student learning, and they offer a means for both instructional designer and teacher to select and organize instructional activities and resources that will facilitate effective learning. Our experience in developing instructional activities for online learners suggests that both the team and faculty approach view instructional objectives as a beginning, not an end. Learners value opportunities that allow them to linger on a subject of interest as long as the discussion remains relevant to the goals of the course. This type of interaction with content and peers is especially pertinent to expert-style learners for whom design flexibility is critical.

8. *Meta-objectives* (writing, numeracy, clarity, analytical skills, search strategies, library use, etc.). Often referred to as standards for graduate level work, these meta-objectives are often as important as content objectives in graduate courses. However, some of these require careful planning for distance delivery and evaluation.

Expanded Faculty Roles in DE Design

Whether a part of the team or working alone, online delivery of courses requires familiar and unfamiliar roles of the faculty-developer. These roles are identified and discussed as they emerge from the study of course development experiences in which both the team and faculty-driven models are applied.

1. *Designer as editor and reviewer of work.* Few faculty or designers are specifically trained to effectively function as text editor and content reviewer. Although many experienced instructional

designers have developed editorial skills and can write effectively, they are not trained editors. Optimal team-based design approaches employ an editor to increase the level and quality of instructional products. But, since the instructional designer is obviously connected to the subject matter expert in key ways during the instructional design and development process, they, too, take on the role of content and structural review of the course materials and content. In some cases, the designer serves as a type of test student by providing feedback to the faculty member or author regarding the clarity and instructional effectiveness of the materials. A single faculty member working alone in this situation relies on his or her best editorial skills in product development, and leaves additional editorial review to the learners.

2. *Designer as surrogate or test student.* In many cases, the instructional designer can serve the role of surrogate student during the course development process. The designer can provide input to sequencing, instructional activities, and assessments that can be helpful. For example, if the instructional designer cannot determine how to proceed on assignments, or cannot answer questions on exams, superficial evidence shows that these course components may not be well designed or written. Obviously, the capacity of the designer to give this type of feedback varies and is a function of the complexity of the design and experience with course content.

3. *Designer as coach to other faculty.* In a fairly comprehensive overview of some of the recent research and evaluation studies on hypermedia in distance education, Dillon and Gabbard (1999) pointed out a serious problem with the ability of these studies to identify learning impacts. Lack of ability to identify impact can most certainly mean the designer/faculty member has little knowledge of what strategies, practices, and processes best service distance learning and instruction. Much of what works in distance learning is procedural knowledge. The proliferation of good practice in online learning requires agents of good practice to share their expertise.

4. *Designer as project manager.* In distance education, the role of the instructor expands to assume the responsibilities of project manager because student interaction with fellow students, the content, and the instructor are priority. In the design process, teaching methods are organized according to the intended instructional outcomes. The instructor rightfully assumes the designer role of identifying any methods, instructor-centered, programmed, or

experiential, effectively engaging the distance learner. And because the world of online learning requires an interaction medium, the instructor must also play a role in determining the media best suited to facilitate chosen teaching methods.

5. *Designer as graphical consultant and media designer.* This category of expertise is usually reserved for professionals in this area. However, ongoing experience helps instructional designers become aware of graphical and media options. In their role, designers should feel confident making recommendations in these areas. Moreover, in some cases they actually become designers through skills in Web page design, multimedia, etc.

6. *Designer as evaluator.* A recent analysis of the literature on distance learning by Wisher, Curnow, and Drenth (2001) indicated that only 21% shows any evidence of systematic evaluation. Unfortunately, distance learning experiences all too often take place unaccompanied by quality evaluation. Evaluation that does take place is generally linked to student assessment and fails to look at other elements of the online delivery environment.

As a part of the design process, evaluation can proceed by first asking illuminative questions that determine if the individual components of the system, such as communication tools and university resource services, are operating. This stage of the evaluation is focused on observing and detecting functional problems. From the illuminative stage, the evaluation evolves to an integrative, summative stage and tends to look at the student learning experience holistically. Learning impact and performance outcomes are relevant at the integrative stage.

From multiple data sources that are both comparison- and criterion-based, evaluation in both the team and faculty design contexts suggest the lens of evaluation can be brought to bear on at least the five following distinct components of the distance learning environment:

- *Infrastructure/System*—examines the compatibility of online learning tools with network speed and connectivity. Technical support systems on either end of the connection are also examined for quality of service to the student/client.

- *Course and program design*—distance learning environments are uniquely situation-dependent and should be examined as such. Instructional sequencing in a project-based curriculum would do well to be world-related. Check for alignment between objectives and assessment activities, and examine the motivational strategies embedded in the instruction.

- *Work Flow*—examines how users navigate and utilize online resources. Do learners progress through their work in a linear fashion (novice-like), or in an opportunistic fashion (expert-like)? Web server log files are generally of excellent help in understanding how students navigate the course Web site. Are directions clear for students and is message redundancy among communication media observed?

- *Interaction*—can take place between instructor and learner, learner and learners, learner/instructor and content, learner/ instructor and technology. Both social and instructional interactions are relevant to evaluation.

- *Impact*—tells designers what influence the learning experience has on learner behaviors. Course performance and learner productivity are two ways to measure impact, as are student retention/attrition. Longer-term impact measures might include self- and supervisor-rated professional performance.

7. ***Designer as student and faculty help-desk consultant.*** Instructional designers are often placed in a role as an on-call consultant during course design, development, delivery, and evaluation. This role is natural in the faculty-driven approach, but atypical in the team-based approach. Rarely do instructional designers work with students directly, but in an unusual design fashion, the MEPP program in Wisconsin closely connected designers to both test students and early cohorts to learn more about the program and course design first-hand. In this case, the connection was an attempt to merge the evaluation and formative design process more closely.

    The help desk function is usually represented by a central phone-in or e-mail in consulting service. Team-based approaches centralize help desk support through computing services related departments. However, many of the questions of students are not well handled by these centralized services and, therefore, the "help desk" style support is required of the program or even within a course. These extra services can be resource-consuming for small-to-moderate programs. The formalized nature of this task is rarely the domain of the instructional designer.

ISSUES WITH ONLINE INSTRUCTION AT THE GRADUATE LEVEL

Although programs vary in their values and views on program and university objectives at the graduate level, experiences working in diverse environments shows that the objectives outlined here are critical to the academic success and integrity of graduate level programs that purport to represent education, distance education, and instructional design (at a minimum). To achieve these "meta-objectives," a program must create both a value system and an infrastructure to allow students and faculty to work toward these goals. Therefore, the integrity of the course content is not exclusively the end goal of the process. Sometimes the above objectives require that a superstructure or infrastructure be in place that allows for these objectives to be met, e.g., a means of interaction in asynchronous and synchronous time, file exchange capability, etc.

CONCLUSIONS

This discussion has elaborated on the role of the faculty member in the many aspects of the course design, development, and delivery, and the availability of support for these processes. Whether the development model is team-based or whether a single faculty drives the development, new design considerations for the faculty member are significant. Both models also suggest that a more involved faculty approach results in serious investment and ownership in the course and learner development process, and online instructional skills are honed in new learner interaction modes.

Quality DE learning experiences take place when new pedagogies are designed to engage the distance learner. The simple conversion of a traditional course to an online format is not advocated here. The online course requires a complete new set of student engagement strategies that do not naturally follow from the face-to-face environment.

Where the design of online learning takes place, further research in this area should study the following:

(a) Design in open versus closed programs
(b) Independent versus group delivered design considerations
(c) Fixed time control versus more individualized control over time and rate of progress.

As a final statement, it should be noted that although distance education is often referred as one type of instructional or teaching method, it is not. Many variations of distance education range from totally individualized instruction to group-based, real-time teaching. In many cases, DE becomes a mixture of both extremes and everything in between the two. The application of instructional design will differ given the DE "plan of attack" selected by the instructor or institution. However, the expanded role of the instructional designer in distance education is clearly called for in most applications.

REFERENCES

Clark, R. (1998). *Building expertise: Cognitive methods for training and performance improvement*. Washington, DC: International Society for Performance Improvement.

Coldeway, D. O., & Spencer, R. E. (1995). Early results on the success of the master of distance education degree program. *Proceedings of the Second Conference on Distance Education: Sharing the Experience II*. Oregon State University Press.

Coldeway D., & Hawkes, M. (2001). *Instructional design in distance delivered graduate education programs*. Presentation at the Distance Teaching and Learning Conference, Madison, WI.

Dillon, A., & Gabbard, R. B. (1999). Prepared to be shocked: Hypermedia does not improve learning. *Proceedings of the Fifth Americas Conference on Information Systems* (pp. 369-371). Milwaukee, WI: Association for Information Systems.

Erdelyi, B., Hoefkens, J., Diening, L., Makino, K., & Berz, M. (2001). The Michigan State University M.S. and Ph.D. online degree programs in beam physics. *Quarterly Review of Distance Education 1*(4). 345-50.

Jonassen, D. H., & Grabowski, B. L. (1993). *Handbook of individual difference, learning, and instruction*. Hillsdale, NJ: Erlbaum.

Jonassen, D. (2000). *Computers as mindtools for schools: Engaging critical thinking*. Columbus, OH: Merrill Prentice Hall.

Wheeler, S. (2000). Instructional design in distance education through telematics. *Quarterly Review of Distance Education, 1*(1), 31-44.

Wisher, R. A., Curnow, C. K., & Drenth D. J. (2001). *From student reactions to job performance: A cross-sectional analysis of distance learning effectiveness*. Presentation at the Distance Teaching and Learning Conference, Madison, WI.

CHAPTER 13

GETTING IT RIGHT GRADUALLY

An Iterative Method for Online Instruction Development

Douglas A. Kranch

Distance education course designers working alone often do not have the luxury of fully developing their instruction before releasing their courses to students. The Individual Iterative Instructional Design (I3D) model is useful for educators who both develop and present their distance learning instructional units in areas ranging from higher education to the K-12 environment. By combining the flexibility of Morrison, Ross, and Kemp's (2003) model, the effectiveness of Gerlach and Ely's (1980) model, and the iterative nature of Sims and Jones' (2002) model, the I3D model adjusts the level of ID effort in each iteration without requiring more resources than individuals working alone could muster. The I3D model's 3-cycle development process also accounts for the varying amount of work instructional design requires during course development.

The Perfect Online Course: Best Practices for Designing and Teaching
pp. 265–273
Copyright © 2009 by Information Age Publishing
All rights of reproduction in any form reserved.

Instructional development (ID) models tend to be rooted in a particular design environment. Gustafson and Branch (2002), for example, divide the models they discuss into those oriented toward classroom instruction, those oriented toward developing instructional products, and those designed by large systems. Other classification schemes could be developed, and certainly models used for instruction could vary widely depending on the intended scope and level as well as the number of people involved in its development. But what about the individual educator, especially those developing and presenting their own online instruction? Can an ID model address their needs and be robust enough to accommodate environments as varied as elementary schoolrooms and university classrooms? The iterative individual instructional development model attempts to be that single model for the individual instructor who is both the developer and presenter of distance instruction.

ID MODELS FOR ONLINE
INSTRUCTIONAL DEVELOPERS/PRESENTERS

While professional instructional developer/presenters may have varying amounts of outside assistance from their institutions, for this model they are considered solely responsible for developing, delivering, and assessing their instruction. Instructional environments differ from the prescription of outcomes in public schools to the more general freedom to specify outcomes in higher education. They also differ in the length of the instructional module that is the focus of the ID effort. Elementary school instructional cycles tend to center on the weekly lesson plan, so that focus shifts from the lesson of the moment to the planned outcomes for the week. The success of the previous day's and week's lessons influences the instructional development of the following lessons. In higher education, while attention is given to the lessons being taught at the moment, it is also drawn towards the fit of each day's lessons into the goals of the entire course. The learning cycles expand to entire course offerings and the fit of the lesson in the course considered as a whole.

Several instructional models could be applied to the varied settings of individual developer/presenters. The first is Morrison, Ross, and Kemp's model (Morrison, Ross, & Kemp, 2003; Gustafson & Branch, 2002), which breaks up what Morrison et al. (2003) call the "four fundamental components [of] learners, objectives, methods, and evaluation" into nine nonlinear developmental "elements" (p. 7). Key features of this model are its nonlinearity, which allows instructional designers to enter the development process at any of the nine elements, and its emphasis on continual assessment and development. This model's comprehensiveness seems more appropriate for designing large online instructional modules and too unwieldy for developing short, single-purpose lessons. It also assumes a constant level of development effort throughout the instructional cycle.

Gerlach and Ely's instructional design model as described by Gustafson and Branch (2002) is described as suitable for the K-12 classroom. It takes the instructional designer/presenter through five phases of ID in a linear, stepwise manner. The first phase involves specifying both the objectives and the content of the instruction. Gerlach and Ely see this as a natural beginning point and indicate that objectives and content should be considered together. They next assess the entering behaviors of the learners to identify learning gaps that instruction will need to address. Gerlach and Ely combine into the next phase (a) determining the instructional strategies to employ (ranging from lecture to discovery), (b) the organization of the students during their activities (from group work to individual work), (c) how time will be budgeted among the activities, (d) where the activities will take place (including work outside the classroom), and (e) the instructional resources needed to assist in the learning. Gerlach and Ely bypass instructional delivery and skip to assessing the instruction both in terms of student learning and the "effectiveness and efficiency of the instruction" (Gustafson & Branch, 2002, p. 22). This assessment is used as feedback to alter the instructional objectives and content. This relatively simple model could be used by developer/presenters in a wide variety of environments; however, it seems too rigid and assumes the same amount of workload for both new units and units that have been taught several times.

The Three Phase Design model of Sims and Jones (2002), intended for producing large-scale Web-based learning modules, conceives of the ID process as phases during which the instructional unit becoming gradually more settled and fixed; that is to say a process of "iterative development or successive approximations" (p. 4). The first iteration is a "prototype" used to "test the water" or see that the instruction being developed is on target before investing heavily into resources for the course. After the prototype is tested, the second phase expands the course into full functional mode that is released to students. The course is again evaluated and a third phase refines the course to its relatively permanent final form. During these phases, Sims and Jones assume a number of professionals are involved in the ID.

The Morrison, Kemp, and Ross model provides robustness while the Gerlach and Ely model provides simplicity and low overhead. The Sims and Jones model adds the element of changing design focus during successive developmental iterations. A combination of these three design theories should provide a satisfactory basis for instructional design by designer/presenters in online learning environments.

AN INDIVIDUAL ITERATIVE INSTRUCTIONAL DESIGN MODEL

The idea of successive iterations in the ID process and of changing the focus of development as the instructional unit passed from initial development to refinement has intuitive appeal. Iterative development is fundamental to any type of repeated instruction such as that delivered in both colleges and K-12 institutions. A school or college unit lasting several weeks may undergo several changes while it is being offered as developer/presenters continuously evaluate the effectiveness of the unit. Between course offerings or school years, the effectiveness of units previously taught is re-evaluated before they are taught again. Creating a new instructional unit is at an entirely different level of effort from revising and refining that unit, although many of the same steps are involved.

The Iterative Individual Instructional Development Model (I3DM) is meant to model the instructional development process of those who develop and present instructional units, online and face to face, that are repeated with different learners over time. The model as diagrammed in Figure 13.1 is built on three developmental iterations (development, major revision, and confirmation) and a fourth iteration (tweaking) that repeats as often as the fully developed instructional unit is taught. At the end of each iteration the question is asked whether there has been a "major change" in the content or teaching method. Such a change could be a result of a curriculum revision or a fundamental change in teaching methods, such as converting from a face-to-face to an online course. When the answer is "Yes," ID returns to the beginning of the entire process for a complete redesign.

The Model in Detail

Each iteration is divided into three phases: analyze content, apply content, and assess content. Each box in the diagram represents an ID process. The open-ended boxes coming off the right of process boxes contain activities that could occur during that process. There is no implied order or hierarchy in this list of activities, which is loosely based on early activities presented in the Gerlach and Ely and the Morrison, Ross, and Kemp models.

The *analyze content* phase includes analyzing the learning aims of the instruction and developing the instructional assessments. Analyzing the learning aims is accomplished by performing task analyses, developing objectives, and identifying outcomes. With these identified the methods for assessing them can be addressed. These two steps are joined by a double headed arrow indicating that they are mutually dependent upon one another and occur in tandem. Specifically, assessment instruments evolve

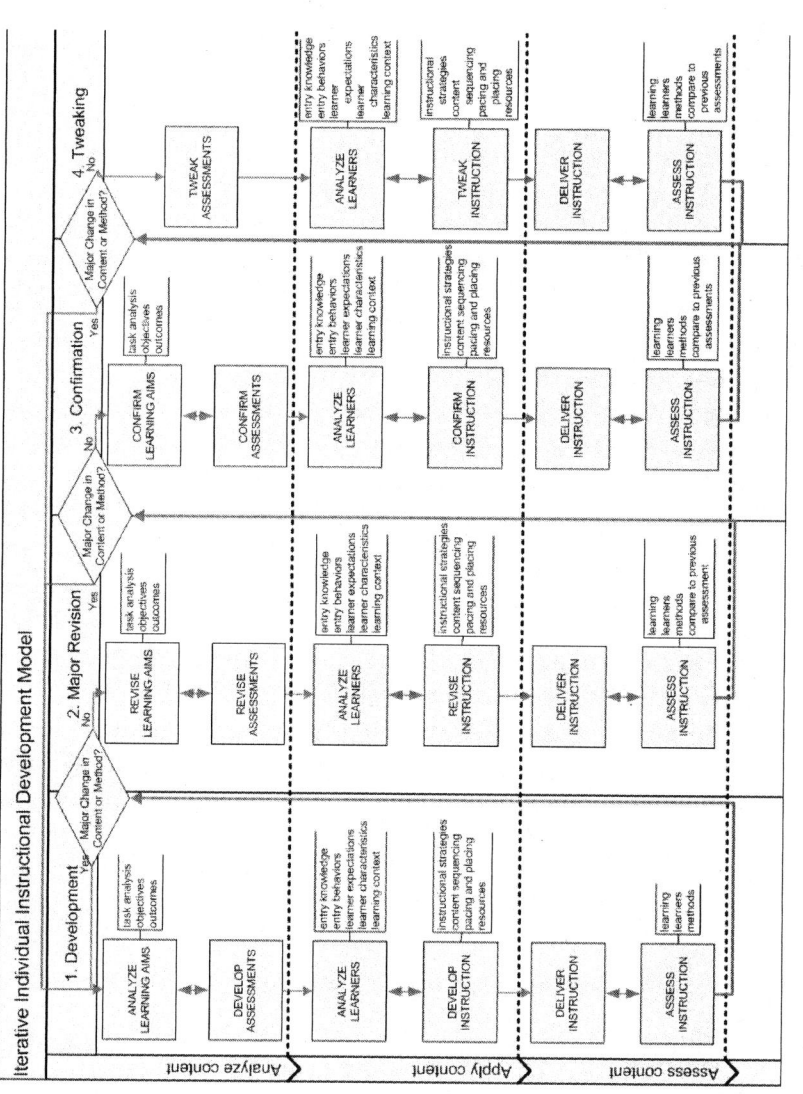

Figure 13.1. Iterative Individual Instructional Development Model

out of task analyses, objectives, and outcomes, while selecting realistic and appropriate assessment methods introduces a powerful means for keeping objectives, tasks, and outcomes within the realm of the doable. Implicit within this analysis phase is a needs assessment that continually evaluates (a) whether the needs that are revealed are addressable via the proposed instruction, and (b) the scope of the instruction as new needs surface to prevent the unit from expanding to an unreasonable size.

During the *apply content* phase, the instructional goals and their assessments are applied to specific target groups. The learners are analyzed during the first step in this phase by (a) identifying their expected entry knowledge and behaviors, (b) identifying their characteristics (e.g. age and cultural background) and expectations (willingness to learn and what they hope to get from the instruction), and (c) examining the learning context (e.g., the environment in which learning will take place, organizational support for the learning, learning criticality, and the time allotted for it). During the second step of this phase, the instruction is developed by (a) selecting instructional strategies (e.g., mnemonics, paraphrasing, outlining, and diagramming), (b) sequencing the content in a way that best allows the strategies to be applied (e.g., by difficulty level, familiarity, expected interest of the learners, some special property of the content, or by an imposed unifying concept), (c) fitting the pacing of content delivery to the ability of the learners, and (d) selecting the supporting resources for the learning. These two steps are joined by a double headed arrow in the diagram to indicate their reciprocal relationship: As the learners are analyzed, the instructional methods used in the classroom will change, and the instructional methods chosen will foreground different learner characteristics.

The *assess content* phase consists of delivering and assessing the instruction. Although many instructional models omit instruction delivery, this model sees it as a vital part of instructional assessment and hence of instructional design. The I3DM is intended to be used to develop units of learning that could occur during a time span reaching several months, during which instructional delivery is a prolonged activity punctuated throughout with assessments that give critical feedback that changes instruction as it is being delivered. Instructional methods may change because of the assessment results, causing a need to change or add assessment instruments to the course that measure the results of the altered methods.

The Iterations

The I3DM is characterized by permanent iterations that are increasingly damped. During the first three iterations of the I3DM, the same six processes are carried out, but the intensity of the scrutiny to which the instructional unit is subjected and the corresponding degree of change made decreases with each iteration. The model expresses this by changing the wording of the verb used in the processes to "revise" in the second iteration and "confirm" in the third. The major commitment in time and mental energy to produce the original instructional unit is replaced in the second iteration with a critical eye toward systematically revising the unit by rethinking the learning aims, assessments, and instructional methods based on the first delivery of the instruction to real learners. The learners still need to be assessed (as they do in all iterations), and the revised instruction is delivered and assessed. In the third iteration, practically all of the needed changes should have been made, and the instructor simply confirms that the instructional aims and methods and the assessment instruments are satisfactory. Thereafter, the three iterations and their six steps are continually repeated during the life of the instructional unit, with only minor changes in method and content expected from each iteration.

This is not to say that the unit will cease to evolve. This gradual adjustment of the unit over time is referred to in the diagram as "tweaking." Note that there is no process in the Tweaking iteration regarding the learning aims. The model assumes that these aims have been well established and will not change unless there is a major change in the unit content. However, instructors will continue to "tweak" the assessment instruments and the instruction, and learners will continue to need analysis to help decide what "tweaking" is needed. This tweaking iteration will be repeated each time the unit is taught; thus, the unit will be revised in some manner each time it is offered.

The I3DM allows the instructional unit to be completely overhauled. The model assumes that such an overhaul will not occur in the middle of instructional delivery, but will occur after the unit has completed its current iteration. This need for an overhaul is shown in the model by the diamonds at the top between iterations asking the question, "Has there been a major change in the content or method?" Whether a change in content or method is major is a judgment call. If it is, no matter how many iterations the unit has undergone, it returns to the initial iteration to receive a comprehensive revision.

While K-12 developer/presenters may have a plan for instructional delivery of material that is spaced out over the entire year (or have a plan that is formulated for them by the state or school district), their instructional development centers on the weekly plan. During the first iteration of this instruction, teachers must develop instructional methods for their various subjects that present a week's worth of information for all subjects. This material is delivered and assessed during the week, and occasionally over the course of 9 weeks to half a year. Course materials may be offered only once in each academic year. Thus, it may require three academic years for the same materials to be offered to students and the material to be fully developed. This has two implications. First, the I3DM model requires that developer/presenters take diligent notes about how well the instruction worked and what should be changed the next time a unit is offered. Second, at any time during those 3 years, curricula could change, forcing the developer/presenter to begin the ID process again with the new curricula. Since the amount of ID work required in this model is greatest during the first iteration and decreases significantly thereafter, institutions that change their curricula often subject their developer/presenters to a far heavier ID workload than those in institutions in which the curriculum remains fixed for at least 3 years.

CONCLUSION

The I3D model is designed specifically for modeling instructional design in formal education environments, where learning units are typically constructed by individual instructors. It is designed to be simple and flexible enough for a single educator to use while reflecting the real-world needs of the full-time teaching environment. The I3D model can guide developer/presenters in a wide variety of educational environments to develop their own instructional units. It sees ID as an iterative process that does not wait for the design process to finish before using the product, but refines the instructional unit through use as it works its way to completion. The five or six processes in each iteration are readily understood and form a simple model that adjusts the scope, aim, and effort of ID as the instructional unit matures. The refining iterations in this model indicate that developer/presenters change their focus as their courses mature. If they are using a course that is already well developed, instructors can enter the model at the second, third, or fourth iteration. The level of ID effort lowers in each successive pass through the model to match the need for further refinement. It should serve well the individual developer/presenter in all areas of education.

REFERENCES

Gerlach, V. S., & Ely, D. P. (1980). *Teaching and media: A systematic approach* (2nd ed.). Englewood Cliffs, NJ: Prentice Hall.

Gustafson, K. L. & Branch, R. M. (2002). *Survey of instructional development models.* Syracuse, NY: ERIC Clearinghouse on Information Technology.

Morrison, G. R., Ross, S. M., & Kemp, J. E. (2003). *Designing effective instruction* (4th ed.). New York: Wiley.

Sims, R., & Jones, D. (2002). Continuous improvement through shared understanding: Reconceptualising instructional design for online learning. In A. Williamson, C. Gunn, A. Young, & T. Clear (Eds.), *Winds of change in the sea of learning. Proceedings of the 19th Annual Conference of the Australian Society for Computers in Learning in Tertiary Education (ASCILITE)* (pp. 1-10). Auckland, NZ: UNITEC Institute of Technology. Retrieved October 7, 2006, from http://www.ascilite.org.au/conferences/auckland02/proceedings/papers/162.pdf

CHAPTER 14

TOWARD A PERSON-CENTERED MODEL OF INSTRUCTION

Can an Emphasis on the Personal Enhance Instruction in Cyberspace?

Christopher Miller and Joan M. Mazur

A person-centered instructional design model has been developed for virtual, Web-based environments. This model, based on the work of Carl Rogers attempts to address several issues raised in the literature regarding (a) the changing role of instructors and students; (b) the broadening of the notion of learning outcomes; (c) the isolation and dissatisfaction of students in dispersed locations; and d) problems with authenticity and individualization of experience. A person-centered instructional model is described and contrasted with instructionalist (Dick & Carey, 1996) and constructivist (Jonassen, 1999) approaches. In conclusion, theoretical and practical issues with the person-centered model are explored.

The Perfect Online Course: Best Practices for Designing and Teaching
pp. 275–296
Copyright © 2009 by Information Age Publishing

INTRODUCTION

Virtual, Web-based environments, while attractive in their potential to widen the scope of users' experiences for communication, collaboration, and access to resources, can also create artificial and possibly depersonalizing social circumstances. A person-centered model of instruction has been developed for use in designing instruction in virtual, Web-based environments. The model, grounded in the person-centered theory of Carl Rogers (1961), attempts to address several issues raised in the literature regarding the changing role of instructors and students, the broadening of the notion of learning outcomes, the isolation and dissatisfaction of students in dispersed locations, and problems with authenticity and individualization of experience. How should instructional designers confront these issues that arise in distributed, virtual instructional environments?

We posit that Rogers' work can be used as a basis to design instruction for virtual Web-based environments and we offer a conceptual analysis upon which to base this claim. A person-centered instructional model is described and contrasted with instructionalist (Dick & Carey, 1996) and constructivist (Jonassen, 1999) approaches. A discussion of theoretical and practical issues of the person-centered model concludes the article.

DEFINING VIRTUAL ENVIRONMENTS

As with any new technology, definitions that are complementary, mutually exclusive, subsuming, and directly contradictory seem to proliferate as fast as the innovation itself. Virtual reality and its many applications are no exception. In this section, we give an overview of prominent definitions and select one to be used for purposes of analysis in this article.

Virtual reality (VR) is, quite literally, an analogous reality to our own but with one significant difference—it occurs in a computerized and/or networked electronic environment. Definitions of VR range from "one part computer simulation and one part consensual hallucination" (Biocca & Levy, 1995; Gibson, 1984 p. 54) to a computer-created sensory experience that completely engulfs participants so they believe and barely distinguish a "virtual" experience from a real one (Franchi, 1994).

Types of VR applications tend to fall into two general categories: immersion and simulated environments. VR immersion environments use specially designed computer hardware, worn by a user as a data glove or head-mounted display, for example, that creates digital versions of external optics and haptics (Biocca, 1992a). These sensory stimuli are chimera, but are processed by the brain as input that makes the person feel as if they are located spatially and temporally in the illusory environment—in a cyberspace (Biocca, 1992b; McCauley & Sharkey, 1992). In contrast, in VR simulated environments, the user experiences a particular context or situation in a much less sensory and more cognitive way, by accessing software applications on a networked hyperspace—such as the World Wide Web. These simulated types of Web virtual environments depict qualities of the actual place or situation using computer graphics, audio, or video as stimuli that mimic the physical or conceptual dimensions of a representative environment. They can be cognitively distinguished from an actual sensory experience. Users can take simulated tours of online museums or other remote locations such as strolling around virtual parks or navigating to selected locations via a virtual map of particular areas. Another common VR simulation environment—the chat room—provides tools for participants to talk with people at geographically dispersed locations in real-time conversations in "rooms" graphically represented as space on a computer screen. These kinds of simulated virtual spaces have been adapted for use in instructional settings. According to Mason (1996), the many virtual classrooms and universities can be characterized by three broad categories of delivery systems:

1. Text-based systems wherein the learning environment includes electronic mail, computer conferencing, real-time chat systems, MUDs/MOOs[2], and other Web applications;
2. Audio conferencing wherein the learning environment includes audiographics and real-time audio over the Internet; and
3. Videoconferencing, wherein the learning environment includes one-way and two-way, software driven videoconferencing and other Web-based visual media.

Because simulated types of VR environments require less hardware and technical commitment, they are more practical for widespread use and have begun to flourish in educational settings. Thus, in the present discussion, it is this latter definition of a virtual environment we use to discuss a person-centered model of instruction.

Virtual education purportedly differs from traditional education in less obvious ways than the presentation mode. Chalmers (1997) asserted that a virtual educational space can offer increased levels of interactivity and the development of learning communities because of the use of a particular learning environment delivery system as described by Mason. One example of this increased activity level is apparent in a text-based interactive learning environment: PuebloMOO (http://www.pc.maricopa.edu/community/pueblo/). This is a multi-layered environment where the students are free to explore a world created completely in the computer, to interact with other people, and to make choices regarding their virtual identity (called an avatar) in the simulated environment.

Potentially, the opportunity to personalize one's role in a virtual environment could be beneficial because the learner can meld learning with recreation, socialization, and personal development activities in a single interactive experience. However, virtual environments, while attractive in their potential to support a variety of users' interactions, also have the potential to create artificial and possibly depersonalizing social circumstances.

DEHUMANIZING EFFECTS OF VIRTUAL ENVIRONMENTS

Concerns associated with the dehumanizing effects of mass-produced, one-size-fits-all instruction are framed by the largely European debate of *Fordist, Neo-Fordist* and *Post-Fordist* approaches (Campion, 1995). These three approaches contrast sharply in defining the role of the learner, the instructional context, and valued learning outcomes. However, they share implicit epistemological assumptions that warrant further scrutiny. On a continuum from maximum central control, low skill, and little learner responsibility (Fordism) to less managerial control, high skill, and responsibility for learning (Post-Fordism), each position implies that control emanates from the point of instruction (or the instructor) and is not shaped through negotiations between the instructor and learner. In other words, though the debate addresses issues that arise from the social interaction aspects of learning, the underlying epistemological assumptions of the positions specifically exclude such key principles as the social negotiation of learning (Vygotsky, 1962).

While the Fordist debate is less publicly articulated in the United States, it is important to note how often disgruntled distance education students report feelings of alienation and dissatisfaction with online learning (Biner et al., 1994). Students at the so-called "remote sites" complain of a lack of co-presence with the instructors and other students. In fact, the only consistently reported benefit is "convenience." American educators claim that students in online learning situations particularly value interaction and personalized instruction. (Simonson et al., 2000, p. 41). In fact, instructors in online courses report students expect increased access to instructors and have higher expectations of on-going interactions with the instructor as well as with peers (Harasim, 1990). However, reports of distance learning experiences show these dimensions of instruction are less often achieved in actual practice. What if course designers want to address the problems created by the efficiency approach of delivering mass-produced, homogeneous online instruction?

We now have delivery systems and technologies that can support increased levels of interactivity and learner control. However, are the current instructional design models adequate? We contend that current models lack components that specifically incorporate opportunities for learners to participate in ways that address issues related to the kinds of dehumanizing effects highlighted in the Fordist debate. The person-centered model of instruction we propose is designed to begin to address these issues. Prior to articulating the model, we turn first to a discussion of salient concepts related to designing instruction in online settings.

TRANSACTIONAL DISTANCE, INTERACTION, CONTROL, AND SOCIAL CONTEXT

Articulating theoretical concepts that are applicable to the task of designing instruction for virtual environments presents several problems. The literature on distance education is broad and spans a 200-year history of instruction in which the instructor and student were in separate locations (McIsaac & Gunawardena, 1996). A recent analysis of distance education research (Anglin & Morrison, 2000) has shown the preponderance of work has been descriptive or survey based research that falls into three categories:

1. conceptual and theoretical papers describing such topics as definitions of terms, cost-benefit analyses, emerging delivery technologies, policies, and specific programs at universities;
2. reviews of the literature focusing on topics such as faculty resistance to professional development, computer based instruction, or instruction in other countries or the military; or
3. evaluation studies that yield "lessons learned" or information regarding student or instructor issues or preferences.

Moore (1989) claimed, and Anglin and Morrison concurred that there is a need for integrated programs of theory-based research that "explore beyond the primary setting" (Anglin & Morrison, 2000). We would add that most models of instruction are not specifically designed for virtual environments. The fact that the models of instruction may be inadequate has the potential to confound the research agenda Morrison and Anglin suggested.

Keegan (1980), in his foundational work on describing the distance education circumstances, discussed six key elements:

1. separation of teacher and learner;
2. influence of educational organization;
3. use of media to link teacher and student (and we would include other students);
4. two-way exchanges of communication;
5. learners as individuals rather than grouped; and
6. education as an industrialized form.

These elements are intended to be descriptive, but they suggest problems that may arise when considering the design of instruction for any distance education setting, and can thus be extended to apply to virtual environments as well. For example, what issues do the separation of teacher and learner create? What issues arise when learners are individuals rather than in a classroom group? In the literature, four issues have been articulated that relate to Keegan's elements, and they are central to our argument for the need for a person-centered model of instruction. These concepts are transactional distance, interaction, control, social context.

Transactional distance as defined by Moore (1989) and Saba and Shearer (1994), referred to the amount and structure of dialogue between participants in an educational relationship. Clearly, transactional distance has been a problem in distance settings where students feel cut off from either the instructor or other students. The availability of chat rooms or MOOs in simulated virtual environments may affect transactional distance, and the design of instruction needs to take into account how to incorporate these features of virtual systems.

Moore (1989) and Hillman et al., (1994) characterized four dimensions of interaction.

1. Learner interaction refers to dialogue with the instructor that is a source of motivation.
2. Learner-content interaction is the process of intellectual engagement with materials and subject matter.
3. Learner-learner interaction occurs among students as they exchange information and ideas (Moore, 1989).
4. Finally learner-interface interaction (Hillman et al., 1994) involves the notion that technology is not neutral and its use affects the learning context.

Much dissatisfaction with online learning environments relates to the lack of interaction. Instruction needs to be designed to specifically incorporate and capitalize on the potential for various dimensions of interaction in virtual environments. Interactive, two-way environments imply an element of control. Related to the need for interaction is the need for opportunities to control aspects of the interactive environment.

The discussion of control in distance education draws on the extensive literature ranging from the seminal locus of control work done by Rotter (1989) to Baynton's (1992) model of control based on a factor analysis. Baynton's analysis revealed that for control to be empowering independence (opportunities for real choice), competence (ability and skill), and support (materials, technology, and human) are required. Many of the issues raised within the Fordist debate and by students who feel powerless and stuck in "remote" locations at distance learning sites relate to perceptions of control. Students often report feeling cut off from the instructor and other students when they are not empowered to participate meaningfully in their own learning experience.

The social context is the milieu of people, relationships, technologies, materials, and interactions that surround the learning experience. Distance education researchers are just now beginning to identify social context factors in cyber-environments. Within these environments, gender, race, and physical features of participants have been identified as contextual demographic factors. In terms of social learning and learner support, the effects of using text-based chats for those whose learning styles are more visual or kinesthetic or, specifically relevant to distributed virtual environments, co-presence or social presence, are among contextual factors recently investigated (Wagner, 1997). Co-presence is defined by reading the sociolinguistic cues in social situations and how immediacy and intimacy are affected. Particularly in computer-mediated situations, co-presence is often affected negatively by the capacity of the delivery system. Technical issues such as bandwidth transmission problems can create situations where audio is out of sync with video or slow download times. Such technical problems are compounded by the fact that many instructors lack skill with the apparatus of instructional delivery (Mazur, 2000). For example, students report that instructors who cannot zoom in on responding students or needlessly pan the classroom in two-way video transmissions create additional distractions and impede the instructional flow.

The challenges of designing instruction to minimize transactional distance, support the four types of interaction, and enable empowering control in the social context of learning in a virtual environment are many. The model of person-centered instruction presented in this paper, derived from the work of Rogers, attempts to address these issues by specifically laying out a series of steps to design instruction to support learning when these problems in a virtual learning context are likely exist.

IN SEARCH OF THEORY-BASED INSTRUCTION
FOR VIRTUAL, WEB-BASED ENVIRONMENTS

The introduction of any new interactive technology inevitably affects the learning arrangement. In virtual environments, both the role of the instructor and the form of instruction will change dramatically. A central change will be less control for the instructor, coupled with more opportunities for learner-selected and controlled exploration and interaction. Indeed, unbeknownst to the instructor at any given time, students may be logging in and participating actively. Directive, didactic forms of instruction will need to be modified in interactive virtual settings to include the learner more actively. Instruction that is shaped and enhanced by facilitation will be key to accommodating increased learner control (Salmon, 2000). Students will clearly need specialized guidance exploring their online learning opportunities and the design of instruction will need to take into account the special nature of asynchronous interaction supported by web-based virtual environments. MOOs, MUDS, chats, and threaded discussion lists would be good examples. We hypothesize these shifts in the roles of instructors and learners are radical and signal significant changes in many of the basic assumptions of instructional design for non-cyber venues. Perhaps most significant among these assumptions will be reconceptualizing instruction as primarily facilitation and designing for that condition. The work of Rogers, with its emphasis on facilitation, empowerment, and self-actualization offers many principles upon which to develop a model of instruction that will be suited to the new roles, approaches, and issues that are present in virtual learning situations.

When Rogers wrote *Freedom to Learn* (1994), he was focused on traditional schools but saw that the person-centered educational approach developed its strongest roots in alternative schools and what he presciently called "universities without walls." While many instructional theories focused on the learner's achievement of specific learning objectives, Rogers' instructional theory focused on the goal of teaching the learner how to learn. It is because of this focus that Rogers felt the learner would become a freely functioning, self-enhancing, self-actualizing, creative, and dependable person.

Rogers revealed that he developed his person-centered learning theory because we live in a constantly changing world and people in such continually evolving contexts needed to be flexible thinkers adapting easily to change. More importantly, he claimed that change is a constant in today's world and students need to be prepared to adapt. In online instructional settings where the roles of students are changing, adaptation means "learning how to learn" within the different types of environments now available. Rogers boldly suggested the facilitator should encourage the learners to charge off in new directions dictated by their own interests and to unleash a student's sense of inquiry and exploration (Rogers & Freiberg, 1994). How can the design of instruction support such learner-directed activity? What, if any, will be the outcomes of such instruction (how will learning be defined) and how can evaluation take place (how will learning be measured)? Will assessment be mutual or individual? What kinds of performance are desirable? Will learner development and satisfaction lead to outcomes that will be valued personally and publicly?

The strategy in this article will be to discuss the utility of the person-centered instructional theory, based on Rogers' work, for designing instruction in virtual environments based on both a conceptual and a comparative analysis. The conceptual analysis focuses on outcomes ascribed to Web-based learning from the literature framed by specific aspects of Rogers' learning theory. These outcomes, such as personal development and learners' self-actualization, broaden more traditional notions of learning outcomes as content objectives. Next, we present a model of person-centered instruction synthesized from Roger's principles and compare it to two prominent instructional approaches. Finally, a discussion of issues related to the use of the model concludes the article.

A CONCEPTUAL ANALYSIS OF ROGERS' PERSON-CENTERED INSTRUCTIONAL THEORY USING AN EPISTEMOLOGICAL HEURISTIC

The foundational conceptual analysis for our investigation of the utility and robustness of Rogers' work as it may be applied to online, virtual learning environments must begin with a sound epistemological analysis of his theoretical perspective. In order to accomplish this goal, we employed the "structure of knowledge" approach developed by Gowin (1981). This heuristic approach seeks to elucidate underlying epistemological elements and has been used to conceptualize design for interactive learning programs (Gay & Mazur, 1989). Gowin's framework is particularly appropriate to the task because it is inquiry-based—the analysis proceeds from central questions emanating from a learning event (in our case the event is "instruction in a Web-based environment"). Central "focus questions" are "What are the epistemological elements (world view, principles, concepts) of Rogers' theory?" and "How can these be applied to instructional design in virtual environments?" Gowin's heuristic details how the underlying epistemological elements such as world view, core principles, and concepts relate to a specific learning event and the various knowledge claims and value to the learner. A complete explication of this epistemological analysis is detailed elsewhere (Miller & Mazur, 2000), however, a summary of that analysis salient to the present discussion follows.

CARL ROGERS AND PERSONCENTERED LEARNING: CENTRAL CONCEPTS AND PRINCIPLES

Freely Functioning Creative Learners

Rogers developed a system of non-directive psychology called client-centered therapy that allows the client, who knows what hurts, to marshal the resources of personal experiences and discover his or her own meanings. The client learns through such reflective experience and uses it to grow as a person. Rogers hypothesized that core concepts of client-centered psychology could be applied analogously toward a person-centered education.

Rogers theorized that a person emerging from therapy or from a productive educational situation has experienced optimal psychological growth (Rogers & Freiberg, 1994). Specifically, the person is able to function freely—realizing his or her potentials, striving to be self-enhancing, continuing to develop, and always seeking newness in each moment—resulting in a self-actualized person. Maslow (1970), described this self-actualized person as someone who has developed or is developing into the full stature of personal capability. Of importance is that learners continue to learn creatively through life rather than becoming automatons reciting the information provided to them (Patterson, 1973). Rogers himself tied self-actualization to creativity with these words:

> The mainspring of creativity appears to be the same tendency which we discover so deeply as the curative force in psychotherapy—one's tendency to actualize oneself, to become one's potentialities ... the urge to expand, extend, develop, mature—the tendency to express and activate all the same capabilities of the organism. (Davis, 1992 p. 3)

Building on Rogers, Davis claims creativity involves developing one's talents; learning to use one's abilities; exploring new ideas, places, activities; and developing a sensitivity to problems of others and humankind (Davis, 1992 p. 7). In a person-centered approach, instructional design links self-actualization, freedom, and creativity. By linking these elements, learners will be empowered by the design of instruction to take advantage of the many learner-controlled options in virtual environments in ways that support developing new understandings (self-actualizing activities) rather than random "surfing" for information.

Davis (1992) elaborated on the notion of creativity in terms of what he called the "4P's": The creative person, process, product (Barron, 1988), and press (Isaksen, 1987; Mooney, 1963; Taylor, 1988). Davis further defined the creative person as the individual in the creative environment, moving through the process of creativity, or having developed the creative product. The creative process is the steps taken to solve real problems in ingenious or innovative ways (Davis, 1992). The creative product is the outcome of the creative process. Creative outcomes emphasize originality and multiplicity of viewpoints or approaches and include the development of a sense of value for the newly created idea or product (Davis, 1992). Davis used the rather awkward term "creative press (as in pressure)" to describe the social and psychological factors affecting any other aspect of the creative person or process.

Instructor as Facilitator

While the development of self-actualized, creative people who are lifelong learners is clearly a commendable goal, how can this goal actually be achieved? First, an instructor should realize that self-actualization cannot be taught and that the student reaches the goal of becoming a self-actualized person through his or her own individualized learning experience. Second, the instructor needs to be self-actualized in order to foster these qualities in the students (Patterson, 1973). In fact, when Rogers and Freiberg (1994) talked to students, they found many of the same qualities required to become a facilitator were also wanted by students. They found students want trust and respect, freedom, a caring environment where people are concerned and attentive, choices, and teachers who help them succeed (Rogers, 1961). In a person-centered educational experience, not only will the learner produce a creative product from the learning experience, but the learner's increased self-actualization is also considered a creative product. As a learner becomes more self-actualized, the learner will be able to perceive reality more accurately; accept him or herself and others; understand varying views and perspectives; and become more spontaneous, independent, and creative (Davis, 1992; Maslow, 1970).

There are several tasks for an instructor wishing to move into a person-centered facilitation role. The facilitator should first set the mood for the environment (the creative press). There should be a sense of cooperation and trust within the group rather than competitive attitudes, which will disrupt the sense of trust and cooperation, thus creating a negative creative press on the experience. The instructor as facilitator becomes one of many resources of information rather than the main source of information for the students. Most importantly though, the instructor as facilitator should be genuine and strive for awareness of personal attitudes, thus developing an authentic relationship with the students (Rogers, 1961).

The Role of the Learner and "Significant" Learning

In *Freedom to Learn*, Rogers suggested that for clients to have successful learning experiences and become self-actualized, they must largely direct their own experiences. This key tenet in Rogers suggests the primary role of the student in a person-centered model. Not only is the student's activity the central element as it is in many student-centered approaches (e.g. anchored instruction), but in a person-centered approach the student will actually initiate needs based on his or her own interests and self-determined level of competence (in consultation with the expert/instructor). "Significant learning" was coined by Rogers as the learning outcome of such learner-directed approach. Significant learning is related to the presence of facilitation. In contrast to didactic instructional methods in which the instructor provides information to the learner, the instructor in a person-centered environment becomes a facilitator of a largely student-conducted learning experience. Such a facilitated experience is termed "significant learning" because the individual initiates it, and exerts a high degree of personal control because the element of self-directed learning is built into the whole experience (Sahakian, 1970). The responsibility for defining as well as meeting learning goals shifts primarily to the learner. To monitor the development and achievement of goals Rogers stressed the importance of the contract. The learner clearly and specifically defines and commits to achieving the articulated goals, projects, activities, and assessments. Also, perhaps related to the benefits of group therapy and peer feedback, Rogers also stressed that peer evaluation is as powerful a tool for assessment as is the input of an expert. Rogers stressed that these were not better, but rather different avenues for obtaining credible, useful, and varied information on performance. Moreover, in the course of this self initiated experience, the learner becomes "the creative person" engaged in a creative process.

A PERSON-CENTERED MODEL OF INSTRUCTION

Elements of a Person-Centered Model of Instruction

Based on the previous conceptual analysis, a model of instructional design can be established that includes the following elements:

1. learner analysis with an emphasis on the learners' interests, personal ability, and prior knowledge of a given topic;

2. formation of tasks based on an integration of the learners' knowledge and interests, and the principles of content or discipline;

3. selection of a non-competitive environment to support cooperative learning and allow learner control;

4. development of learner goals and objectives based on the learners' interests and abilities that is *contracted* by each learner with the instructor;

5. development of individualized forms of self-evaluation;

6. organization of areas to interest in the topic and the sequencing of the topics;

7. identification and selection of resources to enhance the learning experience; and

8. the implementation of the learners' self-evaluation.

By utilizing these eight elements of the person-centered model of instruction, three outcomes can be achieved. The outcomes that would be achieved include the development of an innovative and original creative product; an increase in the self-actualization of the individual learners; and significant learning, which is not only an accumulation of knowledge on a topic but also a sense of satisfaction in the learning; a desire to master the experience; and a greater understanding of the problem and potential resolutions of the problem. As the development of a creative product is an outcome of the person-centered model of instruction, it is important to understand how the creative process operates within the model. Table 14.1 graphically represents the person-centered model and illustrates how Davis' "4-Ps" of creativity operate within the model.

Comparison of the Person-Centered, Instructionalist, and Constructivist Approaches

There are a variety of instructional design models currently in use for designing instruction, the instructional environment, and the evaluation of instruction. Two prominent approaches, representing dichotomous ends of the design spectrum, can be characterized as instructionalist and constructivist approaches. Paradigm exemplars of each approach have been selected as a basis for comparison to the person-centered model described above. We recognize the inherent issues problematic in such comparisons. One-to-one correspondence of elements is often neither possible nor desirable. Underlying epistemological or axiological issues can exist and confound the viability of the comparative effort. For example, emanating from these foundational differences can be fundamental

Table 14.1.   Person-Centered
Instructional Design Model to the "4-Ps" of Creativity

Person-Centered Instruction (Rogers)	*"4-Ps" of Creativity*
Learner Analysis Emphasis is on the learners' interests, personal ability, and prior knowledge of a given topic.	*Creative Person* Emphasis on the person.
Task Formation Task formation proceeds through an analysis of integrating students knowledge and interests around the principles of the content or discipline.	*Creative Person* Focus on developing tasks centered around the person
Learning Environment Selection Select a non-competitive environment that supports cooperative learning and allows the learner to take responsible control over it.	*Creative Press* Creating a social/psychological environment to support the person, process, and product
Develop Learning Goal Develop individual achievable objectives within the context of the learning experience based on the students' interests and abilities and contract with the instructor.	*Creative Process* Process of selecting a goal (creative product)
Individualized Assessment Development Work with students to develop forms of self-evaluation.	*Creative Process* Develop ways to test goal achievement
Reciprocal Teaching Organize the areas of interest to cover in the topic and sequence in a format to maximize the learning potential.	*Creative Process* Organizing the process of the experience
Selection of Instructional Resources Identify and select resources to enhance the learning experience and present them to the students. The teacher presents himself or herself as a resource.	*Creative Process and Press* Selecting resources to support the process and teacher taking role of a resource to support the social/ psychological environment
Learner's Self Evaluation Learners conduct self-evaluation based on the contract of the level of personal involvement, self-initiated involvement, and pervasiveness, which shows the significance of the learning experience.	*Creative Process* Testing and evaluating the process and the creative product
Outcomes of Process 1. Significant learning 2. Self-actualization 3. Creative product (The learner will show not only an accumulation of knowledge of the topic but also satisfaction in the learning, desire to master the experience, and a greater understanding of the problem, and potential resolutions)	*Creative Product* Learning, self-actualization, and a product emphasizing the originality of the person are created.

conceptual discrepancies in the purpose and outcomes of instruction. Moreover, the comparative position of elements is necessarily reductionist and affected by the selection of those elements. Thus the comparative process can (indeed will) leave out nuances, refinements, and complexities within each of the models used for the comparison. With these caveats in mind, we find it useful to compare any new model to existing approaches for two reasons. First, the newly developed model can be situated within the existing norms of the discipline. Secondly, the comparative effort illuminates not only differ ences between the models but also theoretical and practical issues within the new model for future discussion and explication.

For purposes of this discussion, the Dick and Carey systems approach model (1996) serves as a paradigm case of the instructionalist approach and Jonassen's (1999) constructivist model is used as a paradigmatic example of the constructivist approach. In Table 14.2 we provide a comparison of the person-centered model with these instructionalist and constructivist design approaches.

DISCUSSION

To what extent can the person-centered model presented here address the problems of related to transactional distance, interaction, control and social context described in the distance education literature?

Transactional distance. The person-centered model changes the roles of instructors and students by decreasing the transactional distance through a requirement of high interaction, dialogue and negotiation between learner and instructor in shaping the instructional goals. Goals are based on students' interests as mediated by the expertise of the instructor in the knowledge domain.

Interaction. Within the person-centered model interaction is not simply increased, it is *required* along all four dimensions of interaction noted by Hillman et al. (1994) in order for instruction to proceed. Learner interaction occurs through the initial dialogue with the instructor to determine learner interests and goals and provide intrinsic motivation necessary in person-centered situations, which requires responsibility on the part of the learner. In order to continually assess progress and maintain motivation, learner-content interaction is achieved and active learning is facilitated through the thoughtful selection of resources by the facilitator. Self-evaluation, peer review, and contracting provide opportunities for learner-learner interaction. Learner interaction with the interface occurs obviously as a function of utilizing the particular cybertools in the virtual

Table 14.2. Comparison of Instructional Design Models

Instructionalist Design (Dick and Carey)	Constructivist Design (Jonassen)	Person-Centered Instruction
Needs Assessment Determine what is the optimal situation and the actual situation. Find what change is needed to fill the gap between the situations. This will identify the instructional goal.	*Problem Definition* Define how the problem is represented and the manipulation space.	*Learner Analysis* Emphasis is on the learners' interests, personal ability, and prior knowledge of a given topic.
Task Analysis Determine step by step how the students will accomplish the goals.	*Determine Problem Dimensions* Determine what is needed to resolve the problem.	*Task Formation* Task formation proceeds through an analysis of integrating students knowledge and interests around the principles of the content or discipline.
Learning Environments No focus on developing a learning environment.	*Describe Learning Environment Supports* Determine the cases, resources, and tools needed to provide support for the learning environment.	*Learning Environment Selection* Select a non-competitive environment that supports cooperative learning and allows the learner to take responsible control over it.
Performance Objectives Development Write performance objectives of what students will be able to do upon completion of the instruction.	*Goals and Constraints Are Unstated* Uncertainty is a plus. Offer no rules for predicting the outcome.	*Develop Learning Goal* Develop individual achievable objectives within the context of the learning experience based on the students' interests and abilities and contract with the instructor.
Assessment Instrument Development Develop assessment instruments to measure task achievement.	*Alternative Assessments Development* Provide opportunities for flexible, creative demonstrations of student understanding.	*Individualized Assessment Development* Work with students to develop forms of self-evaluation.
Instructional Strategy Sequence and organize the information as an instructional strategy for delivery.	*Instructional Strategy* Coaching, modeling, and scaffolding support and challenge the learner to succeed.	*Reciprocal Teaching* Organize the areas of interest to cover in the topic and sequence in a format to maximize the learning potential.

Selection of Instructional Resources
Develop and select instructional resources.

Evaluation of Learning
Design and conduct a formative evaluation to determine the effectiveness of the instruction. Conduct a summative evaluation to verify the effectiveness of the instructional event.

Outcome of the Process
Based on assessment scores, formative evaluation, and summative evaluation achievement of the goal can be determined.

Provide the Problem Manipulation Space
Include objects and tools that are required for the learner to manipulate the environment.

Evaluation of Learning
Evaluate the problem solving process and viability of the solution.

Outcome of the Process
Outcomes are understanding and further inquiry.

Selection of Instructional Resources
Identify and select resources to enhance the learning experience and present them to the students. The teacher presents himself or herself as a resource.

Learner's Self-Evaluation
Learners conduct self-evaluation based on the contract of the level of personal involvement, self-initiated involvement, and pervasiveness, which shows the significance of the learning experience.

Outcomes of Process Significant Learning
Self-actualization creative product (The learner will show not only an accumulation of knowledge of the topic as well as a creative product but also satisfaction in the learning, desire to master the experience, and a greater understanding of the problem, and potential resolutions)

environment that support dialogue, peer interaction and the selection and exploration of resources.

Control. Baynton's (1992) notion that control is an empowering element if independence (opportunities for real choice), competence (ability and skill), and support (materials, technology and humans) are extant is enabled by the person-centered approach. Primarily this is because the learner is genuinely involved in the design and assessment of the instruction by defining self-initiated goals based on interest and contracting to achieve them. Competence and ability are empowering components that are integral to the negotiation process between knowledgeable facilitator (expert instructor) and the learner in developing learning goals. It is incumbent on the instructor to bring to the negotiation the goals that constitute competence in the knowledge domain, and to shape and customize those goals with the interests and skills of the learner. The learner must honestly assess his or her ability to meet the standards of competence and begin at a point that is reasonable.

Social Context. The social context issues may be most significantly addressed through the use of the person-centered model because the complex of people, relationships, technologies, and materials must all be considered as the learning is designed through negotiation. Indeed, through dialogues with students and facilitators, all parties become aware of the learning issues, the skills required, the technological tools, and the range of materials. The design of instruction requires participation by all parties in defining and carrying out assessments (self, peer, external).

What are the potential benefits and drawbacks of using a person-centered model of instructional design? It is obvious to anyone who has implemented a Web-based course or used these simulated VR tools and/or environments that our students are "out there" independently exploring and shaping their own experiences, sometimes to the detriment, sometimes to the gain, of actual learning and skill acquisition. Web-based instruction is inherently "person-centered" and located at distributed rather than localized classroom group situations in which the instructor controls the environment. By incorporating concepts and principles from Rogers' approach, the person-centered model capitalizes on the distributed and individualistic nature of instruction in virtual settings by redefining roles, instructional procedures, and assessment in ways that accommodate rather than antagonize the learner. Additionally, by emphasizing students' interests and abilities, courses taught in virtual environments such as certain applications delivered via the Web can create an atmosphere of mutual participation and allow for the accommodation of various skill and ability levels. Students can exercise the freedom to choose which is encouraged by user-controlled virtual learning environments. By utilizing the person-centered approach for instructional design, students and instructor can take full advantage of the very features of virtual environments that are thought to promote engagement and enhance learning. In other words, the instruction developed using a person-centered model of design is a good fit with user-controlled, choice-laden instructional virtual environments.

QUESTIONS FOR FURTHER RESEARCH

The person-centered model is new, and many questions can be raised regarding its application. The elements promoting the success of such an approach—learner responsibility, ability to be self-assessing and proactive in learning—are the very elements, when lacking, that will result in an instructional experience that is non-productive at best and frustrating at worst. For example, how will students who have incorrectly assessed their abilities fare in such a free choice environment? Indeed, what kinds of self-assessment tools will be needed for students (and instructors) to make such appraisals of skill and knowledge? What opportunities or interim assistance are needed to aid these students in fully participating in the course and learning the material? Will students who often expect to obtain course material via lecture and didactic instruction feel cheated if the instructor relies on them to shape their own course experiences? What is the proper role of the instructor—how much facilitation/guidance is needed or appropriate?

There are certainly logistic issues, which arise from the implementation of the person-centered approach. Will courses have no design until learners sign up for them? How can instruction be so customized and learner interests assessed? (especially when learners may be unprepared to accurately detail their interests in cogent ways). Will assessment be credible? How can learners be prepared for their new role as mutual participants in the design and assessment of learning?

We believe that some of these concerns, while valid, can be overcome through the thoughtful application of the person-centered model in ways that keep in mind the spirit of the concepts and principles of Rogers' work. There will be course design, but it will be focused on the negotiation of goals within a knowledge domain and competencies tailored to the learner's facilitated self-assessment. The purpose of this article has been to articulate the theoretical underpinnings of the model. Specific procedures and processes for engaging the learner in dialogues that result in the articulation of interests need to be more clearly articulated. Case studies of courses that use the model will be particularly helpful for understanding the practical issues related to using this approach. Moreover, students will have to understand, acknowledge, and accept their new roles as mutual participants, and this new role will augment the well-documented need for activity and participation in meaningful learning.

Issues of dehumanization raised by the Fordist debate as well as problems relating to transactional distance, interaction, control, and social context, which have been documented in the distance education literature, are in evidence (and in some cases augmented) in newer, virtual online instructional environments. A consideration of the person-centered model of instruction described in this paper is clearly in a nascent stage. However, we believe its emphasis on the personal attempts to address several issues raised in the literature regarding the changing role of instructors and students, the broadening of the notion of learning outcomes, the isolation and dissatisfaction of students in dispersed locations, and problems with authenticity and individualization of experience. Though there are unanswered questions regarding implementation of the model, the primary purpose of this paper has been to articulate concepts and principles from Rogers' work that can be applied to designing instruction in online courses where the roles, expectations, and delivery systems are changing radically. New models and approaches will be needed, and the person-centered model is presented to provoke thought and spur further discussion on how instructional design must change to accommodate the challenges posed by the proliferation of online courses and virtual instruction.

NOTES

1.   The term developed by William Gibson (1984) in his book *Neuromancer* which generally refers to any computerized environments

2.   Text-based online collaborations between many people allowing users to communicate with each other, move around, and manipulate objects in virtual environments (Downing, Covington, & Covington, 1996; Syverson, 2000).

REFERENCES

Anglin, G. J., & Morrison, G. R. (2000). An analysis of distance education research: Implications for the instructional technologist. *Quarterly Review of Distance Education, 1*(3), 189-194.

Barron, F. (1988). Putting creativity to work. In R. J. Sternberg (Ed.), *The nature of creativity: Contemporary psychological perspectives*. Cambridge: Cambridge University Press.

Baynton, M. (1992). Dimensions of control in distance education: A factor analysis. *Journal of Distance Education, 6*(2), 17-31.

Biner, P. M., Dean, R. S., & Mellinger, A. E. (1994). Factors underlying distance education satisfaction with televised college-level courses. *The American Journal of Distance Education, 8*(1), 60-71.

Biocca, F. (1992a). Virtual reality technology: A tutorial. *Journal of Communication, 42*(4), 23-72.

Biocca, F. (1992b). Will simulation sickness slow down the diffusion of virtual environment technology? *Presence: Teleoperators and Virtual Environments, 1*(3), 334-343.

Biocca, F., & Levy, M. (Eds.). (1995). *Communication in the age of virtual reality.* Hillsdale, NJ: Erlbaum.

Campion, M. (1995). The supposed demise of bureaucracy: Implications for distance education and open learning--More on the post-Fordism debate. *Distance Education, 16*(2), 192-216.

Chalmers, J. (1997). *Virtual education,* [Website]. J. Chalmers. Available: http://www.musenet.org/~bkort/EdMud.html [1998, January 13].

Davis, G. A. (1992). *Creativity is forever.* (3rd ed.). Dubuque, IA: Kendall/Hunt.

Dick, W., & Carey, L. (1996). *The Systematic Design of Instruction.* (4th ed.). New York: HarperCollins.

Downing, D., Covington, M. A., & Covington, M. M. (Eds.). (1996). *Dictionary of computer and Internet terms* (5th ed.). Hauppauge, NY: Barron's Educational Series.

Franchi, J. (1994, January/February). Virtual reality: An overview. *Tech Trends.*

Gay, G., & Mazur, J. (1989). Conceptualizing the design of a hypermedia program for language learning. *Journal of Research on Computing in Education, 22*(2), 119-126.

Gibson, W. (1984). *Neuromancer.* New York: Ace Books.

Gowin, D. B. (1981). *Educating.* Ithaca, NY: Cornell University Press.

Harasim, L. M. (1990). *Online education: Perspectives on a new environment.* New York: Praeger.

Hillman, D. C., Willis, D. J., & Guawardena, C. N. (1994). Learner-interface interaction in distance education: An extention of contemporary models and strategies for practitioners. *The American Journal of Distance Education, 8*(2), 30-42.

Isaksen, S. G. (1987). Introduction: An orientation to the frontiers of creativity research. In S. G. Isaksen (Ed.), *Frontiers of creativity research: Beyond the basics.* Buffalo, NY: Bearly.

Jonassen, D. H. (1999). Designing constructivist learning environments. In C. M. Reigeluth (Ed.), *Instructional-design theories and models: A new paradigm of instructional theory*(2nd ed., pp. 215-240). Mahwah, NJ: Lawrence Erlbaum Associates.

Keegan, D. J. (1980). On defining distance education. *Distance Education, 1*(1), 13-36.

Maslow, A. H. (1970). Motivation and personality (2nd ed.). New York: Harper & Row.

Mason, R. (1996). *Anatomy of the virtual university,* [Web Site]. Available: http://www.edfac.unimelb.edu.au/virtu/info/robin.html [1998, January 26].

Mazur, J. M. (2000, June). *Applying insights from* film theory and cinematic technique to create a sense of community and particiaption in a dis*tributed video* *environment*, [WWW]. Annenberg School for Communication, University of Southern California. Available: http://www.ascusc.org/jcmc/vol5/issue4/mazur.htm [2000, December 14].

McCauley, M. E., & Sharkey, T. J. (1992). Cyber-sickness: Perception of self-motion in virtual environments. *Presence: Teleoperators and Virtual Environments, 1*(3), 311-318.

McIssac, M. S., & Gunawardena, C. N. (1996). Distance education. In D. H. Jonassen (Ed.), *Hand*book of research for educational *communications and technology* (pp. 403-437). New York: Simon & Schuster Macmillian.

Miller, C. T., & Mazur, J. M. (2000). Towards a person-centered model of instruction: Can an emphasis on the personal enhance instruction in cyberspace? In M. Crawford & M. Simonson (Eds.), *23rd Annual proceedings of selected research and development papers presented at the annual convention of the Association for Educational Communications and Technology* (Vol. 23, pp. 293-299) Denver, CO: Association for Educational Communications and Technology.

Mooney, R. L. (1963). A conceptual model for integrating four approaches to the identification of creative talent. In C. W. Taylor & F. Barrons (Eds.), *Scientific creativity: Its recognition and development* (pp. 331-340). New York: Wiley.

Moore, M. G. (1989). Three types of interaction. *The American Journal of Distance Education, 3*(2), 1-6.

Patterson, C. H. (1973). *Humanistic education*. Englewood Cliffs, NJ: Prentice-Hall.

Rogers, C., & Freiberg, H. J. (1994). *Freedom to learn* (3rd ed.). New York: Merrill.

Rogers, C. R. (1961). *On becoming a person*. Boston: Houghton Mifflin.

Rotter, J. (1989). Internal versus external control of reinforcement. *American Psychologist, 45*(4), 489-493.

Saba, F., & Shearer, R. (1994). Verifying key theoretical concepts in a dynamic model of distance education. *The American Journal of Distance Education, 2*(1), 36-59.

Sahakian, W. S. (1970). *Pyschology of learning: Systems, models, theories* (2nd ed.). Chicago: Rand McNally College.

Salmon, G. (2000). *E-moderating: The key to teach ing and learning online*. London: Kogan Page.

Simonson, M., Smaldino, S., Albright, M., & Zvacek, S. (2000). *Teaching and learning at a distance: Foundations of distance education*. Upper Saddle River, NJ: Merrill.

Syverson, P. (2000, July 19). *Moo information* [Website]. Pe Syverson. Available: http://www.cwrl.utexas.edu/~syverson/basicinfo/moos.html [2000, October 22].

Taylor, C. W. (1988). Various approaches to and definitions of creativity. In R. J. Sternberg (Ed.), *The nature of creativity: Contemporary psychological perspectives*. Cambridge, England: Cambridge University Press.

Vygotsky, L. (1962). *Thought and language*. Cambridge, MA: MIT Press.

Wagner, E. (1997). Interactivity: From agents to outcomes. In T. Cyrs (Ed.), *Teaching and learning at a distance: What it takes to effectively design, deliver, and evaluate programs* (pp. 19-25). San Francisco: Jossey Bass.

CHAPTER 15

ENHANCING WEB-BASED INSTRUCTION USING A PERSON-CENTERED MODEL OF INSTRUCTION

Christopher T. Miller

This study compared the implementation of a person-centered model of instruction to non-person-centered instruction in Web-based courses. Three questions were posed regarding the outcomes of the person-centered model of instruction: Is it possible to increase the self-actualization, or striving for individual achievement from learners in a Web-based course using a person-centered model of instruction? Could instructors in a Web-based course receive original and useful creative products from students experiencing person-centered learning that exceeded the quality of products in similar Web-based courses? Finally, would Web-based instructors see an increased striving for individual achievement within their students experiencing a person-centered learning experience?

The Perfect Online Course: Best Practices for Designing and Teaching
pp. 297–310
Copyright © 2009 by Information Age Publishing
All rights of reproduction in any form reserved.

INTRODUCTION

Web-based instruction is a popular method of delivering instruction to people, but are tried-and-true instructional models such as objectivist and constructivist models the most appropriate for online learning? One instructional model designed specifically with Web-based learning in mind is Miller and Mazur's (2001) person-centered model of instruction based on the humanistic learning theory of Carl Rogers. The person-centered model of instruction integrates the humanistic learning theory of Rogers (1957; Rogers & Freiberg, 1994) by focusing the instruction on the needs, interests, and skills of the learners. Miller and Mazur (2001) theorized when they designed this instructional approach the following three outcomes: the development of a creative product that is original and useful; significant learning as described by Rogers and Freiberg (1994) as an accumulation of knowledge and satisfaction with the learning experience, a desire to master the experience and a greater understanding of the problem and its potential solutions; and, finally an increase in self-actualization, which is a striving for individual achievement, through learning and development of interests (Rogers uses the term "perfection" in his definition of self-actualization, but the term "individual achievement" is being substituted as a more appropriate term in an educational context). Similar outcomes may be described by other instructional models, but the person-centered model of instruction stands out because it not only focuses on achieving a learning goal but also on enhancing the striving for individual achievement or personal perfection of the learners.

A study was conducted to explore the differences between Web-based courses taught by the same instructor. This particular case study explored the different learning outcomes between courses taught using a non-person-centered instructional (non-PCI) approach and a course taught using the person-centered model of instruction. This case study would also be the first implementation of the person-centered model of instruction testing the viability of the instructional model and its outcomes. Three questions were of interest within this study: Is it possible to increase the striving for individual achievement from learners in a Web-based course using a person-centered model of instruction? Could instructors in a Web-based course receive original and useful creative products from students experiencing person-centered learning that exceeded the quality of products in similar Web-based courses? Finally, would Web-based instructors see an increased striving for individual achievement within their students that experienced a person-centered learning experience?

BACKGROUND ON THE
PERSON-CENTERED MODEL OF INSTRUCTION

The PCI model of instruction was designed for use in Web-based instructional settings to enhance the learning that occurs at a distance. While there are many different instructional models that can be implemented in an online environment, the PCI model of instruction focuses on moving control to the learner and allowing the instructor at a distance to take on a more facilitative role in the learning environment. The PCI model of instruction is based on a humanistic psychological approach to education. This approach focuses on the learner learning how to learn and instilling an interest in continuing to learn (Kolesnik, 1975). Specifically, the person-centered model is based on the humanistic learning theory of Carl Rogers (Rogers & Freiberg, 1994). Rogers believed that for individuals to have successful learning experiences they must have significant learning (Rogers, 1969). Significant learning, as used by Rogers is the outcome of a learner-directed approach to instruction in which students engage in directing their own learning experience based on their knowledge, skills, and interests. Within this learning experience the instructor takes on the role of facilitator of both the learning and the learning environment. The person-centered model of instruction, developed by Miller and Mazur (2001), focuses on the learner and instructor as facilitator implementing eight instructional design elements. These elements include the following: learner analysis using interests, skills, and prior knowledge; task formation based on the learner analysis and instructional topic; selection of environment to maximize learning; development and contracting of learner goals and objectives developed with the instructor; development of self-evaluation; development of instructional sequencing; identification and selection of resources; and implementation of learning and learner's self-evaluation. It was hypothesized that following this model of instruction within a Web-based course could lead towards the outcomes of a creative product, Rogers' significant learning, and an increase in the striving for individual achievement.

While this is a new model of instruction, it is not intended as a replacement for other instructional models. The purpose for this model of instruction was to enhance the instructional opportunities provided to educators and learners in the realm of Web-based instruction. Web-based instruction has a primary difference from face-to-face instruction in that the locus of instructor control can be difficult to maintain due to the transactional distance of learner to instructor. This instructional model flips the locus of control from the instructor to the learner so that learners can become more active in the development of their learning. While learners become more actively engaged in controlling their learning experience, the instructor takes on the role of providing resources and becoming a resource to the learners through their personalized learning experiences.

DESCRIPTION OF THE CASE STUDY

Although the principles of the person-centered model of instruction appeared sound, the instructional model needed to be implemented in an instructional setting to evaluate the predicted outcomes. Also, the initial application of the instructional model would provide an opportunity to discover problems with successful application as well as potential solutions. The initial application occurred in a graduate-level Web-based education course at a regional university. Two courses using a non-PCI instructional approach were used as a basis for comparison. All three courses were taught by the same instructor. A total of 60-75 students were anticipated to participate in the study, but due to unforeseen complications of administrative errors in course enrollment and low course enrollment numbers, only 42 participants volunteered for the case study. Table 15.1 describes the three classes used in this case study.

The intervention group (PCI group, $n = 20$) consisted of graduate students enrolled in the spring 2002 Reading in the Elementary School course. The PCI group experienced instruction using the person-centered model of instruction. Comparison group 1 (CI_1, $n = 12$) was comprised of graduate students enrolled in the fall 2001 Reading in the Elementary School course. This course was the same as that used in the PCI group except that the instructor used their traditional non-PCI instructional approach. Comparison group 2 (CI_2, $n = 10$) consisted of graduate stu-

Table 15.1. Sample Group Enrollments

Sample Group	Abbreviation	Education Course	Sample Group Enrollment
Intervention Group (Person-centered instruction)	PCI	Spring 2002 Reading in the Elementary School	20
Comparison Group 1 (non-PCI instruction)	CI_1	Fall 2001 Reading in the Elementary School	12
Comparison Group 2 (non-PCI instruction)	CI_2	Fall 2001 Elementary School Curriculum	10
Instructor	I		1

dents enrolled in the fall 2001 Elementary School Curriculum course. This course was taught to the same population of students and addressed some similar content to the Reading in the Elementary School but was a more broad-based focus on elementary school curriculum. It was taught by the same instructor using their traditional non-PCI instructional approach. To achieve the needed power for analysis of the Personal Orientation Inventory, a quantitative data collection tool used in this case study, the comparison groups CI_1 and CI_2 were pooled (CI_p, $n = 22$).

DESCRIPTION OF DATA COLLECTION AND ANALYSIS

Data were gathered from multiple sources. These sources included the Personal Orientation Inventory (POI), creative products developed by the students in the PCI group, and instructor interviews.

The Personal Orientation Inventory (POI) was provided to the participants as a pretest and posttest measure of striving for individual achievement through the learning and development of interests of the participants in the three sample groups. The POI was developed by Shostrom (1966) as a measure of values and behavior. The POI has been implemented as a measure of individual achievement for close to 40 years with studies conducted testing content validity (Fox, Knapp, & Michael, 1968; Shostrom, 1964), criterion validity (Bouverat, 1970; Jury, Willower, & DeLacy, 1975; Rizzo & Vinacke, 1975), construct validity (Knapp, 1965; Shostrom & Knapp, 1966), and the measure's resistance to faked scores (Braun & Asta, 1969; Braun & La Faro, 1969; Foulds & Warehime, 1971). The POI is made up of 150 two-choice comparative value and behavior judgments providing two major scales and 10 subscores. The subscores were used to measure various aspects of individual achievement in this study. Analysis of the POI pretest and posttest differences were conducted using a Wilcoxon signed-rank test, which is a nonparametric measure for two variables to determine if they have the same sample distribution.

The creative products were collected from the students in the PCI group for evaluation as evidence of creative products developed by participants that experienced the person-centered model of instruction. The creative products were analyzed using a qualitative content analysis (Merriam, 1998).

Instructor interviews were conducted before and after the two control group courses (CI_1 and CI_2) were taught in the fall 2001 semester and before and after the intervention group course (PCI) was in the spring 2002 semester. An additional instructor interview was conducted midway through the spring 2002 semester when the person-centered model of instruction was implemented.

Table 15.2.   Research Design for Data Collection

	Description of Treatment		
Sample Group	Preinstructional Experience	Instructional Experience	Postinstructional Experience
PCI (person-centered instruction)	POI administered	• Read scaffolding chapter in textbook • LAQ administered • Participants develop learning contract • Participants negotiate learning contract • Participants complete and submit the project	POI administered
CI₁ (non-PCI instruction)	POI administered	• Critique textbook reading • Critique three model teaching videos • Write 20-minute scaffolding lesson plan • Videotape the lesson • Submit lesson plan and video to the instructor	POI administered
CI₂ (non-PCI instruction)	POI administered	• Develop a term paper focusing on a content area subject • Submit the term paper to the instructor	POI administered
Instructor	• Fall 2001 preinstruction interview • Spring 2002 preinstruction interview	• Spring 2002 postnegotiation interview	Fall 2001 postinstruction interview Spring 2002 postinstruction interview

PROCEDURES

The procedures for this study occurred over two academic semesters (fall 2001 and spring 2002). The procedures during the fall 2001 semester involved the CI_1 and CI_2 groups. The procedures during the spring 2002 semester involved the PCI group. Table 15.2 describes the research design used in this case study.

The study began with the CI_p group (CI_1 + CI_2) receiving the POI. The participants in the CI_1 group (fall 2001 Reading in the Elementary School) completed the POI pre-test and began their non-PCI instructional experience regarding the topic of scaffolded reading experiences. The participants wrote a critique of their textbook reading and three model teaching videos focused on scaffolded reading. The participants completed a project that entailed developing a 20-minute lesson plan focusing on scaffolded reading experiences and videotaping the teaching of the lesson plan. The CI_1 participants received the POI posttest after their project was submitted at the end of the semester.

The participants in CI_2 group (fall 2001 Elementary School Curriculum) completed the POI pretest and began their non-PCI instructional experience. The CI_2 group participants submitted a term paper focusing on a content area subject. The CI_2 participants received the POI posttest after their term paper was submitted at the end of the semester.

The PCI group participants (spring 2002 Reading in the Elementary School) received the POI pretest and were assigned to review the textbook chapter focused on scaffolded reading experiences. The participants then completed a Learner Analysis Questionnaire (LAQ), which was used to help the participants identify their needs, skills, and interests relating to scaffolded reading experiences. The LAQ was based on a content analysis of the textbook chapter focusing on scaffolded reading experiences. Participants then completed a learning contract to develop a personalized learning experience based on their needs, skills, and interests relating to scaffolded reading experiences. The contracted project was to demonstrate the participants' level of mastery of a scaffolding instructional technique on which they focused and a form of self-assessment of their project. The participants then submitted their completed contract to the instructor and negotiated the terms of the contract. The participants also had the opportunity to contact the instructor throughout the experience and renegotiate any needed modifications. The participants submitted their completed project to the instructor and then completed the POI posttest.

In addition to procedures relating to the students, five interviews were conducted with the instructor. Two interviews were conducted during the fall 2001 semester and three interviews were conducted during the spring 2002 semester. A preinstruction instructor interview was conducted each semester once the POI pretest was made available to each group. A postinstruction instructor interview was subsequently conducted each semester after the POI posttest was made available to each group. A postnegotiation instructor interview during the spring 2002 semester was conducted midway through the person-centered learning experience after the contract negotiations with the PCI group participants were completed.

FINDINGS

Several interesting findings were uncovered in this case study. A primary finding of the study was that participants experiencing the person-centered model of instruction (PCI group) demonstrated statistically significant positive changes in the mean scores on 4 of the 10 subscales between the pre- and posttests of the Personal Orientation Inventory (POI). The four subscales with significant changes were feeling reactivity or sensitivity to one's own needs, synergy, acceptance of one's natural aggression, and the capacity for intimate contact. Also, a nonsignificant but positive trend was found on the POI subscales self-actualizing value and spontaneity for the participants in the PCI group, while participants in the CI_p experienced a nonsignificant negative trend. The participants in the combined comparison group (CI_p) did not show any significant changes, but nonsignificant negative trends were found for seven of the 10 POI subscales. Table 15.3 lists a brief description of the subscales and the difference in significance levels between the PCI and CI_p groups.

Additional findings were the creative products developed by the PCI group experiencing the person-centered model of instruction in the spring 2002 Reading in the Elementary School course. Typically, the projects submitted in previous semesters of the Reading in the Elementary School course included a set of lesson plans accompanied by a videotape of the lessons as they were taught to elementary students. The participants in the PCI group developed course projects demonstrating their mastery over their selected scaffolded reading experiences topic. Each project was based on the contracts negotiated by each PCI group participant and the instructor. Although the project was intended to be completed by each participant, two participants negotiated with the instructor to develop a joint project.

Participants were primarily interested in studying the use of one of the scaffolded reading experience phases (prereading, during reading, or postreading activities). Although most of the participants focused on the scaffolded reading experience phases, each project was unique. It was also found that participants utilized a variety of different project formats as well as multiple project formats to present their work. Table 15.4 lists the various project focuses and formats.

A final set of findings was from the instructor interviews. The instructor was asked to rate the quality of the creative products received from the students at the end of both the fall 2001 semester (CI_1 group) and the spring 2002 semester (PCI group). The instructor described the work delivered during the fall 2001 semester by the CI_1 group as fitting within a continuum of high quality work and minimum quality work. The instructor considered high quality work as teaching beyond the textbook

Table 15.3. Significance Scores
on the POI Subscale Pre- to Posttest Scores

POI Subscale and Description*	PCI Group (Intervention) Significance Scores**	CI$_p$ (Combined Comparison Group) Significance Scores**
Self-actualizing value: values of a self-actualizing person	.12	.44
Existentiality: ability to react without rigid adherence to principles	.23	.08
Feeling reactivity: sensitivity to one's own needs and feelings	.02***	.62
Spontaneity: freedom to react spontaneously	.46	.79
Self-regard: affirmation of self because of worth or strength	.97	.58
Self-acceptance: acceptance of self in spite of weakness or deficiencies	.94	.70
Nature of man: degree of constructive view of the nature of man	.38	.56
Synergy: ability to be synergistic	.04***	.22
Acceptance of aggression: ability to accept one's natural aggressiveness	.02***	.78
Capacity for intimate contact: ability to develop intimate relationships with other human beings	.04***	.86

Notes: *POI descriptions were developed by Shostrom (1966). **$p \leq 05$. ***Items with significant p values

and beyond the normal class expectations. The minimum quality work was described as someone teaching from the textbook for basic understanding. While most of the work fit within the instructor's continuum of high quality of work there were approximately six students that only met the instructor's minimum quality of work.

A different finding occurred with the PCI group. The instructor stated, "I felt my students [in the PCI group] were more precise in what they were doing." The instructor believed that he received more specific work related to strategies and activities targeted to reaching particular students. The instructor also felt that the contracting and decision making that occurred before the participants began the work on their project helped them become more focused, strategic in their implementation, and precise.

Table 15.4.   Focus of Projects and Formats for PCI Group Participants

Participant	Project Focus	Project Format
1	Prereading activities for motivation and comprehension	Research paper, PowerPoint
2	Using prereading activities to enhance the lesson	Video, lesson plans, reflection paper
3	Postreading activities	Video, reflection paper
5	Fostering reading comprehension skills	Lesson plans, reflection papers, digital pictures, PowerPoint
6	Which is more effective reading recovery or accelerated reader	Research paper
8	Importance of reading aloud to children.	Research paper, lesson plans, PowerPoint
9	Prereading activities	Video, reflection paper
10	Postreading activities	Research paper, lesson plans, digital pictures
11	Purpose of prereading activities	Research paper, lesson plans
12	Establishing forms of building text specific knowledge	Lesson plans, PowerPoint
13	Integration phase activities	Lesson plans, PowerPoint
14	Guided reading activities and setting schemata	Video, lesson plans, reflection paper
16	Postreading activities	Video, lesson plans
17	Strategies to teach context clues	Research paper, lesson plans
18	Four-block method	Lesson plans, PowerPoint
19	Four-block method	Lesson plans, reflection paper, audio tape
20	Modifying text with special education students	Research paper, lesson plans
7 and 15	Using the four-block method	Research paper, lesson plans, digital pictures

DISCUSSION OF FINDINGS

Three questions were posited in this article. Is it possible to increase the striving for individual achievement from learners in a Web-based course using a person-centered model of instruction? Could instructors in a Web-based course receive original and useful creative products from students experiencing person-centered learning that exceeded the quality of products in similar web-based courses? Finally, would Web-based instructors see an increased striving for individual achievement within their students that experienced a person-centered learning experience?

Three courses were focused on in this study. One course was taught using a person-centered model of instruction, while the other two courses were taught using a non-PCI instructional approach. Data from the Personal Orientation Inventory, projects developed by PCI group participants, and instructor interviews were analyzed to answer the questions of this study. Based on the results of this study, the outcomes of a person-centered model of instruction described by Miller and Mazur (2001) appear to be supported. When compared to a non-PCI instructional approach, several differences were found.

First, a difference in the striving for individual achievement difference scores between the POI pre- and posttests was found between the PCI and the CI_p groups. A positive trend in the difference scores on the POI was found for the PCI group with significant differences on the four subscales of feeling reactivity, synergy, acceptance of aggression, and capacity for intimate contact. Also, there were nonsignificant positive changes on the self-actualizing value and spontaneity subscales. A nonsignificant negative trend was found for the CI_p group on seven of the ten POI subscales. This data suggests that individuals experiencing a person-centered model of instruction in this case study experienced an increase in their striving for individual achievement.

A difference was also found in the products developed by participants experiencing person-centered instruction (PCI group) compared to the participants receiving non-PCI instruction (CI_1 group). The participants in the CI_1 group were required to develop a 20-minute lesson plan and video tape that lesson on scaffolded reading experiences. Participants in the PCI group were given the opportunity to control their learning and demonstration of their learning mastery. When given this opportunity, the PCI group participants developed a wide variety of projects and utilized multiple formats for presenting their mastery of their selected learning topic. Comparing the results from both groups the data shows that individuals experiencing person-centered learning produce creative products with a quality that exceeds the quality produced by individuals in similar courses that use a different instructional approach.

A final difference was found between the two groups based on the instructor interviews. The same instructor for both groups (CI_1 and PCI) who participated in the Reading in the Elementary School course rated the quality of the creative products differently. The instructor found a continuum of work from high quality to minimum quality from participants in the CI_1 group. A different rating from the instructor was provided for the PCI group. The instructor described the PCI group's work as more precise, focused, and strategic. The instructor also described the quantity of work produced by the PCI group as much larger than had been received in the past. The interview data present a different view of the instructor regarding the quality of work from the CI_p participants. This could suggest that individuals involved in person-centered learning demonstrate an increased striving for individual achievement through the products they create.

Overall, a difference was found between the group having PCI experiences and those having non-PCI learning experiences. The participants who experienced PCI demonstrated a higher quality of work in the course projects compared to the non-PCI participants, as well as mastering their learning topics based on the instructor's evaluation. Also, participants having PCI experiences demonstrated increases on the Personal Orientation Inventory, whereas participants having non-PCI experiences demonstrated primarily decreases on the Personal Orientation Inventory. The data in this particular case study suggest that participants experiencing person-centered instruction produced creative products, experienced significant learning, and increased their striving for individual achievement.

CONCLUSIONS

The data found in this study show that the outcomes predicted for the person-centered model of instruction by Miller and Mazur (2001) were appropriate outcomes within the context of this case study. There are two possible reasons for why the outcomes of the person-centered model of instruction were reached in this case study. First, the PCI group participants were given control over their own learning experience. The participants were able to focus on a topic that was of direct interest to them and could be applied within their classes. Another possible reason is the motivating factor. While many learners are motivated by some type of extrinsic motivation such as a grade, the person-centered learning experience provided more intrinsic motivation. The intrinsic motivation could have been the inherent satisfaction of the learning as described by Ryan and Deci (2000) or the motivating factors of challenge, curiosity, and control described by Malone and Leeper (1987).

The outcomes of the person-centered model of instruction did occur and there are possible reasons for the occurrence, but additional testing of the model needs to occur. Additional studies need to be conducted with multiple instructors in a variety of Web-based learning situations to determine if the predicted outcomes consistently occur as well as the reasons for the occurrences.

Additional questions could also be asked in regards to this instructional model. Would this instructional model be appropriate for application with undergraduate or P-12 learners? Could this instructional model be implemented in other types of distance learning environments, such as instructional television? Could this instructional model be applied in a face-to-face instructional environment? What types of differences would occur in the comparison of the person-centered model of instruction in a Web-based course and a face-to-face course? Finally, what is the impact of the person-centered model of instruction on the instructor due to the changes in the control of the instructional environment? As with any new instructional model, only time and further testing will tell if students will go beyond the instructor's expectations when placed in person-centered learning experiences.

REFERENCES

Bouverat, R. A. (1970). *A study of self-actualization and perceptions of teaching roles of prospective teachers of young children.* Unpublished doctoral dissertation, The Ohio State University, Columbus, Ohio.

Braun, J. R., & Asta, P. (1969). A comparison of "real" vs. "ideal" self with a self-actualization inventory. *Journal of Psychology, 72,* 159-164.

Braun, J. R., & La Faro, D. (1969). A further study of the fakability of the Personal Orientation Inventory. *Journal of Clinical Psychology, 25*(3), 296-299.

Foulds, M. L., & Warehime, R. G. (1971). Effects of a "fake good" response set on a measure of self-actualization. *Journal of Counseling Psychology, 18*(3), 279-280.

Fox, J., Knapp, R. R., & Michael, W. B. (1968). Assessment of self-actualization of psychiatric patients: Validity of the Personal Orientation Inventory. *Education and Psychological Measurement, 28*(2), 565-569.

Jury, L. E., Willower, D. J., & DeLacy, W. J. (1975). Teacher self-actualization and pupil control ideology. *Alberta Journal of Educational Research, 21*(4), 295-301.

Knapp, R. R. (1965). Relationship of a measure of self-actualization to neuroticism and extraversion. *Journal of Consulting Psychology, 29*(2), 168-172.

Kolesnik, W. B. (1975). *Humanism and/or behaviorism in education.* Boston: Allyn & Bacon.

Malone, T., & Lepper, M. (1987). Making learning fun: A taxonomy of intrinsic motiations of learning. In R. E. Snow & M. J. Farr (Eds.), *Aptitude, learning, and instruction: Cognative and affective process analyses* (Vol. 3, pp. 223-253). Hillsdale, NJ: Erlbaum.

Merriam, S. B. (1998). *Qualitative research and case study applications in education* (2nd ed.). San Francisco: Jossey-Bass.

Miller, C. T., & Mazur, J. M. (2001). Towards a person-centered model of instruction: Can an emphasis on the personal enhance instruction in cyberspace? *Quarterly Review of Distance Education, 2*(3), 293-299.

Rizzo, R., & Vinacke, E. (1975). Self-actualization and the meaning of critical experience. *Journal of Humanistic Psychology, 15*(3), 19-30.

Rogers, C. R. (1957). Personal thoughts on teaching and learning. *Merrill Palmer Quarterly, 3*, 241-243.

Rogers, C. R. (1969). *Freedom to learn*. Columbus, OH: C. E. Merrill.

Rogers, C. R., & Freiberg, H. J. (1994). *Freedom to learn* (3rd ed.). New York: Merrill.

Ryan, R. M., & Deci, E. L. (2000). Intrinsic and extrinsic motivations: Classic definitions and new directions. *Contemporary Educational Psychology, 25*, 54-67.

Shostrom, E. L. (1964). An inventory for the measurement of self-actualization. *Educational and Psychological Measurement, 24*(2), 207-218.

Shostrom, E. L. (1966). *EdITS manual for the Personal Orientation Inventory*. San Diego, CA: Educational and Industrial Testing Service.

Shostrom, E. L., & Knapp, R. R. (1966). The relationship of a measure of self-actualization (POI) to a measure of pathology (MMPI) and to therapeutic growth. *American Journal of Psychotherapy, 20*(1), 193-202.

CHAPTER 16

EVALUATING COLLEGE STUDENTS' EFFORTS IN ASYNCHRONOUS DISCUSSION

A Systematic Process

Dave S. Knowlton

This article delineates a systematic process for integrating evaluation of students' efforts into asynchronous discussion. Specifically, this process depends on establishing clear criteria as a basis for evaluating students. These criteria should be educationally useful to students and consistent with the types of discourse found in online discussion. Also, the process is based on formal self- and peer-evaluations as a precursor to professor-centered evaluations. Within this process, professors also should offer formative feedback throughout a discussion. This formative feedback becomes a basis of summative evaluation and grading. Importantly, while practical, this process is grounded in cognitive theories of learning. This process also is grounded in the writing-across-the-curriculum literature. At the end of the article, the author offers implications for further theory development and empiricism.

The Perfect Online Course: Best Practices for Designing and Teaching
pp. 311–326
Copyright © 2009 by Information Age Publishing

INTRODUCTION

Whether distributed as a listserv or centrally-located on a bulletin board, asynchronous computer-mediated discussion can be a valuable component of the higher education classroom. Superficially, in Web-based instruction, asynchronous discussion serves as a reminder to students that they aren't alone in the educational process (Weiss, 2000). More substantively, through asynchronous discussion, students have an opportunity to develop a more thorough understanding of course content. As students share their ideas, perspectives, and experiences, they are broadening their classmates' frame of reference for interpreting course content (Jonassen, Davidson, Collins, Campbell, & Haag, 1995; Morrison & Guenther, 2000). As Hacker and Neiderhauser (2000) note, this type of collaboration makes learning more "deep and durable" (p. 53) and can increase student motivation.

However, evaluating students' efforts in online discussion is sometimes awkward. After all, a valuable online discussion is based on students' initiative—their willingness to share their understandings of course content and react to their classmates' understandings—so it should be no surprise that students view professor-centered evaluations as antithetical to the very types of initiative that make online discussions educationally sound. Also, evaluating students' efforts is awkward because online learning environments don't always "support" authentic assessment (Marra, 2002). Because of the limitations of many online learning environments, evaluation does not happen naturally in asynchronous discussion. Rather, designers of online environments and professors who use asynchronous discussion must integrate evaluation strategies into asynchronous discussion.

In this article, I offer a process-based framework for evaluating students' efforts in online discussion. Importantly, this framework is systematic in that it is based on inputs and corresponding outputs (see Table 16.1 for a summary). These inputs and outputs create a cyclical process. Professors' and students' inputs lead to analysis of evaluation criteria and application of those criteria. Analysis and application lead to outputs, which can further inform students' participation in the asynchronous discussion itself. Thus, evaluation is not tacked on to the end of the discussion; it is integrated into the discussion process and designed to improve the quality of the discussion itself (see Figure 16.1 for a summary of this cycle). Both the systematic and cyclical elements of this process are derived from a variety of already-existing literature—including articles dealing with assessment theory, writing-across-the-curriculum literature, cognitive learning theory, and constructivism.

Table 16.1. Inputs and Outputs of Asynchronous Discussion Evaluation

Professor's Inputs	Students' Inputs	Education Outputs
• Criteria for evaluating students' efforts in online discussion	• Negotiating meaning of abstract criteria	• Operationalized criteria
• Resources for helping students understand criteria	• Completing checklists for self and peer evaluations	• Broadened understanding among students of the educational value of discussion
• Design of activities for helping students understand criteria	• Synthesizing students' own contributions to online discussion with evaluation criteria through generative self evaluations or "tags"	• Meta-discussion that can provide insights into students' ontological and epistemological stances
• Dichotomous and Likert-scale checklists that can serve as the basis of self and peer evaluation	• Describing a plan for improving their own discussion contributions	• Data defining students' views of the value of various discussion contributions
• Generative self-evaluation assignments	• Evaluating peers' contributions in the context of peer feedback groups	• Formative data describing professors' reactions to students' contributions
• Creation of peer feedback groups		• Completed rubrics
• Resources that can foster students' understanding of peer feedback		

I begin by delineating criteria for evaluating students' contributions to an online discussion. I then describe processes for implementing student-centered evaluations and professor-centered evaluations. Throughout this article, implications for online pedagogy will be relatively obvious; so, in the last section of this article, I offer implications for future theoretical and empirical endeavors.

CRITERIA FOR EVALUATING STUDENTS' CONTRIBUTION TO ASYNCHRONOUS DISCUSSION

Professors should establish criteria for evaluating students' efforts in online discussions and communicate those criteria to students. Professors sometimes assume that criteria and standards for evaluation are self-evi-

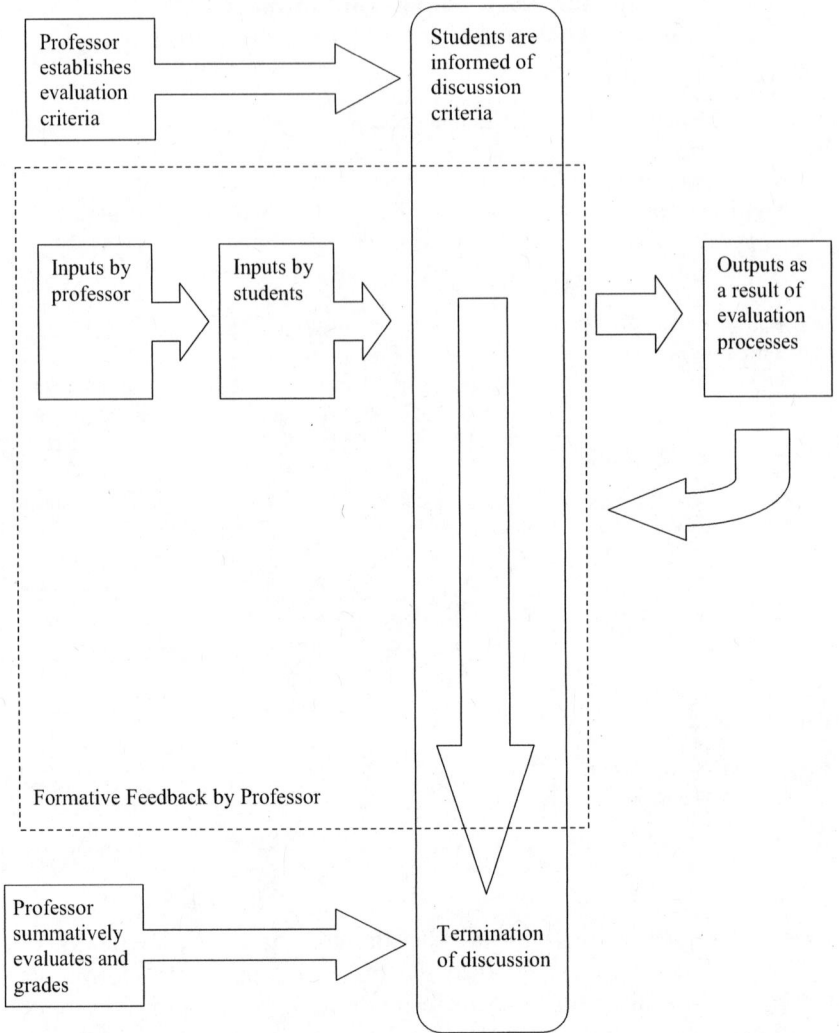

Figure 16.1.

dent (Speck, 1998); this assumption is problematic. When professors fail to communicate standards for participation, students have no choice but to revert to their own past experiences to help them define acceptable levels of performance (Knowlton & Knowlton, 2001). Therefore, professors must establish clear criteria that can serve as the basis of student-centered and professor-centered evaluations, which will be discussed later in this paper. But what criteria should professors rely on for evaluating the products of online discussion? I begin this section by discussing two mistakes that professors routinely make when determining criteria as a basis for evaluation. Then, I offer criteria that can become a basis for evaluating students.

Mistakes in Selecting Criteria

The first mistake that professors often make when selecting criteria as a basis for student evaluation is that they confuse research rigor with pedagogical rigor. This tradeoff of privileging criteria based in research rigor instead of criteria that are pedagogically useful can be destructive. Evaluating students, for example, from a linguistic perspective (cf. Baym, 1996; Murray, 2000) or assessing students based on cultural (cf. Herring, 1999) or social (Rourke, Anderson, Garrison, & Archer, 1999) factors is instructive for researchers and theorists. But these same criteria are relatively useless for students who are trying to determine if their contributions to an asynchronous discussion evidence an understanding of key concepts that are specific to a discipline, like literature, engineering, or biology.

In pointing to the need for professors to develop criteria that are pedagogically useful, I am not suggesting that research is unnecessary. I am not even suggesting that criteria related to linguistics, culture, or social factors are useless. After all, such criteria can provide students with opportunities to think metacognitively about their participation in asynchronous discussion—a topic addressed later in this article. I am suggesting that the primary criteria that will become the basis of student evaluation should be useful to students as they evaluate the degree to which they understand the content of a course, not the linguistic, cultural, or social cyber-milieu of the discussion itself.

A second mistake that professors often make when selecting evaluation criteria relates to the consistency between the criteria and the nature of online discourse. For example, Bauer and Anderson (2000) suggested that professors focus on the degree to which a student "uses complex, grammatically correct sentences on a regular basis." They also urge professors to consider whether or not a student "expresses ideas clearly, concisely, cogently, in a logical fashion" (p. 68). These criteria suggested by Bauer and Anderson imply that contributions to an asynchronous discussion will be revised and polished into formalized writings, but online discourse is more similar to conversation than to formal writing. Students rarely engage in substantive revision when participating in online discussion. Typically, students write a contribution for the discussion, perhaps read over it once, and submit it to a discussion forum. In some respects, then, Bauer and Anderson's criteria are not consistent with online discussion contributions.

Similarly, Morrison and Ross (1998) argue that points should be deducted for off-topic comments. But online discourse is a type of writing in which students often learn about their own perspectives as they write. When they begin a contribution to an online discussion (and sometimes even as they end one), students may not know their own exact point. They are engaged in a type of "writing to learn" (see Lindemann, 1995, and Adams & Hamm, 1990, for a discussion of "writing to learn"). In fact, the more text students generate in a contribution to discussion, the more likely those students will generate ideas from which they can learn. Therefore, criteria for evaluating students' contributions to online discussion should encourage students to explore their ideas in writing even if the exploring creates digressions and seemingly off-topic comments. In other cases, the relevance and scope of asynchronous discussion emerge as different students contribute. In asynchronous discussion, knowledge is collectively created and socially distributed (Moller, 1998). To penalize individual students for seemingly off-topic comments, then, is to undermine the collective and social nature of knowledge.

Determining Appropriate Criteria for Evaluation and Communicating Criteria to Students

As I've argued, criteria for evaluating students' contributions to asynchronous discussion should provide students with an understanding of the degree to which they understand key course concepts. Criteria for evaluation also should be consistent with the "rough draft" nature of most discussion contributions and enhance the opportunity for relevance to emerge throughout the course of a discussion. Even with this consideration of consistency, though, criteria may be idiosyncratic to specific professors and disciplines. So, the criteria in this section can serve as a starting point for consideration, not as a definitive list of criteria that will work as a basis for all asynchronous discussions. After outlining criteria for asynchronous discussion, I describe cognitive approaches for helping students understand and internalize the criteria.

Criteria for Asynchronous Contributions and Replies

When writing initial contributions to a discussion, professors might urge students to consider the following questions:

- Is the contribution mechanically clear enough for readers to understand your points?
- Does the contribution cite assigned readings or other resources as a means of addressing the specific topics and/or questions?
- Does the contribution seem to be based on factually-correct ideas that are generally accepted as discipline "truths"?
- Does the contribution contain "critical thinking" that is indicative of the paradigms in the field?

Because replies in asynchronous discussion are unique in their educational purpose, a separate set of criteria should govern their quality. For evaluating responses to classmates, professors might suggest that students consider the following criteria:

- Does the content of the reply adopt a respectful tone towards the ideas in the contribution to which you are replying?
- Does the reply inspire further discussion among the class?
- Does the reply develop the scope of the discussion in a meaningful way?

Strategies for Promoting Understanding and Internalization of Criteria

Clearly articulating the criteria may not be enough; professors may need to provide resources or facilitate educational activities that will help students understand the nature of the criteria. For example, critical thinking is abstract, and students may not know how to operationalize and apply it in their discussion contributions. Professors, therefore, may need to provide a resource that would help students with their applications. A discipline-based heuristic that defines critical thinking can help scaffold students' thinking about course content. In economics, for instance, Gwartney and Stroupe's (1995) eight guideposts for economic thinking can help students gauge the degree to which they are thinking "like an economist."

Sometimes, though, a resource may not be enough; students may need to participate in activities to gain a more full understanding of evaluation criteria. For example, in teaching an online English composition course, I required students to participate in an online discussion that developed strategies for including critical thinking in their contributions. Some strategies that students developed were relatively obvious, but they introduced some novel strategies, as well. One education major, for example, introduced the class to Bloom's cognitive taxonomy (Bloom, Englehart, Furst, Hill, & Krathwohl, 1956). She suggested—and her classmates and I agreed—that contributions on higher levels of the taxonomy (application, analysis, synthesis, and evaluation) might be more indicative of critical thinking than contributions that only demonstrated knowledge and comprehension of course content. To some extent, then, these students were able to operationalize the criteria to meet their own needs. Through trying to understand a criterion like critical thinking, students renegotiated the scope of that criterion. Anderson (1998) has suggested the value of this type of negotiation. Involving participants in discussions about criteria and their scope can help those students understand the ways that educational goals can be met through online discussion.

STUDENT-CENTERED EVALUATIONS

Professors should actively engage students in evaluation processes. Students should not only be recipients of evaluations, but also they should serve as evaluators. In this section, I describe processes for students' self-evaluations and peer evaluations. Within each, I discuss professor inputs that likely will promote productive student-centered evaluations.

Self-Evaluation

Self-evaluation provides students with an opportunity to critically re-examine their own contributions to an asynchronous discussion. Self-evaluations are only successful when students understand the criteria and practice applying the criteria to their work (Knowlton & Knowlton, 2001). Two strategies are particularly useful for helping students evaluate their own contributions to a discussion. The first is the use of checklists. The second is the use of generative self-evaluations.

First, both Likert-scale and dichotomous checklists can help students evaluate their own contributions to a discussion. For example, by marking a scale ranging from "strongly agree" to "strongly disagree," a student can react to a criterion statement: "My contributions to the discussion contain critical thinking." Or, by simply marking a "yes" or "no," students can check that they referenced assigned readings in their contributions. Checklists can be advantageous because they help students focus specifically on the salient criteria. That is, the close-ended nature of the checklists can help students evaluate their contributions in narrow and discrete terms. A disadvantage of checklists, though, relates to this same close-ended nature. Students easily can become entranced with simply checking positive responses, without closely analyzing the fit between their contributions to the discussion and the criteria (Knowlton, 2001).

Second, students can be asked to complete a generative self-evaluation. Because generative self-evaluations take more time than completing a checklist, they should be used sparingly. But, at key points during the span of a discussion, professors might require students to write a paragraph demonstrating how they met each criterion in past discussions or how they will change their participation to better meet that criterion in future discussions. Professors even might require students to cut and paste excerpts from their contributions as evidence of meeting the evaluation criteria. Similarly, some discussion environments might allow students to "tag" their discussion contributions with additional comments—similar to the "comment" function in word processing. This type of tagging would create a type of meta-discussion that could be seen easily by both students and the professor. A generative self-evaluation moves students beyond passively marking a checklist. Generative self-evaluations obligate students to actively synthesize their own contributions to a discussion with evaluation criteria.

Lin (2001) argued the need for strategy training as a means of promoting metacognition among students. I am arguing that a generative self-evaluation is one such strategy that would be useful in online discussion. Generative self-evaluations can extend students' thinking beyond the immediate content and engage them in issues of ontology and epistemology. They consider what they really do know and how they have come to know it. As students engage in generative self-evaluations, they are thinking about their own thinking. This approach is consistent with Prestera and Moller's (2001) discussion of evaluation because it forces students to examine their own process, not just their products. Such an approach is also consistent with Marra's (2002) vision that online discussion has "the potential to call into question learners' existing epistemic beliefs" (p. 23).

Peer Evaluation

Online discussion creates a self-contained rhetorical context (Anderson, Benjamin, Busiel, & Parades-Holt, 1998) and gives students an authentic audience (Fabos & Young, 1999) that can provide feedback in ways not typical of other writing contexts (Kemp, 1998). To some extent, then, the natural development of an online discussion is a form of peer evaluation. By reading responses to their contributions, students learn about the quality of their own ideas and gain insights into how others receive those ideas.

Though online discussion does have a type of built-in peer feedback mechanism, students also can benefit from more formalized peer evaluations that require students to focus specifically on the pre-established evaluation criteria. Obviously, checklists similar to those described for self-evaluation can be used for peer evaluations. Also, students could be required to complete a generative analysis by answering open-ended questions about their classmates' participation. But, peer evaluation in itself should involve discussion and significant exchange of ideas. For example, professors can create "peer feedback groups" to allow participants to achieve more depth in evaluating each other's contributions to asynchronous discussion. The smaller the peer feedback groups, the stronger the opportunity for obtaining depth in peer evaluations; the more often professors require students to participate in peer feedback group, the more specifically students will be able to refine their own understanding of how to contribute to asynchronous discussions.

As professors themselves give feedback in online discussion—a topic discussed in the next section of this article—they certainly should act as model evaluators. Students can learn how to give feedback by being the recipient of carefully-constructed feedback. Beyond modeling, though, professors might find it helpful to scaffold students' abilities to give constructive feedback to their peers. For some students, direct practice of peer evaluation can be useful. To this end, professors can ask students to evaluate fictional students' contributions to a discussion as a means of providing non-threatening practice for peer evaluation.

More directly relevant to the task of peer evaluation, professors might consider giving students a job aid that offers guidelines for productive peer evaluations. Students can gain insights from simple advice for avoiding personal attacks and ideas for using Socratic questioning as a part of peer evaluations. Effective job aids also might guide students through the peer evaluation by including specific questions for students to consider. These questions might be fairly straightforward, such as asking students to identify three strengths and three weaknesses of contributions written by classmates in their peer feedback group. But, these questions, though, might be much more specific and ask students to pick a contribution of a classmate and evaluate it based on each discussion criterion.

Professor-Centered Evaluations

Though self-evaluation and peer-evaluation are important processes that can add considerable depth to the quality of online discussion, the professor holds the ultimate responsibility of grading. Often, students view a grade—and the anticipation of receiving a grade—as punitive. Therefore, professors should consider offering meticulous formative feedback throughout the span of a discussion. Formative evaluations will better establish a context for summative evaluation.

Formative Feedback

As shown in Figure 16.1, professors should offer formative feedback throughout the online discussion, even as students are engaged in student-centered evaluations. This placement of formative feedback within the evaluation system is consistent with the notion that professors have the responsibility to "frame" students' online activities (cf. Knowlton, 2000, p. 11). Formative feedback should not only be a preliminary judgment of students' contributions, but also formative feedback should offer students advice for improving their contributions. A simple letter grade, number, or other marking (like a check mark) does not serve the function of giving students insights into the strengths and weaknesses of their own contributions. To help students see strengths and weakness in their contributions, professors should explain to students how they reacted—as an authentic reader—to the student's contribution. For example, professors might describe how a student's discussion contribution inspired them to think more (or differently) about the topic. Or, the professor might offer feedback that suggests different connections to course readings. The professor can describe how a consideration of a specific reading could add to the discussion in substantive ways.

My experiences suggest that students initially will be overwhelmed by authentic feedback from a professor. Students often aren't accustomed to professors treating their work with legitimacy. They are more accustomed to professors handing down clear-cut judgments that culminate in a grade. Therefore, students initially may find the authentic feedback to be esoteric and needlessly obtuse. Over time—perhaps the course of a semester, for example—students will become more adept with using authentic reactions from a professor to improve their contributions to the discussions.

Summative Evaluations

Professors should meticulously connect the grade to established discussion criteria, evaluations from peers, and formative feedback from the professor. One way to help students see the relationship between pre-established criteria and a grade is to use grading rubrics. For example, in one class that I taught, I used online discussion as an impetus for connecting textbook readings with students' real world experiences. The criteria used were similar to the criteria described in section one of this article. Table 16.2 shows the rubric that I used for summative evaluation of students' initial contributions to a particular discussion about the text.

**Table 16.2. Rubric for Evaluating
Students' Initial Contributions to a Discussion**

Points	Description
10	All of the listed criteria are clearly met, and the insights provided by the discussion contribution offer profound insights into reading assignments or the implications of the reading assignments.
7-9	All of the listed criteria are met to some degree. Insights into the reading assignment are offered, but those insights could be more substantive by applying one of the critical thinking strategies developed early in the semester.
5-6	Most of the listed criteria are met. The contribution to the discussion does a good job of summarizing the key issues in the text, but it stops short of going beyond summary. That is, the contribution does not contain clear evidence of critical thinking.
2-4	Several of the listed criteria are not met.
1	The contribution does not make clear points. Weaknesses in the mechanics of writing are substantive enough to impede readers as they try to understand your contribution.
0	The post was not on time.

Notably, the issue of a contribution being "on time" is evident in the rubric. The particular course in which I used this rubric was divided into weekly modules. Each discussion lasted the span of one or two weeks. So, if students waited until late in the week to offer their contribution to the discussion, other students didn't have time to respond. That is, the deadlines ensured opportunities for interaction among students.

In this same course, I used a separate rubric to summatively evaluate students' replies within a discussion. This rubric can be found in Table 16.3. Importantly, in this particular course, students were required to offer a minimum of three replies per week. So, a minimum number of replies is an additional criteria listed in this particular rubric but not discussed earlier in this article. As I've noted, criteria may be idiosyncratic to particular professors and courses.

IMPLICATIONS AND CONCLUSIONS

Establishing clear criteria, creating opportunities for self-evaluation, facilitating peer evaluation, and offering formative feedback can form the cornerstones of strong evaluation procedures for online discussion. Notably, constructivist, metacognitive, and generative principles of learning theoretically frame the evaluation system that I've described in this article.

Table 16.3.   Rubric for Evaluating Students' Replies to a Discussion

Points	Description
10	All of the listed criteria are clearly met, and the insights provided by the reply add further legitimacy to the original contribution and the direction of the discussion. For example, the reply encourages the original writer to clarify or elaborate on the point being made, or the reply adds a unique application of the content that has not previously been considered in the discussion.
7-9	All of the listed criteria are met to some degree. The reply does inspire further discussion to some extent, but the level of analysis of the reply could be stronger.
4-6	At least three replies were made, but it's unclear how the reply relates to an original post or the general direction of the discussion.
2-3	Less than three replies were made. But, the replies that were offered added to the discussion in a meaningful way.
1	There was some "activity" in terms of a reply or follow-up, but the reply did not adequately meet most of the listed criteria.
0	The replies were not posted on time.

Perhaps more substantively, this article connects asynchronous discussion to the writing-across-the-curriculum literature by introducing the idea of pre-established evaluation criteria, self-evaluation, and peer evaluation. This article seems to be one of the first to implement connections between the constructivist nature of online discussion and principles from the writing-across-the-curriculum movement into a systematic approach to evaluation.

Pedagogically, the approach described in this article allows evaluation to become an integral component of the learning process in online discussion. No longer is evaluation tacked on to the end of a discussion; evaluation contributes to students' learning and becomes a part of the educational experience. This idea of integration of evaluation into discussion should be useful to designers, professors, and faculty development specialists. Beyond the immediate pedagogical implications, the process of evaluation described in this article raises questions that should be addressed in future theory and through empiricism.

Theoretical Development

In articulating the role of self-evaluation, peer evaluation, and professor-centered evaluations, I am making the assumption that the evaluation process will engage all students; but just as some students have the propensity to lurk in online discussion, students may tend to lurk during peer evaluation. As Lave and Wenger (1991) have noted, legitimate reasons may exist for participants to stay on the periphery of educational activities. What are those reasons? Can learning theory account for them? Can instructional prescriptions guide students toward more active participation throughout the evaluation process? Theoreticians need to address many questions about the behavior of passive participants. Theoretical connections between current learning theory and asynchronous discussion can begin this question-answering process.

Another area for theoretical investigation relates to how these evaluation processes transcend disciplinary lines. My pedagogical experiences are mostly in social sciences and humanities. Does this process that I describe apply equally well to online discourse in the hard sciences? Are self-evaluations and peer evaluations appropriate in business courses? I argue that they are, but I would suspect that the processes manifest themselves slightly differently in various disciplines. Theorists across disciplines should offer prescriptions for implementing self-evaluation and peer evaluation into online discussion.

Empirical Implications

The systematic evaluation process that I describe in this article is based on the assumption that more evaluations in different varieties will result in improvements to the quality of the discussion. But, does *more* evaluation necessarily equal a stronger quality of discussion? Admittedly, quantity is probably not the issue; the specific self-evaluation and peer evaluation strategies that are used are probably a stronger predictor of improvements in discussion quality. Which self- and peer-evaluation strategies promote the greatest improvement in students' contributions to asynchronous discussion? Quantitatively, different peer evaluation and self-evaluation strategies need to be compared. Are dichotomous checklists, for example, any less effective than generative evaluations?

Qualitatively, researchers should examine students' understandings of formative evaluation. Do they understand the formative feedback? Do they know how to use it toward the goal of improving their own work? What types of feedback do they view as helpful? Part of this type of empirical investigation should focus on students' metacognitive competence. But, part of this investigation might depend on gaining an understanding of students' perceptions of the role of a professor in online discourse. Rhetorical analysis, students' personal narratives, and case studies would be useful in understanding students'perspectives.

REFERENCES

Adams, D. M., & Hamm, M. E. (1990). *Cooperative learning: Critical thinking and collaboration across the curriculum*. Springfield, IL: Charles C. Thomas.

Anderson, D., Benjamin, B., Busiel, C., & Parades-Holt, B. (1998). *Teaching online: Internet research, conversation, and composition*. New York: Longman.

Anderson, R. S. (1998). Why talk about different ways to grade? The shift from traditional assessment to alternative assessment. In R. S. Anderson & B. W. Speck (Eds.). *Changing the way we grade student performance: Classroom assessment and the new learning paradigm* (pp. 5-16). San Francisco: Jossey-Bass.

Bauer, J. F., & Anderson, R. S. (2000). Evaluating students' written performance in the online classroom. In R. E. Weiss, D. S. Knowlton, & B. W. Speck (Eds.), *Principles of effective teaching in the online classroom* (pp. 65-72). San Francisco: Jossey-Bass.

Baym, N. (1996). Agreements and disagreements in a computer-mediated discussion. *Research on Language and Social Interaction, 29*(4), 315-345.

Bloom, B., Englehart, M., Furst, E., Hill, W., & Krathwohl, O. (1956). *Taxonomy of educational objectives: The classification of educational goals: Handbook 1. The cognitive domain*. White Plains, NY: Longman.

Fabos, B., & Young, M. D. (1999). Telecommunications in the classroom: Rhetoric versus reality. *Review of Educational Research, 69*(3), 217-260.

Gwartney, J. D., & Stroup, R. L. (1995). *Economics: Private and public choice*. New York: Dryden.

Hacker D. J., & Niederhauser, D. S. (2000). Promoting deep and durable learning in the online classroom. In R. E. Weiss, D. S. Knowlton, & B. W. Speck (Eds.), *Principles of effective teaching in the online classroom* (pp. 53-64). San Francisco: Jossey-Bass.

Herring, S. C. (1999). The rhetorical dynamics of gender harassment on-line. *The Information Society, 15*(3), 151-167.

Jonassen, D. H., Davidson, M., Collins, M., Campbell, J., & Haag, B. (1995). Constructivism and computer-mediated communication in distance education. *The American Journal of Distance Education, 9*(2), 7-26.

Kemp, F. (1998). Computer-mediated communication: Making nets work for writing instruction. In J. R. Galin & J. Latchaw (Eds.), *The dialogic classroom: Teachers integrating computer technology, pedagogy, and research* (pp. 133-150). Urbana, IL: National Council of Teachers of English.

Knowlton, D. S. (2000). A theoretical framework for the online classroom: A defense and delineation of a student-centered pedagogy. In R. E. Weiss, D. S. Knowlton, & B. W. Speck (Eds.), *Principles of effective teaching in the online classroom* (pp. 5-14). San Francisco: Jossey-Bass.

Knowlton, D. S. (2001, April). Promoting durable knowledge construction through online discussion. In *The Proceedings of the Mid-South Instructional Technology Conference*. Murfreesboro, Tennessee: Middle Tennessee State University. Available: www.mtsu.edu/~itconf/proceed01/11.html

Knowlton, D. S., & Knowlton, H. M. (2001). Evaluating students' writing: Contextual tensions and practical resolutions. *The Journal for the Art of Teaching, 8*(1), 81-91.

Lave, J., & Wenger, E. (1991). *Situated learning: Legitimate peripheral participation.* Cambridge, MA: Cambridge University Press.

Lin, X. (2001). Designing metacognitive activities. *Educational Technology Research and Development, 49*(2), 23-40.

Lindemann, E. (1995). *A rhetoric for writing teachers* (3rd ed). New York: Oxford University Press.

Marra, R. M. (2002). The ideal online learning environment for supporting epistemic development: Putting the puzzle together. *Quarterly Review of Distance Education, 3*(1), 15-31.

Moller, L. (1998). Designing communities of learners of asynchronous distance education. *Educational Technology Research and Development, 46*(4), 115-122.

Morrison, G. R., & Ross, S. M. (1998). Evaluating technology-based processes and products. In R. S. Anderson & B. W. Speck (Eds.), *Changing the way we grade student performance: Classroom assessment and the new learning paradigm* (pp. 69-77). San Francisco: Jossey-Bass.

Morrison, G. R., & Guenther, P. (2000). Designing instruction for learning in electronic classrooms. In R. E. Weiss, D. S. Knowlton, & B. W. Speck (Eds.), *Principles of effective teaching in the online classroom* (pp.15-22). San Francisco: Jossey-Bass.

Murray, D. E. (2000). Protean communication: The language of computer-mediated communication. *TESOL Quarterly, 34*(3), 397-421.

Prestera, G. E., & Moller, L. A. (2001). Exploiting opportunities for knowledge-building in asynchronous distance learning environments. *Quarterly Review of Distance Education, 2*(2), 93-104.

Rourke, L., Anderson, T., Archer, W., & Garrison, D. R. (1999). Assessing social presence in asynchronous text-based computer conferences. *Journal of Distance Education, 14*(3), 51-70.

Speck, B. W. (1998). Unveiling some of the mystery of professional judgment in classroom assessment. In R. S. Anderson & B. W. Speck (Eds.), *Changing the way we grade student performance: Classroom assessment and the new learning paradigm* (pp. 17-24). San Francisco: Jossey-Bass.

Weiss, R. E. (2000). Humanizing the online classroom. In R. E. Weiss, D. S. Knowlton, & B. W. Speck (Eds.), *Principles of effective teaching in the online classroom* (pp.47-52). San Francisco: Jossey-Bass.

CHAPTER 17

PRAGMATIC METHODS TO REDUCE DISHONESTY IN WEB-BASED COURSES

Newell Chiesl

The Internet, coupled with technology, has enabled institutions of higher learning to offer online distance education classes to a worldwide student body at an increasing rate. In the next 5 years it is estimated that nearly 90% of universities will offer online classes. Unfortunately, the news is not all that good. Students are now cheating at an all time rate. The very nature of distance learning appears to actually nurture academic dishonesty on the part of its students. This article will present some practical suggestions to reduce the occurrence of cheating by students enrolled in online higher education classes.

INTRODUCTION

According to the United States Department of Education, the growth of online distance education courses offered by universities in the United States experienced rapid growth in the 1990s (U.S. Department of Education, 2003). Actual enrollment for distance education courses approached 3 million during the 2000-01 academic year (Kiernan, 2003). Continuing

The Perfect Online Course: Best Practices for Designing and Teaching
pp. 327–339
Copyright © 2009 by Information Age Publishing

education and distance learning will grow 10 times faster than on-campus growth over the next 10 years (Burns, 2006).

The reasons for the increased popularity of online distance education courses have been well documented, and include:

- Universities offer a wide range of subject areas online from art to zoology;
- Classes are accessible when students have available time, for example, students are not required to be at a specific class at 8 A.M. (this eliminates the time-bound requirement for students);
- Online learning does not require physical attendance at a specific geographical location (this solves the problem for place-bound students);
- Courses are available 24/7, allowing students to study at home, work, or on the road (World Wide Learning, 2006).
- The final reason for online popularity, "on the road," is best confirmed by the recent emergence of students enrolled in the numerous online MBA degree programs being offered all across the country (Beal, 2003; Fisher, 2003; Gale Group, 2003).

Although positive benefits accrue from students taking e-learning courses, there are some significant drawbacks. The most noted include: some students might be technophobic; students lack the required technologies; and, more importantly, students experience a reduction in social interaction, the suppression of communication mechanisms, and the elimination of peer-to-peer learning (Kruse, 2002). Perhaps the largest drawback to online learning is the possibility of academic dishonesty on the part of the students enrolled in class.

ACADEMIC DISHONESTY

In grade school we heard the axioms, "Honesty is the best policy" and "Cheaters never win, and winners never cheat." But this is today, how many college students have actually cheated on an exam during their undergraduate work? Apparently, the majority of college students cheat. These are the findings presented from the first comprehensive study on cheating by college students. The study concludes, "Academic dishonesty, or cheating, is a ubiquitous phenomenon in higher education" (Bowers, 1964). Thirty years later, the next major comprehensive study reported that 70% of the students surveyed, cheated on a test at least once (McCabe, 1993). Student cheating is definitely a concern on college campuses. Other studies have reported between 30% and 70% of students cheated on at least one examination (Baird, 1980; Collision, 1990; Davis, Grover, Becker, & McGregor, 1992; Innerst, 1998; Kritz & Newman, 1991; Maramark & Maline, 1993; Wellborn, 1980).

Cheating Rationale

On children's soccer fields all across America, parents now shout today's axioms: "Winning is everything," and "Nice guys finish last." Winning and being a success are the battle cry of too many parents; being a good sport and having fun receive less attention. When parents cheat by driving too fast or by going through a yellow light, they are teaching their children to cheat (Cummins, 2000). Children observe their parents' actions. Small behavioral actions, regardless of how trivial they might seem to be, however, have a cumulative lasting effect on a child's life long perception of norms. A mom fibbing about her age, or a father's bravado over exaggerated income tax deductions are examples of how parents teach their children to cheat. As if these parents' initial indiscretions alone were bad enough, the problem becomes more profound with their futile attempts at rationalization. Parents respond with the following inept rationalizations: "Everyone lies about their age, and doesn't everyone cheat on their income tax?" Thus, our children learn to cheat, and the rationalization process begins early in a child's life (Murdock, 1999; Whitley & Keith-Spiegel, 2001).

Many studies have documented the reasons why students cheat, including: fear of failure, desire for a better grade, pressure from parents to do well in school, unclear instructional objectives, and being graded on a curve (Evans & Craig, 1990). Other studies report: Everyone else is doing it; I see others cheating; It helps me get better grades, a good job, or admitted to graduate school; I see no reason not to cheat; There is little or no chance of getting caught. There is little, or no, punishment if I did get caught (Alschuler & Blimling, 1995). Students believe few cheaters are caught, and that punishments for cheating are generally lenient (Bowers, 1964).

And finally, one professor notes: "In one of my interviews, a student wrote that anything worth having is worth cheating for" (Whitley, & Keith-Spiegel, 2001).

Reducing Classroom Dishonesty

There are many methods used to reduce the amount of student cheating. Diligent professors can virtually eliminate cheating using multiple versions of the same test, having additional proctors oversee the classroom, and by giving verbal warnings about cheating. Using tenured or tenure-track faculty tends to reduce cheating. Using only teaching assistants in a classroom will increase the amount of cheating (Kerkvliet & Sigmund, 1999). Additional research has reported colleges having a strict honor code, coupled with solid pressure from their student peers will discourage students from breaking the rules; and parents and teachers communicating early with students of grade school age will reduce the amount of student dishonesty (Anderson & Obenshain, 1994; Bowers, 1964; Gomez, 2001; McCabe, 1993; McCabe & Bowers, 1994; McCabe & Trevino, 1993; Newstead, Franklin-Stokes, & Armstead, 1996; Whitley & Keith-Spiegel, 2001).

Some experts say reducing competition among students will reduce student cheating, because the pressure to succeed clouds the judgment of many students, making cheating easy to justify and hard to resist. Other suggestions for professors to reduce the amount of student cheating include: affirm the importance of academic integrity. Encourage students to ask questions if they don't understand the material in class. Establish an honor code (Fishbein, 1993, 1994; Jendrek, 1989; Lathrop & Foss, 2002).

Reducing Distance Learning Dishonesty

Unfortunately, cheating also occurs by students enrolled in online distance education classes. According to research conducted, 64% of university professors perceive that it would be easier for students to cheat during online exams. Similarly, 57% of students also believe it is easier to cheat on exams offered in online classes (Kennedy, Nowack, Raghuraman, Thomas, & Davis, 2000).

Several suggestions have been offered to reduce academic dishonesty in Web-based courses (Christe, 2003; Kelley & Bonner, 2005; Olt, 2002). However, many of these suggestions are simply not practical, too time consuming, require technical expertise, and are somewhat costly for the average professor at a state university. This article presents a more pragmatic approach for the university professor, requiring only a few mouse clicks on a PC.

SUGGESTED PRAGMATIC APPROACHES
TO REDUCE ACADEMIC DISHONESTY

Four practical courses of action are suggested for professors to reduce the amount of cheating by online students: (1) disseminate information to distant students; (2) change the process used by students to turn in written assignments; (3) change the process by which exams are administered; and (4) create a nonsequential chapter assortment of questions.

Disseminate Information to Distant Students

This section summarizes the research reviewed earlier in this article. The following straightforward methods are easy to implement into online higher education classes:

- Inform students by using emails, posting announcements, and incorporating into a syllabus that honesty is the best policy.
- Using the same dissemination methods, notify students that cheating will not be tolerated.
- Professors should warn students that there are strict penalties for cheating.
- Provide a link to a student honor code document.
- Inform students of the professor's qualifications, degrees, consulting work, *pro bono publico*, community leadership roles, grants received, and vita accomplishments.
- Post clear cut course learning objectives. From the first day of class, professors need to communicate to the students an exact list of the requirements necessary to obtain a specific grade for the course.
- Reduce the pressure to get grades. One way to reduce the pressure to get a good grade is not to "curve" student grades. Many professors curve their grade distribution so that a certain percentage of students will receive A's, B's, C's, D's, and F's. If students perceive a class to be too competitive, the propensity of cheating increases. Therefore, in order to limit academic dishonesty, professors could develop a point system of grading. For example an A grade is equaled to 900 points or more.

Change the Process Used by
Students to Turn in Written Assignments

The incidence of plagiarism will theoretically be reduced by changing the process used by students to turn in assignments. Instead of handing in printed hard copy assignments, students should be required to hand in their assignments electronically. Professors then submit the electronic versions to a plagiarism recognition software product. Professors using Blackboard have an available tool called Turnitin to identify plagiarized work (Blackboard, 2007). To detect plagiarism, Turnitin software compares an individual student paper with Web pages, past student papers, newsworthy articles, and academic publications (Turnitin, 2007).

Change the Process by Which Exams are Administered

The third course of action a professor could easily incorporate into an online class would be to change how students take the exams. The newest version of Blackboard's Web site course development system enables a professor to change how students take exams online. A professor teaching an online course has several Blackboard options that predetermine how students will take exams. The first step consists of importing a course cartridge into a Blackboard class Web site. Course cartridge modules are offered directly from the publishers of most textbooks. The course cartridge developed by the publisher contains the usual material found on their CDs, such as key terms, definitions, study guide, cool Web links, and a computerized test bank. It is an effortless task—simply type in the course module code when prompted in the control panel. The course module is then uploaded automatically to a professor's Web site.

The second step is to create an exam from a "pool" of potential questions from the cartridge. This is easily done using Blackboard by going to the control panel, clicking creating an exam, and selecting the type of questions desired from a pull-down menu. For example, exam 1 may be composed of 40 multiple choice questions selected randomly from a publisher's pool of questions, covering chapters 1 and 2.

The next step configures how the exam will be taken by students. Blackboard's Web course development system offers several test options. The suggested options to include are:

1. Select the tightest time frame possible for students to complete each exam. Most professors have suggested to me, depending on the nature of the questions and the difficulty of the subject material, 40 questions in 40 minutes. I disagree. I suggest 40 questions in 30 minutes. (You will need to perform some trial-and-error exam attempts, with last year's students, to determine the least amount of time allotted for the exam.) A tight time frame will discourage students from cheating. Students will barely be able to

complete the exam and will not have time to thumb through the text looking for answers.

2. Select the option "show one question at a time to the student." This will discourage students from conducting a "copy and paste" into a document and then printing out the entire exam. Copying and pasting one question at a time will be very tedious and time consuming task. Plus, students will go beyond the allotted exam time period.

3. Select "no backtracking" on the part of the student. Once a student has selected an answer, do not allow him or her go back and see the prior questions.

4. Select "randomizing" the exam from a pool of questions.

5. Select allow the exam to be taken for an entire week. This reduces the time pressure to cheat.

6. Create a large number of exams to be taken during the semester— for example, 10 exams. Yes, perhaps a student will persuade a sibling or friend to take an exam and cheat for him or her once. But, will the sibling or friend agree to take 10 exams?

7. Set a low point value for each exam; say, 5% of the total semester points for each exam. This will reduce the pressure to cheat on an exam since the exam is not worth a large percentage of their grade.

8. Finally, select "allow multiple attempts" by students to take the exam. Students are allowed to take each exam as many times as they wish during an entire week, but each time they retake the exam, a new set of randomized questions appear. An additional bonus, for students taking the exams as many times as they wish, will be learning.

Create a Nonsequential Chapter Assortment of Questions

The final suggested method to reduce Web cheating is based on the sequencing order of questions. The nonsequential exam method is a system of staggering exam questions by chapters in a nonpredictable assortment. This is accomplished by importing more than one course cartridge from the publisher of the text used by the class.

Without the nonsequential exam method, the professor will usually import one course cartridge from a textbook publisher into the Web site powered by the Blackboard Academic Suite. The learning cartridge contains, among other items, a pool of exam questions developed for each chapter of the textbook. After a successful importation into the Blackboard Learning System, the professor creates an exam by one of several methods. The random block is one potential method used by a professor that desires granting students the ability to take an exam a multiple number of times. The professor selects the chapters to be covered in the exam. For example, exam 3 might contain 60 questions covering chapters 5, 6, and 7. Each time the student repeats exam 3, the exam will randomly generate a new set of questions from the exam pool. The new exam usually has a mix of questions from the previous exam and new questions from the pool. During the exam creation process the professor will request 20 questions from chapter 5, 20 questions from chapter 6, and 20 questions from chapter 7. When the exam is taken, the student will be presented with the same sequential order of questions: 20 questions from chapter 5; 20 questions from chapter 6; and 20 questions from chapter 7. The above-noted procedure, using only one cartridge, will tempt the student to open their textbook and follow along the exam by the sequential chapters.

To reduce academic dishonesty, the professor needs to import multiple course cartridges from the textbook publisher. The procedure is as follows. A professor using the Blackboard Learning System as the software platform to drive the Web course will click the control button and request the course cartridge three times. Usually within about a day, the Web site will be populated with three duplicate exam pools of questions. For the same hypothetical exam 3 containing 60 questions, the professor might select, for example, 5 questions from chapter 6, 7 questions from chapter 5, 6 questions from chapter 7, 4 questions from chapter 5, 6 questions from chapter 7, 9 questions from chapter 6, 8 questions from chapter 7, 9 questions from chapter 5, and 6 questions from chapter 6. It does sound complicated but, in reality, the nonsequential chapter exam method takes only a couple of extra minutes and is as easy as click, click, and click. The nonsequential chapter exam method is perhaps more easily understood by perusing Table 17.1. Obviously, there are numerous other potential nonsequential exam method variations available that can be used to construct exams.

FEEDBACK

In an effort to determine the merit of the suggested pragmatic methods, a survey of Web-based students was implemented. During a 3-year period, 149 students were asked to complete an online survey asking questions concerning their online experience. By using Blackboard's survey feature, their identities were hidden from the professor. Assurances were also given to students guaranteeing their anonymity.

Table 17.1. The Nonsequential Chapter Exam Method to Reduce Academic Dishonesty by Web Students

Chapter	Number of Questions Selected	Cumulative Amount or Each Chapter
6	5	5
5	7	7
7	6	6
5	4	11
7	6	12
6	9	14
7	8	20
5	9	20
6	6	20

Exam 3, 60 questions from Chapters 5, 6, and 7.

The overall results of the student feedback survey were extremely favorable. For the first question in the survey, 81% of the students reported taking each exam two to four times, whereas 10% indicated that they take each exam more than four times. The next survey question showed, on average, that 70% of students increased their exam scores in a range from 10-20 points (exam = 100 points). Table 17.2 presents the results to the next question, "How important to you, is the ability to take an exam as many times as you wish during the semester?" Students reported: 63% very important, it really helps; 23% important; 8% neutral, it does not help, or hurt; 4% slightly not important; and 2% not important. As seen in Table 17.2, an overwhelmingly high amount, 86% of the Web students, reported a positive observation of being allowed to take each exam multiple times.

Presented in Table 17.3 are the equally positive results concerning the quality of learning as perceived by the Web students. Only 8% of the students reported a less-than-average learning experience, while the majority, 63%, reported a very positive learning experience, as compared to other Web classes.

Tables 17.4 and 17.5 report the students' perceptions of cheating in a Web class that has implemented the pragmatic methods to reduce Web course dishonesty, as suggested in this article. As seen in Table 17.4, "Cheating in this web class compared to classroom courses," 17% of the students reported that the average student will cheat more in this Web class than most classroom courses, while 42% of the students reported that the average student will cheat less than most classroom courses. Table

Table 17.2.   Importance of Taking Multiple Exam Attempts

How important to you, is the ability to take an exam as many times as you wish during the semester?

Very important it really helps	Slightly important	Neutral, it does not help, or hurt	Slightly not important	Not important
63%	23%	8%	4%	2%

Table 17.3.   Student Learning

Because I am able to take an exam as many times as I wish to improve my score, I receive instant feedback and learn the material. (Compared to other web courses), my learning increased in this class:

Less than most web courses	Slightly less than most web courses	About the same	Slightly more than most web courses	More than most web courses
4%	4%	29%	40%	23%

Table 17.4.   Cheating in This Web Class Compared to Classroom Courses

As compared to other classroom courses, do you think the average student, in this Web course, can cheat:

More than most classroom courses	Slightly more than most classroom courses	About the same	Slightly less than most classroom courses	Less than most classroom courses
2%	15%	41%	10%	32%

Table 17.5.   Cheating in This Web Class Compared to Other Web Courses

As compared to other Web courses, do you think the average student, in this Web course, can cheat:

More than most web courses	Slightly more than most web courses	About the same	Slightly less than most web courses	Less than most web courses
1%	2%	27%	17%	53%

17.5 compared cheating in this Web class compared to most Web courses. The results of Table 17.5 indicate only 3% of the students reporting cheating more (in this Web class) than most Web classes, while a great percentage, 70%, reported that the average student can cheat (in this Web class) less than in most Web courses.

SUMMARY AND CONCLUSIONS

The foundation of this article has been to report the increasing enrollments in online distance education courses, document the occurrence of academic dishonesty by college students, offer the rationale given as to why students cheat, and present suggestions to reduce cheating in both classroom and online higher education courses. After the groundwork for this article had been established, an easy-to-use pragmatic method to reduce academic dishonesty was then proposed.

In an effort to evaluate the pragmatic method, feedback was obtained from students through the use of an anonymous online survey. Overall, the results were very constructive. Students were satisfied with the amount of the learning they achieved. Students appreciated the ability to take each exam multiple times. Most importantly, students reported a lesser incidence of online cheating compared to other Web classes. The results presented in Tables 17.4 and 17.5 reported a lesser perception of cheating in online classes compared to previous research (Kennedy et al., 2000). This tends to confirm the merit of the pragmatic method to reduce online cheating.

Widespread student academic dishonesty is an unfortunate situation faced by university professors. Nonetheless, professors developing online courses might reduce student cheating by following the recommended pragmatic methods suggested in this article.

REFERENCES

Alschuler, A. S., & Blimling, G. S. (1995). Curbing epidemic cheating through systemic change. *Colleges Teaching, 43*(4), 123.

Anderson, R. E., & Obenshain, S. S. (1994). Cheating by students: Findings, reflections, and remedies. *Academic Medicine, 69,* 323-332.

Baird, J. S. (1980). Current trends in college cheating. *Psychology in the Schools, 17,* 515-522.

Beal, E. (2003). Plenty of players in MBA game. *Crain's Cleveland Business, 24*(35), 15-15.

Blackboard. (2006). Retrieved September 7, 2007, from http://www.blackboard .com/products

Bowers, W. J. (1964). *Student dishonesty and its control in college.* New York: Bureau of Applied Social Research, Columbia University.

Burns, E. (2006). *Continuing education drives distance-learning enrollment.* Retrieved July 17, 2006, from http://www.clickz.com/stats/sectors/education/article.php/ 3605321

Christe, B. (2003). Designing online courses to discourage dishonesty. *Educause Quarterly, 4,* 54-58.

Collison, M. (1990). Apparent rise in students cheating has college officials worried. *The Chronicle of Higher Education, 36*(18), 33-34.

Cummins, C. (2000). *Are you teaching your children to cheat?* Retrieved July 17, 2006, from http://www.educationreportcard.com/columns/2000

Davis, S. F., Grover, C. A., Becker, A. H., & McGregor, L. N. (1992). Academic dishonesty: Prevalence, determinants, techniques, and punishments. *Teaching of Psychology, 19*, 16-20.

Evans, E. D., & Craig, D. (1990). Adolescent cognitions for academic cheating as a function of grade level and achievement status. *Journal of Adolescent Research, July*, 325-345.

Fishbein, L. (1993). Curbing cheating and restoring academic integrity. *The Chronicle of Higher Education, 40*(15), 52.

Fishbein, L. (1994). We can curb college cheating. *Education Digest, 59*(7), 58-61.

Fisher, A. (2003). Will I end up getting scammed if I pursue an online MBA? *Fortune, 148*(6), 170.

Gale Group. (2003). The e-MBA: More MBA students are getting their degrees without ever stepping into the classroom. *Business and Management Practices: Inside Business, 5*(7), 53.

Gomez, D. S. (2001). Putting the shame back in student cheating. *Education Digest, 67*(4), 15.

Innerst, C. (1998). Students are pulling off the big cheat. *Insight on the News, 14*(9), 41.

Jendrek, M. P. (1989). Faculty reactions to academic dishonesty. *Journal of College Student Development, 30*, 401-406.

Kelley, K. B., & Bonner, K. (2005). Distance education and academic dishonesty: Faculty and administrator perceptions and responses. *Journal of Asynchronous Learning Networks, 9*(1), 43-52.

Kennedy, K., Nowak, S., Raghuraman, R., Thomas, J., & Davis, S. F. (2000). Academic dishonesty and distance learning: Student and faculty views. *College Student Journal, 34*(2), 309-314.

Kerkvliet, J. R., & Sigmund, C. (1999). Can we control cheating in the classroom? *Journal of Economic Education, 30*(4), 331-343.

Kiernan, V. (2003). A survey documents growth in distance education in late 1990s. *The Chronicle of Higher Education, 49*(48), 28.

Kritz, F. L., & Newman, R. J. (1991). Campus cheats. *U.S. News and World Report, 11*(24), 71.

Kruse, K. (2002). *The benefits and drawbacks of e-learning.* Retrieved July 17, 2006, from http://www.e-learningguru.com/articles/art1_3.htm

Lathrop, A., & Foss, K. (2002). Student cheating and plagiarism in the Internet era. Englewood, CO: Libraries Unlimited.

Maramark, S., & Maline, M. B. (1993). *Academic dishonesty among college students.* Washington, DC: Division of Higher Education and Adult Learning, Office of Research, U.S. Department of Education.

McCabe, D. L. (1993). Faculty responses to academic dishonesty: The influence of student honor codes. *Research in Higher Education, 34*(5), 647-658.

McCabe, D. L., & Bowers, W. J. (1994). Academic dishonesty among males in college: A thirty year perspective. *Journal of College Student Development, 35*, 3-10.

McCabe, D. L., & Trevino, L. K. (1993). Academic dishonesty: Honor codes and other contextual influences. *Journal of Higher Education, 64*(5), 522-538.

Murdock, T. B. (1999). Discouraging cheating in your classroom. *Mathematics Teacher, 92*(7), 587.

Newstead, S. E., Franklin-Stokes, A., & Armstead, P. (1996). Individual differences in student cheating. *Journal of Educational Psychology, 88*, 229-241.

Olt, M. R. (2002). Ethics and distance education: strategies for minimizing academic dishonesty in online assessment, *Online Journal of Distance Learning Administration, 5*(3).

Turnitin. (2006). Retrieved September 7, 2007, from http://turnitin.com/static/index.html

U. S. Department of Education (Ed.). (2003). *Distance education at degree-granting post-secondary institutions: 2000-2001.* Washington, DC: Author.

Wellborn, S. N. (1980). Cheating in college becomes an epidemic. *U.S. News and World Report, 89*(20), 39-42.

Whitley, B. E., Jr. & Keith-Speigel, P. (2001). *Academic dishonesty: An educator's guide.* Mahwah, NJ: Erlbaum.

World Wide Learning. (2006). Retrieved July 17, 2006, from www.worldwidelearn.com/elearning/elearning-benefits.htm

CHAPTER 18

ORGANIZING INSTRUCTIONAL CONTENT FOR WEB-BASED COURSES

Does a Single Model Exist?

Joi L. Moore, Ricard E. Downing, and David L. York

Instructors are organizing course materials based on their mental models of organization and their interpreted meaning of textual organization labels. A chi-square analysis was conducted between students and instructors. The difference in placement of 3 of 14 course materials was statistically significant. Qualitative methods, such as interviews and concept analysis, were also used for data collection. There is dissonance between students and instructors concerning the placement of certain course materials under static headings. Moreover, there is no consistent agreement among students as a group or instructors as a group regarding such placement. General recommendations for alleviating student confusion are provided.

The Perfect Online Course: Best Practices for Designing and Teaching
pp. 341–358
Copyright © 2009 by Information Age Publishing
All rights of reproduction in any form reserved.

INTRODUCTION

Although the notion of Web-based (for the purposes of this study, the terms Web-based and online, as they refer to courses, are interchangeable) courses is not new, the increase in student enrollment within these courses is causing a revolutionary transformation of the typical educational environment that many people experienced before 1995. Because many of the traditional strategies implemented in face-to-face courses are not as effective and in some cases, no longer appropriate, design decisions for Web-based courses are constantly changing. Adapting becomes an ongoing challenge as most institutions rush to keep up with the competition. It seems that little time remains for understanding how Web-based courses should be designed and implemented. In particular, the students' primary medium for connecting with instructors, classmates, course content, and activities has now changed from the face-to-face environment to the course Web site. As a result, students now have a much higher level of responsibility for obtaining and understanding course information that would generally be provided and explained in a face-to-face course by the instructor.

As instructors and students in Web-based courses, the authors have noticed and experienced a dissonance in the Web-based environment that was not as visible in face-to-face environments. This dissonance occurs because an instructor or designer of the Web-based course has a mental model of the Web site that is often different from the students. Within all electronic communications (e.g., discussion boards, emails) as well as the organization of the course Web site, misunderstandings occur often and can eventually cause unnecessary frustrations. Previous findings reveal that the course structure (Romiszowski & Cheng, 1992) and the interface design of a Web-based course (Eastmond, 1995) can have an impact on student satisfaction and learning in these courses. The implications of these findings indicate that students can become lost or confused within Web-based courses.

Currently, there is no standard model for course material organization for Web-based courses that often rely on textual labels for identification. Instructors are organizing course materials based upon their own mental model of organization and their own interpreted meaning of textual organization labels, rather than using research-based standards to organize and label materials. The objective of this study was to determine if a discrepancy exists between how instructors organize materials under specific headings and where students expect to find these materials. We suspected that there is a dissonance between the instructor and students' mental model of Web-based course organization and set out to test this notion.

PERSPECTIVES AND THEORETICAL FRAMEWORK

Instructor-created course materials delivered to students in a print-based format are generally accepted without question. Course textbooks as well as other instructional materials (e.g., syllabus, assignment descriptions, grading rubrics, class hand-outs, etc.) are substantial components of the mental model for the typical face-to-face instructional environment. The authority of these materials is acknowledged because the student has a mental model of what instructional materials should be.

Computers and the Internet provide readers with a newfound power to question the interpreted meaning of the text on the screen. (Bolter, 1991) noted that modern consumers of electronic text are involved in the negotiated meaning of that text. Such a negotiation can become disputed ground between instructor and student. Word meaning is always open to interpretation. "There is no necessary relation between a word and its meaning" (Fiske & Hartley, 1987, p. 39). The meaning of any given textual symbol is based upon both the writer's and the reader's own experiences and the interpretation of those experiences (Bruner, 1966). Larson and Czerwinski (1997) asserted that the semantics and labeling of Web site content should be consistent with the user's understanding of the information space.

Jonassen (1995, para. 9) contended that mental models of course material organization between instructors and students "...usually vary, often significantly, from the cognitive or conceptual model promoted by the designers (*instructors*) because of varying prior knowledge, individual abilities, and different beliefs about the purpose and functions of the system...." Carley and Palmquist (1992) submitted a short list of assumptions regarding mental models that address precisely the point of this research. Three of their assumptions stated (1992):

- Language is the key to understanding mental models; i.e., they are linguistically mediated.
- The meanings for concepts are embedded in their relationships to other concepts.
- The social meaning of concepts is derived from the intersection of different individuals' mental models.

Categorization

According to Estes (1993), organization and categorization of items is one of the basic mental functions of human beings. Categorization is a vital component of navigation for online courses. The organizational schema of the instructor and student can sometimes be markedly dissimilar. Therefore, students are required to decipher the organization and categorization schema of each course in which they enroll. Recall that, in the physical classroom environment, students and instructors do not negotiate categorization rules, whereas, in the Web-based environment, understanding categorization is required whether accomplished subconsciously or through induction. It is quite possible that students in their early Web-based instructional experiences possess no mental prototype or abstract image of the category within which this new information belongs. This phenomenon may cause students to become lost, frustrated, and to ultimately report a less than satisfactory or nonproductive experience in the Web-based instructional environment.

Often, the student navigator will not know what is right until wrong has been defined. A pseudo-experimental situation is frequently created by this confusion. The student is therefore relegated to testing a number of hypotheses to determine the most appropriate navigational path (Elstein, 1998), sometimes by guessing, sometimes by decoding the instructor's organizational schema, and sometimes by spending time wandering through a navigational maze.

Students are often required to decode dramatically different course content categorization schemes for each instructor's Web site. Within the same semester, they are asked to do this decoding process with almost no domain knowledge of the way any given instructor might choose to categorize course content. As Estes (1993) points out, prototype representation has been, in recent years, one of the dominant concepts of the way humans categorize information. An agreed upon prototype does not currently exist among instructors and designers of Web-based courses, which in turn frustrates even good students' best efforts to decode just where an instructor places specific course content. This moving target is simply too flexible for the student to identify.

One must look to research regarding categorization to study the way in which students might become confused about the placement of various course content components. While organization and categorization of items is one of the basic mental functions of human beings, it was not studied with any vigor until the mid-1970s (Estes,1993). Today the impact of previous experience and knowledge on human understanding of new experiences and the assimilation of new information is one of the foundational concepts of constructivist learning theory (Piaget, 1973; Jonassen, 1991; Vygotsky, 1978; Duffy & Jonassen, 1992). "Prior to encountering a task calling for concept formation, the learner must have enough relevant experience to come equipped with a set of hypotheses that need only be heuristically searched to yield the one defining the needed concept"

(Estes, 1993, p.16). Unfortunately, the physical classroom schema is the one most often brought to a Web-based course.

Following Estes (1993), the schema that students most often possess will not contribute to their understanding of content label or organization within a Web-based delivery environment. The aberrant decoding (Lester, 1995) or misunderstanding by the student in the physical classroom environment is not a large issue. When an instructor distributes a syllabus saying, "This is your syllabus," there is no need for the student to understand the way the instructor might categorize this piece of instructional content. While the instructor seldom discusses the categorization process within a physical classroom environment, the meaning of any category that might contain construct Syllabus is negotiated through immediate verbal exchanges in the classroom as the actual document is distributed. Categorization rules for any given course content are rarely communicated in the classroom. If required the instructor provides categorization rules by example rather than negotiation (Estes, 1993). In most cases the instructor does not categorize disparate components of course content and there is actually no need for categorizing the materials for group communication when the course is delivered in a classroom. Each student may define her own categorization of the material in a notebook or file system. A student easily retrieves specific course material because the student established the categorization rule for this material, filing the syllabus under a certain heading for easy access and retrieval.

We describe the negotiated categorization process as an ill-structured problem. Jonassen (2000) defined ill-structured problems as "...(P)osessing multiple criteria for evaluating solutions, so there is uncertainty about which concepts, rules, and principles are necessary for the solution and how they are organized" (p. 67). Categorization is, at its very core, the ability to solve an ill-structured problem utilizing pre-existing knowledge (Bareiss & Slater, 1993). In ill-structured problem solving, when the student approaches the problem state, such as what heading within a course Web site is the category under which the syllabus might be located, there may be no specifically well-defined goal state (Raufaste, 1998). Students are forced to seek the one solution that eventually presents a syllabus.

While the student may have constructed some initial hypotheses or prototypes through observation or experience with other courses, or through discussion during an on-ground class, new data gathered for each Web-course experience may prompt the student to alter or reformulate the hypothesis, or reconfigure the prototype. This strategy is similar to the information foraging theory derived from biology and anthropology and applied to information seeking behaviors. Pirolli and Card (1995) use this theory to understand how people search for and make sense of information on the World Wide Web. According to information foraging theory, the strategies for seeking, gathering, and consuming information on a Web site are adapted to the environment and guided by the information scent (Pirolli & Card, 1991; Larson & Czerwinski, 1997). Information scent reflects the user's value assignment for the presented information based upon the immediate goal. The appearance of the information has a bearing on the level of information scent.

METHODS AND PROCEDURES

We designed two Web-based surveys, one for students and one for instructors. Both surveys required participants to indicate their experience with Web-based courses and a self-rated level of expertise with computers (beginner, intermediate, and advanced), in addition to basic demographic data (i.e., age, gender, academic level for students, and teaching level for instructors). Using a sample of convenience, 57 students and 23 instructors completed the survey. Student participants ranged in age from 21 to 46+ years old, 44 of whom were female and 13 were male. There were 13 female and 10 male instructor participants. Age of the instructors was not collected. All students were enrolled in graduate courses and instructors taught both undergraduate and graduate courses. Participants had varying levels of computer expertise and experience in a Web-based instructional environment as indicated by the number of courses in which they had been a student or for which they had been the instructor.

The surveys provided descriptive information regarding the organization of information in Web-based courses. In the survey, 14 course components (e.g., Syllabus, Course Objectives, Assignments, etc.) were chosen for placement under eight headings (e.g., Course Information, Course Documents, Assignments, Communication, etc.). Headings were derived from Blackboard, a popular course-management tool currently in use in approximately 300 Web-based courses at our own university. Participants were asked to place each course component under one, and only one, heading. They were also asked to indicate whether they believed the course material belonged under more than one heading.

We performed a chi-square analysis of this categorical data with a level of significance for the analysis established as .05. There were a number of cells within the matrix for which the frequency was less than five. In this case, the total was placed in a column called Other. Headings were excluded from the chi-square analysis in those situations in which neither group had a response. For example, neither instructors nor students placed the course material Syllabus under the heading Staff Information. Accordingly, the chi-square analysis for Syllabus did not include the heading Staff Information. Only percentages were calculated for responses to the question regarding placement under more than one heading.

Our research was further informed with qualitative methods to provide in-depth analysis of the instructors' and students' mental model for the organization of course material. The qualitative data were coded using the constant comparative method to identify key issues or recurrent events that became categories of focus (LeCompte & Preissle, 1993). As data were collected, field notes were examined and written comments were made to note emerging theories and to identify patterns and relationships.

We examined the placement and organization of course materials within Web-based courses and interviewed the instructors of these courses. Our interview questions focused on the instructor's rationale for the organization and structure of their Web-based course. We interviewed instructors individually, in their offices, at separate times. An audio tape recorder captured each of the approximately one hour-long interviews for transcription and further analysis. These interviews followed a semi-structured interview protocol that begins with standard questions such as "What part of the course Web site do you update frequently?" We generated the remainder of the questions from the evaluation of the instructor's Web-based course; For example, "Tell me why you placed the material in more than one location on your Website?" Most of the questions allowed for open-ended comments.

The students' mental model of Web-based course organization was important to this study. Therefore, we gathered data by implementing a concept analysis task with ten students enrolled in an advanced Web design and development course. The students had experience with several Web course management tools and Web-based courses. For a concept analysis the users categorize each node (i.e., course material) according to the label or heading that is the best fit (Bernard, 2000). When this task was complete the entire class was used as a focus group, wherein each team provided their rationale for their decisions and discussed other problems with the course headings.

RESULTS

Quantitative Analysis

Results of the survey data analysis were mixed (see Table 18.1). There was no statistically significant difference between instructors and students regarding the placement of the majority of course materials (11 of 14) including: Syllabus, Policies and Procedures, Lecture Notes, Staff Infor-

**Table 18.1.   Chi-Square Analysis
of Course Materials and Headings Between Groups**

Course Materials	Headings	Instructor	Student	Total
Syllabus	Course Information	19	29	48
($N = 71, p \leq 1$)	Course Documents	3	13	16
	Other	1	6	7
	Total	23	48	71
Course Objectives	Course Information	22	39	61
($N = 72, p \leq 1$)	Course Documents	1	7	8
	Other	0	3	3
	Total	23	49	72
Policies & Procedures	Course Information	18	39	57
($N = 72, p \leq 1$)	Course Documents	4	4	8
	Other	1	6	7
	Total	23	49	72
Lecture Notes	Course Information	18	29	47
($N = 70, p \leq 1$)	Course Documents	5	12	17
	Other	0	6	6
	Total	3	47	70
Staff Information	Course Information	5	3	8
($N = 73, p \leq 1$)	Course Documents	18	45	63
	Other	0	2	2
	Total	23	50	73
Assignments	Course Information	5	11	16
($N = 70, p \leq 1$)	CourseDocuments	16	34	50
	Other	2	2	4
	Total	23	47	70
Tests/Exams	Course Information	5	6	11
($N = 70, p \leq 1$)	Course Documents	17	34	51
	Other	1	7	8
	Total	23	47	70
Required Reading/Text	Course Documents	5	18	23
($N = 72, p \leq .20$)	Assignments	12	24	36
	Course Information	6	4	10
	Other	0	3	3
	Total	23	49	72
Course Schedule*	Announcements	1	6	7
($N = 72, p \leq .05$)	Course Information	16	13	29
	Course Documents	3	7	10
	Assignments	2	18	20
	Other	1	5	6
	Total	23	49	72
Required Reading/Web	Course Documents	5	21	26
($N = 73, p \leq 1$)	Assignments	11	21	32
	External Links	4	8	12
	Other	2	1	3
	Total	22	51	73

(Table continues on next page)

Table 18.1.   (Continued)

Course Materials	Headings	Instructor	Student	Total
References and	Course Documents	4	17	26
Supplemental Reading*	Assignments	2	9	32
($N = 73, p \leq .05$)	External Links	6	16	12
	Other	11	8	3
	Total	23	50	73
Grades*	Course Documents	7	6	13
($N = 69, p \leq .01$)	Assignments	3	5	8
	External Links	6	33	39
	Other	7	2	9
	Total	23	46	69
Class Discussion	Communication	21	46	67
($N = 74, p \leq 1$)	Other	2	5	7
	Total	23	51	74
Class Changes	Announcements	19	43	62
($N = 72, p \leq 1$)	Other	4	6	10
	Total	23	49	72

Note: *Indicates a significant difference.

mation, Assignments, Course Objectives, Tests/Exams, Required Readings/Text, Required Readings/Web, Class Discussion, and Class Changes ($N = 69\text{-}74, p \leq 1$). However, there was a statistically significant difference between groups for the remaining course materials. Instructors and students disagreed on where they expected 3 course materials to be placed: Grades ($N = 69, p \leq .01$), Course Schedule ($N = 72, p \leq .05$), and References and Supplemental Readings ($N = 73, p \leq .05$).

There were approximately five to seven instances (8%–12%) per course material in which there was No Response by a participant. This phenomenon could be caused by a participant's relative lack of experience or it could be based upon the survey or question format. Participants disagreed in their response as to whether the course material belonged under more than one heading. For example, all participants indicated that Class Discussion should be under the heading Communication. However, 20% of students and 50% of instructors believed Class Discussion also belonged under more than one of the headings. That is, while there was agreement about the heading under which Class Discussion should be placed, participants did not agree that Communication was the only heading under which it should be placed.

In our survey, one of the course content listings was Assignments and one of the course headings was Assignments. One could reasonably assume that all participants would agree on the heading under which this course material should be placed. However, 20% of students and 14% of instructors believed Assignment materials should be placed under the Course Information heading. In addition 54% of students and 60% of instructors indicated the Assignment materials could have been placed under more than one heading while 46% of students and 40% of instructors indicated it belonged under only one heading.

Qualitative Analysis

Instructor and student interviews along with course Web site evaluations provided data relating to Web-based course design issues. Course organization and labeling decisions were typically not based on any recommendations or guidelines, but from what seemed logical to the designer at the time of design. These decisions often lead to inconsistencies relating to course content and label meanings.

Design Decisions

Many of the interface design decisions for the courses were influenced by the designer's intuition and experience with online courses, or the capabilities and limitations of the course management tool. Instructors used their own perceptions of the label meanings for categorization decisions. In addition, most universities have a Web-based course management tool to assist instructors with the development and implementation of their courses. These tools, however, can have limited choices for navigation labels. For example, Blackboard provides a selection of labels that can be used but designers are not allowed to create new ones whereas WebCT allows more creative freedom with label names. In addition, some metaphors that are used with the tools, such as documents and folders, create a more compartmentalized perspective of the data that often lead to Web sites with larger depth than breadth.

Previous experience with Web-based courses was another factor in design decisions. Instructors applied feedback from previous implementations of the course to their design. For example, if students indicated that assignment information should be in Course Documents, then the instructor might make certain that the information could be accessed from that specific location as well as the current location. Identical course material in multiple locations, however, is often difficult to synchronize. Sometimes instructors did not make changes to material in both locations causing confusion for students. Another design strategy was to place summary information in one location and specific details in another. For example, Assignments would provide general information for the course assignments, but actual details were located in another section of the Web site, often under a different heading.

Consequently, multiple locations for information can require more work for the instructor when modifications are needed and can lead to student confusion when they notice multiple occurrences of identical course material. The student must then compare the information in both locations to ensure they capture accurate information. Both Blackboard and WebCT allow designers to create hypertext anchors and internal links to material within different sections of the Web site, but internal navigation within these tools may make navigation more confusing for the student. In addition, some instructors indicated that they lacked technical skills required to create custom internal navigation and therefore relied upon the standard capabilities of the course management tool. One instructor with Web development experience suggested that the course management tools should provide a way that is "easier in general to link between the sections, ... because it's difficult in terms of setting it up and it's kind of cumbersome."

Instructors used a combination of strategies for organizing and labeling, such as creating labels on the main Web page for materials or tasks that must be accessed first and/or most often, in addition to organizing similar content under the same label. This often leads to an ambiguous organization scheme that reflects categorization and labels that defy exact definition and are bundled in the ambiguity of language as well as human subjectivity (Rosenfeld & Morville, 1998). Given these ambiguous organization schemes, it was not surprising that one instructor reported that he received more questions relating to the course interface than the course design, content, or instructor expectations.

In several of the courses, Course Documents was a heading used for placing material such as assignment information, syllabi, lectures, and readings. This heading takes on different meanings depending upon the design of the course Web site. Some instructors interpreted it to mean any document other than a Web page, whereas others used it for placement of material that did not fit in the other categories. According to Webster's the term document implies anything that is written, printed, and/or relied upon to record or prove something (Agnes, 1996). In essence, the typical forms of course content and materials (i.e., Web page, pdf file format, and word processing file) are all considered documents. Thus, Course Documents could actually serve as the heading for the entire course Web site.

Another example of label ambiguity was the use of Links as a heading. One instructor used this heading for accessing Web pages outside of the course Web site that contained supplemental material. The instructor indicated that Links was common terminology for navigation to outside Web sites when referring to hyperlinks for Web locations not in the course folder. He knows, at least based on his assumptions, that students will understand the meaning. This instructor's course Web site also contained internal links and anchors for navigating throughout the course Web site. In addition, there were links to password-protected material on an external Web site, but these links were located in a section labeled "Readings" rather than "Links."

Concept Analysis

Ten students organized into two teams in an advanced Web design and development course were provided with descriptions of course content and material, which were identical to the information on the surveys. For approximately 20 minutes the two teams organized and grouped the course content for the major headings in Blackboard. Observations revealed that students within the groups had a difficult time agreeing to the placement of several materials. Table 18.2 provides a summary of the final organization schemes for both teams. The content for Course Information, Course

**Table 18.2. Concept Analysis
of Content Placement Within Course Headings**

Course Headings	Team A	Team B
Announcements	Class changes	Class changes *Make this heading a node within Communication
Course Information	Syllabus Course Objectives Policies & Procedures Calendar/Schedule	Assignments Descriptions, Guidelines, & Evaluation Criteria Course Objective Policies & Procedures
Staff Information	Information about the instructor	Information about the instructor
Course Documents	Required Readings (print) Reference/Supplementary Resources Lecture Notes	Syllabus Lecture Notes Calendar/Schedule
Assignments	Assignments Descriptions, Guidelines, & Rubrics Tests/Quizzes Required Readings (Print)	Assignments Descriptions, Guidelines, & Rubrics Tests/Quizzes Required Readings (print) *Make this heading a node within Course Documents
Communication	Class Discussion	Class Discussions
External Links	Required readings (Web based) Reference/Supplementary Resources	Required readings (Web based) Reference/Supplementary Resources
Student Tools	Grades/Assessment	Grades/Assessment

Documents, and Assignments headings had the most overlap in comparison to the other headings. In addition, there were two instances wherein a team wanted to move a heading to a node within another heading. Team B indicated that Announcements should be within Communication and Assignments should be within Course Documents.

DISCUSSION

The level of dissonance among members of the two groups (instructors and students) as well as between groups poses significant challenges in Web-based instructional environments. Usability of any Web site is an important design factor that can affect the level of dissonance. Bernard (2000) provided the following usability attributes of a well-designed Web site: layout is easy to learn; information retrieval task is small, efficient, and easy to remember; information is up-to-date and accurate; and the user is satisfied with the Web site. Organization and labeling are important design decisions, which can have a direct impact on the Web site usability (Larson & Czerwinski, 1997) and ultimately, the student's satisfaction and success with the course. This leads to the major issue from this study, the information architecture of the Web site, which relates to the strategies for navigation, labeling, organization, indexing, searching, and the use of metaphors (Rosenfeld & Morville, 1998). Based on the results of this study, labeling and organization strategies were the major issues affecting the dissonance within these Web-based courses.

Labeling in Course Web Sites

Bailey (1997) identified three common labeling problems for Web sites: a label is vague and misleading and may provide content not expected by the user; a label used on the main page does not match the title or header on referring pages; and a label is puzzling when it does not relate to the content in any manner. Many of the instructors in this study labeled the content based on their own perspective rather than the users. Bailey notes, however, that labels and labeling schemes are languages that are often different, depending upon the audience.

Organization Strategies in Course Web Sites

Typically, the designer's organization strategies were based upon a combination of past experience, student suggestions, and personal intuition. Within any given Web-based course, some content was organized by task, whereas others were organized by the instructor's understanding of the content meaning. The combination of these two within the same course often leads to placement of identical information in different locations. This phenomenon occurs frequently as designers attempt to match the Web site organization to the retrieval strategies that may differ from student to student. One instructor noted that it is difficult to anticipate the strategies of the students because there are "a lot of different learners and expectations and probably no matter what you do, you'll have some people who think it just doesn't make sense." Unfortunately, when designers try to accommodate the needs of all users, the Web site organization scheme becomes "fuzzy" and leads to an ambiguous organization scheme.

Capabilities of the course management tools also influenced the organization of Web-based courses. At the time of this study, Blackboard offered only eight headings for placing of course content. Eight headings on the home page follows the standard conventions for course Web site breadth as recommended by Web usability research (Miller, 1981; Kiger, 1984), but we discovered that instructors increased the depth within each section because they were concerned about excessive scrolling.

Multiple Course Phenomenon

Given the level of dissonance in the expectations for placement of course content within a Web-based instructional environment, students spend an inordinate amount of time seeking specific course content. Students must repeat the acclimation process for each Web-based course at the beginning of a semester. This notion of a unique acclimation period for each course brings forth a situation we have called the *multiple course phenomenon*. This is a case in which a student enrolls in more than one Web-based course in a given semester or academic period. Essentially, the student must learn the course structure for each Web site because there are inconsistencies between instructors in the placement of course materials such as the syllabus and the description of assignments. Our examination of the course Web sites used by the instructors in this research supports the existence of *multiple course phenomenon*. We believe the magnitude of confusion caused by the dissonance between the instructor's and student's mental model of Web-based course organization cannot be underestimated and we have concluded that there is always at least some dissonance between students and instructors concerning the placement of certain course materials under static headings. Moreover, there seems to be no consistent agreement among students as a group or instructors as a group regarding such placement.

Recommendations

Based on the results of this exploratory study, we have developed some recommendations that can assist designers of Web-based learning environments with creating effective interfaces. Furthermore, our experience as instructors and students within these environments provide practical knowledge of the issues that often occur.

- Syllabus—Students are familiar with this label because of its use in face-to-face settings as a document that provides course information. This should be one of the main links on the Web site.
- Introduction Quiz—At the beginning of the course, it is useful to require students to take a course introduction quiz. Quiz questions relate to critical information within the course, such as the evaluation criteria, due dates, and assignment descriptions. A good strategy is the use of a scavenger hunt, wherein answers can be retrieved through the navigation of the course Web site.
- FAQ (Frequently Asked Questions)— Adding to FAQs is an ongoing process as the course evolves. All instructors recognize that if one student has a question, another student in that semester, or perhaps in a later semester, may have the very same one.
- Scope Notes—These are very brief descriptions of each navigational button or link on the main or home page of a Web site. "(W)hen a user first encounters these navigational labels on a site's main page, he or she will get a sense of their meaning from their accompanying descriptions " (Rosenfeld & Morville, 1998).
- Course Schedule— Many students suggested that all of the assignments and their due dates should be in one location. Typically, this will be located in the syllabus. For quick access, however, a course schedule on the Web site is an effective method.
- Assignments versus Course Documents—In many cases, these two sections are the same. Create an Assignments section that contains all of the instructions and assessment tools for each assignment and eliminate the use of the term Course Documents.

EDUCATIONAL IMPORTANCE OF THE STUDY

Findings of this study are limited in generalizability. Our sample size was small; we used a sample of convenience, and the survey provided only categorical data, thus limiting the depth of our analysis. The results of this study, however, identify a clear and pervasive problem of substantial magnitude, which underscores an urgent need for the development of research-based conventions for organizing course materials within a Web-based instructional environment. Confusion with the Web-based course interface could lead to time away from learning or can potentially lead to a negative effect on overall student satisfaction with both the course and the instructor.

Is this a big problem? There are currently 300 courses listed using the same Web-based course development tool at the university where we conducted this study. Assuming 20 students per course, this dissonance is affecting approximately 6000 students and some 250 to 300 instructors at just one university. The manufacturer of one Web-based course management tool states that their software is installed in 3300 institutions. What are the implications?

If we extend the results of this survey to the 300 courses and 6000 students at this single university, approximately 1500 students will look for their assignments under a heading other than Assignments and they will not find the assignments. How will they usually seek to resolve their problem? One possible solution is to send an email to the instructor requesting the location of the assignments. That means 1500 students will send a note that requires instructors to respond to 1500 emails for a combined total email traffic of 3000 messages for one misplaced course component. Given the dissonance of the placement of course materials as described in this study, we believe that the 3000 messages described in this simple scenario represent just the beginning of the problem. The magnitude of confusion caused by a lack of research-based standards for the organization of Web-based courses cannot be underestimated.

Given that most Web-based course management tools are textually based, our findings are not surprising. Would a detailed email (i.e., roadmap) from the instructor at the beginning of the course mitigate some of the confusion surrounding course material organization for students? Perhaps. Interviews with faculty who deliver instruction in a Web-based environment point to a more abiding need for a set of research-based conventions for course material organization. Many instructors are drawing upon extensive teaching experience to achieve a "best guess" method of organization. Scope of personal and professional experience varies for instructors as well as students. The mental model for the Web-based instructional environment is not consistent. Furthermore, from a student perspective, course material organization appears arbitrary and therefore confusing, which can result in students perceiving instructors as disorganized.

Merrill and the ID2 Research Group suggest a need for "transaction shells" (1996, p. 36) or a sort of standard for instructional design in a Web-based environment. They define these transaction shells as "a set of instructional algorithms" consisting "of rules for selecting and sequencing knowledge objects" (p. 36). Perhaps, development of similar "transaction shells" for the organization of Web-based course material may direct the actions of instructors who teach in a Web-based environment. It may also limit the early semester confusion and the flurry of discussion list postings or email explanations for all parties in a Web-based instructional environment.

The information architecture and task flow may vary from site to site based upon the Web site's purpose and nature of the information. It would be difficult to standardize Web site design, but we should be able to reach some minimal design conventions (Nielsen, 1999). Rosenfeld and Morville (1998) suggest that to design toward usable Web based courses; we need to escape from our own understanding of content labels and organization, and acknowledge the student's mental model. Therefore, we see a need for more research on matching course content labeling and categorization to the student's understanding and mental model for courses. This research, we believe, has provided a foundation for alleviating student confusion as they attempt to navigate and access critical course content within a Web-based instructional environment.

REFERENCES

Agnes, M. (Ed.). (1996). *Webster's new world dictionary.* New York: Macmillan.

Bailey, S. (1997). Web Architect—Love your labels. *Web review: Cross Training for Web Team.* Retrieved November 26, 2001 from http://www.WebReview.com/1997/02_21/Webauthors/02_21_97_3.shtml

Bareiss, R., & Slator, B.M. (1993). The evolution of a case-based computational approach to knowledge representation, classification, and learning. *The Psychology of Learning and Motivation, 29,* 157-186.

Bernard, M. (Winter/2000). Constructing user-centered websites: The early design phases of small to medium sites. *Usability News.* Retrieved November 26, 2001, from http://wsupsy.psy.twsu.edu/surl/usabilitynews/2W/Webdesign.htm

Bolter, J. D. (1991). *Writing space: The computer, hypertext, and the history of writing.* Hillsdale, NJ: Erlbaum.

Carley, K., & Palmquist, M. (1992). Extracting, representing, and analyzing mental models. *Social Forces, 70*(3), 601-636.

Duffy, T. M., & Jonassen, D. (Eds.). (1992). *Constructivism and the technology of instruction: A conversation.* Hillsdale, NJ: Erlbaum.

Eastmond, D. V. (1995). *Alone but together: Adult distance study through computer conferencing.* Cresskill, NJ: Hampton Press.

Elstein, A. S., Ahulman, L. S., & Sprafka, S. A. (1978). *Medical problem solving: An analysis of clinical reasoning.* Cambridge, MA: Harvard University Press.

Estes, W. K. (1993). Models of categorization and category learning. *The Psychology of Learning and Motivation, 29,* 15-56.

Fiske, J., & Hartley, J. (1987). *Reading television.* New York: Methuen.

Jonassen, D. H. (1991). Objectivism vs. constructivism: Do we need a new philosophical paradigm? *Educational Technology Research and Development, 39(3),* 5-14.

Jonassen, D. H. (1995, October). *Operationalizing mental models: Strategies for assessing mental models to support meaningful learning and design-supportive learning environments.* Paper presented at the Computer Support for Collaborative Learning '95 Conference, Indiana University, Bloomington, IN. Retrieved July 23, 2000, from http://www.civa.indiana.edu/cscl95/jonassen.html

Jonassen, D. H. (2000). Toward a design theory of problem solving. *Educational Technology Research & Design, 48(4),* 63-85.

Kiger, J. I. (1984). The depth/breadth tradeoff in the design of menu-driven interfaces. *International Journal of Man-Machine Studies, 20,* 201-213.

Larson, K., & Czerwinski, M. (1997). Web page design: Implications of memory, structure and scent for information retrieval. *Proceedings of the ACM CHI '97 Conference: Human Factors in Computing Systems,* (pp. 111-117). Retrieved November 26, 2001, from http://www.research.microsoft.com/users/marycz/chi981.htm

LeCompte, M. D., & Preissle, J. (1993). *Ethnography and qualitative design in educational research* (2nd ed.). San Diego, CA: Academic Press.

Lester, P. M. (1995). *Visual communication: Images with messages.* Belmont, CA: Wadsworth.

Merrill, M. D., & ID2 Research Group. (1996). Instructional transaction theory: Instructional design based on knowledge objects. *Educational Technologies, 36(3),* 30-37.

Miller, D. P. (1981). The depth/breadth tradeoff in hierarchical computer menus. *Proceedings of the Human Factors Society,* 296-300.

Piaget, J. (1973). *To understand is to invent* (G. -A. Roberts, Trans.) New York: Grossman.

Pirolli, P., & Card, S. (1995). Information foraging in information access environments. *Proceedings of the Conference on Human Factors in Computing Systems, CHI '95* (pp. 51-58). Denver, CO: ACM Press.

Raufaste, E., Eyrolle, H., & Marine, C. (1998). Pertinence generation in radiological diagnosis: Spreading activation and the nature of expertise. *Cognitive Science, 22(4),* 517-546.

Romiszowski, A. J., & Cheng, E. (1992). Hypertext's contribution to computer-mediated communication: In search of an instructional model. In M. Giardina (Ed.), *Interactive multimedia learning environments.* Berlin: Springer.

Rosenfeld, L., & Morville, P. (1998). *Information architecture for the World Wide Web.* Sebastopol, CA: O'Reilly & Associates.

Vygotsky, L. S. (1978). *Mind in society.* Cambridge, MA: Harvard University Press.

CHAPTER 19

AN INSTRUCTIONAL DESIGN APPROACH FOR EFFECTIVE SHOVELWARE

Modifying Materials for Distance Education

Gary R. Morrison and Gary J. Anglin

There has been a rapid proliferation of online courses and shareable content objects. These courses often include a vast array of information, yet they are not instructionally sound. The primary purpose of this article is to provide a procedure (tool) that will help instructional designers determine if existing e-learning courses and sharable content objects are well designed instructionally, or primarily a collection of information posted as a "course" (shovelware). The procedure employs a reverse engineering approach to produce an analysis of the content and instruction. An instructional design model is then used to determine the instructional adequacy of the materials.

The Perfect Online Course: Best Practices for Designing and Teaching
pp. 359–375
Copyright © 2009 by Information Age Publishing
All rights of reproduction in any form reserved.

AN INSTRUCTIONAL DESIGN APPROACH
FOR MODIFYING MATERIALS FOR DISTANCE EDUCATION

E-learning solutions are rapidly becoming an integral part of many university courses, continuing education programs, and training programs in business, government, and the military. A number of experts predict that, in the training area, the number of courses delivered by technology will increase. Cone and Robinson (2001) suggested that the number of e-learning courses was expected to double by the year 2003. Rosenberg (2000) suggested that the expenditures for courses and programs delivered using technology have increased 66% during the previous 5 years. In the private sector a number of companies are reporting the economic benefits of e-learning. As a result of e-learning solutions, IBM saved $20 million in 1999, while Ernst and Young reduced the cost of training by 35% (Strother, 2002). Strother also makes a strong case that corporations are increasing their emphasis on e-learning solutions.

We believe that is necessary to assure that e-learning trainees and students receive courses and training experiences that are well designed from an instructional standpoint. Cone and Robinson (2001) have identified two problems with e-learning, including "poorly designed e-learning" and "insufficient focus" (p. 2).

In this article we will focus on the problem of poor design or lack of instructional design in e-learning materials. In many cases: (a) training courses, college courses, and other traditional instructional packages are repurposed for use on the Web, or (b) faculty/trainers develop a new course for Web delivery that does not provide adequate instructional support. What really happens in practice? We believe that, for both repurposed courses and newly-developed courses, frequently *information* is collected and assembled in the form of online course syllabi, class schedules, course notes, assignments or projects, PowerPoint slides, or course module. This information is then posted to the Web using software such as WebCT, Blackboard, Lotus Learning Management System, or other software designed for the purpose of delivering e-learning instruction. In addition, threaded discussions, chats, and e-mail are also incorporated as a strategy. We believe that "courses" delivered in this manner are not necessarily instructional, and that they should really be labeled "Web-based information." Little or no instructional design may have been done ensuring that sound instructional strategies are embedded in the instructional materials. Such materials are labeled as shovelware. Shovelware is defined as "content taken from any source and put on the Web as fast as possible with little regard for appearance and usability" (whatis.techtarget.com). For example, an instructor can collect information and shovel it into an application such as Blackboard or a learning management system to create a "course." The key to high-quality instruction rests with effective instructional strategies developed in the context of a sound instructional design model. Good strategies are typically missing from shovelware courses.

The primary purpose of this article is to provide a tool that will help instructional designers determine if existing e-learning courses and sharable content objects are well-designed instructionally, or primarily a collection of information posted as a "course" (shovelware). (We will use the term "course" to refer to modules, sharable content objects, and other forms of instruction.) In addition, we will discuss how the tool can be used to evaluate the instructional soundness of a traditional course that is being repurposed for Web delivery. We label the tool the *instructional disassembler*. We believe that the instructional disassembler tool will help developers ensure that existing e-learning courses are instructionally sound and not just collections of information presented in an e-learning environment. The instructional disassembler tool will also help designers repurpose traditional courses for e-learning environments. In particular, instructional designers can use the instructional disassembler tool to identify the component parts of a course in order to describe the content included and if strategies are incorporated in an existing e-learning course or an existing traditional course. Specifically, the tool will allow the instructional designer to disassemble and examine the content, information, and instructional components included in the course. The designer can then determine if additional or initial instructional design work is required. We will first emphasize the importance of defining the construct of distance education and briefly discuss issues concerning distance education in higher education, business, and the military.

DISTANCE EDUCATION IN HIGHER EDUCATION AND BUSINESS

Distance education has several different definitions that can include either synchronous and/or asynchronous communications. We are using Keegan's (1996) definition in which he makes a distinction between distance education and virtual education. Keegan's definition of distance education separates the learner and instructor in time and location on a quasi-permanent basis. Keegan allows for two-way communication and occasional meetings, but places a greater emphasis on asynchronous communications. When synchronous communications, such as two-way video and audio or satellite delivery systems are the dominant mode of delivery, Keegan labels the delivery as a virtual system rather than a form of distance education. Our focus in this article is on asynchronous distance education courses that require the development of materials *prior* to the start of the course offering and allow for anytime/anywhere learning.

Higher Education

Universities are striving to increase their online offerings to remain competitive in a market that is no longer defined by geographic boundaries between universities. The competition and search for students goes beyond trying to fend off other universities who establish a regional center in your own "backyard" to attract students. Today, a student can take a course from a university located almost anyplace in the world without leaving home. In recent years, we have seen many universities increase their online offerings or create a separate entity for delivering distance education courses. In 1997-1998, there were approximately 50,000 college-level credit courses offered in the United States via distance education (National Center for Educational Statistics, 1999). In 2000-2001, there were approximately 3.1 million enrollments. The number of post-secondary schools offering distance education courses has doubled since 1995 (National Center for Educational Statistics, 2003).

One strategy seen in university courses is the adaptation of existing classroom courses for Web-based delivery. Central to most university-level courses are textbooks that form the basis for many courses. The lectures, exercises, and readings are often wrapped around the textbook to provide a course of instruction. Individualization models such as Keller's Personalized System of Instruction (PSI) often used the textbook as the primary source of information. Similarly, the University of Mid-America and Coast Community College often "wrapped" a distance education course around an existing television program. For example, their introductory psychology course was based on a series of *Psychology Today* films, the poetry course *Anyone for Tennyson* was based on Nebraska Educational Television series by the same title, and the *American Nationalism* radio course was based on series of lectures by Henry Steele Commager. In the last two examples, textbooks were developed to support the television and radio content. Given these examples, it is clear that instructional designers in higher education have repurposed traditional courses and information for distance education delivery for a number of years.

Business and the Military

In business and the military, there is a trend to move instruction from the classroom to the Web by converting the classroom materials for an e-learning environment. One reason for this move to convert traditional courses to Web-based courses is to increase effectiveness (Cone & Robinson, 2001) and to reduce costs (Strother, 2002). Like higher education, businesses often convert traditional courses or simply information into Web-based courses. There are several references on the Internet that describe the conversion of traditional classrooms to e-learning courses in the private sector (e.g., http://www.learningcircuits.org/may2000_elearn.html). Similarly, there is a move in the military to use e-learning as the primary means of course delivery. The U.S. Army lists over 1,500 e-learning courses for training (http://usarmy.skillport.com/).

The Result

Course conversions from the traditional classroom to a Web-based format can take different approaches. For example, rather than providing a lecture, an instructor might provide lecture notes or a PowerPoint presentation on a Website. Another instructor might provide a streaming video of the lectures. Similarly, classroom exercises might be converted to readings rather than attempting to provide an interactive exercise online.

As a result, Web-based courses may include a considerable amount of *information*. The information is accurate and includes much if not most of the information needed by the student. This information, however, is not always "*instructional*." It may not be structured for optimal learning. The instructor and students typically provided the instruction in these courses as they interacted in the classroom. For example in Keller's Personalized System of Instruction (PSI) course, the instructor and tutors provided the additional instruction to help the learner grasp and understand the content. Simply placing the textbook in the hands of the student and the tests online with automatic scoring would neglect the instructional component of the classroom-based course. In some cases, the classroom course was not well designed in the first place. Cone and Robinson (2001) suggest that the failure of many e-learning courses to meet expectations is due to the poor design of the course.

Many e-learning courses are composed simply of information that is stored online using course management software. Is there a way to determine if e-learning courses are instructionally sound or if they are simply shovelware? Is there a way to use an instructional design model to design effective e-learning instruction rather than producing shovelware? How can we as designers improve the effectiveness of instruction that is based on existing print materials without incurring significant costs? In this article, we will describe an instructional design tool that an instructional designer can use to evaluate the instructional components of existing e-learning materials, and convert existing traditional courses and instructional materials for Web-based instruction.

E-LEARNING AND THE ID PROCESS

We believe that traditional instructional design approaches and models have much to offer designers of e-learning courses. One approach is to modify the traditional ID model, which starts with front-end analysis. In a traditional routine use of an instructional design model, initially, a front end analysis is completed and the designer and subject-matter expert work together to define the instructional goals and to define the content needed for the course. The most important aspect of this analysis is the task analysis step, which may seem superfluous with content that is already defined by an existing course. We are proposing a modification of the traditional instructional design model to increase the functionality when evaluating existing e-learning courses and when repurposing traditional courses for Web delivery.

Although the existing course materials already include the content for repurposing to a Web-based course, we cannot neglect the task analysis step. Task analysis helps the instructional designer identify the structure of the content for both traditional and e-learning courses so that appropriate strategies can be developed. However, the traditional task analysis process of working with the subject-matter expert may not be appropriate when repurposing traditional course materials or existing Web-based instruction for e-learning. A process is needed that will help designers determine the content structure of the materials and if the existing content is adequate.

Reverse Engineering the Content

How do we determine if the content of existing traditional courses and print materials is instructionally sound, including the critical information and strategies needed for learning? Reverse engineering is a term used to describe the analysis of an existing product (i.e., a toaster oven) or software to determine the component parts and the function of each. As instructional designers, we suggest using a reverse engineering process to determine the structure of existing e-learning courses as well as materials that will be repurposed for e-learning delivery. "Reverse engineering is the process of analyzing a subject system to (i) identify the system's components and their interrelationships and (ii) create representations of the system in another form or a higher level of abstraction" ("Bibliographic references: Terminology," 1997). A subpart of the reverse engineering process is design recovery that adds domain knowledge and fuzzy logic to the reverse engineering analysis to identify higher abstractions ("Bibliographic references: Terminology," 1997).

Programmers use disassemblers to reconstruct the commands, flow, and logic of compiled programs. This disassembly process is referred to as reverse engineering. A similar process of reverse engineering can be applied to existing instructional materials to identify the structure, information included, and the sequencing of the instruction. This process is a form of task analysis that operates on existing materials rather than the traditional approach in which a subject-matter expert is interviewed.

Reverse Engineering and Existing Task Analysis Models

Jonassen, Tessmer, and Hannum (1999) identified three task analysis methods that have potential for use as reverse engineering tools. These three methods are described in the following paragraphs.

Decompose, Network, and Assess (DNA). The DNA approach is a cognitive task analysis process for eliciting knowledge and skills from experts (Jonassen et al., 1999). The DNA methodology requires a software program that interacts with an expert to decompose the domain knowledge. The elements identified through the decomposition process are then ordered and linked in the networking module. Finally, other experts validate the analysis in the assess module.

DNA is not practical for reverse engineering the existing content, as it depends on interaction with an expert who actively answers questions. Attempting to do the task manually on printed materials would appear to be an extended process with unpredictable results.

Matrix Analysis. This methodology was first introduced as a task analysis method for developing programmed instruction (Evans, Homme, & Glasser, 1962). Thomas, Davies, Openshaw, and Bird (1963) further developed matrix analysis as a reverse engineering process with procedures for analyzing programmed instruction. This process was further refined by Davies (1973). Matrix analysis involves four general steps (see Figure 19.1). First, a rule set is constructed by analyzing each frame of the programmed instruction. Second, the rules are numbered and the numbers are recorded on a diagonal or both axis of a large piece of graph paper (an alternative approach is to use an application such as Excel and shade the cells). Third, each rule is compared to each of the other rules. If a relationship exists between the two rules, then the two cells representing the intersection of these two rules are shaded. Fourth, the matrix is then analyzed to identify content structures such as chains, discriminations,

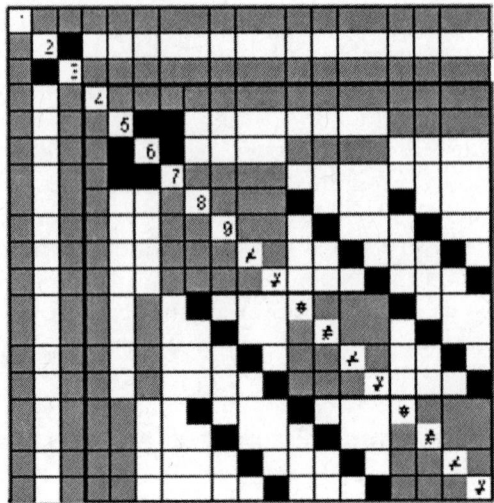

Source: Courtesy of Howard Kalman.

Figure 19.1.   Sample matrix analysis.

concepts, and principles based on the visual pattern created by the shading of the cells.

Although matrix analysis was developed for use with programmed instruction, it may have potential with other types of instructional materials. However, its application may be more difficult due to the lack of the frame structure prevalent in programmed instruction. A drawback to using matrix analysis is the tedious and complex nature of the matrix for complex material.

Syntactic Analysis.   Syntactic analysis is one of the few methods developed to analyze existing materials. Syntactic analysis was developed for analyzing reading and linguistic information. While there are no examples of its application for task analysis (Jonassen et al., 1999), it may have potential as a task analysis method. This method is used to identify tasks and objects (i.e., subject, verb, and modifiers related to the task). The analysis can produce a database of the task units and the related objects. One can then manipulate the database to identify relationships and structures between the subjects, verbs, and modifiers of the various tasks.

Syntactic analysis may reduce the information to too fine of a level for the purpose of task analysis. The value of specifying the subject, verb, and modifiers of each task statement is not readily clear for the purpose of task analysis.

INSTRUCTIONAL DISASSEMBLER TOOL

DNA, matrix analysis, and syntactic analysis all appear to be adaptable to a reverse engineering approach. However, we feel that each of these approaches adds an additional level of complexity. This complexity can translate into additional analysis time and resources that may not be available to the instructional designer or design team working on a shovelware project. We are proposing a simpler approach that we believe can be as effective for the design of Web-based instruction. This approach, the Instructional Disassembler, is used to reverse engineer instructional content or information.

Designers can use the instructional disassembler to determine the content and strategies used in an existing e-learning course or traditional course that will be repurposed as an e-learning course. For example, "shovelwared" courses may or may not include instructional strategies that facilitate learning. Similarly, the content may not be adequate for teaching a concept or principle. The instructional disassembler is a tool for reverse engineering the course into smaller units for identification of the content and strategies. Once disassembled, a designer can determine the effort needed to improve the quality of the course.

Instructional Disassembler. The instructional disassembler is used to break down the existing content in existing e-learning courses, traditional courses, and materials including textbooks or study guides used in a course into component parts. Designers can then analyze the content to determine if adequate information is provided. For example, Tennyson and Cocchiarella (1986) suggest that to teach a concept one needs to include the label (i.e., category name), definition, and one best example. By examining the disassembled content, the designer can determine if these three elements are included for each concept. If they are missing, modifications or additional information can be added, such as a supplemental material.

The effectiveness of this method is highly dependent on the instructional designer. It is assumed that the designer has the expertise to identify content structures such as facts, concepts, principles, rules, and procedures. The designer must also be familiar with strategies one might use to facilitate student learning for each structure. If two or more designers disassemble the same content, we would expect them to negotiate differences in their interpretations.

Using the Instructional Disassembler

Disassembling content, information, and instruction involves three steps. *First* is the disassembly of the content. *Second* is identifying content structures. *Third* is analyzing the instructional adequacy of the content. The following sections detail each of these steps.

Disassembly of Content. Disassembling content, information, and instruction are all done using the same approach. This step of the process is similar to the traditional task analysis used when designing instruction. However, disassembly is done on *existing e-learning or traditional course* materials rather than starting with a blank slate and querying a subject-matter expert. The process starts by breaking the content into the smallest units possible (we are using the term content to include instruction, content, and information). These units or phrases are then recorded in a traditional outline format. Major sections such as first-level headings are assigned to the highest level (i.e., I, II, III) of the outline. Information within the section is then placed in the sublevels of the outline (i.e., A, B, C, 1, 2, 3).

The following are heuristics for disassembling the information.

1. Break each idea into its simplest form. Disassembling should result in phrases or single idea units rather than complex sentences. That is, a single sentence might be reverse engineered into several smaller idea units.

2. The outline produced by the disassembling does not need to reflect the same sequence as the information. Idea units may be reordered to reflect "raw" content that is organized around knowledge structures rather than instructional strategies or elaborated writing.

Consider the following example concerning the concept "loan discount" that includes the disassembly of the content information. First, the "raw" content is presented. Second, the disassembled content for "loan discount" is listed.

Loan Discount ("raw" content): Also often called "points" or "discount points," a loan discount is a one-time charge imposed by the lender or broker to lower the rate at which the lender or broker would otherwise offer the loan to you. Each "point" is equal to one percent of the mortgage amount. For example, if a lender charges two points on a $80,000 loan this amounts to a charge of $1,600. (U.S. Department of Housing and Urban Development, 1997)

C Loan Discount (disassembled content)
    1. A one-time charge imposed by lender or broker
        a). Lowers rate of the loan
    2. Often called points or discount points
        a). Each point is equal to 1 percent of the mortgage amount

3. Example
   a). Lender charges two points on a $80,000
    loan
    (1). The charge is $1,600

Notice how the first sentence, "Also often called 'points' or "discount points,' a *loan discount* is *a one-time charge imposed by the lender or broker* to *lower the rate* at which the lender or broker would otherwise offer the loan to you," was disassembled into three idea units.

Another example of content disassembly is presented in Tables 19.1 and 192. In Table 19.1, selected content information included in a document describing how to buy a home is presented (U.S. Department of Housing and Urban Development, 1997). The disassembled content for the mortgage document is presented in Table 19.2.

An examination of element B, loan origination, illustrates the guidelines presented. First, the complex sentences are disassembled into individual idea units. Second, the disassembling organizes the information in a logical manner *rather* than the sequence used to present the content. By following a logical sequencing, we can group related idea units that will make it easier to identify the content structures.

The two remaining steps to complete are "Identifying Content Structures" and "Determining the Adequacy of Instruction."

Identifying Content Structures

Once the content is dissembled, the designer can identify the content structures in the instruction. The Instructional Disassembler uses the con-

Table 19.1. Buying Your House Document

Buying your Home (Mortgage Document)

800. Items Payable in Connection with Loan: These are the fees that lenders charge to process, approve and make the mortgage loan:

801. Loan Origination: This fee is usually known as a loan origination fee but sometimes is called a "point" or "points." It covers the lender's administrative costs in processing the loan. Often expressed as a percentage of the loan, the fee will vary among lenders. Generally, the buyer pays the fee, unless otherwise negotiated.

802. Loan Discount: Also often called "points" or "discount points," a loan discount is a one-time charge imposed by the lender or broker to lower the rate at which the lender or broker would otherwise offer the loan to you. Each "point" is equal to one percent of the mortgage amount. For example, if a lender charges two points on a $80,000 loan this amounts to a charge of $1,600.

Table 19.2.   Disassembly of Document on Buying a House

Mortgage Document Disassembled

I. Items payable in connection with load
   A. Fees lenders charge to
      1.) Process
      2.) Approve
      3.) Make the mortgage
   B. Loan Origination fee
      1.) Known as loan origination fee
         a.) Sometimes called point or points
         b.) Often expressed as a percentage of the load
         c.) Fee varies among lenders
      2.) Covers lenders administrative costs of covering the load
      3.) Generally buyer pays the fee
         a.) May be negotiated
   C. Loan Discount
      1.) A one-time charge imposed by lender or broker
         a.) Lowers rate of the loan
      2.) Often called points or discount points
         a.) Each point is equal to 1 percent of the mortgage amount
      3.) Example
         a.) Lender charges two points on a $80,000 loan
            (1.) The charge is $1,600

tent structures from Morrison, Ross, and Kemp's (2004) expanded performance-content matrix to identify the content structures. The following explains each of these structures.

Expanded Performance-Content Matrix. The matrix (Morrison et al., 2004) identifies six types of content. First are facts that are associations between two items. For example, C is the chemical symbol for carbon is a fact with an arbitrary association between C and carbon. Second are concepts that are categories of similar things. Gloves, doors, windows, and torts are examples of concepts that encompass similar things. The third category consists of rules and principles that express a relationship between concepts or direct behavior, such as prediction. Fourth are procedures that are a sequence of steps for accomplishing a goal, such as calculating the square footage of a room or how to apply varnish. The fifth category encompasses interpersonal skills, such as correct procedures for answering the telephone and communication with one or more other individuals. Sixth are attitudes which are a predisposition to respond to in a consistent manner (Fishbein & Ajzen, 1975), such as one's attitude towards taking company office supplies.

Identifying Text Structures. The next step is to identify these six content structures in the content disassembly outline. This process requires the instructional designer to chunk the content and identify examples of these structures. When a content structure is found, it is labeled on the outline. After the disassembly of the content and identification of the content structures, an analysis of the instructional adequacy of the content is conducted.

Analyzing the Adequacy of the Content

The next step is to determine the instructional adequacy of the content for the distance education environment. To accomplish this task, we will use the design strategies from Morrison et al. (2004). Designers are not limited to this model for determining the instructional adequacy of the content. They can select any instructional design model or set of heuristics that provide detailed instructional strategies.

Before we can begin to determine the instructional adequacy of the content, we must define the objectives for the materials. These objectives can be stated as either behavioral or cognitive objectives.

In this section, we will describe the minimum content required to teach each of the structures (e.g., facts, concepts, principles, etc.). The requirements are divided into two categories (Morrison et al., 2004). The first structure is the presentation or initial presentation in which the content is presented to the learner. Second is a generative strategy or practice that helps the learners integrate the new information into their existing schema. The following paragraphs describe the minimum content requirement for each of the content types.

Facts. Facts are associations that are taught at the recall level. There are two minimum requirements for teaching a fact. First is a concrete representation of the fact through either direct experience, such as visiting a fire station or by stating an abstract fact such as "Nashville is the capital of Tennessee" by creating a map with a star indicating Nashville. Second is rehearsal and practice or a generative strategy such as a mnemonic device.

Concepts. The minimum requirements for teaching concepts are described by Tennyson and Cocchiarella (1986). First, the presentation of the concept must include the concept name, definition, and best example. Second, a generative strategy such as generating new examples and nonexamples is needed.

Principles and Rules. There are two approaches to presenting a principle or rule to a learner. First is the Eg-Rule approach that provides the learner with several examples and then asks the learner to state the rule. Second is Rule-Eg that presents the learner with the rule and then illustrates the rule with several examples (Markle, 1969). Examples of appropriate generative strategies needed to teach principles and rules include paraphrasing and elaboration strategies.

Procedures.   Procedures are a series of ordered steps one must complete to do either a cognitive or psychomotor task. The presentation consists of a model of the performance, which could vary from a live or videotape demonstration to printed materials illustrating the steps with pictures and text. As an example, Sweller and Cooper's (1985) worked examples are often used to model procedures. The generative strategy involves having the learner develop a mental model of the procedure and then practicing the procedure.

Interpersonal Skills.   Interactions between two or more people are examples of interpersonal skills. Bandura's (1977) social learning theory describes the four minimum requirements for instruction on interpersonal skills. First is providing the learner with a model of the interaction. This model might include a live or videotape example, a role-play, or case study. Second is encouraging the learners to develop a verbal and imaginal model of the interaction. Third is providing the students with a scenario for mental rehearsal. Fourth is overt practice through such activities as role-playing or supervised interactions.

Attitudes.   The minimum requirements for teaching attitudes are the same four criteria as for interpersonal skills: model, develop verbal and imaginal mode, mental rehearsal, and practice.

Determining the instructional adequacy of the content requires the evaluation of each content structure identified in the previous step. Using the minimum criteria stated in the previous paragraphs, the designer determines the adequacy of each occurrence of each content structure. Notes are made indicating any inadequacies in the presentation or generative strategy.

USING THE DISASSEMBLER TOOL
TO EVALUATE EXISTING E-LEARNING MATERIALS

The Instructional Disassembler can also be used to evaluate existing instructional materials. For example, a designer who incorporates sharable content objects might use the Instructional Disassembler to analyze and evaluate an object. An instructional designer can use the same process to determine the adequacy of the content and the appropriateness of the instructional strategies. Evaluating instruction with the Instructional Disassembler is a three-step process. First, the instruction is disassembled into the smallest parts. Second, the content structures are identified in the disassembled content. Third, the instruction is evaluated for adequacy and appropriateness. The designer must use a design model as previously described to determine if minimum content to teach the content structures (e.g., fact, concept, principle, etc.) are present in the task analysis. Then, the instructional strategies for teaching the content are evaluated for accuracy against the prescriptions the designer has developed or that are provided as part of an instructional design model. Another application of this process is to construct metadata ("Scorm Best," 2003) for sharable content objects. The analysis produced by the disassembler will identify the key points of the object that can then be use to create the metadata.

USING THE DISASSEMBLER TOOL
TO REPURPOSE EXISTING INSTRUCTION

The results of the instructional disassembly form the basis for making instructional design decisions for the new delivery method. There are two approaches to improving the adequacy of the content and instruction.

First, if the designer has control of the original documents, that is, they were produced by an instructor, subject-matter expert (SME), or design team, then the documents can be modified. Additional content can be added to improve the content quality and appropriate instructional strategies can be integrated to improve the instructional adequacy of the material.

Second, if the content is part of a book or other copyrighted material that cannot be modified, then supplementary materials similar to a study guide are needed to improve the content and instructional adequacy of the materials. For example, a study guide approach might direct the students to read a few pages in the book. Or, an additional online book could be produced that summarizes the text information and includes discussion questions. Then, the learner's attention is redirected to the study guide where additional content and/or instructional strategies are presented to supplement the book.

SUMMARY

In this article we have presented a tool for instructional designers to use when determining if existing e-learning "courses" and materials or traditional courses that are to be ported to the Web are sound from an instructional design perspective. The tool allows the instructional designer to disassemble the content, identify the content structure, and analyze the adequacy of the content and instructional strategies. While this approach is detailed and time consuming, it provides a more thorough instructional design evaluation than a simple of review of the materials by subject-matter experts.

ACKNOWLEDGMENTS

The authors would like to thank Katherine M. Kuhn and Howard Kalman for their comments on the manuscript.

REFERENCES

Bibliographic references: Terminology. (1997). Retrieved from http://www.cc.gatech.edu/reverse/bibliography/terminology.html

Bandura, A. (1977). *Social learning theory*. Englewood Cliffs, NJ: Prentice-Hall.

Cone, J. W., & Robinson, D. G. (2001). The power of e-performance. *Training and Development, 55*(8), 32-41.

Davies, I. K. (1973). *Competency based learning: Technology, management, and design*. New York: McGraw-Hill.

Evans, J., Homme, L., & Glasser, R. (1962). The RULEG system for the construction of programmed verbal learning sequences. *Journal of Educational Research, 55*(9), 513-518.

Fishbein, M., & Ajzen, I. (1975). *Belief, attitude, intention, and behavior*. Reading, MA: Addision-Wesley.

Jonassen, D. H., Tessmer, M., & Hannum, W. H. (1999). *Task analysis methods for instructional design*. Mahwah, NJ: Erlbaum.

Keegan, D. (1996). *Foundations of distance education* (3rd ed.). London: Routledge.

Markle, S. (1969). *Good frames and bad: A grammar of frame writing*. New York: Wiley.

Morrison, G. R., Ross, S. M., & Kemp, J. E. (2004). *Designing effective instruction* (4th ed.). New York: Wiley.

National Center for Educational Statistics. (1999). *Distance education at postsecondary education institutions: 1997-98*. (No. NCES 2000-013). Washington, DC: U.S. Department of Education.

National Center for Educational Statistics. (2003). *Distance education at degree-granting postsecondary institutions: 2000-2001*. Retrieved February 2005, from http://nces.ed.gov/pubsearch/pubsinfo.asp?pubid=2003017

Rosenberg, M. (2000). E-learning: strategies for delivering knowledge in the digital age, New York: McGraw-Hill.

Scorm best practices guide for content developers. (2003). Retrieved February, 2005, 2005, from http://www.lsal.cmu.edu/lsal/expertise/projects/developersguide

Strother, J. (2002). An assessment of the effectiveness of e-learning in corporate training programs. *International Review of Research in Open and Distance Learning*. Retrieved July 17, 2002, from http://www.icaap.org/iuicode?149.3.1.x

Sweller, J., & Cooper, G. (1985). The use of worked examples as a substitute for problem solving in algebra. *Cognition and Instruction, 2*, 59-89.

Tennyson, R. D., & Cocchiarella, M. J. (1986). An empirically based instructional design theory for teaching concepts. *Review of Educational Research, 56*, 40-71.

Thomas, C., Davies, I., Openshaw, D., & Bird, J. (1963). *Programmed learning in perspective: A guide to programmed writing.* Chicago: Educational Methods.

U.S. Department of Housing and Urban Development. (1997). *Buying your home: Settlement costs and helpful information.* Retrieved October 24, 2001, from http://www.pueblo.gsa.gov/cic_text/housing/settlement/sfhrestc.html

whatis.techtarget.com. (n.d.). Retrieved October, 2001, from http://whatis.techtarget.com /definition/0,sid9_gci212982,00.html

CHAPTER 20

INVESTIGATING THE USE OF ADVANCE ORGANIZERS AS AN INSTRUCTIONAL STRATEGY FOR WEB-BASED DISTANCE EDUCATION

Baiyun Chen, Atsusi Hirumi, and Ning Jackie Zhang

It is synthesized that advance organizers (AOs)—an effective orienting device in traditional classroom instruction—may enhance students' information literacy in self-directed online classes. The current study investigated 2 types of advance organizers, graphic and text, in a fully Web-based undergraduate course of health care ethics. Both the short-term and long-term effects were examined. Although the results failed to find a statistically significant difference regarding learning performance among treatment groups and the control group, additional qualitative data indicated that students held overwhelmingly positive attitudes toward using AOs, especially the graphic AOs, in online learning. The analyses and results of this study added new empirical evidence for the use of AOs in Web-based distance education and posited new directions for further research.

The Perfect Online Course: Best Practices for Designing and Teaching
pp. 377–388

In fully Web-based courses, the use of multimedia resources often brings challenges of cognitive overload and learner disorientation (Dias & Sousa, 1997). While learners enjoy the flexibility and abundance of Internet resources, they may also be overwhelmed with multiple tasks and sources of information. Effective online teaching and learning strategies have been widely perceived as potential solutions to the learning challenges (Bonk & Dennen, 2003). These strategies include, but are not limited to, advance organizers, debate, cases, scavenger hunt, and guest experts. However, there is limited research on integrating teaching and learning strategies in fully Web-based environments. While many studies have shown no significant difference between online courses and traditional face-to-face courses, applying traditional learning strategies at a distance leaves a great deal of uncertainty (Howell, Williams, & Lindsay, 2003).

PURPOSE OF THE STUDY

The present study investigated short-term and long-term effects of two kinds of advance organizers (AOs) in a fully Web-based course. A concept map was used as a visual AO, and an outline was used as a text AO. Students' learning achievement in knowledge acquisition and application was tested both immediately and 4 weeks after the experiment. Specifically, this study is designed to explore the effectiveness of AOs in improving students' learning performance in a fully Web-based course.

THEORETICAL FRAMEWORK

The rationale for using AOs is rooted in cognitive learning theories. Cognitive theories state that learning performance depends on processing capacity and prior knowledge (Driscoll, 1999). With the aid of AOs, learners are able to link what they already know to new information and apply it to new contexts.

Ausubel first introduced the concept of advance organizers in his assimilation theory of meaningful learning and retention. Based on Ausubel's theory and the later studies on AO (Ausubel, 1968; Kenny, 1993; Mayer, 1979; Stone, 1983), a framework has been synthesized to predict the effectiveness of AOs. The theoretical framework includes the following key propositions: students given advance organizers should perform better in tests on the material to be learned than students in control groups; the advance organizer effect should be at least as great in longer studies as in shorter ones; the graphic advance organizers should be at least as effective as the text advance organizers.

Extensive research was conducted on the effectiveness of using AOs in classroom teaching from the 1960s to the 1990s. The research evidence concerning any facilitative effect of AOs upon learning and retention is variable, but positive in general. Although Ausubel's early experiments supported the effectiveness of AOs with significant increasing learning achievement (Ausubel, 1968), later studies failed to show a consistent positive facilitative effect (Barnes & Clawson, 1975; Luiten, Ames, & Ackerson, 1980; Mayer, 1979; Stone, 1983).

In the 1990s and 2000s, many researchers began to conduct studies on AOs in a variety of formats, such as visual AOs (DaRos & Onwuegbuzie, 1999; Herron, Hanley, & Cole, 1995; Hirumi & Bowers, 1991; Millet, 2000) and multimedia AOs (Calandra, Lang, & Barron, 2002; Hale, 2003; Minchin, 2004; Tseng, Wang, Lin, & Hung, 2002; Yeh & Lehman, 2001). Failing to generate statistically significant results on effectiveness of AOs, most researchers continued to suggest a mild but positive effect of AOs on learning and retention. The statistical nonsignificance of the research might be attributed to imprecise construction of organizers, short duration of treatment, inadequate research control, and insufficient instruction on how to use AOs (Kenny, 1993; Luiten et al., 1980; Mayer, 1979).

HYPOTHESES

Two hypotheses were posited for this study.

Hypothesis I.   There is no difference in the short-term knowledge-based and performance-based learning achievements among students in the concept map, outline, and control groups.

Hypothesis II.   There is no difference in the long-term knowledge-based and performance-based learning achievements among students in the concept map, outline, and control groups.

METHODS

Subjects

The population of this study consisted of 164 undergraduate students enrolled in a fully Web-based, health-related ethics class at the University of Central Florida. The students were largely between the age of 21-23, in

$R E_1$	X_1 (Graphic Organizer)	O_1	O_2
$R E_2$	X_2 (Text Organizer)	O_3	O_4
$R C$	(No Advance Organizer)	O_5	O_6

Figure 20.1.   Research design diagram.

either their junior or senior years. The enrolled students were asked to participate in this study on a voluntary basis. Sixty-three of the total 164 students voluntarily participated in the experimental activities.

Research Design

This study used an experiment-control posttest-only design with random assignment to examine the effects of AOs on learning achievements, as illustrated in Figure 20.1.

R indicated that all participants were randomly assigned to three groups, two treatment groups (E_1 and E_2) and one control group (C). AOs were the intervention in this experimental design. The experimental group (E_1) reviewed a concept map, a form of graphic AO, before reading the textbook. The comparison group (E_2) reviewed a text AO, and the control group (C) did not read any AO before textbook reading. During the course of the study, all three groups completed an immediate posttest (O_1, O_3, and O_5) and a delayed posttest (O_2, O_4, and O_6).

Dependent and Independent Variables

One of the dependent variables in this study is students' learning achievement, encompassing their short-term (O_1, O_3, and O_5) and long-term knowledge acquisition and application learning achievements (O_2, O_4, and O_6). The short-term and long-term knowledge acquisition was tested with two corresponding 12-item knowledge quizzes. The short-term and long-term knowledge application was tested with problem-based scenario essay questions.

The independent variable is the treatment of AOs (X_1 and X_2). The three groups had the same instruction, except for the treatment of AOs. The experimental group was intervened with a concept map (X_1); the comparison group was intervened with a textual outline (X_2); and the control group had no AO exposure before textbook reading.

Time is a confounding variable for the research which has been used to distinguish the short-term and long-term impacts of AOs. It is assumed that the time factor might influence students' learning achievement over a period of 4 weeks' time.

Advance Organizers

Two forms of AOs were designed respectively for the experimental and comparison groups. The construction of the AOs followed a series of research-based procedures (Bricker, 1989; Mayer, 1979; West, Farmer, & Wolff, 1991). Students were instructed to review the AOs before they read the textbook. The graphic AO is a flash-based interactive concept map. The text AO presents the same concepts and explanation as the concept map. Both AOs are linked to the instruction page of module 2. The only difference between the two organizers is the presentation of the relationship among the concepts. The concept map illustrates the relationship visually in a nonlinear way, and the textual outline presents it textually in a linear way. The validity of these AOs was tested and confirmed by expert reviews from both the instructor and the outside instructional designers, and modifications were made based on their suggestions.

INSTRUMENTS

This study utilized three major instruments: posttest I, posttest II, and a student survey. Posttest I and II are parallel in content and format, with a 12-question, multiple-choice quiz examining concept acquisition and three open-ended questions based on a scenario, testing knowledge application. Posttest I measured students' short-term learning achievement, and posttest II measured their long-term learning achievement. The student survey contained 18 multiple-choice questions on students' prior online learning experience, study environment, use of concept maps, use of quiz, and demographic information. One additional open-ended question collected further comments from student participants.

PROCEDURES

This study lasted for 6 weeks. During the first week of the 2006 Spring semester, participants were randomly assigned to three groups. Each group was provided with one version of module 2 during week two. In the course module, the students were suggested to first review the AOs to gain an overall idea of the key concepts and issues covered in this module, if they had one available in their group. The students in the experimental group reviewed the multimedia concept map before reading the book. The students in the comparison group reviewed the text outline before reading the book. The students in the control group were not given an AO, and they proceeded directly to textbook reading.

After textbook reading, the students were instructed to complete all the assignments on the assignment page, including the two parts of the post-test I. The knowledge quiz of posttest I was a timed WebCT quiz. The students had 15 minutes to complete 12 multiple-choice questions and they could access and submit the quiz only once. However, as this was a fully Web-based course, the quiz was not proctored and students had the flexibility to do the quiz at their convenience during the instruction week. For the second part of posttest II, the students completed three questions based on a scenario using Microsoft Word and submitted the assignment to the WebCT Assignment tool by the next Monday morning. Also during this week, students filled out an online survey to report their background information and their uses of AOs.

Four weeks after module 2, in week six, posttest II was administered through WebCT. Together with all the other assignments for module 6, posttest II, including a quiz and three scenario questions, was open for the students. It was stated in module 6 that both the quiz and scenario questions of posttest II were part of the voluntary research. The students completed this posttest with the knowledge they had learned in module 2.

ANALYSES

Statistic procedures, including descriptive analysis, one-way analysis of variance (ANOVA), and repeated-measure regression were performed to study the research findings. Descriptive analysis was used for scores in the posttests. Means, standard deviations, and effect sizes of students' learning achievement scores were computed for each quiz and scenario questions of posttest I and II. The assumptions of the analysis, including the homogeneity of variance and the normality of population distributions, were examined using the Levene's test and the Q-Q plot procedures. Descriptive analysis was also used to calculate the frequencies which describe how students had used and liked the advance organizers.

To test the two hypotheses, ANOVA was used to compare the mean scores of the posttests among the three groups. In combination with the AO effects, this study examined other factors that might influence students' learning achievement using repeated-measure analysis of covariance (ANCOVA). These factors include students' weekly study time, study place, gender, academic status, ethnicity, grade point average, and so forth.

FINDINGS

Hypothesis I

In posttest I, students of group 1 using a concept map had the highest mean score (36.25) in the knowledge quiz 1, compared with those of the other two groups. In the performance-based scenario questions, there was little difference in the mean scores of the three groups. Table 20.1 illustrates the detailed means and standard deviations of students' learning outcomes in posttest I.

Hypothesis I suggests that students who were exposed to a concept map AO or an outline AO would show no difference, in both the short-term knowledge-based and performance-based learning achievements, from those who were not exposed to an AO. Table 20.2 shows that there is no statistically significant difference among the three groups in either the knowledge quiz ($F_{2, 122} = 1.130$, $\alpha > 0.05$) or the performance scenario

Table 20.1.   Means and Standard Deviations of Posttest I Scores

		Group				
		1	2	3	Total	Full Score
Quiz 1	M	36.25	32.67	33.89	34.15	60
	SD	9.59	11.46	10.60	10.64	
Scenario 1	M	22.55	22.87	22.28	22.55	25
	SD	2.43	2.33	2.25	2.33	

Note: Group 1—Experimental group with concept map; Group 2—Comparison group with outline; Group 3—Control group.

Table 20.2.   Tests of Between-Subject Effects in Posttest I

Source	Type III Sum of Squares	df	Mean Square	F	P value	Partial Eta Squared
Quiz 1	255.452	2	127.726	1.130	.327	.018
Scenario 1	63.326	2	31.663	.412	.664	.009

Table 20.3.   Means and Standard Deviations of Posttest I Scores

		Group				
		1	*2*	*3*	*Total*	*Full Score*
Quiz 2	*M*	29.04	30.95	30.76	30.36	60
	SD	11.32	6.86	8.40	8.71	
Scenario 2	*M*	23.29	22.23	24.10	23.17	25
	SD	3.62	5.57	2.77	4.21	

Note: Group 1—Experimental group with concept map; Group 2—Comparison group with outline; Group 3—Control group.

Table 20.4.   Tests of Between-Subject Effects in Posttest II

Source	*Type III Sum of Squares*	*df*	*Mean Square*	*F*	*P value*	*Partial Eta Squared*
Quiz 2	63.326	2	31.663	.412	.664	.009
Scenario 2	37.13	2	18.565	1.051	.356	.034

questions ($F_{2, 137}$ = 0.412, α > 0.05). Also, the effect sizes for AOs in both tests are relatively low. Only 1.8% of the differences in quiz 1 scores can be explained by the treatments of AO among the groups. Less than 1% of the difference in scenario 1 scores can be explained by the use of AO.

Hypothesis II

In posttest II, there are little variations in the mean scores in either quiz 2 or scenario 2 questions. The control group outscored the AO treatment groups by less than 1 point in both tests. Table 20.3 shows the means and standard deviations of the students' learning outcomes in the delayed posttest.

Similar to the findings in the short-term learning achievement posttest I, the difference in posttest II is not statistically significant in either the knowledge-based quiz ($F_{2, 95}$ = 0.412, α > 0.05) or the performance-based scenario questions ($F_{2, 60}$ = 1.051, α > 0.05). The effect size of AO in quiz 2 is below 1%. The effect size of AO in scenario questions 2 is 3.4%, far below 20%, which is indicative of a small effect by the Cohen's convention.

DISCUSSIONS

The research findings show that there is no difference in either the short-term or long-term learning achievements among students in the concept map, outline, and control groups. According to Ausubel's assimilation theory, students given AOs should perform better on tests on the material to be learned than students in control groups (Ausubel, 1968). In the current study, students in the concept-map group outscored the other groups by 3-4 points out of a total 60 points on average in the immediate knowledge quiz (posttest I). The difference in performance-based scenario questions was small among the three groups. The full score for the scenario questions was 25, and the mean scores for all of the groups were around 22.5, indicating a ceiling effect that the assessment instrument may lack sensitivity and discrimination in measuring learning outcomes. The control group scored at an average of 22.28 out of 25 on the scenario questions. There was less than 3 points (12%) of improvements for the treatment groups to achieve. Similar to the historical studies on AOs in face-to-face classes, no statistically significant difference was found in either the knowledge-based or the performance-based tests in this Web-based AO study.

It is speculated that the AO effect might be more observable in longer period of study time, especially in the ones over 10 days, than in shorter ones (Ausubel, 1968; Luiten et al., 1980; Stone, 1983). However, this study failed to prove a greater AO effect on students' learning achievements in a delayed posttest (posttest II) 4 weeks after the AO intervention. The differences in both the knowledge-based and the performance-based tests were trivial, and the effect sizes were considered to be small and below 0.05 by the Cohen's convention. Similar to posttest I, a lack of differentiation might be one of the reasons that attribute to the nonsignificant result in posttest II. Also, in the posttest, students reported a shortage of time during the quiz, and over 50% of the students made errors in the last two quiz questions. Therefore, speeding effect, where students did not have sufficient time to answer all questions, might be another factor that seriously affected the measuring error of the quiz instrument.

Most of the students found using AOs, especially the concept map, helped them scaffold the learning materials. Their feedbacks in the survey indicated how they used AOs in learning. The majority of the students would read AOs before they read the textbook. They spent, on average, 6-10 minutes reading the concept map, and would usually refer back to the concept map during or after they read the textbook. For the text outline, the student would spend 1-5 minutes reading, and read it only once. According to the survey results, this study demonstrated how AOs could be integrated in Web-based distance learning, and the concept map was better received by the students compared with the text outline.

IMPLICATIONS AND RECOMMENDATIONS

This study is an attempt to validate Ausubel's AO theory in fully Web-based learning environment. However, the findings did not support Ausubel's proposition that students given AOs performed better in tests than students in the control group. Moreover, the AO effect in long-term tests of this study was not as great as in shorter ones, as Ausubel had predicted. On the other hand, the graphic AO was as effective as the text AO in this study, which evidenced one of Ausubel's propositions. Specifically, students using a concept map (graphic AO) consistently achieved higher scores than those using a text outline (text AO). Students and the instructor also preferred the concept map to the outline, despite that the contents for both AOs were identical. The visual elements and interactivity of the concept map were favored by students in Web-based learning, and the outline was regarded as static and linear.

The practical significance of this study lies in that it has updated and improved the AO conceptual framework to fit the new Web-based learning environment. The original Ausubel's model was first developed for the face-to-face classroom setting where the blackboard is the main teaching medium. The framework had been constantly modified by later researchers to further investigate the methods for constructing and applying an AO in a computer-based instruction environment in the late 1980s and early 1990s. In the new century, school learning is enhanced and optimized with the explosive development of emerging Internet technologies and diversified digital media. However, the research on AOs in fully Web-based learning is very limited. The current study expands the AO framework to a fully Web-based environment. The use of advance organizers is a good teaching and learning practice in the context of self-paced online learning. Students will benefit from using AOs not only in a traditional classroom, but also in the ever-growing Web-based learning environment.

In retrospect, this study might have been improved. The statistical insignificance of students' performance between AO groups and the control group might be due to several reasons. One of the issues that the researcher found is that an online quiz is difficult to monitor. Though the quizzes had been designed as closed-book tests and test questions were randomized, it was possible that students still referred to their lecture notes and the textbook while they took the quizzes. This might seriously threaten the validity of the test instruments. An important implication for further research is to develop measures to prevent students from referring to other assistant materials. Another reason for the nonsignificant result might be the lack of measurement of students' analytical and critical thinking abilities. Future studies should develop stricter rubrics to differentiate students' learning outcomes in the assessment instruments. Also, the limited intervention time might be a factor that negatively influenced the effectiveness of AO. The current AO intervention was one week. For future studies, longer intervention time is highly recommended.

The participatory AO (student-generated AO) is the new direction for future studies on AOs in Web-based learning. Students might interact with the material to be learned more in depth with the help of participatory AOs, thus making the materials easier for them to comprehend and use. Recently, new instructional concept mapping tools have become available for instructors and students to create digital organizers in computer-assisted instruction and online education. For example, the Visual Understanding Environment (VUE) and the C-Map are two free information management applications that provide an interactive concept mapping interface. Future Web-based AO research studies can take advantage of these free AO tools, focus on helping students generate their own advance organizers, and measure the effectiveness of participatory AOs in both face-to-face and Web-based educational settings.

REFERENCES

Ausubel, D. P. (1968). *Educational psychology: A cognitive view.* New York: Holt, Rinehart, & Winston.

Barnes, B. R., & Clawson, E. V. (1975). Do advance organizers facilitate learning? Recommendations for further research based on an analysis of 32 studies. *Review of Educational Research, 45,* 637-659.

Bonk, C. J., & Dennen, V. (2003). Frameworks for research, design, benchmarks, training, and pedagogy in Web-based distance education. In M. G. Moore & W. G. Anderson (Eds.), *Handbook of distance education* (pp. 331-348). Mahwah, NJ: Erlbaum.

Bricker, E. J. (1989). *The effect of advance organizers in the teaching of science.* Unpublished masters thesis, Kean College, NJ.

Calandra, B. D., Lang, T. R., & Barron, A. E. (2002, February). *Assessing Holocaust education: Preservice teachers' knowledge and attitude.* Paper presented at the annual meeting of the Eastern Educational Research Association, Sarasota, FL.

DaRos, D., & Onwuegbuzie, A. J. (1999). The effect of advance organizers on achievement in graduate-level research methodology courses. *National Forum of Applied Educational Research Journal-Electronic, 12E*(3), 83-91.

Dias, P., & Sousa, A. P. (1997). Understanding navigation and disorientation in hypermedia learning environments. *Journal of Educational Multimedia and Hypermedia, 6*(2), 173-185.

Driscoll, M. P. (1999). Meaningful learning and schema theory. In M. P. Driscoll (Ed.), *Psychology of learning for instruction* (2nd ed., pp. 113-151). Needham Heights, MA: Allyn & Bacon.

Hale, J. B. (2003). *The effect of two graphic organizers on learning performance and computer anxiety in a Web-enabled training lesson for navy enlistees.* Unpublished doctoral dissertation, University of South Alabama.

Herron, C. A., Hanley, J. E. B., & Cole, S. P. (1995). A comparison study of two advance organizers for introducing beginning foreign language students to video. *The Modern Language Journal, 79*, 387-395.

Hirumi, A., & Bowers, D. R. (1991). Enhancing motivation and acquisition of coordinate concepts by using concept trees. *Journal of Educational Research, 84*(5), 273-279.

Howell, S. L., Williams, P. B., & Lindsay, N. K. (2003). Thirty-two trends affecting distance education: An informed foundation for strategic planning. *Online Journal of Distance Learning Administration, 6*(3).

Kenny, R. F. (1993, January). *The effectiveness of instructional orienting activities in computer-based instruction.* Paper presented at the Association for Educational Communications and Technology, New Orleans, LA.

Luiten, J., Ames, W., & Ackerson, G. (1980). A meta-analysis of the effects of advance organizers on learning and retention. *American Educational Research Journal, 17*(2), 211-218.

Mayer, R. E. (1979). Twenty years of research on advance organizers: Assimilation theory is still the best predictor of results. *Instructional Science, 8*(2), 133-167.

Millet, C. P. (2000). *The effects of graphic organizers on reading comprehension achievement of second grade students.* Unpublished doctoral dissertation, University of New Orleans.

Minchin, J. I., Jr. (2004). *Meeting needs of information technology students: The development of an in-service training model using graphic and advanced organizers to improve instruction in the information technology classroom.* Unpublished doctoral dissertation, Robert Morris University, Moon Township, PA.

Stone, C. L. (1983). A meta-analysis of advanced organizer studies. *Journal of Experimental Education, 51*(4), 194-199.

Tseng, C., Wang, W., Lin, Y., & Hung, P. -H. (2002, December). *Effects of computerized advance organizers on elementary school mathematics learning.* Paper presented at the International Conference on Computers in Education.

West, C. K., Farmer, J. A., & Wolff, P. M. (1991). *Instructional design: Implications from cognitive science.* Boston: Allyn & Bacon.

Yeh, S. -W., & Lehman, J. D. (2001). Effects of learner control and learning strategies on English as a foreign language (EFL) learning from interactive hypermedia lessons. *Journal of Educational Multimedia and Hypermedia, 10*(2), 141-159.

CHAPTER 21

STREAMLINING THE ONLINE COURSE DEVELOPMENT PROCESS BY USING PROJECT MANAGEMENT TOOLS

M'hammed Abdous and Wu He

Managing the design and production of online courses is challenging. Insufficient instructional design and inefficient management often lead to issues such as poor course quality and course delivery delays. In an effort to facilitate, streamline, and improve the overall design and production of online courses, this article discusses how we implemented Microsoft Project 2003, based on our online course development framework and online course development approaches. This article represents an attempt to approach online course development from a systematic perspective, using Microsoft Office Project Server 2003 (Enterprise Project Management) in a higher education environment.

INTRODUCTION

According to the latest Sloan-C annual report (Allen & Seaman, 2006), more than 96 percent of large institutions have some online offerings

The Perfect Online Course: Best Practices for Designing and Teaching
pp. 389–399

(with more than 3.2 million students). Online course delivery has become a key alternative to face-to-face delivery. With students expecting and demanding anytime, anywhere access to courses, higher education institutions are increasing and diversifying their course offerings by combining hybrid, online, and face-to-face courses to attract nonresidents and adult learners. In order to be responsive to students and to market needs, and yet remain competitive and forward-looking, universities are investing heavily in the design and production of online courses (Bartolic & Bates, 1999).

However, design and production of quality online courses requires a streamlined workflow and the collaboration of several specialists (subject-matter, instructional, technical) working together in a team environment (Phillips, 2005). There are many requirements and concerns related to the design and production of online courses including time management, resource assignment, formative evaluation, quality control, and revision of courses (Chao, Saj, & Tessier, 2006). Thus, managing efficiently and effectively the design and production of a large number of courses is challenging and sometimes daunting. Furthermore, when planning the delivery of online courses, the issue of course quality remains a major concern for many colleges and universities (Chao et al., 2006). Insufficient instructional design and inefficient management of the design and production process of online courses often lead to issues such as poor quality course design, unavailable resources, budget shortfall, and course delivery delay. Hence, to be successful, establishing an effective and efficient management process to produce online courses is crucial.

In response to these management challenges and in an effort to facilitate, streamline, and improve overall design and production of online courses, we developed an online course development framework and identified four different approaches for online course design and production. This framework and theses approaches are based on an extensive literature review, expert evaluations, and years of experience in designing and developing hybrid, synchronous, asynchronous, CD-ROM, two-way video, and online courses. Furthermore, to manage these four approaches in a systematic way and to address issues such as planning, collaboration, quality, resources, and time management, we integrated the four approaches with the Microsoft Office Project Server 2003 (Enterprise Project Management or EPM) based on our practical online course development framework. The purpose of this article is to share our experience in streamlining and systematizing online course design and production by blending project management practices with a comprehensive online course development framework and operational course development approaches (Kenny, Zhang, Schwier, & Campbell, 2005; Layng, 1997; Litchfield & Keller, 2002).

By opting for a systematic approach to planning, designing, and producing online courses facilitated by EPM, we anticipate that our approach of blending project management and online course development practices will position us to reach the following goals:

1. Increase our unit's ability to keep up with the ever-increasing demands for online course/program development, regardless of their size, duration, and complexity, and to eventually shorten the current course development cycle;

2. Optimize the resource usage by creating a common course development framework and project workspace, as well as standardized managing, reporting, and tracking processes across all our project teams;

3. Transform our unit into a learning organization by creating a body of knowledge around online course development (e.g., content collection templates, production toolkit, and quality assurance checklists);

4. Facilitate knowledge transfer (Disterer, 2002) among projects by retaining past project lessons and easily retrieving/reusing them in future projects in order to refine and improve our internal processes;

5. Use EPM as an enabling tool to promote organizational culture change (Partington, 1996) and thus transform our staff into reflective practitioners (Crawford, Morris, Thomas, & Winter, 2006) able to learn, adapt and progress in their daily tasks and routines.

ONLINE COURSE DEVELOPMENT FRAMEWORK

Our project management methodology was developed based on the work of a number of researchers and acknowledges the cyclical nature of online course development (Jiang & Heiser, 2004; Phillips, 2005). A significant benefit of this approach is that it provides an opportunity for all stakeholders to understand their responsibilities and roles. This lifecycle approach is translated into the diagram below, which outlines the phases, roles, assumptions, and risks associated with online course design and production. Our online course development framework identifies seven sequential/iterative phases broken down into subtasks:

1. Preplanning (Project Definition): during this phase the project director clarifies the project scope, deliverables, and expectations. This phase requires senior leadership involvement and approval to

specify the foundations, support, and resources for subsequent phases.

2. Planning: in this phase the project manager (Instructional Designer) works closely with faculty to clarify roles, time commitment, expectations, and risks.

3. Analysis: this phase is dedicated to completing the course requirements and readiness analysis. Several premade templates are used during this process to facilitate content collection and to ensure consistency between projects.

4. Design and Prototype: during this phase the emphasis is on finalizing the interface and completing a representative prototype to assist in producing the course content. This phase requires intensive communication among all the team members to ensure a rigorous testing and quality assurance process. In our approach, quality assurance is an iterative and ongoing process built in to each phase of the development, using tailored checklists.

5. Production: this phase is the longest period of the process. After testing and approving the prototype, team members produce the course content incrementally or simultaneously. Each segment is produced, reviewed, and approved by faculty and the project manager.

6. Postproduction: this phase prepares faculty to teach online by attending workshops and seminars and by preparing course delivery documentation. In addition to this, this phase provides the opportunity to identify, capture, and document lessons learned and to review and update project templates.

7. Delivery: in the last phase, faculty and student feedback about the course, the content, the layout, and the activities is collected. This feedback is used to improve future course offerings and development.

In addition to outlining the subtasks of each phase, this diagram is designed to summarize our unit's overall conceptual and operational framework. This framework is extremely useful in presenting and sharing our processes and assumptions with university administrators, faculty and staff involved in online course development. By sharing up-front our development timeline (6 months), roles, assumptions, risks (lack of content, nonrespect of timeline) and expectations, we reduce miscommunication and contribute to the success and completion of the program/course development.

ONLINE COURSE DEVELOPMENT APPROACHES

As a learning organization, the Center for Learning Technologies enjoys the reputation of gathering under the same umbrella a pool of talent and experts in online course design and development. Our extensive experience includes designing and producing dozens of courses for a variety of delivery modes (hybrid, synchronous, asynchronous, CD-ROM, two-way video). To capture our experience in a systematic way, we conducted a number of weekly meetings with instructional designers, instructional technologists, graphics designers, multimedia designers, and video production managers to identify and capture their knowledge and experiences with the design and production of online courses. Drawing from this pool of talent and after going through several iterations of reviews and improvements, we identified four different approaches to online course development. These approaches are categorized with relevance to complexity of overall instructional design and multimedia production. Depending on the pedagogical goals and requirements of each online course, we work together with faculty to decide the choice of the approaches. Our objective is to reach the highest level of both faculty and student satisfaction with online courses, based on the available resources we have. As shown in the table, the shift of requirements between instructional design and multimedia development is dictated by the level of effort required for each approach. For example, approach D generally requires more time and higher effort than other approaches for online course development such as the creation of syllabus, course introduction, course objectives, learning activities and interaction.

By presenting this matrix, we are able to share with our faculty and administrators another tool that clarifies our quality, commitment, and workload requirements.

MICROSOFT OFFICE PROJECT SERVER (EPM)
AS A MANAGEMENT TOOL

Along with EPM, there are several project management software programs on the market such as BaseCamp (http://www.basecamphq.com/), GForge (http://gforge.org/), and Maven (http://maven.apache.org/). However, we decided to use EPM because it is widely used in business and industry. Many organizations shared successful experiences for deploying and implementing this tool. In their study about the factors influencing the usage and selection of project management software in industry, Liberatore and Pollack-Johnson (2003) mentioned that Microsoft Project was

Online Program/Course Development A Non-Linear, Cyclical, Iterative, and Dynamic Process: Timeline, Phases, Roles and Risks

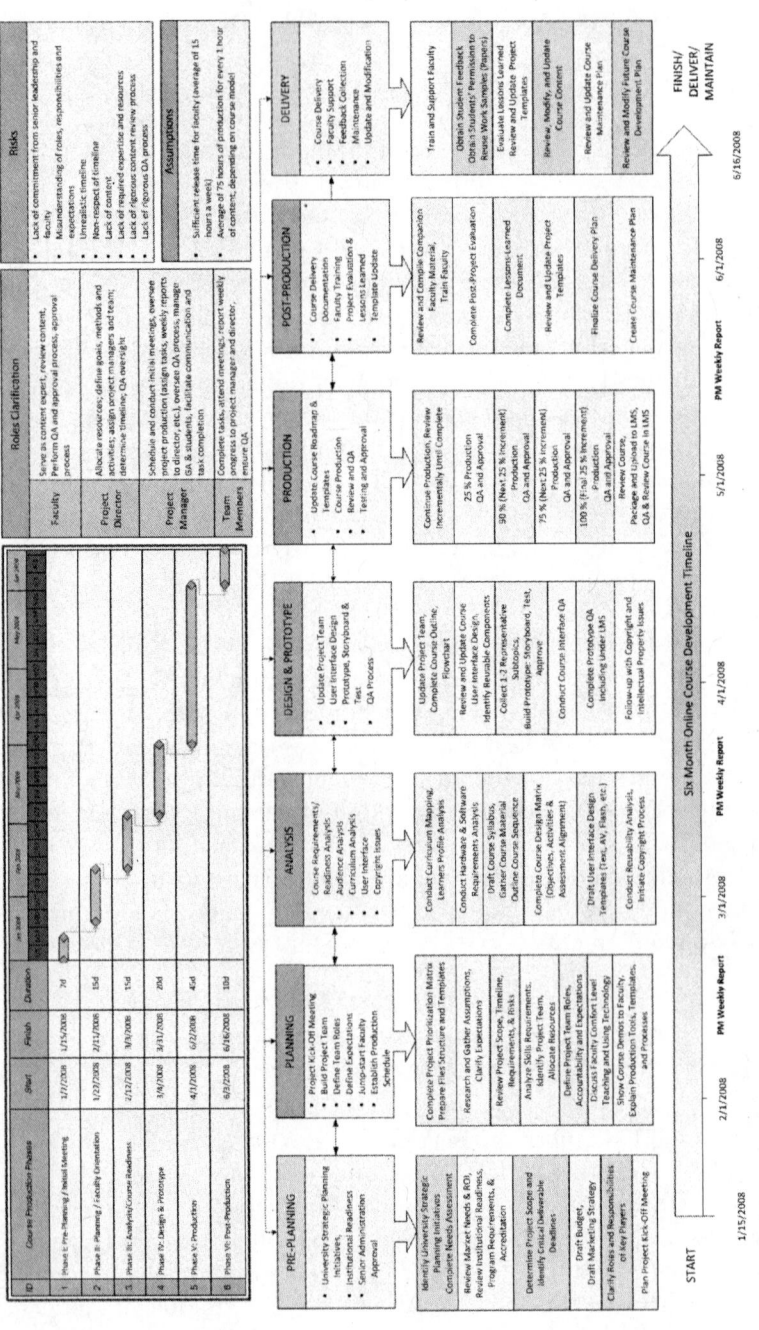

Figure 21.1.   Online course development framework.

Course Components	Approach A			Approach B			Approach C			Approach D		
	ID	TG	A/V,A	ID	TG	A/V,A	ID	TG	A/V,A	ID	TG	A/V,A
Syllabus	Low	Minimal	Minimal	Low	Low	Low	Low	Low	Medium	High	Low	Medium
Course Introduction	Low	Minimal	Minimal	Low	Low	Low	Low	Low	High	High	High	High
Course Schedule	Minimal	Minimal	No	Low	Low	No	High	Low	No	High	Medium	No
Course Objectives	Minimal	Minimal	No	Low	Low	No	Medium	Low	Low	High	Medium	Medium
Modular Content Presentation	Minimal	Low	Minimal	Low	Low	Low	Medium	Medium	Medium	High	High	Medium
Learning Activities(e.g.,)	Minimal	Low	Minimal	Low	Low	Low	Medium	Medium	Medium	High	Medium	Medium
Interaction (student/student and student/content)	Minimal	Minimal	No	Low	Minimal	No	Medium	Low	Low	High	Medium	Medium
Interaction (student/instructor)	Minimal	Minimal	No	Low	Low	No	Medium	Low	Low	High	Medium	Medium
Assessment	Minimal	Minimal	No	Low	Low	No	Medium	Medium	Medium	High	Medium	Medium
Reflection by whom?	Minimal	Minimal	No	Low	Low	No	Medium	Low	No	High	Medium	Medium
Relevance to what?	Minimal	Minimal	No	Low	Low	No	Medium	Low	No	High	Medium	Medium
Resources	Minimal	Minimal	Minimal	Low	Low	Low	Low	Medium	Medium	High	Medium	Medium
Estimated Development Time	1.5 months			2 months			4 months			6 months		

Legend:

(empty circle)	(quarter-filled circle)	(half-filled circle)	(three-quarter-filled circle)	(filled circle)
No effort	Minimal Effort	Low Effort	Medium Effort	High Effort

ID:	TG:	A/V,A:
Instructional Design	Text & Graphic	Audio/ Video & Animation

Figure 21. 2. Online course development approaches by level of efforts.

used by nearly 50% of respondents, followed by Primavera Project Planner (P3) at 21%, all others at 5% or less.

EPM is project management software designed to assist project managers to develop plans and timelines, assign resources to tasks and, more importantly, track progress, manage budgets, and track team members' workload. Although project management as a field of practice has accumulated an extensive body of knowledge and wide industry-based experience, it is still largely absent from higher education institutions (Shenhar, 1999). Wierschem and Johnston (2005) note that academia has historically lagged behind in the adoption of new information technology products such as project management. In this regard, we posit that the organizational culture of higher education institutions and the disconnection between instructional design models and project management practices are among the barriers that impede the adoption and the integration of EPM solutions in higher education.

Guided by our online course development framework and the level of effort associated with each approach, we created a project plan template for each approach. As a first step, new courses are categorized under one of the four approaches (Approach A, B, C, or D), based on the pedagogical goals and requirements, course timeline, and budget and administrative support (individual versus departmental). Following this, we select the appropriate project plan template, detailing the tasks associated with each phase. Each heading is broken into subtasks, displaying information about: task identification number, indicators (related information), task names, task duration, task start and finish dates, task relationships, and team members assigned to the task.

Team members use a Web interface where they can view and update their tasks and progress on a weekly basis. Project managers review project status and progress reporting by task or resource for a selected period. Basically, the Web project space provides a shared space for project templates and related documents.

PRELIMINARY LESSONS LEARNED

Informed by the above online course development framework, four online course development approaches, and strong project management tool, we believe our approach to streamlining and systematizing online course development is innovative and promising. Our framework, approaches, and EPM implementation are still permeating our organization's processes and practices. However, we have gained some valuable insights and learned some early lessons. We believe that sharing these lessons will be useful for those practitioners who are considering using EPM in a higher education environment.

Senior Leadership Support

By expressing strong commitment and support to our EPM implementation, our senior leadership contributed greatly to the creation of a supportive organizational culture and environment. Indeed, He, Means, and Lin (2006) report that having a supportive organizational culture and environment is vital for the success of project implementation. However, we are mindful that change management requires attentive listening and consideration to staff involved in the implementation. As Folger and Skarlicki (1999) point out, change usually generates skepticism and resistance in personnel, making it sometimes difficult or impossible to implement organizational improvements. Consequently, before designing the system, we spent considerable effort in cultivating the support of the staff members by continuously meeting to develop common understandings, listening to feedback, and addressing specific benefits, issues, and concerns. These regular meetings with stakeholders kept the implementation of the EPM on track and alleviated several predictable concerns about the viability of the project management solution.

Staff Training

In addition to the staged approach of the implementation, staff training was at the center of our implementation process. Using EPM causes a somewhat steep learning curve at the beginning. We therefore organized several training sessions targeting users' categories (project managers and team members). In addition, we provided several handouts and tutorials, while encouraging all staff members to share their experiences and knowledge using EPM.

Server Configuration, Documentation, and Backup

Setting up and configuring the project server properly is a time-consuming and complex process. EPM installation requires specialized skills in Web server administration and server and database administration (Microsoft Windows Server, Internet Information Services, SharePoint Services, and Microsoft SQL). After several failed installations, we decided to document every step of our installation, particularly the customized changes and fixes gathered through the different newsgroups. In addition to this, we made a backup of the server after each installation milestone.

CONCLUSION AND FUTURE WORK

By blending a systematic approach to planning, designing, and producing online courses with EPM, we consider our approach to be robust and promising. We expect to transform our unit into a flexible learning organization capable of building flexible knowledge both on streamlining and on producing high quality online courses in an efficient and effective way. Early results indicate a high level of student and faculty satisfaction with our online courses. In this regard, and from a research perspective, this article highlights the need for research to investigate the efficacy of our integrative approach and, in particular, the efficacy of project management practices in improving the overall efficiency and effectiveness of online course development. In addition to this, research is needed to investigate the validity of our online course development approaches. Finally, our article is also intended to initiate a discussion about using EPM as a management tool for online program development.

REFERENCES

Allen, I. E., & Seaman, J. (2006). *Making the grade: Online education in the United States, 2006*. Retrieved February 12, 2007, from http://www.sloan-c.org/publications/survey/pdf/making_the_grade.pdf

Bartolic, S., & Bates, A. (1999). Investing in online learning: potential benefits and limitations. *Canadian Journal of Communications, 24*, 349-366.

Chao, T., Saj, T., & Tessier, F. (2006). Establishing a quality review for online courses. *Educause Quarterly, 29*(3).

Crawford, L., Morris, P., Thomas, J., & Winter, M. (2006). Practitioner development: From trained technicians to reflective practitioners. *International Journal of Project Management, 24*, 722–733.

Disterer, G. (2002). Management of project knowledge and experiences. *Journal of Knowledge Management, 6*(5), 512-520.

Folger, R., & Skarlicki, D. (1999). Unfairness and resistance to change: hardship as mistreatment. *Journal of Organizational Change Management, 12*(1), 35-50.

He, W., Means, T., & Lin, G. (2006). Tracking and Managing Field Experiences in Teacher Development Programs. *International Journal of Technology in Teaching and Learning, 2*(2), 134-147.

Jiang, B., & Heiser, D. (2004). The eye diagram: A new perspective on the project life cycle. *Journal of Education for Business, 80*(1), 10-16.

Kenny, R. F., Zhang, Z., Schwier, R.A., & Campbell, K. (2005). A review of what instructional designers do: Questions answered and questions not asked. *Canadian Journal of Learning and Technology, 31*(1), 9-26.

Layng, J. (1997). Parallels between project management and instructional design. *Performance Improvement, 36*(6), 16-20.

Liberatore, M., & Pollack-Johnson, B. (2003). Factors influencing the usage and selection of project management software. *IEEE Transactions on Engineering Management, 50*(2), 164-174.

Litchfield, B. C., & Keller, J. M. (2002). Instructional project management? In R. A. Reiser & J. V. Dempsey (Eds.), *Trends and issues in instructional design and technology* (pp. 168-182). Columbus, OH: Merrill.

Partington, D. (1996). The project management of organizational change. *International Journal of Project Management, 14*(1), 13-21.

Phillips, R (2005). Pedagogical, institutional and human factors influencing the widespread adoption of educational technology in higher education. In H. Goss (Ed.), *Balance, fidelity, mobility? Maintaining the momentum? Proceedings of the 22nd ASCILITE Conference*. Brisbane, Australia: Queensland University of Technology. Retrieved February 16, 2007, from www.ascilite.org.au/conferences/brisbane05/blogs/proceedings/62_Phillips.pdf

Shenhar, A. J. (1999). Strategic project management: The new framework. *Management of Engineering and Technology, 1999. Technology and Innovation Management. PICMET '99. Portland International Conference* (Vol. 382, pp. 382-386).

Wierschem, D., & Johnston, C. (2005). The role of project management in university computing resource departments. *International Journal of Project Management, 23*, 640-649.

CHAPTER 22

THE LEARNING CONTRACT PROCESS

Scaffolds for Building Social, Self-Directed Learning

Naomi R. Boyer

The advent of online learning has created a demand for structures to facilitate the construction of knowledge, the formation of learning communities, and the reinforcement of adult learning pedagogies. Therefore, this study investigates the instructional design necessary to develop social, self-directed learning processes in an online course. Educational Leadership master's students (81 subjects) participated in this 3-phase action research study. Self-directed learning tools, learning styles, meta-cognitive approaches, and specialized content framed the virtual, social learning experience. Using scaffolds to assist with an autonomous group learning process was found to be very successful, increasing student satisfaction and overall learning outcomes.

The Perfect Online Course: Best Practices for Designing and Teaching
pp. 401–422
Copyright © 2009 by Information Age Publishing

INTRODUCTION

This article focuses on the online classroom space in which social, self-directed learning scaffolds were used to improve course outcomes, enhance student satisfaction, and extend course impact. Social learning theory emphasizes the import of the contextual social environment and the exchange that occurs between an individual, his or her surroundings, and other people (Berk & Winsler, 1995). Learning is not only tied to the context in which it is embedded, but also to relationships with others. The act of knowing in social learning theory becomes mediated by the competences that are displayed in social communities (Wenger, 2000). Communities have also been found to be contextual in nature, varying from setting to setting involving attitude, thought, and interest.

While many have noted the benefits of interaction and social exchange in online courses, the integration of tools associated with self-directed, adult learning philosophies have been relatively ignored. Therefore, the defining question for research is as follows: What content framework is conducive for developing social, self-directed learning processes in an online course? An action plan was established and continually revised during three consecutive semesters in a master's level course, "EME 6425: Microcomputer for School Managers," offered by the University of South Florida, Lakeland, to investigate the facilitation of social, cooperative development; online engagement; and self-directed learning philosophies. Within course iterations, new tools were added to better scaffold the experience, raise expectation, and allow for personal exploration.

The Virtual Classroom

Virtual learning has been built on the foundation of "anytime/anyplace" and, while some learning experiences can be developed along these lines, most courses require timelines and assignments. Realistically, students can work from anywhere in the world in an online class at any time during the day that they choose (unless there is a pre-determined synchronous "real-time" portion of the course). However, in some circles "anytime/anyplace" has been interpreted as an independent learning experience; one in which students only have to follow a scripted experience and complete all assignments by the end of a specified time frame. Timelines, interaction, and goal orientation are often an integral part of a learning experience and therefore virtual structures cannot be non-existent and limitless. When interaction and group involvement are integrated into an online course, students become responsible for both their own learning and assisting in the learning of others (Harasim, Hiltz, Teles, & Turoff, 1995).

The infusion of a collective focus into the instructional design and learning experience can reinforce the walls of the virtual classroom. The development of collaborative learning, "an interactive group knowledge-building process" (Harasim et al., 1995, p. 4) that assists learners in actively constructing knowledge in conjunction with the views and perspectives shared by others is being instituted in many online environments. Learning in this manner is often quite discombobulating and requires strong safety measures to secure all members of the experience. The use of community can also negate the isolation that often accompanies many independent, correspondence courses (Brown, 2001).

The safety paraphernalia required within a virtual construction learning zone are usually established by the instructor or facilitator of the course. Role designation, interaction guidelines, respect, and trust all act as safety and security elements, reinforcing the fundaments necessary for higher levels of learning. Role designations or role discussions are often advisable for online classes to limit logistical difficulties in certain non-visual, asynchronous environments that tend to be characteristic of the virtual classroom (Harasim et al., 1995). Guidelines for interaction can provide a listing of expectations while expressing the import of interchange within the isolation of virtual learning activities. As stated by Harasim et al. (1995), "Group learning and the obligations it entails may not be familiar or comfortable at first.... A positive attitude and considerate behavior will generally help all students become productive group members in the online environment" (p. 207). Learning communities thrive in settings where there are feelings of belongingness and a sense of trust (Rovai, 2002).

Interaction has also been found to be critical to community building online. Being engaged has been conceptualized as a mode of belonging and interaction as a medium for active involvement (Brown, 2001; Wenger, 2000). Curtis (2001) has conceptualized successful collaboration in face-to-face settings as possible in an online learning environment. Interaction in an online course is developed by instructor-created pedagogical structures that guide student learning. Therefore, interaction becomes hinged on course design and intended outcomes rather than the virtual medium by which the curriculum is shared (Rovai, 2002). Interaction online becomes the means of vital perspective sharing, product development, and connectedness to the greater learning objective.

Virtual Community Creation

Group learning, learning communities, and collaborative environments have become a necessary fundament of increased productivity in the business sector, education and other fields. The age of knowledge has mandated the need for greater intellectual problem-solving capacity than exists within the individual. The power of many can accomplish more than the power of one, with diverse perspective and unprecedented ingenuity. To this end, community and community learning have become the focus of much attention. Community has been hypothesized to be context specific, adapting, and mutating based upon the setting and purpose (Hill, 1996; White & Weight, 2000). Therefore, the assumption that online communities are distinct from in-person communities can also be made.

What are classroom/learning communities? According to Rovai (2002), classroom communities can be defined as having spirit, displaying trust, engaging in interaction, and sharing learning experiences. These components can be replicated, given the appropriate course/learning structure, in virtual settings as well as in the physical environment. "Experienced online instructors can also build and sustain levels of community that are at least equal to those experienced in traditional classrooms" (Rovai, 2002, p. 52). Of course, factors such as student personalities and individual input agents mediate overall learning outcomes, but providing guiding structure for community development forces a collective element into the learning process.

Positive virtual classroom communities have the following components according to Collison, Elbaum, Haavind, and Tinker (2000): participants post regularly, members' needs are accommodated and honest opinions are expressed, teaching occurs, participant-to-participant collaboration with spontaneous moderation emerges from a variety of roles, reasonable venting is acceptable, and participants show concern and support for the community. Instructors and course designers need to provide the structures for these elements to develop (Brown, 2001; Ko & Rossen, 2001; Palloff & Pratt, 2001). Expecting these characteristics to emerge naturally is unrealistic and akin to starting a construction project without a basic set of blueprints to guide the process. "Constructing a course that allows these naturally occurring processes to unfold greatly enhances the learning outcome and the process of community building" (Palloff & Pratt, 2001, p. 33). One way to encourage the creation of online communities is to provide collaboration-type learning goals for groups to explore together as well as require joint learning outcomes rather than independent assignments.

Communities of practice have been described by Wenger (2000) as the building blocks of a social learning system. Within communities of practice, competence is linked to a shared sense of completion and accountability, establish mutually accepted relationships that are transmitted through interaction, and share a culture of resources, language, routines, etc. (Wenger, 2000). To prepare a structure open enough for individual exploration yet closed enough for the establishment of communities of practice, a scaffold must be applied to the overall learning experience that allows for the development of adult competencies through a means that enhances cooperative thought and action. This scaffold must also be flexible and adaptive enough to allow for student socio-cultural/socio-cognitive development.

Within the designed framework, the support structure for individual *and* collective growth potential must also accommodate assessment procedures that measure collective learning objectives. As stated by Derry and DuRussel (2000), "much of the work within learning communities is project-oriented and inquiry based rather than curriculum driven, the goals of instruction are variable across individuals and groups and are largely determined by learners themselves" (p. 2). Sharing information and resources created by group endeavor increases the capacity for self-assessment (White & Weight, 2000). The conceived framework not only supports the building of social learning, but also specifies the measurement of outcomes for competence, usability, and overall completion of the intended objectives.

Self-Directed Learning and the Virtual Classroom

Knowles (1975) defined self-directed learning as "a process in which individuals take the initiative, with or without the help of others, in diagnosing their learning needs, formulating learning goals, identifying human and material resources for learning, choosing and implementing appropriate learning strategies, and evaluating learning outcomes" (p. 18). Key components of Knowles' (1986) adult learning concept of andragogy are interaction, task centeredness, individualization, and self-directedness (Lane, 1997), and are applicable regardless of the learning setting.

Self-direction has been considered to be a function of the "socially-independent or isolated learner, to distance education methods, and to the techniques employed as well as the psychological process" (Long, 2000, p. 22). Blending andragogy and self-direction with a group focus is an interesting concept given the specific focus on individualization and self-directedness. White and Weight (2000) note, "Working adults may be self-directed, but they also value the exchange of ideas and meaningful relations" (p. 43).

Knowles (1986) has suggested that adults have a deep psychological need to be self-directing and designing educational programs toward this end increases the ownership of the learning experience. Evidence indicates that when "adults learn on their own initiative they learn more deeply and permanently than what they learn by being taught" (Knowles, 1986). Experienced educators have noted in a study by Schrum (2002) that providing flexibility within online courses can help students be responsible for their own learning. Students who become empowered to control their own learning experience become transformed as individuals and therefore more engaged in their own learning process (Moore & Kearsley, 1996; Lane, 1997; Palloff & Pratt, 1999).

The architecture of the virtual classroom appears to be more aesthetically pleasing and more structurally satisfying to learners who are more mature and self-directed (Moore & Kearsley, 1996; Palloff & Pratt, 2001). However, along with the non-traditional nature of the learner who is successful and satisfied with the online setting comes the need for an upheaval of traditional classroom hierarchies. Encouraging adults to plan and complete educational experiences modifies traditional role schematics (Harasim et al., 1995; Palloff & Pratt, 1999, Schrum, 2002). The role transition of instructor position provides the opportunity to incorporate adult learning frameworks within the online experience.

The Scaffold: Platform for the Learning Structure

As a group of learners construct a learning experience, it must be remembered that each of the individuals is in control of his or her own engagement, and yet the overarching project must be formed from the juncture of commonality. To frame the social experience, a loose-fitting structure must be applied that illuminates the style of each learner, sets a course of action, and specifies what successful completion entails. The term "scaffolding" has been used by scholars (Berk & Winsler, 1995) to describe teaching pedagogies that focus on the zone of proximal development (ZPD), as introduced by Vygotsky (1978). The ZPD can be defined as the discrepancy between current level of psychological and cognitive functioning and the potential level that can develop with expert guidance (Hung, 2002). This concept was originally developed in regard to children; however, it has bridged age delimitations into adult learning schematics (Alfred, 2002). The establishment of scaffolds to support novice learners coupled with a steady progression to remove structure as students gain knowledge, confidence, and skills can increase independence and encourage self-regulated patterns (Dabbagh, 2003). Scaffolding can be established as a support system within the virtual classroom, to assist learners in moving from one level to the other.

The learning contract process suggested by Knowles (1986) provides the basic platforms for structuring individual learning. There are eight steps to the learning contract process: diagnose learning needs, specify learning objectives, specify learning objectives and resources, specify evidence of accomplishment, specify how the evidence will be validated, review of the contract, carry out the contract, and evaluation of overall learning. Each of these levels of planning, action, and review, coupled with an instructor-provided supply of general content objectives, tools, guidance when needed, and materials or resources can be established as a framework for learning in online environments. The use of learning contracts can reduce some of the difficulty faced by instructors that attempt to design online programs that are more self-directed rather than control oriented (Moore & Kearsley, 1996).

While traditionally this learning design has been formulated as part of individual experience, it is equally valuable to a joint learning encounter. Learning contracts have been used in a conventional manner in a variety of disciplines including but not exclusive to: nursing programs, adult education programs, independent studies, social work, staff development programs, clinical learning, organizational learning, and management development. The use of learning contracts has been found to be highly effective in face-to-face settings that promote an individualistic approach to the learning experience (Knowles, 1986; Huff, 1998; Beitler, 2000; Waddell, 2000).

Learners may need to diagnose their own learning interests, but the juncture where a group's needs meet is the foundation for the community project. The struggle through course material and medium can actually enhance the group buy-in and connectedness (Palloff & Pratt, 1999). The initial process of the learning contract construction, particularly the diagnosing of needs, objective selection, strategy identification, and product designation are critical to the process, and it is suggested here that these steps be completed during a face-to-face orientation session rather than in the virtual classroom space.

The Scaffold: Connecting Content to the Learning Process

The platforms provided by the learning contract process must be connected together, in order to provide a stable footing and general understanding for the self-directed learner. Understanding of self and others can provide a conduit to higher levels of interaction and group learning.

Schrum (2002) noted that "Individuals must be able to recognize their own abilities and styles, in order to ask or modify the learning necessary for online environments" (p. 61). Developing a basic reference of how the individual members of a learning community conceptualize information and are motivated to make decisions (this includes values and emotional preferences), makes it possible for the collective to accommodate the individual (Palloff & Pratt, 2001). Utilizing an ongoing meta-cognitive awareness process for continually adjusting personal learning styles to group dynamic can be valuable for online learning.

Knowledge of learning style issues also allows instructors to prepare materials and resources that provide a means for all learning preferences to thrive. For example, those learners who love the structure and step-by-step guidance of clear directions and expectations can have a choice of prescriptive activities from which to select. Others may prefer to learn through trial and error and exploration or to receive excessive information for internalization. According to Palloff and Pratt (2001), "Because it is difficult for an instructor to know the learning styles of his or her students in advance, creating a course that is varied in its approaches can help to motivate all students and keep them involved" (p. 112). When groups establish their own objectives and plan products through the learning contract process, the use of learning style information can then connect the course content to a group's overall creation of learning, support without controlled prescription.

Researching a Work in Process

Investigating the success of the scaffold suggested above as a means of providing a global overall structure to a social, online learning experience requires the use of research techniques that can be integrated into the learning process. "Action research aims at solving specific problems within a program, organization, or community" (Patton, 2002, p. 221). The problem presented as part of this research project was reconciling the concept of self-directed philosophies with collaborative groups in an online environment. Therefore, active investigation of created content, learning structures, context, learning outcomes, community dynamic, successes, and challenges are necessary. The online environment is appropriate for the ongoing nature of action research, where iterative design decisions can be used to enhance online learning community environments (Lock, 2003).

Data collection, data analysis, evaluation of results, and further planning is ongoing throughout an action research project (Razik & Swanson, 1995). The researcher during the action research process is a practitioner and member of the activity being researched (Glickman, Gordon, & Ross-Gordon, 1995). A collaborative classroom environment with clear focus of problem, continuous data collection, and reflective evaluation could be considered appropriate for action research opportunities. The virtual classroom then becomes a logical application of action research possibilities.

METHODS

As previously mentioned, action research provides an ongoing emergent view of the constructed learning process that is as critical as the individual data analyses. The general focus of this study was to address the lack of available research on the integration of self-directed learning tools in online settings that encourage socio-cultural learning opportunities. The defining question for research follows: What content framework is conducive for developing social, self-directed learning processes in an online course? The research, which included three phases, began in January, 2002 and ended in December, 2002. The participants in this research selected the course "EME 6425: Microcomputers for School Managers" as part of their master's program in Education Leadership. A few selected the course for credentialing or continuing education purposes. The student group was primarily made up of teachers, school district administrators and school specialists. Students were asked to sign consent forms acknowledging participation in the research, and video consents were also obtained. Any student who chose not to participate was removed from the data set and was not penalized in any way.

Each of the three phases (phase duration was equivalent to semester time blocks) included a face-to-face full-day orientation meeting (9:00-4:00), closing half day meeting (9:00-12:00), and Web-based instruction. Orientation provided an overview of the courseware package, learning styles instrument and information, self-selected group formation, and group exchange to determine objectives and build cohesiveness. The final face-to-face meeting included time for product sharing, group reflection, and course closure (completion of paperwork).

A learning style instrument, the Learning Combination Inventory (LCI) was given to students during different points in the semester and evaluated as to information effectiveness. The LCI assists participants in identifying natural talents and provides information that can enhance cooperative learning relationships. The data from the LCI was collected and students were given a brief presentation on how to conceptually consider the learning style categories and how each of the categories related to one another.

The face-to-face classes were videotaped during phase 2 and phase 3 to provide record of the group dynamic, cues to individual satisfaction, and overall success of the scaffolding structure. Discussion transcripts and e-mail records were downloaded each semester and reviewed to determine level of interaction, student engagement, and knowledge outcomes. Students also submitted personal reflections, either during or at the end of the semester, on course effectiveness, group work process, and overall learning accomplishment. End-of-the-semester course evaluations prepared by the professor provided information about course structures and the impact on student learning and satisfaction.

The tools and scaffolding also furnished evidence of individual and joint learning outcomes and learning process. Learning contact documents were required for phases 2 and 3. Along with these learning contracts, a diagnostic instrument, grading contract, and online participation rating form were also used to scaffold the student experience. Students completed a self-rated diagnostic instrument assessing current topic knowledge and professional competency needed on all course objectives, integrating the learning contract process into the course. This method was also used by Knowles (1986) in his work with adult education students. Areas that were selected as important by students, both on an individual and learning community basis, were then transferred to the learning contract. These objectives identified the major areas of content that must be covered per University standards; however, unique objective requests that were appropriate to the course were explored with the learner.

Within the learning contract, students listed the objectives that were identified on the diagnostic instrument described above. They then specified strategies and resources that would be used to achieve knowledge about the self-specified (individual and learning community) objectives. Online course materials provided support activities resources and skill checklists that could be used as self-determined by the students, but students could also self-create learning experiences. Creative ways of learning were encouraged to be explored. The students also set dates for themselves to have specific objectives completed. Students specified evidential products that would show gained knowledge and demonstrate outcomes. Finally, students were asked to specify authentication activities on the learning contract, listing who would be providing feedback on the quality and content of their work, and how this person or persons would be communicating their feedback to the group or individual. The person(s) authenticating the project must have knowledge and competence in the particular subject area, integrating work product into the real context and thereby extending learning impact. For instance, if a learning community project was to create an "ideal" technology plan, then the group may have their respective four administrators evaluate the project and rate the project on a group-supplied evaluation form. The professor in this scenario would also receive a copy of the completed project and authenticating documents for accountability, record-keeping purposes, and verification of basic skills.

The grading contracts and online participation rating form, completed at the end of the semester, provided information on students' self-reflection, personal feedback on objective completion, course engagement and interaction, and personal impacts of the course and course tools. These additional forms also provided accountability measures for students to conscientiously recognize personal contribution and commitment to self-prescribed learning activities and outcomes.

RESULTS

Phase One

During this initial pilot phase, none of the self-directed tools (learning contracts, diagnostic instruments, or reflective components) were utilized to guide groups. This phase included 28 student participants and was designed primarily as a conventional online course that also utilized learning communities. There was no student attrition during this semester. Included in the original course structure were ten content modules to be completed by students during the 15-week semester. Early in the semester, students communicated that the workload was too extensive and a content adjustment was made; learning communities were advised to select 5 of the 10 overall content modules. Although this self-selection allowed for choice of modules, each individual module remained highly structured, prescribing specific learning activities to be completed for credit. While the reduction in workload was appreciated, when asked in the final evaluation whether increased face-to-face contact would be helpful, 11 students responded "yes," indicating that directions often remained unclear. Following are examples of their comments:

Sometimes the instructions are confusing and one needs someone to explain if there is any question[s].

Sometimes you need somebody to actually see what you've done to see if you are on the right track.

Because it is important that there is congruence with the instructions, etc.

I think it would help to keep everyone on track. Some people aren't prepared to work independently for an entire course.

Although increasing face-to-face opportunities might prove helpful, these statements seemed more indicative of issues with self-direction and personal comfort that would require further enhancements in future semesters. The online nature of the course is an integral aspect of the course content designed to intentionally foster the use of hardware, software, and other computer media and materials. Therefore, adapting the course structure made more sense than altering the overall course delivery.

During this phase, the LCI was administered at the conclusion of the semester in order to better understand the learning preferences of the students. As is common with action research, the decision to administer this instrument was determined at the mid-semester point and, therefore, was not given at the beginning of the semester. The majority of students in this group (21) had a high degree of sequence guiding their learning profile, suggesting that they enjoyed planning, working neatly, and requiring a clear sense of direction (see Table 22.1). Ironically, although the content modules were highly structured and prescribed, those with high sequence desired more clearly defined directions, requesting that future semesters involve additional face-to-face contacts.

Approximately half of the students (16) were also driven by a precise style, meaning that they sought extensive information, enjoyed writing, sharing details, and questioning others. The other two learning style domains were represented less significantly by the students, with 10 scoring high in technical qualities (therefore they enjoy relevant meaningful tasks, hands-on activities, and privacy and independence in thought), and 6 individuals who presented as highly confluent (creative, intuitive thinkers, risk-takers, and tending to make unique connections). While this diagnostic process recognizes that all individuals possess combinations of each of the four learning patterns, the driving force among this group was sequential processing. The information in Table 22.1 represents the class averages of LCI scores in each phase.

Table 22.1.   Average LCI Scores by Phase

	Class Averages		
	Phase 1	Phase 2	Phase 3
Sequence	26.7	23.8	27.1
Precision	24	25.3	24.7
Technical reasoning	23.3	22.2	21.3
Confluence	21.8	23.9	22.5

Phase 2 (Summer Semester, 2002)

As a summer course, this phase was only ten weeks in duration. There was no student attrition during this phase of the course. Based on an analysis of the overall experience in Phase 1, several actions were taken to enhance student learning, integrate the curriculum within the online course delivery model, and increase aspects of social, self-direction. First, the learning styles analysis was completed at the onset of the semester in order to enhance understanding of both individual and group learning patterns (see Table 22.1 for results). Second, although the content remained unchanged, ten-module format, frameworks supporting social, self-direction were provided for the first time. These frameworks for scaffolding learning included the self-rated diagnostic instrument, learning contracts, grading contracts and an online discussion rating form. Learning contracts were submitted initially in draft format and were altered based upon instructor feedback. The learning contract process operated much like a negotiation between the instructor and the group or individual. Instructor approval (usually the second week of class) meant that the learning contract represented an acceptable level of work and learning "if" contracts were completed to specification. The students were free to adapt the contract as necessary in collaboration with the professor. These documents were considered a living and breathing representation of the learning process.

Students were asked to self-organize into learning communities and complete a diagnostic instrument designed to evaluate personal knowledge of course objectives. The results then became the basis for planning a learning contract, requiring a minimum of five goals (to coincide with choosing at least five modules). In order to encourage social learning, at least three of the five goals were to be learning community goals. However, all groups did have the option of completing all five goals jointly. Extra credit was offered for completion of additional goals. Final approval of all learning contracts was negotiated with the instructor for both group and individual goals.

A final addition to the course delivery involved the use of self-evaluation. At the end of the semester, students were asked to complete a grading contract, designed to provide the opportunity to self-evaluate their own attainment of goals. Additionally, each student was asked to submit a self-evaluation of their online participation throughout the semester.

Although the learning styles instrument was administered at the start of the course, due to time constraints during the initial face-to-face meeting, only individual interpretation was completed. Very little attention was devoted to the utilization of results for the enhancement of group effectiveness. In the final evaluation, some students expressed a need for further integration of learning styles into course design and group coordination.

Students directly addressed the issue of learning contracts and other tools in the end of the course evaluations. Of the 21 students enrolled in the course during the second phase, 20 submitted these instructor-designed evaluations. On questions about the level of relevancy of the course and the positive aspects of the course, students responded as follows:

> I was able to incorporate the knowledge of subject matter with the learned technology to create a high interest student project.

> We were allowed to use our personal needs to drive our learning. I thought I was fairly versed on the computer, but I found I had lots to learn.

Other students also indicated that the learning contract and resulting strategies and project work were helpful tools in the learning process. Every student completed their agreed upon contracts. Final course products included presentations on a variety of technology topics utilizing appropriate software applications, design of Web pages and Web animations, database creation and manipulation, virtual research, Internet usage and research evaluations, brochures on topics such as networks and technology usage with visually impaired populations, and extensive technology curriculum integration projects. All of these products were planned and completed by the individual groups using the provided content and the course objectives.

However, despite the general interest in use of the scaffolding format, some students expressed concerns about the flow of the material and discomfort with this "non-traditional" format. Comments on the course evaluation which indicated these issues are as follows:

> The only draw back to this course was that there was so much information it took me a while to figure out how it was all organized and the expectations.

> I feel like I am much better prepared for a course like this than when we started. The learning contracts and other elements were confusing.

> Amount of content: The module structure threw me at first and didn't seem consistent with the encouragement to develop our own projects

While it appeared that some students were uncomfortable with the course structure that required student-driven objectives and products, the value of such tools appeared greater than returning to a traditional course format. The modules appeared confusing to the contract development since the resources did not effectively align to the diagnostic instrument that was completed at the beginning of the semester. This premise is based on the course evaluation data (5 of the 20 responses), discussion/e-mail transcript information, personal conversation, and feedback from students to the instructor. Therefore, the research team decided to continue with the use of the self-direction frameworks, but instead modify the content, provide a more specific face-to-face training experience and re-state in a variety of ways the course expectations to clearly identify student and instructor roles.

In this second iteration of the course, only four students suggested that the course should require additional face-to-face work. This number is significantly decreased from the previous phase when 11 responded that they felt more face-to-face work would be beneficial. Those who indicated that they would prefer more face-to-face linked their responses to their individual learning style and personal readiness for self-directed experiences. For instance, one student wrote, "The best way to learn technology is to have an expert standing by you to help when things go wrong." Clarity was not an issue that was linked to the need for further face-to-face teaching experiences during this semester. There were also only a few students who were still unclear as to the overall expectation and expressed a lack of understanding of the "self-directed" model that they were asked to use.

Phase 3 (Fall, 2002)

Phase 3 ran for the duration of 15 weeks and included 27 student participants, all of whom successfully completed the course. Expectations of student work remained consistent with the previously stated requirement of three learning community objectives and two individual objectives for course completion.

Based on the feedback from Phase 2, course content and curriculum resources were aligned and redesigned to reflect the objectives listed as part of the diagnostic instrument. Each of the modules became a part of a "resource pack" that students could, but did not have to, utilize in the design of their learning contracts. The resource packs included four major sections, directions, guidelines (activities), skills, and materials, which were available to students online in Web-based format. These resource packs were introduced as materials that provided information about each of the objectives in the initial diagnostic instrument, but use of these materials were not required.

Students indicated on the final evaluation that the detailed syllabus, resource packs, and associated matrices were helpful in their work. When responding to the question about the helpful aspects/activities of the course, one student responded, "The best is the materials online associated with each learning objective. The resources, articles, references, websites, etc. [are] awesome and I have referred to that material many times even for personal/professional use outside of this class." Others concurred on the course evaluation and through personal discussion with the instructor. Those students who did not take advantage of these resources reported a lack of clarity and/or discomfort with the format of the course. Grades in the course were dependent upon online participation, the completion of learning contract objectives, the submission of the forms (learning contract, grading contracts, online discussion rating forms), completion of a student homepage, and participation in the last class face-to-face session. Therefore, students were never penalized if they made the choice not to actively engage with the available materials.

To attend with the issue of unclear expectation that was expressed during Phase 2, students were given a detailed brochure titled, "Tips to Online Success and Satisfaction," which listed the following four tips with detailed explanation of the item of importance: stay engaged, use the tools available to plan for you, ask for what you need, and structure comes in many shapes and sizes. This brochure was reviewed during the face-to-face orientation class to eliminate any confusion over individual student expectation. In fact, this brochure accompanied a detailed syllabus clearly outlining course tools, grading procedures, and instructor/student roles. Despite the distribution of this brochure, there were still two students who did not actively engage throughout the entire 15-week semester.

Once again, all students completed their self-designed learning contracts. Products during this semester included: presentations utilizing the appropriate software, covering a variety of technology topics, active research in schools assessing student technology preferences and usage, technology plan development, video presentations/lesson plans for hardware usage, Website development, spreadsheet and database projects, research evaluations and video-conferencing/communication tool demonstrations. The authentication sequence of the learning contract extended learning outcomes into the natural work environments, increasing the level of impact of learning experiences. Students reported sharing learning products and new knowledge with administrators, district supervisors, colleagues, and other experts in the field, infusing product development into authentic work settings.

Unfortunately, during the face-to-face orientation meeting of this phase, facility issues disrupted the flow of the experience, minimizing the amount of time that was spent integrating the online course content with the joint learning contracts the self-selected groups attempted to create.

This led to a continued sense of initial disequilibrium at the onset of the course. As students delved into the course materials, discussions reflected the need for further structured review. Students also wanted some indication of the priority of the objectives and importance to the roles they were to assume as future administrators. It was planned that further review of these materials would be done during the initial orientation for future phases.

As previously mentioned, each phase included a final, face-to-face meeting at which students shared their assignments and learning throughout the semester. During the second phase, this was hampered by the facility accommodations due to the need for multiple computers. While the technology was readily available, as is standard in most computer labs, computers were placed in rows minimizing the amount of flow and movement in the room. The final day of sharing was student-designed to be in a conference style, different stations arranged around the room displaying student products. While the physical environment of the final meeting did not interfere with the learning during the semester, it did seem to reduce the effectiveness of this last class experience.

In preparation for the next semester, this issue was addressed through the purchase and implementation of a wireless laptop cart that could be brought to any traditional classroom. In phase 3, a large meeting room where tables were rearranged and multiple wireless laptops and projectors were stationed around the room was used. In addition, Internet connections (wireless) were established that allowed students to display their work products and encourage other groups to interact with and explore the final projects, many of which were in the form of Websites. These alterations to the physical space and enhancement of technologies proved to be highly beneficial to the intent of the last face-to-face experience.

Based upon comments listed in the course evaluations, fewer students recommended changes to the course to improve the learning of material. Although enrollment increased this semester, the number of students requiring additional face-to-face work decreased even more. Only two students indicated that they would prefer to meet more often, and these responses were expressed as being tied to interpersonal reasons, rather than issues of clarity.

At the onset of the course, the students were presented with a more extensive overview of the learning style process, emphasizing the meta-cognitive analysis aspect and the application for enhancement of group dynamics. Immediately following the first meeting, they were asked to write a brief reflective response to the process, focusing on how the knowledge affected them personally and how it might be used during their coursework. Early in the semester, the research team provided LCI data back to the students in the form of class averages and group profiles. In addition, as the semester progressed, groups were asked to utilize their knowledge of learning patterns to reflect on their group process.

From their responses to the reflection questions, the highly sequential nature of many of the students was evident. Most comments were favorable toward the self-directed nature of the course, learning contracts, the diagnostic guide, and the structured modules. Individuals whose lead pattern was sequence described how they were able to use their skills to help their group develop a plan quickly and efficiently. Several whose lead pattern was technical reasoning appreciated the opportunity to link coursework to relevant problems within their schools. In their reflections about group process, several individuals discussed how knowledge and understanding of learning patterns helped enhance group function by encouraging patience and sensitivity to different needs and styles. Following are some of their comments:

> I found that I needed to adjust my normal learning patterns to coincide with the group's needs . . . As a group member I felt it was my responsibility to be as flexible as possible to make the group function productively. Often this entailed me beginning assignments earlier than normal and spending more time reviewing completed assignments.

> I believe that my learning pattern has impacted my participation in this class. I am a very sequential person. The structure of this class is very frustrating for me because I seek clear directions and plans.... If I am given a task with a deadline, I will meet that goal and produce a product that is neatly and completely done. When my group split up tasks for each member to do, I finally felt a sense of relief.

> I scored very high in the sequential area and I think this best describes me. I do like everything to be planned out and I think this is what made me LOVE the learning contract. It was a great way to know everything that needed to happen throughout the semester and allowed plenty of planning/ organizing time ... I would often catch myself flipping through our contract to see what was next. I do sometimes get carried away with the agenda and I have to be aware of this trait.

The enhanced meta-cognition described in the statements above provided two benefits. First, students were able to reflect on their own work process and group dynamic to alter role adoption and individual behaviors. Secondly, these meta-cognitive reflections provided valuable information to the researchers on what was working for students and what needed adaptation in the course design in future semesters.

CONCLUSIONS

While self-directed learning allows for the development of individual interests in a manner that is aligned to the learning patterns of the student, this does not necessarily mean a lack of overall structure. Students in virtual groups appear to thrive on a clear expression of guiding concepts and the provision of helpful resources along with frameworks and scaffolding for obtaining knowledge. Lock (2003) described the following metaphor that directly supports the scaffolds that were used in this research:

> A building contractor begins a construction project by carefully studying blueprints as a guide to laying the groundwork and building the foundation for the project. The careful installation of footings, the use of supports and careful construction provide a solid foundation for what is to be constructed on this base. The same is true in laying the foundation for the creation of online learning communities. The foundation needs firm footings and structures in place to allow for future scaffolding and the building of community. (p. 403)

The self-directed learning framework provided by Knowles (1975) can be used with groups to provide a structure that facilitates the acquisition of knowledge without collapsing the adult quest for meaningful experience and relevance. Rather than controlling the mechanisms of learning and disseminating knowledge, the online professor then begins to construct scaffolds through the facilitation of process, provision of opportunity, attention to both group and individual requests, and learning styles.

Introducing the self-directed tools to mature students proved to be initially intimidating and overwhelming. Due to the online nature of the class, maximizing face-to-face time and hands-on experience around learning contract activities was imperative to the productive nature of group and individual planning. The "newness" of the self-directed tools had students stretched beyond their comfort zones and therefore expressing a bit of disequilibrium at the outset. Most students expressed increased comfort and understanding as learning contracts were submitted for instructor approval and as time elapsed during the semester. Instructor feedback and responsiveness and clearly defined expectation were critical to developing the learning contract process. This process built an atmosphere of instructor/student trust within the learning environment.

The high expectation, high quality, and diverse product that were a result of the learning contract process were amazing. The final results far exceeded professor expectations in both overall knowledge acquisition and outcomes-based evidence. The few groups that had difficulty aligning the independent nature of online work with the group "social" design of the course were guided by the professor through feedback and reiteration of the self-specified learning contract objectives and tasks.

Despite positive student feedback and general understanding of the learning contracts, phase 2 and phase 3 had about two students each semester who expressed extensive dislike and discomfort with the course structure and use of the learning contracts. While suggestions were taken from these students, it is essential to consider certain facets about student satisfaction in relation to course design. Some of these students were not prepared or "ready" for self-directed frameworks and others preferred to expend less effort designing their own learning. Another influencing factor could be tied to the expectations and roles that these individuals assume. Years of experience within traditional educational systems has prepared most adults for a format of instructor-control and dissemination of knowledge. Therefore, a small percentage of students will need additional time, investment, and learning maturation to move toward deliveries that reflect self-directed philosophies. In fact, there will be some students who will not be pleased regardless of the instructional method or delivery system.

At the end of each semester, there were a number of students who felt that they were now better prepared to explore further learning in this format. This course, however, was offered in isolation and therefore was not part of a larger program. Program development, using the suggested framework, which would incorporate both individual and group intellectual development, could be easily adapted from this material to provide a comprehensive approach to the learning process.

The action research methods that were employed as an initial frame to the study will be adapted to accommodate a more rigorous, comprehensive approach. Design-based research will be utilized to further involve theory development, model replication, and empirical emphasis in the investigation of the innovated scaffolds for facilitating the social, self-directed phenomena. The design-based research format incorporates collaboration, model verification, complex system investigation, diverse data collection techniques, and reform (Cobb, Confrey, diSessa, Lehrer, & Schauble, 2003; Shavelson, Phillips, Towne, & Feuer, 2003, Sloane & Gorard, 2003). Therefore, the global emphasis of this research will shift to encompass this educational inquiry paradigm.

Future semesters of this course will be taught with further modifications based upon the findings listed above. The next term will include a content activity allowing groups to explore the materials more fully before writing the initial draft of the group learning contract. Use of the LCI as a meta-cognitive analysis tool will continue to be part of the initial

face-to-face session, with encouragement for students to use the knowledge in their learning communities while developing goals, identifying
strategies, and assigning responsibilities. At several points during the
next semester they will be asked to respond to reflective questions about
their use of the meta-cognitive aspects.

REFERENCES

Alfred, M. (2002). The promise of sociocultural theory in democratizing adult
    education. *New Diesctions for Adult and Continuing Education, 96*(Winter), 3-13.
Beitler, M. A. (2000). Contract learning in organizational learning & management
    development. In H. B. Long & Associates (Eds.), *Practice & theory in
    self-directed learning* (pp. 143-150). Schaumburg, IL: Motorola University
    Press.
Berk, L. E., & Winsler, A. (1995). *Scaffolding children's learning: Vygotsky and early
    childhood education.* Washington, DC: National Association for the Education
    of Young Children.
Brown, R. E. (2001). The process of community-building in distance learning
    classes. *Journal of Asynchronous Learning Networks, 5*(2), 28-35.
Cobb, P., Confrey, J., diSessa, A., Lehrer, R., & Schauble, L. (2003). Design experi-
    ments in educational research. *Educational Researcher, 32*(1), 9-13.
Collison, G., Elbaum, B., Haavind, S., & Tinker, R. (2000). *Facilitating online learn-
    ing: Effective strategies for moderators.* Madison, WI: Atwood.
Curtis, D. D. (2001). Exploring collaborative online learning. *Journal of Asynchro-
    nous Learning Networks, 5*(1), 21-34.
Dabbagh, N. (2003). Scaffolding: An important teacher competency in online
    learning. *TechTrends, 47*(3), 39-49.
Derry, S. J., DuRussel, L. A. (July, 1999). *Assessing knowledge construction in on-line
    learning communities.* A paper presented at the Conference of the Interna-
    tional Society for Artificial Intelligence in Education, Le Mans, France
Glickman, C. D., Gordon, S. P., & Ross-Gordon, J. M. (1995). *Supervision of instruc-
    tion: A developmental approach.* Boston: Allyn & Bacon.
Harasim, L., Hitz, S. R., Teles, L., & Turoff, M. (1995). *Learning networks: A field
    guide to teaching and learning online.* Cambridge, MA: MIT Press.
Hill, J. L. (1996). Psychological sense of community: Suggestions for future
    research. *Journal of Community Psychology, 24*(4), 431-438.
Huff, M. (1998). Empowering students in a graduate-level social work course.
    Journal of Social Work, 34(3), 375-385
Hung, D. W. L. (2002). Bringing communities of practice into schools: implica-
    tions for instructional technologies from Vygotskian perspectives. *Interna-
    tional Journal of Instructional Media, 29*(2), 171-183.
Knowles, M. S. (1986). *Using learning contracts.* San Francisco: Jossey-Bass.
Knowles, M. S. (1975). *Self-directed learning.* New York: Association Press.
Ko, S., & Rossen, S. (2001). *Teaching online: A practical guide.* Boston: Houghton
    Mifflin.

Lane, C. (1997) Technology and systemic educational reform. In P. S. Portway & C. Lane (Eds.), *Guide to teleconferencing and distance learning* (pp.179-226). Livermore, CA: Applied Business teleCommunications.

Lock, J. V. (2003). Laying the groundwork for the development of learning communities within online courses. *Quarterly Review of Distance Education*, *3*(1), 395-408.

Long, H. B. (2000). Understanding self-direction in learning. In H. B. Long & Associates (Eds.), *Practice & theory in self-directed learning* (pp. 143-150). Schaumburg, IL: Motorola University Press.

Moore, M. G., & Kearsley, G. (1996). *Distance education: A systems view.* Belmont, CA: Wadsworth.

Palloff, R. M., & Pratt, K. (1999). *Building learning communities in cyberspace: Effective strategies for the online classroom.* San Francisco: Jossey-Bass.

Palloff, R. M., & Pratt, K. (2001). *Lessons from the cyberspace classroom: The realities of online teaching.* San Francisco: Jossey-Bass.

Patton, M. Q. (2002). *Qualitative research & evaluation methods* (3rd ed.). Thousand Oaks, CA: SAGE.

Razik, T. A., & Swanson, A. D. (1995). *Fundamental concepts of educational leadership and Management.* Englewood Cliffs, NJ: Prentice-Hall.

Rovai, A. A. P. (2002). A preliminary look at the structural differences of higher education classroom communities in traditional and ALN courses. *Journal of Asynchronous Network Learning*, *6*(1), 41-56.

Schrum, L. (2002). Dimensions and strategies for online success: Voices from experienced educators. *Journal of Asynchronous Network Learning*, *6*(1), 57-67.

Shavelson, R. J., Phillips, D. C., Towne, L., & Feuer, M. J. (2003). On the science of education design studies. *Educational Researcher, 32*(1), 25-28.

Sloane, F. C. & Gorard, S. (2003). Exploring modeling aspects of design experiments. *Educational Researcher, 32*(1), 29-31.

Vygotsky, L. S. (1978). Mind in society: The development of higher psychological processes. Cambridge, MA: Harvard University Press. (Original work published in 1934)

Waddell, D. (2000). Use of learning contracts in a RN-to-BSN leadership course. *The Journal of Continuing Education in Nursing, 31*(4), 179-184.

Wenger, E. (2000). Communities of practice and social learning systems. *Organization, 7*(2), 225-246.

White, K. W., & Weight, B.H. (2000). *The online teaching guide: A handbook of attitudes, strategies, and techniques for the virtual classroom.* Boston: Allyn & Bacon.

PART IV

BEST ENGAGEMENT STRATEGIES

CHAPTER 23

INTERACTION IN ONLINE LEARNING ENVIRONMENTS

A Review of the Literature

Constance E. Wanstreet

This article reviews research related to the construct of interaction in the educational technology and distance education literature. The review is limited to higher education and includes theories and empirical research that inform the construct of online interactions. Conceptual and operational definitions of *interaction* are categorized from 3 frameworks emerging from the review: interaction as an instructional exchange, interaction as computer-mediated communication, and interaction as a social/psychological connection. Gaps in the research are identified and similarities that inform practice in designing and teaching in online learning environments are presented to provide linkages from research to practice.

Researchers and practitioners are in general agreement that interaction is a key variable in learning and satisfaction with distance education courses (Fulford & Zhang, 1993; Gunawardena & Duphorne, 2001; Swan, 2001). Yet, the term is defined in so many different ways in the distance educa-

The Perfect Online Course: Best Practices for Designing and Teaching
pp. 425–442

tion literature as to be practically useless unless specific distinctions can be defined and generally agreed upon (Moore, 1989). Promoting common definitions and interpretations is even more challenging when the educational technology literature is considered. Bannan-Ritland (2002) calls for the fields of educational technology and distance education to define various forms of interaction better to ensure that appropriate interactions occur online and lead to improved learning. Nevertheless, little has been done to synthesize related literature on interaction in online learning environments (Hirumi, 2002).

The purpose of this review is to build a bridge between the educational technology and distance education literatures by clarifying terminology related to the construct of interaction in the context of online learning environments, meaning those that are Web-based or Web-enhanced. The focus of this review is limited to higher education and includes theories and empirical research that inform the construct of online interactions. The review process generally followed Cooper's (1998) stages of problem formulation, data collection, data evaluation, analysis and interpretation, and presentation of results.

In light of multiple meanings and conceptual confusion related to interaction in online learning environments, the study was designed to answer this primary research question: How is the term *interaction* defined conceptually and operationally in the educational technology and distance education literature? Secondary research questions are, What similarities are found in the definitions that inform practice in designing and teaching in online learning environments? What constructs span the boundary between face-to-face and virtual interactions?

METHOD

This study is a comprehensive review of journal articles published between 2000 and 2004, with a selected sample of work described in the paper. As a starting point, the main educational technology and distance education journals identified by Wallace (2003) and Lee, Driscoll, and Nelson (2004) were assessed for impact in an attempt to confirm their status as primary journals. They were supplemented by additional journals known to the author. Acceptance rates, representation in appropriate abstracting services and citation indices, and whether the journals are peer-reviewed were among the criteria used to determine impact (Thyer, 1994).

After discussions with two reference librarians, the assessment included reviewing Cabell and English's directories (2003a, 2003b) and the Social Sciences Citation Index for the journals' inclusion, and searching the following online databases deemed most representative for distance education and educational technology for the number of citations of each journal's name: EBSCOhost's Academic Search Premier and Computer Source, Education Abstracts, Educational Resources Information Center (ERIC), and PsycINFO. The database searches were conducted on January 28, 2005. The results are summarized in Table 23.1.

The top five journals in each field with the most articles available through the abstracting services were chosen for this review. The distance education journals chosen for this review are the *American Journal of Distance Education, Distance Education,* the *Journal of Distance Education, Open Learning,* and the *Quarterly Review of Distance Education.*

The educational technology journals are the *British Journal of Educational Technology, Educational Technology Research and Development,* the *Journal of Computers in Mathematics and Science Teaching,* the *Journal of Educational Computing Research,* and the *Journal of Research on Technology in Education* (formerly the *Journal of Research on Computing in Education*).

One limitation of this approach to determining the leading journals in the field is the exclusion of online journals widely regarded as reputable despite not being indexed by the major database services. The *Journal of Asynchronous Learning Networks (JALN)* is an example of a respected journal whose articles are not included in a review such as this, which is limited to documents abstracted in academic databases. *JALN* is not indexed by those services since it is freely available online (J. Moore, personal communication, February 1, 2005).

Data Collection

Four databases were used to identify articles addressing interaction in online learning environments in higher education: Academic Search Premier, Education Abstracts, ERIC, and PsycINFO. EBSCOhost's Computer Source was eliminated at this stage because eight of the 10 journals are not included in that database, and records for one journal are duplicated in Academic Search Premier, another EBSCOhost database.

Descriptors used were *interaction* and *higher education* or *colleges and universities,* combined with each journal's name. All databases and each descriptor set were searched by date: 2000-2004 and pre-2000. All database searches were conducted on January 30, 2005, and resulted in 125 articles distributed as follows: 73 educational technology articles (32 published between 2000 and 2004; 41 published before 2000), and 52 distance education articles (28 published between 2000 and 2004; 24 published before 2000). Table 23.2 shows frequencies by journal and database.

It was expected that the most recent 5-year period would adequately reflect the multiple meanings of *interaction* in higher education online

Table 23.1. Peer-Reviewed Journal Selection Criteria

Field/Name	Listed in Cabell's	Included in Social Sciences Citation Index	Acceptance Rate	Number of Records in Database				
				Education Abstracts	ERIC	Psyc-INFO	Academic Search Premier	Computer Source
Educational Technology								
• British Journal of Educational Technology	yes	yes	11-20%	1,258	593	132	585	0
• Educational Technology Research & Development	yes	no	11-20%	556	350	188	30	0
• Internet and Higher Education	yes	no	21-30%	0	122	0	118	0
• Journal of Educational Computing Research	no	no	15%	578	511	554	0	99
• Journal of Research on Technology in Education	yes	no	28%	607	338	0	501	501
• Journal of Computers in Mathematics and Science Teaching	yes	no	0-5%	820	591	50	0	0
• Journal of Technology and Teacher Education	yes	no	15%	202	170	0	0	0
Distance Education								
• American Journal of Distance Education	yes	no	11-20%	74	172	0	78	0
• Journal of Asynchronous Learning Networks	no	no	<25%	0	0	0	0	0
• Journal of Distance Education	no	no	40%	110	233	0	131	0
• Distance Education	yes	no	21-30%	760	745	0	605	0
• Open Learning	no	no	25%	0	214	0	167	0
• Quarterly Review of Distance Education	no	no	50%	0	127	0	112	0

learning environments and yield a sufficient number of articles to review. Therefore, this review was restricted to articles published between 2000 and 2004.

Table 23.2.   Search Results for *Interaction* and *Higher Education* by Journal and Database

Journal	Academic Search Premier		Education Abstracts[1]		ERIC		PsycINFO		Total	
	pre-2000	2000-2004	pre-2000	2000-2004	pre-2000	2000-2004	pre-2000	2000-2004	pre-2000	2000-2004
• British Journal of Educational Technology	0	2	0	6	7	6	0	1	7	15
• Educational Technology Research & Development	0	0	1	3	4	1	0	0	5	4
• Journal of Educational Computing Research	0	0	3	4	11	5	0	0	14	9
• Journal of Research on Technology in Education	0	0	2	2	6	2	0	0	8	4
• Journal of Computers in Mathematics and Science Teaching	0	0	2	0	5	0	0	0	7	0
• Educational Technology Journals Subtotal									41	32
• American Journal of Distance Education	0	1	0	3	6	5	0	0	6	9
• Journal of Distance Education	0	0	1	9	10	4	0	0	11	13
• Distance Education	0	0	0	1	4	0	0	0	4	1
• Open Learning	0	0	0	0	3	2	0	0	3	2
• Quarterly Review of Distance Education	0	0	0	0	0	3	0	0	0	3
• Distance Education Journals Subtotal									24	28
Total	0	3	9	28	56	28	0	1	65	60

Note: [1]Descriptors were *interaction* and *colleges and universities*.

Data Evaluation

The database search resulted in 60 articles about interaction and higher education published between 2000 and 2004. Duplicate titles were eliminated, which resulted in 48 articles to review: 24 from the distance education journals and 24 from the educational technology journals. Abstracts were scanned to narrow the records to those relevant to the construct of interaction in online learning environments. This eliminated articles that identified statistical interactions between independent variables, such as the statistical interaction of computer experience with gender, as well as studies of interaction in distance courses that used audio and video technology but had no online component. The number to review was thus further reduced to 42 articles: 20 in distance education and 22 in educational technology.

Of the 42 articles reviewed, 76% (32) were research studies and 24% (10) were conceptual articles that included primarily theoretical positions, lessons learned, and other non-empirical writings.

Of the total 42 articles, 93% (39) explicitly articulated a conceptual definition of interaction through terminology either in the articles' theoretical background or research questions or implicitly conceptualized the construct through the presentation of results. Three conceptual frameworks permeate the discussion:

1. Interaction as an instructional exchange between these entities: learner-content, learner-instructor, and learner-learner (Moore, 1989) as well as learner-interface (Hillman, Willis, & Gunawardena, 1994). A variation of learner-content interaction is included: learner-information (Sabry & Baldwin, 2003), which accounts for information specific to the course material as well as information relevant to the learning task but not specific to the content, such as learning how to conduct a Web search when creating a Webquest about the Electoral College, for example.

2. Interaction as communication facilitated by networks of computers (Jonassen, Davidson, Collins, Campbell, & Bannan Haag, 1995). Computer-mediated communication technologies support synchronous and asynchronous conversation and collaboration among learners separated by space.

3. Interaction as a social and psychological connection that fosters learning as problem solving in collaboration with capable peers (Vygotsky, 1978).

A few articles combine these conceptual frameworks, such as learner-instructor interaction and Vygotsky's (1978) zone of proximal develop-

**Table 23.3. Number of Articles by Field
That Include a Conceptual Definition of Interaction**

Conceptualization of Interaction	Educational Technology Articles	Distance Education Articles
Learner-learner exchange	12	11
Learner-instructor exchange	12	8
Learner-content or learner-information exchange	6	4
Learner-interface exchange	6	4
Computer-mediated communication	2	10
Social and psychological connection	7	4

ment, in which the instructor acts as a bridge between what the learner knows and can do and what the learner needs to be able to know and do (Ng'ambi & Hardman, 2004).

The largest category of interaction type—learner-learner—is addressed in 23 articles followed by learner-instructor interaction in 20 articles, learner-content interaction in 10 articles, and learner-interface interaction in 10 articles. Interaction was conceptualized as computer-mediated communication in 12 articles and as a social and psychological connection in 11 articles. Table 23.3 summarizes the conceptual frameworks authors used by field.

Of the total 42 articles, 76% (32) included an operational definition of interaction, primarily through the instruments used to measure the construct. These are discussed below and representative definitions are summarized in the Appendix.

The term *interaction* was not often used interchangeably with *interactivity*, as is generally asserted (Roblyer & Weincke, 2003). Wagner (1997) made a distinction between *interaction* as a desired quality of instruction to change learners and move them toward an action state of goal attainment and *interactivity* as machine attributes, or characteristics of instructional delivery systems. That distinction held with only two exceptions—one from each field (Sims, 2003; Volery, 2001).

RESULTS AND ANALYSIS

Multiple operational definitions exist within the conceptual frameworks of online interaction. The following selective citations are representative of the empirical research comprising this review.

Instructional Exchange

Interaction as an instructional exchange between entities was the predominant framework in both the distance education and educational technology fields (Chen, 2001, ET[1]; Gauss & Urbas, 2003, ET; Lee, 2002, ET).

Learner-Learner Interaction

Articles in distance education journals defined learner-learner interaction as reciprocal communication, and articles in both fields defined it as a learning style preference (Brace-Govan & Clulow, 2000, DE; Chen & Paul, 2003, ET; Lamy & Hassan, 2003, DE; Oriogun & Cook, 2003, DE).

Lee and Gibson (2003, DE) reported on a graduate-level course that used computer conferencing as an instructional strategy almost exclusively. They defined interaction as reciprocal communication and analyzed three weeks' of transcripts for evidence of initiation (encouraging new topics or encouraging discussion and having a response), explicit response (direct response to a previous message), and implicit response (expanding on a previous message).

Ronteltap and Eurelings (2002, DE) also analyzed initial messages and reactions to them among students in a law school class and a medical school class in the Netherlands. They defined interaction as the ratio between reactions and initial documents. Weller (2000, DE) defined learner-learner interaction in an entry-level computer course simply as participation in conferences that relate to course readings and in support conferences where students could ask for specific help from peers and tutors.

Three studies operationalized interaction as a learning style preference. Bradley and Lomicka (2000, ET) asked students in a language learning lab their feeling about working with others in the lab and their preference about working individually, with student peers, or in combination. Litchfield, Oakland, and Anderson (2002, DE) asked students in a dietetic training program whether they preferred to work with others, on their own, or with the instructor; and Sanders and Morrison-Shetlar (2001, ET) asked engineering students to rate their level of comfort in posting and answering questions through the Web and in talking to people in chat rooms.

Learner-Instructor Interaction

As was the case with learner-learner interaction, reciprocal communication and learning style preferences help define learner-instructor interaction (Lee & Gibson, 2003, DE; Litchfield et al., 2002, DE). Other studies approached the construct from either the learner perspective or the instructor perspective. For example, instructors in a distance education graduate program in the United Kingdom were expected to send eight motivational messages to learners, including a welcome letter, assignment deadline reminders, and exam advice (Visser, Plomp, Amirault, & Kuiper, 2002, ET). The second way of defining level of interaction was through answers to a multiple choice question that was part of a survey of all students enrolled in a university's online courses. The question asked learners whether they had "a great deal," "sufficient," "insufficient," or no interaction with their instructors.

Learner-Content Interaction

Learner-content interaction in an entry-level computer course was assessed through logs of simulations, animations, and assessment tools; completion of a Web site development assignment; and creation of an online journal with hypertext links (Weller, 2000, DE).

Content quality in a large Web-based introductory psychology course was assessed by survey questions about the "likeability" of working with animations, drag-and-drop options, hyperlink boxes to other references, and images and photos available for the course (Harris, Dwyer, & Leeming, 2003, ET).

Learner-Interface Interaction

The definitions for this type of interaction address preferences for technology, how it is used, and the ease of use (Lehtinen, 2002, DE). Bradley and Lomicka (2000, ET) asked learners to describe their relationship to the computer in a language learning lab. Their interviews also addressed learner experiences with software programs and with technology in general in foreign language classrooms.

A second analysis involved the World Wide Web as an interface as well as a content resource in an educational technologies course (Greene & Land, 2000, ET). Students were observed following a "think aloud" technique while they used a Web browser in a demonstration of learner-interface interaction. They then used the Web as the main resource for content to complete class projects in a demonstration of learner-content interaction.

Survey questions were developed to examine expectations and preferences for computer use as part of a "climate of interaction" questionnaire (Mitra, 2002, ET). And Dooley, Kelsey, and Lindner (2003, DE) interviewed doctoral students in agricultural education about ease of use and adequacy of training related to technology.

Computer-Mediated Communication

Researchers in this category evaluated mediated communication behaviors because of their role in establishing an environment for involvement or projected ways that communication technologies integrate learning and doing (Levin, 2002, DE; Wertsch, 2002, DE). Effective use of computer-mediated communication was operationalized in this literature through text messages. In two studies, the number of messages between learners served as an indicator of collaboration (Cunningham-Atkins, Powell, Moore, Hobbs, & Sharpe, 2004, ET; Orrill, 2002, DE). Articles also went beyond counting to examine the sequence of messages and learner perceptions of messages. Russo and Campbell (2004, DE) asked students in two communication technology and organizational change courses their perceptions of message frequency, style, and responsiveness, while Jeong (2003, DE) studied sequences of messages that increased business administration students' participation in course discussion boards.

Social/Psychological Connection

Researchers defining interaction as a social and psychological connection that fosters learning approached the construct from two directions: from a learner perspective or an instructor perspective. Sonnenwald and Li (2003, ET) operationalized the construct in terms of social interaction learning style preferences—competitive, cooperative, or individualistic—among students majoring in the natural sciences. Bernard, Brauer, Abrami, and Sturkes (2004, DE) defined learners' desire for interaction in terms of their ability to collaborate online and their enjoyment with group work. Other studies defined interaction as social construction by analyzing the messages of learners who participated in discourse to see how topics were tied together during online discussions, how learners made conversation, and how they requested peer support (Bielman, Putney, & Strudler, 2003, ET; Ge & Land, 2003, ET; Liu, Chen, Wang, & Lu, 2002, ET).

INTERPRETATION

Despite scholars who bemoan multiple definitions of interaction (Bannan-Ritland, 2002; Moore, 1989), this review of the literature has shown that there is a great deal of agreement on the conceptual definitions of the term. The preponderance of articles in both fields conceptualized interaction in terms of learner-learner or learner-instructor exchanges. Studies about both types of interaction were fairly evenly distributed between the educational technology and distance education journals. However, research into learner-content and learner-interface interactions was underrepresented in these journals. In addition, only one article addressed the perceived relationship of the learners to their computers (Bradley & Lomicka, 2000, ET).

Differences among the journals emerged when conceptualizing inter-action as computer-mediated communication or as a social and psychological connection. Computer-mediated communication research was not in evidence in the educational technology literature, while studies of the role of peer collaboration in scaffolding learning were barely reported in the distance education literature. However, research articles about both interpretations were meager.

Among other measures, scholars in both the educational technology and distance education fields operationalized interaction in terms of learning styles (Bradley & Lomicka, 2000, ET; Litchfield et al., 2002, DE), frequencies (Cunningham-Atkins et al., 2004, ET; Orrill, 2002, DE), and actions by agents (Lee & Gibson, 2003, DE; Visser et al., 2002, ET). Again, there was a fair amount of agreement in how the operational definitions were approached, yet too much emphasis was placed on frequency counts and not enough on quality measures.

Regarding application to practice, Moore (2001) wrote that it is pointless for instructors to use an interactive medium if they do not structure and encourage interaction. Yet having the opportunity for interaction is not enough; the effort must be seen as leading to a valuable outcome (Anderson, DuPlessis, & Nickel, 2001). This requires instructors to induce knowledge through an activity-based learning environment that leaves learners with latitude and initiative to pursue their own goals in the context of the broad goals of the course (Carr-Chellman & Duchastel, 2000). Theory-based rubrics such as that developed by Roblyer and Wiencke (2003) to assess the interactive qualities in distance courses provide practical guidelines to make the construct of interaction measurable and useful to instructors.

In many respects, constructivist online learning environments are not different from face-to-face environments when considering educational interactions. Learner-learner, learner-instructor, and learner-content interactions increase student involvement and enhance the sense of belonging to a learning community (Scagnoli, 2001). And social scaffolding by instructors or capable peers—in person or online—helps learners expand or refine their thinking (Greene & Land, 2000). Yet Barnes (2000) considers face-to-face and online interactions in the context of affordances—the opportunities for action each presents and the appropriate medium to enhance learning—and warns of limitations for each. She asserts that educators do not yet know what forms of interaction people need, want, or expect to support their learning; and until we fully understand what it is about face-to-face interactions that enhance learning, we cannot know what features are required for an online system. It is hoped that this review moves the educational technology and distance education fields closer to an answer.

APPENDIX:
SELECTED OPERATIONAL DEFINITIONS OF INTERACTION BY FIELD

Field[1]	Citation	Operational Definition
Learner-Learner Exchange		
ET	Bradley & Lomicka (2000)	Observation of learner-learner behaviors in computer lab and answers to interview questions: • How do you feel about working with others in the lab? • How would you describe your experience collaborating on assignments, activities, or tasks with student peers in the computer lab? • If you had a choice, what would you do: work with others or individually or in combination?
ET	Sanders & Morrison-Shetlar (2001)	Answers to three questions on a 19-question attitude scale: • I am uncomfortable answering questions through the Web • I prefer talking to people in person rather than through a chat room • I would rather post questions through the bulletin board than ask them during class
DE	Lee & Gibson (2003)	Reciprocal communication: encouraging new topic or discussion and having a response; expanding on previous message; direct response to previous message
DE	Litchfield, Oakland, & Anderson (2002)	Self-reported learning style preference (working on own, working with others) and frequency of visits to WebCT tool pages
DE	Ronteltap & Eurelings (2002)	Ratio between reactions and initial documents
DE	Weller (2000)	Observation of computer conferencing
Learner-Instructor Exchange		
ET	Visser, Plomp, Amirault, Kuiper (2002)	Eight motivational messages sent to learners by instructors, including welcome letter, encouragement to discuss problems, assignment deadline reminders
ET	Carswell, Thomas, Petre, Price, & Richards (2000)	All electronic communication between students and tutors (both tutorial interactions and queries); speed of feedback on assignments
DE	Lee & Gibson, 2003	Reciprocal communication: encouraging new topic or discussion and having a response; expanding on previous message; direct response to previous message
DE	Litchfield, Oakland, & Anderson (2002)	Self-reported learning style preference (working with instructor) and frequency of visits to course management tool pages
DE	Swan (2001)	Answer to multiple choice question on whether learners had "a great deal," "sufficient," "insufficient," or no interaction with their instructors

(continues on next page)

Field[1]	Citation	Operational Definition
Learner-Content Exchange		
ET	Harris, Dwyer, & Leeming (2003)	Answers to survey questions about "likeability" of animations, drag-and-drop options, hyperlink boxes to other references, and images and photos
DE	Weller (2000)	Use of simulations, animations, and assessment tools; completion of Web site development assignment; creation of online journal with hypertext links
Learner-Interface Exchange		
ET	Bradley & Lomicka (2000)	Answers to interview questions: • Describe your relationship to the computer in the lab • Tell me about your experience with the writing assistant software, e-mail, and the World Wide Web in terms of frequency of use, how they were used, and possible advantages and disadvantages • What are your experiences with technology in foreign language classrooms?
Learner-Interface Exchange (continued)		
ET	Greene & Land (2000)	Observations of a "think aloud" technique while students used a Web browser
ET	Mitra (2002)	Researcher-developed "climate of interaction" questionnaire subscale, including: • I prefer classes in which I get to use computers • I prefer classes with hands-on computer experiences • I expect that I will be required to use the computer
DE	Dooley, Kelsey, & Lindner (2003)	Answers to telephone interview questions: • is the balance between synchronous (lecture) and asynchronous learning time appropriate? • any difficulty managing the technology? • did you receive adequate training for using technology?
Computer-Mediated Communication		
ET	Cunningham-Atkins, Powell, Moore, Hobbs, & Sharpe (2004)	Number of messages sent by each student and the number of messages read
DE	Orrill (2002)	Number of messages sent by students to other students
DE	Russo & Campbell (2004)	Learner perceptions of frequency of interaction, responsiveness, message style, and instructor's use of non-verbal channels
DE	Jeong (2003)	Patterns in interactions that support group discussions and promote critical thinking

(continues on next page)

Field[1]	Citation	Operational Definition
Social and Psychological Connection		
ET	Sonnenwald & Li (2003)	Competitive, cooperative, and individualistic scores on social interaction learning style preference questionnaire
ET	Bielman, Putney, & Strudler (2003)	Interaction units in transcripts of online discussions
ET	Liu, Chen, Wang, & Lu (2002)	Analysis of discussion activity in a Web portfolio system, including incidents of peer support
DE	Bernard, Brauer, Abrami, and Sturkes (2004)	Researcher-developed "desire for interaction" questionnaire subscale including: • as a student, I enjoy working with other students in groups • I can work in a group during Internet activities outside of class • I can collaborate with other students during Internet activities outside of class • I feel that face-to-face contact with my instructor is necessary for learning to occur
DE	Roblyer & Weincke (2003)	Rubric item outlining highest level of social/rapport-building designs for interaction: in addition to providing for exchanges of personal information among students, the instructor provides at least one other in-class activity designed to increase communication and social rapport among students.

Note: [1]DE = Distance Education; ET = Educational Technology.

ACKNOWLEDGMENT

My thanks are due to Professor Suzanne K. Damarin for encouragement and advice while this article was being developed.

REFERENCES

Anderson, E. C., DuPlessis, J., & Nickel, T. (2001). Participation in international teleconferences and discussions: Implicit assumptions. *Educational Technology Research and Development, 49*(3), 119-123.

Bannan-Ritland, B. (2002). Computer-mediated communication, elearning, and interactivity: A review of the research. *Quarterly Review of Distance Education, 3*(2), 161-179.

Barnes, S. (2000). What does electronic conferencing afford distance education? *Distance Education, 21*(2), 236-247.

Bernard, R. M., Brauer, A., Abrami, P. C., & Sturkes M. (2004). The development of a questionnaire for predicting online learning achievement. *Distance Education, 25*(1), 31-47.

Bielman, V. A., Putney, L. G., & Strudler, N. (2003). Constructing community in a postsecondary virtual classroom. *Journal of Educational Computing Research, 29*(1), 119-144.

Brace-Govan, J., & Clulow, V. (2000). Varying expectations of online students and the implications for teachers: Findings from a journal study. *Distance Education, 21*(1), 118-135.

Bradley, T., & Lomicka, L. (2000). A case study of learner interaction in technology-enhanced language learning environments. *Journal of Educational Computing Research, 22*(3), 347-368.

Cabell, D. W. E., & English, D. L. (Eds.). (2003a). *Cabell's Directory of Publishing Opportunities in Educational Psychology and Administration* (6th ed.). Beaumont, TX: Cabell.

Cabell, D. W. E., & English, D. L. (Eds.). (2003b). *Cabell's directory of publishing opportunities in educational curriculum and methods* (6th ed.). Beaumont, TX: Cabell.

Carr-Chellman, A., & Duchastel, P. (2000). The ideal online course. *British Journal of Educational Technology, 31*(3), 229-241.

Carswell, L., Thomas, P., Petre, M., Price, B., & Richards, M. (2000). Distance education via the Internet: The student experience. *British Journal of Educational Technology, 31*(1), 29-46.

Chen, S. Y., & Paul, R. J. (2003). Editorial: Individual differences in web-based instruction—An overview. *British Journal of Educational Technology, 34*(4), 385-392.

Chen, Y. -J. (2001). Dimensions of transactional distance in the World Wide Web learning environment: A factor analysis. *British Journal of Educational Technology, 32*(4), 459-470.

Cooper, H. (1998). *Synthesizing research: A guide for literature reviews* (3rd ed.). Thousand Oaks, CA: SAGE.

Cunningham-Atkins, H., Powell, N., Moore, D., Hobbs, D. & Sharpe, S. (2004). The role of cognitive style in educational computer conferencing. *British Journal of Educational Technology, 35*(1), 69-80.

Dooley, K. E., Kelsey, K. D., & Lindner, J. R. (2003). Doc@distance: Immersion in advanced study and inquiry. *Quarterly Review of Distance Education, 4*(1), 43-50.

Fulford, C. P., & Zhang, S. (1993). Perceptions of interaction: The critical predictor in distance education. *The American Journal of Distance Education, 7*(3), 8-21.

Gauss, B., & Urbas, L. (2003). Individual differences in navigation between sharable content objects: An evaluation study of a learning module prototype. *British Journal of Educational Technology, 34*(4), 499-509.

Ge, X., & Land, S. M. (2003). Scaffolding students' problem-solving processes in an ill-structured task using question prompts and peer interactions. *Educational Technology Research and Development, 51*(1), 21-38.

Greene, B. A., & Land, S. M. (2000). A qualitative analysis of scaffolding use in a resource-based learning environment involving the World Wide Web. *Journal of Educational Computing Research, 23*(2), 151-179.

Gunawardena, C. N., & Duphorne, P. L. (2001, April). *Which learner readiness factors, online features, and CMC related learning approaches are associated with learner satisfaction in computer conferences?* Paper presented at the annual meeting of the American Educational Research Association, Seattle, WA.

Harris, R. N., Dwyer, W. O., & Leeming, F. C. (2003). Are learning styles relevant in Web-based instruction? *Journal of Educational Computing Research, 29*(1), 13-28.

Hillman, D. C. A., Willis, D. J., & Gunawardena, C. N. (1994). Learner-interface interaction in distance education: An extension of contemporary models and strategies for practitioners. *The American Journal of Distance Education, 8*(2), 30-42.

Hirumi, A. (2002). A framework for analyzing, designing, and sequencing planned elearning interactions. *Quarterly Review of Distance Education, 3*(2), 141-160.

Jeong, A. C. (2003). The sequential analysis of group interaction and critical thinking in online threaded discussions. *American Journal of Distance Education, 17*(1), 25-43.

Jonassen, D., Davidson, M., Collins, M., Campbell, J., & Bannan Haag, B. (1995). Constructivism and computer-mediated communication in distance education. *American Journal of Distance Education, 9*(2), 7-26.

Lamy, M. -N., & Hassan, X. (2003). What influences reflective interaction in distance peer learning? Evidence from four long-term online leaners of French. *Open Learning, 18*(1), 39-59.

Lee, I. (2002). Gender differences in self-regulated on-line learning strategies within Korea's university context. *Educational Technology Research and Development, 50*(1), 101-111.

Lee, J., & Gibson, C. C. (2003). Developing self-direction in an online course through computer-mediated interaction. *American Journal of Distance Education, 17*(3), 173-187.

Lee, Y., Driscoll, M. P., & Nelson, D. W. (2004). The past, present, and future of research in distance education: Results of a content analysis. *American Journal of Distance Education, 18*(4), 225-241.

Lehtinen, E. (2002). Developing models for distributed problem-based learning: Theoretical and methodological reflection. *Distance Education, 23*(1), 109-117.

Levin, J. (2002). A 2020 vision: Education in the next two decades. *Quarterly Review of Distance Education, 3*(1), 105-114.

Litchfield, R. E., Oakland, M. J., & Anderson, J. A. (2002). Relationships between intern characteristics, computer attitudes, and use of online instruction in a dietetic training program. *American Journal of Distance Education, 16*(1), 23-36.

Liu, C., Chen, G., Wang, C., & Lu, C. (2002). Student performance assessment using Bayesian network and Web portfolios. *Journal of Educational Computing Research, 27*(4), 437-469.

Mitra, A. (2002). Toward developing questionnaire items to measure effectiveness of computers in teaching. *Journal of Educational Computing Research, 26*(4), 381-394.

Moore, M. G. (1989). Three types of interaction. *The American Journal of Distance Education, 3*(2), 1-6.

Moore, M. G. (2001). Surviving as a distance teacher. *American Journal of Distance Education, 15*(2), 1-5.

Ng'ambi, D., & Hardman, J. (2004). Towards a knowledge-sharing scaffolding environment based on learners' questions. *British Journal of Educational Technology, 35*(2), 187-196.

Oriogun, P. K., & Cook, J. (2003). Transcript reliability cleaning percentage: An alternative interrater reliability measure of message transcripts in online learning. *American Journal of Distance Education, 17*(4), 221-234.

Orrill, C. H. (2002). Supporting online PBL: Design considerations for supporting distributed problem solving. *Distance Education, 23*(1), 41-57.

Roblyer, M. D., & Wiencke, W. R. (2003). Design and use of a rubric to assess and encourage interactive qualities in distance courses. *American Journal of Distance Education, 17*(2), 77-98.

Ronteltap, F., & Eurelings, A. (2002). Activity and interaction of students in an electronic learning environment for problem-based learning. *Distance Education, 23*(1), 11-22.

Russo, T. C., & Campbell, S. W. (2004). Perceptions of mediated presence in an asynchronous online course: Interplay of communication behaviors and medium. *Distance Education, 25*(2), 215-232.

Sabry, K., & Baldwin, L. (2003). Web-based learning interaction and learning styles. *British Journal of Educational Technology, 34*(4), 443-454.

Sanders, D. W., & Morrison-Shetlar, A. I. (2001). Student attitudes toward Web-enhanced instruction in an introductory biology course. *Journal of Research on Computing in Education, 33*(3), 251-262.

Scagnoli, N. I. (2001). Student orientation for online programs. *Journal of Research on Technology in Education, 34*(1), 19-27.

Sims, R. (2003). Promises of interactivity: Aligning learner perceptions and expectations with strategies for flexible and online learning. *Distance Education, 24*(1), 87-103.

Sonnenwald, D. H., & Li, B. (2003). Scientific collaboratories in higher education: Exploring learning style preferences and perceptions of technology. *British Journal of Educational Technology, 34*(4), 419-431.

Swan, K. (2001). Virtual interaction: Design factors affecting student satisfaction and perceived learning in asynchronous online courses. *Distance Education, 22*(2), 306-331.

Thyer, B. A. (1994). *Successful publishing in scholarly journals.* Thousand Oaks, CA: SAGE.

Visser, L., Plomp, T., Amirault, R. J., & Kuiper, W. (2002). Motivating students at a distance: The case of an international audience. *Educational Technology Research and Development, 50*(2), 94-110.

Volery, T. (2001). Online education: An exploratory study into success factors. *Journal of Educational Computing Research, 24*(1), 77-92.

Vygotsky, L. S. (1978). *Mind in society: The development of higher psychological processes* (M. Cole, V. John-Steiner, S. Schribner, & E. Souberman, Eds. & Trans.). Cambridge, MA: Harvard University Press.

Wagner, E. D. (1997). Interactivity: From agents to outcomes. In R. J. Menges (Series Ed.) & T. E. Cyrs (Vol. Ed.), *New directions for teaching and learning* (Vol. 71, pp. 19-26). San Francisco: Jossey-Bass.

Wallace, R. M. (2003). Online learning in higher education: A review of research on interactions among teachers and students. *Education, Communication & Information, 3*(2), 241-280.

Weller, M. J. (2000). Creating a large-scale, third generation, distance education course. *Open Learning, 15*(3), 243-252.

Wertsch, J. V. (2002). Computer mediation, PBL, and dialogicality. *Distance Education, 23*(1), 105-108.

CHAPTER 24

INTERACTION ONLINE

A Reevaluation

John Battalio

Instructors commonly assume that the successful online course must replicate its live counterpart by including a variety of interactions among student, instructor, and computer. Given the changing lifestyles prompted by
an evolving Internet, an increasing student need for autonomy, and student
learning styles, highly interactive courses may not necessarily be the best
online approach. In this article, I review research dealing with interactive
environments, present the results of my own interaction study, and propose
an integrative approach for the use of interaction that sees it in light of the
increasing integration of the Internet into students' daily lives.

In order to conserve resources and provide additional options and opportunities for students, many universities provide salary or course-reduction
incentives for instructors to convert at least one section of their courses
for distance delivery via the Internet. The need to provide these incentives stems from the general skepticism that a computer environment can
ever replicate the live class. In early conversions from live to online environments, the general consensus was that, for online courses to be suc-

The Perfect Online Course: Best Practices for Designing and Teaching
pp. 443–462
Copyright © 2009 by Information Age Publishing

cessful, that is, for them to have student experiences and outcomes equivalent to those of live courses, the online environment must replicate the live class as much as possible (Coppola, 2005; Gilbert & Moore, 1998). And because classroom instructors often believe that the live class is the right way, or, as Wagner (1994) puts it, "the real thing" (p. 9), they attempt to duplicate the experience online by providing written lectures, tests, and quizzes, class discussions, in-class exercises, and collaborative projects. As a result, incorporating a variety of interactions among students and instructor has become an expected feature of the online classroom.

Berge (1999) presents a perhaps representative argument for the incorporation of interaction into Web-based Internet courses. Though recognizing the widely held belief that high levels of interaction are desirable, he acknowledges the lack of evidence supporting the use of interaction for improving the quality of learning for distance-education students. Referencing instead studies of student satisfaction and persistence, and arguing that interaction is "central to the *expectations* of teachers and learners," he concludes that "interaction will continue to be seen as a critical component of formal education, regardless of whether there is research showing a direct link to increased effectiveness" (p. 5).

As a result, the process of converting live courses to Internet offerings often involves trying to figure out how to preserve the same kinds of experiences online as in the campus classroom by forcing technology to conform to traditional environments (Wagner, 1994, pp. 8-9). Consequently, instructors attempt to provide the multiple forms of interaction usually found in the live class. Even courseware developed since 2000 has modeled itself after its brick-and-mortar ancestors.

In a recent article in the *Quarterly Review of Distance Education*, Reisetter and Boris (2004) shed a different light on the place of interaction online. Their study of graduate student perceptions of effective online practices found not only that these students emphasized the importance of student-instructor interaction, but also that, contrary to widely held belief, students devalued peer interaction, somewhat uncharacteristic for graduate students. They suggest that students' preferred mode of learning online content may have "less to do with the dynamic of a learning community than it does with learning course content well on their own" (p. 289) and call for a reconsideration of online learning communities and the extent to which this type of online interaction is needed.

In this article, I try to respond to this request. After describing the forms of interaction available to the Internet instructor, I review the literature showing the traditional consensus that a variety of interaction is essential to success in online courses. I next present a number of research studies questioning the necessity of providing such variety and offer my own study as another example. Pointing out the effects that rapidly evolving technology has had on students' daily lives, I propose an integrative approach to online interaction and offer two suggestions for a realistic approach to incorporating interaction into distance education courses.

FORMS OF INTERACTION

Although support for online interaction has been commonplace, the exact meaning of the term *interaction* varies from one research study to the next. The review of research by Bannan-Ritland (2002) has described the many, varied, and sometimes contradictory definitions of interactivity used by researchers. Hirumi (2002), on the other hand, has attempted to put these definitions in perspective by proposing a framework to describe the interrelationship among the various types of interaction.

Consequently, I begin briefly by defining the term *interaction* as used here. For my naming convention, I have adopted the common practice of focusing on the main players, that is, instructor and learner. But I use two terms, *peer* and *student*, to identify the learner in order to distinguish the more authoritarian relationship implicit in student-instructor interaction. In addition, because an entirely different dynamic occurs when students interact to share thoughts in open discussion as opposed to collaborating for a grade, I use the term *collaborative group interaction* to refer to the latter. Therefore, the term interaction as used in this article is meant as a general term for a variety of interactivities: (1) student-instructor; (2) peer-to-peer; (3) peer-to-peer-to-instructor (as, for instance, in discussion board threads); (4) collaborative group; and (5) interaction with technology.

STUDIES SUPPORTING HIGHLY INTERACTIVE ENVIRONMENTS

In recent years, learning models have emphasized the necessity of social interaction in completing the learning process (Garrison, 2000; Gilbert & Moore, 1998; Swan et al., 2000; Tu & Corry, 2002). In fact, since the late 1990s, when distance education began its rapid rise on university campuses across the country, there has been much published research documenting the importance of collaborative interaction and learning communities in providing successful online experiences for distance education students, so much so that both peer and instructor collaboration is generally a "given" in distance education (see Hillman, Willis, & Gunawardena, 1994, p. 31).

After analyzing a number of studies on interaction published in the 1990s, Arbaugh (2000) concludes that "instructors need to emphasize each of the three dimensions of interaction [that is, student-instructor, peer-to-peer, and interaction with technology] within their Internet-based courses and develop methods to facilitate them" (p. 15). In another, more comprehensive survey of research into interaction during the 1990s, Roblyer and Wiencke (2003) find, among other things, that social variables enhance interaction in distance courses and that collaborative experiences enhance online student engagement. As a result, their resulting rubric for assessing interaction in distance courses privileges student-student and group collaboration. Perhaps as a result of these and similar studies, the Council of Regional Accrediting Commissions released in March 2001 its guidelines for evaluating distance education courses. Among its recommendations, the Council set interactivity standards higher than for the traditional classroom, such that online courses have to be "more interactive" than their live counterparts (Carnevale, 2000). Among the values the Council felt essential in distance education is the concept that "learning is dynamic and interactive, regardless of the setting in which it occurs" (Council of Regional Accrediting Commissions, 2001, p. 2).

Mabrito (2001) followed the council's lead, focusing on what he termed "collaborative interactivity" by promoting various forms of online discussions and collaborative activities to "more closely simulate the face-to-face classroom experience" (p. 86) by enabling both student-instructor and peer-to-peer interaction. Although Benbunan-Fich and Hiltz (2003) find no significant differences in the perception of learning by students in 17 undergraduate information systems courses regardless of the presentation mode, the researchers did see significant relationships between learning perception and the amount of student-instructor and group interaction for online courses. The researchers conclude that "measures of collaborative learning and active participation online ... [are] strong mediators of the outcomes of online courses" (p. 310). Lee and Gibson (2003) report similar results in a content analysis of asynchronous communication in an online graduate education course. Group, peer-to-peer, and student-instructor interaction were all important in developing self-direction, that is, "taking control and responsibility for one's own learning" (p. 185). Northrup (2002) has found that her online graduate students preferred to have interactive elements that simulate a campus-based class.

STUDIES QUESTIONING THE VALUE OF HIGH INTERACTIVITY

Although it has generally been assumed that interaction in all of its forms is an essential component of distance courses, it should be noted that Moore's popular classification did not assume learner-learner interaction a "given" in every situation (1989). And some more recent studies have begun to shed a different light on interaction in online education. Mehlenbacher, Miller, Covington, and Larsen (2000) posit that a student's learning style may determine the amount and forms of interaction required for success online. In particular, reflective learners may be hindered by synchronous interactions, interactive Web interfaces, and other instantaneous environments that do not "necessarily facilitate reflection or a careful examination of all the materials and tasks" (p. 177).

Perhaps highly interactive environments for everyone may not be the answer. Studying two contrasting Internet-based course designs, one a presentational or independent study design and the other an interactive design that involved both student-instructor and peer-to-peer interaction, Cook (2000) found that either design is acceptable, depending on the outcomes desired. Students in both designs achieved "multiple literacies" and "produced rhetorically effective, competently written documents" (p. 108).

Despite the positive findings for peer-to-peer and group interaction by Benbunan-Fitch and Hiltz (2003), the perception of group collaboration by students in fully online modes was the lowest of the modes studied (p. 307). Concluding their study, the researchers called for more research into the effects of collaborative learning, adding that "collaborative learning in online courses is a complex construct whose effects on outcomes are not always consistently positive" (p. 310). Swan et al. (2000) also reported negative findings regarding collaborative work: the more students' grades depended on collaboration, the less students thought they learned. Hawisher and Pemberton (1997) have documented students' negative reactions toward collaborative postings, and Thurmond, Wambach, Connors, and Frey (2002) found similar dissatisfaction among students participating in team/group work. Although Berge (1999) supports interaction in Web-based instruction, he acknowledges that inappropriate methodological approaches may lead to "loss of the student's attention, boredom, information overload, and frustration" (p. 9). Given such mixed messages, MacKinnon (2002) rightly concludes that interactivity is no panacea for online courses.

In fact, Palloff and Pratt (1999) describe successful online students as more introverted, intrinsically motivated, and self-disciplined than typical students, a characterization that more aptly fits the reflective learners described by Mehlenbacher et al. (2000). Collins (1996) describes the major costs of high interactivity: "a lack of thoughtfulness by the student because things move fast, and a lack of problem finding and construction by students because everything they do is responsive to some situation" (p. 352). He suggests instead a mixture of highly interactive and less interactive environments. And, in fact, the benefits Collins attributes to high interactivity, that is, immediate feedback, motivation, and employment of different skills and strategies, may all be accomplished in a highly interactive student-instructor environment (see Moore, 1989).

A STUDY OF STUDENT ATTITUDES ABOUT INTERACTION

When I first began teaching online courses in 1997, I assumed that my Internet class needed to replicate the activities I had found successful in live versions of the class. However, based on my own 8 years of teaching in this environment and on my research into my students' attitudes and preferences, I now believe that online courses need not, of necessity, include a variety of interaction, as shown in the study described below.

During summer 2004 and 2005, in an attempt to determine the importance of interaction in my Internet courses, I experimented with the delivery of four summer sections. The courses were sections of our undergraduate service course in technical communication, which consists primarily of a proposal and technical report, in addition to a number of other smaller assignments, including memo and instruction writing. I created two versions of the course: an interactive section and a self-directed section in which required interaction was kept to a minimum. I taught two sections of each version that summer.

In addition to some individual assignments, the interactive sections consisting of 31 students incorporated a variety of forms of interaction, including peer-to-peer and peer-to-peer-to-instructor interaction, as well as two major collaborative projects. Students were given weekly overviews and assignments, which were customized to that particular section. Applying the rubric proposed by Roblyer and Wiencke (2003) for assessing interactive qualities, this section had high levels of interactive qualities for the social/rapport-building and instructional design elements. Interactivity of technology resources had moderate qualities only because teleconferencing was not available.

In contrast, the self-directed sections had low to minimum interactive qualities for the three interaction elements. In these sections, which consisted of 28 students, all weekly overviews, assignments, and quizzes were made available the first day of class. The primary interaction was via e-mail between student and instructor, although students were asked to post discussion-board messages consisting of the drafts of their two major assignments. However, there was no interaction among students for this drafting. The purpose was to make available student examples for the class to review and to enable students to read instructor comments about each of the drafts.

To gather information about the student population taking the courses and to understand the effectiveness of these versions, I gave students the following two surveys: (1) an 11-question demographic questionnaire that solicited information about students' computer experience; prior experience with technical documents; educational preferences; and employment status, distance from campus, and age range; and (2) an end-of-semester opinion questionnaire to determine students' satisfaction with the course and their attitudes toward interaction. The response rates were between 85% and 100% for all eight surveys.

I obtained the following class profiles from the demographic questionnaires. This was the first Internet class for between 40% and 50% of those responding; most of the rest had taken one or two other online courses. Almost all students had prior experience with the courseware. Approximately two thirds of the students worked full time, a fourth part time. A somewhat smaller percentage of the self-directed students lived close to campus and were slightly younger than those from the interactive section. Because the questionnaire results for both sections were very similar, differences in students' attitudes toward either the course or interaction do not appear attributable to the demographic features surveyed.

When asked about their attitudes toward interaction, students in the interactive sections responded by a two-thirds margin that peer-to-peer interaction was more difficult online; yet they split about evenly as to whether or not participating in class discussions (that is, peer-to-peer-to-instructor interaction) and student-to-instructor interaction was more difficult online. However, regardless of the amount of class interaction, all but five, or approximately 90%, of the 55 respondents from all sections combined were satisfied with the course, despite the fact that two thirds of them said they preferred working on their own, rather than interacting with others. At least with these sections of students, it does not appear that the amount, or even presence, of a variety of forms of interaction played a significant role in student perceptions about the success of the course. This study at least does not appear to support the thesis that providing a variety of forms of interaction, that is, to replicate the campus class experience, will give students a greater sense of security and presence, thus giving them a more satisfying, and consequently more successful, experience. In fact, 60% of those responding (range = 50% to 83%) preferred Internet courses without student interaction, whether it be peer-to-peer or group collaboration (response rate = 55%, $n = 59$).

Finally, regarding interaction with technology, survey results of students' experience with, usage of, and attitudes toward technology mirror more recent studies refuting any significant influence of technology on the successful completion of online courses. Most students considered themselves at least average computer users, and between 50% and 60%

labeled themselves as "above average." The wide variety of Internet activities, from e-mail to chat rooms, videoconferencing, and instant messaging, and the frequency of usage, seem to verify students' self-classifications. When asked about the influence technology had on the course, three-fourths of the students felt that the quality of the course was unaffected by its being taught online. Likewise, the majority of students believed that the course was neither more difficult (65%) nor took more time (81%) than if they had taken it on campus. However, self-directed students were somewhat more evenly split when asked about the time involved: 72% said that time was not a factor, in contrast to 89% of students in the interactive sections—a logical contrast given the nature of self-direction. These results add to the evidence that most students are now comfortable with electronic environments and do not need online experiences that replicate either the campus classroom experience or the interactive methodologies associated with live courses.

TWENTY-FIRST CENTURY TECHNOLOGY AND ATTITUDES

What are the reasons for the contradictions in research findings concerning the need for a variety of interaction in distance courses? Because of the many personnel, time, and budgetary constraints in conducting human-subject research within educational contexts, published research in distance education commonly analyzes outcomes based on student opinion questionnaires, which may be easily obtained without significant administrative overhead. For instance, of the 27 research studies I reviewed on the topic of interaction published since 2000, 75% of them rely—many almost exclusively—on student preference and/or opinion surveys in drawing conclusions about their data, just as I have here. So to answer the question about the changing nature of research into interaction as a central component in the distance class, one must look at the evolution in the way the general public views and uses the Internet because student perceptions will naturally be affected by students' attitudes about and usage of distance education's primary delivery medium. Reisetter and Boris (2004) argue that the "effects of technology in computer-mediated communication" (p. 289) may be responsible for the changing nature of group interaction, but I suggest that evolving technology forces us to reconsider our overall implementation of online interaction.

Twenty-first century attitudes and behaviors are evolving at an exponential rate, as shown by the following facts and events.

1. Internet connectivity continues to rise, up from 33% of the popula-
    tion in 2000 to 68% in 2005 (Miniwatts Marketing Group, 2006).

2. An increasing number of homes have upgraded to high-speed
    broadband cable and DSL lines, 53% of home-Internet users in
    2005, up from 35% in 2003, according to the Pew Research Center
    Internet Project (Horrigan, 2005), with the rise expected to con-
    tinue (Miniwatts Marketing Group, 2006). Consequently, Internet
    access is now more efficient and reliable than ever before for mil-
    lions of Americans. Even for those who cannot afford this more
    expensive mode, there is more often than not high-speed access at
    universities and businesses.

3. Wireless mobile technology now allows instant access to the Inter-
    net via Internet cafes, and the technology is now evolving not only
    to create both free and subscriber Internet hotspots across an
    entire city (see jiwire.com), but also to interconnect these hotspots
    among cities. Called WiMAX, this new wireless technology enables
    fiber-optic and microwave broadband connections over long dis-
    tances and may be the answer to enabling high-speed Internet
    access in rural areas across the country. Even without this technol-
    ogy, rural adoption of broadband is still increasing, with the gap
    between rural and nonrural cut in half within the last 2 years (Hor-
    rigan & Murray, 2006).

4. In addition, increasing numbers of people consider the Internet an
    important information source; see, for instance, the declining tele-
    vision news ratings, thought to be caused at least in part by the
    Internet (Project for Excellence in Journalism, 2004). The video
    streaming of news clips and events is now a commonplace substi-
    tute for television news stories. Consumer surveys in 2005 by Jupi-
    terResearch found that 50% of online adults use the Internet for
    their daily news ("Internet Growing," 2005). Note also the rise of
    the blog phenomenon in the past year as the latest Internet news
    source. By mid-July 2005, Wired News reported about 12 million
    blogs, with 10 more created every second (Penenberg, 2005). By
    early 2006, the blog search engine Technorati was indexing over
    27 million of them.

5. Sales of information appliances, that is, Internet-capable handheld
    devices like PDAs and cell phones, have risen exponentially in
    recent years. Worldwide PDA sales increased 25% to 3.4 million,
    just for the first quarter of 2005 (Lemon, 2005). eTForecasts, a
    market research and consulting company, projects communications
    sales, a category dominated by Web-enabled cell phones, to grow

from over 10 million in 2002 to 65 million in 2008 (eTForcasts, 2003).

6. E-commerce continues to expand far beyond the online shopping malls that first appeared in the mid 1990s. More services than ever are available online, among them major consumer services like banking, bill-pay, and long-distance telephone.

7. The multimedia use of the Internet for work and play continues to evolve: with the continued expansion of high-speed Internet, videoconferencing will eventually become commonplace in the home; and the release of first-run movies on the Internet now seems practical.

Considering recent technological change, Garrison (2000) wonders if distance education theory has "kept pace with new, affordable applications of communications technology and the changing educational needs of a learning society" (p. 2). Although his answer is to privilege transactional theories that adopt collaborative approaches, is this answer simplistic?

The point is that our mental model of the Internet does not envision a specific place and time, and does not have the physical restrictions associated with a traditional classroom. The Internet is a technology that has increasingly pervaded our lives and will continue to do so, and the primary demographic leading this evolution is the younger population, our major student audience. Not unexpectedly, a Pew Internet Project survey found the most active group of Internet users to be between ages 12 and 29 (Fox & Madden, 2005).

Consequently, today's students often see the opportunity to take a class on the Internet as a means to integrate their learning experiences into their daily schedules, not the other way around. Student preferential surveys, including my own, support this view. Online students consistently say that they have chosen this mode of instruction because they believe it will save them time and will be more convenient for them (Arbaugh, 2001; Johnson, 1999, p. 166). Many students opting for online courses are nontraditional students who must manage full- or part-time jobs and families. Consequently, attending traditional courses at specific times and places, especially those in which the formation of collaborative online communities is a priority, is problematic for them. Commenting on changing student demographics, Kanuka (2001) describes an even more radically different university student: "Many adult learners view themselves as customers, rather than students, and demand readily accessible learning services that are tailored to their needs" (p. 51).

AN INTEGRATIVE APPROACH TO INTERACTION

Roblyer and Wiencke (2003) have commented that interaction has "come to be considered a sine qua non for successful distance courses" (p. 77). But exactly what kind of interaction should instructors strive for? This new twenty-first century lifestyle requires that we take a different approach to incorporating interaction into the distance education experience—referred to here as an integrative approach—by incorporating interaction into the seamless interface that is evolving between twenty-first century technology and people's daily lives. Today's students need course materials, assignments, and instructors that are easily accessible on the fly whether by workstation or handheld device, whether at home or in the office.

It also means that issues related to interaction with technology have faded into the background, even though the implementation of technology has not. Although studies prior to 2000 often found student comfort with and/or use of technology an important factor in the success of or satisfaction with the online course (Scott & Rockwell, 1997; see also the meta-analysis by Allen, Bourhis, Burrell, & Mabry, 2002), recent studies have not found similar associations (Stein, Wanstreet, Calvin, Overtoom & Wheaton, 2005; Swan et al., 2000), most likely because of students' increasing familiarity with computers and the Internet, although some cite the results as evidence of adaptive structuration, where technology becomes subservient to users' adaptations of it (Poole & DeSanctis, 1990). In any event, whether or not an online class can use videoconferencing, video streaming, Macromedia Flash presentations, and Java applets depends largely on connectivity speed, rather than on technological expertise—most of these interfaces now function seamlessly.

Thus, an integrative approach to interaction suggests that instructors consider how to integrate interactivity such that it accommodates students' needs. Given students' evolving attitudes and experiences with the Internet and technology, and the mixed results of research into online interaction, here are two suggestions that provide a more accommodating approach to online interaction.

Student-Instructor Interaction as the Only Required Interaction

Despite the conflicting research surrounding peer and group interaction, and the diminishing need to assist students with technology, one type of interaction continually rates high in online research studies: student-instructor interaction. Certainly, busy students, for whom the online class is only one part of their Internet existence, need guidance through the course and assurance that they are progressing successfully. In this type of environment, social interaction may no longer be considered the primary means through which learning evolves.

The study by Swan et al. (2000) of 264 online courses offered through the SUNY Learning Network finds only three factors contributing significantly to the success of online courses—one of them student-instructor interaction. The researchers conclude that "an instructor who interacts frequently and constructively with students" (p. 379) is important to course success. The study by Arbaugh (2001) of online MBA students also finds student-instructor interaction a predictor of student learning. Instructor immediacy behaviors, such as use of personal examples and humor, encouragement of student ideas, and calling students by name, were found to be important factors in the study's findings (pp. 44-46). Only instructors can provide the encouragement, guidance, and reassurance that online students need to be assured they are progressing successfully. Volery (2001), studying the factors contributing to the success of online learning, found that instructor-student interaction is critical for course success to the extent that today's technology cannot substitute for an effective instructor. However, the researcher suggests a role change from lecturer to "learning catalyst," that is, as an enabler who can empower students to "discover their own learning" (p. 90). Grady and Davis (2005) use the concept of scaffolding to show the many ways instructors function as catalysts. Most recently, Stein et al. (2005) have identified the importance of "instructor-initiated interaction in the form of guidance and encouragement" in overall student satisfaction (p. 115).

A variety of communication opportunities, both traditional and Internet, enable instructors to integrate student-instructor interaction into distance courses. Telephone access, live office hours, online office hours in a chat room or via instant messaging, and e-mail are all ways to provide multiple means of access for students.

Different Versions of Courses
With Varying Degrees of Interaction

The influential theory of transactional distance proposed by Moore (1991) supports the concept of offering a variety of course formats to distance students. Theorizing that variations in the amount of dialogue (that is, instructor-student interaction) and structure (that is, the course design) influence psychological and communications gaps, he concludes that "much care should be given to determine both the structure of the program and the nature of the dialogue that is sufficient and appropriate for each set of particular learners and, ideally, each individual learner," that is, according to the amount of autonomy each learner has (p. 5). A number of recent studies support his theory. For instance, in a study of seven Web-based courses, Thurmond et al. (2002) find not only that students prefer a variety of ways to assess learning, but also find it to be the strongest predictor of student satisfaction. Allen et al. (2002), in reflecting upon the results of their meta-analysis of 25 student-satisfaction studies, suggest the "need for diagnosis [of student learning style] or providing a course in multiple formats" (p. 92).

And as I argue here, the use of the Internet as the primary distance delivery mode also requires a different, more integrative approach to interaction, one that offers more than one version of the same course, varying the amount and variety of online interaction accordingly. Experienced instructors will find that, once these versions are set up, they are no more time-consuming to teach than the traditional approach because, where one version may require more of an instructor's attention, the other requires less.

We know the importance of interacting with others in the workplace, but students see things differently. Unless we can accommodate their own needs as well, the resulting dissatisfaction will likely reduce the chances for effective learning outcomes. The challenge then is to find a middle ground where we provide interactive opportunities while still accommodating students' needs. Here are three possible ways to accomplish this goal.

Versions for Self-Directed and Interactive Learning Styles

Research into the influence of learning styles on online student success may be a key to determining the kinds of required online interaction. In the mid 1970s, as part of a research project to test his theories about distance learning, Moore (1984) studied the influence of cognitive styles on student learning in independent study environments, finding a positive relationship between field independence and distance study. Field-independent students typically are self-directed, prefer self-evaluation, are task oriented, and are less affected by social stimuli. Harrison and Bergen (2000) likewise describe successful online students as self-motivated and independent.

As part of a more recent study comparing learning in Web-based versus conventional courses, Mehlenbacher et al. (2000) included a learning styles inventory questionnaire as one means of comparing student performance in the two course designs. The researchers found that learning style did affect student performance. Reflective learners preferred environments that encourage reading to learn and act, as opposed to highly interactive interfaces, whereas reflective global learners more readily understood instructional goals and course content, thereby decreasing the amount of student-instructor interaction. In a similar approach, studies by Irani, Telg, Scherler, and Harrington (2003) and Soles and Moller (2001) suggest a relationship between success in distance education and students' personality traits, such as extrovert, introvert, sensing, and thinking. The meta-analysis by Allen et al. (2002) notes that any given population of students may contain those with learning styles that favor distance education, while others prefer face-to-face environments. Like Mehlenbacher et al., Aragon, Johnson, and Shaik (2002) found online students to be more reflective, and additionally found them to prefer abstract conceptualization (learning by thinking) (p. 236). While they report no significance difference in the learning styles of their live versus online students, the use of online lectures to conduct the distance course certainly played a role in the outcome. Students encountering the same type of instructional methods would likely use similar learning strategies.

Versions for College-Age and Nontraditional Students

Although college-aged students, particularly those on small or rural campuses, may find online learning communities attractive, non-traditional students, especially those with families and full-time employment, will not be able to devote the time required for multi-level interaction. As the number of nontraditional students continues to rise due to economic and societal pressures and the need for retraining (Turner, 2003), universities will need to find ways to integrate this growing student population into online courses.

Graduate and Undergraduate Versions

Of the 25 recent research studies I reviewed for this article, 18 (72%) used graduate students as subjects. Graduate seminar courses, for instance, tend to be more theoretical than undergraduate courses. Consequently, peer-to-peer-to-instructor interaction may be necessary for encouraging the exploration of ideas and knowledge building that comes only through the development of a learning community. For instance, the syllabi used by Palloff and Pratt (1999) to describe their approach are examples of such courses. Many such graduate courses are highly interactive, whereby students may experience the dynamic, ephemeral nature of communication (Zachry, 2005). That research tends to show a preference for interactive learning may be the result of the large number of studies using graduate students as their subjects.

The study by Kanuka (2001) is particularly relevant here because it compares both graduate and undergraduate students' perceptions of the same subject matter taught by distance. The study found that undergraduates had a much greater need for "structure, motivational techniques, and guided study" (p. 65) than graduate students and concludes that, for Web-based learning, dialogue (interaction) and structure are most effective when matched with students' "needs and ability to be autonomous learners" (p. 69). A more recent study of both undergraduate and graduate student satisfaction by Stein et al. (2005) echoes this finding. Researchers concluded that the amount of course interaction should be fluid so that "autonomous learners can identify their learning needs" (p. 116).

CONCLUSION

This reevaluation of interaction online provides a contemporary perspective of how extensively online interaction in all its forms can be used. Informed by 25 of the most recent studies into interaction online, and including an additional study of its own, it is an up-to-date review for instructors and researchers wishing to explore the options that interaction offers. More importantly, however, it informs the body of research into interaction online by placing this research into the broader context of twenty-first century technology and the students who use it, providing insight into the sometimes conflicting research into the amount of interaction required for successful online instruction. The question is not whether highly interactive environments are educationally sound but rather whether the context in which distance education is delivered affects the amount of interactivity needed. In describing the state of twenty-first century technology and its relationship to today's online learners, the article offers a realistic set of options for integrating varying amounts and types of interaction into today's online courses, while at the same time recognizing the importance of interaction in the learning process.

If the integrative approaches to interaction online as described in this article are adopted, distance-education researchers are among the benefactors. The wide array of evolving electronic technologies provides researchers the means for designing numerous studies to assess the technologies that best help instructors accomplish the goals of effective teaching and learning in the twenty-first century. In fact, Levin (2002), considering the exponential evolution of electronic technologies, envisions higher education by the year 2020 as a "seamless integration" between learners and their electronic environment, which at least for introductory courses may consist largely of interaction with computer-based intelligent systems. In the meantime, this integration is beginning to take various forms. For instance, a number of universities are now encouraging the instructor to integrate iPods into the classroom by enabling downloads of course content ("Rural," 2006). In particular, XML technology with single sourcing and dynamic content delivery may be the most promising means to provide limitless ways for learning, customized for multiple learning styles. RSS technology may be yet another means for pushing course information to students in real time.

However, the greatest beneficiaries of the integrative approaches advocated in this article are the students who strive to pursue their educational goals online. By providing students different versions of courses with varying degrees of interaction, instructors will more likely ensure that online students have a positive, rewarding experience. As Fahy and Ally (2005) suggest, if instructors do not allow students to participate according to their individual styles and preferences, "the requirement for online interaction may ironically become a potential barrier to learning" (p. 19). Consequently, the calls by Levin, Levin, and Waddoups (1999) for multiple ways of learning online and by Kanuka, Collett, and Caswell (2002) for flexibility in adapting methodologies that accommodate learner autonomy seem sensible.

Still, as numerous authors point out, not all students can be successful online. Some students will continue to need the reinforcement that comes only from meeting and working with people face to face, thus the recent rise in popularity of hybrid courses—that is, at least until technology makes commonplace videoconferencing, the interactive leveler that has the greatest potential to replicate the various forms of classroom interaction without the pitfall of artificiality. As a result, the future holds much in store for us as we explore the various ways that modern technology may facilitate effective interaction online.

REFERENCES

Allen, M., Bourhis J., Burrell, N., & Mabry, E. (2002). Comparing student satisfaction with distance education to traditional classrooms in higher education: A meta-analysis. *The American Journal of Distance Education, 16*(2), 83-97.

Aragon, S. R., Johnson, S. D., & Shaik, N. (2002). The influence of learning style preferences on student success in online versus face-to-face environments. *The American Journal of Distance Education, 16*(4), 227-244.

Arbaugh, J. B. (2000). How classroom environment and student engagement affect learning in Internet-based MBA courses. *Business Communication Quarterly, 63*(4), 9-26.

Arbaugh, J. B. (2001). How instructor immediacy behaviors affect student satisfaction and learning in Web-based courses. *Business Communication Quarterly, 64*(4), 42-54.

Bannan-Ritland, B. (2002). Computer-mediated communication, elearning, and interactivity: A review of the research. *Quarterly Review of Distance Education, 3*(2), 161-179.

Benbunan-Fich, R., & Hiltz, S. R. (2003). Mediators of the effectiveness of online courses. *IEEE Transactions on Professional Communication, 46*(4), 298-312.

Berge, Z. L. (1999). Interaction in post-secondary Web-based learning. *Educational Technology, 39*(1), 5-11.

Carnevale, D. (2000, August 11). Accrediting bodies consider new standards for distance-education programs. *Chronicle of Higher Education Online.* Retrieved April 21, 2006, from http://chronicle.com/free/2000/08/2000081101u.htm

Collins, A. (1996). Design issues for learning environments. In S. Vosniadou, E. De Corte, R. Glaser, & H. Mandl (Eds.), *International perspectives on the design of technology-supported learning environments* (pp. 347-361). Mahwah, NJ: Erlbaum.

Cook, K. C. (2000). Online professional communication: Pedagogy, instructional design, and student preference in Internet-based distance education. *Business Communication Quarterly, 63*(2), 106-110.

Coppola, N. W. (2005). Changing roles for online teachers of technical communication. In C. H. Sides (Series Ed.) & K. C. Cook & K. Grant-Davie (Vol. Eds.), *Online education: Global questions, local answers* (pp. 89-99). Amityville, NY: Baywood.

Council of Regional Accrediting Commissions. (2001, March). *Statement of commitment by the regional accrediting commissions for the evaluation of electronically offered degree and certificate programs.* Retrieved November 11, 2006, from http://www.wcet.info/services/publications/accreditation/

eTForecasts. (2003, 11 March). *Information appliances: Computer platforms invade electronic devices.* Retrived February 3, 2006, from http://www.etforecasts.com/products/ES_infoappsv3.htm

Fahy, P. J., & Ally, M. (2005). Student learning style and asynchronous computer-mediated conferencing (CMC) interaction. *The American Journal of Distance Education, 19*(1), 5-22.

Fox, S., & Madden, M. (2005, December). *Pew Internet & American life project: Generations online.* Retrieved February 3, 2006, from http://www.pewinternet.org/pdfs/PIP_Generations_Memo.pdf

Garrison, R. (2000, June). Theoretical challenges for distance education in the 21st century: A shift from structural to transactional issues. *International Review of Research in Open and Distance Learning 1*(1). Retrieved November 14, 2006, from http://www.irrodl.org/index.php/irrodl/article/view/2/333

Gilbert, L., & Moore, D. R. (1998). Building interactivity into Web courses: Tools for social and instructional interaction. *Educational Technology, 38*(3), 29-35.

Grady, H. M., & Davis, M. T. (2005). Teaching well online with instructional and procedural scaffolding. In C. H. Sides (Series Ed.) & K. C. Cook & K. Grant-Davie (Vol. Eds.), *Online education: Global questions, local answers* (pp. 101-122). Amityville, NY: Baywood.

Harrison, N., & Bergen, C. (2000). Some design strategies for developing an online course. *Educational Technology, 40*(1), 57-60.

Hawisher, G. E., & Pemberton, M. A. (1997). Writing across the curriculum encounters asynchronous learning networks or WAC meets up with ALN. *Journal of Asynchronous Learning Networks, 1*(1), 52-72.

Hillman, D. C. A., Willis, D. J., & Gunawardena, C. N. (1994). Learner-interface interaction in distance education: An extension of contemporary models and strategies for practitioners. *The American Journal of Distance Education, 8*(2), 30-42.

Hirumi, A. (2002). A framework for analyzing, designing, and sequencing planned elearning interactions. *Quarterly Review of Distance Education, 3*(2), 141-160.

Horrigan, J., & Murray, K. (2006, February). *Pew Internet and American life project: Rural broadband Internet use.* Retrieved February 27, 2006, from http://www.pewinternet.org/pdfs/PIP_Rural_Broadband.pdf

Horrigan, J. B. (2005, September). *Broadband adoption at home in the United States: Growing but slowing.* Paper presented at the 33rd Annual Telecommunications Policy Research Conference, Arlington, VA. Retrieved April 10, 2006, from http://www.pewinternet.org/pdfs/PIP_Broadband.TPRC_Sept05.pdf

Internet growing as main source of news among online adults. (2005, April 26). *TechWeb Technology News.* Retrieved January 26, 2006, from http://www.techweb.com/rss/161600643

Irani, T., Telg, R., Scherler, C., & Harrington, M. (2003). Personality type and its relationship to distance education students' course perceptions and performance. *Quarterly Review of Distance Education, 4*(4), 445-453.

Johnson, J. L. (1999). Distance education and technology: What are the choices for higher education? *Journal of Educational Computing Research, 21*(2), 165-181.

Kanuka, H. (2001). University student perceptions of the use of the Web in distance-delivered programs. *The Canadian Journal of Higher Education, 31*(3), 49-72.

Kanuka, H., Collett, D., & Caswell, C. (2002). University instructor perceptions of the use of asynchronous text-based discussion in distance courses. *The American Journal of Distance Education, 16*(3), 151-167.

Lee, J., & Gibson, C. C. (2003). Developing self-direction in an online course through computer-mediated interaction. *The American Journal of Distance Education, 17*(3), 173-187.

Lemon, S. (2005, May 4). PDA sales increase sharply. *PC World.* Retrieved February 3, 2006, from http://www.pcworld.com/news/article/0,aid,120698,00.asp

Levin, J. (2002). A 2020 vision: Education in the next two decades. *Quarterly Review of Distance Education, 3*(1), 105-114.

Levin, J., Levin, S. R., & Waddoups, G. (1999). Multiplicity in learning and teaching: A framework for developing innovative online education. *Journal of Research on Computing in Education, 32*(2), 256-269.

Mabrito, M. (2001). Facilitating interactivity in an online business writing course. *Business Communication Quarterly, 64*(3), 81-86.

MacKinnon, G. R. (2002). Practical advice for first time online instructors: A qualitative study. *Journal of Instruction Delivery Systems, 16*(1), 21-25.

Mehlenbacher, B., Miller, C. R., Covington, D., & Larsen, J. S. (2000). Active and interactive learning online: A comparison of Web-based and conventional writing classes. *IEEE Transactions on Professional Communication 43*(2), 166-184.

Miniwatts Marketing Group. (2006). United States of America Internet usage and broadband usage report. *Internet World Stats.* Retrieved January 26, 2006, from http://www.internetworldstats.com/am/us.htm

Moore, M. (1984). On a theory of independent study. In D. Sewart, D. Keegan, & B. Holmberg (Eds.), *Distance education: International perspectives* (pp. 68-94). London: Croom Helm.

Moore, M. G. (1989). Editorial: Three types of interaction. *The American Journal of Distance Education, 3*(2), 1-6.

Moore, M. G. (1991). Editorial: Distance education theory. *The American Journal of Distance Education, 5*(3), 1-6.

Northrup, P. T. (2002). Online learners' preferences for interaction. *Quarterly Review of Distance Education, 3*(2), 219-226.

Palloff, R. M., & Pratt, K. (1999). *Building learning communities in cyberspace: Effective strategies for the online classroom.* San Francisco: Jossey-Bass.

Penenberg, A. L. (2005, July 14). Technorati: A new public utility. *Wired News.* Retrieved January 26, 2006, from http://www.wired.com/news/culture/1,68204-0.html

Poole, M. S., & DeSanctis, G. (1990). Understanding the use of group decision support systems: The theory of adaptive structuration. In J. Fulk & C. Steinfield (Eds.), *Organizations and communication technology* (pp. 173-193). Newbury Park, CA: Sage.

Project for Excellence in Journalism. (2004). *The state of the news media 2004: An annual report on American journalism.* Retrieved January 26, 2006, from http://www.stateofthenewsmedia.org/narrative_networktv_intro.asp?cat=1&media=4

Reisetter, M., & Boris, G. (2004). What works: Student perceptions of effective elements in online learning. *Quarterly Review of Distance Education, 5*(4), 277-291.

Roblyer, M. D., & Wiencke, W. R. (2003). Design and use of a rubric to assess and encourage interactive qualities in distance courses. *The American Journal of Distance Education, 17*(2), 77-98.

Rural college pushes ipod use for lectures. (2006, March 20). *Education with Student News.* Retrieved March 21, 2006, from http://www.cnn.com/2006/EDUCATION/03/20/ipod.university.ap/

Scott, C. R., & Rockwell, S. C. (1997). The effects of communication, writing, and technology apprehension on likelihood to use new communication technologies. *Communication Education, 46,* 44–62.

Soles, C., & Moller, L. (2001). Myers Briggs type preferences in distance learning education. *International Journal of Educational Technology, 2*(2). Retrieved March 18, 2006, from http://www.ao.uiuc.edu/ijet/v2n2/v2n2articles.html

Stein, D. S., Wanstreet, C. E., Calvin, J., Overtoom, C., & Wheaton, J. E. (2005). Bridging the transactional distance gap in online learning environments. *The American Journal of Distance Education, 19*(2), 105-118.

Swan, K., Shea, P., Fredericksen, E., Pickett, A., Pelz, W., & Maher, G. (2000). Building knowledge building communities: Consistency, contact and communication in the virtual classroom. *Journal of Educational Computing Research, 23*(4), 359-383.

Thurmond, V. A., Wambach, K., Connors, H. R., & Frey, B. B. (2002). Evaluation of student satisfaction: Determining the impact of a Web-based environment by controlling for student characteristics. *The American Journal of Distance Education 16*(3), 169-189.

Tu, C., & Corry, M. (2002). eLearning communities. *Quarterly Review of Distance Education, 3*(2), 207-218.

Turner, S. E. (2003, May). *For-profit colleges and non-traditional students: Responses to cyclical shocks.* Paper presented at the NCSPE Conference on Markets, For-Profits and Higher Education, New York, NY. Retrieved March 17, 2006, from http://www.ncspe.org/publications_files/turner.pdf

Volery, T. (2001). Online education: An exploratory study into success factors. *Journal of Educational Computing Research 24*(1), 77-92.

Wagner, E. D. (1994). In support of a functional definition of interaction. *The American Journal of Distance Education, 8*(2), 6-29.

Zachry, M. (2005). Paralogy and online pedagogy. In C. H. Sides (Series Ed.) & K. C. Cook & K. Grant-Davie (Vol. Eds.), *Online education: Global questions, local answers* (pp. 177-190). Amityville, NY: Baywood.

CHAPTER 25

ONLINE LEARNERS' PREFERENCES FOR INTERACTION

Pamela T. Northrup

The purpose of this study was to investigate types of interactions that students perceived to be important for elearning. Interaction attributes studied in this investigation included content interaction, conversation and collaboration, intrapersonal/metacognitive skills, and need for support. This study was an initial investigation of learner perceptions of online interaction. Data were collected through the administration of the Online Learning Interaction Inventory (OLLI) to 52 graduate students in an online masters program. Online learners reported that flexibility ($M = 4.65$, $SD = .74$) and convenience ($M = 4.13$, $SD = 1.14$) were the two primary reasons why they selected to learn at a distance. Indicators of interaction were noted in each of the four interaction attribute areas. However, the idea of self-regulating learning ($M = 4.58$, $SD = .72$) and having timely feedback from the instructor ($M = 4.48$, $SD = .64$) was reported as most valued by participants.

Interaction has been defined from many perspectives. Most simply stated *interaction is engagement in learning* (Hillman, Willis & Gunawardena, 1994). It is agreed that interaction must be designed into an instructional

The Perfect Online Course: Best Practices for Designing and Teaching
pp. 463–473

program and that it is an important variable for online learning. Berge (1999) suggests that interaction is important to learner satisfaction and that it assists in maintaining student persistence in courses. With retention in online learning programs being as low as 50% in some cases and course completion rates in traditional courses at 10-20 percentage points higher than in online courses (Carr, 2000), learner satisfaction is a key variable. With interaction being a component of overall student satisfaction, interaction should be considered when trying to increase retention in online courses. However, from the online learners point of view, too much interaction may be perceived as busywork and lead to frustration, boredom, and overload (Berge, 1999); while too little interaction may result in student isolation. Both are considered frustrating and a balance has to be found.

The term interaction has been classified using many frameworks and taxonomies over the years. The most notable is Moore's (1989) communications framework classifying engagement in learning through (a) interaction between participants and learning materials, (b) interaction between participants and tutors/experts, and (c) interaction among participants. Interaction between participants and learning materials may take many forms and may be as simple as a student logging onto an online course and reading the weekly text. Or, it may be more complex with students engaged in an individual WebQuest (Dodge, 2001). Interaction between participants and experts likely would include participant to instructor dialog over an assignment communicated via email, chat room, or some other asynchronous method. Moore's third classification, interaction among participants may include collaboration among teams of online students discussing the problem of the week through a threaded discussion or on a group listserv. All three of the classifications of interaction are very open-ended, allowing for much flexibility in the design of engaging, interactive online learning.

Another approach to classify interaction is Gilbert and Moore's (1998) approach, dichotomizing it as content or social interaction. Content interaction is always directed at attaining the specific learning outcomes or goal of the instruction. Although a broad category, the notion is that any type of interaction directed at achieving instructional success would be classified as content interaction. Social interaction on the other hand, provides opportunities for peers to connect in non-task specific conversation (Northrup, 2001a). At least initially, this should be intentionally designed into the course. As a course evolves, this type of dialog will continue on its own. By the very nature of social interaction, learners will be able to directly foster content interaction (Liaw & Huang, 2000). Typically both content and social interactions are interwoven into highly interactive online courses.

Sorting through interaction frameworks to determine the most appropriate interactions for given learning outcomes is difficult at best. Northrup (2001a) provides a set of interaction attributes that can be used to select strategies and tactics to facilitate online interaction. The attributes encompass levels of content interaction, types of dialog through communications and collaboration, levels of student self-directedness, and types of support for the learner anytime, anyplace.

With most research on interaction focused on classifying the types of interactions or building frameworks from which designers would select appropriate interactions for given learning outcomes, it seemed apparent that there should be an upper and lower limit to the types of interactions used for a given set of instruction. Additionally, with *student perception of interaction being complete* as such an important variable for ongoing participation in the course (Zhang & Fulford, 1994), the relationships of student perception to the attributes of interaction should be considered.

PURPOSE OF THE STUDY

The purpose of this study was to investigate the types of interactions that students perceived to be important for online learning. The interaction attributes investigated included content interaction, conversation and collaboration, intrapersonal/metacognitive skills, and need for support. Also investigated were reasons why learners were taking online courses. It was presumed that students taking courses for convenience, flexibility, or preference would likely be more pleased with interaction in online course than those required to take an online course because it wasn't offered on campus. This study was an initial investigation of learner perceptions of online interaction. Data were collected through the administration of the Online Learning Interaction Inventory (OLLI) (Northrup, 2001b).

METHOD

Participants

This study consisted of 52 graduate students in an online masters program in instructional technology. Thirty-four of the students were female and 18 were male. Participants ranged in their experiences with online learning with 14 students in their first online course, 24 have taken 2-4 online courses, 10 have taken 5-8 online courses, and 4 have taken 9 or more online courses. The majority of students (27) were in the 36-50-age range, with 18 students in the 26-35-age range. The remainder of the students were under the age of 25 (5 students) or over the age of 50 (2 students). Students were selected to participate in this study based on where they were in the program of study. Intact classes of students were selected from two courses at the beginning of their online learning sequence and two courses at the end of their online learning sequence.

Instrumentation

The instrument used for this study was the Online Learning Interaction Inventory (OLLI), with a reliability coefficient of .95. The OLLI focused on the four interaction attributes of content interaction, conversation and collaboration, intrapersonal/metacognitive skills, and need for support. Each of the attributes of the OLLI were designed around the indicators for interaction (Table 25.1).

The OLLI was divided into six sections with a total of 50 items. Section 1 dealt with demographic information. Section 2 included five questions on reasons why students selected to take an online course. Section 3-6 addressed each of the interaction attributes and were rated on a five point Likert scale with 1 representing strongly disagree to 5 representing strongly agree. Section 3 dealt with *Content Interaction*. There were 13 items relating to the indicators of content interaction. Section 4 addressed *Conversation and Collaboration* with 14 items relating to the indicators of interaction. Section 5 addressed *Intrapersonal/Metacognitive Skills* with 7 items relating to the indicators of interaction. Section 6 addressed *Support* with 7 items relating to the indicators of interaction.

Procedure

The Online Learning Interaction Inventory was pilot tested with 26 students during the semester prior to implementation of this study. Students from two online classes in the masters program in instructional technology were sent a detailed email stating that the purpose of the OLLI was to test the instrument and to gather information about interaction and online learning. Students selected for the pilot test were in their last sequence of courses in the online program. Students had one week to complete the online instrument. Based on the pilot study, some items were reworded, two demographic identifier questions were added, and the classification of interaction attributes were clustered from five to four areas. In the pilot study, collaboration and communication were individual attributes. When updating the instrument, collaboration and communication were clustered into one attribute.

Table 25.1.   Indicators of Interaction

Variable	Indicator
Content interaction	Level of structure
	Level of pacing
	Learning from multiple mediums
	Learning using interactive strategies
Conversation and collaboration	Peer relationships
	Participation in learning community
	Peer discussion
	Teaming
	Peer tutoring
	Feedback from peers
	Feedback from instructors
	Learning using interactive strategies
Intrapersonal/metacognitive	Self-monitoring of progress
	Structure of embedded cognitive strategies
	Posted times for getting online
	Instructor encouragement/guidance
	Advance organizers
	Notetaking guides
Support	Timeliness of responses
	Mentoring
	Tutorials
	Peer tips
	Corresponding with instructor

In the current study, students from four online classes were sent a detailed email stating that the purpose of the Online Learning Interaction Inventory (OLLI) was to gather information to continue to make the online courses and the program more appropriately interactive. The email indicated that data would be reported and used as research as well as be used for formative evaluation purposes. Students were provided with the URL to take the OLLI online. In two of the four courses, the OLLI was posted as a weekly assignment. In the other two courses taking the OLLI was optional. Students were provided with one week to complete the 50-item instrument.

Data Analysis

Data were analyzed by item using frequency, means, and standard deviations to report areas of interaction that are perceived to be valuable or a hindrance to success for online learning. Research questions for the study are as follows:

- Question 1: Why do students learn online?
- Question 2: What interaction attributes do students perceive as important for online learning?

RESULTS AND DISCUSSION

Data collected from the OLLI were analyzed by attribute, with frequency, means and standard deviations reported. Reported first will be responses from the first research question related to students learning online. The second research question related to the interaction attributes will be reported by each of the four interaction attributes.

Learning Online

Learning online is related to the first research question, *Why do students learn online?* The majority of students selected to take online courses for convenience ($M = 4.13$, $SD = 1.14$) and flexibility ($M = 4.65$, $SD = 1.33$). Most of the students reported that they could attend school even if the course was campus-based ($M = 3.58$, $SD = 1.58$), indicating that many of the students lived close enough to the campus to take campus-based courses. Only 12 students (23%) reported that it would be impossible to take the course if it were not offered online.

Interaction Attributes

There are four interaction attributes related to the second research question. Attributes included content interaction, collaboration and conversation, intrapersonal/metacognitive strategies, and support. Responses are included by attribute for the following research question: *What interaction attributes do students perceive as important for online learning?*

Content Interaction

In general, it appears that students agree that interacting with the content is important to their online learning experiences. Overall, they report that they like partially individualized courses with some instructor direction ($M = 3.77$, $SD = .85$). Participants also reported a desire to interact with content delivered via audio-narrated online presentations ($M = 3.65$, $SD = 1.22$). Interacting with innovative instructional strategies also was reported to be important to their online experience. Strategies such as case studies ($M = 2.83$, $SD = .92$); structured games ($M = 3.10$, $SD = 1.11$); and readings followed by online discussion ($M = 4.56$, $SD = 1.09$) were all rated popular with participants. Interestingly, participants expressed strong frustrations about being required to participate in too many interactive assignments in a weekly segment of the course ($M = 4.08$, $SD = 1.06$).

Interacting with the content is a major component of an online course and the primary location where new knowledge, skills, and abilities are presented. Typically instruction online is presented as instructor-centered or student-centered. Both are appropriate given the learning outcome and topics of the course content. Students in this study seem to prefer a variety of techniques, yet seem to feel most comfortable with the "feeling" of a traditional class. With the highest reported perceptions of positive interaction in the areas of audio-narrated presentations and readings text followed by discussion. The lecture itself (the audio-narrated presentations) can provide a foundation for other attributes of interaction including conversation, collaboration and informal discussion.

Conversation and Collaboration

Results of the interaction attribute of conversation and collaboration indicated that participants rely on their peers and their instructor in forming and maintaining the online learning community. The majority of participants ($M = 4.94$, $SD = 1.06$) reported that it is essential to build a community of learners in the online environment. Participants reported liking to discuss ideas and concepts with peers ($M = 4.00$, $SD = .71$) and also perceive that sharing information with peers is important ($M = 3.83$, $SD = .71$). In relationship to teaming, participants reported that working in teams was difficult for them ($M = 3.08$, $SD = 1.19$) and that once a team is formed, they prefer to maintain the same team for the entire semester ($M = 3.62$, $SD = 1.05$). In terms of innovative instructional strategies for interacting online, participants reported liking online debates ($M = 3.04$, $SD = 1.12$) and posing questions to experts ($M =$

4.02, *SD* = 1.02). Students weren't as receptive to the idea of posing as the guest presenter in class (*M* = 2.71, *SD* = 1.18). Finally, in terms of feedback from the instructor, participants reported that it is important to them (*M* = 4.35, *SD* = .76) and that the instructor should make every attempt to provide some kind of feedback to them at least two times per week (*M* = 3.77, *SD* = .85). Interestingly, participants reported that it was unnecessary for instructors to provide feedback on a daily basis (*M* = 4.25, *SD* = .84).

Promoting collaboration and conversation online is an attribute of online learning that participants considered important. Overall, forming the community of learners, collaborating with peers, and getting feedback from the instructor were the most highly rated indicators of this attribute. Given that groups of students do not just become collaborative because they are assigned together (Johnson & Johnson, 1994) means that designers and instructors should provide clear expectations for collaboration online.

Interestingly, note the positive responses on innovative instructional strategies. The variety of strategies presented within the confines of a course appears to yield positive perceptions among students. Providing both synchronous and asynchronous conversation and communication online can extend learning and at the same time motivate the learner (Sherry, 2000).

Intrapersonal/Metacognitive Skills

Analysis of items related to intrapersonal/metacognitive skills suggest that self-directedness and embedded cognitive strategies designed into the online learning environment are perceived to be important to participants. Participants reported that it is important to monitor their own progress each week (*M* = 4.58, *SD* = .72). With regard to embedded cognitive strategies, participants reported that it is important to have structured times that assignments are due (*M* = 4.33, *SD* = .83), to have an advance organizer to assist them through the assignments each week (*M* = 4.10, *SD* = 1.00), to provide graphical representations of the steps that should be taken to complete assignments (*M* = 3.96, *SD* = 1.31), and to have note-taking guides to accompany audio-narrated presentations (*M* = 4.04, *SD* = 1.12).

Overall, self-regulating one's own learning is an important aspect of online learning. Not only do students need to monitor their progress in an ongoing fashion and adjust their strategies for learning based on their progress, they also need to maintain a time management schedule in order to complete online learning activities in the allotted timeframes. To assist and guide learners through online learning, strategies like advance organizers and graphical representations are used to guide the learner through assignments, while note-taking guides and posted times for assignment due dates are also included.

Support

Results indicate that support is also a key attribute in the success of online learning. Designing online learning with a solid support system in place enables timely responses to questions, mentoring, tutorials, and tips from peers. This support system may very well provide a foundation for successful learning. Participants report that timeliness of response ($M = 4.48$, $SD = .64$) is a major indicator of support. Most participants reported also that having a mentor in place to provide assistance is also important ($M = 3.52$, $SD = 1.35$). Participants also reported that having tutorials available as needed ($M = 3.12$, $SD = 1.55$) will assist them in performing tasks such as being in a chat room, posting to a threaded discussion, etc. And no surprise, participants report that when the technology doesn't perform as intended, they are extremely frustrated ($M = 4.17$, $SD = 1.15$).

Overall Perceptions of Interaction

Overall, participants provided the reasons why they chose to take courses online. They also rated items in each attribute of online interaction as important to their success as online learners. The top reason for taking a course online was the flexibility ($M = 4.65$, $SD = .74$) followed closely by convenience ($M = 4.13$, $SD = 1.14$). With regard to the interaction attributes, Intrapersonal/Metacognitive had the most highly rated indicators with self-monitoring of individual progress ($M = 4.58$, $SD = .72$) rated at the highest frequency. The support attribute also rated at the top with timely responses by the instructor ($M = 4.48$, $SD = .64$) rated as the number two indicator of an interactive online course. Table 25.2 notes the frequency, means, and standard deviations of the top rated indicators for each of the four interaction attributes of online learning. Although indicators exist in each of the interaction areas, the idea of self-regulating learning and having timely feedback from the instructor was reported as most valued by participants.

CONCLUSION

In conclusion, it is agreed that interaction should be designed into online instruction. It is also agreed that interaction is an important variable for learning, primarily because it is important to learner satisfaction and

**Table 25.2.   Means and Standard Deviations
of Reported Interaction on Highly Rated Attributes and Indicators**

Attribute	Indicator	M	SD
Content Interaction	Mixture of individualized And guided activities	3.77	.85
	Learning from Audio-Narrated presentations	3.65	1.22
Conversation & Collaboration	Peer Discussions	4.00	.71
	Sharing ideas with peers	3.83	.71
	Teaming with same partners	3.62	1.05
Intrapersonal /Metacognitive	Monitoring own progress	4.58	.72
	Structuring online time	4.33	.83
	Advance organizers	4.10	1.00
	Notetaking guides	4.04	1.12
Support	Timeliness of response	4.48	.64
	Corresponding with instructor	4.25	.84
	Peer tips	3.87	1.07

Note: 1 = *strongly disagree* to 5 = *strongly agree.*

motivation (Berge, 1999). In this study, online learners echo the importance of interaction by requesting interactive elements in their online experiences. Participants in this study are still most comfortable with the idea of simulating a campus-based class online, as reflected in their statements regarding the desire for instructors to use online audio-narrated lectures, provide note-taking guides, and discuss learned experiences in some type of online conversation. Although their comfort is with the "known," they still favorably rated using more innovative strategies in the online environment including case studies, debates, role-plays, and gaming. The foundation of the online learning environment however, included the notion of solid student support and self-directedness. Participants strongly stated that the need for timely responses from peers and from their instructor was of utmost importance. They also indicated that it was essential for students to self-monitor their progress for survival in the online course.

This study was an initial investigation into the perceptions of online learners' interaction needs. Future studies should consider other variables that may affect the individual learner, the learning environment, and instructional strategies that may be most appropriate for specific learning outcomes.

REFERENCES

Berge, Z. (1999, January/February). Interaction in post-secondary web-based learning. *Educational Technology, 39*(1), 5-11.

Carr, S. (2000, February 11). As distance education comes of age, the challenge is keeping the student. *Chronicle of Higher Education.*

Dodge, B. (2001, October 27) *WebQuest Web Site.* San Diego State University. Retrieved November 24, 2001, from http://edweb.sdsu.edu/webquest/webquest.html

Gilbert, L., & Moore, D. L. (1998, May/June). Building interactivity into web courses: Tools for social and instructional interaction. *Educational Technology, 38*(3), 29-35.

Hillman, D. C., Willis, D. J., & Gunawardena, C. N. (1994). Learner-interface interaction in distance education. An extension of contemporary models and strategies for practitioners. *The American Journal of Distance Education, 8*(2), 30-42.

Johnson, D. W., & Johnson, R. T. (1994). *Learning together and alone: Cooperative, competitive and individualistic learning* (4th ed.). Boston: Allyn & Bacon.

Liaw, S. & Huang, H. (2000, January/February). Enhancing interactivity in web-based instruction: A review of the literature. *Educational Technology, 39*(1), 41-51.

Moore, M. G. (1989). Three types of interaction. *The American Journal of Distance Education, 3*(2), 1-6.

Northrup, P. T. (2001a). A framework for designing interactivity into web-based instruction, *Educational Technology, 41*(2), 31-39.

Northrup, P. T. (2001b). *The online learning interaction inventory (OLLI).* Unpublished document, University of West Florida.

Sherry, L. (2000). The nature and purpose of online discourse: A brief synthesis of current research as related to the WEB project. *International Journal of Educational Telecommunications, 6*(1), 19-51.

Zhang, S., & Fulford, C. P. (1994). Are interaction time and psychological interactivity the same thing in the distance learning classroom? *Educational Technology, 34*(6), 58-64.

CHAPTER 26

LEARNER SUPPORT NEEDS IN ONLINE PROBLEM-BASED LEARNING

Steve Wheeler

This article describes how online discussion groups and visual collaboration can be used in combination to build and support a virtual community of learners. Data derived from several online discussion groups are presented, and the support needs of learners are highlighted as a key factor of success.

MOTIVATION, SUPPORT NEEDS, AND LEARNING DOMAINS

It is widely acknowledged that attrition rates in distance education are generally greater than those in traditional higher education and may be as high as 50% (Moore & Kearsley, 1996; Ross, Morrison, Smith, & Cleveland, 1990). Distance learners tend to require more support than their classroom-based counterparts (Gibson, 1996, 1998), and support needs in distance education link directly to individual motivation (Osborn, 2001). Motivation is a key factor in any learning enterprise, and in distance education, it appears to be particularly crucial. Social isolation poses a signif-

The Perfect Online Course: Best Practices for Designing and Teaching
pp. 475–486

icant problem for some distance learners, as does the reduction in motivation normally engendered within traditional student communities (Yorke, 1999). Motivation contributes to success, along with a number of other critical factors, including maintenance of attention and the will to complete; social support, including mutual encouragement, sharing of ideas, problems, and triumphs; and ready access to resources, the tutor, and the peer group. Lack of any will guarantee that online learning environments will not provide the easiest route to obtaining postgraduate qualifications.

Many distance education students are mature, with full-time jobs, domestic commitments, and other agendas that compete with the amount of time available during a standard week (Willis, 1993). Students often cite time taken up by family and tiredness after work for nonattendance at tutorials (Fung & Carr, 2000). These factors highlight the importance for distance learners to receive support throughout their programs of study. Student support may therefore be the most important issue affecting the success or failure of online learning.

Carnwell (2000) has categorized learning support in distance education into the three discrete areas of academic, emotional, and technical-practical support. Academic support naturally maps across the cognitive domain originally described by Bloom (1956), as shown in Figure 1. Students are anxious to know how they can pass their assessments, and where they need to go to access the reading materials needed to understand the subject they are studying. The emotional needs of the learner are affective in nature, and thus fall into this learning domain as classified by Krathwohl, Bloom, and Masia (1964/1972).

The technical-practical support that students require is located within the skills (or psychomotor) domain. Students may, for example, forget

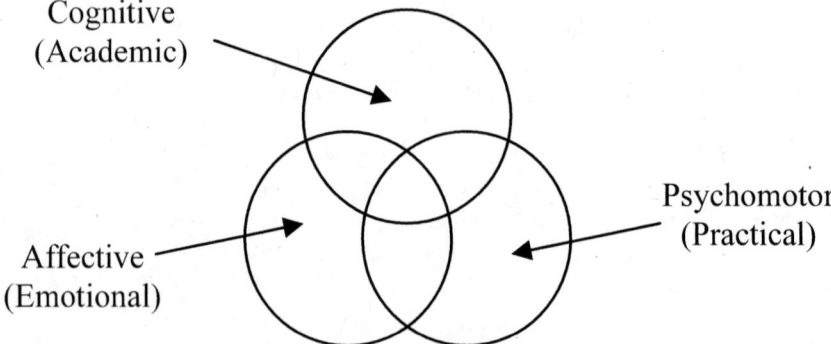

Figure 26.1.   Three domains of learning and support needs.

their password, or find difficulty downloading a file they require to complete an assignment. If help is not quickly forthcoming, students may become frustrated and reject the technology (Wheeler, 1993) and some students may terminate their studies. Support of a practical nature may be pitched at a lower level than the support offered in the other two domains, but may nevertheless be just as crucial to the learner's success. The manner in which online learning is designed and delivered will usually determine the method through which students can be supported. Support can be provided by the tutor or subject specialists, but also by the student peer group, or in some cases through the structure and content of the learning material, or through software features.

PROBLEM-BASED LEARNING

Problem-based learning (PBL) methods emerged as a means of promoting deeper cognitive engagement. PBL strongly promotes the development of skills through the use of complex, real-life problems, motivating students to generally approach learning in a deeper manner (Duch, Groh, & Allen, 2001), facilitating critical thinking, cooperative working, verbal and written communication skills, and lifelong learning skills.

Distributed PBL (dPBL) is a version of PBL that can be offered to distance learners. Learning is mediated through computer technology, and a shared, "virtual" distributed learning environment is used to enable students to collaborate. A powerful PBL utility enables teachers to present students with authentic problems they might encounter in the "real world." Students must also practice problem-solving skills while reading more widely and investigating more deeply the structure and context of the presented problem. To facilitate this, tutors must act as guides and facilitators in the process, and may even adopt a learning role themselves (Roblyer, Edwards, & Havriluk, 1997). The learning group is encouraged to collaborate as a team with each member monitoring the progress of others whilst simultaneously assessing their own (Barrows, 2002). This distributed community of practice therefore encourages a self-regulating and autonomous body of students. Online collaborative knowledge building approaches have previously been used to promote effective learning in in-service teacher training (Ahlberg, Kaasinen, Kaivola, & Houtsonen, 2001) and to establish communities of practice in CMC-based initial teacher training (Clarke, 2002; Tsui & Ki, 2002).

THE ONLINE MODULE

The online module, titled "Information and Communication Technologies in Teaching and Learning: Theoretical Perspectives," is presented in dual-mode format. Perhaps more accurately, it utilizes a number of modes, so it is in fact "multiple-mode," incorporating face-to-face and technology-mediated modes, synchronous and asynchronous media, and encouraging both independent and collaborative study (see an elaboration of this in Wheeler, 2001). This is reflected in face-to-face teaching and learning (lectures, seminars, group work, and discussion), online delivery (electronic resources, online discussion, problem-based learning scenarios, and online multiple response question assessment), videoconferencing and dual mode tutorial support (synchronous via telephone, asynchronous via e-mail). The multi-modal characteristics of the course combine with the problem-based learning materials to endow the course with its power and flexibility.

Successful completion of the module earns students 30 credits toward a master's degree in education, constituting 25% of the taught element of the degree. If they successfully complete a second related independent study module, students earn another 30 credits, thereby completing half the taught portion of the degree. A differentiated assignment at the end of the course contributes toward the mandatory assessment of each student's learning. Differentiated assessment allows the learner to select a form and focus of assignment relevant and applicable to his or her professional practice from a range of assignment options. A large proportion of the course is delivered on the Web through a specialized platform known as MTutor. Before MTutor is described, it is important to review the limitations of computer-based learning (CBL).

"MINDTOOLS" FOR LEARNING

Jonassen, Peck, and Wilson (1999) have argued that CBL has fallen short of its optimum value due to misapplication of its potential and have called for a radical change. Indeed, Jonassen has recently argued that most online learning does little more than replicate face-to-face lectures (Jonassen, 2002). He argues that, in traditional forms of CBL, computers are expected to "do the teaching," while students are expected to "memorize" the materials. This represents a linear "drill and practice" approach to teaching based on the knowledge transmission model, and fails to support meaningful learning, because computers can store information more efficiently than humans, and humans can teach better than computers. Jonassen and his colleagues have called for a reversal of these functions, where computers are used for what they do best, liberating the student to explore, discover, and create personal meaning from diverse sets of material in an active manner.

Technology, they argue, should be used to engage the student in thinking and knowledge construction rather than merely as an information transmitter. Jonassen and his colleagues call for the computer to be used as a "mindtool" to promote open-ended learning. The mindtools approach challenges the established "computer-based learning approach" in which knowledge resided in the machine and was systematically delivered to the student. Instead, students bring their knowledge to the computer, which provides a fertile environment within which the student can construct new knowledge through proactive exploration and collaboration with others. MTutor can perform these mindtool functions by providing the remote student with a combination of meaningful, open ended learning in the form of PBL, and a flexible, nonlinear environment within which to study.

DISTANCE LEARNING

MTutor is a Web-based system into which a range of problem-based activities, scenarios, and online resources can be assembled and presented. It also houses a comprehensive discussion group facility and a range of multiple-choice and multiple-response question options. It uses specialist (common gateway interface) software to facilitate the presentation of online survey questionnaires for evaluation purposes. MTutor has previously been used successfully to support problem-based learning in health studies, engineering, and psychology (Culverhouse & Burton, 1998, 2001), although each of these had been implemented within a networked campus-based environment. Now, in order to deliver the new module, MTutor is being used for the first time as a platform for a truly distance-based course. Web-based learning appears to lend itself readily to dPBL, and the next section of this article discusses these possibilities.

PROBLEM-BASED LEARNING

Problem solving is probably one of the most important skills students can acquire, because it enables generalizability across diverse problems encountered in everyday life. We encounter problems every day, some of which merely take a minute or two to solve. Others take days or even years to circumvent, and then often with no guarantee of success. Problem solving is therefore a key component of the lifelong learning process, involving many cognitive resources and much commitment and practice.

Problem-based learning can be characterised as learning that is based on the thinking-through of real life problems or, to use a more appropriate term, situated cognition. Of course, everyday problems are rarely clear-cut in nature, as many have no structure and may bear no similarities to previously-encountered problems.

ILL-STRUCTURED PROBLEMS

The presentation of ill-defined or ill-structured problems has a number of advantages but, according to Simon (1973), they are primarily representative of real-life situations and thus can have practical outcomes. Simon (1978) has argued that ill-structured problems exhibit three key characteristics. First, they are more complex and have less-definite criteria for determining when the problem has been solved. Second, not all the information has been provided in the presentation of the problem, leaving several gaps for the learner to fill in. Finally, ill-defined problems have no apparent "rules" that can be immediately applied. It is also conceivable that ill-structured problems offer better generalizability potential across diverse problem types. Nevertheless, the extent to which a problem is ill-structured may depend on the skills and knowledge that the learner brings to bear on the problem.

Learners with the requisite knowledge may perceive a problem to be better-defined than those with no, or little, knowledge (Frederiksen, 1984). Moreover, student-centred learning can be supported using ill-structured problem solving. Kahney, for example, has asserted that ill-structured problems tend to encourage learners to define the problem themselves (Kahney, 1994). This leads, in turn, to greater motivation and, ultimately, the construction of personal meaning within individualised contexts.

The online element of the module is problem based, enabling students to immerse themselves within situated aspects of the theory, such as real-purpose tasks and transformed teacher roles (Jonassen, 1996). Ill-structured problems of this nature are presented for them to address. The first scenario, for example, takes the form of a heated debate between two teachers in the staff room. One teacher is opposed to the use of in formation and communication technology (ICT) across the curriculum, while the other is a strong advocate. Their polemic is analyzed by the students, and a range of theoretical and practical issues are teased out which they later discuss online with their peers and the tutor.

DISCUSSION AS LEARNING SUPPORT

Generally, each student will abstract the meaning he or she feels to be uppermost in the presented dialogue, and this will invariably be an issue or set of issues that impact on his or her own professional practice in some way. Humans are social beings who depend on feedback from their peers to validate their own beliefs (Jonassen, 1998) and online discussions are ideal environments within which this kind of learning can be propagated. The argumentative nature of the ensuing online discussion encourages each student to further construct, deconstruct, and reconstruct their own personal meaning from the problem and its implications. Yet, within the argumentative nature of the dialogue, cooperative processes have been seen to emerge. Cooperative dialogue can occur, for example, when students "take sides" during online discussions, or where they work together to justify a particular position adopted. Incidentally, Ravenscroft (2001) suggests that such cooperative dialogue can be achieved as effectively through an intelligent computer system as through a human tutor. However, this notion of machine intervention must at present be little more than a utopian ideal for the vast majority of educational providers and so remains little more than an application for future use.

Thus, for each learner and over a period of time, a mutual climate of support is developed as the learner's cognitive development is incrementally shifted through a process of negotiation and cooperation in dialogue.

ACADEMIC SUPPORT

As previously stated, academic support is directly related to the cognitive development processes of learning. Academic support need not always originate from the tutor or course team, but can just as easily be provided by more knowledgeable students within the group. Online groups quickly discover which members have the best skills and experience for each emergent task or problem, usually through a degree of self disclosure, as highlighted in the following posting about technophobia and computers (Note: all names are pseudonyms to maintain participant anonymity.)

> [3 December 20:12] Grace: I have submitted my "How I Done It", This tells that I used my experience of adult learning and fears and related it to the topic under investigation.... I had ten 11-12 year old children. I got them to create a little web page on WORD. They loved it but the teachers were clearly shocked that these children had created these pages. I also detected fear.

Grace reveals that she has had experience teaching both 11-12 year olds and adults. Later in the module, if either of these topics arises, other members of the group may remember her expertise and ask her directly for her opinion, thereby tacitly requesting support within their own zone of proximal development. An exemplification of this occurs during an online dialogue about computer-mediated communication (CMC). One student offers help following the request of another group member, and this help derives from his greater knowledge of available resources:

> [4 January 22:09] Sylvia: Many of my students have learning and/or physical disabilities. Any suggestions over the best way to make CMC accessible to such people?

> [5 January 20:23] Colin: Sylvia, there's a good article on this in a newsletter I found on a Hong Kong Web site recently— address as follows: [he provides the Web address]

EMOTIONAL SUPPORT

Emotional support is arguably the most vital support for learning in online environments, as distance learning is generally devoid of face-to-face support, and students often have problems understanding course information (Baker, 1986). This deficit can lead to frustration, anxiety, and other negative emotional responses. Negative emotions also result when students cannot gain easy access to course materials. The following exchange on a course discussion group starts off as a nervous plea for technical support and then generates its own humour and emotional support:

> [19 November 20:14] Sophie: Steve, this is Monday and I have come expectantly onto [name of the course Web site] to have a look at the second tutorial, but no Devon version available. I even tried to log onto the old Jersey version but it won't accept my name/password. So I've resorted to coming back to this discussion group even though it has officially closed! I'm feeling exceptionally asynchronous!

Sophie's plea for help is confirmed by other students within 11 minutes of her posting her discussion contribution:

> [19 November 20:25] Andrew: As with Sophie, I too have been refused entry into Tut2. Only a blip to be sure but it shows that we're ready and willing! (-} anonymous chat room lurker.

> [19 November 23:00] Gina: *me too - we must be realy sad*

Within 24 hours, several other students have joined in the exchange, with one providing the solution:

[20 November 18:53] Jack: It is there—I have been on it!!! Instead of going into WiP (work in progress), click on the students button. This gives a list of all the current tutorials—scroll down the list and there it is!!! Jack.

[21 November 12:11] Andrew: Well spotted Jack. Thanks.

[21 November 21:16] Rachel: well I've done all those things and it won't let me in.

[21 November 21:26] Jack: Were you clicking the tutorials listed for the Devon group? It is directly below the Jersey group—with identical tutorial lists!

[22 November 21: 22] Rachel: yes but nothings happening!

At this point, with the frustration mounting, the tutor intervenes and provides practical (technical) support for the group. Once technical issues are resolved, the frustration subsides and emotional support is no longer high on the agenda. In another recent publication (Wheeler, Kelly, & Gale, 2005) a fuller analysis of online dialogue was presented, including analysis of post-module student interviews.

EVALUATION METHODS

Throughout each module delivery, five methods are employed to enable as full- and wide-ranging an evaluation as possible. The first method involves the automatic tracking of student activities within the MTutor Web-based learning environment. This enables the tutor to provide students with support in the form of remedial help if required, and will indicate how each individual student reaches or approaches expertise within each discrete problem space.

The second method of evaluation is a two-part paper-based questionnaire completed by each student at the start and the end of the course, to determine changes in learning style, preferred approaches to learning, and a measure designed to elicit student perception of transactional distance (see Moore & Kearsley, 1996; Wheeler, 2000; 2002). Transactional distance is the psychological distance perceived by students when separated from their teacher and peers. The manner by which teachers use technology to mediate communication over distance may have the potential to reduce as well as amplify any misunderstandings and other negative effects associated with transactional distance (Wheeler, 2002, 2004) .

Third, a questionnaire presented on screen at the conclusion of the online delivery gathers data from each student on technical and logistical operations. This includes, for example, how quickly each student has been able to adapt to the new way of learning, how difficult each has found the problem spaces, the appearance of the material, ease of navigation around the Web-based learning environment, and how well the material has been sequenced and presented.

The fourth method of evaluation is a quantitative record of each e-mail and telephone call initiated by students to the tutor. This is complemented by a content analysis of each e-mail communication, the results of which will be presented in other papers.

Finally, for the fifth evaluative method, each student is asked to keep a reflective diary of his or her experiences, which will include verbal feedback from a focus group at the conclusion of the course. Attrition rate and completion data will complete the picture of the success of the course. The online student contributions data provide an analysis of the efficacy of dPBL approaches. Names of contributors have been changed to protect identities.

REFLECTIONS ON SUPPORT NEEDS

The first two deliveries of the online module yielded rich data about the success of the course and the satisfaction levels of the students. Generally, students reported that they appreciated the opportunities to collaborate together through discussion groups. It was considered an important social support structure, scaffolding their academic thinking through problem solving. Emotional support was forthcoming between group members, in various forms, including encouragement and humour.

As time passed and the group members began to develop interpersonal relationships, the use of emoticons gradually decreased, indicating that the use of such symbols may initially have been a device employed to minimise any potential misunderstandings. Practical support was also given freely by group members at early technical problem stage, but when students reached the limit of their knowledge, the tutor and the course team intervened.

CONCLUSIONS

Distributed problem-based learning is a reworking of the established case study approaches familiar to the medical profession. It is a nascent online method, mediated by technologies that are still unfamiliar to many. Thus, a great deal of opportunity exists to research the effectiveness of dPBL and its place specifically in postgraduate studies and generally in distance learning.

REFERENCES

Ahlberg, M., Kaasinen, A., Kaivola, T., & Houtsonen, L. (2001). Collaborative knowledge building to promote in-service teacher training in environmental education. *Technology, Pedagogy and Education, 10*(3), 227-238.

Baker, K. (1986). Dilemmas at a distance. *Assessment and Evaluation in Higher Education, 11*(3), 219-230.

Barrows, H. (2002). Is it truly possible to have such a thing as dPBL? *Distance Education, 23*(1), 119-122.

Bloom, B. S. (Ed.). (1956). *Taxonomy of educational objectives. Handbook 1: The cognitive domain.* New York: Longman.

Carnwell, R. (2000). Approaches to study and the impact on the need for support and guidance in distance learning. *Open Learning, 15*(2), 123-140.

Clarke, L. (2002). Putting the "C" in ICT: Using computer conferencing to foster a community of practice among student teachers. *Technology, Pedagogy and Education, 11*(2), 163-180.

Culverhouse, P. F., & Burton, C. J. (1998, March). *MTUTOR: A tutorial shell for supporting problem solving.* Paper presented at the Bringing Information Technology to Education (BITE) Conference, Maastricht, Holland.

Culverhouse, P. F., & Burton, C. J. (2001). Learning best-practice in design and problem skill development: MTutor—A Web-based distance learning tool. *Quarterly Review of Distance Education, 2*(3), 221-232.

Duch, B. J., Groh, S. E., & Allen, D. E. (2001). *The power of problem based learning.* Stirling, VA: Stylus.

Frederiksen, N. (1984). Implications of cognitive theory for instruction in problem solving, *Review of Educational Research, 54*(3), 363-407.

Fung, Y., & Carr, R. (2000). Face-to-face tutorials in a distance learning system: Meeting student needs. *Open Learning, 15*(1), 35-46.

Gibson, C. C. (1996). Academic self concept: Its nature and import in distance education. *The American Journal of Distance Education, 10*(1), 23-36.

Gibson, C. C. (1998). *Supporting the distance learner in context.* Keynote speech to the 2nd Turkish Distance Education Symposium. Ankara, Turkey.

Jonassen, D. H. (1996). *Computers in the classroom: Mindtools for critical thinking.* Englewood Cliffs, NJ: Prentice Hall.

Jonassen, D. H. (1998). Designing constructivist learning environments. In C. M. Reigeluth (Ed.), *Instructional design theories and models: Their current state of the art* (2nd ed, pp. 215-239). Mahwah, NJ: Erlbaum.

Jonassen, D. H. (2002). Engaging and supporting problem solving in online learning. *Quarterly Review of Distance Education, 3*(1), 1-14.

Jonassen, D. H., Peck, K. L., & Wilson, R. G. (1999). *Learning with technology: A constructivist perspective.* Columbus, OH: Merrill Prentice Hall.

Kahney, H. (1984). *Problem solving: Current issues* (2nd ed.). Buckingham, United Kingdom: Open University Press.

Krathwohl, D. R., Bloom, B. S., & Masia, B. B. (Eds.). (1972). *Taxonomy of educational objectives. Handbook 2: The affective domain.* New York: David McKay. (Original work published 1962)

Moore, M. G., & Kearsley, G. (1996). *Distance education: A systems view.* Belmont. CA: Wadsworth.

Osborn, V. (2001). Identifying at-risk students in videoconferencing and web-based distance education. *The American Journal of Distance Education, 15*(1), 41-54.

Ravenscroft, A. (2001). Designing e-learning interactions in the 21st century: Revisiting and rethinking the role of theory. *European Journal of Education, Research, Development and Policies, 36*(2), 133-156.

Roblyer, M. D., Edwards, J., & Havriluk D. M. (1997). *Integrating educational technology into teaching.* Upper Saddle River, NJ: Prentice Hall.

Ross, S. M., Morrison, G. R., Smith, L. J., & Cleveland, E. (1990). *An evaluation of alternative distance tutoring models for at-risk elementary school children. Computers in Human Behaviour, 6,* 247-257.

Simon, H. A. (1973). The structure of ill-structured problems. *Artificial Intelligence, 4,* 181-201.

Simon, H. A. (1978). Information processing theory of human problem solving. In W. K. Estes (Ed.) *Handbook of learning and cognitive processes: Vol. 5. Human information processing* (pp. 271-296). Hillsdale NJ: Erlbaum.

Tsui, A. B. M., & Ki, W. W. (2002). Teacher participation in computer conferencing: Socio-psychological dimensions. *Technology, Pedagogy and Education, 11*(1), 23-44.

Wheeler, S. (1993). Ensuring psychological safety in computer studies. *Information Technology in Nursing, 5*(1), 10-12.

Wheeler, S. (2000). Instructional design in distance education through telematics. *Quarterly Review of Distance Education, 1*(1), 31-44.

Wheeler, S. (2001, November). *Dual-mode delivery of problem based learning: A constructivist perspective.* Paper presented at the New World Learning Symposium, Royal College of Physicians, London.

Wheeler, S. (2002). Student perceptions of learning support in distance learning. *Quarterly Review of Distance Education, 3*(3), 419-430.

Wheeler, S. (2004). *Transactional distance and the mediating influence of telematic technologies in distance education.* Unpublished doctoral thesis, University of Plymouth.

Wheeler, S., Kelly, P., & Gale, K. (2005). The influence of online problem based learning on teachers' professional practice styles. *Association for Learning Technologies Journal: ALT-J, 13*(2), 125-137.

Willis, B. (1993) *Distance education: A practical guide.* Englewood Cliffs NJ: Educational Technology Publications.

Yorke, M. (1999). *Leaving early: Undergraduate non-completion in higher education.* London: Falmer.

CHAPTER 27

DEEP LEARNING

The Knowledge, Methods, and Cognition Process in Instructor-Led Online Discussion

Byron Havard, Jianxia Du, and Anthony Olinzock

A structure for online discussion within a framework for deep learning provides three strategies for dynamic online discussion; flexible peer, structured topic, and collaborative task discussion. This article examines the discussion structure and the 3 separate roles demonstrated by the instructor in the promotion of deep learning through the use of online discussion. The roles of the instructor are critical in the implementation of discussion strategies and design of student tasks for significant learning in online collaborative environments. This article has theoretical and practical implications for instructors in designing and facilitating asynchronous and synchronous discussion.

Many online courses are discussion oriented. The popular use of course management systems in online courses has resulted in research on its effects on learning processes and outcomes. Major variables investigated

The Perfect Online Course: Best Practices for Designing and Teaching
pp. 487–502

include participation, interaction, critical thinking, knowledge construction, and social, cognitive, and metacognitive elements (Rourke, Anderson, Garrison, & Archer, 2001). Deep learning leads to understanding and long-term retention of information through the critical analysis of new ideas and may be defined as "learning that promotes the development of conditionalized knowledge and metacognition through communities of inquiry" (Weigel, 2001, p. 5). It is the holistic acquisition of higher order skills such as analyzing, interpreting, and evaluating (Entwistle & Ramsden, 1983). New learning is combined with existing knowledge for problem solving in unfamiliar contexts. Asynchronous online discussion is believed to support critical thinking and deep learning, as it provides a learner-centered environment and allows time for learners to reflect and respond to issues being discussed. As a result, students construct an understanding of new information through interactions with peers and the instructor. However, it does not mean that the discussion will necessarily engender deep learning. It is important for the instructor to facilitate the online discussion and promote deep learning: knowledge, methods, and cognition, which are essential for learners in a constructive, inquiry-focused online learning environment. This article examined the effects of the instructor role on the promotion of deep learning in asynchronous and synchronous online discussion. It has theoretical and practical implications for online instructors in the design and facilitation of dynamic online discussion.

Several researchers have contributed to the effort of understanding the learning process. Their conclusions can help in the process of developing models for analyzing the distance learning process. One particular model was developed to emphasize five dimensions of the learning process exteriorized in the message: participation, interaction, social, cognitive, and metacognitive dimensions (Henri, 1992). Henri's model provides information on the participants as learners and on their ways of dealing with a given topic. Oliver and Mcloughlin (1996) suggested some changes to Henri's analytical model. They recognized five kinds of interactions:

1. *Social:* teacher and student dialog establishing and developing rapport;
2. *Procedural:* teacher and student dialog involving exchange on course requirements and procedures;
3. *Expository:* student or teacher demonstrating knowledge or skill in response to a direct request from another;
4. *Explanatory:* teacher using student responses to explain knowledge and develop content; and

5. *Cognitive:*   teacher providing constructive feedback to a student response causing the student to reflect and to consider an alternative perspective/reality (p. 118).

Oliver and Mcloughlin's model has been used for analyzing the different kinds of communication in distance learning and in traditional teaching, and served as the foundation for the framework presented in this article.

A FRAMEWORK FOR ANALYSIS OF THE DEEP LEARNING PROCESS

The framework of deep learning for distance education is established through the categorization of the five kinds of interactions proposed by Oliver and Mcloughlin; social, procedural, expository, explanatory, and cognitive, into three general processes; methods, information, and cognition (Du & Havard, 2003). The first stage of integrating these learning processes is the acquisition of knowledge, representing a surface level of understanding. Skill development, the second stage of the framework, is often accomplished through drill and practice. Students operating at these two levels develop a *know-how* of the material, but on a very limited basis. The third stage represents cognition in which the student begins to conceptualize and apply learning to solve problems. A deeper understanding of the material fosters creative use of the subject content. New and innovative types of assignments that require students to apply their recently acquired skills and knowledge encourage higher-order thinking. Without deep learning, students will simply imitate the instructor, rather than apply their learning to new problems (see Figure 27.1).

Two fundamental concepts inherent in the proposed framework are adopt and adapt. Students with a surface understanding of material can effectively adopt what the instructor does, but are unable to adapt their learning to unique situations because they have not developed a deeper learning of the material. They lack the strong grasp of the material required in adapting to a complex learning environment. Assignments familiar for the student measure surface learning while new and innovative assignments measure the student's deep learning. Adopt and adapt become very important when change is introduced in the distance learning environment regarding the material students are learning. It is not enough to adopt what the instructor teaches. Encouraging students to effectively adapt to changes in the distance learning environment requires students to think for themselves rather than rely on learning guidance from the instructor (Brookfield, 1982). In this type of distance learning environment, the instructor acts as a facilitator, requiring students to take

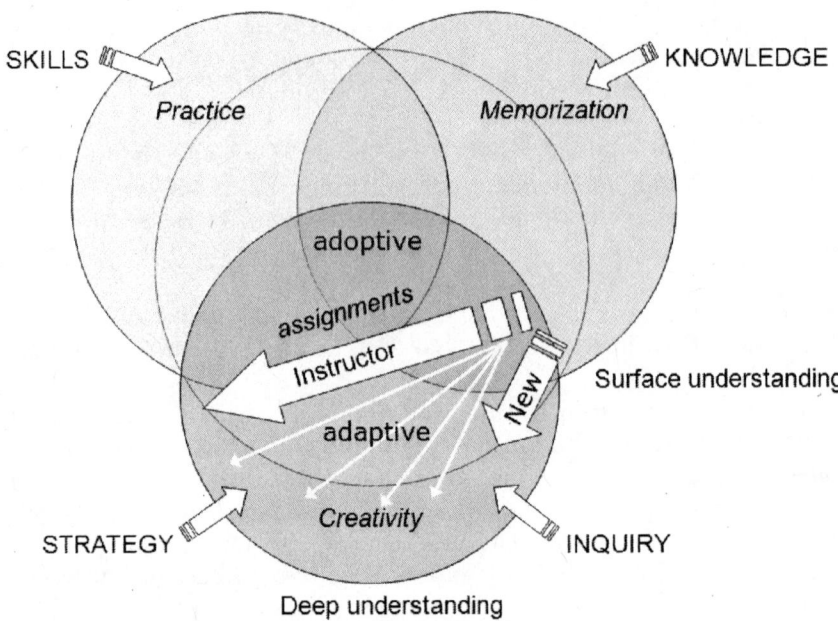

Figure 27.1.   Deep learning process: Developing deeper learning through assignments that encourage inquiry and creativity.

more responsibility in the learning process. The role of facilitator is complex, but through the proposed framework, techniques and student activities are diagramed to assist in reducing this complexity.

FRAMEWORK APPLICATION
IN INSTRUCTOR-LED ONLINE DYNAMIC DISCUSSION

Distance education requires special course design techniques, special methods of communication, as well as special organizational and administrative arrangements (Moore, 1989). To further explore the framework of deep learning for online discussion, we applied the framework during two semesters of a graduate level multimedia design for instruction course. This multimedia design for instruction course is required for all students enrolled in the Master of Science in Instructional Technology (MSIT) program. Students enrolled in the MSIT program and in this course represent a wide range of diverse backgrounds. They reside throughout the state of Mississippi, and in Tennessee and Alabama. Each semester approximately 30 students are enrolled in this course. The purpose of this course is to provide students with an overview of hypermedia/interactive multimedia technology through working with various hypermedia/multimedia tools. Students are introduced to the design and production process of developing multimedia applications and are provided the opportunity to learn various tools concentrating on different aspects of the technology: text, graphics, audio, animation, and video. Through working with these tools, students are expected to develop an understanding and the skills required for the creation of instructional tools for application in education and industry settings. Students are required to apply design principles necessary for the creation of hypermedia/multimedia when developing multimedia-based applications.

The course simulates practices in the multimedia industry. Students work in groups and take on different roles in the multimedia development process. The contexts for learning in this course are primarily interactive, collaborative, multidisciplinary, and student centered. Students are required to actively participate in weekly discussions regarding specific multimedia development topics. Assignments on learning different tools are given to assess application skills. Students must write a research and reflective paper on hypermedia/interactive multimedia instruction. Group projects for the semester both develop and assess students' ability to comprehensively apply the theoretical and technical requirements for multimedia design for instruction. Through these activities we have observed students developing deep thinking in higher-order problem solving, from the foundation of surface understanding to deeper understanding exhibited by problem resolution.

ONLINE ENVIRONMENT CREATED BY INSTRUCTOR

The online learning environment for this course is created in WebCT (see Figure 27.2). WebCT is a database-driven Web-based course management system designed to support online learning environments (Hutchins, 2001). We have been using WebCT in our university teaching for several years now and recognize that one of the major benefits of the use of this technology is the facility it provides to incorporate learning activities that help to develop students' deep learning and understanding, exhibited through higher-order problem solving and inquiry (Tiene, 2002). The database elements available in WebCT enable the instructor to record, manage, and support the activities and interactions of a large number of students. There are several important aspects about this environment regarding skill development, theoretical and technical issues, and the application of skills and knowledge toward the successful development of

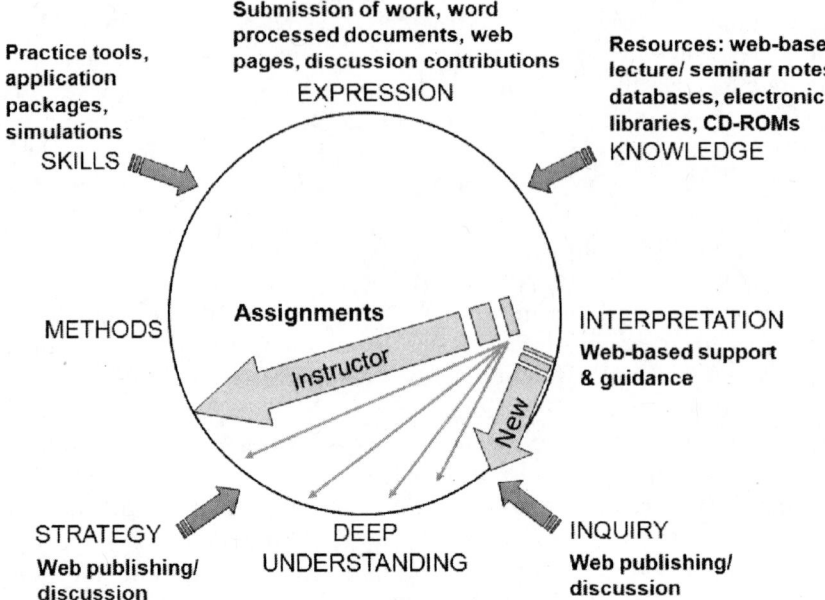

Figure 27.2.   Mapping online discussion features onto the deep learning framework.

a comprehensive multimedia instructional tool (Popolov, Callaghan, & Luker, 2002). Through online group communication using the asynchronous discussion feature and synchronous chat available through WebCT, students' skills and knowledge regarding multimedia development are enhanced. The social aspect of the learning environment is critical (Vygotsky, 1978). This requires focused attention by the instructor, as knowledge is socially constructed and enhanced through peer-to-peer and instructor-to-peer communication (Boud, Cohen, & Sampson, 1999; Kitchener, 1983; Kitchener & King, 1981).

The strategies used through framework application may assist others in implementing the framework within their own distance learning environments. Application of the framework within the context of a distance learning environment will be described. The methods, knowledge, and cognition framework serves to foster and encourage learning, and specifically deep learning in an online environment. Through implementation of the three-stage framework, we have established a learning environment that encourages deep learning with synchronous and asynchronous tools for students to collaborate on set problems, share resources, post solutions, and compare and review answers from other groups (Popolov et al., 2002).

ONLINE DISCUSSION: INSTRUCTOR ROLE

A structured and moderated online discussion may be defined as a Web-based bulletin board for peer learners to communicate and collaborate, where the instructor takes active responsibility to structure, scaffold, and moderate the collaboration. The structure of the bulletin board is divided into the three processes related to the proposed framework of methods, knowledge, and cognition. Through this structure, a number of key skills are demonstrated by students in the higher-order problem solving process; from surface understanding to deeper understanding.

Students complete assignments requiring them to apply their surface learning and develop their deeper learning. The difficulty of the assignments progresses, challenging students to hone their abilities and problem-solving skills. Scaffolding is important throughout the process and is most pronounced during the first two assignments. As students' deep learning develops and their competence to accomplish the assignments increases, the necessity to scaffold is reduced (Gredler, 1997). The assignments in this course consist of two technical projects: a theoretical research paper and a comprehensive technical and theoretical final group project. The purpose of these assignments and their structure is to scaffold students' learning from surface to deep. Online discussion is used extensively in this course as a means to develop deeper learning. The WebCT bulletin board is composed of three categories; technical, theoretical, and comprehensive, corresponding to the three general process of the framework; methods, information, and cognition.

Flexible Peer Discussion—Instructor as Class Member

Students use Macromedia Dreamweaver and Macromedia Fireworks as the two main multimedia development tools for this course. Within the technical category of the bulletin board, discussion points are further categorized into topic technical issues, practice issues, and peer discussion. Students are presented two questions per week within the topic technical issues related to the technical aspects and use of Dreamweaver and Fireworks. Students must respond to the question presented and must also critique one other peer's response. Students are also presented with weekly practice assignments progressing in difficulty from relatively simple at the beginning of the semester. As they work through the assignments, they must post one question regarding an issue they encountered while working on the assignment. They must also answer at least one peer's question that was posted. The peer discussion category of the bulletin board is available for open discussion about Dreamweaver and Fireworks, and students are required to post at least one new item they learned while using either of these multimedia development applications. If a student posting is unclear or needs refining, the instructor may question the post for clarification. All students are encouraged to seek clarity on bulletin board postings. The instructor models the behavior for seeking this clarity, and students soon follow this behavior. For example, the instructor may post a question regarding topics such as form creation, tables, or layers in Dreamweaver. Students respond to this question and soon learn to post questions and insight on their own.

Structured Topic Discussion—Instructor as Initiator

The theoretical category of the bulletin board consists of three questions posed by the instructor to the students over a 3-week period prior to the middle of the semester. Through focused and concise answers, students are able to develop the foundation for their theoretical research paper. Students are encouraged to discuss the question and offer opinions on how the question may be addressed. Responses do not occur immediately; instead, students spend time clarifying the questions among themselves. Discussion occurs during the week. Toward the end of the week, students begin to formulate and post their responses. Discussion continues as students submit their responses. Students must also critique two other peers' responses each week. In the critique, students must provide constructive criticism and assist in further developing each peer's topic further. The questions are meant to be a guide to assist students in topic development for the individual paper assignments. The first question guides students toward describing how the specific multimedia development tools used in the course may be used. They must cite their reading assignments within their response to support their claims. An example of the first topic question posted by the instructor for the students follows:

> In what ways do you see how the authoring tools (e.g., Flash, Fireworks, Dreamweaver) can be used to create interactive multimedia instruction? (a) Discuss the special features and functionalities for each authoring tool. (b) Explain how those features and functions can be used to enhance meaningful and effective instruction. (c) Give examples for item (b) responses. (d) Use citations from the course readings to support your arguments.

The second question focuses on instructional design principles. There are two required textbooks for this course, and relevant articles provided by the instructor, posted online, which serve as additional reading. Students must describe how instructional design principles are applied in an actual multimedia development project, including details related to the learner and context. The second topic question posed to students by the instructor follows:

> What have you learned about instructional design principles? First, recall what you have learned from this class, the textbooks and additional readings about (a) needs analysis, (b) designing instructional strategies, and (c) developing instructional multimedia? Second, describe how you can apply those design principles in a real-world multimedia design project. Be very specific about the learner, context, subject content, and the needs for multimedia instruction.

The third question requires students to propose a group project they will collaborate on and submit as their final comprehensive project. Their responses must include details regarding the learner, instructional context, subject content, and the needs for the proposed multimedia instruction. They must provide a rationale for the development tools they wish to use. They must also describe the instructional strategy they will use and describe why they chose that particular strategy. The third question posted by the instructor within the structured topic discussion portion of the bulletin board follows:

> Based on what you have learned about the authoring tools and the instructional design principles in this class, propose a group project that you may want to collaboratively work on. (a) Again, be very specific about the learner, instructional context, subject content, and the needs for multimedia instruction. (b) Propose the authoring tools you are going to use and explain why you are going to use these tool(s). (c) Propose the instructional strategies that you are going to implement for the project.

After thorough discussion of the topics and submitting responses to all three questions, students must then complete a theoretical reflective paper. The instructor provides guidelines for the reflective paper, due 2 weeks after the conclusion of the structured topic discussion. The guidelines posted by the instructor regarding the paper follow:

> Based on the three online discussions, write a 6-8-page reflective paper on your knowledge construction process, for example:
>
> What have you learned through the online discussion about learning, instruction, and instructional design? Please list all that you have learned *and* describe in detail. (b) What issues about instructional design have you found yourself lacking? Please list and describe in detail. (c) What have you found that you need to learn more about in your future pursuit as an instructional technologist? How are you going to do it? Please describe in detail.

Collaborative Task Discussion—Instructor as Discussant

The outcome of the comprehensive final project is a Web-based instructional tool. The project combines the technical aspects and theoretical issues discussed online during the semester. The groups must apply instructional design principles toward the development of a "real" Web-based educational product. There are three progress points during final project development that are meant to focus students toward the desired outcome in a professional manner. These points consist of a proposal presentation, a progress report, and a final project and presentation with documentation. The groups are composed of five students, with one serving as the coordinator. Asynchronous and synchronous discussion occurs among the groups. The bulletin board is used by the group for introductions. The group must decide which member will accomplish what task, based on the proposed project. The topic is decided on through discussion and deliberation among the group members. Each member proposes a topic and must negotiate online to determine which topic the group will agree on for the final product. As group members begin gathering information on their chosen topic, they post this for other group members. Discussion and clarification is often necessary as the information is refined (Flynn & La Faso, 1972). Synchronous chat offers the group opportunities to discuss issues in real time. Specific chat dates and times are decided on through the bulletin board. Students meet in their group's chat room to discuss issues with the instructor and to present their proposal and progress report. Each group conducts their final presentation through chat with the instructor present. At each progress point, the instructor serves as a discussant, judging the students' work, and providing insight regarding improvements or enhancements as necessary. Students receive immediate feedback from the instructor and must respond to questions posed by the instructor regarding the final product.

The proposed framework and the design of the discussion activities applied within the framework provide students both adoptive and adaptive learning opportunities. The technical and theoretical discussion aspects occur as students complete the first two assignments. This provides a strong surface level of understanding regarding the multimedia development tools used in this course. The theoretical portion of the discussion, as students respond and critique one another's responses to the three questions posed by the instructor, provides students with a strong surface understanding of the instructional design principles for multimedia development. Students begin moving toward adaptive learning as they begin focusing their efforts on the final comprehensive project. Through asynchronous and synchronous discussions regarding the development of the instructional product, students move from surface to deep learning. The instructor role in online discussion is vital and the three functions—class member, initiator, and discussant—are important in cultivating deep learning in online discussion. The learning, enhanced through the role served by the instructor, is adaptive as students are creating a product to fulfill an instructional need where no one correct or true answer exists.

OUTCOMES

It is patently clear to us that the methods, knowledge, and cognition framework provides very powerful contexts for learning the course content. The online discussion environment and assignments designed by the instructor encourage students to interact with the course content, to read and explore beyond the immediate setting, and to reflect on what is being read (Warschauer, 1997). At the same time, the discussion and assignments encourage and support many other useful skills, including negotiation, written communication, diversity, constructive criticism, strategy development and execution, and reflection.

When the assignments undertaken by the students exposed to this form of learning environment are examined in the light of a framework proposed by Bennett, Dunne, and Carre (1999), its capacity to support students achieving deep understanding level immediately becomes evident. Based on the framework we have proposed, the distance learning setting helped and encouraged students to practice and develop higher order thinking across the full range of methods, knowledge, and cognition. The following major points, based on our experiences, emphasize the importance of the instructor role in designing the discussion environment and assignments in an online course. It is our intent to further investigate each of these points to substantiate our claims.

1. The assignments, and specifically the discussions, required learners to plan their steps, explore the domain, and work toward a goal. Similar to Fenwick, students perceived their most valuable learning was related to two main areas: group process and self-knowledge (Fenwick, 2002). Regarding group process, students needed to confront unexpected outcomes and hurdles, reflect and judge their progress, and use a variety of learning strategies to develop their solution. In the group setting, students were required to work with others and maintain a good working relationship throughout the semester. On a day-to-day basis, they needed to be cooperative and attentive to the group's needs, defend their own stance, negotiate, and give and accept criticism.

2. The assignment discussions regarding the assignments required students to apply various technologies available to them in the learning environment. These include e-mail, chat, and the bulletin board. Through the strategies for dynamic discussion, students consolidated large amounts of information obtained and discussed how to delineate the importance and value of the information toward assignment completion. They needed to interpret the information and balance the multiple perspectives presented. Succinct summaries of the information required reflection and critical thinking.

3. Students' reflections on the course based on e-mail, collaborative discussion, and chat demonstrate their positive attitudes regarding the course. Their satisfaction with the structure of the online environment was expressed in the individual student evaluations gathered at the end of the semester. Through their final documentation submitted with their final product, students described their appreciation for their diligent work.

4. Finally, in terms of managing assignments, these activities compelled students to identify subtasks and to conceptualize the problem they were required to solve and how it could best be managed. The activities required the students to formulate a plan and execute the course of action and to reflect on the directions and outcomes. Each member of the group takes on specific responsibilities, executes tasks to benefit the group, and works together with team members towards achieving a common goal. This finding is similar to other research (Dehler & Parras-Hernandez, 1998; Hinds & Weisband, 2003). Amid differing opinions and perspectives, groups were highly capable of resolving the problems assigned throughout the course.

CONCLUSIONS

The three roles of the instructor in online discussion presented in this article identify critical elements for creating a discussion environment for deep learning. Each distinct role—class member, initiator, and discussant—and the corresponding discussion type—flexible peer, structured topic, and collaborative task—provided students with an interactive task-oriented discussion environment as shown in Figure 27.3. In the beginning of the semester, during flexible peer discussions on technical issues, the instructor models the desired discussion behavior. Students begin to adopt this behavior and actively discuss the issues presented by the instructor. As the instructor initiates structured topic discussion regarding theoretical issues, the discussion behavior now demonstrated by the students continues, creating a supportive learning environment. Finally, as

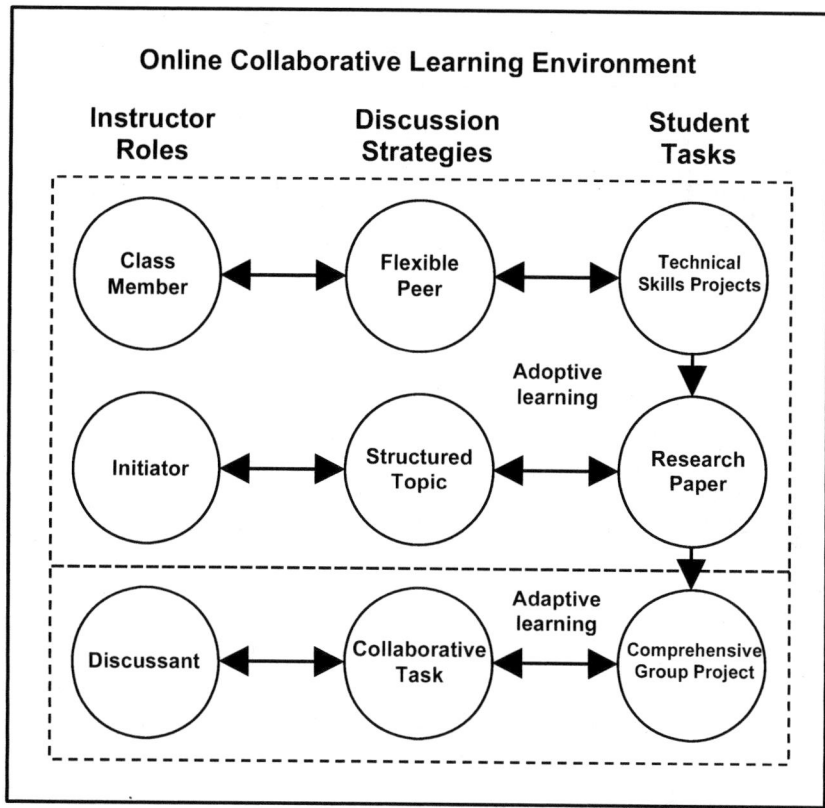

Figure 27.3.   The three instructor roles, discussion strategies, and student tasks within the collaborative learning environment.

students are engaged in the collaborative task discussions, their adaptive learning is enhanced and challenged. They must be able to respond succinctly and concisely to questions and react promptly to specific project and process focused questions posed by the instructor. Adoptive learning gradually transforms into adaptive learning exhibited by higher order problem solving skills.

Online discussion strategy is imperative for student learning; however, further investigation is necessary in order to determine the effect of the multiple instructor roles has on student learning. What is the specific impact of the instructor roles (class member, initiator, and discussant) on student learning outcomes? Future research guided by this question may assist in addressing why many distance-delivered courses experience high attrition rates that result from factors such as students feeling isolated, unmotivated, overwhelmed, or unchallenged. Based on the framework and the dynamic discussion strategy proposed, student participation is encouraged in all aspects of the requirements for course completion. Students are made to feel as if they are part of a community, where their input is valued by their peers and where their suggestions are encouraged, a conclusion similar to that of Blumenfeld, Marx, Soloway, and Krajcik (1996). The supportive environment created in a dynamic discussion serves to assist students who may feel overwhelmed by the course requirements. Motivation to learn and share ideas is encouraged and evolves naturally as the course progresses. Continuous peer review of posted responses to items challenges each student to provide their best input for the learning community created through dynamic discussion.

Dynamic discussion is an integral part of an online course. However, the amount of time and percentage of the course spent in a particular discussion environment has yet to be explored with the proposed framework. As students work through the assignments, the importance of discussion, the sharing of ideas and opinions, cannot be ignored. The assignments in this course require extensive peer-to-peer discussion throughout the semester in order to achieve the desired outcomes for the course. Through the structure of the dynamic discussion presented in the framework, students engage in discussion as part of assignment completion. In a sense, the discussion and the assignment cannot be separated; both act as a means for attainment of the course goal. Future study questions that address the relationship of dynamic online discussion with the overall course learning experience will be posed. The nature of online interactions and communications must be understood by both instructors and instructional designers (Pincas, 1998). The strategies we have proposed for creating dynamic discussion serve to facilitate online interactions among diverse learners and assist in effective interactions for assignment completion.

Providing students with a learning environment that will assist them in achieving the course goal is important, but we must look beyond the boundaries of a single course. The framework proposed and the strategies for dynamic discussion provide an environment in which students may learn beyond the course goal. Future study addressing how deep learning evolves through the proposed framework will provide insight regarding transfer of problem solving ability to ill-structured problems and unfamiliar environments. Initially it appears students build on the adoptive learning taking place through assignments designed to promote adaptive learning and challenge their cognitive abilities resulting in deep learning. Students' cognitive process is challenged through learning to use collaborative tools, learning to work collaboratively on complex learning assignments, and learning how to collaborate at a distance both asynchronously and synchronously.

Three strategies for dynamic online discussion—flexible peer, structured topic, and collaborative task discussion—were presented. This article examined these discussion structures and the three distinct roles—class member, initiator, and discussant—demonstrated by the instructor in the promotion of deep learning through the use of online discussion. The roles of the instructor are critical in the implementation of discussion strategies and design of student tasks for significant learning in online collaborative environments. While research will continue, this article has theoretical and practical implications for instructors in designing and facilitating asynchronous and synchronous discussion.

REFERENCES

Bennett, N., Dunne, E., & Carre, C. (1999). Patterns of core and generic skill provision in higher education. *Higher Education, 37*(1), 71-93.

Blumenfeld, P. C., Marx, R. W., Soloway, E. & Krajcik, J. (1996) Learning with peers: From small group cooperation to collaborative communities. *Educational Researcher, 25*(8), 37-42.

Boud, D., Cohen, R., & Sampson, J. (1999). Peer learning and assessment. *Assessment and Evaluation in Higher Education, 24*(4), 413-426.

Brookfield, S. (1982). Independent learners and correspondence students. *Teaching at a Distance, 22*, 26-33.

Dehler, C., & Parras-Hernandez, L. H. (1998) Using computer-mediated communication (CMC) to promote experiential learning in graduate studies. *Educational Technology, 38*(3), 52-55.

Du, J. X., & Havard, B. (2003). A framework for deep learning in distance education. *Delta Pi Epsilon, 45*(3), 204-214.

Fenwick, T. J. (2002). Problem-based learning, group process and the mid-career professional: Implications for graduate education. *Higher Education Research & Development, 21*(1), 5-21.

Flynn, E. W., & La Faso, J. F. (1972) *Group discussion as a learning process*. New York: Paulist Press.

Entwistle, N., & Ramsden, P. (1983). *Understanding student learning*. London: Croom Helm.

Gredler, M. E. (1997). *Learning and instruction: Theory into practice* (3rd ed). Upper Saddle River, NJ: Prentice-Hall.

Henri, F. (1992). Computer conference and content analysis. In A. Kaye (Ed.), *Collaborative learning through computer conferencing* (pp. 117-136). Berlin, Germany: Springer-Verlag.

Hinds, P., & Weisband, S. (2003). Knowledge sharing and shared understanding in virtual teams. In C. B. Gibson & S. G. Cohen (Eds.), *Virtual teams that work:*

Creating conditions for virtual team effectiveness (pp. 21-36). San Francisco: Jossey-Bass.

Hutchins, H. M. (2001). Enhancing the business communication course through WebCT. *Business Communication Quarterly, 64*(3), 87-94.

Kitchener, K. S. (1983). Cognition, metacognition, and epistemic cognition: A three-level model of cognitive processing. *Human Development, 26*, 222–232.

Kitchener, K. S., & King, P. M. (1981). Reflective judgment: Concepts of justification and their relationship to age and education. *Journal of Applied Developmental Psychology, 2*, 89-116.

Moore, M. (1989). Three types of interactions, *The American Journal of Distance Education, 3*, 1-6.

Oliver, R., & Mcloughlin, C. (1996). *An investigation of the nature and form of interactions in live interactive television.* Melbourne, Australia: Australian Society for Educational Technology. (ERIC Document Reproduction Service No. ED396738)

Pincas, A. (1998) Successful online course design: virtual frameworks for discourse construction. *Educational Technology and Society, 1*(1), 14-25.

Popolov, D., Callaghan, M., & Luker, P. (2002). Tying models of learning to design of collaborative learning software tools. *Journal of Computer Assisted Learning, 18*(1), 46-47.

Rourke, L., Anderson, T., Garrison, R., & Archer, W. (2001). Methodological issues in the content analysis of computer conference transcripts. *International Journal of Artificial Intelligence in Education, 12*, 8-22.

Tiene, D. (2002). Exploring current issues in educational technology using a problem-based approach to instruction. *Educational Technology, 42*(1), 14-22.

Vygotsky, L. S. (1978). *Mind in society.* Cambridge, MA: Harvard University Press.

Warschauer, M. (1997) Computer-mediated collaborative learning: theory and practice. *Modern Language Journal, 81*(4), 470-481.

Weigel, V. (2001). *Deep learning for a digital age: Technology's untapped potential to enrich higher education.* San Francisco: Jossey-Bass.

CHAPTER 28

IT'S THE SAME
ONLY DIFFERENT

The Effect the Discussion Moderator
has on Student Participation
in Online Class Discussions

Vance A. Durrington and Chien Yu

Online discussions are an effective method used to enhance interactions among learners and the instructor. The study examined the differences in communication based on whether the discussions were instructor-moderated or peer-moderated and based on whether the classes consisted of undergraduate or graduate students. Results indicate that student classification had no significant effect on the level of participation in the online discussions. However, there were significant differences in the amount of student participation in the discussions that were moderated by their peers rather than the instructor.

The development of online courses has the potential to change our educational learning environment and has caused many educators to integrate

The Perfect Online Course: Best Practices for Designing and Teaching
pp. 503–519
Copyright © 2009 by Information Age Publishing
All rights of reproduction in any form reserved.

technology into their courses for learning effectiveness. Courses offered via the Internet provide learning opportunities for those who have difficulty accessing traditional classrooms (Koszalka & Bianco, 2001). Students can now access courses for college credit anytime, anywhere.

The National Center for Education Statistics (1999) reported that 44% of two- and four-year degree-granting institutions offered distance education courses in 1997-98, and the number of online courses is still on the rise. Developing and delivering courses at a distance depends on faculty members' ability to use technology to enhance the teacher/learner process, and overcome barriers to implement distance education courses and programs.

Perrin and Mayhew (2000) indicate that distance education courses might not be able to create the level of interaction achieved in face-to-face courses. However, Miller and Webster (1997) found that faculty teaching distance education courses could provide their online students with levels of interaction similar to their on-campus students. The need to pay close attention to online interaction has been emphasized in many studies (Gunawardena & Zittle, 1997; Haythornthwaite, 2001; Vrasidas & McIsaac, 1999). Moore (2001) indicated that in order to successfully deliver online courses, faculty must allow student-to-student interaction with minimal faculty intervention; engage students in regular assignments in order to monitor progress and intervene when needed; provide specialized attention to students with low levels of self-directedness; and help students become more self-directed. Current research is examining not only student-to-instructor interactions, but also student-to-student interactions. Student-to-student online interactions have become as important as student-to-instructor online interactions and in some cases are more important (Driver, 2002; Wegerif, 1998). The purpose of this study was to examine the amount of discussion that occurs when the online class discussions are instructor-moderated and when they are student-moderated, to determine if there is a significant difference in student participation based on the discussion moderator. This study was conducted using both graduate and undergraduate students, so the discussions were also examined to determine if the students' classification (undergraduate/graduate) had a significant impact on the amount of student participation in the online class discussions. The results of this study will provide information that will aid in making online courses more learner-centered.

LITERATURE REVIEW

One of the main characteristics of distance learning is the separation of instructor and learner by time and geography. For distance education programs to be successful, Murphy (1997) indicated that they must provide "for appropriate and sufficient synchronous and asynchronous inter-action between faculty and students and among students" (p. 8). Relan and Gillani (1997) pointed out that the asynchronous, virtual, and net-work features of Web-based instruction can facilitate constructivist learn-ing approaches. Koszalka and Bianco (2001) stated that this support of the learning process can be achieved by providing multiple means of pre-senting instruction, information, and activities. The achievement of this variety in instructional design can best be accomplished through instruc-tor involvement and intervention.

Online Interaction

Effective learning environments often require some type of social inter-action. A number of studies (Moore, 1989; Northrup & Rasmussen, 2000) classified interaction as engagement in learning through

1. interaction among students, which refers to the student's relation-ship with other students in the class,
2. interaction between students and instructor, which refers to inter-action between the learner and the creator of the subject material, and
3. interaction between students and content, which refers to the stu-dent's relationship with the course materials.

While many studies have focused on one or the other type of interac-tion, Fulford and Zhang (1993) concluded that "overall interaction dynamics may have a stronger impact on learners' satisfaction than strictly personal participation. Vicarious interaction may result in greater learner satisfaction than would be the divided attention necessary to ensure the overt engagement of each participant" (p. 9). Their findings may suggest that students perceive interaction as a general characteristic of a class that could be attained in a variety of ways, with some ways being more effective than others. The level of interaction among students and between students and their instructors has a major impact on the quality of Web-based instruction and, therefore, it is crucial that distance educa-tors have a clear understanding of how to promote interactivity in their online courses.

Different levels of interactivity are embedded within both content and social interaction (Gilbert & Moore, 1998). Increasingly, studies have emphasized linking online communication technology with the context of learning (Crook, 1994). For example, online discussion technology can be a major means for fostering the development of collaborative skills among learners (Harasim, 1993; Kaye, 1995). To create instructionally sound collaborative tasks for online use, Bernard, Rubalcava, and St-Pierre (2000) indicated that several factors must be taken into account. Bernard and Lundgren-Cayrol (2001) indicated the need to "create positive interdependence among students, which is also a necessary ingredient for successful collaborative learning" (p. 244). Hiltz and Wellman (1997) recommended that optimal Web-based learning environments "create the feeling of a true 'class' or group of people learning together ... and support carefully planned collaborative learning activities" (p. 47). The moderator plays an important role in the successful development of the collaborative learning environment (Rohfeld & Hiemstra, 1995).

Discussion Moderators

There is a limited amount of research that examines the use of student moderators, and comparisons between student-moderated discussions and instructor-moderated discussions are even more limited. Jordan (1999) examined the use of student moderators within a listserv discussion. Student moderators were not actual students in the course and the listserv was open to anyone who wanted to join, so the online discussion wasn't a structured element of the specific course examined in the study. Students indicated that serving as the discussion moderator was a rewarding experience. Jordan's findings prompt speculation that if the moderating experience was rewarding for students not enrolled in the class, then the experience might be even more rewarding for students who are enrolled in the class. Jordan concluded that student moderators can provide technical leadership and create a welcoming online environment as new members enter the discussion.

Requiring students to serve as moderators can positively effect online discussions (Cifuentes, Murphy, Segur, & Kodali, 1997; Poole, 2000; Tagg, 1994). Rohfeld and Hiemstra (1995) argued that the effectiveness of online discussions is dependent on the instructor and student being involved in both the teaching and learning. The role of the moderator is to maintain the flow of the discussion. Tagg found that the instructor and student moderators complemented one another. Using Feenberg's (1989) typology of moderator functions (Table 28.1), Tagg delineated between the moderating functions that were more appropriate for student moderators and those functions that were more appropriate for the instructor. Student moderators were given the responsibility of opening the discussion and setting the agenda, both contextualizing functions, while the instructor was better suited to perform the monitoring functions of encouragement and guidance. Even though the students served as mod-

Table 28.1.   Summary List of the Contextualizing and Monitoring Moderator Functions Identified by Feenberg

Contextualizing Functions

- **Opening Discussion:** Carefully designed opening comments should announce the theme of discussion, and identify any shared experiences or symbols that can clarify content and purpose
- **Setting Norms:** A familiar communication model should be selected to establish tacit expectations about conference behavior, and to suggest rules of behavior.
- **Setting Agenda:** The moderator controls the order and flow of discussion topics, and generally shares part or all of the agenda with participants at the outset

Monitoring Functions

- **Recognition:** The moderator refers explicitly to the participants to assure them that their contribution is valued and welcome, or to correct any misapprehensions about the context of discussion
- **Prompting:** To solicit comments from participants, either publicly or through private mail messages; might be formalised as "assignments" in some conferences

Meta Functions

- **Meta-commenting:** To remedy problems in context, norms or agenda, clarity, irrelevance, and information overload
- **Weaving:** To summarize the state of the discussion and to find unifying threads in participants' comments; it encourages these participants and implicitly prompts them to pursue their ideas

Source: Feenberg (1989, p. 35).

erators, there was still an obvious instructor presence in the discussions, such that there was an instructor-student team approach to discussion moderation.

Poole (2000) also examined the role of student moderators with a class that met completely online. The instructor presented material on a course topic and then students completed a quiz related to the topic. After completion of the quiz, a student moderated an online discussion on the topic just completed. So the instructor performed the contextualizing functions that the student moderators performed in Tagg's (1984) study. In Poole's study, the student moderators were given the responsibility of performing the monitoring functions, which Tagg described as instructor functions. Poole found that the discussions moderated by students created a more learner-centered environment and also empowered the students. The number of discussion postings also exceeded expectations, but one potential confounding factor was the creation of a fictitious class member. This fictitious class member usually posted content that "generated lots of discussion among class members" (p. 173). Therefore, it is unclear what role the peer moderators played and what role the fictitious class member played in generating the greater than expected number of postings. Yet, Poole did conclude that the moderator role enhanced the sense of community among the students, because all students served in the moderator role.

By moderating discussions, students take an active role in the course and it forces the instructor to move away from the role of teacher (Poole, 2000; Tagg, 1994). But, in all of these studies, the instructor is still playing an outward role either in the discussions or the introduction of the discussion material. It is still unclear what effect peer moderation has on the level of discussion when the peer moderator is responsible for performing both the contextualizing and monitoring functions.

METHODOLOGY

This research study was carried out using undergraduate and graduate technology education courses offered at a major southeastern university. These courses were offered online and there were no face to face components in any of these courses. One of the undergraduate courses dealt with the use of telecommunications in the K-12 classroom. The other undergraduate course was an office systems technology course related to effective online communications. The graduate course dealt with issues in distance education. All of these courses were offered using the WebCT courseware package. All three courses were taught by the same instructor. As part of the course, a number of discussions related to the course content served as required elements of the course. Some of these discussions were moderated by the instructor and others were moderated by the students in the class. As a required element of the courses, each student was required to select and introduce a topic related to the course curriculum and moderate an online discussion related to the selected topic. Rather than provide students with a list of topics to choose from, students were responsible for determining the topic they would introduce and discuss, the only criteria being that the topic had to be related to the course curriculum and it had to have the instructor's approval. The approval of the instructor was necessary to make sure that students had selected a topic that related to the course and to make sure the topic could be researched and developed into an online discussion. Some of the instructor-led discussion topics included social equality online, Internet privacy, and learning styles in distance education. Examples of discussion topics that students selected to moderate included technology course requirements for undergraduates, women on the Internet, and distance learning and disabilities. The instructor was also a participant in the student-moderated discussions. Each student moderated only one discussion per class and the instructor moderated six discussions in each class. Initially, the instructor-moderated discussions were the only discussions occurring. Student-moderated discussions began during the fourth week of classes. There were times when only student-moderated discussions were occurring, and other times when both student-moderated and instructor-moderated discussions were occurring.

The purpose of this study was to determine if there was a difference in the frequency of student contributions when the discussions were instructor-moderated versus when the discussions were peer-moderated. As mentioned previously, in Tagg's (1994) study, the students were responsible for performing Feenberg's (1989) contextualizing functions, because he indicated that the instructor is more adept at carrying out the monitoring functions of encouragement and guidance. Poole (2000) took the opposite approach in her study, because the instructor performed the contextualizing functions. In this study, the peer moderators were expected to perform both the contextualizing and monitoring moderator functions. Demographic information as well as student reflections related to the course and online discussions were also gathered.

Characteristics of Students

There was a total of 61 students in the three classes. In the two undergraduate courses there were 37 students (20 in the education oriented class and 17 in the office systems-oriented class) and 24 students in the graduate course. Even though the two undergraduate classes were oriented toward a certain degree program, students pursuing other degrees were permitted to enroll in these classes (Table 28.2). The majority of the participants were female (82%); more specifically, approximately 88% of the graduate students were female and approximately 78% of the undergraduate students were female. In terms of ethnicity, 62% of the students identified themselves as Caucasian, while 35% of the students identified themselves as Black, and one student was identified as American Indian/Alaskan Native. The ethnic composition of the undergraduate students was 68% Caucasian and 32% Black, while the ethnicity of the graduate students was 54% Caucasian, 42% Black, and 4% American Indian/Alaskan Native.

The majority of students in the three classes fell into three age categories: under 23 (21%), 23-27 (26%), and over 42 (26%). These same three age categories also made up the majority of the undergraduate students,

Table 28.2.   Demographic Data of Participants

General Characteristics	Undergraduate	Graduate
Gender		
Female	29	21
Male	9	3
Ethnicity		
Caucasian	25	13
Black	13	10
American Indian/Alaskan Native	0	1
Age		
Under 23	12	1
23-27	9	7
28-32	2	2
33-37	4	3
38-42	2	3
Over 42	8	8
GPA		
4.0-3.51	11	18
3.50-3.01	8	3
3.00-2.51	9	2
2.50-2.01	8	1
2.00-1.51	1	

where 32% of the students were under the age of 23, 24% of the students were in the 23-27 age range, and 22% of the students were over 42. Among the graduate students, the two main age groupings were the 23-27 age range (29%) and the over 42 age group (33%). The grade point average of the undergraduate students was relatively evenly distributed ranging from 2.01 to 4.00, with one student falling below this range. The majority of the undergraduate students were majoring in either office systems and technologies or elementary education (Table 28.3). The majority of the graduate students were working toward a master's degree (58%). Instructional technology was the most prominent concentration for the master's students. All of the doctoral students were pursuing PhD degrees in education with an emphasis in educational technology.

Table 28.3.   Program of Study by Classification

Undergraduate Program of Study	
Office Systems & Technologies	10
Elementary Education	9
Business Information Systems	5
Interdisciplinary Studies	5
Technology Teacher Education	2
Undeclared	2
Secondary Education	1
Sociology	1
Computer Science	1
Gen Business Admin	1
Graduate Program of Study	
Masters	
Instructional Technology	9
Technology	3
Undecided	1
Education Specialist	1
Doctor of Philosophy	10

FINDINGS

Within the three classes there was a total of 2,326 postings with an average of 38 postings per student and 31 postings per discussion. Each discussion averaged 9.8 discussion threads and each discussion thread averaged 2.1 levels. Initial t-tests were performed to examine differences in computed means for the total number of postings, the total number of original postings, and the total number of follow-up postings based on classification (Table 28.4) and discussion moderator (Table 28.5). The t-test analysis based on classification indicated that there was no significant difference in the frequency of overall postings based on classification. In addition, the test indicates that there wasn't a significant difference between the two groups in terms of initiating discussions and following-up or replying to the postings of their peers.

The t-test analysis comparing the discussion moderators (Table 28.5) indicated that there was a significant difference in the number of postings between instructor-moderated and student-moderated discussions. Stu-

Table 28.4.   T-Test Analysis of Postings Based on Classification

Postings	Undergraduate		Graduate		t value	p
	M	SD	M	SD		
Total number of postings	40.49	35.36	41.75	36.60	-0.133	0.894
Total number of original postings	14.32	9.94	15.25	7.51	-0.389	0.693
Total number of follow-up postings	26.19	32.39	26.50	34.43	-0.36	0.972

Table 28.5.   T-Test Analysis of Postings Based on Discussion Moderator

Postings	Instructor-led		Student-Led		t-value	p
	M	SD	M	SD		
Total number of postings	9.23	8.55	18.00	19.51	-3.22	0.002**
Total number of original postings	5.25	3.05	3.95	5.73	1.56	0.122
Total number of follow-up postings	3.98	7.40	14.05	18.94	-3.87	0.000***

Note: **$p < .01$. ***$p < .001$.

dents participated significantly more when the discussions were student-moderated as opposed to instructor-moderated ($p < .01$). Analysis related to differences in original postings and follow-up postings indicated that there was no significant difference in the number of original postings based on the discussion moderator. However, students responded to each other significantly more in the student-moderated discussions as opposed to the instructor-moderated discussions ($p < .001$).

A multivariate analysis of variance was used to explore the interaction between student classification and moderator leader with respect to the number of total postings, the number of original postings and the number of follow-up or reply postings. Significant multivariate effects were obtained for discussion (Pillai's Trace $= 0.124$, $F(2, 117) = 8.297$, $p < .01$) and for the interaction effects of discussion and classification (Pillai's Trace $= 0.124$, $F(2, 117) = 8.288$, $p < .002$). Analysis of the univariate effects demonstrated a significant effect for the discussion moderator on the total number of postings ($F(1, 118) = 6.978$, $p < .01$), the number of original postings ($F(1, 118) = 5.697$, $p < .05$), and the number of follow-up postings ($F(1, 118) = 11.863$, $p < .001$). In addition, the interac-

**Table 28.6.   Two-Way ANOVA for
Classification and Discussion Moderator on Total Number of Postings**

Source of Variation	Sum of Squares	df	Mean Square	F	Sig.
Classification	1.036	1	1.036	0.005	0.945
Discussion moderator	1518.719	1	1518.719	6.978	0.009**
Classification * disc. mod.	1536.293	1	1536.293	7.059	0.009**
Error	25681.458	118	217.639		

Note: **$p < 0.01$.

**Table 28.7.   Two-Way ANOVA for Classification and
Discussion Moderator on Total number of Original Postings**

Source of variation	Sum of squares	df	Mean square	F	Sig.
Classification	40.359	1	40.359	2.133	0.147
Discussion moderator	107.775	1	107.775	5.697	0.019*
Classification * disc. mod.	1536.293	1	1536.293	7.059	0.009**
Error	2232.260	118	18.917		

Note: *$p < .05$. **$p < .01$.

**Table 28.8.   Two-Way ANOVA for Classification and
Discussion Moderator on Total Number of Follow-Up Postings**

Source of Variation	Sum of Squares	df	Mean Square	F	Sig.
Classification	28.463	1	28.463	0.139	0.710
Discussion moderator	2435.640	1	2435.640	11.863	0.001**
Classification * disc. mod.	541.608	1	541.608	2.638	0.107
Error	24227.766	118	205.320		

Note: **$p < .01$.

tion between classification and discussion moderator was found to have a significant effect on the total number of postings ($F(1, 118) = 7.059, p < .01$) and the number of original postings ($F(1, 118) = 13.403, p < .001$). The interaction did not indicate a significant effect on the number of follow-up postings. In addition, classification had no significant effect on any of the posting categories examined (Tables 28.6-28.8).

Based on these results, whether the students were graduate students or undergraduate students had no significant effect on the number of postings made by an individual student during the course discussion. This may be due to the fact that distance learners are found to be highly motivated (Simonson, Smaldino, Albright, & Zvacek, 2003). However, who the moderator is does appear to have a significant effect on not only the total number of postings, but also on the number of original and follow-up postings made by students. Interestingly, the students tended to have more overall postings and follow-up postings in the student-moderated discussions, but had more original postings in the instructor-led discussions. This could indicate that there are fewer and longer discussion threads in the student-moderated discussions, but further research will need to be completed to determine if this is the case. The findings do indicate that students preferred posting and responding in the student-moderated discussions as opposed to the instructor-moderated discussions.

In examining the postings of the student moderators, the researchers looked for examples of Feenberg's (1989) moderating functions. One moderator began her discussion with confusion, before setting the context. In her moderation of a discussion on spam, "Diane" intentionally posted a message that appeared to be unrelated to the discussion topic (italicized text indicates author changes to maintain anonymity):

Posted by *Diane*
Subject spam
Just heard a way I could sign up for classes and get a guaranteed A, so since this is an on line communication class I felt obligated to share this with my classmates. I didn't realize our *university* would approve something like this but I have checked it out. Here's the site and pass it along. gradshif.xom Another thing that hits college students and working folks, bad credit occasionally, get your debts wipe away at nucredlife.xom Just thought before I get into my subject on spam, I would let my hard working friends in on these secrets. Let me know how you come out once you check out the sites. I'll check back and don't forget to pass the info around. You wouldn't want your friends to miss out on a chance of being Suma Cum Laude, would you?

As she expected, the students began posting messages indicating they weren't able to access the sites indicated, in desperation one student finally posted:

Posted by *Peggy*
Subject Re: spam
Diane, I think we are all screaming HELP! It seems that nobody can get into those sites.
Peggy

Then later that day, another student caught on to what Diane had done:

> *Diane,*
> HA hahahaha.... I love it. I got half way through your message and realized what you had done. Brilliant example! Reads just like all those messages I get in my junk mail.
> It's very easy to get sucked into spam messages, especially when they come from friends. You will be thinking you got a real message from them and it turns out to be some advertisement that was forwarded to you just to keep the e-mail alive.
> Jeff

After Jeff's posting, the discussion on spam took off and Diane proceeded to provide background information and asked her peers to identify their experiences with spam. Diane's opening and subsequent postings demonstrate them as contextualizing functions identified by Feenberg, which Tagg (1994) indicated as functions well suited for student moderators.

Tagg (1994) indicated that peer moderators couldn't perform the monitoring functions effectively. Analysis of the discussion postings also showed clear examples of student moderators performing monitoring functions. Travis was moderating a discussion on partnerships in distance education and had raised the issue of funding for such endeavors. A fellow student related her personal knowledge and experiences related to the funding issue and Travis replied:

> Posted by *Travis*
> Subject Re: Collaboration
> *Carol*:
> You possess some insight that I do not, which is not unexpected since I am not from *this state*. Did you happen to discuss distance learning with any officials at *university X*? Did they give you any idea as to what their future plans are for distance learning?
> For the rest of you, I sense that some of you are K-12 teachers. Are you aware of collaborations existing at that level in distance learning. One thought that I had along those lines (and I realize this is not distance learning) regards my profession of law enforcement. I am seeing many regional jails where counties are combining to share resources and operate one jail for several counties. Do you envision something similar happening in distance education between county school boards?
> Regards, *Travis*

In this posting, Travis clearly displays an example of Feenburg's (1989) monitoring functions by referring explicitly to the participant and recognizing the backgrounds of other participants in the discussion (recognition) Travis then develops the discussion further by soliciting comments from other discussion participants about what they envision for the future in their professional arenas (prompting) related to funding.

In discussing the moderating functions, Feenberg (1989) indicated the importance of having one person be responsible for performing these functions in order to keep the discussion alive, but he also indicated that "discussions are most absorbing and successful when the members of the group share these functions with the moderator" (p. 36). When analyzing the postings, there were indeed examples of discussion participants also performing moderating functions. Below is an example of a discussion thread related to the effectiveness of distance education, which wasn't posted by the student moderator. The first posting beginning the thread is an example of a contextualizing function and then the peer's response to this new thread is an example of a monitoring function:

Posted by *Kayla*
Subject First Discussion Topic
I feel that some courses would be quite difficult to take through a distance learning environment. For example more difficult courses such as engineering, harder mathematic courses, etc. that require a lot of explanation. I also feel that it takes a very special type person to do well in an online course. They have to be a student that can organize their time wisely and most of all not be the type person to procrastinate.

I feel that your performance in an online situation can be just as effective, if not more effective, as your performance in a traditional classroom. Actually, in an online setting, you are able to work at your own pace and it probably wouldn't be as stressful as if you were in a traditional classroom setting with limited class time and the stress caused by knowing that someone is monitoring you constantly.

Also, in numerous readings that I have come across, they say that females tend to perform better and are much appreciative of online classes than males.

Posted by *Tanner*
Subject Re: First Discussion Topic
Kayla:
Your post triggered a thought that we haven't really discussed here. What if a particularly difficult course is offered and the student needs tutoring on the side. How will that be accomplished? On campus, it's relatively easy to find upper classmen (pardon the term) or graduate students willing to tutor. However, when you live In The Middle Of Nowhere, USA, that may not be available.
Regards, *Tanner*

Kayla has added a new element to the effectiveness of distance education, by introducing the topic of whether some content areas lend themselves more to the distance learning environment than others (contextualizing function). Tanner then responds to Kayla's posting by specifically addressing her by name and then expanding on her thought by bringing up the topic of accessing tutoring for courses (contextualizing & monitoring functions). The use of contextualizing and monitoring functions among not only the moderators, but also the discussion participants as well, may help to explain the significant differences found in the amount of discussion. This would be consistent with Wegerif's (1998) research on the importance of the social dimension in online learning.

CONCLUSIONS

Despite the increasing asynchronous and synchronous avenues of communication, a major concern is the lack of personal interaction between the professor and student (Roberson & Klotz, 2002). Hiltz and Wellman (1997) spoke of the importance of planned collaborative learning activities for class or group identity. The use of student-moderated discussions can be one way of developing planned collaborative learning activities for an online class. Further research needs to be completed to identify other factors that can contribute to and enhance online discussion, such as possible predictors that contribute to the amount of discussion. In addition, a content analysis of discussions in future classes where this technique is used will help us to attain a better understanding of the dynamics of the online discussions that are occurring. The content analysis will help us obtain a better understanding of the context in which postings, both original and follow-up occur. Along these same lines, a sequence analysis of messages and responses similar to the one performed by Jeong (2003), shows great promise in helping to develop a greater understanding of what people are saying and how they are saying it in online discussions. Jeong's Discussion Analysis Tool has the potential to provide new insight into the different levels of the threaded discussions. The state transitional diagram combined with social network theory also has the potential to further analyze the flow of the online discussions. The rapid advancement in technology and communications has changed the way we teach and the opportunities students have for learning. As a result, distance education has deeply affected the form and structure of our teaching and learning in both the face-to-face and distance education environments as we strive to effectively use these communication and learning avenues to promote collaborative learning.

REFERENCES

Bernard, R. M., & Lundgren-Cayrol, K. (2001). Computer conferencing: An environment for collaborative project-based learning in distance education. *Educational Research and Evaluation, 7*(2-3), 241-261.

Bernard, R. M., Rubalcava, Beatriz Rojo de, & St-Pierre, D. (2000). Collaborative online distance learning: Issues for future practice and research. *Distance Education, 21,* 260-277.

Cifuentes, L., Murphy, K. L., Segur, R., & Kodali, S. (1997). Design considerations for computer conferences. *Journal of Research on Computing in Education, 30,* 177-201.

Crook, C. (1994). *Computers and the collaborative experience of learning.* London: Routledge.

Driver, M. (2002). Exploring student perceptions of group interaction and class satisfaction in the web-enhanced classroom. *The Internet and higher Education, 5*(1), 35-45.

Feenberg, A. (1989). The written world: On the theory and practice of computer conferencing. In R. Mason & A. Kaye (Eds.), *Mindweave: Communication, computers, and distance education* (pp. 22-39).

Fulford, C. P., & Zhang, S. (1993). Perceptions of interaction: The critical predictor in distance education. *The American Journal of Distance Education, 7*(3), 8-21.

Gilbert, L., & Moore, D. L. (1998). Building interactivity into web courses: Tools for social and instructional interaction. *Educational Technology, 38*(3), 29-35.

Gunawardena, C. N., & Zittle, F. J. (1997). Social presence as a predictor of satisfaction within a computer-mediated conferencing environment. *American Journal of Distance Education, 11*(3), 8-26.

Harasim, L. (1993). Collaborating in cyberspace: Using computer conferences as a group learning environment. *Interactive Learning Environments, 3*(2), 119-130.

Haythornthwaite, C. (2001). Exploring multiplexity: Social network structures in a computer-supported distance learning class. *The Information Society, 17,* 211-226.

Hiltz, S. R., & Wellman, B. (1997). Asynchronous learning networks as a virtual classroom. *Communications of the ACM, 40*(9), 44-49.

Jeong, A. C. (2003). The sequential analysis of group interaction and critical thinking in online threaded discussions. *The American Journal of Distance Education, 17,* 25-43.

Jordan, K. (1999). "Can anybody get the ball rolling?" The roles of a student moderator. *English in Australia, 124.* Retrieved April 11, 2003, from http://www.aate.org.au/E in A/April99/991jord. html

Kaye, A. (1995). Computer supported collaborative learning. In N. Heap, R. Thomas, G. Einon, R. Mason, & H. Mackay (Eds.), *Information technology and society: A reader* (pp. 192-210). Newbury Park, CA: SAGE

Koszalka, T. A., & Bianco, M. B. (2001). Reflecting on the instructional design of distance education for learners: Learning from the instructors. *Quarterly Review of Distance Education, 2,* 59-70.

Miller, W. W. & Webster, J. (1997). *A comparison of interaction needs and performance of distance learners in synchronous and asynchronous classes.* Paper presented at the American Vocational Association Convention, Las Vegas, NV. (ERIC Dcoument Reproduction Service No. ED415411)

Moore, M. G. (1989). Three types of interaction. *The American Journal of Distance Education, 3*(2), 1-6.

Moore, M. G. (2001). Surviving as a distance teacher. *The American Journal of Distance Education, 15*(2), 1-5.

Murphy, T. H. (1997). Five factors to evaluate distance education programs. *NACTA Journal, 42*(3), 6-10.

National Center for Educational Statistics. (1999). *Distance Education by Postsecondary Faculty.* Retrieved September 5, 2002, from http://nces.ed.gov/programs/coe/2001/section5/indicator49.html

Northrup, P. T., & Rasmussen, K. L. (2000). *Designing a web-based program: Theory to design.* Paper presented at the annual conference of the Association for Educational Communications and Technology, Long Beach, CA.

Perrin, K. M., & Mayhew, D. (2000). The reality of designing and implementing an Internet-based course. *Online Journal of Distance Learning Administration, 3*(4). Retrieved April 11, 2003, from http://www.westga.edu/~distance/ojdla/winter34/mayhew34.html

Poole, D. M. (2000). Student participation in a discussion-oriented online course: A case study. *Journal of Research on Computing in Education, 33*, 162-177. Retrieved April 11, 2003 from Academic Search Elite database.

Relan, A., & Gillani, B. (1997). Web–based instruction and the traditional classroom: Similarities and differences. In B. Khan (Ed.), *Web-based instruction* (pp. 41-46). Englewood Cliffs, NJ: Educational Technology Publications.

Roberson, T. J., & Klotz, J. (2002). How can instructors and administrators fill the missing link in online instruction? *Online Journal of Distance Learning Administration, 5*(4). Retrieved April 11, 2003 from http://www.westga.edu/~distance/ojdla/winter54/roberson54.htm

Rohfeld, R. W., & Hiemstra, R. (1995). Moderating discussions in the electronic classroom. In Z. L. Berge & M. P. Collins (Eds.), *Computer mediated communication and the online classroom: Vol. 3. Distance education* (pp. 91-104), Cresskill, NJ: Hampton Press.

Simonson, M., Smaldino, S., Albright, M., & Zvacek, S. (2003). *Teaching and learning at a distance: Foundations of distance education.* Upper Saddle River, NJ: Pearson Education.

Tagg, A. C. (1994). Leadership from within: Student moderation of computer conferences. *The American Journal of Distance Education, 8*, 40-50.

Vrasidas, C. & McIsaac, M. S. (1999). Factors influencing interaction in an online course. *American Journal of Distance Education, 13*(3), 22-36.

Wegerif, R. (1998). The social dimension of asynchronous learning networks [Electronic version]. *Journal of Asynchronous Learning Networks, 2*(1), 34-49.

CHAPTER 29

DOES SENSE OF COMMUNITY MATTER?

An Examination of Participants' Perceptions of Building Learning Communities in Online Courses

Xiaojing Liu, Richard J. Magjuka,
Curtis J. Bonk, and Seung-Hee Lee

Using a case study approach, this study explored the participants' perceptions of building learning communities in online courses in an online MBA program. The findings suggested that students felt a sense of belonging to a learning community when they took online courses in this program. The study found positive relationships between sense of learning community and perceived learning engagement, course satisfaction, and learning outcomes. In addition, interview findings revealed mixed perceptions of both online instructors and students with regard to the values and strategies for building learning communities in online courses. Many instructors have a weak awareness of online community and low value of its learning impact. The existing technology may still be a barrier without the supportive structure to enhance bonding within the online community. To design online courses for a learning community, the results suggest a more systematic

The Perfect Online Course: Best Practices for Designing and Teaching
pp. 521–543

instructional plan needs to be adopted to integrate elements of a learning community across different levels.

INTRODUCTION

Over the past decade we have witnessed exponential growth of online courses through a variety of educational or corporate settings. In line with this trend, there is an increased discussion with regard to building online communities in Web-based courses. This increased interest is primarily a reaction to two major concerns related to Web-based education: retention and quality (Rovai, 2002b). In online environments, the reduced social and visual cues might expose online learners to a risk of feeling isolated and disconnected. Studies found a weak sense of social cohesiveness could result in increased drop-outs of online students if they feel isolated and stressed (Eastmond, 1995). It is expected that an online community helps establish social connectedness among online instructors and students and thus reduces the potential attrition rates of online students (Rovai, 2002). Additionally, it is believed that the "social capital" (Schwier, 2004) derived from online communities—such as mutual understandings and shared values and behaviors—will eventually benefit online learners through the availability of greater support and socioemotional well-being (Rovai, 2001).

While there is a growing body of literature emphasizing the importance of building learning communities in online courses, clear directions based on empirical studies in this area are lacking and there is neither an accepted set of rules or strategies (Lock, 2002) nor clearly defined road maps or steps in the development of online communities (Bonk, Wisher, & Nigrelli, 2004). In addition, the research on the effects of online communities on learning is mixed. A few scholars criticize existing research for failing to demonstrate the role of community in learning through rigorous empirical studies. Although several studies claim to have found positive relationships between higher sense of community and enhanced learning experiences, those studies often fail to separate the effect of sense of community from other confounding factors or are unable to demonstrate a cause-effect relationship between the role of community and learner performance (Chao, 1999; Misanchuk, 2003; Moller, 2000).

Many existing studies seem to be based on the basic assumption that having a feeling of community is always likable by its members. However, several studies indicate that this might not be the case (Brown, 2001; Misanchuk, 2003). For example, Brown found that whether a student can find a community in a class appears to be an individual phenomenon based on personality, time, interaction, and level of participation and engagement.

As a result, community will not happen unless the participants want it and make it happen. As in Brown's study, a significant portion of the participants were resistant to membership in a community and intentionally avoided community activities. In addition to the problems of resistance, there are also concerns regarding the cost involved in maintaining and participating in a learning community, especially in a virtual environment. And, a couple of studies note problems or risk when replacing academic rigor with an emphasis on social relationships and community building (Chao, 2001; Misanchuk, 2003).

If the building of a learning community is not always readily accepted practice and we have yet to prove the direct learning benefit through facilitating a sense of community in online courses, then it is important to examine the perceptions of online students and instructors on whether it matters to build a learning community in online courses, as well as the effective ways to build a sense of community. The empirical research is extremely lacking in this respect (Brown, 2001). Such examinations will provide insights into the factors that can facilitate or hinder community building in online education. Driven by this overarching research purpose, this exploratory study attempts to answer following specific research questions:

1. Do students feel a sense of community in online courses? How is the sense of community related to learner engagement, perceived cognitive learning, and satisfaction?
2. What are some communication and collaboration strategies used in online courses, and how do the participants perceive these strategies in facilitating community development in online courses?
3. What are student and instructor perceptions of factors affecting building communities in online courses?

LITERATURE

Definitions

Many definitions of learning communities are discussed in the professional literature. For example, Misanchuk and Anderson (2001) defined online learning communities as "a bounded group of students involved in cooperative learning online" (p. 3). Using social constructivist interpretations of online learning, Schwier (2002) defined the virtual learning community as a particular online environment where individuals willingly "take advantage of, and in some cases invent, a process for engaging ideas, negotiating and learning collectively" (p. 8).

Although online learning communities have been defined in different ways, the majority of the definitions share common elements such as shared goal, membership, trust, connectedness, collaboration, and community boundaries (Shea, Li, Swan, & Pickett, 2002). In this chapter, an online class learning community is considered to occur when participants of an online course have "a feeling that members belong to each other, a feeling that members matter to one another and to the group, and a shared faith that members' needs will be met through their commitment to be together" (McMillan & Chavis, 1986, p. 9).

Strategies to Facilitate Community Building

Community is defined by the relationships and interactions between and among people who gather together (Riel, 1996). Research suggests that once a reliable technology system is in place, course design and pedagogy plays more significant roles in facilitating community building than the e-learning system itself (Rovai, 2002a, 2002c). Interaction is often encouraged to promote the identity and autonomy of community members (Schwier, 2002). Rovai (2001) suggested using two kinds of interactions that have different roles in facilitating a sense of community. From his perspective, task-driven interactions facilitate the goal of learning, whereas socioemotional driven interactions facilitate social well-being of members and helps develop friendships. A sense of community is affected by the quality and quantity of both types of online interactions. An online discourse constructed on shallow interactions or lacking an in-depth dialogue is unlikely to foster a sense of community in online courses (Liu, 2006).

Misanchuk and Anderson (2001) similarly suggest strategies to promote online learning communities through increasing levels of communication and interaction. Drawn from a comprehensive literature review, they particularly noted strategies that had students interact at high levels of communication, cooperation, and collaboration. Examples of these strategies include: (1) noninstructional strategies, such as designing an onsite orientation that quickly bonds students with each other, encouraging students to post personal profiles, and incorporating an online café for off-topic discussions; and (2) strategies for learning tasks, such as encouraging high quality discussion through assessment and peer critique, designing content-based group projects that require extensive negotiation and modeling of effective communication skills in online discussion.

As one of the ways to promote interaction, there is consensus that collaboration plays a key role in facilitating high levels of interaction in online courses. A positive and collaborative culture can provide a community with opportunities to learn from each other, accommodate diverse membership, contribute to others' learning, and nurture the authentic expression of multiple perspectives (Wilson, Ludwidg-Hardman, Thornam, & Dunlap, 2004). Studies have also found that intentionally building collaborative assignments and electronic sharing activities fosters a sense of belonging together with a shared experience (Barab, Thomas, & Merrill, 1999). Rice-Lively (1994) found that even with simple tasks such as requiring students to post regularly to a newsgroup or participate in a decision making on communication rules or protocols can assist in facilitating a sense of community.

A few scholars suggest developmental stages for building online communities (Brown, 2001; Palloff & Pratt, 1999). For example, Brown (2001) argued that community could be experienced at any of three levels: making online friends or acquaintances through frequent interactions, feeling part of an online classroom community, and enjoying camaraderie. Brown also asserted that the students' interpersonal relationships could be amplified through enrolling in multiple courses together and, thus, feeling higher levels of community. She encourages organizations to consider using strategies to strengthen such relationships beyond the course and program level.

Technology

Technology can moderate the growth of a learning community. Since technology essentially provides a gathering and communication space for members, the accessibility and effective use of technology for online discourse facilitates virtual learning communities (Schwier, 2002). A prerequisite for facilitating a virtual community is to provide a technology environment that is "glitch" free and has flexible access for community members. Frequent technical failures or connectivity issues may leave members out of the community gathering place and thus hinder the development of a sense of community (Hill, 2001; Kearsley, 2000; Lock, 2002).

A variety of technologies have the potential to aid in the development of a learning community. For instance, a Web site can provide a central space for people to gather as well as archived histories of the people who participated as well as showcases for "best practices." Further, asynchronous and synchronous discussion forums enable information sharing, idea exchanges, and mentoring (Bonk et al., 2004).

Empirical evidence suggests that both synchronous and asynchronous communication strategies foster virtual community building, but in different ways. Synchronous communications, text-based chat discussions, and video conferencing have been found to foster social interaction in online courses as well as contribute to the continuity of the class, whereas asynchronous communications foster deeper dialogue and continuous discourse without time or geographical limitations (Duffy, Dueber, & Hawley, 1998; Schwier & Balbar, 2002). For example, a study found that asynchronous computer conferencing can enhance a sense of community through developing camaraderie, connectedness, and sense of accomplishment among military students (Phelps, Ashworth, & Hahn, 1991, as cited in Bonk, Wisher, & Nigrelli, 2004). Another study revealed that using synchronous instant messaging in Web-based courses simplified communication and enabled more venues for informal and social communication. Consequently, students felt a stronger sense of community among each other than students who chose not use the tool (Nicholson, 2002).

Communities of learners will not occur just because of the use of the technology itself. The role of technology in community building will be enhanced through careful planning and designing a psychologically safe, open, and inviting environment for information sharing and knowledge construction (Barab et al., 1999; Moller, 1998). A few researchers have emphasized the design of technological attributes to foster community development. For example, Preece (2000, as cited in Lock, 2002) believed that a technology-enriched environment needs to address sociability (social interaction) and usability (focus on human computer interaction) of the system.

Instructor's Role

Previous research indicates a close relationship between teacher behaviors and the development of virtual learning communities in online courses (Shea et al., 2002). Shea et al.'s study indicates that perceived teaching presence is associated with students' sense of learning community. A majority of the variance in students' perceptions of the sense of learning community can be explained by the students' sense of their instructors' teaching presence, defined as effective instructional design, organization, and "directed facilitation" (p. 62) of discourse (e.g., presenting content and questions, directing and summarizing discussion, and injecting knowledge from diverse resources).

Among Berge's (1995) four dimensions of online instructor roles, an important role is to promote a friendly environment and community that supports student cognitive learning processes. From a constructivist perspective, online social roles require the instructor to develop nurturing skills for creating a context conducive to knowledge construction by encouraging participation, giving ample feedback and reward, attending to individual concerns, and using a friendly, personal tone (Kerr, 1986). Not only do the instructors need to establish a leader role in nurturing a sense of community, they also are expected to model the social roles for online students to motivate and engage students in a community of inquiry (Anderson, Rourke, Archer, & Garrison, 2001).

Despite these fairly commonsense findings, empirical studies indicate that social roles and activities of online instructors are not always acknowledged by online instructors. Studies have indicated that virtual learning community instructors who are new to teaching online may have difficulty getting used to the concept of community (Bonk, 2000; Conrad, 2004).

METHODOLOGY

The case study approach is often considered appropriate for exploratory research that examines the perceptions of participants in an online program. Such an approach can also be beneficial in providing better understanding of a complex system like the one studied here (Stake, 1994).

The field setting selected was an accredited online MBA program in a top-ranked business school at a large Midwestern university. The program was designed for professionals who wished to continue their employment while earning their MBA. Full-time, tenured faculty members were chosen for the faculty pool from various departments of the business school to teach in the program. Some faculty members had more years of teaching experience than others, since the program had grown to more than 1,000 students in just a few years. The researchers believed that such a rapidly expanding program would best illustrate the complexities of a social system and provide a rich context for participants' perceptual change.

For the purposes of this particular study, 28 faculty members and 20 second-year MBA students within this program were interviewed in a one-on-one format. Importantly, the subject areas of the faculty participants related to all the major disciplines offered in this program. Each interview took approximately 45 to 75 minutes and about 20 semistructured questions were asked. The interview questions primarily related to students' online learning experiences and sense of community.

Program evaluation survey data related to students' perceptions of their online learning experiences was used to assess students' satisfaction with online learning experiences and their sense of online community. The student survey instrument consisted of 65 questions. The 65-item survey questionnaire contained 5-point scale Likert type questions about their overall student perceptions and attitudes toward learning online. One hundred and two second-year MBA students responded to program evaluation survey data. The internal reliability of the survey, Cronbach's alpha, was reported at .91.

Twenty-seven online MBA courses across a wide spectrum of business disciplines were then selected for content analyses. The content coding scheme was a list of online collaboration, communication, and social interaction strategies drawn from the professional literature that were believed to facilitate community building in online courses (Misanchuk & Anderson, 2001; Rovai, 2001). Descriptive data were obtained by counting the frequencies of occurrences based on the coding scheme. Importantly, the intercoder agreement was 81%.

The present study employed Strauss and Dorbin's constant comparative method (Merriam, 1998) to triangulate the data from different interview transcripts and to identify emerging themes related to learning communities in online courses. To ensure intercoder reliability, two interview transcripts were coded initially and the intercoder agreement achieved 89%. The researchers then continued coding independently and discussed their coding decisions with each other until a common set of codes based on all the transcripts were determined. All data were recoded again using the ATLAS.ti qualitative analysis software program to determine the frequencies of the different coding categories. Member checking was also used after the interviews to ensure the trustworthiness of the findings. At the later stages of this analysis, themes from different data sources (i.e., survey, interviews, and content analyses) were merged to obtain a more in-depth understanding of the emerging issues.

FINDINGS

Sense of Community

In general, students felt a sense of belonging to a learning community for the online courses in this program. About 90% of the respondents ($N = 102$) agreed or strongly agreed that they felt part of a learning community when taking online courses ($M = 4.27$, $SD = 0.72$, where $1 = strongly$ $disagree$ and $5 = strongly\ agree$). About 60% of the students never felt lonely while taking the classes. However, about 25% did, in fact, feel isolated.

Correlation analyses were conducted between student feelings of sense of learning community with other items in the survey (see Table 29.1). Positive correlations were found between feelings of belonging to the learning community with learning engagement ($r = .62$, $p < .01$), feelings of having learned a lot ($r = .60$, $p < .01$), and overall satisfaction with the quality of online courses ($r = .61$, $p < .01$). This result indicates close rela-

Table 29.1. Correlation Matrix of Sense of Belonging to a Learning Community With Other Variables Based on Student Survey

	1	2	3	4	5	6	7	8	9	10	11
1. Sense of belonging to a learning community	1										
2. Learning engagement	.62**	1									
3. Feeling of having learned a lot	.60**	.56**	1								
4. Overall satisfaction	.61**	.65**	.73**	1							
5. Perceived familiarity with other students	.44**	.36**	.27**	.39**	1						
6. Not feeling isolated	.41**	.29**	.33**	.40**	.34**	1					
7. His or her comfort level with reading messages or materials online	.42**	.29**	.31**	.33**	.24*	.30**	1				
8. Perceived emotional presence of other students through online interaction	.31**	.29**	.25*	.24*	.33**	.21*	.32**	1			
9. Instructor offering regular feedback	.46**	.33**	.42**	.35**	.43**	.24*	.40**	.29**	1		
10. The perceived helpfulness of the instructor's facilitation	.50**	.42**	.37**	.47**	.45**	.16	.37**	.28**	.43**	1	
11. Informative feedback on learning performance	.44**	.30**	.48**	.43**	.31**	.35**	.26**	.33**	.50**	.36**	1
12. Intention to drop out of the program	-.47**	-.40**	-.51**	-.51**	-.34**	-.30**	-.40**	-.28**	-.35**	-.51**	-.43**

Note: *p < 0.05. **p < 0.01.

tionships exist between the sense of learning community in this environment and the perceived learning outcomes and quality.

In addition, moderately positive relationships were found between feelings of belonging to the learning community with several items (item 5, 6, 7, 8) related to social presence in online courses as shown in Table 29.1.

The results also showed that sense of belonging to a learning community was positively related to the behavior of instructor presence and facilitation (item 9, 10, 11) as shown in Table 29.1. Such findings indicated that aspects of teaching presence, such as facilitation and feedback, were linked to students' feeling of a sense of community.

Additionally, only 9% of the students surveyed responded that they ever thought about dropping out of the online MBA courses. Equally interesting, a correlation analysis revealed that the student's intention to drop out of the program was negatively correlated with the perceived helpfulness of the instructor's facilitation ($r = -.51$), the student's sense of community in the class ($r = -.47$), his or her comfort level with reading messages or materials online ($r = -.40$), and the student's engagement in learning ($r = -.40$), where the significance level was .05.

INTERACTION STRATEGIES USED IN ONLINE COURSES

As we have discussed in the literature review, strategies to promote collaboration, instructor presence, and social interaction have the potential to foster a sense of learning community. Table 29.2 displays the frequencies of major strategies used in online courses related to collaboration and interaction.

The content analysis suggested that compared with synchronous text-based forums that were in low to moderate use (41%), asynchronous discussion forums were employed in the vast majority of online courses (85%). Interview findings revealed that many instructors preferred asynchronous conferencing discussions over synchronous communication to facilitate online discussion due to the flexibility of accessing online discussion forums and the capability of this communication mode to mediate a learner-centered cognitive discourse and knowledge negotiation. For example, one instructor commented, "The discussions helped [building a sense of community] and I thought people were very cordial toward each other." Several instructors noted the effectiveness of asynchronous discussions in engaging online learners in a professional dialog. For example, one instructor noted, "One of the things that I found that I think was pretty effective was when we got off script on occasion and talked about particular issues that were more practitioner oriented."

On the other hand, the low use of synchronous chat was attributed to a lack of typing or facilitation skills and, more importantly, the inflexibility

**Table 29.2.   Frequencies of
Collaboration and Interaction Strategies in 27 Online Courses**

Instructional Activities	Instructional Activities	Percentage of Usage (N=27)
Collaborative discourse	Asynchronous class conference	85%
	Synchronous class conference	41%
	Participation in online discussions as part of assessment	67%
Instructor presence	Course announcement	100%
	Email communications with students	100%
	Instructor's active participation in class discussions	44%
	Instructor participation in team discussions	4%
	Virtual office hours	11%
Virtual team	Team-based learning activities	81%
	Team deliverable	78%
	Small team discussions	41%
	Interteam feedback/critique	15%
	Peer evaluation	19%
	Team membership change	7%
Social interactions	Personal profile	100%
	Student online coffee house	7%
	Student introduction forum	7%
	Bulletin board to express student expectations	15%

Note: "Instructor's active participation in class discussions" was defined as posting at least two responses in each discussion forum.

of real-time interaction that might result in limited online member participation due to the difficulty of scheduling a time that accommodated all the students. For example, one instructor voiced his concern in the following comment: "My understanding of the chat rooms is that's more real time discussion and we just really had a group of people that it was difficult to get all at one time." However, several students' comments suggested that effective use of chat rooms in several courses enhanced the sense of community in online courses. For example, one student noted that "Only in the Quantitative [Analysis] course, professors used to hold lectures (literally) in chat rooms at specified times. That was the only real learning community experience so far."

The results indicated that all instructors (100%) seemed to highly prefer personalized e-mail communication in providing feedback and answering questions over other forms of communication with students. Announcements were used in all the courses (100%), most frequently to broadcast course related news. The survey results confirmed that regular course announcements and feedback was positively correlated with the feelings of sense of community ($r = 0.46$, $p < .01$). As noted subsequently in interviews, online instructors strongly valued the immediacy of providing just-in-time feedback through e-mail. Compared to personalized e-mail interaction, the rate of instructors' participation in class discussion was relatively low. Only slightly more than half the courses that used asynchronous discussion forums had the presence of online instructors.

Virtual team activities (81%) were used in the majority of courses. The majority of courses (78%) used common team deliverables to encourage shared goals and close collaboration. However, the majority of the courses (93%) that used virtual teaming did not change team membership throughout the quarter, and few courses (15%) used strategies to promote classwide team interactions. (As we will discuss in detail in the section on qualitative findings, encouraging group work experience through a common goal or deliverable did promote a stronger sense of community in the working group but not necessarily at the class level.)

Compared with more content-based online discourse, extremely few courses used non-content-related strategies to establish familiarity and social bonding among online learners. For example, social icebreakers were used in 7% of the courses. Similarly, only 7% of course instructors provided an online coffee house for informal discussion. Fifteen percent of the courses used bulletin boards as a place for members to express course expectations. Interview findings from students and instructors supported the usefulness of social interaction strategies in boosting interpersonal relationships and positive interactions among students. For example, one instructor stated, "I had an introduction forum at the very beginning of the course where people wrote in and introduced themselves and so forth, and then several other discussions where I saw that they were talking to each other."

Participants' Perceptions of Community Building in Online Courses

Necessity to Build Learning Communities. There was a wide range of attitudes toward the importance of establishing a learning community in these online MBA courses. Overall, most instructors were not community-minded. They did not recognize the role of having a sense of community in their online courses. Corroborating with our content analysis results, the interview findings indicated that instructors strongly preferred to use e-mails or phone calls to provide personalized assistance to online learners instead of taking a progressive role in facilitating a community of learners wherein collaboration and the learner-centered process is the key to learning. For example, one instructor commented, "So I really encouraged the students to contact me in any way that they felt comfortable. I sort of gave them many options. But as far as creating a sense of we're all here at this moment, I did not." Another instructor said similarly, "Well, I think it's important [to building a sense of community] ... The teams provide an opportunity to do that, whether or not it has to move to the class level, I'm not so sure. It probably is useful, but I'm just trying to think about why that would help beyond."

A few instructors did not think that a sense of community is a relevant concept for online learning because they believed that the advantages of online learning are flexibility and self-paced learning. Considering the students' multiple responsibilities, putting effort into building a sense of community seemed to be an extra burden on both the students and instructors. For example, admitting that he did not feel a sense of community in his course, one professor commented on the necessity to build a sense of community in online courses: "It's not necessary. It's irrelevant. Most of these [students] are people working by themselves. They are people who hold down a regular job; they're really not interested in trying to build social connections or anything like [that]. It just gives me what I need to know, I don't have time for that stuff." Another instructor was concerned about the extra time and effort community building required. He stated, "I certainly don't want to do any more; even if they offered me to do more I wouldn't do it. All of those kind of interactive stuff is time that we can spend doing other work."

On the one hand, a few instructors were well aware of the needs of creating learning communities in online courses and indicated it was important for students to engage in a constant idea exchange and dialogue to understand the complexities of business issues. Those instructors usually seemed to demonstrate a strong empathy to the social needs of online students. One instructor had this to say: "What I have found is that they crave being a class. They crave thinking of themselves as a group studying this together, so I will be using their names to either applaud or not, thank you, Rich, for saying that, or Bless you, Irene, finally somebody has said this. They will come up and do the same, so they'll be complimenting one another, while I'm not there, complementing one another."

Students' perceptions of the role of learning communities in online courses also showed variance. Many students desired to get to know their peers better so they could obtain social and academic support when needed. A few others seemed unconcerned about interacting with other students. Their attitudes seemed to be associated with the lowered social expectations when studying online and also personality differences.

For example, the following quote demonstrates the importance of shared experiences in an online program: "I think it is very important that students feel they are in it together, for both emotional and academic support. It is not easy to get through this program since it is very demanding. And only students who are in the same program would understand the difficulties."

However, some students perceived the lack of interaction as an expected tradeoff of online learning experiences. For example, one student commented, "I'm not having as much fun as I would at a regular program, and, again, that's only revolving around social activities, that's really it. I feel like networking goes along with that. I think you meet some really neat and interesting people, and I'm passing some of that up, but, at the same time, I still get to work and continue my career, so what I'm passing up is justified."

It should be noted that both instructors and students seemed to have narrowly defined learning community as purely social network or social "buddies" that were established among students but did not necessarily influence the overall learning outcomes.

Preexisting Community. Many instructors noted that students had a strong desire to work together with people from previous communities. For example, even though a professor did not think it was necessary for building community in online course, he did feel that the students would like to work with members of their previous social network. He commented on this,

"So there are some students that do like to work together but normally they're people who know each other before they come to class. Other than that the class is just give me what I need to know as quickly as possible."

Another instructor mentioned the students from the same corporation who had previously worked with each other requested to work with these same members. He said, "But, that I can see now is a potential issue, they are comfortable doing this in a cohort, they want to be able to talk to their group of 30 or 32 ... it's easier to teach students who come in with a sense of community because they feel as if, I think, they are part of a team, whether or not they're actually a group in my class, they're part of a team from [company name] and they want to do well."

Students' interview results showed existing social networks that were either from their previous work company or from prior group work experience in online courses were key sources of gaining academic or emotional support.

Social Presence in Online Courses. The majority of online instructors regarded the low social presence afforded by the asynchronous technology as a barrier to establishing social rapport in online courses. The instructors were frustrated with impersonal environments that were deprived of tacit social and visual cues in an online environment. Such environments made it difficult to form an impression of online participants, thus making it almost impossible to establish intimacy among students and instructors. For example, one instructor expressed his concerns in the following comment: "That's one of the difficulties. It's a very impersonal environment whereas the face-to-face is much more personal. You can develop a rapport with a student. You see the interaction that's going on between people and you can use that in a teaching environment. That's much more difficult to do in an online environment and that's one of the things that I feel is missing from the online environment."

A few instructors recommended the improvement of existing technology to build technological attributes to promote social identity in the online learning space although they realized that it might not be a perfect solution. For example, one instructor stated, "But, [in]conversation with him directly or indirectly, cued the thought of sort of talking heads—just animation graphics, maybe—and that would be artificial but nevertheless if we could inject something like that then peer team level meetings would appear to install identity maybe a little bit more robustly. Deeper, it's still pseudo-personal but maybe just a little more personal."

The student survey results suggested that the social presence and familiarity among the students in these online courses was not very high. Almost half of the students (49%) could not saliently feel the emotions or feelings of other students in their online courses. The majority of the students (over 70%) indicated they did not really know their fellow students and the instructors well when taking online courses. The interview findings of students revealed that a low sense of social presence created barriers for online interaction and collaboration, as noted in the following comment: "Because we don't understand each other's personalities and we've only had a very short amount of time to meet one another, so for me the most difficult part of, and the worst part, the hardest part, is to try and understand who these other people are."

However, as noted subsequently, students seemed to have higher tolerance of the impersonal nature of online media itself, but attributed the low social presence to the lack of social structures to promote identity formation and socioemotional ties in the online courses. As the following quote indicates, several students recommended intentionally designing social interaction strategies and allocating a sufficient amount of time to establish familiarity and interpersonal relationships. For instance, one student stated that "I think one of the biggest things that could be done is to either extend the length of the in-residence or do a lot more ice breaking activities because there is a lot of ice."

Importance of Group Work. Both students and instructors agreed on the importance of group work in building learning communities. Although online MBA instructors preferred to use virtual teams for reasons such as simulating the real business world and developing real skills, they did not intentionally structure any team interactions for community building purposes. However, retrospectively they thought they helped build a sense of community among online learners by encouraging group learning experiences through a shared task goal. For example, one instructor commented as follows about group works: "In some cases, they're from the same company and the same location, but in other cases, they're in the same company and they're in totally different parts of the world. So I don't know whether they know each other or not. But at least with the teams I create a sense of community with four or five people."

Student survey results also showed the positive impact of teamwork on their learning experiences online. Eighty percent of students felt that group work was helpful for their learning ($M = 4.22$, $SD =0.91$). Approximately 93% of the respondents felt that sharing information and giving peer feedback on team projects contributed to student learning ($M = 4.17$, $SD = .63$). Approximately 86% of the respondents felt collective knowledge is created through group work in taking online courses ($M = 4.18$, $SD = 0.8$). Students frequently mentioned that they felt a sense of community within their work groups. However, they did not think that a sense of group community can be projected as a sense of community across an online course because there are few extensive interactions with the rest of one's classmates outside of the group members. For example, one student's comments related to this issue is included here: "I think we're all going through the same thing in the course and in reading what the other classmates are thinking, whether it's different or the same, it kind of, yeah, it forms a kind of community, but I think the major community that we do form is with our own team members."

Further analysis of students' interview findings suggested that sometimes the small group community was highly task oriented. Camaraderie and trust might never develop in such highly task-oriented settings and within the short duration of most online courses.

DISCUSSION

The present study revealed evidence of a significant relationship between sense of community and perceived learning engagement, perceived learning, and student satisfaction. In addition, the study also found a relationship between students' sense of community and lowered feelings of isolation as well as reductions in likelihood that they will drop out of their online courses. These results are consistent with the findings from previous studies that also found a significant relationship between classroom community and perceived learning (Rovai, 2002c). This study also added to the evidence that supports the importance of community in reducing course attrition rates (Rovai, 2002a, 2002c; Tinto, 1993).

As noted subsequently, in addition to this relationship between sense of community and learning quality, several important themes emerged from this study.

Community Awareness

The findings of this study suggested a weak awareness of online community and low value on its learning impact. This result was highly similar to those of Conrad's (2004) study. As with her work, there was limited awareness of the possible value of learning community to online learning and a general lack of an active social role of online instructors in facilitating a learning community. In the present study, the weak community awareness seems to have resulted in a low level of social presence in online courses as reported in the survey of online students.

This result indicated that although the concept of a sense of community is widely acknowledged in online education research, its value may not be as readily accepted in the reality of existing practices in many online programs. With both online instructors and learners having competing roles within their respective lives, they need to be convinced that the benefits of a learning community are worth the extra time to invest in their creation and maintenance. Not too surprisingly, existing research with regard to the benefits of community seems to be mixed and in need of further large-scale testing (Misanchuk, 2003). Data from the present study indicated a need to further explore the relationship between actively facilitating learning communities in online courses and high quality learning.

Technology Versus Pedagogy

An interesting finding from this study is that both students and instructors felt a low level of social presence in online courses due to the nature of asynchronous text-based technology. However, instructors seemed to resort to technology as a solution, whereas the students stressed the importance social activities as a solution to heighten the level of social presence and collegiality in online courses. The dichotomy of technical solutions and social solutions to the development of online learning communities is worth noting. It seemed that at first glance, a high media-rich technology can immediately raise the level of social awareness by exposing the image or identity of online learners. However, this solution may be cost prohibitive for most online programs and, worse still, may be highly superficial.

As we discussed, a deep trust or spirit of community lies in the commitment and mutual engagement of community members. Fundamentally it lies in the pedagogical or socially supported interactions rather than in technology itself. The present study found that many features of the available online technologies were not sufficiently explored to promote such social presence using established pedagogical practices. For example, a simple opening activity that asks students to introduce themselves and their previous experience may help establish the familiarity among students. A social acknowledgement in online conferencing such as "Hello" or "Glad you could join us" can help students feel part of a learning family. However, our content analysis indicated that there was a lack of such social prompting in the online discourse in general. This result also indicated an urgent need to develop social skills of online instructors if a community of learners is planned.

Social Skills

The present study indicated several limitations related to the social skills of online instructors. Similarly, Wilson et al. (2004) noted that it is important for online instructors to "model community participation skills and values, including turn-taking, netiquette, thoughtful responses to peer's posts, and organization and facilitation of community events and chat. They should actively monitor the community discussions to answer questions, resolve conflicts, and guide discussion as needed." However, in this study, we found such roles were absent in half of the online courses. During the interviews, we asked how instructors would facilitate online discourse. Somewhat surprisingly, many instructors admitted that they lacked skills in facilitating an interactive online discussion and creating a sense of class community.

In addition, the facilitation of class community may be limited by the instructors' lack of using strategies for cross-pollinating virtual teams for a classwide interaction. Without cross-team interaction, it is unlikely students will naturally feel connections to other students when they mainly interacted within one team during the course. Although maintaining one team throughout the course is a reasonable strategy for semester-long projects, other strategies such as classwide discussion or ad hoc groups should be used to connect students with other class members other than those in the working groups.

Different Levels of Community

Although the survey results indicated that students in general felt a sense of community in their online MBA courses, the interview findings suggested that the sense of community may come from the group or program level rather than from the course level. The findings of the present study also confirmed Brown's (2001) study that found different levels of community existing in online courses. Students may feel a strong sense of community at the group level through extensive team collaboration but not feel a sense of community at the course level. This study also corroborated Hill, Raven, and Han's (2002) study findings—that the impact of community building strategies seemed to occur more readily and faster in small teams. Students may have much stronger relationships with small collaborative groups and virtual teams than with the larger class group. Such team bonding and social networking may be due to the close networks and shared knowledge that forms for building joint products and supporting each other to complete challenging tasks.

Both Brown (2001) and Wilson et al. (2004) stressed the importance of considering larger contextual factors such as students belonging to a program. They argued that although it may be difficult to establish a deep sense of community due to the brief duration of an online course, the sense of learning community is worth pursuing, as the process of building community itself enhances effective collaboration and communication, learner engagement, and social networking that will eventually benefit both participants as well as the online program.

Based on our findings and discussions, we believe that to design online courses for a learning community, a more systematic instructional plan needs to be adopted; one that integrates learning community across different levels.

CONCLUSION

This study added further evidence that the there are positive relationships between sense of community and perceived learning gains, learner engagement, and satisfaction. Moderate relationships were also found between sense of community and social interaction activities. The interview findings revealed mixed perceptions with regard to the values and strategies for building learning communities in online courses. For both online students and instructors, it seemed that there was no uniform agreement regarding the necessity to build communities in online courses. The existing technology may still be a barrier without the supportive structure to enhance the bonding within the online community. This study also confirmed that three levels of community—group, class, and beyond class—exist in online courses.

The results of this study remind online educators that building learning communities in online courses may not be as intuitive as advocates and promoters might suggest. Communities cannot develop on their own without careful planning, continued support, and intentional tasks and activities. Instructors may fail to value the role of online community either within the present class or for long-term relationships, student satisfaction with the program, and overall persistence to complete it. Findings from this study indicated a need for a systematic effort to build a sense of learning community, starting from perceptual changes from online instructors to providing substantial training support and best practices for community building to programmatic plans for three levels of community building.

The results of this study highlight several areas for future research. First, there is a need to conduct similar studies in other online programs or disciplines. Understanding the perceptions of online participants toward community building is important to get them to buy into community building goals and activities. Second, there is a need to examine the interaction effect of technology and pedagogy within community building since there is a dearth of research on the technological and pedagogical variables necessary to foster virtual communities (Bonk et al., 2004). Third, there is also a need to understand the development of the three levels of communities (group, class, and beyond class). How do they interact? Which level is most important? By answering such questions, we will be better able to understand the complexities of community building in online courses and provide enhanced strategies, advice, and training for online instructors to plan and facilitate community building.

This study has several key limitations. First, the participants of this study were limited to one online MBA program and only a small sample of participants from that program were selected for interviews. As a result, generalizations of the findings presented here to other online programs or disciplines should be cautious. Second, the correlation analyses of this study (e.g. the relationship between sense of community and learning engagement) should not be misconstrued as causal relationships between a sense of community and other variables in the study. Correlation is not causality. As a result, controlled experimental studies that examine the causal effects of a sense of community would strengthen the findings of the present study. Third, the time duration of this study was too short and limited to thoroughly investigate a complex sociocultural phenomenon such as a sense of community in online environments. A longitudinal study could be conducted to examine whether perceptions of sense of community is associated with change in time. Fourthly, the study used a program evaluation survey to measure students' perceptions of sense of community. A more vigorous and valid instrument could be employed in the future to measure sense of community as a multidimensional construct.

In summary, as a program level study, the generalizations from the results in this study may be limited. However, the analysis of emerging issues and recommendations raised in this study provide highly valuable information and insights to assist distance educators and policy makers to make educational policies and practices for successful and engaging online learning experiences. We hope we have shed some light on variables that can positively influence the sense of community in online environments.

REFERENCES

Anderson, T., Rourke, L., Archer, W., & Garrison, R. (2001). Assessing teaching presence in computer conferencing context. *Journal of Asynchronous Learning Networks, 5*(2), 1–17. Retrieved October 20, 2005, from http://www.sloan-c.org/publications/jaln/v5n2/v5n2_anderson.asp

Barab, S. A., Thomas, M. K., & Merill, H. (1999). *Online learning: From information dissemination to building a shared sense of community.* Unpublished manuscript, Indiana University Bloomington.

Berge, Z. L. (1995). Facilitating computer conferencing: Recommendations from the field. *Educational Technology, 15*(1), 22–30. Retrieved October 20, 2005, from http://www.emoderators.com/moderators/teach_online.html

Bonk, C. J. (2000). My hat's on to the online instructor. *e-Education Advisor: Education Edition, 1*(1), 10–13.

Bonk, C. J., Wisher, R. A., & Nigrelli, M. L. (2004). Learning communities, communities of practice: Principles, technologies, and examples. In K. Littleton, D. Miell, & D. Faulkner (Eds.), *Learning to collaborate, collaborating to learn* (pp. 199-219). Hauppauge, NY: NOVA Science.

Brown, R. (2001). The process of community building in distance learning classes. *Journal of Asynchronous Learning Networks, 5*(2), 18–35.

Chao, C. (2001). *Toward an understanding of sense of community and meaningful learning experiences in an on-line language education course.* Unpublished doctoral dissertation, Indiana University, Bloomington.

Conrad, D. (2004). University instructors' reflections on their first online teaching experiences. *Journal of Asynchronous Learning Networks 8*(2), 31–44. Retrieved October 20, 2005, from http://www.sloanc.org/publications/jaln/v8n2/v8n2_conrad.asp

Duffy, T. M., Dueber, B., & Hawley, C. L. (1998). Critical thinking in a distributed environment: A pedagogical base for the design of conferencing systems. In C. J. Bonk (Ed.), *Electronic collaborators: Learner-centered technologies for literacy, apprenticeship, and discourse* (pp. 51-78). Mahwah, NJ: Erlbaum.

Eastmond, D. V. (1995). *Alone but together: Adult distance study through computer conferencing.* Cresskill, NJ: Hampton Press.

Hill, J. R. (2001). Building community in web-based learning environments: Strategies and techniques. Retrieved November, 23, 2005, from http://ausweb .scu.edu.au/aw01/papers/refereed/hill/paper.html

Hill J. R., Raven R., & Han, S. (2002). Connections in web-based learning environments: A research based model for community building. *Quarterly Review of Distance Education, 3*(4), 383-393.

Kearsley, G. (2000). *Online education: Learning and teaching in cyberspace.* Belmont, CA: Wadsworth.

Kerr, E. (1986). Electronic leadership: A guide to moderating online conferences. *IEEE Transactions on Professional Communications, 29*(1), 12-18.

Liu, X. (2006). *The socio-cultural factors affecting the success of an online MBA course: A case study viewed from activity theory perspective.* Unpublished dissertation transcripts, Indiana University Bloomington.

Lock, J. V. (2002). Laying the groundwork for the development of learning communities within online courses. *Quarterly Review of Distance Education, 3*(4), 395-408.

McMillan, D. W., & Chavis, D. M. (1986). Sense of community: A definition and theory. *Journal of Community Psychology, 14*(1), 6-23.

Merriam, S. B. (1998). *Case study research in education: A qualitative approach.* San Francisco: Jossey-Bass.

Misanchuk, M. (2003). *Sense of community, satisfaction, and performance in a distance education program.* Unpublished dissertation transcripts, Indiana University Bloomington.

Misanchuk, M., & Anderson, T. (2001). *Building community in an online learning environment: Communication, cooperation and collaboration.* Paper presented at the Mid-South Instructional Technology Conference, Murfreesboro, TN. Retrieved November 20, 2004, from http://www.mtsu.edu/~itconf/proceed01/ 19.html

Moller, L. (1998). Designing communities of learners for asynchronous distance education. *Education Technology Research and Development, 46*(4), 115-122.

Nicholson, S, (2002). Socialization in the "virtual hallway": Instant messaging in the asynchronous Web-based distance education classroom. *The Internet and Higher Education, 5,* 363-372.

Palloff, R., & Pratt, K. (1999). *Building learning communities in cyberspace: Effective strategies for the online classroom.* San Francisco: Jossey-Bass.

Phelps, R. H., Ashworth, Jr., R. L., & Hahn, H. A. (1991). *Cost and effectiveness of home study using asynchronous conferencing for reserve component training* (U.S. Army Research Institute for the Behavioral Sciences Technical Report 1602). Alexandria, VA: U.S. Army Research Institute for the Behavioral Sciences.

Preece, J. (2000). *Online communities: Designing usability and supporting sociability.* Chichester, United Kingdom: Wiley.

Rice-Lively, M. L. (1994). Wired warp and woof: An ethnographic study of a networking class. *Internet Research*, 4(4), 20-35.

Riel, M. (1996). *The Internet: A land to settle rather than an ocean to surf and a new "place" for school reform through community development*. Retrieved April 27, 2006, from http://www.gsn.org/gsh/teach/articles/netasplace.html

Rovai, A.P. (2001). Building classroom community at a distance: A case study. *Educational Technology Research and Development*, 49(4), 33-48.

Rovai, A. P. (2002a).Building sense of community at a distance. *International Review of Research in Open and Distance Learning*, 3(1). Retrieved January 10, 2005, from http://www.irrodl.org/content/v3.1/rovai.html

Rovai, A. P. (2002b). Development of an instrument to measure classroom community. *Internet and Higher Education*, 5(3), 197-211.

Rovai, A. P. (2002c). Sense of community, perceived cognitive learning, and persistence in asynchronous learning networks. *The Internet and Higher Education*, 5(4), 319-332.

Schwier, R. (2002). *Shaping the metaphor of community in online learning environments*. Retrieved online on October 20, 2006, from http://cde.athabascau.ca/ISEC2002/papers/schwier.pdf

Schwier, R. A., & Balbar, S. (2002). The interplay of content and community in synchronous and asynchronous communication: Virtual communication in a graduate seminar. *Canadian Journal of Learning and Technology*, 28(2). Retrieved April 27, 2006, from http://www.cjlt.ca/content/vol28.2/schwier_balbar.html

Shea, P., Li, C. S., Swan, K., & Pickett, A. (2002). Developing learning community in online asynchronous college courses: The role of teaching presence. *Journal of Asynchronous Learning Networks*, 9(4), 59-82.

Stake, R. (1994). Case studies. In N. K. Denzin & Y. S. Lincoln (Eds.), *Handbook of qualitative research* (pp. 435-454). Thousand Oaks, CA: SAGE.

Tinto, V. (1993). *Leaving college: Rethinking the causes and cures of student attrition* (2nd ed.) Chicago: University of Chicago Press.

Wilson, B. G., Ludwig-Hardman, S., Thornam, C., & Dunlap, J. C. (2004). Bounded community: Designing and facilitating learning communities in formal courses. *The International Review of Research in Open and Distance Learning*, 5(3). Retrieved April 27, 2006, from http://www .irrodl.org/index.php/irrodl/article/view/204/286

CONCLUSION

CHAPTER 30

DESIGNING THE "PERFECT" ONLINE COURSE

Michael Simonson

Dictionary definitions of the word *perfect* are universally similar: without defect, faultless. Certainly it is foolish to try to quickly define the perfect online course; a course without defect and faultless. However, with the current "rush to go online," many instructional designers, distance educators, and training directors and being asked to design just such a course—an effective, rigorous, yet interesting online course—a "perfect" online course.

So, for the sake of the naiveté of those asking and the motivation of many distance educators to want to help, let us examine what the best practices literature seems to be indicating about online courses—good, if not perfect ones—and make a recommendation. (Actually, the components of an online course summarized in this chapter are derived from the recent edition of *Teaching and Learning at a Distance: Foundations of Distance Education*)

When designing an online course, there are three organizational categories to consider: course structure, course contents, and artifacts of learning. It might also be informative to look at the organization of the major subdivision of a typical online course: the course unit.

The Perfect Online Course: Best Practices for Designing and Teaching
pp. 547–550
Copyright © 2009 by Information Age Publishing
All rights of reproduction in any form reserved.

COURSE STRUCTURE

The typical college course is a three-semester, 15-week course with a title something like "Management of Service Centers," or "Introduction to Educational Statistics." Certainly most educators know that a three-credit college course will meet about three times a week for the 15 weeks of the semester, or for about 45 class sessions. And, for every hour a student is in class he or she should expect to spend about 2 hours outside of class preparing, reading, or studying, for a semester total of somewhere between 100 and 140 hours.

What about a class that does not have class sessions—an online class? If the course designer applies the same logic to an online class as to a traditional class, then, in an online course an average student should expect:

- Between 100 and 140 hours of "work" during the semester, or about 7-9 hours per week. This time would be spent reading, studying, writing, posting, viewing, listening, and chatting.
- A course that is organized around three major units, each with about five modules. Modules would be studied for about a week.

And, the instructor should also expect to devote between 100 and 140 hours of effort, organizing, posting, reading, grading, and interacting, or between 7-9 hours per week.

COURSE CONTENT

Effective online courses emphasize instructional content that presents in a variety of ways what students should learn. The key organizational document for the online course is the syllabus that gives most, if not all, the important information about the course content and organization. The syllabus contains the sequence of topics, course objectives, assignments, rubrics, reading and viewing lists, and other information needed by the student to "keep up and stay informed."

Additionally, the perfect online course would use a course management system. It is hard to imagine an online course, especially a "perfect" one, without a course management system. The course management system would be a meeting place, a virtual classroom, and the venue where instruction and learning interact.

Next, the online course must have a considerable amount of instructor involvement—even presentations, although lecturing by the instructor of the online course is probably not conducive to perfection. The instructor should introduce himself or herself, distribute periodic and regular organizational e-mails, personally contact individual students, make postings to threaded discussions, participate in chats, both spoken and typed, and make short and on-target presentations—single concept lectures.

Textbooks and other reading materials remain the mainstay for delivering content in most courses, including the online course. The average for a typical online course is two to three textbooks. The modern, well-chosen textbook can provide the content information for most courses.

Finally, the online course should have single-concept videos, audio explanations or descriptions, narrated visuals, and other multimedia content. Also of importance are the contents of the virtual portion of the course—chats and threaded discussions, for example—that are built and constructed during the course.

ARTIFACTS OF LEARNING

Some would probably choose a different phrase than "artifacts of learning," but most who study online education look for observable objects, things, and artifacts that are evidence of student learning. A comprehensive investigation of online courses yields the following general set of expectations for student assignments:

- Three major graded assignments, usually one for each major unit of the course. These major assignments can be exams, problem/scenario solutions, research papers, group projects, or media productions.
- Approximately 10 minor graded assignments, such as discussion postings, chat participations, e-mails, wiki input, or blog postings.

These artifacts, or learning outcomes, are at the core of the perfect online course (and at the heart of almost any course, as instructional designers often tell us).

If the typical course is examined in more detail, and the major building block of the course—the unit—is examined, its organization might look like this:

- A video introduction to the unit produced by the instructor that in 5 minutes or less explains what this unit is "all about."
- An audio explanation of the major assignment for this unit, made by the instructor and posted online as an audio file; this explanation would supplement the syllabus explanation and would be what students are referred to when they ask "what am I supposed to do?"

Obviously, the assignment rubric would be explained in this "pod-cast."

- A reading assignment of several hundred pages from one or more of the course textbooks, or a series of readings from the Web or from a course packet.

- A few short video viewings that highlight key ideas or that demonstrate important processes.

- A series of threaded discussion questions that build on one another to provide a sequenced construction of information that supports the unit's final assignment. Instructors are actively involved in discussions early in the unit, but reduce their involvement as students begin to grasp the content more completely.

- Chats, mostly between students working as individuals or in teams, in which between-student interaction is stressed. Instructors monitor chats, but are not overly involved.

- A few instructor presentations, either prerecorded or presented live using voice-over-Internet technologies.

This typical unit would last about 5 weeks, and would build on previous units of study and contribute to subsequent units. The three units in a typical online course would be the "three-legged stool" supporting the overall purpose of the course.

And finally, let us not kid ourselves; the perfect online course is a pipe dream—according to the dictionary again, a pipe dream is the result one gets from smoking one of those funny pipes, so let us be more realistic (and legal). The key to an effective course is the direct, purposeful involvement of a knowledgeable teacher; one with content knowledge, teaching skills, and design experience.

REFERENCE

Simonson, M., Smaldino, S., Albright, M. & Zvacek, S. (2009). *Teaching and learning at a distance: Foundations of distance education* (4th ed.). Boston: Pearson.

AUTHOR AFFILIATIONS

M'hammed Abdous
Old Dominion University

Gary J. Anglin
University of Kentucky

John Battalio
Boise State University

Danilo M. Baylen
University of West Georgia

Curtis J. Bonk
Indiana University

Greg Boris
South Dakota Voices for Children

Naomi R. Boyer
University of South Florida

Baiyun Chen
University of Central Florida

William N. Chernish
University of Houston

Newell Chiesl
Indiana State University

Dan O. Coldeway
Dakota State University

Agnes L. DeFranco
University of Houston

Kim E. Dooley
Texas A&M University

Richard E. Downing
Rockhurst University

Jianxia Du
Mississippi State University

Vance A. Durrington
Mississippi State University

Byron Havard
University of West Florida

Mark Hawkes
Dakota State University

Wu He
Old Dominion University

Atsusi Hirumi
University of Central Florida

Terry L. Hudgins
Nova Southeastern University

Dave S. Knowlton
Southern Illinois University

Douglas A. Kranch
North Central State College

Seung-hee Lee
Indiana University

James R. Lindner
Texas A&M University

Xiaonjing Liu
Indiana University

Richard J. Magjuka
Indiana University

Joan M. Mazur
University of Kentucky

Angelene C. McLaren
Wayne State University

Christopher T. Miller
Morehead State University

Joi L. Moore
University of Missouri - Columbia

Gary R. Morrison
Old Dominion University

Pamela T. Northrup
University of West Florida

Anthony Olinzock
Mississippi State University

Anymir Orellana
Nova Southeastern University

Marcy Reisetter
University of South Dakota

Sorel Reisman
California State University - Fullerton

Alaa Sadik
South Valley University, Egypt

Charles Schlosser
Nova Southeastern University

Michael Simonson
Nova Southeastern University

Sharon Smaldino
Northern Illinois University

Christine K. Sorensen
University of Hawaii - Manoa

Richard T. Walls
West Virginia University

Constance E. Wanstreet
The Ohio State University

Steve Wheeler
University of Plymouth, UK

David L. York
Johnson County Community College

Chien Yu
Mississippi State University

Ning Jackie Zhang
University of Central Florida

Jinsong Zhang
Stevenson University

Lihua Zheng
Hebei Teachers' University, China

ORIGINAL PUBLICATIONS

The original publication of each chapter is noted below.

PART I: INTRODUCTION

1. Simonson, M., & Schlosser, C. (2004). We need a plan: An instructional design approach for distance education courses. *Distance Learning, 1*(4), 29-38.

2. Chernish, W. N., DeFranco, A. L., Lindner, J. R., & Dooley, K. E. (2005). Does it matter? Analyzing the results of three different learning delivery methods. *Quarterly Review of Distance Education, 6*(2), 87-95.

PART II: BEST GUIDELINES AND STANDARDS

3. Hirumi, A. (2005). In search of quality: An analysis of e-learning guidelines and specifications. *Quarterly Review of Distance Education, 6*(4), 309-329.

4. Sorensen, C. K., & Baylen, D. M. (2004). Learning online: Adapting the seven principles of good practice to a Web-based instructional environment. *Distance Learning, 1*(1), 7-17.

5. Zhang, J., & Walls, R. T. (2006). Instructors' self-perceived pedagogical principle implementation in the online environment. *The Quarterly Review of Distance Education, 7*(4), 413-426.

6. Zheng, L., & Smaldino, S. (2003). Key instructional design elements for distance education. *Quarterly Review of Distance Education, 4*(2), 153-166.

7. Orellana, A. (2006). Class size and interaction in online courses. *Quarterly Review of Distance Education, 7*(3), 229-248.

8. Reisetter, M., & Boris, G. (2004). What works: Student perceptions of effective elements in online learning. *Quarterly Review of Distance Education, 5*(4), 277-291.

9. Sadik, A., & Reisman, S. (2004). Design and implementation of a Web-based learning environment: Lessons learned. *Quarterly Review of Distance Education, 5*(3), 157-172.

10. Hirumi, A. (2002). A framework for analyzing, designing, and sequencing planned e-learning interactions. *Quarterly Review of Distance Education, 3*(2), 141-159.

11. McLaren, A. C. (2008). Designing effective e-learning: Guidelines for practitioners. *Distance Learning, 5*(2), 47-57.

PART III: BEST INSTRUCTIONAL METHODS AND MODELS

12. Hawkes, M., & Coldeway, D. O. (2002). An analysis of team vs. faculty-based online course development: Implications for instructional design. *Quarterly Review of Distance Education, 3*(4), 431-441.

13. Kranch, D. A. (2008). Getting it right gradually: An iterative method for online instruction development. *Quarterly Review of Distance Education, 9*(1), 29-34.

14. Miller, C., & Mazur, J. M. (2001). Towards a person-centered model of instruction: Can an emphasis on the personal enhance instruction in cyberspace? *Quarterly Review of Distance Education, 2*(3), 193-207.

15. Miller, C. T. (2007). Enhancing Web-based instruction using a person-centered model of instruction. *Quarterly Review of Distance Education, 8*(1), 25-34.

16. Knowlton, D. S. (2003). Evaluating college students' efforts in asynchronous discussion: A systematic process. *Quarterly Review of Distance Education, 4*(1), 31-41.

17. Chiesl, N. (2007). Pragmatic methods to reduce dishonesty in Web-based courses. *Quarterly Review of Distance Education, 8*(3), 203-212.

18. Moore, J. L., Downing, R. E., & York, D. L. (2002). Organizing instructional content for Web-based courses: Does a single model exist? *Quarterly Review of Distance Education, 3*(3), 269-281.

19. Morrison, G. R., & Anglin, G. J. (2006). An instructional design approach for effective shovelware: Modifying materials for distance education. *Quarterly Review of Distance Education, 7*(1), 63-74.

20. Chen, B., Hirumi, A., & Zhang, N. J. (2007). Investigating the use of advance organizers as an instructional strategy for Web-based distance education. *Quarterly Review of Distance Education, 8*(3), 223-231.

21. Abdous, M., & He, W. (2008). Streamlining the online course development process by using project management tools. *Quarterly Review of Distance Education, 9*(2), 181-188.

22. Boyer, N. R. (2003). The learning contract process: Scaffolds for building social, self-directed learning. *Quarterly Review of Distance Education, 4*(4), 369-383.

PART IV: BEST ENGAGMENT STRATEGIES

23. Wanstreet, C. E. (2006). Interaction in online learning environments: A review of the literature. *Quarterly Review of Distance Education, 7*(4), 399-412.

24. Battalio, J. (2007). Interaction online: A re-evaluation. *Quarterly Review of Distance Education, 8*(4), 339-352.

25. Northup, P. T. (2002). Online learners' preferences for interaction. *Quarterly Review of Distance Education, 3*(2), 219-225.

26. Wheeler, S. (2006). Learner support needs in online problem based learning. *The Quarterly Review of Distance Education, 7*(2), 175-184.

27. Havard, B., Du J., & Olinzock, A. (2005). Deep learning: Knowledge, methods and cognition. *Quarterly Review of Distance Education, 6*(2), 125-135.

28. Durrington, V. A., & Yu, C. (2004). It's the same only different: The effect the discussion moderator has on student participation in online class discussions. *Quarterly Review of Distance Education, 5*(2), 89-100.

29. Liu, X. (2007). Does sense of community matter? An examination of participants' perceptions of building learning communities in online courses. *Quarterly Review of Distance Education, 8*(1), 9-24.

CONCLUSION

30.   Simonson, M. (2008). And finally ... Designing the "perfect" online course. *Distance Learning, 5*(3), 82-84.